Retrieving Sāṁkhya History

An Ascent from Dawn to Meridian

Contemporary Researches in Hindu Philosophy & Religion, no. 11

Retrieving Sāṁkhya History

An Ascent from Dawn to Meridian

by

Lallanji Gopal

D.K.Printworld(P)Ltd.
NEW DELHI - 110 015

Cataloging in Publication Data — DK

Gopal, Lallanji, 1934-1999.
Retrieving Sāṁkhya history.
(Contemporary researches in Hindu philosophy & religion, no. 11).
Includes bibliographical references (p.).
Includes index.

1. Sankhya. 2. Philosophy, Hindu. I. Title.
II. Series: Contemporary researches in Hindu philosophy & religion, no. 11.

ISBN 81-246-0143-7

First Published in India in 2000

Published and printed in India by:
D.K. Printworld (P) Ltd.
Regd. office: '*Sri Kunj*', F-52, Bali Nagar
New Delhi-110015
Phones: (011) 545-3975, 546-6019; *Fax* : (011) 546-5926
E-mail: dkprint@4mis.com

Contents

1

Prologue

(A) A PLEA FOR THE HISTORY OF SĀṀKHYA

History and Philosophy

THE progress of culture and civilisation consists essentially in acquisition, aplication and preservation of knowledge. The edifice of knowledge rests on the four pillars of scientific method, mathematics, philosophy and history. All other disciplines and branches of learning are the offshoots or projections of these four, or else they result from a combination of two or more of these or their sub-branches. History is one of the four basic sciences. It is generally identified with its contents in the form of information relating to certain aspects of the past of societies and communities. But history is not restricted in its scope and contents. Its real significance does not lie in the found of information it collects. History is important for its methodology, its approach, its way of looking at facts. It has a developmental approach. It does not view things as fixed, static or dead. It considers them in the process of change and development. It studies their background, their genesis and the stages in their growth, including the influences which have shaped them. This gives the whole picture and the correct in understanding.

History is the lamp which illumines other branches of knowledge. It is not restricted to its own specialised areas. It has an equal applicability to all spheres of information and all branches of learning. All branches of knowledge gain by the use of the historical method and approach. The information acquires a new dimension, a fullness and a correctness. It is viewed in its proper perspective and its totality.

History and philosophy combine wonderfully. They are supplimentary to one another. Philosophy is helpful in historical analyses. History, for a meaningful understanding, requires to be philosophically interpreted. Philosophy, in its turn, when subjected to the process of historical analysis, unfolds its meaning better. The philosophy of history and a history of philosophy offer a happy and healthy blending.

In practice, however, the followers of the two disciplines do not combine to the extent desirable. They consider the other one to be beyond their scope and interest. A historian generally refrains from philosophising. A philosopher, likewise, is absorded with his concepts, their meaning and validity. He generally does not bother about their genesis and growth. He takes the developed concepts in their finished form and studies them. History, to him, does not serve much useful purpose. In the case of India the separation of the two has affected them adversely. Knowing well that any generalisation on such issues can be objected to by citing exceptions, we would submit that it is seldom that a historian takes interest in the problems of philosophies, and a philosopher presenting his study of a philosophical system as a history is not met generally. Here we propose to study Sāṁkhya through the historical method to understand the scope of possibilities and the nature of problems.

History of Saṁkhya

Sāṁkhya enjoys a high respectability among the philosophical systems. It is considered to have been the oldest philosophy. It was given a honoured position as characteristic of the philosophical thought in early periods. Sāṁkhya has had a glorious history. In the beginning it signified philosophical thought in general. Later it became synonymous with philosophy and finally came to stand for a philosophy. Sāṁkhya influenced the growth of philosophy. Through a process of interaction it contributed to the development of philosophical thought in other systems also. Its views on metaphysics and epistemology receive a respectful consideration from other systems. Sāṁkhya is noteworthy for keeping philosophy separate and distinct and not mixing it with the requirements of religion. The Sāṁkhya dualism is a happy combination of pragmatic realities and spiritual orientation. The world cannot be dismissed as unreal. It is to be understood. But materiality yields primacy to the spiritual element. Sāṁkhya is a philosophy of hope for spiritual advancement leading to emancipation. Many theistic sects, even when adopting a Vedāntic cover, subscribe to the Sāṁkhya dualism. Sāṁkhya finds a prestigious recognition in the *Gītā* and many Purāṇas. In Indian aesthetic tradition, in literature and are alike, the Sāṁkhya speculations are accepted as the basis. Sāṁkhya provides the philosophical support to the system of *Āyurveda*.

Some scholars have traced the historical development of the Sāṁkhya system, G.J. Larson[1] has attempted a judicious and critical appraisal of all earlier studies on the subject. He does not analyse the work done by P. Chakravarti[2] and the Hindī publications of U.V. Shastri[3] and A.P. Mishra,[4] possibly because they emphasise the development through the texts concerned and not in terms of the concepts and principles.

Larson is himself cautious and does not determine stages in the history of Sāṁkhya. He speaks broadly of three periods of Ancient speculations, Proto-Sāṁkhya and Classical Sāṁkhya. Larson considers only the third, the Classical Sāṁkhya, as Sāṁkhya. In his recent work *Sāṁkhya*[5] he does not admit the first two as being Sāṁkhya and does not give any space to them. He modifies his view about the *Sāṁkhyakārikā*. He splits the Classical Sāṁkhya into two phases: the pre-*Kārikā* and and the *Kārikā*. He includes

---

1. *Classical Sāṁkhya*, pp. 15-74.
2. *Original and Development of the Sāṁkhya System of Thought*. •
3. *Sāṁkhya-darśana kā Itihāsa*.
4. *Sāṁkhya-darśana kī Aitihāsikha Paramparā*.
5. C. Larson and R.S. Bhattacharya, *Sāṁkhya (Encyclopedia of Indian Philosophies)*, ed. by K. H. Potter, Vol. IV, pp. 3-41.

Paurika, Pañcādhikaraṇa, Patañjali and Vārṣagaṇya in the pre-*Kārikā* phase. The *Kārikā* phase is represented by the followers of Vārṣagaṇya. In this category he includes both Vindhyavāsin and Īśvarakṛṣṇa. Thus, the *Sāṁkhyakārikā* represents not the beginning of Classical Sāṁkhya, but its culmination.

The survey attempted by Larson exposes the inadequacy of the earlier studies. Beside the paucity of evidence and the non-availability of original texts, the reconstructions suffer from misconceptions about the chronology of texts and assumptions about the nature of Sāṁkhya and the importance of the *Sāṁkhyakārikā*. This necessitates fresh attempts at retrieving Sāṁkhya history by reappraising available evidence and utilising new sources of information. The validity of the assumptions taken for granted is to be looked into. The historical approach is expected to throw welcome light on many an obscure and debated point.

(B) SAṀKHYA HISTORY IN REVERSE GEAR

Īśvarakṛṣṇa and the History of Sāṁkhya

IMPORTANCE OF ĪŚVARAKṚṢṆA

The *Sāṁkhyakārikā* of Īśvarakṛṣṇa in the most celebrated Sāṁkhya Text. It systematised the Sāṁkhya system with the result that subsequently scholars belonging to the Sāṁkhya tradition as well as those connected with other systems took his formulation to be the standard form of Sāṁkhya. Al-Bīrūnī (eleventh century), who relies on the most authoritative text of a system for presenting its salient features, uses the *Sāṁkhyakārikā* in describing the Sāṁkhya philosophy.[6] Likewise, Mādhava (fourteenth century), in his *Sarvadarśanasaṁgraha*, presents Sāṁkhya doctrines solely using the *Sāṁkhyakārikā*.[7] Modern authorities on Sāṁkhya aptly describe the *Sāṁkhyakārikā* as representing the Classical Sāṁkhya.

But, the outstanding contribution made by Īśvarakṛṣṇa has not

6. E. Sachau, *Alberuni's India*, pp. 226-7, 30, 40-9, 62, 132.
7. Mādhava, *Sarvadarśanasaṁgraha*, tr. by E.B. Cowell and A.E. Gough, pp. 221-30.

been without some bad effects. The high respect earned by the *Sāṁkhyakārikā*, on account of its systematic and unambiguous formulation seems to have pushed into the background earlier writings on Sāṁkhya, which were relegated into oblivion in course of time.

PROBLEMS OF PRE-ĪŚVARAKṚṢṆA HISTORY

The absence of independent Sāṁkhya texts and the standardised formulation in the *Sāṁkhyakārikā* have created in the minds of modern scholars certain assumptions which have affected the study of Sāṁkhya.

As the *Sāṁkhyakārikā* is the earliest known Sāṁkhya text and as subsequent writers only attempted commentaries on it, it has been inferred that the Sāṁkhya system has not undergone any basic change in its history. Any formulation of the Sāṁkhya system, showing any point or aspect apposed to the *Sāṁkhyakārikā*, it is assumed to be a later development. Such texts or passages are given a later date and, if this involves serious chronological difficulties, efforts are made to explain them as influences of other systems or as attempts to accomodate differring systems and to synthesise them with Sāṁkhya.

But, in spite of several scholarly studies we have not been able to delineate the history of Sāṁkhya in pre-Īśvarakṛṣṇa times. It is shrouded in the mist of mythology and controversies. On account of the non-availability of authentic information we cannot say anything definite about Kapila, the founder of the Sāṁkhya system, his life and contributions, his philosophical ideas, and writings. The deft fingers of time have been busy weaving around him a cob-web of legends transforming him into a mythological figure. Some scholars suspect the historicity of Āsuri and even of Pañcaśikha. Even in the case of Vārṣagaṇya, Vindhyavāsin and other predecessors of Īśvarakṛṣṇa the known facts about their life and views are disgustingly few and far from being meaningful.

Another difficulty is the absence of Sāṁkhya text which can be definitely placed in this period. The claims of *Sāṁkhya-*

pravacanasūtra and *Tattvasamāsasūtra* to be recognised as ancient texts have been challenged. We have some passages, quoted in a few later texts, which give Sāṁkhya principles or accounts revealing Sāṁkhya elements or influences.

Garbe[8] and Ottamare[9] do not contemplate any major change in the Sāṁkhya system in the course of its long history. According to them, the original formulation of the system by Kapila contained all the important features of the system, and the *Sāṁkhyakārikā* does not mark any significant departure from the earlier accounts.

Other scholars do not openly subscribe to the view of the Sāṁkhya system remaining static, but seem to work under that unconscious impression. They limit their task to discussing the origin of the Sāṁkhya and to delineating the sources, trends or traditions which have contributed to the formation of the Sāṁkhya system. The best illustration of this type of study is to be found in the scholarly work of S.N. Dasgupta.[10]

Many scholars have attempted a reconstruction of the history of Sāṁkhya in pre-Īśvarakṛṣṇa times.[11] But no unanimity has been reached even on some important issues. The origin of Sāṁkhya is bedated: whether it is from Vedic or non-Vedic or folk stream. The original meaning of the term Sāṁkhya, relevant to the nature of Sāṁkhya in earliest stages, is not beyond the pale of controversy. The chronology of the earliest Sāṁkhya philosophers and their contributions, their philosophical ideas and their writings are not known for definite. Many later Sāṁkhya philosophers are mere names. We are not sure about the relative chronology of these philosophers, what to say of their exact dates. As a result of these dark areas in our knowledge of pre-Īśvarakṛṣṇa Sāṁkhya, we cannot determine the stages through which Sāṁkhya principles came to acquire their form recorded by Īśvarakṛṣṇa.

8. Garbe (ed.), *Sāṁkhya Sūtra Vṛtti*, p. iv.
9. P. Oltramare, *L'Histoire des Idées Théosophiques dans L' Inde*, Vol. I, pp. 219f.
10. S.N. Dasgupta, *A History of Indian Philosophy*, Vol. I, pp. 211-21.
11. G.J. Larson, *Classical Sāṁkhya*, pp. 17-72, 245-56.

SAṀKHYAKĀRIKĀ AS THE BASIS FOR RECONSTRUCTION

We are of the opinion that for this work also the *Sāṁkhyakārikā* must form the basis of our enquiry and reconstruction. This is the earliest complete work on Sāṁkhya principles. Īśvakṛṣṇa makes a pointed reference to his familiarity with the early history of Sāṁkhya. He mentions its original formulation by Kapila and its being handed down through Āsuri and Pañcaśikha. He also refers to the Sāṁkhya doctrine being transmitted through a succession of teachers and disciples (*śiṣya-paramparā*). He was familiar with the writings of many Sāṁkhya philosophers who preceded him.

Īśvarakṛṣṇa was well acquainted with the rich, vast literature produced by his predecessors. He unequivocally admits that he has presented the doctrine only in a summarised form (*saṁkṣiptam*) and has avoided referring to the illustrative tales and criticism of the point of view of opponents (*ākhyāyikāvirahitaḥ paravādavivaritaścā'pi*). In a concluding verse preserved in the *Māṭharavṛtti* Īśvarakṛṣṇa describes his own account of Sāṁkhya as briefly expounded (*tasmāt samāsadṛṣṭam śāstram*). On account of its vastness the Sāṁkhya literature is difficult to understand, hence Īśvarakṛṣṇa puts forward the claim that he has fully comprehended the system (*samyag vijñāya siddhāntam*).

From Īśvarakṛṣṇa's own assertion it can be deduced that the system did not have a monolithic form. It seems that the writings of his predecessors contained differing versions on several important points. Īśvarakṛṣṇa is at pains to establish that he is faithful to the Sāṁkhya tradition and has not done injustice to its earlier accounts. He claims to have fully comprehended the Sāṁkhya system. He asserts that whatever principles are enunciated in the whole of the *ṣaṣṭhitantra*, they all are found in his presentation in seventy verses (*karikā* 72). In the concluding verse of the *Sāṁkhyakārikā*, found only in the *Māṭharavṛtti* (*kārika* 73), Īśvarakṛṣṇa claims that his presentation is not defective in its meaning or essence (*arthataḥ*); it is like the reflection reproduced in a mirror of the big form of the *tantra*.

In the *Sāṁkhyakārikā* the verses significant for the

reconstruction of the early history of Sāṁkhya are *kārikās* 69 to 73. The introductory two *kārikās* also contain some useful references, particularly about the original nature and goal of Sāṁkhya.

With the help of these *kārikās* we may try to determine the broad outlines of the early history of Sāṁkhya. For the sake of convenience we will process the account in the reverse gear.

CONTRIBUTIONS OF ĪŚVARAKṚṢṆA

Let us begin with Īśvarakṛṣṇa himself. Though Īśvarakṛṣṇa enjoys a pre-eminent position in the history of Sāṁkhya and the credit for establishing the classical Sāṁkhya, he himself does not claim much glory for himself. In *kārikā* 71 Īśvarakṛṣṇa is described as *āryamati* (noble-minded). This type of adjective need not be on insertion by a devoted disciple; the author himself could have used it without incurring the criticism for self-glorification. Īśvarakṛṣṇa asserts that he has presented Sāṁkhya principles in a summarised manner. The one new features is the use of *āryā* metre (*āryābhiḥ*).

Another significant feature of his account is that Īśvarakṛṣṇa does not give any place to illustrative tales and criticism of the point of view of other systems, thus suggesting that he has confined himself to the undisputed and commonly accepted principles.

We have pointed out the emphasis which Īśvarakṛṣṇa gives to his account being in full consonance with the Sāṁkhya system. He makes a pointed reference to the *ṣaṣṭhitantra*. Of the various accounts of the system, the one associated with *ṣaṣṭhitantra* was widely respected as the most prominent stream of Sāṁkhya thought. Īśvarakṛṣṇa mentions Kapila, Āsuri and Pañcaśikha alone. Possibly the main tradition in Sāṁkhya, known as *ṣaṣṭhitantra* came through the line of Kapila, Āsuri and Pañcaśikha. After Pañcaśikha there was no outstanding scholar to maintain this tradition. Its prominence was possibly over-shadowed by a crowd of philosophers subscribing to differing principles. Īśvarakṛṣṇa can be given credit for re-establishing the supremacy of the *ṣaṣṭhitantra* version. Thus, Īśvarakṛṣṇa restored the ancient links of Sāṁkhya.

Īśvarakṛṣṇa does not seem to have added any new principles. The claim for presenting a summarised account does not provide much scope for this. Of course, it can be admitted that, in his effort to present a coherent account, he made improvements by way of a better style, a more appropriate expression, and a more apt analogy.

But, it can be expected that in the process of summarising and, introducing coherence and compactness, Īśvarakṛṣṇa minimised the importance of certain principles and details and in some cases omitted them altogether.

Īśvarakṛṣṇa made a significant deviation in his account of the *ṣaṣthitantra*. The way he emphasises the fact that his account faithfully represents the Sāṁkhya principles, that all the *artha*s (*padārtha*s or *tattva*s) in the *ṣaṣthitantra* are enunciated in his own text and that, though summarised, they mirror the original is a clear indication that there were differences between his account and the version generally associated with the *ṣaṣthitantra*. The sixty principles cotemplated by the *ṣaṣthitantra* considered of ten *mūlikārtha*s and fifty *pratyaya-sarga*s. We find that the *Sāṁkhyakārikā* (*kārikā*s 46-47) enumerates the fifty *pratyaya-sarga*s but does not mention the ten *mūlikārtha*s. It was to cover up this change, of omitting the ten *mūlikārtha*s that Īśvarakṛṣṇa was pleading for his faithfulness to the original *ṣaṣthitantra*. Possibly he meant to canvas that by omitting the ten *mūlikārtha*s he has not caused any harm to the original *ṣaṣthitantra* and that the purpose served by the ten *mūlikārtha*s has been adequately covered by him. If we have to list the main contributions of Īśvarakṛṣṇa, then possibly the omission of the *mūlikārtha*s will figure in it.

RICHNESS OF PRE-ĪSVARAKṚṢṆA SĀṀKHYA

The period after Pañcaśikha but before Īśvarakṛṣṇa was a long one. It produced a line of distinguished Sāṁkhya philosophers. Though no single text composed in this period is available, we do get stray quotations from these works. Some of the names of the Sāṁkhya philosophers are those of renowned sages, but others distinctly were historical individuals. It may be sugested that in view of their known reputation the sages were associated with Sāṁkhya. Another possibility is that some person belonging to their school or lineage contributed to the enrichment of the Sāṁkhya tradition. But the fact that a limited few and not a large number of sages are thus associated with the Sāṁkhya makes a case for the genuineness of their Sāṁkhya association.

Īśvarakṛṣṇa says that there was a continuous living tradition about the Sāṁkhya philosophers. A long line of teacher-student tradition (*śiṣya-paramparā*) had preserved the principles and writings of these philosophers.

The Sāṁkhya literature produced in this period was voluminous indeed. This is evident from Īśvarakṛṣṇa's own admission that he presents a summarised account of the principles.

If seems that the presentation of Sāṁkhya principles by their earlier sages and texts was not rigidly uniform. There was a baffling variation in the enunciation of many principles by various schools and philosophers making it difficult to comprehend clearly the essentials of the system. Īśvarakṛṣṇa makes a bold claim that he clearly understood the principles of the system.

It is not possible to identify all the important principles enunciated by the earlier philosophers. Later tradition shows how on some basic points Sāṁkhya philosophers upheld widely divergent views, sometimes violently opposed to the generally accepted notions about Sāṁkhya. The quotations from the writings of these philosophers, which occur in later works, cannot be expected to cover even the important principles enunciated by them. But they do indicate the range of variation and some important and characteristic principles enunciated by them.

From the *Sāṁkhyakārikā* we learn about three important features of the Sāṁkhya writings in this period.

Form of Writing

The first relates to the form of these writings. Īśvarakṛṣṇa takes legitimate pride in presenting the principles in *āryā* metre. This would suggest that earlier the Sāṁkhya philosophy was not versified in *āryā*; possibly it was in prose and not in verses. But, this does not completely rule out the use of verses. Verses could have occurred occasionally. It is also not unlikely that some text was versified, though not in *āryā* metre. But the use of prose was not necessarily confined to the employment of *sūtras*. Some philosophers could have expounded their principles through analysis, elaboration, discussion and analogy. In the surviving extracts we find passages with these characteristics.

Īśvarakṛṣṇa says that he omitted *ākhyāyikās* and *paravāda* from his text. By implication these two formed the characteristics of the Sāṁkhya literature before his times. The richness and volume of the earlier Sāṁkhya writings was possibly largely due to these two features.

Ākhyāyikā

In Sanskrit literature the term *ākhyāyikā* is used in a technical sense. It is differentiated from *kathā*, which, in popular usage, has a similar import. Ancient authorities on *Kāvyāśāstra* list the points of differences between the two. Bhāmaha, in his *Kāvyālaṁkāra*,[12] and Daṇḍin, in his *Kāvyādarśa*,[13] describe the characteristic features of the two. Later texts, the *Agni Purāṇa*,[14] the *Kāvyālaṁkāra*[15] of Rudraṭa, the *Dhvanyāloka*[16] of Ānandavardhana and the *Sāhityadarpaṇa*[17] of Viśvanātha point out minute differences between the two. But these are evidently elaborations deduced from the two compositions of Bāṇa, the *Harṣacarita* and the *Kādambarī*, which were taken to be classic examples of *ākhyāyikā*

12. The use of the word *artha* here may refer to *padārthas* or *tattvas* in Sāṁkhya. In *kārikā* 72 *arthaḥ* used twice has the same sense.
13. I.23-30.
14. I.25-9.
15. Ch. 337, 13-7.
16. XVI.20-7.
17. III.

and *kathā*. The original and the basic difference between the two is the one mentioned in the *Amarakośa*[18] which possibly was adopted by the *Alaṁkāra-saṁgraha*.[19] According to Amarasiṁha, the *ākhyāyikā* is written on the basis of a well-known subject-matter, whereas the *kathā* is the creation of imagination. The *Alaṁkāra-saṁgraha*, in making the difference more explicit, says that, whereas the theme of *kathā* is a conjectured one, the *ākyāyikā* is based on true facts. Thus, the *ākhyāyikā* relates to a theme which is historically correct; the *kathā* is a fiction of imagination.

It must, however, be noted that some authorities maintain that there is no real difference between the two; they are the two names of one and the same literary type. This view was expressed by such an early authority as Daṇḍin.[20]

But we do not know of any *ākhyāyikā* earlier than the *Harṣacarita*. Neither any text, the name of any such text has survived. In such a situation the possibility of an *ākhyāyikā* text numerating or illustrating Sāṁkhya principles is difficult to expect. Then, how are we to explain the reference in the *Sāṁkhyakārikā*? When Īśvarakṛṣṇa aims at a summarised narration, each single expression used by him must have some appropriate relevance. The reference suggests that, if there was no separate text of the nature of *kāvya*, there were certainly works which concerned historical persons belonging to the Sāṁkhya tradition. Possibly here Īśvarakṛṣṇa is referring to the chapters in the Śāntiparva of the *Mahābhārata*, particularly its Mokṣadharmaparva section. Several chapters in this section give an account of Sāṁkhya principles. The enunciation is done through an interlocution between well-known personalities who enjoy a high reputation in the history of Indian thought, specially Sāṁkhya philosophy. These celebrities include the names of Pañcaśikha, Jaigīṣavya, Asita-Devala Yājñavalkya and Janaka. Significantly the author of these chapters presents them as

18. VI.332-6.
19. I.321-2 — *ākhyāyikapalabdhārthā* | *prabandhakalpanā kathā* |
20. *kathā kalpitavṛthāntā satyārthākhyāyikā matā* |

pieces of old history (*itihāsam purātanam*). Thus, it would seem that Īśvarakṛṣṇa, by using the term *ākhyāyikā*, referred to the chapters in the Śāntiparva which present Sāṁkhya principles as interlocution between famous Sāṁkhya scholars. It is not unlikely that there were similar accounts in other texts lost in course of centuries.

Paravāda

The other type of Sāṁkhya writings in times preceding the composition of the *Sāṁkhyakārikā*, scrupulously avoided by Īśvarakṛṣṇa, are mentioned as *paravāda*. Literally the term means the doctrines of others. It includes a criticism of the principles of other schools of philosophy and a reply to the points of criticism raised by the opposing philosophers. Indian systems of philosophy do not confine themselves to an enunciation of their own principles. They often present as *pūrva-pakṣa* the criticism raised against their philosophy as also points which possibly could be raised, and then meet them to establish their own point of view. This type of literature assumed volumnious proportion in later periods. There are indications that even before the times of Īśvarakṛṣṇa some Sāṁkhya philosophers went beyond the work of presenting Sāṁkhya principles. They argued in favour of the Sāṁkhya view and against the criticism by other systems. It is this type of literature that has suffered most by the standardisation and summarisation enforced by Īsvarakṛṣṇa. The quotations from the writings of Sāṁkhya philosophers of this phase of Sāṁkhya history, surviving in later commentaries, contain passages which may be classed as *paravāda* mentioned by Īśvarakṛṣṇa.[21]

FIRST PHASE OF SĀṀKHYA HISTORY

The first phase in the formulation and evolution of Sāṁkhya principles covers the lives and works of Kapila, Āsuri and Pañcaśikha. As in the case of the two characteristics of a later period covered above, here also we will confine ourselves to information recorded by Īśvarakṛṣṇa.

---

21. *Kāvyādarśa*, I.28 — *tatkathākhyāyiketyekā jātiḥ sañjñādvayāṅkitā* ।

Kapila

The *Sāṁkhyakārikā* (*kārikā* 69) says that this secret knowledge about *prakṛti* functioning for the sake of *puruṣa*, wherein is deliberated the existence, origin and extinction of all beings, was expounded by the greatest sage. In the following *kārikā* the sage is referred to as *muni* and Sāṁkhya is described as pure and foremost.

Here the adjective *agryam* does not refer merely to the excellence of the doctrines but also suggests the chronological position of Sāṁkhya. Sāṁkhya is generally taken to be the earliest system of philosophy to emerge in India. Īśvarakṛṣṇa is possibly alluding to the respect which Sāṁkhya enjoyed as the oldest system of philosophy. The honour, which it enjoyed, is also communicated by the adjective *pavitram* used for it.

The *Sāṁkhyakārikā* refers to Sāṁkhya as *guhyam* which means secret or mysterious. According to Īśvarakṛṣṇa, Kapila duly expounded this secret knowledge. This provides an interesting information about the origin and early formulation of Sāṁkhya principles. It seems that even before Kapila gave the first systematic exposition of Sāṁkhya, it circulated long as the characteristic philosophy of a closed group. Possibly during the early period, when the Vedic cult of sacrifice was the dominant religion, a class of thinkers applied themselves to a deliberation of deeper problems of life. This tradition existed as a system of thought as distinguished from the cult of sacrificial rituals.

The *Sāṁkhyakārikā* refers to Kapila as *parama ṛṣi* and *muni*. In the vedic literature we meet the terms *yati* and *muni*. Scholars generally take them to represent a tradition different from the Vedic one. Often they are described as belonging to the Śramaṇa tradition. This tradition was concerned with a deliberation of deeper problems of life.

Īśvarakṛṣṇa does not mention Kapila by name. He uses the words *parama ṛṣi* and *muni* to refer to him. This does not make Kapila a mythical feature. On the contrary, it indicates that Īśvarakṛṣṇa regarded him as a historical person commanding great respect. By making a specific reference to his philosophical contribution Īśvarakṛṣṇa removes all suspicious about the historicity of Kapila.

It would appear from the *Sāṁkhyakārikā* that the philosophy expounded by Kapila was basically concerned with the nature of the mysterious phenomena of life and death, the creation of the works and its dissolution, problems which are the starting point of philosophical investigation in any period and in any country. Basically, Sāṁkhya, as expounded by Kapila, was an enquiry into the phenomena of creation, existence and dissolution. Īśvarakṛṣṇa does not give details about the philosophical principles expounded by Kapila. The only point mentioned is that it was aknowledge of the concept of *puruṣārtha*. This was the main thrust of Kapila's philosophy. It implies other connected principles, the principle of *prakṛti* and of its functioning for the sake of *puruṣa*. We can speculate that the exposition possibly referred to the transformation or evolution of *prakṛti*. *Prakṛti* does so that *puruṣa* achieves its liberation. A knowledge of the separateness of *puruṣa* and *prakṛti*, of *prakṛti* functioning for the sake of *puruṣa*, is the means to realise emancipation.

Possibly Sāṁkhya in this period was not identifies with an enumeration of a specific number of categories (*tattva*s or *padārtha*s). Īśvarakṛṣṇa does not refer to this characteristic of Sāṁkhya in mentioning the Sāṁkhya principles of Kapila.

In referring to the exposition by Kapila the *Sāṁkhyakārikā* employs the expression *samākhyātam*. Considering the compact style of Īśvarakṛṣṇa, for presenting in a summarised form the entire Sāṁkhya philosophy, it seems that he was very careful in choosing words and expressions. Hence the expression *anākhyātam* could not have been without significance. There is some controversy about the original nature of Sāṁkhya and the original meaning of the word *sāṁkhya*. Some scholars derive the word *sāṁkhya* from *saṁkhyā* (number) on account of the system presenting its principles through a fixed number of *tattva*s or *padārtha*s, or from *parisaṁkhyāna* because it is characterised by an enumeration of its principles. Some others derive the name *sāṁkhya* from *saṁ* or *samyak khyāti* or a proper exposition. Sāṁkhya was so named because it presented its principles in a proper and reasonable manner. This type of controversy is not confined to modern scholars; even ancient and medieval authorities participated in it. In this context the use of the expression *samākhyātam* is meaningful. Īśvarakṛṣṇa possibly used it deliberately to express his view about the original meaning of the term *sāṁkhya* and the original nature of the Sāṁkhya system. It may be suggested that according to Īśvarakṛṣṇa, the presentation of the Sāṁkhya principles by Kapila was not characterised by an enumeration of *tattvas* or categories.

The only other information about Kapila, in the *Sāṁkhyakārikā*, is that he compassionately gave his system of philosophy to Āsuri. We do not learn anything about the text composed by Kapila. Actually the *Sāṁkhyakārikā* is silent about the question whether Kapila composed a text or merely formulated his principles orally. Modern scholarship is seriously concerned about the name of the text written by Kapila. Some scholars ascribe the *Tattvasamāsasūtra* and the *Sāṁkhyapravacanasūtra* to Kapila, though admitting that they have been revised by subsequent hands. In view of what Īśvarakṛṣṇa says about the contribution made by Pañcaśikha, it may be surmised that Kapila presented his ideas orally and briefly, and if in the form of a text, then possibly in *sūtras*.

Āsuri

The *Sāṁkhyakārikā* (*kārikā* 70) does not attribute any specific contribution to Āsuri but even then mentions his name for receiving the Sāṁkhya system from Kapila and passing it on to Pañcaśikha. This fact ordinarily will not be enough to merit a mention in a list of only three celebrated names. Āsuri possibly made a more tangible contribution. We may suggest, on the basis of the reference in the *Sāṁkhyakārikā*, that he reduced to writing the exposition which Kapila had communicated to him.

Pañcaśikha

Īśvarakṛṣṇa assigns to Pañcaśikha a place of high importance in the history of Sāṁkhya next only to that of its founder Kapila. He says that Pañcaśikha expanded the doctrine. The commentators give different meanings to the line *tena ca bahudhā kr̥taṁ tantram*. Modern scholars are also not unanimous in interpreting this reference. *Bahudhā* can be variously interpreted to mean modified, diversified, and expanded. *Tantra*, likewise, can mean a system or a book. In any case the line would refer to the elaboration and expansion of the Sāṁkhya philosophy brought about by Pañcaśikha. It may signify that whereas Kapila and Āsuri had presented a brief account, Pañcaśikha offered an elaborate treatment. But, possibly it was not a case of merely elaborating the original account. Pañcaśikha seems to have introduced a more vital change, without altering the original base. It was he who first presented Sāṁkhya through sixty items. This possibly the meaning of the reference to his increasing or elaborating the *tantra*. This was a major change or improvement. There is evidence to indicate that in earlier stages of its history Sāṁkhya was known as *ṣaṣṭhitantra*. *Ṣaṣṭhitantra* meant the presentation of Sāṁkhya through an enumeration of ten *mūlikārtha*s and fifty *pratyaya-sarga*s.

It is quite reasonable to suggest that Pañcaśikha composed a text to present his account. The text also was possibly known as the *Ṣaṣṭhitantra*. It is not available, but numerous quotations in later works do not leave any doubt about it.

The claim of Pañcaśikha for the authorship of the *Ṣaṣṭhitantra* is disputed by some modern scholars who plead in favour of Āsuri. The question has been confused by evidence which attributes *Ṣaṣṭhitantra* to Vārṣagaṇya.[22] If not mistaken, the reference would indicate that Vārṣagaṇya chose to name his own composition after the title of the great work written by Pañcaśikha.

From references in the Mokṣadharmaparva of the Śāntiparva and quotations in later works it is clear that Pañcaśikha deeply influenced the history of Sāṁkhya. But the *Sāṁkhyakārikā* does not give details about all his contributions. Īśvarakr̥ṣṇa indicates

---

22. *Infra* chapter 17.

that Pañcaśikha and his *Ṣaṣṭhitantra* represented the main line in the rich Sāṁkhya tradition.

ADDITIONAL VIEW

B.M. Barua (*A History of Pre-Budhist Philosophy*, pp.) in tracing the history of Sāṁkhya relies on the evidance of the *Sāṁkhyakārikā*. In this text there are only four names associated with Sāṁkhya: Kapila, Āsuri, Pañcaśikha and Īśvarakṛṣṇa. Barua takes these four to represent four stages in the history of Sāṁkhya. According to Barua, the first stage is represented by the *Puruṣasūkta* in the *Ṛgveda*, the second by the *Puruṣavidha Brāhmaṇa* in the *Bṛhadāraṇyaka Upaniṣad*, the third by Pañcaśikha's views in the Śāntiparva and the fourth by Īśvarakṛṣṇa's views in the *Bhagavad Gītā*.

In restricting the history of Sāṁkhya to the four names known from the *Sāṁkhyakārikā*, Barua ignores the contributions of other teachers of Sāṁkhya. He confines himself to one particular line in Sāṁkhya and thus does little justice to the rich and varied growth of Sāṁkhya. He emphasises the earliest period to which belonged Kapila, Āsuri and Pañcaśikha and than jumps to Īśvarakṛṣṇa. The long period of several centuries is not taken into consideration.

Barua tacitly assumes the Vedic connections of Sāṁkhya. He traces the history of Sāṁkhya in the Vedic tradition and does not consider the possibility of an independent history of its own. But the Sāṁkhya tradition does not claim such origins for itself.

Barua's efforts to link the first two stages with the Vedic literature is conjectural and without any cogent reason. He attributes the first stage of the *Puruṣasūkta* to Kapila. He argues that traditionally Nārāyaṇa is taken to be the author of the *Puruṣasūkta* and that Nārāyaṇa stands for Kapila. To attribute the *Puruṣasūkta* to Kapila is far-fetched. The Vedic tradition does not associate Kapila with this *sūkta*.

The suggestion of Āsuri being the author of the *Puruṣavidha Brāhmaṇa* in the *Bṛhadāraṇyaka Upaniṣad* is completely conjectural. There is no evidence to confirm it.

Methodology — Sources and Approaches

UPANIṢADS AND ORIGIN OF SĀṀKHYA

The non-availabality of authentic accounts of Sāṁkhya in an early period has led scholars to indulge in scholarly speculations. There is an apparent contradiction in these studies. Whereas Sāṁkhya is often described as being non-Vedic in its origin, efforts are made to trace elements of Sāṁkhya in the *R̥ksaṁhitā*, the *Brāhmaṇas*, *Āraṇyakas* and Upaniṣads.

We find a strange misconception about the origin of Sāṁkhya. Sāṁkhya is treated as evolving out of these early references. Sāṁkhya, thus, becomes a *tabula rasa* receiving impressions from diverse sources. But, Sāṁkhya is not patchwork created by the scissor and paste method. It is not a mosaic assimilating diverse elements. It is not a caravan which is formed by people coming and joining it. This strangely implies that Sāṁkhya did not have anything of its own. Sāṁkhya history is thus, reconstructed by identifying elements in other sources. Sāṁkhya is taken to have emerged only when sufficient details are found in these sources. Texts, which have only partial details, are explained as earlier phases leading to the final emergence of Sāṁkhya. On the basis of references in the Upaniṣads scholars have determined the stages in the emergence of Sāṁkhya. Thus, it is said that the first clear references to Sāṁkhya ideas and terminology are found in the *Kaṭha Upaniṣad*, composed in the fourth century BC, and that the *Śvetāśvatara Upaniṣad*, placed around the third century BC, represents a later stage of thought.[23]

But, this is a misconceived approach. It implies a wrong expectation from the Upaniṣads. The Upaniṣads are neither encyclopaedias or digests of philosophical views. They were not required to record the Sāṁkhya principles in their fulness. If any principle or aspect of Sāṁkhya is not mentioned in any particular Upaniṣad, it does not mean that it had not originated by that time.

23. Larson, *Classical Sāṁkhya*, pp. 95-105.

The Upaniṣads have their own philosophical views to expound. They mention only those details which are compatible with their own ideas or are relevant to them.[24] The Upaniṣadic evidence only indicates a lower limit for those principles. They had originated before these texts, but how much earlier is to be determined independently.

SĀṀKHYA SOURCES

In delineating the history of Sāṁkhya there has been a forced reliance on sources which do not belong to the Sāṁkhya stream. These sources view Sāṁkhya from their standpoint and in the light of their interest. They cannot be expected to be exhaustive in their account. Though they may be critical of the Sāṁkhya principles, they possibly could not have a sympathetic understanding of them. As a matter of methodology the Sāṁkhya principles are to be delineated primarily on the basis of sources belonging to the Sāṁkhya tradition itself.

The methodological approach has not been implemented on account of the non-availability of original Sāṁkhya works written before the *Sāṁkhyakārikā*. But, there has been no serious effort to tap the available material, with all its limitations of form and style.

There are indications that Sāṁkhya had a rich literature in the earlier period. The evidence for attempts at standardisation and systematisation of Sāṁkhya principles made several times is an admission of the vast and varied nature of Sāṁkhya expositions. The *Devaladharmasūtra* refers to serious and voluminous texts of Sāṁkhya which it summarised to present a systematic account.

In this connection we would like to refer to two Sāṁkhya texts — the *Sāṁkhyapravacanasūtra* and the *Tattvasamāsasūtra*. In their present form the texts are dismissed as later works with little value for the early history of Sāṁkhya. But, it is admitted that, along with some portions of an evidently later period, they have much information which seems to refer to an early period. Some

---

24. See *infra* chapter 3.

scholars attribute the texts to the earliest Sāṁkhya *ācāryas*, Kapila or Pañcaśikha. Though the inscription may not find many supporters, the early elements in the texts are to be treced.

A significant new source on Sāṁkhya is the *Devala-dharmasūtra*.[25] U.V. Shastri had collected extracts from this text. But no effort has been made to analyse the passages and determine its importance for the history of Sāṁkhya. Devala gives a systematic and complete account of Sāṁkhya and helps identify some of the early stages in Sāṁkhya history. Devala represents a stage when the two enunciations of Sāṁkhya, in terms of sixty principles and twenty-five categories, circulated together. Devala described Sāṁkhya through both the traditions, but, it seems that by his time the enunciation of twenty-five categories had gained precedence over the earlier tradition. Though Devala enumerates sixty principles, he does not refer to them as such. He mentions them in the form of fifty *pratyaya-sargas* and ten *mūlikārthas*.

The *Yuktidīpikā* is a very useful document for the history of Sāṁkhya. It is unique among the commentaries on the *Sāṁkhyakārikā* in mentioning earlier Sāṁkhya celebrities and also recording some of their important views. These *ācāryas*, from the manner of their reference in the *Yuktidīpikā*, apparently preceded Īśvarakṛṣṇa. But, there is no clear evidence to determine the dates of these *ācāryas* and calculate the time-gap separating Īśvarakṛṣṇa from them. Larson and Bhattacharya,[26] who place Īśvarakṛṣṇa in AD 350-450, describe Paurika, Pañcādhikaraṇa and Patañjali as the early *ācāryas* and place them as also Vārṣagaṇya in the slab AD 100-300.[27]

BUDDHACARITA, CARAKASAṀHITĀ AND MOKṢADHARMAPARVA

In reconstructing the history of Sāṁkhya the evidence of three sources, the *Buddhacarita* of Aśvaghoṣa, the *Caraksaṁhitā* and

---

25. See *infra* chapter 12.
26. *Sāṁkhya*, p. 13.
27. *Ibid.*

the Mokṣadharmaparva in the Śāntiparva of the *Mahābhārata*, has not been properly utilised. They are not specific works of Sāṁkhya but contain useful material on Sāṁkhya. Of these the Mokṣadharmaparva section has been analysed by many scholars, but the other two have been late in receiving attention and even now require a critical study.

These texts have suffered from the domination of the *Sāṁkhyakārikā* as the standard work of Sāṁkhya and the identification of its exposition as Sāṁkhya. This naturally created a disinclination to treat any deviation from it as Sāṁkhya. These accounts of Sāṁkhya have been labelled as Proto-Sāṁkhya. It has not been realised that the exposition of Sāṁkhya could not remain fixed and static over long centuries. The elaboration and change in later times do not mean that earlier expositions were not Sāṁkhya.

The misconceptions about the date of these texts has stood in the way of a proper evaluation of the evidence supplied by them. By a strange coincidence all the three are located around the first century of the Christian era. There has been no attempt to scrutinise the internal evidence to find out the actual period to which their accounts look back.

The *Buddhacarita* of Aśvaghoṣa is datable. Being associated with the Kuṣāṇa king Kaniṣka, Aśvaghoṣa is generally placed in the first century of the Christian era. Aśvaghoṣa is the author of the text, hence the views expressed in it are associated with him. But, generally it is not emphasised that in the text he attributes the presentation to Arāḍa. Buddha, before his enlightenment, had approached Arāḍa for receiving knowledge. Arāḍa, after expounding his principles, observed that similar views were held also by Jaigīṣavya, Janaka and Vṛddha-Parāśara. Aśvaghoṣa, thus, presented the principles of the system as advocated by Arāḍa, a pre-Buddha Sāṁkhya teacher.[28]

A similar misconception has persisted about the date of the *Carakasaṁhitā*. On the basis of a reference in the Chinese translation of *Tripiṭaka* to the court physician of Kaniṣka being

---

28. See *infra* chapter 7.

named as Caraka, the text is dated in the first century. But the text, in its present form, was not composed at one date. According to the text, itself, it was revised twice. The original composition by Agniveśa was revised by Caraka; later Dṛḍhabala restored chapters which had been lost. The chapters, containing accounts of Sāṁkhya principles, are those associated with the names of Agniveśa and Caraka. It is very difficult to apportion chapters and passages to Agniveśa and Caraka. The very fact that the name of Agniveśa was retained even after the revision made by Caraka shows that the revised text preserved much of the original composition by Agniveśa. The present text evidently has much older material and also earlier style and expressions. Agniveśa records many views expressed by his teacher Ātraya. We have argued that Agniveśa and Caraka are to placed respectively around 800 BC and 500 BC.

The encyclopedic *Mahābharata* is described by the tradition as having grown in three stages. Modern scholarship also believes that it has received its present form as a result of accretions over centuries. Winternitz proposed the rough time-bracket of fourth century BC to fourth century AD for the text,[29] which was narrowed to 300-100 BC by Hopkins.[30] Later researches have shown that by the first century of the Christian era the text had acquired its known form and size. The Śāntiparva is generally considered to have been among the latest portions inserted into its body. The evidence shows that the chapters in the Śāntiparva are generally to be dated before the first century. They belong to an earlier period and had been incorporated into the work before this date. But, by an inexplicable logic the latest date has been foisted on the Śāntiparva and its Mokṣadharmaparva section. Here also the internal evidence of the relevant chapters has not been looked into. Some of the chapters are introduced as *itihāsam purātanam*. Evidently, their authors considered them to contain authentic, details of a known past. There are, no doubt, some chapters which have been given a mythological colour. But in others the historical core is evident. The

29. See *infra* chapter 6.

30. *A History of Indian Literature*, Vol. I, p. 465.

Sāṁkhya *ācāryas* are associated with historical personalities who can be identified and dated. Thus, according to the authors of the chapters in the Mokṣadharmaparva, the Sāṁkhya accounts refer to known Sāṁkhya *ācāryas* who belonged to a datable past. The accounts have been affected by the format and style of the authors/compilers of the chapters. But that need not cast any doubt about the historicity of the Sāṁkhya *ācāryas* and the kernel of their expositions. Within the limitations of the presentation we have to recognise in them principles attributed to Sāṁkhya *ācāryas* of an earlier period. On account of their differences from the *Sāṁkhyakārikā* they need not be dubbed as proto-Sāṁkhya. They were Sāṁkhya expositions in a specific period and had their own distinguishing features.

APPROACHES TO THE HISTORY OF SĀṀKHYA

Beginnings

We want to emphasise that the general view, identifying Sāṁkhya with a set, fixed and static exposition of principles, does not stand the scrutiny of the historical method. Sāṁkhya has not been a monolithic system, nor has its development been unilinear. Long before the standardisation brought about by Īśvarakṛṣṇa it had a rich literature and a wide variation of exposition of principles. This long period witnessed an interesting history of changes, vital shifts, elaboration and introduction of new details, and debates and difference of opinion. The history of Sāṁkhya had its own course of development. In its growth it gained through new situations and the influence of other systems. But it would be wrong to view Sāṁkhya as the product of the piercing together of other elements or the result of the grafting of ideas received from time to time. Scholars have variously suggested Vedic, non-Vedic and tribal origins for Sāṁkhya. In earlier times also philosophers were at pains pointing out Vedic and non-Vedic features of Sāṁkhya in support of their own views about its origins. Sāṁkhya arose in the Vedic circles, though it did not fully subscribe to the Vedic cult of sacrifices. Sacrifices have a limited efficiency. For freedom from *duḥkha* and for emancipation the Vedic circle had a distinct class of thinkers. They were not anti-Vedic. They followed reason. They expounded their views in a well-reasoned manner. Their views circulated in their own closed circles and were not disseminated among the common people.

Early phase

At this stage possibly several slightly differing views were circulating. It was Kapila who formulated an ordered system out of the mass of views. Kapila is said to have enunciated the esoteric knowledge of *prakṛti* being for the sake of *puruṣa* (*puruṣārtha-jñāna*) in which were contemplated the existence, creation and dissolution of the beings. Modern scholars often dismiss Kapila as a mythological figure. This is primarily due to the high veneration given to him in ancient texts. On account of the importance of his contributions posterity raised him to the position of a divine being. It is not possible to identify the text, if any, composed by Kapila.

Āsuri, the immediate successor of Kapila, remains a little known person. The very fact that in his very brief account of the early history of Sāṁkhya, Īśvarakṛṣṇa chose to include his name testifies to his historicity. His most significant role was in receiving the Sāṁkhya principles from Kapila and transmitting them to Pañcaśikha. This would suggest that neither Kapila nor Āsuri put down their formulation in the form of a text. But, a later quotation from Āsuri makes a case for Kapila and Āsuri also having given a concrete shape to their exposition.

Pañcaśikha is to be regarded as the first systematiser of Sāṁkhya. He laid down set principles for Sāṁkhya as a philosophical system. He formulated Sāṁkhya as consisting of sixty principles. In the Jain sources some early references indicate this nature of Sāṁkhya. Pañcaśikha gave a detailed exposition of the Sāṁkhya philosophy. He was possibly the first to offer a standard work on Sāṁkhya. The Sāṁkhya principles included ten *mūlikārtha*s and fifty *pratyaya-sarga*s. Quotations surviving in later texts indicate some of the important points made by him. Though the *Sāṁkhya-pravacanasūtra*, in its present form, seems to contain later accretions as well, possibly in its original form it was close to the Sāṁkhya system as laid down by Pañcaśikha.

Post-Pañcaśikha phase

It is difficult to trace the full history of Sāṁkhya after Pañcaśikha. We have references to a number of Sāṁkhya scholars. Some of these are mere names. In some lists the mythological names are mixed up with historical ones. Establishing sequence in them remains a difficult problem. But some lists retain a distinctly historical appearance. Who among these *ācārya*s first formulated Sāṁkhya philosophy in terms of twenty-five categories cannot be determined. The Sāṁkhya tradition does not contain a specific reference. In course of time it was recognised as the most standard enunciation of Sāṁkhya philosophy. Later tradition, unmindful of the historical evolution of the Sāṁkhya system, attributed the authorship of the twenty-five categories to Kapila, the founder, himself. The testimony of the *Devaladharmasūtra* would indicate that formulation of Sāṁkhya in terms of the twenty-five categories had occurred before this text.

The post-Pañcaśikha period was very creative in the history of Sāṁkhya. It was rich not only in the number of eminent *ācārya*s. It was characterised by a wide variety of expositions in the details of the principles. The terminology had not been finally fixed. The number of categories was still being discussed. The *ācārya*s of the period are venerated as Sāṁkhyavr̥ddhas or Maulikya Sāṁkhyas. The *Carakasaṁhitā* mentions them. The *Yuktidīpikā* refers to some of them. The *Buddhacarita* mentions Arāḍa of this phase. The Mokṣadharmaparva records the names of some of these and certain important features of their thought, though modified by the format of the chapters. This early phase can be roughly placed between 650 and 500 BC.

Īśvarakr̥ṣṇa refers to two important features of the Sāṁkhya literature of the earlier period — *ākhyāyikā* and *paravāda*. *Ākhyāyikā* refers to narrative. The accounts of Sāṁkhya in the Mokṣadharmaparva are often presented in the form of ancient narratives. We are not sure of there were other texts in this form. Īśvarakṛṣṇa refers to these Sāṁkhya narratives which he avoided in his exposition. Whatever be the date of the *ācārya*s represented in them, the composition of the chapters may be placed around 300-200 BC.

Paravāda refers to another important development in Sāṁkhya history. Sāṁkhya in establishing itself as a philosophical system, had to meet the criticism of other systems and to vindicate its own position. This was the period of elaboration of the exposition, of debates and discussion and of arguments in support of the principles. The phase acquired prominence through Vārṣagaṇya and gained force through his followers. Vindhyavāsin was the foremost teacher of this tradition. We place this phase after 300 BC. Some notable Sāṁkhya views of this phase are noted in the writings of other philosophical systems as painstakingly ferretted out by E. Frauwallner and P. Hacker.

The ascent of Sāṁkhya on the philosophical horizon of India, from the colourful richness of the dawn to the shining brilliance of the meridian, is a fascinating travail. Īśvarakṛṣṇa represents Sāṁkhya at its zenith. He himself proclaims his allegiance to the tradition of *ṣaṣthitantra*. For this he names only Kapila, Āsuri and Pañcaśikha. Īśvarakṛṣṇa has monopolised focal attention in Sāṁkhya studies. For this reason we have not attempted a study of Īśvarakṛṣṇa and post-Īśvarakṛṣṇa developments. For the present we have not discussed the *ṣaṣthitantra* tradition of Kapila, Āsuri and Pañcaśikha. We have emphasised schools and *ācārya*s other than these, because their contributions are not duly studied in the history of Sāṁkhya.

Approaches

Before finally attempting the history of Sāṁkhya and the development through stages covering all aspects of the system, including its *ācārya*s, texts and principles, we may approach the subject from different points. In the absence of requisite information about the nature of principles at different stages, we may resort to an analysis of the contributions of various *ācāryas* and the characteristic views of the schools.

(a) Structure: The development can be traced in terms of a number of points. One possible manner is through the structure of the texts. From the *Yuktidīpikā* we learn that initially Sāṁkhya was presented as Tantra. The *Ṣaṣṭhitantra* was possibly the earliest work. The Jain sources mention this name in referring to the early Sāṁkhya system. The prestige accorded to *Ṣaṣṭhitantra* by Īśvarakṛṣṇa is an admission of its being the earliest exposition. This is admitted by Frauwallner when he credits Vāraṣagaṇya with the authorship of the *Ṣaṣṭhitantra*.

Later we find the vogue for presenting Sāṁkhya as *Saptati*. The Jain tradition mentions (*Kanakasaptati*) as an early title in the Sāṁkhya system. We have suggested that it was the composition of Vārṣagaṇya. Vasubandhu, in his attack on the Sāṁkhya position, named his work as *Paramārthasaptati*. In his final exposition Īśvarakṛṣṇa chose to have seventy verses (*satpati*), though naming it as *kārikā*.

(b) Principles: Another approach can be in terms of the principles. In the absence of relevant details it is not possible to present a full account of the various stages in the development of principles. But certain important landmarks can be noted. *Puruṣārthatā* seems to have been an important principle expressed by Kapila. This was elaborated into the concept of ten *mūlikārthas*. Pañcaśikha, in expounding sixty principles (*ṣaṣṭhitantra*), mentioned both the ten *mūlikārthas* and the fifty *pratyaya-sargas*. This was later replaced by the exposition in terms of categories. Twenty-five came to be accepted as the standard number. There was a period when varying numbers of categories were enumerated. We cannot be sure about the author of this system of exposition, but it had emerged before the composition of the *Devaladharmasūtra*.

(c) Relationship with yoga: One significant point for delineating the history of Sāṁkhya is its relationship with the allied system of Yoga. Depending on their views about the changes in the closeness and separation of the two, scholars have determined stages in the history of Sāṁkhya. Larson and Battacharya, in their recent study, have designated the Yoga expounded in the *Yogasūtra* of Patañjali as Pātañjala Sāṁkhya and have allocated a detailed treatment to it as a distinct exposition of Sāṁkhya. The earliest period in the history of Sāṁkhya and Yoga being shrouded in obscurity we cannot assert positively about the history of Sāṁkhya in its correlationship with Yoga. Archaeological evidence suggests the currency of Yoga in the Indus Valley civilisation. The speculative nature of Sāṁkhya system is not expected to receive archaeological confirmation. Sāṁkhya and Yoga are so much allied that they are considered to be twin systems, as two aspects of the same, Sāṁkhya being the speculative basis of the practical Yoga. The two go together as supplimentaries.

We cannot posulate that for the long current *yoga* practices Sāṁkhya was evolved as a philosophical support at a later stage. Possibly the two coexisted but, because of its very nature, Sāṁkhya could receive expression later. Subsequently Sāṁkhya and Yoga started developing in their own spheres. At this stage efforts were made to emphasise the unity of the two. In the Mokṣadharmaparva some Sāṁkhya *ācāryas* are said to have expounded the two together and to have asserted that they are not separate and different. In the *Buddhacarita* also Arāḍa, a pre-Buddha Sāṁkhya teacher, expounds Sāṁkhya and Yoga as two methods of the same system. Thus, the post-Pañcaśikha phase does not represent an effort to fuse two different systems. It asserted the oneness of the two allied systems, which were tending to develop independently. The Sāṁkhya base of Yoga is evidenced from this early period. It need not be postponed to the period of the *Yogasūtra* of Patañjali, which again need not be pushed to a date later than the *Sāṁkhyakārikā*.

(d) Belief in god: Some scholars determine the stages in the history of Sāṁkhya in terms of its belief in the existence of God or rejecting it.[31] The sequence of transformation is presented differently. One formulation is that the originally atheistic Sāṁkhya becomes theistic and finally settles down as atheistic. Another possibility

31. *Epic Mythology*, p. 1.

suggested is that Sāṁkhya was theistic in the beginning, but later developed as atheistic. We suggest that there have been no such radical changes in the Sāṁkhya position. The Sāṁkhya view has been that God has no place in its philosophical scheme. But beyond the philosophical sphere it does not categorically dismiss the existence of god or gods.

(C) CHANGING MEANING OF SĀṀKHYA

Three usages of Sāṁkhya

G.J. Larson and R.S. Battacharya take the term *sāṁkhya* to mean 'relating to number, enumeration, or calculation'. According to them, there are three dimensions of the meaning in the word, which refer to corresponding three identifiable phases if its development. In the first phase, from the Vedic period to the beginning of the Christian era, Sāṁkhya is one of the three traditions of *ānvīkṣikī*. The terms *sāṁkhya, ānvīkṣikī* and *tantra* do not refer to philosophy in its usual sense they are "the first and groping attempts at systematic thinking, which proceeded by determining and enumerating the components of anything". It "could, refer generally to any enumerated set of principles".

In the second phase, from the period of the pre-Buddhistic Upaniṣads, (eighth or seventh centuries BC) reaching into the first centuries of the Christian era, Sāṁkhya is primarily a methodology for attaining salvation by knowledge. It allows for a great variety of philosophical formulations, but does not imply any system of metaphysical truth whatever. What Larson had described as Proto-Sāṁkhya, in his first study, he now terms as Kapila-Pañcaśikha-Sāṁkhya, Kapila-Pañcaśikha-Tantra, or Kapila Tantra.

The third phase extends from about the last century BC through the first several centuries of the Christian era. Now Sāṁkhya becomes a technical philosophical system. The *Kārikā* comes at the end of this normative period of formulation, which is preceded by a pre-*Kārikā* phase. Frauwallner has shown the Sāṁkhya epistemology of this phase. Hacker has reconstructed its ontology-cosmology.

Larson and Bhattacharya proceed by assuming that the term Sāṁkhya means enumeration or calculation. They do not pay attention to the fact that the term has other derivations, which lead to different meanings, nor do they demonstrate the change in its meaning in different phases. They have only indicated the change in the contents and scope of Sāṁkhya, maintaining that in the later phases the original meaning of the term as enumeration or calculation persisted, though it received a changed expression. Without meaning to controvert the main thesis of phases in the development of Sāṁkhya, it may be pointed out that the persistence of the supposed original meaning of the term, through all the stages, is not evidenced. The changes in the nature of the principles expounded and the details of the contents do not by themselves imply that the term had undergone a parallel change in meaning. The fact is not to be assumed, it has to be proved.

The meaning assigned to the term in the first stage does not stand closer scrutiny. It has been suggested that the three terms *ānvīkṣikī*, *sāṁkhya* and *tantra* have the same meaning. The terms are, no doubt, allied and have much in common in their approach and scope. But they are by no means synonymous. They have their specific nature and scope. *Ānvīkṣikī* is a wider term. Sāṁkhya comes under the broad category of *ānvīkṣikī*. It is one of the constituent elements in *ānvīkṣikī*, Tantra signifies a system and also a composition expounding it. Sāṁkhya is one of the earliest systems and was often designated as a Tantra. Some of the early Sāṁkhya accounts were named as Tantras. The rules governing the presentation of the system in a Tantra were designated as *tantra-yukti*. Very early we find the adoption of these rules by the Āyurvedic tradition and the *Arthaśāstra*. The *Yuktidīpikā* was written with the avowed purpose of demonstrating that the *Sāṁkhyakārikā* implements them.

For determining the meaning of *ānvīkṣikī* and *sāṁkhya* the context in the *Arthaśāstra* is to be looked into. The terms occur in chapters 2 to 4 of the first book (*adhikaraṇa*). These chapters (as *prakaraṇa* 1) deal with subjects of knowledge or sciences (*vidyā*). *Ānvīkṣikī* is one of the four *vidyā*s, the other three being *trayī*, *vārtā* and *daṇḍa-nīti*. The four have their own approaches and objectives, but are also identified in terms of their contents, topics or subjects. Thus *trayī* (Vedic love) is defined as including the three Vedas, besides *Atharvaveda* and *Itihāsaveda* and the *Vedāṅgas*. *Vārtā* is constituted of *kṛṣi* (agriculture), *paśu-pālana* (cattle-rearing) and *vāṇijya* (trade). *Ānvīkṣikī* is given a higher importance as the camp of all sciences, as the means of all actions, and as the support of all laws and duties. *Ānvikṣikī* can investigate, by means of reasoning (*hatubhir avnīkṣamāṇa*), the objectives in the other *vidyās*. To describe *ānvīkṣikī* as merely the first attempt at systematic thinking and Sāṁkhya as one of its three traditions is not enough. Realising that the term philosophy has its own implications in the Western tradition, all of which may not be present in the case of India, we have to admit that, with all its distinctive features and limitations *ānvīkṣikī* is to be taken to mean philosophy. It is clear from the reference to *sāṁkhyam*, *yogaḥ* and *lokāyatam* as constituting *ānvikṣkī*. These three are not more three traditions of *ānvīkṣikī* with their distinguishing approaches. If Sāṁkhya is explained as the method of enumeration or calculation, we cannot find a comparable characteristic methodology referring to Lokāyata. The *Arthaśāstra* itself does not give any indication to support the proposed meaning of Sāṁkhya. The passage leads to the natural conclusion that here we have an early reference to the three earliest 'philosophical' systems in India. Sāṁkhya and Yoga are generally recognised as such, and there is evidence to indicate it for Lokāyata also. Without asserting anything about the nature and contents of principles, we interpret the *Arthaśāstra* evidence as an early recognition of Sāṁkhya as one of the three main philosophical systems. In any case the *Arthaśāstra* does not confirm that in that period the term *sāṁkhya* meant any system based on enumeration or calculation.

Sāṁkhya as a system underwent changes in its nature, its objectives, emphasis and principles. The enumeration of categories became one of its distinguishing features. But we cannot categorically assert that this was so in the initial stages. Possibly this feature was identified in course of time. In any case, evidence has not been adduced to show that the term *sāṁkhya* witnessed changes in its derivation and meaning, matching the later phases in its growth culminating in a technical philosophical system.

Derivation From Sāṁkhya

The meaning of the term *sāṁkhya* differs according to the explanation offered for the word *saṁkhyā*, from which it is derived. This, in its turn, varies according to the interpretation offered for the two parts of the word *saṁkhyā*, namely the prefix *saṁ* and the root *khyā*. The differing explanations of the word *saṁkhyā* proposed by ancient authorities are reflected in the interpretations offered by modern scholars, R. Garbe, H. Oldenberg, H. Jacobi and M. Eliade. Edgerton[32] holds that in older texts Sāṁkhya is not a technical designation for a particular system of thought; it signifies its derivative meaning of the method 'based on reason, ratiocination', it is the rationalising, reflective, speculative, philosophical method. He takes it to refer to the method of gaining salvation by 'knowledge'.

The most significant question in this connection is, which of the various meanings of the term *sāṁkhya* is the original and the earliest. Are we to suppose that the term primarily referred to the idea of number of enumeration and hence stood for those which communicated their principles through an enumeration of categories? Or are we to suggest that it signified a rationalising philosophical system or a method of attaining salvation by knowledge? It may be incidentally pointed out that, when Īśvarakṛṣṇa refers to the history of the Sāṁkhya principles, he used the expression *samākhyātam* (expounded) for the presentation of 'this secret knowledge (*guhya*) of other elements being for the sake of *puruṣa*' (*puruṣārtha-jñāna*) by the greatest sage Kapila.[33] We may suggest that the use of the expression *samākhyātam* is not causal. Possibly, Īśvarakṛṣṇa, in referring to the original formulation of the Sāṁkhya principles, deliberately chose it to indicate the original meaning of the term *sāṁkhya*.

---

32. See *infra* chapter 16.

33. *Encyclopaedia of Indian Philosophies*, ed. by K. Potter, Vol. IV — *Sāṁkhya*, pp. 3-14.

Sāṁkhya Meaning Reasoning

The name Sāṁkhya can be derived from *saṁkhyā* but not in the sense of number. The *Amarakośa*[34] paraphrases *saṁkhyā* to mean discussion and investigation. This usage is confirmed by the *Amarakośa*,[35] when later it gives *saṁkhyāvān* as one of the synonyms of *vidvān*.

Raghunātha Tarkavāgīśa (nineteenth century)[36] seems to have followed Amara when he explains *saṁkhyā*, from which *sāṁkhya* is derived, as meaning consideration (*vicāra*). Śrīdharasvāmī and Sūryapaṇḍita[37] paraphrase *saṁkhyā* to mean right (*samyak*) knowledge. Devatīrthasvāmin (1772-1852) elaborates *samyak* as meaning 'enunciation in an order' or 'consideration in an orderly manner'.[38]

It would be pertinent to find out if this usage has the sanction of a reference in an early text. In the *Arthaśāstra*[39] of Kauṭilya as we have seen, both Sāṁkhya and Yoga, along with Lokāyata are mentioned as being the discipline (*vidyā*) of *ānvīkṣikī*. *Ānvīkṣikī* is interpreted as meaning logic or metahysics. The rational approach characterising it is implied in the root *ikṣā* 'to see', from which it is formed. R.P. Kangle translates *ānvīkṣikī* as philosophy. P. Chakravarti justifiably explains it as 'the system which tries to establish the validity of its tenets by the process of logical reasonings'.[40] The *Arthaśāstra* makes the approach of *ānvīkṣikī*

---

34. *Beginnings of Indian Philosophy*, pp. 35-7.
35. *Sāṁkhyakārikā*, 69.
36. I.5.2 — *carcā saṁkhyā vicāranā* ǀ
37. II.7.5 — *vidvān . . . sāṃkhyāvān paṇḍitaḥ kaviḥ* ǀ
38. *Sāṁkhyatattvavilāsa — pañcaviṁśatitatvānāṁ saṁkhyā vicāraḥ* ǀ *tamadhikṛtya kṛto granthaḥ sāṁkhya iti sāṁkhyapadavyutpattiḥ saṁgacchate* ǀ
39. Śrīdharasvāmin (*Sudodhinī* on *Gītā*) and Sūryapaṇḍita (*Paramārthaprapā*) — *sāṁkhya samyag jñānam*.
40. *Sāṁkhyataraṅga — samyak kramapūrakaṁ khyānaṁ kathanaṁ yasyāṁ as saṁkhyā kramapūrvā vicāraṇā. yat tāmadhikṛtya kṛtaṁ tasmāt sāṁkhyamityucyate śāstram* ǀ

clear by observing that by investigation (*anvīkṣamāṇā*) by means of reasoning (*hetu*) the relative strength and weakness of the other three sciences, it confers benefit on the people, keeps the mind steady in adversity and in prosperity and brings about proficiency in thought, speech and action. It is described as the lamp (*pradīpa*) of all sciences.[41]

This is quite in line with the testimony of chapter 320 in the Śāntiparva of the *Mahābhārata*. The chapter, which is in the form of an interlocution between Sulabhā and Janaka, contains an exposition of Sāṁkhya principles. It is significant that here the term *sāṁkhya* is used not in the sense of a system of philosophy, it signifies one of the five meaningful characteristics of a sentence.[42] It is defined as the enunciation of the defects and merits by proper analysis with a view to establishing a particular meaning.[43]

The *Yuktidīpikā* commentary on the *Sāṁkhyakārikā* brings out the characteristic of Sāṁkhya in establishing its view with the help of reasoning. It compares Sāṁkhya to an elephant, who roams in the forest of *pakṣatā* (subjectness) and has the *vīta* (positive) and *avīta* (negative) forms of inference as its tasks, and for it the *pravādas* (points of disputes) are perishable like the cluster of *śallakī* trees.[44] *Pakṣatā* or *pakṣadharmatā* is called the *pratijñā* (thesis) in the five-membered syllogism. It is what is to be proved by means of inference. It is the psychological condition of inference, the absence of uncertainty and a desire to know.

This shows that the method of reasoning was considered to be the distinguishing feature of Sāṁkhya. P. Chakravarti[45] is of the view that at the time of the composition of the *Brahmasūtra*

---

41. I.2.10 — *sāṁkhyaṁ sogo lokāyataṁ cetyānvīkṣikī* |
42. *Origin and Development of Sāṁkhya System of Thought*, p. 41.
43. I.2.11-12.
44. XII.320.79 — *saukṣmyaṁ sāṁkhyakramau cobhau nirṇayaḥ saprayojanaḥ* |
pañcaitānyarthajñānṁ vākyamityucyate nṛpa |
45. XII.320.82 — *doṣāṇāṁ ca guṇānāṁ ca pramāṇaṁ pravibhāgataḥ* |
kaṁcidarthamabhipretya sā saṁkhyetyupadhāryatām |

Saṁkhya was 'famous for its rationalism'. He bases this view on the fact that the *Brahmasūtra* 'which is always very keen to refute the doctrine of Sāṁkhya speaks of the *prakṛti* as the *anumāna* or *ānumānika* (lit. based upon inference).[46]

Sāṁkhya as Spiritual Discipline — Parisaṁkhyāna

In earlier times Sāṁkhya does not seem to signify a system of philosophy with twenty-four or twenty-five categories. In the absence of clear statements about the meaning of the term Sāṁkhya in those times and the characteristic principles to which it subscribed, we can have only vague ideas about its connotation. There are indications that the term *sāṁkhya* was used to signify spiritual discipline. According to the *Śvetāśvatara Upaniṣad*[47] one achieves the supreme reality through Sāṁkhya and Yoga. It is significant that in the *Mahābhārata*[48] Droṇa, before breathing his last is said to have been established in supreme Sāṁkhya.

An early definition of Sāṁkhya, recorded in the *Vyāsasmṛti*,[49] describes it as the knowledge of the principle of true self (*śuddhātmattva-vijñāna*). The traditions in the Yoga school use the term *parasaṁkhyāna* in the sense of supreme knowledge. This usage is found in the *Yogasūtra*[50] of Patañjali and is maintained in the *Yoga-sūtra-bhāṣya* of Vyāsa. The *Yogasūtra* says that a *yogī*, who even after acquiring *parisaṁkhyāna* does not desire to possess its results (*akusīda*) and receives the discerning knowledge (*viveka-khyāti*), reaches the concentration (*samādhi*) named Dharmamegha. The use of the form *parisaṁkhyāna* for higher level of knowledge in Yoga, an allied system of Sāṁkhya, is significant. Further, in the *sūtra* we find that the term *khyāti* (having the same derivative meaning as *saṁkhyā*, *sāṁkhyāna* and *sāṁkhya*) is used to refer to

---

46. *vītāvītaviṣāṇasya pakṣatāvanasevinaḥ* ।
pravādāḥ sāṁkhyakariṇaḥ śallakīṣaṇḍabhaṅguraḥ ।
47. *Op. cit.*, p. 41.
48. I.1.18; I.3.3; I.4.1; II.2.1.
49. VI.13.
50. VII.192. 49—*droṇo'pi śastrāṇyatsṛjya paramaṁ sāṁkhyamāṣṭhitaḥ* ।

the knowledge of the *yogī* possessing *parisaṁkhyāna*.

The technical usage of the terms *parisaṁkhyāna* and *khyāti* in *Yogasūtra* supports the interpretation of Sāṁkhya originally as reasoned knowledge. Vyāsa, in his commentary,[51] brings out this meaning of *parisaṁkhyāna*. He refers to those who see the defects of objects (*viṣaya-doṣa*) using *prasaṁkhyāna*, to the afflictions (*kleśa*) being reduced by the fire of *prasaṁkhyāna*, to the contemplation (*dhyāna*) of *prasaṁkhyāna* and to the seeds of afflictions (*kleśa*) being burnt by *prasaṁkhyāna*. The use of *prasaṁkhyāna* in Yoga is significant, because a verse in the *Mahābhārata*[52] unequivocally describes Sāṁkhya-*darśana* as *parisaṁkhyāna-darśana*.

This usage of *prasaṁkhyāna* is also found in the *Ahirbudhnya-saṁhitā* of the Pañcarātra sect. In it Kapila is said to bestow the divine highest *siddhi* (spiritual power) full of *prasaṁkhyāna*,[53] which will have to be explained as referring to the exposition of knowledge. Another passage in the same text says that the *śāstra*, which Kapila proclaimed, became the Sāṁkhya *śāstra* devoted to *prasaṁkhyāna*.[54]

---

51. Śaṅkara's Commentary on *Viṣṇusahasranāma* quoted by Hall, *Sāṁkhyasāra*, p. 5 — *śuddhātmatattvavijñānaṁ sāṁkhya-mityabhidhiyate iti vyāsasmṛteḥ* । Śrīdharasvāmī (*Subodhinī* on *Gītā* II.39) followed by Sūryapaṇḍita (*Paramārtha-prapā*) seem to have adopted it — *sāṁkhyā samyag jñānam* । *tasmin prakāśamānam* (*prakāśyam* by Sūryapaṇḍita) *ātmatatvaṁ sāṁkhyam* ॥

52. IV.29 — *prasāṁkhyane'pyakusīdasya sarvathā vivekakhyāter-dharmameghaḥ samādhiḥ* ।

53. I.15 — *viṣayadoṣadarśinaḥ prasaṁkhyānabalāt . . . vairāgyam* ।

II.2 — *prasaṁkhyānāgninā pratanūkṛtān kleśān* ।

II.11 — *prasaṁkhyānena dhyānana hātavyaḥ* ।

II.13 — *prasaṁkhyānadagdhakleśabijabhāvaḥ* ।

54. XII.306.42 — *sāṁkhyadarśanametāvat parisaṁkhyāna-darśanam* । Suryanarayan Sastri (*Sāṁkhyakārikā*, Introduction, p. 9) confuses the significance of the passage by interpreting *parisaṁkhyāna* as meaning abandonment. The interpretation, as remarked by L.D. Barnett (Review in *JRAS*, 1931) is not at all convincing and is without any support.

The term Sāṁkhya in Caraka-saṁhitā

The *Caraka-saṁhitā* provides an interesting support for our suggestion that Sāṁkhya acquired its name because it was originally a system of reasoned exposition of knowledge. In one verse[55] there is a clear reference to Sāṁkhya as a system of philosophy, because it mentions Yoga also. Here the Sāṁkhyas are described as *saṁkhyāta-dharmas*. *Saṁkhyāta* means 'expounded well' it cannot signify 'enumerated', because there is no question of an enumeration of *dharma*.[56] The interpretation of *saṁkhyāta* as derived from *saṁkhyā* in the sense of reasoned exposition is confirmed by another verse in the *Caraka-saṁhitā*.[57] Here Sāṁkhya does not stand for Sāṁkhya thinkers, but for experts of *Āyurveda*, who are thus described as 'having good knowledge'. The Sāṁkhyas are mentioned as *saṁkhāta-saṁkhyeyas*, which is to be interpreted as those who have well expounded subjects which are to be expounded well. Clearly all these three terms *sāṁkhya*, *saṁkhyāta* and *saṁkyeya* can be explained by taking the basic term *saṁkhyā* to mean exposition. This is significant because Caraka seems to be well acquainted with the Sāṁkhya system.[58]

Sāṁkhya and Khyāti

All doubts about the derivation of the term Sāṁkhya and its original meaning are set at rest by a *sūtra* quoted by Vyāsa in his *Yogabhāṣya*.[59] It says that there is only one *darśana*, *khyāti* alone

---

55. 56.31 — *siddhiṁ dadāti yo divyāṁ prasaṁkhyānamayīṁ parām* |
devaḥ siddhipradārṇena kapilaḥ sa nigadyate ||

56. XI.58 — *tatakṣa kapilaḥ śāstrādyavadaṁśamudāradhīḥ* |
tatsāṁkhyamabhavacchāstraṁ prasaṁkhyānaparāyaṇam ||

57. *Śārīra*, I.150 — *ayanaṁ punarākhyatametad yogasya yogibhiḥ* |
saṁkhyātadharmaiḥ sāṁkhyaiśea muktairmokṣasya cāyanam ||

58. In the first line of the verse the word *ākhyāta* is used to mean 'described' or 'designated', which supports the interpretation of *saṁkhyāta* offered by us.

59. *Sūtra* XIII.3 — *saṁkhyaiḥ saṁkhyātasaṁkhyeyaiḥ sahāsīnaṁ punarvasum* |
jagaddhitārthaṁ papraccha vahniveśaḥ svasaṁśayam |

is the *darśana*. Here the expression is *khyāti* and not *sāṁkhyāti* or *sāṁkhya*. *Khyāti* means exposition. It shows that in *saṁkhya* the root is *khyā* with the *upasarga saṁ* prefixed to it to indicate 'proper' (*samyak*). The term *sāṁkhya* hence originally was not derived from *saṁkhyā* meaning number.

Changes in the Derivative Meaning of Sāṁkhya

A passage in the *Mahābhārata*[60] seems to represent a stage of transition in the meaning of the term *sāṁkhya* from its original usage to the new one imposed on it. Here both the meanings are mixed up. *Saṁkhyā* refers to reasoned exposition, but there is a reference to the number of the *tattvas*. The passage says that reasoned exposition (*saṁkhyā*) is done and *prakṛti* is expounded and the *tattvas* are said to be twenty-four. Hence the expounders are described as Sāṁkhyas. The dual usages of Sāṁkhya is repeated in another passage of the *Mahābhārata*.[61] It describes Sāṁkhya as the *darśana* of *parisaṁkhyāna*. The reasoned exposition is done and *prakṛti* is described and twenty-four *tattvas* also for a proper exposition (*parasaṁkhyāya*) according to the *tattvas*; the Sāṁkhya philosophers (*sāṁkhyāḥ*) mention along with *prakṛti* the *nistattva* (or *puruṣa*) as the twenty-fifth. The parallels in the expressions in the two passages indicate that they look back to a common source. On account of the irregular expressions in the verses, which possibly could not be touched by the compiler, the true significance of the original meaning of Sāṁkhya, as expressed in *parisaṁkhyāna* and *parisaṁkhya*, is not properly communicated by the expression *saṁkhyā*.

In the *Bhāgavata Purāṇa*[62] we find the expression *tattvānāṁ saṁkhyātā*. This can be explained either way, to the exposition of the *tattvas* and to the enumeration of the *tattvas*. Vallabhācārya, in his commentary, maintains the ambiguity and does not commit

60. See *infra* chapter 6.

61. I.4—*tathā ca sūtram ekameva darśanaṁ khyātireva darśanam* | Also *Yuktidīpikā* on *Sāṁkhyakārikā* (p. 41).

62. XII.31.12 — *saṁkhyāṁ prakurvate caiva prakṛtiṁ ca pracakṣate* | *tattvāni ca caturviṁśat tena sāṁkhyāḥ prakīrtitāḥ* ||

himself to any of the two. He refers to the background of the uncertainty about the *tattvas* (*tattvānāṁ sandigdhatvāt*) and paraphrases *tattvasaṁkhyātā* as *tattvasaṁkhyāna-karttā*; but substituting *sāṁkhyātā* by *sāṁkhyānakarttā* does not help the matter, because the verb *saṁkhyā* and its derivative noun *sāṁkhyāna* can have either of the two explanations.

Possibly even after the Sāṁkhya had acquired its characteristic feature of enumeration of twenty-five *tattvas*, its original nature as expounding reasoned knowledge persisted.

It is only Śrīdharasvāmi, in his commentary on the *Bhāgavata Purāṇa* passage, who makes an unambiguous assertion that *saṁkhyātā* means one who counts or enumerates (*gaṇaka*).[63] Grammatically the term *sāṁkhya* can be derived from *saṁkhyā* meaning number. Patañjali[64] uses *sāṁkhya* to mean something pertaining to number. He does it so only to illustrate the grammatical rule. There is absolutely no indication that Sāṁkhya here refers to a philosophical system.

An Ignorant Explanation

Guṇaratna's commentary on the *Ṣaḍdarśana-samuccaya*[65] gives a strange explanation of the name Sāṁkhya. Relying on an ancient tradition (*vṛddhāmnāya*), it says that the Sāṁkhya system was also known as Sāṁkhya. According to Guṇaratna, there was in early times a man of special qualities, named as Śaṅkha. His descendants, his grandsons and others were designated as *śāṁkhyāḥ* by suffixing *yañ pratyaya*. The system propounded by them is known as *sāṁkhya* or *śāṁkhya*. Guṇaratna's assertion is not valid.

63. XII. 306. 42-3—*sāṁkhyadarśanametāvadparisaṁkhyānadarśanam* ǀ
saṁkhyāḥ prakurvate caiva prakṛtiṁ ca pracakṣate ǀǀ
tattvāni ca caturviṁśat parisaṁkhyāya tattvataḥ ǀ
sāṁkhyāḥ saha prakṛtyā tu nistatvapaṁcaviṁśaka ǀ

Sāṁkhyāḥ in v. 42 is a mistake for *saṁkhyām*.

64. III.24.36 — *etanme janma loke'smin mumukṣūṇām durāśayāt* ǀ *prasaṁkhyānāya tattvānāṁ saṁmatāyātmadarśane* ǀǀ See also III.25.1.

65. *tattvānāṁ saṁkhyātā gaṇakaḥ sāṁkhyapravartaka ityarthaḥ* ǀ

We have no evidence about the system being designated as Śāṁkhya. In all the sources it is always named as Sāṁkhya. In the unnamed source, relied upon by Guṇaratna, the name of the original founder of the system is not given. It is attributed to an anonymous descendant of Śaṅkha. Guṇaratna does not give any specific, detail, which may help his identification, except saying that he was an eminent man.

Guṇaratna's statement indicates that in later times, when the Jain scholar did not have any access to the Sāṁkhya as a living system, he could not make himself believe either the then current view that Sāṁkhya is so termed because it enumerates the *tattva*s or the other explanation that it is so named because it was based on reasoned exposition, and hence imagined this fanciful explanation. This apparently indicatess his ignorance and is not based on an authentic earlier tradition.

Conclusion

Thus, we see that the original meaning of the term *sāṁkhya* was a reasoned exposition. This usage persisted in later times, even when an alternative derivation from *saṁkhyā* in the sense of number had been coined. Originally Sāṁkhya did not refer to any system of philosophy. It meant philosophy in general. All sorts of philosophical speculations were covered by the term. There was no distinguishing feature of the contents of these speculations, except that they were rationally considered, as contrasted with the way of rituals and sacrifices. It ran parallel to the sacrificial system, which was the predominant form of religious activity of the Vedic people.

There are reasons to believe that this way of knowledge was esoteric in nature confined to its own circle. We do not know anything definite about the nature and composition of this group. We can, likewise, only guess the reasons for keeping their views secret. It is quite likely that such people were limited in number. Considering the general prevalence of the system of sacrifices, they could not dare to make public their differing approach. They possibly followed the sacrificial system, but secretly cultivated their ideas based on a rational exposition of things. It can be imagined that the group could not remain undetected for long, even though their characteristic ideas could not gain much public pronouncement.

In the Vedic literature we find reference to two types of ascetics, the *yati*s and the *muni*s; differentiated from the *ṛṣi*s or Vedic sages. Some scholars identify them as representing the Śramaṇa stream. The antiquity of the Śramaṇa tradition and its various manifestations and their significant contributions to Indian thought and culture are now generally admitted. The Sāṁkhya tradition, committed to speculations and reasoned expositions, was associated with the Śramaṇas.

There is an indication that in between the two stages of Sāṁkhya derivatively signifying reasoned exposition and its subsequent transformation into a philosophical system there was an intermediate stage when it was used as the term for philosophy in general. A *sūtra* noted by us earlier, is ascribed by Vācaspatimiśra[66] to Pañcaśikha. It says that there is only one *darśana*; *khyāti* alone is *darśana*. It seems that Sāṁkhya became a synonym for *darśana*. Sāṁkhya meant philosophy. Later, it was recognised as *the* only philosophy. Thus, Sāṁkhya from siginifying philosophy, came to stand for *the* philosophy. Possibly there were some other expositions also. If the ascription of the *sūtra* to Pañcaśikha is accepted,[67] it will indicate that Sāṁkhya was recognised as the pre-eminent philosophy.

---

66. *Mahābhāṣya* on II.2.24. Under *Vārtika* 8 — *laiṅgāḥ sāṁkhyāśca vidhayo niḥsidhyanti* ।

    Under *Vārtika* 9 —
    sāṁkhyeṣvapyuktam karmādīnāmanuktva ekatvādaya iti kṛtvā sāṁkhyā bhaviṣyanti ।

67. p. 22 — *yadvā tālavyādirapi sāṁkhyadhvanirastīti vṛddhāmnāyaḥ* । *tatra śaṁkhnānāmā kaścidādyaḥ puruṣaviśeṣastasyāpatyaṁ pautrādiriti gargāditvāt yañpratyaye śāṁkhyāsteṣāmidaṁ sāṁkhyaṁ sāṁkhyaṁ va* ।।

2

Sāṁkhya and Vedic Tradition

Introduction

G.J. LARSON, in his classic work *Classical Sāṁkhya*, makes a very judicious and balanced analysis of Sāṁkhya philosophy, making a proper use of earlier studies of the subject. He favours the view that "Sāṁkhya is a derivative and composite system, a product of a wide variety of contexts, both orthodox and heterodox."[1] It is a very reasonable statement. History shows that ideas and institutions have often a composite origin and that their subsequent history is not a unilinear development. They grow and change according to new situations and forces, assimilating some and modifying in reaction to others. He would always like to identify the contributing sources and determine the elements issuing from them, both at the time of the original formulation and later growth. In any case the nature of formulation in the earlier stages has always a distinguishing significance.

Sāṁkhya Speculation in Vedic Literature

Larson identifies six traditions of speculations in ancient texts which were important in the formation of the Sāṁkhya. They are of a mixed nature, including both orthodox and heterodox elements. Of these, five traced in ancient Vedic speculation are: (a) mythological and cosmological passages exphasising order and chaos, *sat* and

---

1. Second edition, 1979, p. 95.

asat, etc., (b) cosmological speculations emphasising a tripartite creation in which the creative force or principle enters into the creation as the first-born, (c) speculations concerning *puruṣa* as the primal sacrifice and emphasising *puruṣa* as the essence or reason for the emergence of the world and of man, (d) speculations concerning the Self (*ātman*) as the radical foundation of subjectivity and consciousness, and (e) passages which set forth various kinds of enumeration some of which contain many *tattva*s of later Sāṁkhya. Larson identifies one such speculation in the non-Vedic doctrines of Jainism and Buddhism, e.g., *kaivalya* and *duḥkha*. The preponderance of speculations appearing in Vedic texts is a clear indication of Larson favouring a Vedic origin for Sāṁkhya. He himself makes it clear when he remarks that the carrying over into Sāṁkhya of some notions of Buddhism or Jainism do not imply that 'Sāṁkhya, arose in some ancient, non-Vedic tradition'.

A number of scholars have traced Sāṁkhya concepts and terms in Vedic literature. They identify passages in the various Upaniṣads, even the early ones. Some have pointed out references in the *Brāhmaṇa*s as well and find a few passages in the *Ṛgveda* itself. 'There are differences in details of the interpretation, which, in some cases, go to the extent of totally negating the view of one scholar about a certain passage. Thus, opinion may differ about the number of such passages and the actual meaning given to them. But scholars generally agree in identifying elements of Sāṁkhya in early Vedic literature beginning with the *Ṛgveda* and coming down to the Upaniṣads, though, leaving aside some later Upaniṣads, none of these passages make an avowed reference to the Sāṁkhya system. On the basis of such references many scholars have proclaimed the origin of the Sāṁkhya from Brāhmaṇical or Vedic tradition.

Joseph Dahlman takes the original form of Sāṁkhya as represented in the philosophical portions of the *Mahābhārata* to be theistic and a natural outgrowth of the speculation found in the *Brāhmaṇa*s and early Upaniṣads.[2] Paul Oltramare restricts the

2. *Die Sāṁkhya Philosophie als Naturlehre und Erlösungslehre*, pp. 1-19.

Vedic context of the Sāṁkhya to the ancient Upaniṣads.[3] Hermann Oldenberg does not differ from this view, when he infers that the Sāṁkhya 'has developed in a direct line out of the *Brahman-ātman* speculation of the old Upaniṣads'.[4] A.B. Keith is convinced about the origin of the Sāṁkhya being within the orthodox Vedic framework. He subjects the Vedas, *Brāhmaṇas* and Upaniṣads to a detailed and in-depth analysis[5] and traces a number of key concepts of Sāṁkhya in the Vedic literature. According to him, Sāṁkhya is most natural derivation, albeit illogical and absurd, of the early speculations in the Vedic literature, but no Upaniṣad gives the full classical system of the Sāṁkhya, because it had not received its final form in that period.[6] Franklin Edgerton holds a similar view about the Vedic connection of Sāṁkhya. According to him, the ancient Sāṁkhya was a method of salvation by knowing and it grew out of the speculations in the Vedas and Upaniṣads.[7] S.N. Dasgupta is also sure about the Sāṁkhya deriving its major ideas and terms from the Vedic-Upaniṣadic tradition.[8] E.H. Johnston also investigates the *Brāhmaṇas* and the Upaniṣads and infers that Sāṁkhya is rooted in the speculations of the *Brāhmaṇas* and the oldest Upaniṣads about the constitution of the individual and that its formulation took place in the interval between the oldest group of Upaniṣads and those of the middle group.[9] P. Chakravarti has also attempted a critical study of the Sāṁkhya elements in the Vedic literature. His treatment of the Upaniṣadic evidence in more definitive in interpreting the passages as containing Sāṁkhya

3. *L'Histoire des Idées Theosophique dans l'Inde*, Tome Premier, p. 222.
4. "Zur Geschichte der Sāṁkhya — Philosophie", *Nachrichten von der Königlichen Gesellschaft der Wissenschaften zu Götingen*, Jahre, 1917, p. 248.
5. *The Religion and Philosophy of the Veda and Upaniṣads*, Vol. 2, pp. 489-551.
6. *The Sāṁkhya System*, pp. 6-23.
7. "The Meaning of Sāṁkhya and Yoga", *American Journal of Philosophy*, XLV, L, No. 177 (1924), pp. 1-46.
8. *A History of Indian Philosophy*, Vol. I, p. 211.
9. *Early Sāṁkhya*, pp. 18-21.

terms and principles.[10] A.P. Mishra scrutinises the ancient as well as modern views about Sāṁkhya elements in the Upaniṣads and concludes that the original (*maulika*) Sāṁkhya emerged in the period between the very old and the less old Upaniṣdads.[11]

The opinion of G.J. Larson is clear from the division of the chapter on 'historical development'. Under 'ancient speculations' he discusses Veda and the oldest Upaniṣads and in the second phase of proto-Sāṁkhya speculations he places *Kaṭha*, *Śvetāśvatara*, *Maitrī* and later Upaniṣads. He is of the view that though the Vedic texts do not confirm the Sāṁkhya system or clear Sāṁkhya terminology, they do indicate doctrines and trends which 'may have later been assimilated into Sāṁkhya'. According to him, the *R̥gveda* and the *Atharvaveda* contain passages relevant to the Sāṁkhya view of creation, evolution, etc., and the *Brāhmaṇa*s and earliest Upaniṣads have passages bearing on Sāṁkhya views on self, knowledge and salvation.

Thus, we can classify the views of scholars about the connection between Sāṁkhya and Vedic tradition broadly into three: (a) those which trace Sāṁkhya ideas and terms in the Upaniṣads, (b) those which trace ideas and terms which led to the formulation of Sāṁkhya system, and (c) those which hold that the Vedic texts have passages with ideas similar to those of the early Sāṁkhya system, but not of the standard form of Sāṁkhya found in the *Sāṁkhyakārikā*.

Sāṁkhya Non-Vedic in Origin and Character

Those, who subscribe to the view that Sāṁkhya had a non-Vedic origin and character, start with the assumption that Sāṁkhya as a system is characterised by features recorded in the *Sāṁkhyakārikā*, without realising that Sāṁkhya has a rich history in which its early forms reveal significant variations. These scholars take Sāṁkhya to be characterised by *puruṣa-prakr̥ti* dualism, plurality of *puruṣa*s, evolution from a material cause (*prakr̥ti*) and atheism. All these

10. *Origin and Development of the Sāṁkhya System of Thought.*
11. *Sāṁkhya Darśana kī Aitihāsika Paramparā*, pp. 20-40.

features are in total opposition to the idealistic monism of the Upaniṣads and hence some scholars find it hard to visualise a Vedic origin for Sāṁkhya and propose alternative origins.

VRĀTYA ORIGIN

J.W. Hauer traces the origin of Sāṁkhya ultimately to the Vrātyas. The Yoga originated with the Vrātyas and Sāṁkhya was a later development of Yoga. The Vrātyas were different from the Brāhmaṇical priesthood. They formed part of the first-wave of Āryans, possibly going back to Indo-Iranian or Indo-Germanic times. Hauer relies on the *Atharvaveda* for the views and practices of the Vrātyas. There is no sound argument for describing Sāṁkhya as a development from the folds of Yoga. Even in the case of Yoga the characteristic practices of the Vrātyas are known to occur in some Brāhmaṇical sources also, suggesting that they were assimilated early in the Brāhmaṇical tradition.

KṢATRIYA ORIGIN

Arguing on the basis of the absence of the distinguishing ideas of standardised Sāṁkhya in the *Brāhmaṇa*s and Āraṇyakas, Richard Garbe postulates a non-Brāhmaṇical origin for Sāṁkhya. According to him, Sāṁkhya arose in kṣatriya circles.[12] In another context Garbe describes Sāṁkhya as a reaction against the idealistic monism of the Upaniṣads.[13] There is a clear incompatibility between the two views. Many earlier scholars forcefully argued for describing Upaniṣads as a product of the kṣatriya tradition. If Sāṁkhya had a kṣatriya origin, how could it originate as a reaction to the Upaniṣads, which were also of kṣatriya origin.

Garbe's arguments for taking Sāṁkhya to be a kṣatriya philosophy are: (a) The *Bhāgavata Purāṇa* describes Kapila as descended from a *rājarṣi*, (b) Sanatkumāra, a Sāṁkhya teacher, is connected with the kṣatriyas, and (c) The Mokṣadharma (Śāntiparāva, *Mahābhārata*) mentions five traditions, Vedic,

12. *Die Samkhya Philosophy*, pp. 12-27.
13. *Encyclopaedia of Religion and Ethics*, Vol. XI, p. 189.

Sāṁkhya, Yoga, Pāñcarātra and Pāśupata, suggesting that Sāṁkhya was different from the Vedic tradition.

The theory of a dichotomy between the brāhmaṇa and kṣatriya traditions of thought, fashionable with earlier Western Indologists, was misconceived and is no longer accepted. Kapila cannot be described as a kṣatriya. On the *Bhāgavata Purāṇa* evidence itself, as the son of Kardama, he is to be treated as a brāhmaṇa. The instance of Sanatkumāra also does not make Sāṁkhya a kṣatriya philosophy. There is a long list of Sāṁkhya teachers, but most of them are not kṣatriyas. Sanatkumāra was neither the most important nor the earliest among Sāṁkhya philosophers. The Sāṁkhya tradition and writings do not give much importance to Sanatkumāra and his views. Kapila, Āsuri and Pañcaśikha are the earliest three Sāṁkhya philosophers, but none of them is known as a kṣatriya. The third argument of Garbe does not show that the Vedic tradition was opposed to the Sāṁkhya. The *Mahābhārata* passage lists five traditions which were respected at that time. They did have their own distinct form but were not necessarily antagonistic to one another. Actually all the five co-existed as equally respected in the Brāhmaṇical circle.

Garbe's second view of Sāṁkhya originating as a reaction to the Upaniṣads has been opposed by Suryanarayan Sastri who says that this view ignores both, the diversified character of the Upaniṣadic teaching and the history of the Sāṁkhya doctrine itself, which in its pre-classical stages seems to have had considerable affinities with Upaniṣadic doctrine.[14]

ANTI-VEDIC FOLK ORIGIN

Here we may refer to the views of Debiprased Chattopadhyaya about the origins of Sāṁkhya and its contacts with the Brāhmaṇical

---

14. *Sāṁkhyakārikā*, Introduction, p. 1, A.P. Mishra, *op. cit.*, pp. 10-12, objects to Sāṁkhya in pre-Classical age being described as having affinities with Upaniṣadic thought, obviously because he identifies Sāṁkhya with its later form in the *Sāṁkhyakārikā* and ignores texts and passages giving an account of early Sāṁkhya.

tradition. Chattopadhyaya emphasises popular folk traditions as against priestly elite traditions. He dismisses Sāṁkhya in the *Sāṁkhyakārikā* as being anti-Vedic and without any claim to represent the orthodox tradition. He trace Sāṁkhya to the archaic agricultural-matriarchal traditions of mother-right which were pre-Vedic. Sāṁkhya originally was a philosophy of monistic materialism of *pradhāna-kāraṇavāda*. Īśvarakṛṣṇa attempted its syncretism with the pastoral patriarchal tradition of male dominance represented by Vedānta idealism and thus created dualism which came to characterise later Sāṁkhya.[15]

This refreshingly new materialistic interpretation is valuable. But, it assumes on the basis of anthropology the very facts for which we would like to have evidence and arguments. Chattopadhyaya does not adduce any evidence in support of an archaic agricultural matriarchal tradition and of the emergence of Sāṁkhya from it. There is no support for it either in the Sāṁkhya texts or traditions opposed to Sāṁkhya. Chattopadhyaya's formulation is highly speculative. Its oversimplification may appear interesting and appealing, but has no factual, historical or philosophical support. As remarked by Larson, it is "clearly an oversimplification that reflects Chattopadhyaya's political ideology more than it does India's ancient cultural heritage".[16]

Our analysis of the Sāṁkhya elements in the Vedas, *Brāhmaṇas* and Upaniṣads, in the light of the evidence about its nature in the early stages of the formulation of Sāṁkhya and also its subsequent transformation and development, provides a historical perspective to our study of the correlation between Sāṁkhya and Vedic tradition. By indicating the Vedic background it serves as a corrective to views, expressed under pre-conceived notions and partisan stands, which may have emerged in ancient times.

---

15. *Lokāyata*, pp. 383-458.
16. *Op.cit.*, p. 65, Larson points out that by his methodology Chattopadhyaya has reversed the Marxist perspective of interpreting 'Social reality with its economic infrastructure' and instead interprets Indian cultural history as 'an on-going conflict on the idealogical level' between Sāṁkhya materialism and Vedānta idealism.

By no means less important are three aspects which are to be investigated: the prestige enjoyed by Sāṁkhya in the circles of the orthodox Brāhmaṇical tradition, the criticism of Sāṁkhya by orthodox thinkers, and Sāṁkhya attitude towards Vedas and other sacred elements in the orthodox tradition.

Sāṁkhya in Authoritative Brāhmaṇical Texts

A.P. Mishra[17] has pointed out that authoritative texts of the Brāhmaṇical tradition, the *Mahābhārata*, *Gītā*, *Rāmāyaṇa*, Smṛtis and Purāṇas, extol the Sāṁkhya system for its excellence and superior merit. The *Bhāgavata Purāṇa*[18] says that one, who listens to the *ātmayoga* of Kapila, attains the feet of the *bhagavān*. In this Purāṇa *bhagavān* Kapila tells his mother that one, who listens with faith to the Sāṁkhya principles even once or recites it to another person, achieves His position.[19] The *Mahābhārata* is replete with passages glorifying. Sāṁkhya as a philosophical system for achieving the *summum bonum*. At one place it is said that the knowledge gained from Sāṁkhya is great (*mahat*).[20] Another passage unequivocally says that there is no knowledge equal to Sāṁkhya.[21] The best testimony to the high regard for Sāṁkhya is provided by the *Gītā*. Its teachings are clearly surcharged with Sāṁkhya principles.[22]

Śaṅkara, the Advaita Vedāntist, is an avowed critic of Sāṁkhya philosophy, but he himself testifies to the high position enjoyed by Sāṁkhya in the orthodox circles. In prefacing his criticism of Sāṁkhya, he mentions the reasons for giving primacy to the controverting of Sāṁkhya texts. He says that Sāṁkhya and Yoga are well known in the world as the means for attaining the highest goal; they are accepted by the cultured people, and are glorified by

17. *Lokāyata*, pp. 8-14.
18. III.33.37.
19. III.32.43.
20. XII.301.109.
21. XII.316.2 — *nāsti sāṁkhyasamaṁ jñānaṁ* ।
22. P. Chakravarti, *Origin and Devlopment of the Sāṁkhya System of Thought*, pp. 58-60.

references in the Śrutis. For the third point, Śaṅkara quotes the passage in *Śvetāśvatara Upaniṣad* (VI.13) which says that one is freed from all the bondages by knowing that divine cause as enunciated by the Sāṁkhya and Yoga.[23] It is clear that Śaṅkara criticises Sāṁkhya to maintain his own philosophical position, but he could not wish away the high regard enjoyed by Sāṁkhya as a spiritual system among the orthodox cultural groups.

Sāṁkhya on its Relationship with the Vedic Tradition

It will be pertinent to know the Sāṁkhya position about its relationship with the Vedic tradition, its views about the authority of the Vedas and the Vedic ideas and systems, and the extent to which it considers its own ideas to be sanctioned by the Vedic texts, being mentioned in them, or being in consonance with them or emanating from them. The difficulty is that we do not have any text belonging to the Sāṁkhya tradition itself, which discusses this issue and belongs to the times before Śaṅkara, the *Sāṁkhyakārikā* and the commentaries on it are not polemical. This holds good about other texts which are known to possess glimpses of Sāṁkhya principles of an earlier period. The *Sāṁkhyapravacanasūtra* and later commentaries of the medieval period are known to adopt a polemical approach and style. But, they are of a very late period, when many compulsions of historical development of ideas and principles influenced them to assume their own stance. Their evidence cannot hold good for the Sāṁkhya view in the earlier stages of its formulation and development.

On this question Śaṅkara provides welcome information. In maintaining his own philosophical stand, he criticises other systems of philosophy. In this regard he shows the highest regard to the Sāṁkhya, criticising it in great details.[24] Śaṅkara, in challenging

---

23. On *Brahmasūtra*, II.1.3 — *sāṁkhyayogau hi paramapuruṣārtha-sādhanatvena loke prakhyātau, śiṣṭaiśca parigṛhītau liṅgena ca śrautenopabṛṁhitau "tatkāraṇaṁ sāṁkhyayogābhipannaṁ jñātvā devaṁ mucyate sarvapāśaiḥ" iti* ||

24. On *Vedāntasūtra*, I.1.5-11, 18; 1.4.1-28; II.1.1-11; II.2.1-10.

the claims of the Sāṁkhya to be authoritative, does not adduce arguments from any earlier Sāṁkhya texts. He, however, presents faithfully the Sāṁkhya point of view as *pūrva-pakṣa*. We can never know if he had polemical Sāṁkhya texts on which he relied, or got information personally from representative Sāṁkhya circles. In any case, the presentation of the Sāṁkhya view, its ciriticism, the Sāṁkhya rejoinder, and its further criticism suggest that Śaṅkara's account of the Sāṁkhya stand is very near to being a faithful representation.[25]

From this the emerging main Sāṁkhya argument seems to be that the principle of *pradhāna* as the cause of the world is consistent with the views of the scriptures (*vedānta-vākya*); that its own views are also expressed in scripture; and that its views are based on Smṛti (authoritative tradition) and *tarka* (reasoning). As analysed by Śaṅkara, for their *śruti* support the Sāṁkhya philosophers rely on *Kāṭhaka*, *Śvetāśvatara* and *Kauṣītaki Upaniṣad*s and certain passages in the *Chāndogya Upaniṣad*, VI (about Śvetaketu), and *Bṛhadāraṇyaka Upaniṣad*, IV.4.17 (about five pentads) and IV.5.6 (Yājñavalkya-Maitreyī dialogue). They further quote the *Gītā*, *Manu-smṛti* and other Smṛtis in their support and claim Smṛti status for their own Sāṁkhya tradition (Kapila-Tantra). They go to the extent of arguing for the primacy of the Smṛti and reasoning, because there are many discrepancies in the Śruti itself about the origin of the world.

Śaṅkara on Sāṁkhya Claim of Śruti Sanction

Though Śaṅkara criticises Sāṁkhya principles on the basis of philosophical reasoning, he is mainly concerned about the argument based on the authority of the Śruti and its sanction. For him the final authority is derived from the scriptures and reasoning, if it is subordinate to scripture. Thus, Śaṅkara scrutinises in great detail the Sāṁkhya claim of Śruti sanction for itself.

Śaṅkara does not challenge those Sāṁkhya principles which are not opposed to the Veda, for example, the concept of self as

25. G.J. Larson, *op. cit.*, pp. 209-35.

nirguṇa (without qualities) and the rules of *yoga*. Śaṅkara argues that the Śruti maintains *Brahman* as *sarvajña* (omniscient) and *sarvaśakti* (omnipotent) cause of the world and rejects as unsupported by Śruti the Sāṁkhya principles of *pradhāna*, *puruṣa-bahutva* (plurality of selves) and *buddhi*, or *mahat*, etc., being derived from *pradhāna*.

Śaṅkara argues that passages in the scripture, which Sāṁkhya supporters mention as upholding their views, mean something other than (*teṣām śabdānām anyaparatvam*) what they claim. Śaṅkara further argues that, in the case of a contradiction among the Smṛtis, those which are in consonance with the Śrutis get precedence (*śrutyanusāriṇyaḥ smṛtayaḥ pramāṇam*) and only that reasoning is to be relied upon which is approved by the Śruti (*śrutyanugṛhīta eva hi tarka*). Śaṅkara demonstrates that the Smṛtis (including the Kapila-Tantra) are not in consonance with the Śruti and the Sāṁkhya arguments are also not supported by Śruti.

Śaṅkara on Śvetāśvatara Upaniṣad Reference to Kapila

The Sāṁkhya philosophers quote in support of their claim for Śruti sanction the passage in the *Śvetāśvatara Upaniṣad* (V.2)[26] referring to the *ṛṣi* Kapila. Śaṅkara rejects the Sāṁkhya claim for Vedic support. He says that by the Śruti passage, which has been quoted to indicate the extreme knowledge of Kapila, faith cannot be reposed in Kapila's principles, which are opposed to Śruti, merely on the basis of the commonness of the name Kapila in the Śruti, because of the tradition of another Kapila, Vāsudeva by name, who burnt the sons of Sagara.[27] According to Śaṅkara, Kapila mentioned in the *Śvetāśvatara Upaniṣad* is not Kapila, the Sāṁkhya expounder; he is to be identified with Vāsudeva, an *avatāra* of Viṣṇu. This point

26. *ṛṣiṃ prasūtaṁ kapilaṁ yastamagra jñānaibibharti jāyamānaṁ ca paśyet* ।

27. On *Brahmasūtra*, II.1.1 — *yā tu śrutiḥ kapilasya jñānātiśayaṁ pradarśayantī pradarśitā, na tayā śrutiviruddhamapi kāpilaṁ mataṁ śraddhātuṁ śakyaṁ, kapilamiti śrutisāmānyamātratvāt, anyasya ca kapilasya sagaraputrāṇāṁ prataptur-vāsudevanāmnaḥ smaraṇāt* ।

has been made clear by Ānandagiri and Govindānanda, the commentators on Śaṅkara. They add that it is erroneous to regard the expounder of Sāṁkhya as Śrauta merely on the basis of the word Kapila. Ānandagiri speaks of two Kapilas. Vasudeva Kapila was *vaidika* and was different from the expounder of Sāṁkhya who was *avaidika*. Govindānanda says that Kapila, the Sāṁkhya expounder, was a dualist (*dvaitavādin*) and hence could not claim omniscience (*sarvajñatva*). The Kapila of *śruti* was endowed with omniscience and was an incarnation (*aṁśa*) of Vāsudeva. He was omniscient (*sarvajña*), because he preached Vaidika Sāṁkhya, characterised by the knowledge of *sarvātmatva*.

In his commentary on the *Śvetāśvatara Upaniṣad* (V.2) Śaṅkara interprets Kapila to stand for Hiraṇyagarbha, taking the word to refer to the tawny gold colour (*kanaka-kapilavarṇa*) of the Hiraṇyagarbha or, on the basis of the Purāṇic statement of Kapila as *agraja* or born in the beginning of the creation, explaining it as an adjective of Hiraṇyagarbha. However, later on in the same context he mentions Kapila as the *ṛṣi* who appeared as an *aṁśa* of *bhagavān* Viṣṇu and describes him as the Sāṁkhya teacher (*sāṁkhyānām kapila devo*). It is to be noticed that in his commentary on the *Brahmasūtra*, II.1.1 Śaṅkara, quite against his stand to differentiate the Kapila of the *Śvetāśvatara Upaniṣad* passage from Kapila of Sāṁkhya and to identify him with Vāsudeva, remarks that in the Upaniṣadic passage the main reference is to the Supreme Soul the omniscience of Kapila is mentioned only causally,[28] thus admitting that Kapila of the passage is the Sāṁkhya teacher.[29]

The above discussion suggests that Śaṅkara was quite conscious of Kapila mentioned in the *Śvetāśvatara Upaniṣad* being the Sāṁkhya teacher, but, for demolishing the Sāṁkhya claim of a Śruti sanction and for rejecting the Sāṁkhya interpretation of the Upaniṣads, he, to maintain his own Vedāntic interpretation, undertook the exercise of identifying Kapila as an *avatāra* of Viṣṇu in one place as Hiraṇyagarbha in another.

---

28. *anyārthadarśanasya ca prāptirahitasyāsadhakatvāt* ।
29. A.P. Mishra, *op. cit.*, p. 50.

Brāhmaṇical Tradition not Favourable to Sāṁkhya

In support of the view that the Sāṁkhya system had a non-Vedic origin one of the arguments is that in some texts of the Brāhmaṇical tradition Sāṁkhya has not been referred to favourably. The *Padma Purāṇa*[30] mentions Kapila along with Jaimini as sages of the *tāmasa* order and their writings are described as atheistic (*nirīśvara*). There is evidence to show that the Sāṁkhya was critical of the efficacy of sacrifices. The *Sāṁkhyakārikā*[31] begins by criticising the revealed or Vedic means of removing suffering (*duḥkha*). They are not final or abiding like the perceptible means. They are impure in character, involve the slaughter of beasts and excesses. A similar criticism of the Vedic sacrifices as resulting in some evil, howsoever trivial, is attributed to Pañcaśikha by Vācaspati.[32] In the *Mahābhārata*[33] we have the episode of a Kapila, who, though not specifically mentioned as the propounder of Sāṁkhya but possibly the same Kapila, disowning any intention to criticise the Vedas, points out the limited merit of sacrificial *karma*.

Sāṁkhya arose in the Vedic Circle

It seems that the Sāṁkhya arose in the Vedic circle itself. It possibly originated in times when the Vedic sacrifices were widely current. Though the Sāṁkhya was not in full support of the sacrificial system, it will be equally wrong to describe it as the result of the reaction against sacrifices. As is well known, in the Vedic circle

---

30. *Padma Purāṇa*.
31. *Kārikā* 1-2 — *dṛṣṭe sā'pārthā cennaikāntātyanto'bhavāt* ।
dṛṣṭavad ānuśravikaḥ sa hyativiśuddhikṣayātiśayayuktaḥ ॥
The *Śataśāstra* of Āryadeva (translated from Chinese sources) expresses an identical view on the authority of the *sūtra*s of the Sāṁkhyas. See P. Chakravarti, *op. cit.*, p. 5, fn. 2.
32. *Yogasūtrabhāṣya*, II.13 — *yatredamuktam*
syāt svalpaḥ saṅkaraḥ sapariharaḥ sapratyavamarṣaḥ kuśalasya nāpakarṣāyālam । *kasmāt? kuśalaṁ hi bahvanyadasti yatrāyamavāpaṁ gataḥ svarge'pi apakarṣamalpaṁ kariṣyati it* ॥
33. XII.268-70.

itself there were voices of protest against sacrifices.[34] The Sāṁkhya system does not represent a total opposition of the sacrifices. It does admit that the sacrifices have their efficacy, but points out that their results are of a limited nature and suffer from other defects. For enduring results and for liberation from *duḥkha* it advocates a different method. There are indications that in the Vedic period itself there were two parallel religious traditions. One, which seems to have been more widely current, subscribed to the system of sacrifices. The other tradition was contemplative; it believed in acquiring a true knowledge through reasoning and analysis. Whereas the sacrificial tradition aimed at worldly gains, the other tradition set as its goal the total innihilation of suffering and complete liberation. The Sāṁkhya system seems to have arisen in the second tradition in the Vedic circle. This possibility can be seen in the episode of Kapila and Syūmaraśmi recorded in the Śāntiparva of the *Mahābhārata*.[35] Kapila, in his criticism of the sacrifices for being of a limited merit and efficacy, holds to his Vedic mooring and asserts his position of not criticising the Vedas. The *Sāṁkhyakārikā*[36] also mentions together two means of removing *duḥkha*: the revealed or Vedic (*ānuśravika*) and another, which is different from it and is superior on account of the discriminating knowledge of the manifest, the unmanifest and the knower. The *Sāṁkhyakārikā*, no doubt, belongs to a late date in the history of Sāṁkhya, but, in view of its tacit admission that it is based on earlier works and presents the principles in a summarised manner,[37] it is not unlikely that here Īśvarakṛṣṇa wants to clarify the origin of Sāṁkhya and its Vedic connexions. Āsuri, the immediate disciple of Kapila, was a staunch believer in the sacrifices, sacrificing for a thousand years (*varṣa-sahasrayājī*). All this shows that the system arose in Vedic circles; it was not totally opposed to sacrifices; for higher goals and results it regarded sacrifices to be of limited merit.

---

34. H.C. Raychaudhuri, *Political History of Ancient India*, p. 315.
35. XII.268-70.
36. *Kārikā* 2.
37. *Kārikā*s 69-71.

Conclusion

To conclude, the Sāṁkhya did not have a non-Vedic origin. It arose in the Vedic circle itself. It believed in reasoned exposition. It regarded the sacrifices to have a limited efficacy. In the beginning it was a system of the knowledge of self (*ātma-jñāna*) which explained the process of creation and, for overcoming the sufferings of human existence and for achieving liberation, expounded the system of spiritual knowledge. In this form the Sāṁkhya gained recognition as the foremost system and was respected and adopted by many sects and disciplines. This position of respect survived in later times when the Sāṁkhya acquired its dualistic emphasis and other associated features. The criticism by Śaṅkara, and those influenced by his thought, originated from antagonism as philosophical system, and, in this process, Sāṁkhya's Vedic sanction was tried to be explained away. But, Śaṅkara himself indicates the high position enjoyed by Sāṁkhya in orthodox circles.

3

Sāṁkhya and the Upaniṣads

Upaniṣadic Evidence for Sāṁkhya History

VIEWS OF MODERN SCHOLARS

GENERALLY scholars studying the origins of Sāṁkhya as a system of philosophy connect it with the Upaniṣads in some way or the other.[1] Garbe, who holds that the Sāṁkhya system has not undergone any remarkable change in the course of its history, places its original formulation in the period between the oldest pre-Buddhistic Upaniṣads and the rise of Buddhism.[2] P. Oltramare places Sāṁkhya in the Brāhmaṇical tradition; it took its birth in the context prepared by the ancient Upaniṣads and represents strong reaction against some of the themes in that tradition.[3] Others have postulated a more direct connexion between the Upaniṣads and Sāṁkhya. They consider Sāṁkhya as the lineal descendant of the ancient speculation which is found in the Vedic-Upaniṣadic texts. According to J. Dahlmann, Sāṁkhya was the first systematic formulation of the ancient speculations found in the *Brāhmaṇas* and early

1. See G.J. Larson, *Classical Sāṁkhya*, pp. 16-72, for a survey of some of the important attempts to reconstruct the history of the pre-Īśvarakṛṣṇa Sāṁkhya.
2. *Die Sāṁkhya Philosophie*, p. 26.
3. *L' Histoire das Idées Theosophiques dans L'Inde*, Tome Premier (*La Theosophie Brahmanique*), pp. 222-3. He considers the basic dualism of Sāṁkhya to be between Being and Becoming.

Upaniṣads, its *puruṣa* and *prakṛti* dualism arising out of the dualism of *ātman* and that which is not *ātman*.[4]

Oldenberg propounded the thesis that Sāṁkhya has developed in a direct line out of the *Brahman-ātman* speculations of the old Upaniṣads.[5] This resulted in a 'pre-classical Sāṁkhya' to be seen in middle and younger Upaniṣads—*Kaṭha*, *Śvetāśvatara*, *Maitrāyaṇī*, etc.[6] This approach has been adopted and elaborated by subsequent scholars. Keith holds that the Sāṁkhya is derived out of the speculations in the Vedas, *Brāhmaṇa*s and Upaniṣads.[7] According to S.N. Dasgupta, the major ideas and terms of Sāṁkhya are received from the Vedic-Upaniṣadic heritage.[8] E.H. Johnston demonstrates that "Sāṁkhya is rooted in the speculations of the *Brāhmaṇa*s and the oldest Upaniṣads about the constitution of the individual."[9] According to him, of the five phases through which early Sāṁkhya speculation developed, the first, an incomplete form of Sāṁkhya, is found in the *Kaṭha Upaniṣad*, the second, a more systematic form of Sāṁkhya emerged in the interval between the *Kaṭha* and *Śvetāśvatara Upaniṣad*s, and the third, a theistic phase, is seen in the *Śvetāśvatara Upaniṣad*.[10]

E. Frauwallner[11] does not take references to Sāṁkhya in the Upaniṣads as actual Sāṁkhya speculation, but as influenced by it. He maintains that the Sāṁkhya arose out of that stream of development which originates in the Fire Theory of the Upaniṣads,

---

4. *Die Sāṁkhya Philosophie als Naturlehre und Erlösungslahre*, pp. 12-13, 180ff, 251ff.
5. "Zur Geschichte der Sāṁkhya-Philosophie", *Nachrichten von der königlichen Gesellschaft der Wissenschaften zu Gottingan*, 1918, p. 248. Other cases of dualism in the oldest Upaniṣads are of unity and multiplicity, subject and object, self and non-self.
6. *Ibid.*, p. 218. *Kaṭha* uses some of the technical terms of Sāṁkhya: *avyakta*, *puruṣa*, *indriya*, *manas*, *buddhi*, etc. See *ibid.*, p. 222.
7. *The Sāṁkhya System*, p. 8.
8. *A History of Indian Philosophy*, Vol. I. p. 211.
9. *Early Sāṁkhya*, p. 21.
10. *Ibid.*, pp. 81-8.
11. *History of Indian Philosophy*, Vol. I, pp. 223, 227-36.

is at the basis of the doctrine of the Buddha, and is found variously in the epic. According to him, the early Sāṁkhya speculation, as found in the original "*Grund* text" in the Mokṣadharmaparva section of the Śāntiparva in the *Mahābhārata*, was a further working out of the doctrine of self in the *Bṛhadāraṇyaka Upaniṣad*.

R.D. Ranade[12] is opposed to Garbe's[13] view that the oldest Upaniṣads do not contain any traces whatsoever of the Sāṁkhya philosophy. He points out that the conception of the three colours in the *Chāndogya Upaniṣad* led to the conception of the tri-coloured *prakṛti* in Sāṁkhya; the *Kaṭhopaniṣad* enunciates the mind (*manas*) and intellect (*buddhi*), the *mahat*, the *avyakta* and the *puruṣa* which formed important categories in Sāṁkhya; and the *Praśnopaniṣad* adumbrates the conception of the *liṅga-śarīra* of Sāṁkhya.[14]

G.J. Larson[15] is cautious. He says that the earliest Upaniṣads, as also the *Ṛgveda*, *Atharvaveda* and the Brāhmaṇas, do not provide a Sāṁkhya system or a clear Sāṁkhya terminology, but contain 'doctrines and trends of thought which may have been assimilated into Sāṁkhya'. He traces the first references to Sāṁkhya-Yoga terminology in the *Kaṭha Upaniṣad*.

ARGUMENTS BASED ON UPANIṢADS

Thus, we see that, broadly speaking, the use of the Upaniṣadic testimony implies two main arguments: (1) the early Upaniṣads, *Chāndogya* and *Bṛhadāraṇyaka*, do not contain any reference to the Sāṁkhya or its doctrines and (2) the middle Upaniṣads, *Kaṭha*, *Śvetāśvatara* and *Maitrāyaṇī*, contain, in varying degrees, principles resembling the Sāṁkhya system.

The inference generally derived from the first argument is that the Sāṁkhya system could not have been formulated before the

---

12. *Survey of Upaniṣadic Philosophy*, (2nd edn.), Preface, p. ix.
13. *Sāṁkhya Philosophie*, p. 27.
14. Ranade, *Loc. cit.*, pp. 134-5.
15. *Op. cit.*, pp. 73, 78-96.

times of the Upaniṣads. Some scholars further infer that Sāṁkhya cannot be taken to have been contemporaneous with the early Upaniṣads. A third inference, suggested by some scholars, would place the origin of the Sāṁkhya principles after the period of the early Upaniṣads.

The second main argument is based on the evidence supplied by the middle Upaniṣads, namely *Kaṭha*, *Śvetāśvatara* and *Maitrāyaṇī*. Scholars have offered different interpretations of the nature of the occurrences in these Upaniṣads, either as referring to the Sāṁkhya principles, or to a form of Sāṁkhya earlier than that of the classical Sāṁkhya. Sometimes the second possibility has been elaborated as indicating that before the atheistic Sāṁkhya as standardised by Īśvarakṛṣṇa, there was an earlier phase, reflected in the middle Upaniṣads, which referred to a theistic form of Sāṁkhya. Some scholars trace development and change within the middle Upaniṣads. They regard the *Kaṭha Upaniṣad* to refer to an earlier and undeveloped form of Sāṁkhya, and take the *Śvetāśvatara* to reflect a slightly developed from of Sāṁkhya.

METHODOLOGICAL REQUIREMENTS

In analysing the Upaniṣadic evidence we have to make ourselves sure about its nature and comparative position. Are we to interpret the Upaniṣadic references as pointing to principles which originated in earlier times or, we suggest that they reflect contemporary views? Scholars have not addressed themselves to this methodological problem. They interpret the Upaniṣadic evidence in their own manner, to suit the convenience of their own formulation of the stages in the origin and development of Sāṁkhya. They have not argued in support of their stand about the chronological significance of the Upaniṣadic reference.

Another methodological problem, which requires to be considered before we evaluate the Upaniṣadic references for determining the history of Sāṁkhya, concerns the identification of the principles mentioned in the Upaniṣads with those of the Sāṁkhya. We have to answer the question whether the references relate to Sāṁkhya or to some other system. The Upaniṣadic texts are themselves silent on the point. If we hold that the Upaniṣads are not referring to Sāṁkhya principles, then we will have to take the position that there was an undefined common stream from which developments in both the Sāṁkhya and the Upaniṣadic channels were diverted. This will have an important bearing on the interpretation of Upaniṣadic evidence for the reconstruction of the history of Sāṁkhya, the nature of the evidence and its chronology.

Generally scholars using the Upaniṣadic evidence for the history of Sāṁkhya have been influenced by two alternative assumptions. They think that Sāṁkhya has borrowed principles from the Upaniṣads and hence its early history is to be delineated on the basis of the references in the Upaniṣads. Those who subscribe to the alternative possibility of connexions of Sāṁkhya references in Upaniṣadic texts with another source, hold that the later development of Sāṁkhya is along lines indicated by the Upaniṣads. They cannot imagine the situation of early Sāṁkhya history being considered independent of Upaniṣadic evidence.

We would suggest a third possibility that the origin and early history of Sāṁkhya be considered independently. It is not necessary to tie Sāṁkhya history inseparably with the Upaniṣads. Whatever its origin, Vedic, non-Vedic or folk streams, Sāṁkhya seems to have followed its own course of development. This development was not conditioned by the Upaniṣads. The Upaniṣads do not have a direct bearing on the history of the Sāṁkhya system. They reflect the Sāṁkhya only marginally. It is not Sāṁkhya in its totality that is recorded in the Upaniṣadic texts. Only those principles of Sāṁkhya are mentioned in the Upaniṣads which are relevant to them.

The total absence of Sāṁkhya principles in the early Upaniṣads and their partial or modified account in the middle Upaniṣads can lead to a compelling inference only when it is demonstrated that a reference to Sāṁkhya principles was binding on the authors of the Upaniṣads. If the subject-matter of the Upaniṣads and some particular passages and contexts in them necessitate a reference to the principles of Sāṁkhya and we do not find any mention, then only the absence will have a meaningful value. The negative evidence by itself cannot lead to a positive inference, because there can be several possible explanations of the absence of the reference.

The Upaniṣads are not in the form of compendiums or digests of views on topics of their interest. Ordinarily the Upaniṣads do not make any effort to collect all the views on any given point. From the contexts in various Upaniṣads we do not see a situation which makes it obligatory on the part of their authors to refer to different views.

The Upaniṣads have a characteristic style. Often the principles are enunciated in course of a dialogue between two persons. An important thinker or philosopher communicates his philosophical ideas to his disciple or to a person seeking enlightenment. Sometimes the teacher himself poses questions and then correcting or improving upon the reply given by the inquirer elaborates his own view. This type of arrangement does not give any scope for the enunciation of the principles of other systems.

In view of the importance of the issue we would discuss in greater details the question of the meaning of the term Upaniṣad, the contents and scope of the Upaniṣads, and the style adopted for presenting principles and views in them.

Meaning and Scope of Upaniṣads

Śaṅkara, the great Advaita philosopher, provides useful information about the scope and contents of the Upaniṣads. In the introductory passages of his commentary on some of the Upaniṣads[16] he discusses the derivation of the word *upaniṣad* and how it indicates the purpose and central theme of the Upaniṣadic texts. He derives the word *upaniṣad* from *kvibanta sadi* with the prefix *upa* and *ni*.[17]

16. *Aitareyopaniṣad, Muṇḍakopaniṣad, Bṛhadāraṇyakopaniṣad* and *Taittirīyopaniṣad.*
17. On *Aitareyopaniṣad — upaniṣadityupapūrvasya sadeḥ kibantasya viśaraṇagatyavasāda nārthasya rūpamācakṣate* ।
On *Bṛhadāraṇykopaniṣad — upanipūrvasya sadestadarthatvāt* ।

Using the component parts of the word *upaniṣad* as basis, Śaṅkara elaborates its scope and meaning. In his commentary on the *Aitareyopaniṣad*[18] he says that those, who with purpose remain near (*upa*) this science of soul, through their soul, are steadfast in the science of soul. The science of soul annihilates (*avasādayati*) or destroys their ignorance, etc., which are the seeds of the cycle of life, leads to the realisation (*nigamayati*) or understading of the supreme soul and cuts asunder (*nisātayati*) conception in the womb, birth, old age, disease, etc., hence it is known as Upaniṣad. In his commentary on the *Muṇḍakopaniṣad*[19] Śaṅkara explains *upaniṣad* as the science of *brahmā* which cuts asunder (*nisātayati*) the collection of evils, such as conception in the womb, birth, old age and diseases, leads to the supreme Brahmā (*gamayati*) or completely annihilates (*avasādayati*) or destroys the causes of the cycle of life, such as ignorance, of those who approach it (*upayānti*) with feelings of self-preceded by faith and devotion. The explanation in the commentary on the *Taittirīyopaniṣad*[20] is not so elaborate. Here Śaṅkara says that Upaniṣad is called a science on account of the cutting asunder (*nisātanāt*) or annihilation (*avasādanāt*) on cenception in the womb, birth, diseases, etc., of those who follow it or their coming closer (*upanigamayitṛtvāt*) to the *Brahman* or the highest good being closely formulated (*upaniṣaṇṇam*) in it. The explanation in the commentary on the *Bṛhadāraṇyakopaniṣad*[21] is a very brief one. It says that this science of *Brahman* is termed *upaniṣad* because it completely annihilates (*avasādanāt*) the cycle

---

18. *ye hyasyomātmavidyāyām tātparyeśā upa ātmatayā vartante ātmavidyāniṣṭhāsteṣāmātmavidyādisaṁ-sārabījamavasādayati vināśayati paraṁ cātmānaṁ nigamayati avabodhayati garbhajanma-jarārogādīṁśca niśātayati ata eyamātmavidyā upaniṣat* ||

19. *ya imāṁ brahmavidyāmupayantyātmabhāvena śradhābhakti-puraḥsarāḥ santasteṣāṁ garbhajanmajarārogādyanarthayūgaṁ niśātayati, paraṁ vā brahma gamayati, avidyādisaṁsārakāraṇaṁ cātyantamavāsadayati vināśayatītyupaniṣat* ||

20. *upaniṣaditi vidyocyate, tacchīlināṁ garbhajanmajarādiniśātanāt tadavasādanād vā brahmaṇo vā upanigamayitṛtvāt upaniṣaṇṇam vā'syāṁ paraṁ śreya iti* |

21. *tatparāṇāṁ sahetoḥ saṁsārasyātyantāvasādanāt* |

of life, along with its cause, of those who follow it.

In his commentary on the *Aitareyopaniṣad*[22] Śaṅkara gives the additional information that the science of *prāṇa*, etc., being auxiliary to the science of *ātman*, also come under the category of Upaniṣad.

Śaṅkara, thus, uses the word *upaniṣad* as signifying a *vidyā*[23] and paraphrases it as *ātma-vidyā*[24] and *brahma-vidyā*.[25] In the commentary on the *Aitareyopaniṣad*[26] the *ātma-vidyā* is designated specially by the word *upaniṣad*. But, in the commentary on the *Bṛhadāraṇyakopaniṣad*[27] Śaṅkara says that the *brahma-vidyā* is designated by the word *upaniṣad*. Śaṅkara introduces another element in his conception of *upaniṣad* as a *vidyā* when he describes it as the science of the identity of *brahman* and *ātman* and as the means of liberation from the cause of the cycle of life.[28]

This analysis shows that Śaṅkara took *upaniṣad* as the science of *ātman*, the science of *Brahman* or, to be more elaborate, the science of the identity of *ātman* and *Brahman*. The science of *prāṇa*, etc., were auxiliary to this science. This science aimed at annihilating the sufferings of life, conception, birth, old age and diseases destroying ignorance and other causes of the cycle of birth, death and leads to a realisation of *Brahman* or to an understanding of the nature of *ātman*.

Śaṅkara adds that the texts which deal with this import of the word *upaniṣad* and also designated as the *upaniṣad*.[29]

---

22. *tadupakārakatvāt prāṇādividyānamapyupaniṣatvam* ।
23. On *Taittirīyopaniṣad-upaniṣaditi vidyocyate* ।
24. On *Aitareyopaniṣad*.
25. On *Bṛhadāraṇyakopaniṣad* and *Muṇḍakopaniṣad*.
26. *viśeṣena copaniṣacchabdavācyā ātmavidyā* ।
27. *seyaṁ brahmavidyā upaniṣacchabdavācyā* ।
28. On *Bṛhadāraṇyakopaniṣad* — *saṁsārahetunivṛtti-sādhanabrahmātmaikatvavidyā* ।
29. On *Aitareyopaniṣad* — *tādarthyāt grantho'pyupaniṣat* ।
    On *Taittirīyopaniṣad* — *tadarthatvāt granthopyupaniṣat* ।
    On *Bṛhadāraṇyakopaniṣad* — *tādarthyād grantho'pyupaniṣaducyate* ।

Problems Considered by the Upaniṣads

R.D. Ranade[30] has aptly summarised the chief problems that are considered by the Upaniṣads. The Upaniṣadic philosophers began with a desire to know the 'arché' of knowledge. Failing to find this in the cosmological sphere, they searched after it in the psychological domain. They explored the transmundane problem of the persistence of the self after death. For them the most central problem was that of the Ultimate, the Real. Its intellectual solution led into the very heart of mataphysics. The effort to attain to that knowledge involved ethics for the norm of conduct to be followed. "Mysticism was the culmination of Upaniṣadic philosophy, . . . the cosmology and the psychology, the metaphysics and the ethics of the Upaniṣads are merely a propaedeutic to their mystical doctrine."[31]

The central point not only of all philosophies, but also of all religions and ethics, has been man's contemplation of himself, the study of the self. This holds good for the Upaniṣads as well. The Upaniṣadic philosopher explores this problem at two levels — the cosmological (*ādhidaivata*) and the psycho-physical (*adhyātma*). Thus, the two concepts of fundamental importance to the Upaniṣads are the *Brahman* and the *ātman*. The unique significance of Upaniṣadic philosophy is its realisation of the identity of the two.

Laxman Shastri Joshi in the *Upaniṣatkāṇḍa* of his monumental work *Dharmakośa* has not discussed the characteristic subject-matter of the Upaniṣads. One may, however, form some idea on the basis of topics on which original passages from the Upaniṣads have been collected by him. But, on account of the concern for giving an encyclopaedic coverage, the main or central points tend to be mixed with others of a secondary nature. In his introductory remarks Joshi[32] emphasises the importance of the conceptions of *ātman* and the *Brahman*. According to him, "At the root of the Upaniṣads lie the eagerness to investigate truth and the intense craving of the

---

30. R.D. Ranade, pp. 44-5.
31. *Ibid.*, p. 45.
32. Pp. 102-3.

heart for liberation. The very desire to find the ultimate reality in the universal phenomena and to determine the highest moral ideals is an ethical motive, and it is the very foundation of the Upaniṣadic philosophy."

Though there is uniformity in regard to the central point or subject-matter of the Upaniṣads, it will be wrong to take all the Upaniṣads as constituting one systematic whole or as advocating one single doctrine.[33] One can notice considerable variations in exposition of principles in the various Upaniṣads. The variation can be seen not only in terms of the particular point or points in Upaniṣadic philosophy selected for exposition, but also in their contents and manner of exposition. Within the broad pattern of principles we can find differences in regard to emphasis, details and method of presentation. Sometimes the views seem to be quite opposed to one another. The impression of uniformity in the Upaniṣadic texts has been strengthened by the later commentators, who in their keenness to support their own philosophical system, have read into the Upaniṣads the principles of their own systems and, through commendable scholarly ingenuity and arguing, have tried to iron out even the most apparent textual differences. The differences could not be appreciated as honest and unavoidable differences resulting from the fact that they were the products of not one but many minds. It is due to the long use of the historical and critical method of studying the Upaniṣadic texts, which has been introduced by the Western scholarship, that justice could be done to the individual character as different from the broad uniform label used for them. The realisation that the Upaniṣadic texts contain the views of many seers, who belonged to different periods, and record principles showing variations, is the result of modern scholarship.

Fallacious Expectations from the Upaniṣads

Two facts are mainly responsible for creating a wrong impression about the position of Upaniṣads in the history of Indian philosophy.

33. R.D. Ranade, *op.cit.*, pp. 131-2.

One is the traditional view describing Upaniṣads as texts belonging to the category of Śruti. The other, which possibly received support from the traditional view, is the assumption on the part of modern historians of Indian philosophy that "the highest philosophic thought in the Upaniṣads was not a gradual development, but was the result of a spontaneous, miraculous and revolutionary inspiration, that it was a phenomenon which had burst itself loose from all old traditions".[34]

R.D. Ranade[35] has suggested a very appealing explanation of the appellation Śruti used for the Upaniṣads along with the Vedas and the *Brāhmaṇas*. The Naiyāyikas explain them as *pauruṣeya* or composed by God; the Mīmāṁsakas regard them as *apauruṣeya* or existing from eternity in the form of sounds. According to Ranade, both these explanations are futile. The Vedāntin explanation of these texts as *apauruṣeya* or inspired by God (*puruṣaprayatnam vinā proktam*) comes nearest to the significance of the word *śruti* used for them. These texts are to "be regarded as having been composed by seers in a state of god-intoxication".[36] In the *Bṛhadāraṇyaka Upaniṣad*[37] the Upaniṣads, along with some other texts, are described as breathed forth by that Great Divinity. Explaining it in the light of some other Upaniṣadic passages, Ranade infers that "the Upaniṣads are regarded by the Upaniṣads themselves as being the work of the inspirational activity of God in human mind".

The assumption on the part of some modern scholars that the Upaniṣadic teachings had a sudden emergence is a historical non-sense. No doubt, the Upaniṣadic principles in their characteristic form find expression only in the Upaniṣads. But, history amply demonstrates that no new principle or change in ideas is completely abrupt. In the case of Upaniṣadic philosophy also we can trace the roots of some of its essential principles in the earlier texts and in

34. L.S. Joshi, *Dharamkośa, Upaniṣatkāṇḍa*, Vol. I, Part I, Preface, p. 9.
35. *Op. cit.*, pp. 6-8.
36. *Ibid.*, p. 7.
37. II.4.10.

many cases we can delineate the line of evolution howsoever dimly. There is a demonstrable continuity of religious practices and philosophical speculation from the *Ṛgveda* to the Upaniṣads. Some scholars trace the seeds of the Upaniṣadic concepts of *ātman* and its identity with *Brahman* in earlier Vedic texts.

Authors and Philosophers of the Upaniṣads

The individual authors of different Upaniṣads will remain hidden from us. The Upaniṣadic texts or later traditions do not provide evidence to identify the authors of these texts and to place them in time an space. It is only in the case of the *Maitrī* and *Śvetāśvatara Upaniṣads* that the names of the propounders of the doctrines have been retained in the names of the texts. It is clear that we cannot apportion all the details of Upaniṣadic philosophy to their individual propounders. In many cases we have a statement of the philosophical views, but its author has unknowingly or deliberately avoided mentioning his name. As remarked by R.D. Ranade,[38] "there must have been many a philosopher who lived, and thought, and died unknown. His work has remained, though his personality has been lost".

Among the names actually occurring in the Upaniṣads[39] there are some which clearly refer to unhistorical or mythological personages, such as Indra, Virocana, Prajāpati, Varuṇa and Yama. R.D. Ranade has noted the names of several philosophers and pointed out their significant views. Among mystical and moral philosophers he names Triśaṅku, Maitrī, Rāthitara, Pauraiśiṣṭi, Nāka Maudgalya, Mahīdāsa Aitareya, Āruṇi, Kauṣītaki, Paiṅgya, Pratardana, Śuṣkabhṛṅgāra and Jaivāli. The cosmological and psychological philosophers listed are Uddālaka, Prācīnaśāla, Buḍila, Śarkarākṣya, Indradyumna, Satyayajña, Raikva, Aśvapati Kaikeya, Satyakāma Jābāla, Gārgya, Ajātaśatru, Pippalāda, Kabandhī Kātyāyana, Bhārgava Vaidarbhī, Kausalya Āśvalāyana, Sauryāyaṇi Gārgya, Śaibya Satyakāma, Sukeśī Bhāradvāja, Bhujya, Vāmadeva,

38. L.C. Joshi, *op. cit.*, p. 31.
39. R.D. Ranade, *op. cit.*, pp. 30-41.

Bhr̥gu, Jitvan Śailini, Udaṅka Śaulbāyana, Varku Vārṣṇa, Gardabhīvipīta Bhāradvāja, Vidagdha Śākalya and Yājñavalkya. Metaphysical philosophers occupy an important position in the Upaniṣadic thought. Of these Śāṇḍilya, Dadhyañc, Sanatkumāra, Āruṇi and Yājñavalkya are the most prominent.

No Sāṁkhya Philosopher in the Upaniṣads

All these names do not include a single Sāṁkhya philosopher. Even though we cannot claim that the names of all the early Sāṁkhya authorities have down to us we are assumed that the prominent among them have been mentioned in one or the other source.[40] It is not without significance that the Upaniṣads do not mention the views of any one of the Sāṁkhya philosophers. There are some contexts where views parallel to those of Sāṁkhya have been expressed. We have some occasions where on particular topics divergent views have been listed.[41] The Sāṁkhya stand would have been relevant here. Most of the names of thinkers whose views are recorded here do not appear from the surviving records to have been notable parsonalities. We do not find support of their eminence and their significant ideas from other texts. In such a situation the absence of a reference to any Sāṁkhya celebrity or his principal principles assumes a greater significance.

We cannot maintain the position that none of the Sāṁkhya philosophers existed before or during the course of the composition of the many Upaniṣadic texts, because this world create serious difficulties in formulating the early history of the Sāṁkhya system and in fixing the date of the formulation of different principles and of the important philosophers.

A reasonable explanation will be that the authors of the Upaniṣads did not consider it necessary to refer to the Sāṁkhya philosophers and their views. They were referring to the views of

40. U.V. Shastri, *Sāṁkhya darśana kā Itihāsa*, pp. 570-645. *See also* H.D. Sharma, "The Sāṁkhya-teachers", *Festschrift Moriz Winternitz*, Leipzig, 1933, pp. 225-31.

41. *Chāndogya*; V.II.1-4, *Praśna*, I.1ff; *Br̥hadāraṇyaka*, IV.1.1-7.

only those philosophers who belonged to the Upaniṣadic circle. The suggestion would emerge that they did not consider the Sāṁkhya philosophers as falling within their own circle and hence did not feel any compulsion to include a reference to them in their texts.

Method and Style of the Upaniṣads

We may investigate how far the method or style of presentation accepted by the authors of the Upaniṣads creates the possibility of an occasion to refer to the views of other systems of philosophy or other philosophers. R.D. Ranade[42] has listed ten different methods resorted to by the Upaniṣadic authors according to the needs of discussion. Of these, five refer to the nature of argument and are not at all conducive to any expectation of the Sāṁkhya system being referred to. The enigmatic method contains engimatic riddles and cryptic expressions or sentences. The aphoristic method adopts the pattern of the later Sūtra texts. The etymological method is in the nature of word puzzles in which different parts in any word are explained as signifying different concepts. In the mythical method parables or myths are used to deduce lessons. The analogual method envisages to explain by images what cannot be done by logic.

The remaining five methods are not so irrelevant to the question under investigation. Here again the monologic method does not appear to be helpful for the nature of reference we are expecting. It is the method of soliloquy; the speaker, after answering to the questioner's problem, is lost in a reverie, thinking aloud about problems beyond the bounds of the original question.

Three other methods would appear to be more relevant in offering a possibility for referring to the views of others. The dialectic method (used in its root sense and not in the Platonic or Hegelian sense) is the method of the dialogue. In the *ad hoc* or temporising method the speakers do not discuss all the aspects of a question. They discuss "the one which is immediately before

42. *Op. cit.*, pp. 23-8.

them, and according to the capacity of the learner". The regressive method "takes the form of many successive questions, every new question carrying us behind the answer to the previous question". But, in all these three methods there is no debate between the supporters of two different systems, one presenting his principles which the other criticises to formulate his own. They are in the form of an interlocution, in which the main speaker asks his disciple or a seeker after truth a question, to which the latter gives a wrong or partially correct answer and then the former explains or elaborates the principle or else the latter poses his problem of enquiry, which is explained by the main speaker. Naturally, the points discussed cannot ordinarily relate to subjects beyond the scope of the main subject-matter of the Upaniṣads; the chances for other systems of thought being discussed in the Upaniṣads do not arise.

Synthetic Method

It is only in the case of the synthetic method that we have the possibility of a number of views being referred to. In this method the speaker, without discussing the different views and their arguments sympathetically, includes them in a higher synthesis. Instances of the use of the method by Aśvapati Kaikeya,[43] Pippalāda[44] and Yājñavalkya[45] are found. This is not the general or most common method adopted by the authors of the Upaniṣads for presenting their views. This type of treatment is to be found only in a few of the many Upaniṣads.[46] Even in these Upaniṣads this method has been followed at a very few places and not throughout the texts.

Evidently, the Upaniṣads are not texts of the nature of a *Sarvadarśana-saṁgraha*, wherein the views of all the important systems or schools of philosophy find representation. They also differ from philosophical texts of later times in which the author establishes the principles of his own system, but presents the views

---

43. *Chāndogya Upaniṣad*, V.11.1-4.
44. *Praśnopaniṣad*, I.1ff
45. *Bṛhadāraṇyaka Upaniṣad*, IV.1.1-7.
46. *Chāndogya*, *Praśna* and *Bṛhadāraṇyaka*.

of other schools as *pūrva-pakṣa*. The authors of commentaries on philosophical texts have also chosen to refer to different views as propounded by various schools to make their account exhaustive and authentic. The Upaniṣads have not assumed any such function for themselves.

We could have expected a reference to Sāṁkhya in the Upaniṣads if they had been cast in the mould of Nibandha texts in the Dharmaśāstra literature or texts dealing with the theory and practice of *Kāvyaśāstra* and its different branches. The former are clearly in the nature of digests or compendiums and the latter reproduce profuse quotations from earlier texts and authorities. Considering their techniques or method the Upaniṣads cannot be compared with these categories of texts.

In cases where the Upaniṣads adopt the synthetic method there is an open and direct reference to the views of others. Here there is no case of the principles of other systems being incorporated unknowingly or without acknowledgement. If the Sāṁkhya ideas had been accommodated in the Upaniṣads, they would have been acknowledged as the views of Sāṁkhya system or one of its philosophers.

Thus, we see that the different methods adopted in the Upaniṣads for propounding views do not provide any compelling occssion for recording the Sāṁkhya views. If the authors of the Upaniṣads actually wanted to refer to the Sāṁkhya views, they would have mentioned them openly and would not have borrowed them without acknowledgement.

Ranade's Criticism

It is interesting to note that R.D. Ranade[47] was aware of the force of the argument we have adopted here and actually applied it in analysing a problem connected with the Upaniṣads. He takes up issue with Hertel[48] for his observation that *Brahman* in the

---

47. *Op. cit.*, Preface, p. xi.
48. *Die Weisheit der Upanishaden, Kenopaniṣad*, Introduction.

Kenopaniṣad is not to be understood as "the World-Soul in which all the individual Souls ultimately merge". Ranade points out that this Upaniṣad aims at describing *Brahman* as a power or a presence, hence "it would be an *ignoratio elenchi* on the part of that Upaniṣad to go into the description of the *Brahman* as a "World-soul in which all the other souls ultimately merge". His methodological argument is that we cannot accuse the Upaniṣad of not having considered a point which is not the point at issue. His logic is that if the context requires a particular type of statement, then only its absence can be used to deduce any inference. Though Ranade uses this argument in a particular case, he does not apply it generally to the Upaniṣads for studying the problem of the origins and antiquity of the Sāṁkhya; he has not applied to the fact that there is a total absence of a reference or that there is only a partial reference to Sāṁkhya in the Upaniṣads the type of logic he used in rebutting Hertel's thesis based on the absence of a reference in the *Kenopaniṣad* to a particular aspect of the concept of *Brahman*.

Chronology of Upaniṣads

A consideration of the question of the connexion between the Upaniṣads and the Sāṁkhya system requires a discussion of the chronology of the Upaniṣads. Even after the scholarly researches of a long line of competent scholars, we cannot determine the exact date of the composition of any of the Upaniṣads. R.D. Ranade[49] phaces thirteen Upaniṣads in the category of Old Upaniṣads which belonged to the Upaniṣadic age to be placed between 1200 BC and 600 BC. He classes these Upaniṣads into five groups:

I. *Bṛhadāraṇyaka* and *Chāndogya*

II. *Īśa* and *Kena*

III. *Aitareya*, *Taittirīya* and *Kauṣītaki*

IV. *Kaṭha*, *Muṇḍaka* and *Śvetāśvatara*

V. *Praśna*, *Maitrī* and *Māṇḍūkya*.

49. *Op. cit.*, pp. 8-10.

But, generally scholars subscribe to a more limited time-bracket for these earlier Upaniṣads, placing their origin between 800 BC and 600 BC and bringing the lower limit down to 400 BC and 300 BC. Likewise, these early Upaniṣads are classified into a more simplified way into Old, Middle and Late Upaniṣads.

The relative chronology of the Upaniṣads and the known texts containing Sāṁkhya terms and ideas no doubt suits the possibility of the Upaniṣads containing the seeds of Sāṁkhya. But, as the dates of the different Upaniṣads are not settled, it will not be possible to dogmatise in favour of or against the possibility of Sāṁkhya evolving out of the Upaniṣadic philosophy or about any effort to determine the different stages in the evolution of Sāṁkhya through different Upaniṣads.

Affinities between Upaniṣads and Sāṁkhya

The Upaniṣads and Sāṁkhya system have some affinities, which may explain the occurrence of some of the Sāṁkhya principles and terms in the Upaniṣads. Both seem to have arisen in the same cultural milieu. They are concerned about similar problems. It was not unlikely that in formulating their views they came to similar inferences and views. The Upaniṣads and Sāṁkhya alike are taken to partake of the broader tradition of thought which is often designated as the Śramaṇa tradition.[50]

Another parallel theory, relevant to our present discussion, envisages a kṣatriya tradition as different from and, to some extent, opposed to the brāhmaṇa tradition. All those ideas institutions, and texts, which do not have a visible connexion with the Vedas and cultural traditions associated with them, are attributed to a different stream. The theory is often advanced with reference to the Purāṇas.[51] Elaborating the hypothesis it has been suggested that the Upaniṣads, Buddhism, Jainism, Sāṁkhya-Yoga and Purāṇas all were the

---

50. G.C. Pande, *Origines of Buddhism*, pp. 258-61, 541-57; *Śramanism and Its Impact on Indian Culture*, Ahmedabad, 1978.
51. Pargiter, *Ancient Indian Historical Tradition*, chapter V. See also V. Gordon Childe, *The Aryans*, p. 32.

creation of this kṣatriya tradition.[52] The theory has been criticised by many scholars.[53] It will not be correct to postulate a dichotomy between brāhmaṇa and kṣatriya traditions. Though there were occasions of clashes of interest between the brāhmaṇa and the kṣatriya in the social and political spheres, we cannot subscribe to the view that there was any fundamental difference between the philosophies and values of the two *varṇas*. But, it has to be conceded that the philosophies and literary traditions mentioned above are not completely compatible with the Vedic tradition and, to that extent, may be given a separate recognition. This would imply that the Upaniṣads and the Sāṁkhya system have certain common features and similarities in their ideas as a result of their being derived from the same broad stream of tradition.

Sāṁkhya Terminology and Principles in the Upaniṣads

The occurrence of Sāṁkhya terminology and Sāṁkhya and semi-Sāṁkhya principles in Upaniṣads can be explained in another manner. As we have suggested earlier, Sāṁkhya tradition had its separate existence free from the Upaniṣadic circles. Sāṁkhya is respected in Indian tradition as the earliest and very ancient system of philosophy. It is not unlikely that the authors of the Upaniṣads could not ignore the Sāṁkhya views and terms. If we postulate that the Sāṁkhya system and Upaniṣads had a common origin from one common and broader stream then the explanation of the occurrence of same terms and similar principles is facilitated.

It can be easily surmised that the terms in currency in the philosophical world of those times were put to handy use by the authors of the Upaniṣads. They do not seem to have acquired definite restricted meaning. It is only when terms get closely

---

52. R. Garbe, "Die Weisheit des Brahmanen oder die Kriegars" *Beitrage zur indischen Kulturgeschichte*, Berlin, 1903, pp. 1ff, E. Frauwallner, *pp. cit.*, pp. 34f.
53. H. Oldenberg, *Die Lehre der Upaniṣaden und die Anfange des Buddhismus*, Gottingen, 1915, pp. 166ff. *See* A.D. Pusalker in *The Vedic Age*, ed. by R.C. Majumdar and A.D. Pusalkar, p. 309.

connected with a particular system, which, thus, imparts a monopolistic connotation to them, that the terms receive a restricted usage. We know of cases where terms having a fixed meaning in the traditions of a particular sect or school have been used by writers outside the narrow circle of that group in a broader, more general or even different sense. But, before these terms receive the label of a particular class or group acquire a fixed meaning they are the common property of all people and can be used by anybody without the least hesitation. We suggest that in the case of terms, which later acquired a close association with Sāṁkhya philosophy, we can offer the same explanation. It seems likely that the terms under reference were in common circulation. They were borrowed by both the Upaniṣads and the Sāṁkhya from the same common source. Another possibility, which has to be recognised, is that though the Sāṁkhya system used these terms, their association with Sāṁkhya was not of such a long duration as to acquire a fixed association and a rigid meaning.

As regards the appearance of Sāṁkhya principles or proto-Sāṁkhya views in the Upaniṣads we have seen that the authors of the Upaniṣads were under no obligation to mention Sāṁkhya views or to quote from Sāṁkhya texts. They had their own pattern or system of thought. They would condescend to borrow from other sources details which could be adopted in their own pattern of thought. Those principles, which could not be accommodated within the Upaniṣadic system of thought, would hardly be expected to find a place in the Upaniṣads. The important question is the relevance of a particular principle or details associated with it to the Upaniṣadic thought. The authors of the Upaniṣadic texts cannot be expected to have been a willing party to the occurrence of irrelevant details or to principles radically opposed to their own finding a mention in the Upaniṣads. Thus, we can suggest that the Upaniṣads, when they refer to Sāṁkhya principles, select only those which were relevant to them and were not opposed to their ideas, omitting in the process other details.

Conclusion

In the light of our discussion we can formulate certain suggestions about the relevance of the Upaniṣadic evidence for delineating the origin and early history of Sāṁkhya.

We have seen that the absence of a reference to Sāṁkhya in the early Upaniṣads does not necessarily mean that the Sāṁkhya philosophy did not exist by the time of the early Upaniṣads. We cannot rule out the possibility that, though Sāṁkhya philosophy had originated, its principles were not considered relevant to be mentioned. Likewise, the reference to some of the Sāṁkhya principles and the occurrence of some of the Sāṁkhya terms in the Middle Upaniṣads does not lead to the inference that Sāṁkhya had developed only partially by that time and that its fuller form emerged after these Upaniṣads. Here also we have to recognise the possibility that Sāṁkhya system had been formulated before the period of the Middle Upaniṣads, but only those principles and terms of Sāṁkhya find mention which seemed to be relevant to the presentation in these Upaniṣadic texts.

The history of Sāṁkhya and the chronological evolution of its principles have to be determined independently, not necessarily on the basis of the presence or absence of references in the Upaniṣads.

4

Sāṁkhya Accounts in the Mokṣadharmaparva

Introduction

THERE is a lamentable dearth of original Sanskrit texts on Sāṁkhya. Besides the *Sāṁkyakārikā* and the two texts of uncertain dates, the *Tattvasamāsasūtra* and *Sāṁkhyapravacanasūtra*, we have only commentaries on these three to determine the nature of the Sāṁkhya system. It is against this background that the chapters in the *Mahābhārata* which expound Sāṁkhya deserve attention.

Difficulties in Using Mahābhārata Evidence

But, the testimony of the *Mahābhārata* chapters has not been duly utilised in presenting an account of Sāṁkhya principles, especially in tracing their historical development. Strangely, many competent scholars did not take this source very seriously. The main reason for this approach is the form of the presentation of these chapters. They have a popular character. They are narratives emboxed within the main story of the Epic. The literary presentation, on the part of the composer, with efforts at embellishment and effect, does not suit the exposition of philosophical principles. Expecting a more sober account befitting philosophy, some scholars have been prone not to treat the *Mahābhārata* chapters on Sāṁkhya as serious philosophies.

The popular interest has resulted in the inclusion of passages in the text which are not amenable to philosophical analysis.

Viewed from the philosophical angle, many passages are incomprehensible. Besides, we find instances of inconsistencies in the exposition of principles. This applies not only to the various chapters attributed to different persons but also to the statements in the same chapter.

A strong reason for scholars to ignore the *Mahābhārata* testimony is the general view identifying the exposition of Sāṁkhya in the *Sāṁkhyakārikā* as the exclusive account of Sāṁkhya. Any deviation from it was not recognised as Sāṁkhya and hence was not subjected to a respectful analysis. The account in the *Mahābhārata* shows major differences with the *Sāṁkhyakārikā*, even on some very vital issues, to the extent of amounting to a negation of its fundamental characteristics.

Methodological Pleading by Johnston

Methodologically, it is E.H. Johnston, who first argued for recognising the *Mahābhārata* chapters as an authentic source of information for the principles of Sāṁkhya. Very succinctly he offered the main arguments in favour of the reliability of the *Mahābhārata* for the philosophical material in it. "The teaching in the Epic is of a semipopular character and is not given with the precision of statement which would be expected of a formal treatise on philosophy. Further it covers a considerable period of time and emanates from many different writers and from several schools; naturally, therefore, there is discordance between different passages. But frequent ambiquity and lack of consistency do not prove that these epic descriptions are not to be taken seriously."[1]

Case of Epic Sāṁkhya

Scholars often speak of epic Sāṁkhya, as if it has its distinctive features and a uniform character, as distinguished from other formulations of Sāṁkhya principles. Some scholars recognised the bewildering differences in the various expositions of Sāṁkhya in the *Mahābhārata*, but try to identify features common in them,

1. *Early Sāṁkhya*, p. 4.

which they project as Epic Sāṁkhya. This creates the impression that the Sāṁkhya in the *Mahābhārata* has a special character.

Sāṁkhya Sections in the Mahābhārata

Two well-known sections dealing with Sāṁkhya principles in the *Mahābhārata* are the Mokṣadharmaparva and the *Gītā*. In dealing with Epic Sāṁkhya scholars generally emphasise these two. A third section, which is only casually noticed in dealing with Epic Sāṁkhya, is the *Anugītā*. In the *Mahābhārata* there are four main sections expounding Sāṁkhya principles: (1) Sanatsujātaparva in the Udyogaparva (V), chapters 41-45, (2) *Bhagavad Gītā* in the Bhīṣmaparva (VI), chapters 25-42, (3) Mokṣadharmaparva in the Śāntiparva (XII), chapters 174-365 and (4) *Anugītā* in the Āśvamedhikaparva (XIV), chapters 16-51. Scholars, who do not take into account all the different portions in the Epic, give only a partial picture of its Sāṁkhya evidence. As against this, some scholars club the evidence of the four sections together, as if they are one. It is often not realised that, though they form parts of the same text, they do not have a unified character. They are to be treated separately, because they were compositions of different periods. A.B. Keith,[2] for example, mentions the differing dates assigned to the four sections. But, in presenting an account of the Sāṁkhya philosophy in the epic, he refers to their testimony together. He brings out the varying shades of opinion on various philosophical issues, especially those considered by Sāṁkhya. It would be better if the nature of Sāṁkhya in the four sections is analysed separately and then a comparative and historical study is attempted. For the purposes of the present study we propose to concentrate on the exposition of Sāṁkhya in the Mokṣadharmaparva to analyse the views of different schools and teachers, and determine if we can speak of an Epic Sāṁkhya as a distinct tradition.

Nature of Sāṁkhya Accounts

In the Mokṣadharmaparva chapters we find discussions about

2. *A History of the Sāṁkhya Philosophy*, pp. 35-6.

various aspects of the subject of emancipation (*mokṣa*), including philosophical views about life and death, human bondage and the path of liberation, creation and dissolution, material world and self. These are presented in the form of dialogues (*saṁvāda*), narratives (*ākhyāna*) and religious poems (*gītā*). Sāṁkhya philosophical principles are often found mixed up with the general discussions on all these subjects, but without any specific reference to their Sāṁkhya associations. Likewise, the account of *adhyātma* in some chapters contains Sāṁkhya views, without formal declaration to that effect. The portions dealing specifically with Sāṁkhya principles as expounded by some sages or teachers are: chapters 182-8 (dialogue between Bhr̥gu and Bharadvāja), chapter 194 (*adhyātma* by Bhīṣma), chapters 201-6 (dialogue between Manu and Br̥haspati) chapters 210-17 (*adhyātma* by Kr̥ṣṇa), chapters 218-19 (*Pañcaśikhavākya*), chapter 299 (dialogue between Jaigīṣavya and Asita-Devala), chapters 236, 247-55 (dialogue between Vyāsa and Śuka), chapters 268-70 (dialogue between Syūmaraśmī and Kapila), chapter 275 (dialogue between Nārada and Asita-Devala), chapter 285 (*adhyātma* by Bhīṣma), chapters 300-1 (Sāṁkhya and Yoga by Bhīṣma) chapters 302-8 (dialogue between Vasiṣṭha and Karāla Janaka), chapters 310-18 (dialogue between Yājñavalkya and Daivarāti Janaka) and chapter 319 (dialogue between Pañcaśikha and Janaka).

Grouping of Sāṁkhya Accounts

We can place these accounts under several groups. First, we have chapters associated with the early Sāṁkhya teachers Kapila and Pañcaśikha. Second, there are chapters relating to other teachers, Jaigīṣavya and Asita-Devala, whose Sāṁkhya associations are known. Third, there are sages, Vasiṣṭha and Yājñavalkya, expounding Sāṁkhya to historical kings. Fourth, we have exposition by mythical and legendary sages, Manu and Bhr̥gu. Fifth, there are accounts given by Vyāsa, the author of the *Mahābhārata*, and Bhīṣma, one of the principal characters in the Epic. Evidently, the accounts in the fourth group do not have a historical basis. Those of the fifth group raise problems when we consider Vyāsa and Bhīṣma as established Sāṁkhya teachers. It is mostly in the case of the teachers in the first three groups that their position as expounders of Sāṁkhya principles is confirmed.

Critical Edition on Mokṣadharmaparva

V.M. Bedekar, who was associated with the work of the preparation of the critical edition of the *Mahābhārata* by the Bhandarkar Oriental Research Institute, in the Introduction to the Śāntiparva has added a lengthy note in accordance with the approach of its editor S.K. Belvalkar. He treats the Mokṣadharmaparva, covering chapters 168 to 353 as a single unit attributing it to its redactor. In the conspectus he analyses the contents of all these chapters. He points out 'the astonishing variety of metaphysical, cosmological, ethical and theological teachings' contained in it. Often 'basically unconnected and disparate with one another', they do not 'constitute any consistent, homogeneous system', nor is these any attempt 'to represent them on the form of a synthesis or digest'. According to Bedekar, the redactor 'had sought to bring together, in one single section, different philosophical teachings and views, which had been sponsored by different teachers in different periods'. He does not make any attempt to determine any chronological sequence, either on the basis of the textual apparatus or a comparative analysis of the philosophical contents. According to him, the doctrines mostly 'belong to a period of thought-ferment whence free-lance thinkers were speculating and setting forth tentative ideas pertaining to a variety of philosophical questions'. They reflect a distinct stage in the evolution of the classical philosophical and religious systems such as the Sāṁkhya, the Yoga, the Vedānta and the Pāñcarātra.

Bedekar presents the philosophical thought of the Mokṣadharmaparva as a whole under five heads: (1) Cosmology and Metaphysics; the soul and *mokṣa*, (2) The Sāṁkhya and the Yoga, (3) *kāla*, *svabhāva* and *niyati*, (4) Theistic ideas, and (5) Ethical ideas. The first receives a detailed treatment, in which fourteen dialogues have been analysed, without any distinction of the persons expounding them. They include many which proclaim to expound Sāṁkhya and Yoga principles.

Bedekar on Sāṁkhya in the Mokṣadharmaparva

In his account of the Sāṁkhya Bedekar notes chapters 211-12 (Pañcaśikha-Janaka dialogue), 222 (Jaigīṣavya), 228 (Vyāsa-Śuka dialogue), 261 (Kapila-Cow dialogue), 289 (Bhīṣma), 294 (Vasiṣṭha-Janaka dialogue), 337-8 (Vaiśampāyana).

Bedekar points out that in the Mokṣadharmaparva Sāṁkhya doctrines are specifically mentioned as such. They are by no means identical with the classical system of Sāṁkhya. He underlines two different sets of passages, in one Sāṁkhya appears merely as 'the way of knowledge characterised by some kind of logical reasoning, which ultimately leads to remuneration', and in the other, 'on account of the enumeration of various entities and principles which are represented as evolving from one another in a specific order, it seems to adumbrate the later classical system'.

According to Bedekar, the accounts though betraying 'an obvious tendency towards a gradual development into the classical Sāṁkhya' differ from it in many respects: (1) They do not always emphasise an absolute and clear-cut dualism; they point at the apex one single principle or entity, (2) They speak of eight *prakṛtis* in place of one, (3) The doctrine of *tanmātras* (subtle elements) is not yet developed, (4) The number, place and functions of the psychic faculties, *manas*, *ahaṁkāra* and *buddhi* have not been fixed, and (5) The source of the five senses of knowledge has not been fixed.

Bedekar depends on the present position of the text of the Mokṣadharmaparva. Though he notices two distinct and widely separated stands of Sāṁkhya exposition, he seems to give all the credit to the redactor of the section. He does not make any effort to determine the views of individual thinkers and schools and underline their differences. Historically the persons expounding the principles belonged to different periods and their views are to be located in their respective periods and not in the times of the redactor. Within the limitations of the textual position and the uniformity and synthesis introduced, this approach is expected to project Sāṁkhya expositions in the Mokṣadharmaparva in their proper form.

Text Group Representing an Early Form

G.J. Larson[3] analyses the chapters in the Mokṣadharmaparva. He attempts both chronological and comparative study. He follows E. Frauwallner and E.H. Johnston, who interpret a text-group in the Mokṣadharmaparva as representing the early form of Sāṁkhya. But, he agrees with J.A.B. van Buitenen in distinguishing two traditions of Sāṁkhya in this text-group.

In the Bombay edition (also Gita Press edition) of the *Mahābhārata* there are three sets of chapters which have common passages: XII.194; XII.247-8; XII.285. In the critical edition they are reduced to two sets XII.187 and XII.239-40. In the critical edition chapter XII.187 includes both chapters XII.194 and XII.285 of the Bombay edition. The three sets of chapters are taken to be based on one common source, which is termed as *Grund* (Ur) text by Frauwallner.

In this text-group van Buitenen[4] points out two distinct traditions on the basis of two usages of the term *bhāva* as (a) sensations, qualities and condition, and (b) successive evolutes of *buddhi*. He himself presents a reconstituted text. Larson[5] carries the argument further. He divides the text-group into two. He terms the reconstituted text of J.A.B. van Buitenen as Text A and the remaining passages as Text B. Text A uses *guṇa* or *bhāva* as referring to varying levels of evolution, whereas in Text B they signify moral or psychic condition or state.

According to Frauwallner, this text-group represents the original formulation of Sāṁkhya characterised by the absence of an evolutionary doctrine and a *guṇa* theory. Johnston also sees in it the original theory of *guṇa* or *bhāva* as psychical qualities. For an early date of this text-group Frauwallner points out that it is highly corrupt. Larson adds the argument of the absence of *ahaṁkāra* for

---

3. *The Classical Sāṁkhya*, pp. 108-27.
4. "Studies in Sāṁkhya", *JAOS*, Vol. 76 (1957), pp. 153-7, L. Rocher (ed.), *Studies in Indian Literature and Philosophy*, pp. 43-52.
5. *Op. cit.*, pp. 110-13.

the early date of the text-group. He describes Text A and Text B in this text-group as proto-Sāṁkhya traditions.

Other Groups

Larson[6] describes the remaining accounts by clubbing them together and listing varying views on different points. He further points out a mechanical difference in a set of passages which are quite unintelligible and probably represent aberrant speculations. The points, on which he records divergent views, are: listing of Sāṁkhya *tattvas*, the meaning of the term *guṇa*, the ultimate material reality, the nature of self or Self, the association with Yoga, and the emphasis on knowledge or 'knowing'. Larson has not attempted to find a system in the accounts of the varying principles and to attribute them to a specific tradition, school or teacher.

This task has been partially attempted by P. Chakravarti.[7] He holds that the *Mahābhārata* records various forms of Sāṁkhya. He identifies them on the basis of their mutual inconsistencies and their differences with the classical or orthodox Sāṁkhya of Īśvarakṛṣṇa. In this connection he refers to the expositions by Pañcaśikha,[8] Asita-Devala,[9] Bhīṣma,[10] Vasiṣṭha[11] and Yājñavalkya.[12] He tries to note the similarities as also differences which their principles have with the orthodox Sāṁkhya. He regards the Epic chapters as representing the atheistic school of Sāṁkhya.

---

6. *Op. cit.*, pp. 113-27.
7. *Origin and Development of the Sāṁkhya System of Thought*, pp. 42-64.
8. XII.219. Chakravarti points out that the account in *Mbh.*, XII.321.96-112 (= Gita Prees edn. XII.320.78-134), attributed by Hopkins, *The Great Epic of India*, p. 172 and Keith, *The Sāṁkhya System*, p. 47 to Pañcaśikha, actually records the views of Sulabhā.
9. XII.275.
10. XII.300-1.
11. XII.302-8.
12. XII.310-18.

Consideration in Evaluating Epic Sāṁkhya

Scholars, who speak of Epic Sāṁkhya, face serious problems, when they attempt to define its nature and spell out its characteristic features in terms of principles common to the various conflicting accounts. Their formulations are conditioned by their views on four vital preliminary issues.

The first point relates to the evaluation of the exposition of Sāṁkhya principles in the *Sāṁkhyakārikā*. Some earlier scholars identified Sāṁkhya with its form in this text. They consider it to be the original Sāṁkhya. Modern scholars modify the position by describing it as representing the orthodox Sāṁkhya or the Classical Sāṁkhya. This leaves open the possibility that there were other formulations of Sāṁkhya principles which differed from that of the *Sāṁkhyakārikā*. If we assume that Sāṁkhya means the principles as expounded by Īśvarakr̥ṣṇa, then our approach to the Epic Sāṁkhya will be conditioned significantly.

This point is of vital importance, with far-reaching implications for the history of Sāṁkhya. If the original Sāṁkhya is the same as expounded in the *Sāṁkhyakārikā*, then the accounts differing from it are to be considered as aberrations not deserving any respect for representing Sāṁkhya. This does not leave any scope for the Sāṁkhya principles changing and evolving in course of centuries. This will be inimical to the need for a serious, critical analysis of the Mokṣadharmaparva chapters.

Scholars, who regard the Sāṁkhya in the *Sāṁkhyakārikā* to be the orthodox Sāṁkhya, accept that there were deviations from this exposition and, even when new and conflicting principles were propounded, the earlier system continued to enjoy respectability as the authentic version. On this basis the Mokṣadharmaparva accounts will be interpreted as modifications mooted in the later history of Sāṁkhya, which were rejected and could not find a place in the sober exposition of Sāṁkhya philosophy.

The approach to the Mokṣadharmaparva accounts is significantly altered when the *Sāṁkhyakārikā* is taken to record the Classical Sāṁkhya. This view admits that Sāṁkhya was not set and fixed from the very beginning; it changed and grew in course of time. This means that passages, in which Sāṁkhya exposition differs from that in the *Sāṁkhyakārikā*, belong to different stages in the growth of Sāṁkhya, before it received a standard and classical formulation. Such an approach will evaluate the Mokṣadharmaparva chapters as recording the rich divergence of views, long before Īśvarakṛṣṇa gave them a standard form.

The third consideration, which conditions the critical assessment of the Mokṣadharmaparva accounts of Sāṁkhya, is the view about the nature of the *Mahābhārata* as a text and the date of its composition. If the *Mahābhārata* is taken to be a unified text composed by a single writer, all its chapters, including those in the Mokṣadharmaparva, will be evaluated as his creation. In that case the Sāṁkyha accounts in the Mokṣadharmaparva will be placed in the times of its author Vyāsa, and the Sāṁkhya teachers and their expositions will then be dated before the composition of the *Mahābhārata*. But, modern scholars generally agree that all the chapters in the text did not form part of it originally. It has acquired its present form as a result of accretions made over a long period of time. The Śāntiparva, including the Mokṣadharmaparva, is taken to have been affected by the insertion of new material. On this ground the Sāṁkhya teachers and their expositions cannot be said to have belonged to the times of the original composition of the *Mahābhārata*; they are to be regarded as later than the times of the characters of the Epic, but earlier than their incorporation in the text.

A fourth consideration to be kept in mind is the fact that all the chapters in the Mokṣadharmaparva are not uniformly of the same date. This is indicated by the critical edition of the text and is also borne out by the internal evidence of the accounts. Serious problems arise when principles expounded in different periods are processed together as if belonging to one single system.

It is in the light of these points that one has to examine the modern studies of Epic Sāṁkhya.

Epic Sāṁkhya the Original Sāṁkhya

GARBE

R. Garbe, who holds Sāṁkhya to have been the creation of one single mind and in vogue before the Epic took its present shape,[13] regards Epic Sāṁkhya to be merely a popularisation and contamination of the true Sāṁkhya and far removed from the precision and the clarity of the true system.[14] Keith and some other scholars criticise the view that the true Sāṁkhya was the creation of a single mind and hold that it was the result of a slow process of development. The true Sāṁkhya as a complete whole did not exist before or in the early period of the Epic.

DAHLMANN — EPIC SĀṀKHYA POST-UPANIṢADIC AND PRE-CLASSICAL

According to J. Dahlmann, the epic, from the beginning, had its present character as esssentially a book of customary law and usage illustrated by its tales. Thus, the epic is to be viewed as a unified text of great antiquity expressing a unitarian philosophy. Dahlmann holds that the epic preserves the original character of the Sāṁkhya and, in its form and expression, is almost identical with the Sāṁkhya in the *Sāṁkhyakārikā*. Originally Sāṁkhya was theistic and was the development of the unsystematic teachings of the early Upaniṣads.[15] It is a science of the *Brahman* (*Brahma-vidyā*), based on logic (*ānvīkṣikī*), though never abandoning its traditional foundations. It investigates the number of principles and their evolution from the Absolute. It accepts the absolute and impersonal *Brahman*, but denies any personal deity. It recognises a material nature as the source of the manifold empiric reality, though which the Absolute becomes multiplied. According to Dahlmann, the logical theory of the *Brahman* in the Epic Sāṁkhya gave up

---

13. R. Garbe (ed.), *Sāṁkhya Sūtra Vṛtti*, Introduction, p. iv.
14. *Die Sāṁkhya Philosophie*, pp. 54-9.
15. *Die Sāṁkhya Philosophie als Naturlehre und Erlösungslehre*, Berlin, 1902, pp. 1-19.

Brahman to become the Classical Sāṁkhya and, by stressing the unreality of the world, led to the illusion theory of Śaṅkara.

Keith[16] very aptly points out the basic mistake in Dahlmann's analysis when he says that 'the attempt to hold that the epic is a unity and that it teaches a unitarian philosophy is one which offends every canon of criticism and common sense, and the main doctrine that the atheistic Sāṁkhya is really a doctrine which accepts the *Brahman*, but denies the personal deity of the Yoga, is a *tour de force*'. It is generally believed that the *Mahābhārata* was not a unified text from the very beginning; it acquired its present form as a result of accretions from time to time. Hence, all the views expressed in different parts of the text cannot be attributed to one single author. Further, it will not be appropriate to single out any particular exposition as representative of the philosophical views of the text. The *Mahābhārata* especially the Mokṣadharmaparva, contains several accounts of Sāṁkhya, which are so much conflicting that their differences cannot be ironed out to present one standard exposition.

Dahlmann's view that the Epic Sāṁkhya represents a development of the principles in the early Upaniṣads underlines similarities with some but not all of the expositions of Sāṁkhya in the Mokṣadharmaparva. The similarities do not necessarily imply that one account was indebted to another. Possibly they were breathing a common intellectual atmosphere. The *Mahābhārata* refers to the expositions as ancient narratives. Though the insertion of the relevant chapters in the *Mahābhārata* occurred much later, the persons participating in the dialogues can be historically identified and are to be located in the times of the Upaniṣads. There is no wide chronological gap between these persons and the Upaniṣads to necessitate the acceptance of the early Upaniṣads as the source of Epic Sāṁkhya.

Historically Dahlmann is correct when he places Epic Sāṁkhya before the Classical Sāṁkhya, but the process of development is not so simple as Dahlmann suggests it to be. Likewise, the view that

16. *Op. cit.*, p. 56.

Śaṅkara's theory of illusion resulted from emphasising the unreality of the world in the epic Sāṁkhya is an over simplification of the issues. The antecedents of Śaṅkara's Advaita Vedānata are well known and have their own line of evolution.

Hopkins — Sāṁkhya Predominance in the Epic

E.W. Hopkins, who appreciates the historical problems about the original nature of the *Mahābhārata* text and its later expansion, is in a better position to analyse the philosophical accounts in it. He does not believe that any single philosophical system is uniformly presented in the *Mahābhārata*. He does not argue that the traditional six systems of philosophy are represented in the Epic. He, however, traces six shades of philosophical ideas. They are not established philosophical systems. They have their distinctive character, but, at the same time, have similarities also. The six systems emphasised by Hopkins are (a) Vedic orthodoxy, (b) Brāhmaṇism (the doctrine of *Brahman*), without, and sometimes, with the illusion theory, (c) the Sāṁkhya, (d) the Yoga, (f) and (g) the Pāśupatas and the Bhāgavatas adopting a good deal of Sāṁkhya-Yoga philosophy.[17]

In this philosophical analysis we can easily see the primacy of Sāṁkhya along with Yoga. Leaving aside Vedic orthodoxy, the remaining five reflect Sāṁkhya affiliation. But significantly there is no common feature of Sāṁkhya in the associated systems. Sāṁkhya and its influence assumes different forms, so that one cannot speak of a uniform system of epic Sāṁkhya. Here besides the exposition of Sāṁkhya and Yoga in their separate forms, we find Sāṁkhya-Yoga philosophy being adopted by the two theistic sects, the Pāśupatas (the worshippers of Śiva) and Bhāgavatas (the worshippers of Viṣṇu). Even the system of Brāhmaṇism, though advocating the principle of *Brahman* as the Absolute at the top, mentions Sāṁkhya principles at the lower stratum. Thus, there is no case of a unitary epic Sāṁkhya in the analysis offered by Hopkins. Hopkins[18] was the first to point out that the three sets of chapters represent the three versions of one text.

17. *Op. cit.*
18. *Op. cit.*

Oldenberg — Developed Pre-classical Sāṁkhya

H. Oldenberg, who is of the view that Sāṁkhya, like all other systems, is the product of development over a long period of time, regards the Mokṣadharmaparva to represent a developed form of Sāṁkhya-like speculations, more developed than the pre-classical Sāṁkhya of the Upaniṣads, but not as yet having the full classical form. This section of the *Mahābhārata* enumerates twenty-five categories, the twenty-fifth comprising of the double notion of the individual *puruṣas* and the cosmic *puruṣa*. The twenty-sixth category refers to the released *puruṣa* as contrasted with the bound *puruṣa*.[19]

The suggestion of Oldenberg that the twenty-fifth category includes both the individual spirits and the absolute spirit is not plausible. If such a distinction was made by the Sāṁkhya, it would have been maintained by enumerating the two categories of spirits separately in the list of *tattvas*. Sāṁkhya in the Mokṣadharmaparva is described as including twenty-five categories, whereas Yoga is said to recognise a twenty-sixth category. This twenty-sixth category of Yoga in the Mokṣadharmaparva is different from Īśvara of the *Yogasūtra*. It, thus, seems that the Mokṣadharmaparva associates the absolute spirit with the Sāṁkhya-Yoga and not with Sāṁkhya proper. The Sāṁkhya, represented in the Epic, as argued by Keith, is a Sāṁkhya without an absolute.

Keith — Genuine Earlier Sāṁkhya

A.B. Keith maintains that the Epic contains many kinds of speculation, including a dominant theistic tinge along with some Vedāntic ideas.[20] According to him, some later portions of the Mokṣadharmaparva are the earliest evidence for a full Sāṁkhya system, but without some of the minor classical doctrines.[21] He

19. "Zur Geschichte der Sāṁkhya-philosophie", *Nachrichten von der königlichen Gessellschaft der Wissenschaften zu Gottingen*, Philologisch-historische Klasse aus dem Jahre, 1917, pp. 218-20, 235-40.
20. *Op. cit.*, pp. 36-7.
21. *Ibid.*, p. 65.

summarises his findings about Sāṁkhya in the Epic:

> It is not a blurred version of the classical Sāṁkhya, nor is there any reason to believe that the classical Sāṁkhya had already been excogitated by this period. On the other hand, it is not a Sāṁkhya which recognises an absolute, and merely denies a personal creator: it is, aprat from efforts made by the epic to torture it into more orthodox pantheism, a system which denies an absolute, and asserts instead a multiplicity of individual souls, but in the epic . . . it is still without some of the more characteristics of its minor doctrines, and has not achieved the completeness and . . . clarity of outline which mark its classical form.[22]

Keith is justified in recognising the epic Sāṁkhya to be a genuine exposition of Sāṁkhya principles representing a stage of development much before the times of the *Sāṁkhyakārikā*. But, in his final analysis he does not underline the conflicting accounts of Sāṁkhya in the epic. He ignores the discordant details and variations presented by the individual teachers and interprets Epic Sāṁkhya to represent a stage in the development of the Sāṁkhya which includes a set and definite exposition of principles.

Dasgupta — Schools of Sāṁkhya

S.N. Dasgupta does not enter into a detailed analysis of the Sāṁkhya evidence in the *Mahābhārata*. He, however, notes that the Epic refers to more than the one school of Sāṁkhya. According to him,[23] *Mahābhārata*, XII. 318 mentions three schools of Sāṁkhya: those who admitted twenty-four categories, those who admitted twenty-five, and those who admitted twenty-six categories. He takes the first school to be represented by Pañcaśikha in *Mahābhārata*, XII.219. He holds that the system of Sāṁkhya Pañcaśikha sketches is the same as that of Caraka and that doctrines similar to this school are referred to in some other chapters, *Mahābhārata*, XII.203, 204.

22. H. Oldenberg, *op. cit.*, pp. 64-5.
23. *A History of Indian Philosophy*, Vol. I, p. 217.

Dasgupta regards the second school admitting twenty-five categories as being the well-known orthodox Sāṁkhya system. The third school admitted as the twenty-sixth category a supreme being in addition to *puruṣa*.

Dasgupta's analysis is sketchy and incomplete, based only on four chapters of the *Mahābhārata*. This gives a very partial picture of Sāṁkhya in the Epic. There is much more diversity of views suggesting many more schools. Dasgupta blacks out the rich variety of Sāṁkhya accounts in the Epic.

Dasgupta associates Pañcaśikha with the school admitting twenty-four categories and brackets him with Caraka. No doubt, there are significant similarities in the expositions of Sāṁkhya by Pañcaśikha and Caraka. But, Pañcaśikha is regarded by Īśvarakṛṣṇa himself as having originally expounded the Sāṁkhya which he presents in the *Sāṁkhyakārikā*.

Dasgupta interprets the reference to twenty-five categories as standing for the classical Sāṁkhya. It is generally believed that the classical Sāṁkhya was formulated later than the Mokṣadharma-parva. The mention of twenty-five categories alone does not mean the formulation of classical Sāṁkhya. There are many other distinguishing features of the classical Sāṁkhya. These have to be confirmed in any account of Sāṁkhya; they cannot be assumed by a mere reference to twenty-five categories.

Dasgupta[24] points out that the third school admitting twenty-six categories agrees with the orthodox Yoga school. He holds it to be the form of Sāṁkhya advocated in the *Mahābhārata*. This is a significant point, but has not been elaborated by Dasgupta. He does not demonstrate whether other chapters in the *Mahābhārata* also subscribe to this view. In the Epic a reference to the twenty-sixth category is made by Vasiṣṭha[25] and Yājñavalkya.[26] There is no reason why this view is to be regarded as typical of Sāṁkhya in the *Mahābhārata*.

24. S.N. Dasgupta, *op. cit.*
25. *Mbh.*, XII. 308.7.7, 11, 16-17, 20-1.
26. *Ibid.*, XII.318.72, 77, 80.

The basic defect in Dasgupta's view is his tracing a reference to three schools of Sāṁkhya in *Mbh*, XII.318.[27] We have discussed elsewhere[28] the passages which are supposed to contain a reference to three Sāṁkhya schools admitting respectively twenty-four, twenty-five and twenty-six categories. The passages actually refer to the twenty-fourth, twenty-fifth and twenty-sixth categories. This does not mean that there were schools believing in twenty-four, twenty-five and twenty-six categories. What we have here is an account of a Sāṁkhya school which admits twenty-six categories; the twenty-fourth, twenty-fifth and twenty-sixth categories are explained in course of the exposition of twenty-six categories. Dasgupta says that 'the schools of Sāṁkhya of twenty-four and twenty-five categories are here denounced as unsatisfactory'. But the relevant passages do not discuss any of these supposed schools. What they denounce is the limited knowledge possessed by the twenty-fourth and twenty-fifth categories, as contrasted with that by the twenty-sixth category.

Merit of Mahābhārata Evidence

JOHNSTON

Johnston recognises the merits of the *Mahābhārata* evidence for the early history of Sāṁkhya. Of the four groups of texts, on which he depends for this, the epic texts are the second, placed after the Upaniṣads but before the *Buddhacarita* and the *Carakasaṁhitā*, with the classical texts of the *Yogasūtra* and the *Sāṁkhyakārikā* belonging to the fourth. In the epic group he mentions the *Anugītā* and the last six chapters in the *Gītā* as being later. In the Mokṣadharmaparva he admits earlier and later portions, the earlier ones being similar in thought to the first twelve chapters in the *Gītā* and to Aśvaghoṣa's *Buddhacarita*. He postulates five phases in the development of Sāṁkhya speculation in terms of the principles. He does refer to the phases represented in the Upaniṣads, but does not

27. He possibly relies on XII.318.72.
28. See *infra* chapters 5 and 10.

spell out the stage recorded by the Epic. He does not analyse the various schools of Sāṁkhya in the Epic, except referring to the views of Pañcaśikha. It seems that he does not take the Epic accounts to refer to one particular stage but to contain evidence for the first-four stages. Thus, Johnston does not assign one unified character to the exposition of Sāṁkhya in the Epic.

FRAUWALLNER

For the history of Sāṁkhya E. Frauwallner[29] considers the Epic evidence to be more relevant and authentic than that of the Upaniṣads, *Buddhacarita* and *Carakasaṁhitā*. He admits that it is impossible to sort out earlier portions from the later ones in many cases. He regards the *Grund* (Ur) text, which formed the basis of three different sets of chapters in the Mokṣadharmaparva, to represent the first stage in the history of Sāṁkhya. According to him, this extremely old tradition originated before the writing of the Mokṣadharmaparva. The second stage of speculation is reflected in the passages recording the questions of Śuka.

Frauwallner has emphasised the importance of the Epic accounts. But, this has led to an overemphasis on this source of evidence and the exclusion of others. He has not given proper allowance to the process of revision and the uniformity introduced by the composer of these chapters. He has not cared to determine the nature of Sāṁkhya system before the stage represented by the *Grund* (Ur) text.

J.A.B. VAN BUITENEN

J.A.B. van Buitenen makes improvement upon Frauwallner's studies. He bases himself on the Epic chapters analysed by Frauwallner. He demonstrates that the development of Sāṁkhya was incredibly complex. In the concerned chapters he reconstructs two passages. One describes an early horizontal theory using *bhāva* to mean moral or psychical quality. The second uses *bhāva* to mean

---

29. *History of Indian Philosophy*, pp. 379-81.

guṇa or 'the tried in which *rajas* figures' and implies a horizontal theory of evolution in which *buddhi* successively evolves into *manas*, senses and elements. van Buitenen does not consider all the various accounts of Sāṁkhya in the Mokṣadharmaparva.

Nature and Complexity Evidence — Sāṁkhya-Yoga School

CHAKRAVARTI

The analysis of Sāṁkhya material in the *Mahābhārata* offered by Chakravarti and Larson mark definite improvement in appreciating the true nature of the evidence and its complexities.

Chakravarti recognises that there are many forms of Sāṁkhya in the *Mahābhārata*, which are not always consistent and do not fully *tally*, with the Sāṁkhya of Īśvarakṛṣṇa. He discusses the different accounts of Sāṁkhya, pointing out their special features and differences with the *Sāṁkhyakārikā* version. He admits that the Epic does not always offer the same exposition in the different chapters, but notes two common points in them, namely, representing the atheistic school as devoid of belief in a supreme God, and describing the organs as material objects. Chakravarti shows that the Epic presupposes the existence of the Sāṁkhya literature. According to him, the *Gītā* reflects the full-fledged Sāṁkhya.

Chakravarti treats the accounts of Sāṁkhya in the Epic as the expositions of the different schools of Sāṁkhya in those days. To gain wide popularity the Epic incorporated the sects and systems prevalent, including the many schools in which Sāṁkhya was divided.

Chakravarti admits that some chapters in the Epic, XII.301 for instance, do not represent the true Sāṁkhya view. Here the sectarian interest is predominant. Terms and tenets of the Sāṁkhya are used, but Nārāyaṇa is mentioned as the Supreme Lord, from whom proceed creation and destruction. Such expositions cannot be regarded as Sāṁkhya accounts. Chakravarti views them as the contamination of the proper Sāṁkhya.

Chakravarti shows that the Epic records a Sāṁkhya school which subscribes to the doctrines of *Brahman*. Accounts mentioning a twenty-sixth category belong to this type. According to Chakravarti, this is not the doctrine of pure Sāṁkhya. He mentions it as the Sāṁkhya-Yoga school of the Epic. It represents a distinguishing feature of the Sāṁkhya accounts in the epic and marks a significant stage in the history of Sāṁkhya. Here Sāṁkhya and Yoga go together and form a single unit.

LARSON

We have already noted the main points in the treatment of Sāṁkhya chapters in the Mokṣadharmaparva offered by Larson. He also argues for a Sāṁkhya-Yoga school being represented in the Epic. But, his interpretation of the distinguishing features of this school differs from that of Chakravarti. He underlines passages which characterise Sāṁkhya and Yoga separately as against those which emphasise their oneness. According to him, Sāṁkhya emphasises knowledge as the best means of salvation. Yoga, generally treated as the method of salvation by 'doing', is used here in the sense of 'a disciplined course of action'. Sāṁkhya-Yoga is a tradition of Yoga which emphasises the discipline of knowledge. According to Larson, this school claimed an independent position apart from the other tradition of undifferentiated Sāṁkhya and Yoga. It emphasised the knowing of the principles and of the distinction between the field and the field-knower (self) more than practice and meditation, and was interested in the enumeration of *tattvas*.

Evaluation of Mokṣadharmaparva Evidence

DIVERSITY OF EXPOSITIONS

Thus, we see that the exposition of Sāṁkhya in the Epic is not of one set type. We cannot identify features which characterise all the accounts. There are several expositions which have their own individuality and differ from one another or many points. The Mokṣadharmaparva section contains a collection of expositions of several schools and individual teachers.

PRESUPPOSES VAST SĀṀKHYA LITERATURE

The Epic presupposes the existence of a vast and varied Sāṁkhya literature. It specifically refers to the vastness of the existing Sāṁkhya literature. It gives a long list of Sāṁkhya teachers from whom Viśvāvasu claims to have learnt Sāṁkhya. Besides a few mythical names, it mentions a number of sages and individuals. It discusses in detail the principles expounded by some teachers. An analysis of the chapters helps identify some of the Sāṁkhya schools.

REPRESENT MORE THAN ONE STAGE

It would not be correct to take all these accounts to represent one particular stage in the history of Sāṁkhya. Though they are known from the Mokṣadharmaparva, which fixes a lower limit to their date, they all originally did not belong to one and the same period. They refer to different periods. Such as a long period, with so many divergent schools and teachers, if to be treated together, has to be divided into sub-phases. There is no one common label to cover all the various shades of Sāṁkhya accounts.

NO CHRONOLOGICAL SEQUENCE

The chapters do not maintain a chronological sequence. They are not incorporated in the order in which the events recorded in them possibly occurred. To illustrate, the chapters in which Vasiṣṭha imparts a knowledge of Sāṁkhya to Karāla Janaka are placed earlier than those in which Yājñavalkya instructs Daivarāti Janaka, though Karāla Janaka came long after Daivarāti Janaka.

EARLY PERIOD OF SĀṀKHYA

The Sāṁkhya accounts refer to an early period, in any case several centuries before the incorporation of the chapters in the Mokṣadharmaparva. This is admitted by the author of these chapters, when he refers to the accounts of the dialogue expounding Sāṁkhya principles as ancient narratives (*itihāsam purātanam*). It is also to be noted that, within the structure of the main story of the Epic, the sages and teachers presenting Sāṁkhya principles are made contemporaries of historical persons who belong to the *Brāhmaṇa*-Upaniṣad period. They are in some cases connected with Pañcaśikha and Jaigīṣavya as contemporaries, senior or junior.

PHILOSOPHICALLY EARLIER

Philosophically also these accounts are to be dated much earlier than the Sāṁkhya of Īśvarakṛṣṇa. They differ from the *Sāṁkhyakārikā* version on many a vital point and imply a long course of evolution to reach the later form. It is clear that the author of the chapters had no knowledge of the characteristic details of the later version. Further, the Mokṣadharmaparva chapters breathe an atmosphere of a very early phase in the development of philosophical thought. It is only the Sāṁkhya and the Yoga which are named here. The other systems of philosophy are conspicuous by their absence. They do not seem to have acquired their separate identity as systems of philosophy. Sāṁkhya and Yoga alone dominate the philosophical horizon. Even those philosophical accounts, which do not claim to expound Sāṁkhya and Yoga, are predominantly Sāṁkhya in form and principles.

SIMILARITIES WITH UPANIṢADS

These accounts of Sāṁkhya have similarities with the philosophical views in the Upaniṣads on many an important point. This has led some scholars to trace the origin of Sāṁkhya to Upaniṣadic speculations. We have elsewhere[30] argued that Sāṁkhya is not the lineal development of Upaniṣadic philosophy. Sāṁkhya had its own independent origin and course of development. Besides similarities in respect of the categories and their evolution, we find resemblance between the two about the general and fundamental approach of *adhyātma*, belief in *Brahman*, and the method of salvation for the individual soul. It is not a case of one borrowing from the other. The ideas were the common features of the intellectual

30. See *supra*, chapter 3.

life of the *Brāhmaṇa*-Upaniṣad period and are to be noticed also in the Sāṁkhya accounts of the period.

STRATIFICATION OF VIEWS

We may not be able to frame a chronological chart of the Sāṁkhya accounts in the Epic and to determine the various stages in the development of their principles. A criterion, followed by some scholars, is the extent of the resemblance of an account with the *Sāṁkhyakārikā* version. But, this cannot be a definite pointer. There are some indications of earlier and later strata in the Sāṁkhya accounts. The similarities in three chapters have been interpreted by Frauwallner to refer to an earlier *Grund* (Ur) text. Following van Buitenen, Larson has distinguished two texts, A and B, even in it. Text A represents philosophical principles of an early date, whereas Text B records principles of a later phase. Likewise, accounts of Sāṁkhya under the name of Sāṁkhya-Yoga also refer to a later period. In an early phase Sāṁkhya and Yoga were undifferentiated. Later they started developing in their own line. This Sāṁkhya school held that Sāṁkhya and Yoga are one and are not to be treated as separate. It emphasised the method of 'knowing' more than that of meditation and 'doing'.

FORM AND STYLE OF PRESENTATION

A seriouss problem arises on account of the form and style of these chapters. They have the same structure of dialogue introduced by Bhīṣma. The versification and style also have a common characteristic. Clearly the accounts are not presented in the form in which the individual teachers expounded them. When and by whom they were included in the Epic cannot be determined. It is generally suggested that they were incorporated at different periods. This does not seem to be very likely. The close similarity in their form and style would indicate that, though the accounts look back to the periods of their original formulation, they were included at one and the same period. In evaluating these accounts we have to give due allowance to the element of uniformity, sometimes involving repetition in verses and expressions, caused by the revising hand of the composer of the chapters.

Conclusion

Thus, we can say that the Sāṁkhya represented in the Epic accounts was genuine Sāṁkhya in a period long before that of the *Sāṁkhyakārikā*. It cannot be dubbed as the vulgarisation of Sāṁkhya or its garbled version. It was as authentic as the later Sāṁkhya system. If the *Sāṁkhyakārikā* account is considered to be Classical Sāṁkhya, then the Epic accounts will be pre-Classical Sāṁkhya. But, this should not lead to a misconceived notion that these accounts are undeveloped Sāṁkhya. This judgement arises from the assumption that the *Sāṁkhyakārikā* represents the true Sāṁkhya.

5

Yājñavalkya — An Independent Sāṁkhya Tradition

Introduction

THE lists of Sāṁkhya teachers found in the commentaries on the *Sāṁkhyakārikā* do not contain the name of Yājñavalkya. The other Sāṁkhya sources also do not mention his name as a Sāṁkhya teacher. It is only in the Mokṣadharmaparva section of the Śāntiparva of the *Mahābhārata*, chapters 310 to 318,[1] that Yājñavalkya is represented as a Sāṁkhya teacher. The *Bṛhadāraṇyaka Upaniṣad* (II.4.1; III.5.1) mentions him as a great philosopher, but there is no reference to his being an authority on Sāṁkhya.

The absence of the name of Yājñavalkya in the lists appended by the commentators on the *Sāṁkhyakārikā* is not surprising. These commentators give the names of Sāṁkhya teachers who belonged to the period of the gap between Pañacaśikha and Īśvarakṛṣṇa. But, as we have demonstrated below, Yājñavalkya flourished before Pañcaśikha, hence he is omitted by the commentators.

Yājñavalkya in Mokṣadharmaparva

The exposition of Sāṁkhya by Yājñavalkya in the Mokṣa-

1. We have consulted the Gita Press, Gorakhpur edition of the *Mahābhārata*.

dharmaparva has not received due importance in the modern studies of Sāṁkhya. Even those scholars, who have analysed the Epic material on Sāṁkhya, have not always cared to notice the distinctive character of the Sāṁkhya principles expounded by Yājñavalkya. P. Chakravarti[2] has analysed the chapters presenting the Sāṁkhya principles of Yājñavalkya. But he concentrates on a few points having parallels with the Sāṁkhya account of Vasiṣṭha.

The chapters in the Mokṣadharmaparva which contain Yājñavalkya views are chapters 310-18. The main principles noticed by U.V. Shastri[3] are those laid down in *Mbh.*, XII. 310.10-18; XII.313.15, 17-28; XII.315.3, 11; XII.318.55, 72-79. The passages emphasised by A.P. Mishra[4] are *Mbh.*, XII.310.10-25; XII.313. 16-28; XII.314.5-12; XII.318.77, 80. He reproduces all these verses, but does not analyse them to present the principles.

The account of Sāṁkhya in the Mokṣadharmaparva has an interesting structural feature. It is emboxed within the general framework of the narrative of the *Mahābhārata* in which Bhīṣma, lying on the bed of arrows in the war, replies to questions raised by Yudhiṣṭhira. Yudhiṣṭhira seeks to be enlightened about the *tattva* which is eternal, indestructible and unchanging, and is free from *dharma* and *adharma*, all doubts, birth and death, and merit and sin. In his reply Bhīṣma narrates the ancient account of the dialogue between Yājñavalkya and Daivarāti Janaka. In this presentation, Yājñavalkya inserts an account of his own exposition to Viśvāvasu, the Gandharva King.

In chapter 310 Yājñavalkya proposes to expound the highest knowledge, particularly the Sāṁkhya. He mentions eight *prakṛtis* — *avyakta*, *mahat*, *ahaṁkāra* and *pṛthivī*, *vāyu*, *ākāśa*, *āpa* and *jyoti* (*agni*). Then he enumerates sixteen *vikāras*, which are rooted in the five elements (*mahābhūtas*). Of these, the five sensations of *śabda*, *sparśa*, *rūpa*, *rasa* and *gandha*, along with the five senses of

2. *Origin and Development of the Sāṁkhya System of Thought*, pp. 49-53.
3. *Sāṁkhyadarśana kā Itihāsa*, pp. 592-3. We have transferred the references to the Gita Press edition.
4. *Sāṁkhyadarśana kī Aitihāsika Paramparā*, pp. 150-2.

actions, are termed as *viśeṣas*, whereas the five senses of knowledge (*buddhīndriyas*) are called *saviśeṣas*. *Manas* is called the sixteenth *vikāra*.

Yājñavalkya arranges the evolution of *tattvas* from *prakṛti* under nine *sargas*: *prādhānika* (*mahat* from *avyakta*), *buddhyātmaka* (*ahaṁkāra* from *mahat*), *āhaṁkārika* (*manas* from *ahaṁkāra*), *mānasa* (*mahābhūtas* from *manas*), *bhautika* (five subjects from *mahābhūtas*), *bahucintātmaka* (five sense-organs), *aindriyaka* (five *karmendriyas*), *ārjavaka* (*prāṇa*, *samāna*, *vyāna* and *udāna* flowing upwards) and again *ārjavaka* (*vyāna*, *udāna* and *apāna* flowing downward).

In chapter 311 Yājñavalkya mentions the time span (*kāla-saṁkhyā*) in terms of day and night of *avyakta*, *mahat*, *ahaṁkāra*, *manas* and subjects (*viṣaya*). He describes the process of creation. The *pratibhuddha* (the Supreme Consciousness) created vegetation (*oṣadhi*) in the beginning. He created Brahmā from the Golden Egg (*hiraṇyāṇḍa*). Brahmā created earth, sky and heaven and four *putras* (*buddhi*, *ahaṁkāra*, *manas* and *citta*), who were the *pitṛs* of the *pitṛs* (creators of the *pañca-mahābhūtas*). The *devas* (sense-organs) are the sons of the *pitṛs* (five *mahābhūtas*). The entire movable and immovable world is covered by the *devas*. The *parameṣṭhin* (*ahaṁkāra*) creates the five elements (*bhūtas*). The *śabda*, *sparśa*, *rūpa*, *rasa* and *gandha* are the special subjects (*viśeṣa*) of the *mahābhūtas*. Yājñavalkya says that *manas* is the foremost among the *indriyas*.

Chapter 312 describes the process of dissolution (*saṁhāra*). It is initiated by the eternal *avyakta Brahman* propelling the personified god *ahaṁkāra* who appears as the sun (*āditya*) and burns all animate and inanimate objects on the earth. The earth is engulfed by water which is destroyed by *kālāgni*. *Kālāgni*, *vāyu*, *ākāśa*, *manas*, *ahaṁkāra* and *buddhi* follow in succession, the succeeding one swallowing the preceding one. The eternal (*ananta*) supreme (*īśvara*), *Brahman* (*mahātmā*) assimilates *buddhi*. At the end He alone remains.

In chapter 313 several items are listed under the classification of *adhyātma*, *adhibhūta* and *adhidaivata*. The *prakṛti* is said to create many *guṇas* (qualities) of a *puruṣa* (individual) which are grouped into three: *sattva, rajas and tamas*. Chapter 314 brings out the difference between *puruṣas* characterised by the three *guṇas*. It also envisages a combination of two or three *guṇas*. *Prakṛti* is *acetana*, but when the *parama tattva* subsists in it, it creates and destroys. Janaka asks significant questions to which Yājñavalkya replies in the following chapters.

Chapter 315 brings out the difference between *prakṛti* and *puruṣa*. The *avyakta prakṛti* is characterised by *guṇas*. The *puruṣa* is *nitya* and *akṣara*. On account of ignorance *puruṣa* gets associated with *guṇas*. *Puruṣa* is called *sarga-dharma*, *yoga-dharma*, *prakṛti-dharma*, *bīja-dharma* and *guṇa-dharma* for considering itself the *kartā* (doer) of *sarga*, *yoga*, *prakṛti*, *bīja* and *guṇa*. *Puruṣa* is *kevala* (unassociated with *prakṛti*. Though *nitya* and *avyakta*, *puruṣa* is described as *anitya* and *vyakta*, because of its association with *prakṛti*. *Prakṛti* is one, but *puruṣa* is plural. With the help of apt analogies the difference as also the relationship between the two are brought out. This account is referred to as the *sāṁkhya-jñāna*. Chapter 316 presents the *yoga-jñāna*. It says that there is no knowledge (*jñāna*) like Sāṁkhya, and no power (*bala*) like Yoga. The two are not separate; they are one. In Yoga the *prāṇa* (*rudra*) has the main importance. Controlling it, one can move in all the ten directions. Yoga is characterised by eight *guṇas*, it leads to eight subtle qualities (*guṇas*). Yoga is of two kinds — *dhāraṇā* is *saguṇa* and *prāṇāyāma* is *nirguṇa*. Practical advice is given for controlling the senses: through a process of controlling *mana*, *ahaṁkāra* and *buddhi* one is to meditate on the *avyaya* Brahmā. In beautiful verses the characteristic qualities of a *yogī* are described.

Chapter 317 describes the fate of the soul according to the part of the body from which it leaves. It mentions the *ariṣṭas* (prognostics) or indications of coming death and advises the course of action to be followed by a *yogī*.

In chapter 318 Yājñavalkya relates how he acquired knowledge through the blessings of Sūrya. He refers to his dialogue with Viśvāvasu, the Gandharva, who was expert in the knowledge of the essence of the Veda (*vedāntajñānakovida*). Viśvāvasu asked him twenty-four questions relating to the Veda and a twenty-fifth on the *ānvikṣikī*. The twenty-four questions related to the meaning of *jñāna, jñeya, jñātā, ajña, ka, tapā, atapā, sūrya, atisūrya, vidyā, avidyā, vedya, avedya, cala, acala, apūrva, akṣaya* and *kṣaya*. Yājñavalkya claims to have churned in his mind in the Upaniṣad with its auxiliary parts and the *ānvikṣikī*. He explains the twenty-four terms as referring to the dichotism between *puruṣa* and *prakṛti*. He refers to this knowledge as *ānvikṣikī*, which leads to emancipation. He who does not understand the *vedya* (the *avyakta*) has not studied the Veda. A knowledge of *puruṣa* and *prakṛti* saves a man from the cycle of birth and death. Giving up the Vedic rites, which are perishable, one should follow the ever-lasting *dharma*. One should realise the twenty-sixth *tattva* (*ṣaḍviṁśam*). The twenty-fifth *tattva* (*pañcaviṁśaka*) is not different from the twenty-sixth. Explaining the essence of knowledge to Viśvāvasu, Yājñavalkya says that the twenty-fifth *tattva* knows *prakṛti*, but *prakṛti* does not know the twenty-fifth *tattva*. *Prakṛti* is also designated as *pradhāna*. The twenty-fifth does not realise the twenty-sixth. The twenty-sixth sees the twenty-fifth and the twenty-fourth. When the twenty-fifth realises its separateness from the twenty-fourth, it realises the twenty-sixth. The twenty-fifth and the twenty-sixth are not different. Yājñavalkya refers to these three as *apratibuddha, budhyamāna* and *buddha*.

Concluding his exposition Yājñavalkya says that *mokṣa* is possible through *jñāna*, which should be received from a person of any *varṇa*, because, being born of Brahmā, all *varṇa*s are brāhmaṇa. The entire world is Brahmā.

Sāṁkhya as expounded by Yājñavalkya

We find several distinctive features in this account of Sāṁkhya. P. Chakravarti[5] points out its principles which tally with the traditional Sāṁkhya: *prakṛti* is constituted of the *guṇa*s; it cannot transcend them; it is devoid of consciousness; being presided over the

5. *Op.cit.*, pp. 51-2.

puruṣa, it creates and destroys. Yājñavalkya describes the characteristics of the *guṇas*. He brings out the difference between *puruṣa* and *prakṛti*; the two exist together but are distinct categories. Similarities on some points are bound to occur in different expositions of Sāṁkhya, in spite of the difference in the approaches of the teachers and the distance of time and space separating them. In the Mokṣadharmaparva account Yājñavalkya proposes to expound Sāṁkhya principles and this unequivocal testimony is to be accepted. The similarities, which have been pointed out, only enforce this natural interpretation.

What is important here is the analysis of the distinctive features of Sāṁkhya in this account, especially its differences with the current standard version.

First, the account does not deal only with Sāṁkhya in its narrow scope. It considers Yoga to be inseparable from Sāṁkhya; the two form a unity. Yājñavalkya gives a clear and authentic account of Sāṁkhya and recognises its importance as a means for achieving *mokṣa*. He deals with Sāṁkhya in its phase of Sāṁkhya-Yoga.

Second, the account does not accept the popular identification of Sāṁkhya with twenty-five *tattvas*. This is not emphasised as the distinguishing feature of Sāṁkhya. In the first instance it mentions only twenty-four categories, eight *prakṛtis* and sixteen *vikāras*. The first *prakṛti* is *avyakta*, the remaining seven are *vyakta*. The *vikāras* are classified into ten *viśeṣas* and five *saviśeṣas* with *manas* as the sixteenth. The evolution of *tattvas* from *prakṛti* is arranged under nine *sargas*. In this scheme *puruṣa* is not mentioned as the twenty-fifth *tattva*.

Third, the account mentions separate time-span for *avyakta*, *mahat*, *ahaṁkāra*, *manas* and subjects.

Fourth, here we find, besides an account of the evolution of *tattvas*, a description of the processes of creation and dissolution. The process of creation is initiated by the *pratibuddha* through Brahmā created from the Golden Egg. The dissolution is initiated by the eternal *avyakta Brahman*, through the god *ahaṁkāra* personified.

Fifth, the classification of *adhyātma*, *adhibhūta* and *adhidaivata* is applied to many objects.

Sixth, *prakṛti* is said to create many qualities in a *puruṣa* which are gouped into three (*guṇas*). *sattva*, *rajas* and *tamas*. *Parkṛti* is *acetana*, but when *puruṣa-tattva* subsists in it, it creates and destroys. The *avyakta prakṛti* is characterised by *guṇa*s.

Seventh, the dichotomy between *puruṣa* and *prakṛti* is brought out. *Prakṛti* is one, but *puruṣa* is many. The account of the difference between *puruṣa* and *prakṛti* and the relationship between the two is the main point in Saṁkhya.

Eighth, it is significant that the account uses a number of terms for both *puruṣa* and *prakṛti*. It seems that the use of the terms *puruṣa* and *prakṛti* had not settled down as the regular terms.

Ninth, the account introduces a twenty-fifth and a twenty-sixth category. *Prakṛti* is the twenty-fourth category. It is called *apratibuddha*. *Budhyamāna* is the twenty-fifth category and stands for the individuals. *Buddha* is the twenty-sixth category and signifies he Supreme Brahmā. A belief in the Supreme Brahmā, besides the *puruṣa* and *prakṛti*, is an important point.

Tenth, the account emphasises the consideration of death, the part of the body through which *prāṇa* goes out, the indications of coming death and the conduct after that.

Yājñavalkya and Daivarāti Janaka Date

According to Bhagavaddatt,[6] Nimi Janaka is the famous Janaka mentioned in the Upaniṣads, Yājñavalkya being his friend and preceptor, who was present in the Mahābhārata War. But, the suggestion is untenable. In the Mokṣadharmaparva it is Daivarāti Janaka, and not Nimi Janaka, to whom Yājñavalkya expounds Sāṁkhya.

6. *Bhāratavarṣa kā Itihāsa* referred to by U.V. Shastri, *op.cit.*, p. 595.

U.V. Shastri[7] points out that in the *Rāmāyaṇa* in the family of Videhan kings, founded by Nimi, the name of Devarāta occurs in the seventh generation. Devarāta's son will be designated as Daivarāti. Shastri identifies Daivarāti with king Bṛhadratha mentioned in the *Rāmāyaṇa.* On the basis of Bhīṣma in the *Mahābhārata* referring to the dialogue between Yājñavalkya and Daivarāti Janaka, as ancient history (*itihāsam purātanam*), Shastri places Yājñavalkya and Daivarāti Janaka in the middle of the *tretā yuga*.

Shastri does not advance any cogent argument for equating Bṛhadratha with Daivarāti Janaka, the contemporary of Yājñavalkya. In the Purāṇic list, compiled by Pargiter, after Devarāta, the sixth king, Bṛhaduktha (and not Bṛhadratha) occurs as the seventh king, but the two were not father and son, Devarāta belonging to the seventeenth generation, whereas Bṛhaduktha was in the twentieth generation.[8] Again, it will not be safe to place Yājñavalkya a few centuries before the Mahāhārata War on the basis of his dialogue with Daivarāti being referred to as ancient history. As we have pointed out,[9] in the parallel case of the dialogue between Vasiṣṭha and Karāla Janaka it was the compiler of the Mokṣadharmaparva in the Śāntiparva who took the narrative to be ancient history. Possibly, it was not ancient history for people of the Mahābhārata War times.

S.N. Pradhan[10] offers a new analysis of the dynastic list of the Videhan kings from Śīradhvaja Janaka (Pargiter No. 23) to Kṛti (Pargiter No. 53). According to him, after Kuni (= Śakuni, Pargiter No. 29) the dynasty branched into two, a collateral branch, consisting of kings (Pargiter No. 31-41) from Kratujit (= Pargiter's Ṛtujit) to Upagupta, and the main line (Pargiter No. 42-53) from Svāgata to Kṛti. Pradhan places the last two names in the main line, Bahulāśva and Kṛti, after the Mahābhārata War. He does not attach much importance to Yājñavalkya-Daivarāti Janaka dialogue in the

7. *Op.cit.*, p. 592.
8. *Ancient Indian Historical Tradition.*
9. See *infra* chapter 10.
10. *Chronology of Ancient India*, pp. 138-44.

Mahābhārata, and says that Kṛti was a contemporary of Janaka Vaideha and Yājñavalkya of the Vedic literature. This would place Yājñavalkya immediately after the Mahābhārata War. Pradhan's suggestion to locate Yājñavalkya a generation after the Mahābhārata War is arbitrary. Pradhan is silent about Yājñavalkya and Daivarāti Janaka equation. He does not find a place for the important king Janaka Vaideha in the history of the main branch of Videhan kings, but instead mentions him as a contemporary of the little known Kṛti. Pradhan's suggestion of the contemporaneity of Kṛti and Janaka Vaideha is presumtuous and cannot be used for placing Yājñavalkya sometime after the Mahābhārata War.

F.E. Pargiter[11] has collected fifty-three names of Videhan kings from the Purāṇas and the *Rāmāyaṇa* representing ninety-four generations. The dynasty was founded by Ikṣvāku's son Nimi. The sixth name in the list is Devarāta belonging to the seventeenth generation. Śīradhvajajanaka, the father of Sītā and a contemporary of Rāma, is no. 23 in the list and belongs to the sixty-fourth generation. The Purāṇic list of Videhan kings does not go beyond the Mahābhārata War. The Videhan monarchy was revived after the War. But, the Purāṇas do not furnish the genealogy of Videhan kings in the post-Bhārata War period.

Y. Mishra has tried to restore order in the history of the Videhan dynasty in this period. He holds that there were twelve generations of Videhan kings in the post-Bhārata War period who ruled for more than two centuries. Of the fifteen names of the kings of Videha mentioned in the *Jātakas*, Mishra[12] prepares a list of twelve belonging to this period. In the *Mahābhārata* he traces the names of nine Videhan kings of the post-Bhārata War period.

According to Mishra,[13] Daivarāti Janaka of the *Mahābhārata*

---

11. *Op.cit.*, P.L. Bhargava, *India in the Vedic Age*, pp. 60-1, gives only fifty-one names of the Videhan kings, omitting no. 9 (Dhṛtimant) and no. 44 (Śruta in Pargiter's list).
12. *Comprehensive History of Bihar*, Vol. I, Part I (ed. by B.P. Sinha), pp. 199-200.
13. *Op.cit.*, p. 201.

(No. 7 in the list) is identical with Mahājanaka II (No. 7 in the list) of the *Jātaka* literature. He further identifies this Videhan king with Janaka Vaideha mentioned in the *Bṛhadāraṇyaka Upaniṣad*. In the philosophical contest at his court, the most prominent figure was Yājñavalkya Vājasaneya, a pupil of Uddālaka Āruṇi. Mishra places this Daivarāti Mahājanaka II-Janaka Vaideha known from three different sources in the last quarter of the ninth century BC (*c.* 825 BC-800 BC). Accordingly the date of Yājñavalkya can be suggested to be *c.* 875-800 BC.[14]

Yājñavalkya's Background

In the Mokṣadharmaparva account Yājñavalkya stands by himself. We are not informed about his teacher, from whom he learnt Sāṁkhya and other philosopical ideas. In chapter 318 he narrates how he acquired, through the blessings of Sūrya, the *Śukla Yajurveda* and composed the *Śatapatha* including *rahasya*, *saṁgraha* and *pariśiṣṭa*. He claims to have learnt the Purāṇas from Romaharṣa. Later, in reply to Viśvāvasu's twenty-four questions, based on the Veda, and the twenty-fifth, about *ānvīkṣikī* he churned in his mind the Upaniṣad, with its *pariśiṣṭa*, keeping an eye on the *ānvīkṣikī*. On this basis, he claims to have expounded his views.

Viśvāvasu gives a long list of famous Sāṁkhya teachers and a few sages reputed for their Sāṁkhya associations, from whom he claims to have learnt Sāṁkhya earlier. His request to Yājñavalkya to expound Sāṁkhya would imply that Viśvāvasu did not consider Yājñavalkya to be idealogically connected with these Sāṁkhya authorities. Thus, Yājñavalkya seems to have enjoyed an independent position through his distinct views on Sāṁkhya topics.

14. For Yājñavalkya in Indian tradition see Kane, *History of Dharmaśāstra* Vol. I, part 1. Our own Foreword to Rajdeo Dubey, *Smṛtikālīna Bhāratīya Samāja evem Saṁskṛti*. He is mentioned in the *ŚatBrā*, IX.7; *Śāṁkyaṇa Āraṇyaka*, XIII.1. The *Isibhāsiyāim*, 12 records the views of Jaṇṇavakka (=Yājñavalkya). Sagarmal Jain *Ṛṣibhāṣita: Eka Adhyayana,* pp. 45-6 points out its close parallels with *BṛUp*, III.5.1 He places the composition of this Jain text between the fifth and third centuries BC.

According to the *Mahābhārata* evidence, Yājñavalkya had a deep knowledge of the fifteen *śākhās* of the *Śukla Yajurveda*, with all their auxiliary parts. He is said to have composed the *Śatapatha Brāhmaṇa*. The *Bṛhadāraṇyakopaniṣad* is the last part of this *Brāhmaṇa*. As he himself observes, Yājñavalkya formulated his Sāṁkhya views on the basis of a deep understanding of the ideas in the Vedic texts he had learnt, and later expounded them to his students. U.V. Shastri[15] supports this evidence and remarks that the philosophical ideas attributed to Yājñavalkya in the *Mahābhārata* have a general agreement with the views expressed in the *Bṛhadāraṇyakopaniṣad*. He says that the Sāṁkhya views of Yājñavalkya mentioned in the *Mahābhārata*, were derived from this *Upaniṣad*, or, in any case, the complier of the relevant chapters in the *Mahābhārata* believed in the idealogical linkage between the two philosophical expositions.

From the Mokṣadharmaparva,[16] we learn that Yājñavalkya had collaborated with several *ṛṣis*, Devala, Sumantu, Paila and Jaimini, in performing a sacrifice for the father of king Daivarāti Janaka. Yājñavalkya refers to his unpleasant relations with his own maternal uncle. But, from this we cannot infer any similarity or difference between the philosophical views of Yājñavalkya and those of the sages named here.

The reference to Yājñavalkya learning Purāṇas from Romaharṣa is not of much historical value for determining the intellectual background of Yājñavalkya. Though *purāṇa* as a genre of writings is evidenced in the Vedic literature, no extant Purāṇa appears to have circulated in that early period. The earliest portions of the available Purāṇas are dated back to third-fourth century BC. The present reference, thus, cannot be construed to suggest Purāṇic influence on Yājñavalkya's view. At best it may indicate that, according to the compiles of the relevant chapters in the Mokṣadharmaparva, there is a compatability between Yājñavalkya's exposition of Sāṁkhya and the treatment of Sāṁkhya in the Purāṇas.

15. *Op.cit.*, pp. 594-5.
16. *Mbh.*, XIII.318.17-20.

Yājñavalkya's Followers

Yājñavalkya possibly did not found a Sāṁkhya school. If he did create a school, it does not seem to have existed long enough to leave a lasting memory. In the Mokṣadharmaparava[17] Yājñavalkya says that he taught the *Śatapatha Brāhmaṇa* to his students and with them performed the sacrifice for the Janaka king. He taught his students the entire *Śatapatha* along with the *saṁgraha*, after which they returned home.

His students are not mentioned in connection with his discourse to Viśvāvasu, the Gandharva king. This would suggest that his students were not present to receive the exposition of Sāṁkhya. The narrative says that after Yājñavalkya's discourse Viśvāvasu went back to the heaven. Viśvāvasu taught this philosophy to Brahmā and other gods, to people living on the earth, and also to those living in the underneath world.

The introduction of Viśvāvasu, a Gandharva, as the medium for the circulation of Sāṁkhya, expounded by Yājñavalkya, was evidently intended to add to its glory. But, this does not rule out real students who promoted the Sāṁkhya teachings of Yājñavalkya. According to the Mokṣadharmaparva, Yājñavalkya preached his philosophical views to king Daivarāti Janaka. After receiving the instructions, Janaka gave the Videha kingdom to his son, but adopting the rules of an ascetic (*yati-dharma*), lived there. Studying the Sāṁkhya philosophy and the *Yogaśāstra* in their fullness, he adopted the correct approach towards *prakr̥ti* and his ownself. In the later part of his life Janaka possibly himself followed Sāṁkhya and Yoga principles and preached them to others. The *Br̥hadāraṇyakopaniṣad* shows that the court of Janaka was a prestigious centre of philosophical discussion in which Yājñavalkya surpassed other contestents. It can be guessed that Yājñavalkya's characteristic philosophical ideas gained currency in the Videhan kingdom. We can concede the possibility that these ideas influenced some of the later philosophers at the Videhan court.

---

17. XII.318.17-18, 24.

In the Mokṣadharmaparva[18] Bhīṣma says that Janaka received the knowledge from Yājñavalkya and that he himself got it from Janaka. There will be no chronological discrepancy in Bhīṣma referring to Yājñavalkya-Daivarāti Janaka dialogue as ancient history and also saying that he himself obtained the knowledge of Sāṁkhya from Janaka; it can be explained as possible, considering the surprisingly long life attributed to Bhīṣma. If, however, Daivarāti Janaka is placed long after Bhīṣma and the Mokṣadharmaparva is taken to reflect the views of its compilers in a late phase of the growth of the *Mahābhārata* text, then the claim of Bhīṣma to have received Sāṁkhya from Janaka cannot be historically valid. This calim was inserted possibly to add to the credence of the account of the Yājñavalkya-Daivarāti Janaka dialogue.

Yājñavalkya and Vasiṣṭha

P. Chakravarti[19] refers to a few points of similarity in the expositions of Sāṁkhya attributed to Vasiṣṭha and Yājñavalkya. Both employ the terms *apratibuddha*, *budhyamāna* and *buddha* and introduce the twenty-sixth category. Both describe the characteristics of the *guṇas* and differentiate the *puruṣa* from the *prakṛti*. Both accept twenty-five categories, but do not speak of the *tanmātras*. Both maintain the dualism of the conscious and the unconscious, but do not always refer to them by the terms *puruṣa* and *prakṛti*. Instead, they use the terms *kṣetrajña* and *kṣetra*, *akṣara* and *kṣara*. Chakravarti explains the introduction of the twenty-sixth category by associating Vasiṣṭha and Yājñavalkya with the Sāṁkhya-Yoga school of the Epic.

There are some other points of similarities between Vasiṣṭha and Yājñavalkya, though they are by no means identical. Both attach importance to creation (*sarga*) and speak of several varieties of *sargas*. Vasiṣṭha classifies them into five, whereas Yājñavalkya describes nine. Both believe that, on account of its association with *prakṛti*, *puruṣa* considers itself to be the doer and enjoyer. Both

18. *Mbh.*, XII.318.109.
19. *Op.cit.*, pp. 49-53.

emphasise the need for a proper understanding of the Veda. Both give separate accounts of Sāṁkhya and Yoga, but maintain that the two are one. Both regard the knowledge of the self as the proper means of *mokṣa*. Both explain the essential point through terms in pairs of opposites.

The similarities are to be seen also in style and presentation, which, in some cases, involve identical lines and expression. Thus, the passage in Vasiṣṭha describing a man who reads the Veda without understanding it as only carrying the load[20] has its parallel in the expression *jñānabhāravaha* used by Yājñavalkya.[21] The passage about Sāṁkhya and Yoga being one are almost identical in the two.[22] Likewise, the passages about the two types of Yogic activities in the two are closely similar, with the difference that Vasiṣṭha has *dhyāna* for *dhāraṇā* in Yājñavalkya.[23]

The similarities in expression can be explained as being due to the style of presentation adopted by the author of these chapters in the Mokṣadharmaparva. But the similarities in principles require a deeper explanation. If one has not been influenced by the other, we have to postulate that the two belonged to the same phase in the development of Sāṁkhya or else the two were connected with the same tradition. As we have seen, whereas Yājñavalkya possibly did not belong to the main line of Sāṁkhya from Kapila to Pañcaśikha, Vasiṣṭha is mentioned as one of the followers of Pañcaśikha. It is, however, to be noted that both were associated with the court of Mithilā and were not far removed in time. It is not unlikely that the principles expounded by Yājñavalkya influenced Vasiṣṭha.

Chakravarti refers to the two Sāṁkhya teachers as belonging to the Sāṁkhya-Yoga school. Both give separate accounts of Sāṁkhya and Yoga, but maintain that they are not separate. It seems that

---

20. *Mbh.*, XII.305.14.
21. *Ibid.*, XII.318.52.
22. *Ibid.*, XII.305.19 (Vasiṣṭha) = XII.316.4 (Yājñavalkya).
23. *Ibid.*, XII. 306-7-8 (Vasiṣṭha) = XII. 316.9-10 (Yājñavalkya). See also the first line in XII.306-18 = XII.316.19.

both belonged to a phase when Sāṁkhya and Yoga had acquired their distinctive form, but attempts were being made to fuse them. Here there are two possibilities. First, Sāṁkhya and Yoga had their separate traditions, which were tried to be integrated. Second, the two were parts or aspects of the same system. In course of time they developed in their own way, but an attempt was made to retain their joint character. There is no definite ground for arguing in favour of either of the two possibilities. It is, however, likely that for long the two existed together, Sāṁkhya concerning more with the philosophical principles and Yoga with the practical aspect. When Yoga started developing separately, some Sāṁkhya teachers asserted their joint character, but maintained the primacy of Sāṁkhya by emphasising that *mokṣa* is possible through *jñāna* and advocating the practice of *yoga* in furthering the approach and attitude resulting from knowledge. Yājñavalkya was among the foremost Sāṁkhya teachers advocating the joint character of Sāṁkhya and Yoga.

We may now attempt placing Yājñavalkya in the history of Sāṁkhya. The Sāṁkhya principles in the *Sāṁkhyakārikā* are taken to represent the standard account. The extent of the closeness of any version of Sāṁkhya with the *Sāṁkhyakārikā* presentation determines its relative chronological position as earlier or later. But, this involves an assumption that the philosophical ideas of a system grows in a strictly unilinear vertical direction. It does not recognise properly the possibility of individual variations, of differing views surfacing at times and coexisting, and of there being no ascertainable and fixed period for their continuance, with the result that we cannot formulate a chronological graph for the life-tenure of the origin and development of any particular idea or principle.

Early Sāṁkhya in Yājñavalkya

In the case of Yājñavalkya also one may trace elements which, for their similarity with the exposition in the *Sāṁkhyakārikā*, would appear to be later developments, and also others so widely different as to be placed in earlier times. In any case, we must admit the possiblity of the presence of elements which were retained in the standardised Sāṁkhya of later times. But, significantly there are several prominent features referring to early stages in the development of Sāṁkhya.

First, the terminology of the categories of *puruṣa* and *prakṛti* had not been standardised. Instead we find several alternative terms being current.

Second, the primacy was of the concepts of *puruṣa* and *prakṛti,* through which the central philosophy of Sāṁkhya is explained. This is characteristic of a very early stage in Sāṁkhya history, when it was expounded through the concepts of *puruṣārthatā* and *daśamūlikārthas*,[24] which emphasise the *tattvas* of *puruṣa* and *prakṛti*, and explain the system through their mutual relationship.

Third, the category of *prakṛti* the evolution of the *tattvas* from it, and the three *guṇas* characterising it do not appear to have been standardised.

Fourth, the account of creation and dissolution, time-span assigned to *prakṛti*, *mahat*, *ahaṁkāra*, *buddhi*, *manas* and the *viṣayas* and the passage of *prāṇa* through particular parts of the body are not philosophically maintainable. They possibly belong to an early period when philosophical principles had not freed themselves from popular ideas.

Fifth, the account breathes an atmosphere of *Brāhmaṇa*-Upaniṣadic ideas. It does not mark a total revolt against the Veda, but criticises the Vedic rites as being of limited efficacy. It emphasises the need for a proper understanding of the Veda. Yājñavalkya is credited with the authorship of the *Śatapatha Brāhmaṇa* and is said to have churned the Upaniṣed for expounding his principles. He asserts that what he says in answering the questions on the Veda is *ānvikṣikī* and represents the essence of the Veda. The use of the term *ānvikṣikī* is significant. The *Arthaśāstra*[25] of Kauṭilya mentions *ānvikṣikī* as one of the four *vidyās*, the other three being

24. See our article "Daśamūlikārtha in Sāṁkhya" in *Indian Historical Review*, Vol. pp.

25. I.2.1.

trayī, vārtā and *daṇḍanīti*. *Ānvikṣikī* contains Sāṁkhya, Yoga and Lokāyata.[26] Thus, the *Mahābhārata* account refers to the teachings of Yājñavalkya as philosopohy in opposition to the Vedic ritualism designated as *trayī*. In ealy stages the term Sāṁkhya did not signify a set of philosophical system. It stood for the method of rational exposition or philosophy, as opposed to the Vedic method of sacrificial rites. Yājñavalkya belongs to the phase of later Vedic texts, of the *Brāhmaṇas* and Upaniṣads, when Sāṁkhya emerged as a method of rational exposition of the problems of human existence.

Sixth, this analysis eminently suits the concept of *budhyamāna* and *buddha* as the twenty-fifth and twenty-sixth categories. *Budhyamāna* or the individual *puruṣa* does not know about the twenty-sixth category, on account of its misconceived relationship with the twenty-fourth category, the *apratibuddha* or *prakṛti*. When it understands its separateness from *prakṛti*, it realises that it is really the twenty-sixth category. The basic point in this account is the essential oneness of *budhyamāna* and *buddha*. This is the cardinal concept of *Brahman* and *ātman*, which had its beginnings in the *Brāhmaṇas* and *Āraṇyakas*, but acquired its charcteristic form and development in the Upaniṣads.

Seventh, the exposition of Sāṁkhya and Yoga categories separately, with the assertion that the two are not different, shows a phase when the two had acquired their distinctive forms but the Sāṁkhya teachers claimed that Yoga was an integral part of Sāṁkhya. This represents the phase of Sāṁkhya-Yoga in the history of Sāṁkhya.

Conclusion

We, thus, find that Yājñavalkya appeared in a very early period in the history of Sāṁkhya. He did not belong to the philosophical lineage of Kapila-Āsuri-Pañcaśikha. He was earlier than Vasiṣṭha, a disciple of Pañcaśikha, but was not far removed from Pañcaśikha. He was possibly earlier than Pañcaśikha and, thus, has to be referred to the Āsuri-Pañcaśikha bracket. The evidence of the

26. *Indian Historical Review*, I.2.10.

Bṛhadāraṇyaka Upaniṣad would suggest that Yājñavalkya was a senior contemporary of Āsuri. In one of the three lists of teachers and pupils in this Upaniṣad[27] Āsuri appears as an immediate successor of Yājñavalkya. Yājñavalkya was, thus, an early Sāṁkhya teacher, independent of the main line of Sāṁkhya and belonged to the times of Āsuri.

27. *Bṛhadāraṇyaka Upaniṣad*, VI.5.2.

6

Sāṁkhya Adoption by Āyurveda Teachers

(Ātreya, Agniveśa and Caraka)

Earlier Studies on Caraka-saṁhitā Evidence

DASGUPTA

S.N. DASGUPTA[1] is the first scholar who paid attention to the refreshing evidence about Sāṁkhya philosophy in the *Caraka-saṁhitā* and analysed it for reconstructing the history of Sāṁkhya. He was followed by Chakravarti,[2] who presented an independent appraisal of the evidence in this text. G.J. Larson[3] has offered his own interpretation of the evidence. No other scholar has attempted a new analysis of the material.

Dasgupta[4] identified six main features of Sāṃkhya as given by Caraka: (1) *Puruṣa* is the state of *avyakta*. (2) The *avyakta* and its later products form a conglomeration which generates the living being. (3) The *tanmātras* are not mentioned. (4) *Rajas* and *tamas* represent the bad states of the mind and *sattva* the good ones. (5) The ultimate state of emancipation is absolute annihilation or

---

1. *A History of Indian Philosopy,* Vol. I, pp. 213-7.
2. *Origin and Development of the Sāṁkhya System of Thought*, pp. 99-110.
3. *Classical Sāṃkhya*, pp. 103-8.
4. *Op. cit.*, p. 216.

characterless absolute existence; it is spoken of as the *Brahman* state; there is no consciousness in this state, for consciousness is due to the conglomeration of the self with its evolutes, *buddhi, ahaṁkāra*, etc. (6) The senses are formed of matter (*bhautika*).

According to Dasgupta, this account of Sāṁkhya agrees with the system propounded by Pañcaśikha in the *Mahābhārata*, XII. 219[5] and represents the earliest systematic doctrine of Sāṁkhya.[6]

Dasgupta refers to the common points in the expositions of Caraka and Patañjali: both accept twenty-four principles, *puruṣa* and *avyakta* being combined into one, both argue for the existence of a self as the basis for moral responsibility: both regard consciousness to be due to the conglomeration of the physical body, mind and *cetas*; both say that suffering arises because the conglomeration is identified with the self; both describe *guṇa*s as good and bad qualities of the mind; both speak of a *kṣetra* (the state of conglomeration); and both describe the last state of salvation as *aliṅga,* to be attained by the doctrine of ultimate renunciation or complete destruction. But, Dasgupta does not carry these points forward to suggest any connection between the two.

CHAKRAVARTI

P. Chakravarti emphasises certain striking similarities between Caraka and Aśvaghoṣa (*Buddhacarita*) in their accounts of Sāṁkhya: both classify the *avyakta* and its evolutes into two groups — the eight-fold *prakṛti*, constituting the *avyakta*, *buddhi*, *ahaṁkāra* and the five gross elements and the *vikāra* (modification) comprising the ten organs, the mind and the five objects of the senses; both count the objects of the senses as *tattva*s, but do not mention the *tanmātra*s; both speak of *kṣetra* and *kṣetrajña* and differentiate the *avyakta* from the *vyakta*; both describe eight factors, which are at the root of worldly existence; and both identify the stage of liberation with *Brahman*, described as indestructible and without attributes.

5. *Classical Sāṃkhya*, p. 216.
6. *Op.cit.*, p. 217.

P. Chakravarti also points out significant differences in the exposition of Sāṁkhya by Caraka and Aśvaghoṣa. Caraka combines *prakṛti* and *puruṣa* into one single principle called *avyakta*, but this is not done by Caraka. Caraka and Aśvaghoṣa differ about the sequence of the eight motive factors at the root of the worldly existence, besides slight variations in their definitions. Caraka differs from Aśvaghoṣa in not defining *sattva* and not discussing the five-fold ignorance (*pañcaparva avidyā*).

On the basis of the similarities in their Sāṁkhya accounts Chakravarti suggests that Caraka and Aśvaghoṣa received their ideas from a common source. He points out that some ideas in the *Buddhacarita* are closely related to the Sāṁkhya passages in the *Mahābhārata* and suggests that Caraka, as also Aśvaghoṣa and the Epic 'were more or less influenced by a common school of Sāṁkhya'. Significantly, Chakravarti does not emphasise similarities between Caraka and Pañcaśikha, though noting the similarities of Caraka with the Sāṁkhya accounts of Vasiṣṭha and Yājñavalkya.

LARSON

Larson brackets Caraka and Pañcaśikha and places Aśvaghoṣa's *Buddhacarita* in a separate category. He reproduces the points of similarities between Caraka and Pañcaśikha, as noted by Dasgupta, but adds that there are also some striking differences. According to him, all the three were influenced by an old common Sāṁkhya-Yoga tradition which was in a fluid or changing condition. He distinguishes the Caraka-Pañcaśikha as more monistic and the *Buddhacarita* as clearly dualistic.

In analysing the passages in the three sources scholars have tended to overemphasise similarities, but have not given due importance to the points of differences, some of which will be weighty considerations in determining the nature of Sāṁkhya in the different accounts. These go against the thesis of a common tradition as origin. The common features may be explained in many ways, not necessarily by a single school or a common tradition. The varying points are the distinguishing features. The tradition, to which Pañcaśikha belonged, is known as that of Kapila and Āsuri. It is difficult to believe that Pañcaśikha derived his ideas from a tradition different from that of Kapila and Āsuri. If Caraka also belonged to this tradition, we cannot explain the absence of his name in the sources naming the teachers of Sāṁkhya. It is more plausible that there were many stages in the growth of the Sāṁkhya system and teachers belonging to one stage shared certain points. These teachers had their own distinctive ideas which on some points differed from the common expositions. They are to be treated as idependent thinkers presenting distinct, separate expositions,which may be related on account of the common points, but are not to be described as issuing out of the same tradition.

Philosophical Portions of Caraka-saṁhita

In studying the Sāṁkhya views of Caraka scholars generally confine themselves to the first chapter in the Śārīrasthāna section of the text. But, there are many other chapters in the text which contain views on philosophical problems. Sūtrasthāna 1, 8, 11, 12, 25, 26, 28 and 30, Vimāna 4 and 8, Śārīra 1, 3, 4 and 5, Cikitsāsthāna 15 and 28, and Siddhisthāna 12. Śārīrasthāna, chapter 1 presents a consolidated account of the Sāṁkhya principles in the form of questions and answers. The other important chapters, which deal with problems connected with Sāṁkhya principles are Sūtrasthāna, 1 (Vaiśeṣika topics *sāmānya*, *viśeṣa*, *guṇa*, *dravya*, *karma* and *samavāya*), 8 (*indriyas*), 11 (*eṣaṇā* and criticism of *nāstika* views with the help of *pratyakṣa*, *anumāna*, *āgama* and *yukti*), 25 (*puruṣa*), Śārīrasthāha 3-5 (transmigration of *ātman* and creation) and 1, 5 (*yoga*). The text refers to Sāṁkhya and Yoga by name. It discusses some topics which are generally considered by Nyāya, Vaiśeṣika, Mīmāṁsā and Vedānta. Whether Caraka discussed these topics as parts of these systems or they were within the original scope of his ideas cannot be decided.

Sāṁkhya Principles in Caraka-saṁhitā

S.N. Dasgupta has not noted several important points in the

account of Sāṁkhya presented by Caraka.[7] Here the *tattvas* are enumerated as being twenty-four in number. *Puruṣa* is described as the conglomeration (*rāśi*) of these twenty-four.[8] *Prakṛti* is not included in the list as the basic *tattva, avyakta. Puruṣa* itself is mentioned as *avyakta*. For the purposes of medicine the *puruṣa* is described as the *saṁyoga-puruṣa,* the fusion of six *dhātus*, the five elements, sky, etc., and *cetanā, brahma* or *avyakta*.[9] Caraka often uses the term *dhātu* in place of *tattva*. In the discussion[10] about *puruṣa* being *nitya* (eternal) or *anitya* (impermanent) it is said that *puruṣa* is *nitya*, as it is without beginning, but *puruṣa*, as a conglomeration, resulting from a cause, is not so. The former is *avyakta* and cannot be conceived; the latter is *vyakta. Avyakta* is also designated as *ātman*, *kṣetrajña*, *śāśvata, vibhu* and *avyaya*. From it issue *buddhi*, *ahaṁkāra*, etc., which are *vyakta*. That which is the subject of senses is *vyakta*; that which is beyond senses and can only be inferred through *liṅgas* is *avyakta*.

Caraka is not ignorant of the term *prakṛti*; he describes *prakṛti* as consisting of eight *dhātus*, which include the five elements, *buddhi*, *avyakta* and *ahaṁkāra*,[11] but, in the direct question about the nature of *prakṛti*,[12] he does not describe it. The classification of twenty-four *tattvas* into two groups, *prakṛti* and *vikāra*, and their enumeration by Caraka[13] different from the account in the standard Sāṁkhya system. The *prakṛti* group includes the five elements, *buddhi*, *avyakta* and *ahaṁkāra*. The *vikāra* group consists of ten organs, *manas*, and five objects of sense-organs. In this account the two terms *mahat* and *pañcatanmātra* are not mentioned.

In many passages Caraka expresses the view that *ātman* is one.

---

7. I have consulted Jyotirmitra, *Caraka evaṁ Suśruta ke Dārśanika Viṣaya kā Adhyayana* with advantage.
8. Śārīra, I.17, 37, 61-4.
9. *Ibid.*, I.85, V.4.
10. *Ibid.*, I.61-2.
11. *Ibid.*, I.17, 63.
12. *Ibid.*, I.4.
13. *Ibid*, I.163. Also Nidāna, VIII.41.

This is in opposition to the well-known Sāṁkhya view about the plurality of *puruṣas*. Caraka says that, on account of the association of *rajas* and *tamas*, *ātman* appears in the form of innumerable individuals; but, with the increase of *sattva*, it is freed from the identity with the conglomeration.[14] In all the beings *ātman* is one (*nirviśeṣa*) and without modification; it appears as individual (*viśeṣa*) on account of the *sattva* and the body.[15] *Ātman* is one, but it appears in all the bodies.[16]

Though Caraka regards *ātman* to be without attributes, attachment and action and to be all-pervading,[17] he describes *puruṣa* as characterised by *guṇas*, because he does not subscribe to the idea of an inactive *prakṛti* having the three *guṇas*. This *puruṣa* enjoys the fruits of his action, acquires knowledge, and suffers from attachment (*moha*), joy and sorrow, and life and death.

Caraka mentions two different courses of evolution (*sṛṣṭi*). The first is in the form of six *dhātus*. Caraka specifically says that the concept of *puruṣa* as the conglomeration of six *dhātus* was propounded by earlier Sāṁkhyas.[18] Possibly, this concept was adopted by Punarvasu Ātreya, but the passage was introduced in the text by Caraka when he revised it.[19] The course of evolution according to this view is explained by Hiraṇyākṣa in symposium.[20] The number of *guṇas* increases from one to five in an ascending order from *ākāśa* to *vāyu, tejas, jala* and *pṛthvī*.[21]

The second course of evolution, in terms of twenty-four *tattvas*.[22]

14. Śārīra, I.36.
15. *Ibid.*, IV.33.
16. *Ibid.*, I.81, II.32.
17. *Ibid.*, I.35.
18. *Sūtra*, XXV.15.
19. Cakrapāṇi on Caraka, Śārīra, I.16, ignorant about the early history of Sāṁkhya, says that this *puruṣa* as expounded by Vaiśeṣika, is the subject of medicine.
20. *Sūtra*, XXV.5.
21. Śārīra, I.28; IV.8.
22. Śārīra, I.36.

is similar to the generally accepted Sāṁkhya view. The only difference is that Caraka traces it from *avyakta* (and not *prakṛti*) and mentions *buddhi* (and not *mahat*) as its first evolute.

As opposed to the generally circulated Sāṁkhya view of *prakṛti* being the material cause of creation, Caraka regards *puruṣa* as the cause. The question is posed how is *puruṣa* the cause[23] and the point is established with the help of arguments.[24] The main reason for this distinctive view is the nature of *puruṣa* expounded by Caraka. Caraka presents two different account of *puruṣa*. As an exclusively *cetanā*, *tattva*, *puruṣa* is beyond the consideration of cause and effect. But *puruṣa*, as a conglomerate of *tattvas*, is characterised by *rajas* and *tamas* undergoes birth and death. It is this *puruṣa* which becomes *vyakta* from *avyakta* and then again becomes *avyakta*, and is regarded as the *kāraṇa*.

In the Classical Sāṁkhya *indriyas* are said to evolve from *ahaṁkāra*. But Caraka regards them as emanating from the five elements.[25] Through analysis the five basic elements are inferred from *kha* (sky), *vāyu*, *jyoti* (*agni*), *jala* and *pṛthivī*. By a combination of the modifications of these elements the five sense-organs are created, which are dominated respectively by one of these elements. The organs are pervasive and receive the subject created by the particular element predominant in them.

Caraka describes eight kinds of miraculous powers acquired by the *yogīs*. These are *āveśa* (entering another's body), *cetasojñānam* (knowing an other's mind) *arthānāṁ chandathaḥ kriyā* (regulating the objects of senses according to will), *dṛṣṭi* (perceiving this beyond eyes), *śrotra* (hearing sounds beyond ears), *smṛti* remembering all ideas), *kānti* (supernatural splendour) and *iṣṭathaḥ adarśanam* (becoming invisible according to will). The *Sāṁkhyakārikā*[26] enumerates eight *siddhis*, beginning with *ūha* (reasoning). The Yogic tradition also mentions eight supernatural powers (*siddhis*

23. Śārīra, I.3.
24. Śārīra, XXXIX-45.
25. *Sūtra*, VIII.14.
26. *Kārikā*, 51.

or *aiśvaryas*), beginning with *aṇimā*, which later acquired a standardised formulation.[27] Caraka's account is distinctive, both in the use of the terms and the nature of the powers referred to.

Sāṁkhya teachers maintain distinctive views about the nature of the subtle body through which *ātman* transmigrates from one birth to another. Caraka says that *ātman* enters the womb in the form of seed made of four elements created by the results of his *karma*.[28]

The knowledge (*jñāna*) which Caraka mentions as instrumental in achieving emancipation, is also of a special nature.[29] According to the *Sāṁkhyakārikā*,[30] the *kevala-jñāna* means the realisation, that I do not exist and there is nothing which is mine. Caraka says that this knowledge is characterised by the realisation that *ātman* pervades the *loka*, and *loka* subsists in the *ātman*.

Caraka does not include *kāla* in his list of *tattvas*, but he does expound the importance of *kāla*.[31] This is significantly opposed to the exposition in the *Sāṁkhyakārikā* which is silent about *kāla*. The non-acceptance of *kāla* has been generally noted as an important feature of Sāṁkhya.[32]

Textual Problems in Evaluating Caraka-saṁhitā Evidence

There are certain basic difficulties which prevent a proper analysis of the Sāṁkhya material in the *Caraka-saṁhitā* for reconstructing the history of Sāṁkhya. It being a classic text on *Āyurveda*, a student of philosophy does not give it the respect parallel to an original text of philosophy. There is also a misconception about the characteristic features of Sāṁkhya and a failure to appreciate the

---

27. Dahlaṇa on *Suśruta*, Cikitsā, XXIX.13.
28. Śārīra, II.35.
29. Śārīra, V.20.
30. *Kārikā*, 54.
31. Vimāna, VIII.125.
32. Vācaspatimiśra, *Sāṁkhyatattvakaumudī* on *Kārikā,* 33. See also *Ratnaprabhā* of *Śāṅkarabhāṣya* on *Brahmasūtra,* II.2.1.

significance of evidence referring to a different account of Sāṁkhya of an earlier period. A third factor is the nature of the text. In its present form it is not a unified text composed by a single author. There are three recognised stages in the growth of the text. It was originally composed by Agniveśa, a pupil of Punarvasu Ātreya. later it was revised by Caraka. A second redaction was attempted by Dṛḍhabala. The fourth difficulty arises because Caraka cannot be identified and his date cannot be determined with certainty.

The name of the text creates an impression that it was the composition of Caraka and hence the views expressed in it are attributed to Caraka.[33] Some scholars, while admitting that it has received its present form in course of time, apportion the main credit to Caraka. The alternative suggestions offered are: (a) the original brief treatise of Agniveśa was completely changed and developed into an altogether new text by Caraka and (b) Caraka has presented a summary of the debates and discussions of sages, experts of *Āyurveda* and assembled in symposia. But the colophon always asserts that the treatise was composed by Agniveśa and revised by Caraka (*agniveśakṛte tantre carakaprati-saṁskṛte*). In the text also Caraka is always referred to as the redactor, but never as author; it is Agniveśa who is mentioned as the author.[34] If Caraka had been the original author, or if he had so completely revised and recast the earlier text as to give it the form of a new text, there will be no justification for associating the name of Agniveśa so prominently. Evidently, even after the revision the text retained much of its orignial form and content.

In the account of Sāṁkhya in the *Caraka-saṁhitā* it is difficult to apportion individual points to Agniveśa, Caraka and Dṛḍhabala.

---

33. G. Haldar, *Vṛddhatrayī* (Calcutta, 1362 Bengal era), pp. 21, 32 postulates two Carakas, the first, the student of Vaiśampāyana wrote the original Saṁhitā, and the second, the physician of Kaniṣka, named as Kapilabala, revised the Saṁhitā partially. According to him, the text was further revised thrice, by the son of Kapilabala by Dṛḍhabala and then by Candraṭa. This is highly speculative and without any textual support.

34. *Caraka*, Siddhi, XII.38, 52.

So far as Dṛḍhabala is concerned, we know, on his own authority, that he completed the redaction of the *Agniveśatantra* by adding to the text prepared by Caraka seventeen chapters in the Cikitsāsthāna and all the twelve chapters in both Kalpasthāna and Siddhisthāna, which had been lost.[35] Of the portions revised by Dṛḍhadbala it is only the last chapter in the Siddhisthāna,which has a connection with Sāṁkhya; it deals with the *tantrayukti*s. But, it will always remain debatable if the *tantrayukti*s were laid down by Sāṁkhya in its early stages.

On the basis of the person expounding Cakrapāṇi[36] classifies the *sūtra*s in the *Caraka-saṁhitā* into four: *guru-sūtra* (that expounded by the teacher), *śiṣya-sūtra* (that expounded by the student), *pratisaṁskartṛ-sūtra* (that expounded by the redactor) and *ekīya-sūtra* (which presents the opinion of one sage). Cakrapāṇi illustrates these four categories. This textual apparatus has not been applied to the whole text to sift passages of the four categories. This cannot be done in all the cases. As a result of the revision, the passages are so mixed up that the specific contributions of Ātreya, Agniveśa and Caraka are difficult to identify. This holds good for passages presenting philosophical views, including Sāṁkhya principles.

The revision has not succeeded in introducing complete uniformity of form and style. Traces of earlier elements are easily discernable in some cases. The prose in the text is similar to that of the *Kṛṣṇa Yajurveda*, its style of presentation follows the *Brāhmaṇa*s, the account of debates and discussions in the *pariṣad*s is nearer to the Upaniṣadic accounts, and the naming of some chapters[37] after the opening expressions is characteristic of early Vedic texts.[38] But, we face real difficulty when we try to distinguish earlier portions in the text from its later ones.

---

35. *Caraka*, Cikitsā, XXX.289-91.
36. *Caraka,* Sūtra, I.1.
37. Sūtra, I.25.
38. Jyotirmitra, *op.cit.*, p. 6.

Ātreya

The introductory sentence in the chapters mentions Ātreya as expounding them.[39] There is evidently no case for the chapters being in the original words of Ātreya. His student Agniveśa presented the exposition and attributed it to Ātreya. This style was retained by Caraka after revision.

The full name of Ātreya appears as Punarvasu Ātreya.[40] He is also named as Cāndrabhāgī or Cādrabhāga.[41] Kṛṣṇātreya possibly refers to his personal name. He is to be distinguished from Bhikṣu Ātreya, as the two are mentioned together in some cases.[42]

It is not possible to give specific details about Ātreya and fix his date. His name implies that Atri was his father. He is sometimes mentioned as Atriputra, Atrisūnu and Atryātmaja. According to Filliozat,[43] Atri, the father of Ātreya, is to be identified with sage Atri, referred to in the *Ṛgveda*.[44]

Merely on the basis of the introductory sentence in the chapters it cannot be dogmatised that all the philosophical principles in the text were originally expounded by Ātreya. We will be on surer grounds about expositions which are attributed to him in the discussions in the *pariṣad*s.

One line of approach can be to infer even vaguely Ātreyas philosophical views from the expositions made by his disciples. According to tradition Ātreya thaught *Āyurveda* to his six disciples, of which three, Agniveśa, Bhela and Hārīta, are associated with

39. *iti ha smāha bhagavān-ātreyaḥ*.
40. This was possibly his *nakṣatra* name.
41. These are taken to refer to his mother or the river or region associated with his birth.
42. *Caraka*, Sūtra, XXV.24. Hoernle, *Studies in Ancient Indian Medicine, Osteology,* pp. 7, 8, identifies the two. For a full discussion see Jyotirmitra, "Ātreya and his Period", *Nāgārjuna*.
43. *The Classical Doctrine of Indian Medicine*, p. 7.
44. Yogendranātha on *Caraka*, Sūtra, I.7 suggests that the name Kṛṣṇātreya refers to his being the son of Kṛṣṇātri, but this is opposed to rules of Sanskrit grammar.

three separate *Āyurveda saṁhitās*. The *Bhīlasaṁhitā* is known from a single manuscript, which is incomplete and faulty. The available *Hārītasaṁhitā* cannot be the composition of a disciple of Ātreya; it was written by a later author who adopted the name of Hārīta. Both the *saṁhitās* are without an account of philosophical views.

We do not find any reference to Ātreya as a Sāṁkhya philosopher, excepting a reference in the account of Sāṁkhya in Guṇaratna's *Ṣaḍdarśanasamuccaya* to *Ātreyatantra* as a Sāṁkhya treatise.[45] Atri is named as a sage who went to Indra and learnt *Āyurveda* from him.[46] We can never know the principles communicated to Atri. We are not sure if this Atri was the father of Ātreya and subscribed to Sāṁkhya views but it may be noted that according to Aśvaghoṣa,[47] Atri did not belong to the discipline of medicine, which was actually propounded by Ātreya.

Agniveśa, as a student of Punarvasu Ātreya, will belong to the same period. This receives support from the fact that he is mentioned in the *Bṛhadāraṇyaka Upaniṣad*[48] and is included in two *gaṇapāṭhas* in the *Aṣṭādhyāyī*.[49]

Agniveśa and Caraka

In the *Caraka-saṁhitā* portions contributed by Agniveśa and Caraka are difficult to separate. Jyotirmitra[50] gives Caraka the credit for the philosophical passages in the text. According to him, Caraka introduced philosophical elements to strengthen the medicinal principles and transformed it into a lasting achievement. But, there is no definite argument in support of this view. The philosophical principles are an intrinsic part of the Āyurvedic

45. P. Chakravarti, *op.cit.*, p. 54 raises doubt about the authenticity of this statement as Guṇaratna himself, in another content, mentions it as a treatise of Vaiśeṣika.
46. *Caraka*, Ciktsā, I.4.3; *Kāśyapasaṁhitā*, Chowkhamba, 1953, p. 61.
47. *Buddhacarita*, I.42.
48. II.6.2.
49. IV.1.105; II.4.68.
50. *Op.cit.*, pp. 7, 20.

system and are the foundations on which the details are built-up in different chapters. The chapters, in which philosophical ideas are expounded, also have the colophon saying that the treatise was composed by Agniveśa and revised by Caraka. The philosophical principles in many cases, are enunciated in the course of discussions in *pariṣads*. The accounts of the *pariṣads* are taken to be among the earliest parts of the text and were probably written by Agniveśa.

Thus, we may conclude that philosophical principles were presented by Agniveśa in the original treatise. Caraka is to be given credit for systematising them and in some cases, elaborating them. We cannot determine the nature and extent of these new features. There is no way to determine the new details added by Caraka.

Date of Agniveśa and Caraka

We will not enter into a full discussion about the possible dates of Ātreya, Agniveśa and Caraka. The date of Caraka continues to be a subject of debate. The Chronology committee of the National Institute of Sciences of India concluded that AD 100 is the date for the composition of the *Caraka-saṁhitā*. This view is based mainly on the reference in the Chinese translation of Buddhist *Tripiṭaka* to a physician named Tehe-lokia (= Caraka) in the court of the Kuṣāṇa king Kaniṣka, whose accession is deated in AD 78. This evidence, first pointed out by S. Levi,[51] has been followed by subsequent writers. But, the internal evidence of the *Caraka-saṁhitā* does not indicate that its author belonged to the first century of the Christian era and was associated with the court of the renowned Buddhist king Kaniṣka.[52] Caraka literally means one who moves about. Possibly it was not a personal name, but referred to a physician who wandered from place to place. Pāṇini mentions a Caraka. Persons with the name of Caraka are referred to in many sources, not necessarily connected with *Āyurveda*. There was a Caraka-śākhā of the *Kṛṣṇa Yajurveda*.

---

51. *Journal Asiatique*, Nov.-Dec. 1886, pp. 451ff; *Indian Antiquary*, XXXII, pp. 382 ff.
52. P.V. Sharma, *Āyurveda kā vaijñānika Itihāsa*, pp. 116-18.

An ancient tradition equates Caraka with Patañjali, to whom are attributed both the *Yogasūtra* and the *Mahābhāṣya* on the *Aṣṭādhyāyī*.[53] Without examining the details of this tradition, we may point out that there are serious objections to the identification of the two Patañjalis, the author of the *Yogasūtra* and the author of the *Mahābhāṣya*. P.V. Sharma[54] raises arguments showing that Caraka of the *Caraka-saṁhitā* could not have been identical with either the author of the *Mahābhāṣya* or with that of the *Yogasūtra*. However, on the basis of an analysis of the internal evidence of the text, he places Caraka in the Śuṅga period or a little earlier, in the period between the Mauryas and the Śuṅgas, i.e., the third century BC.[55]

Some scholars pull Caraka further back, mainly on the basis of the name Caraka occurring in the *Aṣṭādhyāyī*[56] of Pāṇini, R.K. Sharma and B. Dash[57] place Caraka in the eighth century BC. This date will vary according to the date which one accepts for Pāṇini. Jyotirmitra[58] suggests a date around 1000 BC.

A very early date will bring Caraka close to the times of Ātreya and Agniveśa. The need for a revision of the *Agniveśatantra* by Caraka could have arisen only sometime after the original composition. It is to be emphasised that the arguments for placing Caraka much earlier are baced on traces of earlier elements in the text which actually were a survival of Ātreya-Agniveśa times.

The prestige of Agniveśa and his contributions was so great that even after the revision by Caraka his name was retained in the colophon to the chapters. There are indications that up to a late period it was the name of Agniveśa and not that of Caraka which was remembered. Thus, in the *Nāvanītaka* the prescriptions, which are found in the *Caraka-saṁhitā* also, are attributed to Agniveśa

---

53. See Jyotirmitra, *op. cit.*, p. 23.
54. *Op. cit.*, pp. 111-13.
55. *Op. cit.*, pp. 115-19.
57. IV. 3.107.
58. *Caraka-saṁhtā*, Prfeace, p. xxxviii.

and not to Caraka.[59] Some quotations attributed to Agniveśa occur in later writings,[60] which may suggest that in some quarters the original work of Agniveśa survived the revision by Caraka. But, the argument is not compelling. Many quotations from several important texts cannot be traced in the original work. Passages even of authoritative texts are known to have dropped out in course of centuries. Hence, it may be suggested that the quotations in question were intended to be from the revised text of Agniveśa which later came to be known under the name of Caraka.

We cannot fix the date when the text of Agniveśa was named after Caraka. It was possibly quite sometime before Dṛḍhabala. This alone can explain the loss of thirteen chapters in the Cikitasāsthāna and the whole of the Kalpasthāna and the Siddhisthāna, requiring Dṛḍhabala to write them afresh and add them to the text. Dṛḍhabala himself mentions Kapilabala as the name of his father.[61] On the basis of reference to Kapilabala in the *Aṣṭāṅgasaṁgraha* of Vāgbhaṭa and quotations from Dṛḍhabala in it, Dṛḍhabala is taken to have been earlier that Vāgbhaṭa. P.V. Sharma[62] assigns Vāgbhaṭa to the sixth century and hence places Dṛḍhabala in the Gupta period in the fourth century.[63]

Philosophical Contribution of Agniveśa and Caraka

On the question of the specific contributions of the two phases of the text, the original composition and the revision, historians of *Āyurveda*

59. Bāṇabhaṭṭa in his *Harṣacarita* mentions as physicians Paunarvasava (a son or student of Punarvasu), which may refer to Agniveśa.
60. Cakrapāṇi and Vijayarakṣita (twelfth century) as mentioned by Jyotirmitra *op.cit.*, p. 20.
61. *Caraka*, Cikitsā, XXX.289-91.
62. *Op.cit.*, pp. 121-6.
63. According to Jyotirmitra, *op.cit.*, p. 27, Vāgbhaṭa belonged to the fourth century and Dṛḍhabala to the first half of the fourth century. R.K. Sharma and B. Dash, *op.cit.*, p. xxxix place Vāgbhaṭa in AD 300 and Caraka before this date and suggest that Dṛḍhabala may be Caraka, the second, who was the court physician of king Kaniṣka. Hoernle places Dṛḍhabala in the ninth century after Mādhava; but *contra* see P.V. Sharma, *op.cit.*, p. 122, fn. 1.

have not paid serious attention to the evidence of the nature of Sāṁkhya in the text. The text does refer to the views of the early Sāṁkhya philosophers.[64] This apparently came from the pen of Caraka. But, we cannot ferret out all the passages recording the views of early Sāṁkhya teachers. It is to be noted that the Sāṁkhya system in the revised text is earlier than the standardised exposition presented by Īśvarakṛṣṇa. The details, given by Agniveśa initially but allowed to remain in the text, indicate that Caraka also subscribed to them. Thus, the exposition of Sāṁkhya in the *Caraka-saṁhitā* and its expounders Ātreya-Agniveśa and Caraka belonged to an early phase in the history of Sāṁkhya. These Sāṁkhya principles have much in common with the accounts in the Mokṣadharmaparva section in the Śāntiparva of the *Mahābhārata*, particularly those ascribed to Pañcaśikha, and those in the *Buddhacarita* recording the views of Arāḍa. Dasgupta and, following him, other scholars could not evaluate properly the account in the *Caraka-saṁhitā*, because of their fixed view that Caraka belonged to the reign of Kaniṣka. Accordingly they ascribed the Sāṁkhya in the *Buddhacarita* to its author Aśvaghoṣa and not to its proclaimed expounder Arāḍa. Likewise, they dated the Śāntiparva account of Sāṁkhya on the basis of the date assigned to the inclusion of Śāntiparva in the *Mahābhārata*, without realising the force of the argument that there are differences in the accounts of the individual Sāṁkhya teachers, and that they are referrred to as ancient narratives (*itihāsam purātanam*).

Conclusion

Thus, the Sāṁkhya account in the *Caraka-saṁhitā* is to be considered as representing an early phase in Sāṁkhya history, to which belonged other Sāṁkhya teachers, such as Pañcaśikha and Arāḍa, who preceded Buddha. In connection with the history of *Āyurveda*, the evidence is to be interpreted as placing Caraka in the age of the Buddha. We will not be erring much if we place Caraka around 600 BC and Ātreya-Agniveśa around 800 BC.

---

64. Sūtra, XXV-15.

7

Arāḍa — An Ignored Pre-Buddha Sāṁkhya Teacher

Sāṁkhya in the Buddhacarita

THE *Buddhacarita* of Aśvaghoṣa records the philosophical views of a Sāṁkhya teacher, who belonged to the pre-Buddha times. Buddha, before he received enlightenment, approached Arāḍa for the knowledge, which may help him get emancipation from suffering. In reply Arāḍa expounded his philosophy, which is to be found in Canto XII of the *Buddhacarita*.

The *Buddhacarita* does not refer to Arāḍa as a Sāṁkhya teacher, nor does he himself claim to expound Sāṁkhya views. Modern scholars of Sāṁkhya have been so much obsessed with the exposition of Sāṁkhya principles in the *Sāṁkhyakārikā* of Īśvarakṛṣṇa that they have failed to do justice to accounts of Sāṁkhya, which show major deviations on important points. This is the reason why earlier authorities on Sāṁkhya, such as Garbe, A.B. Keith and S.N. Dasgupta, did not take any notice of the account of Sāṁkhya in the *Buddhacarita*.[1]

E. Johnston, who minutely analysed the account in the *Buddhacarita*, demonstrated that it contains genuine Sāṁkhya

---

1. U.V. Shastri and A.P. Mishra in their *Histories of Sāṁkhya Philosophy* (in Hindi) have considered Sāṁkhya views and scholars mentioned in various sources, but are silent about Arāḍa's views in the *Buddhacarita*.

principles.[2] He points out close similarities between the doctrines of Aśvaghoṣa and those of Caraka-Pañcaśikha.[3] P. Chakravarti[4] holds that there was a school of Sāṁkhya which influenced alike Aśvaghoṣa, Caraka, the Epic and the authorities cited in the *Yogabhāṣya*. J.A.B van Buitenen[5] also interprets the account in the *Buddhacarita* as representing a distinct tradition of Sāṁkhya-Yoga. Whereas Sāṁkhya is often viewed in terms of a theory of 'horizontal' evolution of *buddhi* in three *bhāvas* or *guṇas*, the present text represents eightfold *prakṛti*, which later led to a theory of vertical evolution. G.J. Larson[6] argues that Aśvaghoṣa, along with Caraka and Pañcaśikha, represents an old tradition of Sāṁkhya-Yoga, which is yet in a fluid or chaning condition. He finds the account in the *Buddhacarita* to be closer to the doctrines of the Mokṣadharmaparva and the *Gītā*.

An analysis of the account in the *Buddhacarita* shows that, though it differs from the Sāṁkhya system as standardised by Īśvarakṛṣṇa, it represents a particular type of formulation of Sāṁkhya principles. Arāḍa himself alludes to the Sāṁkhya character of his teachings, when he remarks that they have been upheld by Jaigīṣavya, Janaka and Vṛddha-Parāśara,[7] whose identity as Sāṁkhya teachers is confirmed by independent sources. In the narrative Arāḍa uses the expression *ātmacintaka* (those who deliberate upon *ātman*) for those who were proficient in expounding the philosophical system.[8] In some other texts we notice similar terms for teachers of the Sāṁkhya system.[9] It is clear from the account itself that Arāḍa presents the twin systems of Sāṁkhya and Yoga. Thus, after describing Sāṁkhya principles in XII.15-44,

---

2. *Early Sāṁkhya*, p. 8.
3. *Op.cit.*, p. 10.
4. *Origin and Development of the Sāṁkhya System of Thought*, p. 109.
5. *JAOS*, LXXVI (1957), pp. 22-3.
6. *Classical Sāṁkhya*, pp. 106-8.
7. *Buddhacarita*, XII.67.
8. *Ibid.*, XII.20.
9. P. Chakravarti, *op.cit.*, pp. 17-19.

he says[10] that he will now discuss the same *dharma*, but by a different (*anya*) method (*kalpa*). What follows[11] is an account of the Yoga system. Arāḍa makes it clear that he does not lay down a different system; he simply presents an other approach within the system described earlier by him. This suits the relationship between Sāṁkhya and Yoga. They are not two separate systems, but are two different aspects of one and the same system.

Modern researches have exposed the erroneous character of the view the Sāṁkhya was always monolithic in form, with fixed principles which show a unilinear development or elaboration. Scholars have to ferretted out passages referring to Sāṁkhya views earlier than the *Sāṁkhyakārikā*. These sources prove that Sāṁkhya had a long and rich history, which witnessed a wide variety of views on several vital issues. It is clear that an account of philosophical views may differ from the *Sāṁkhyakārikā*, yet it retains its claim to be a Sāṁkhya system. This is the case with the account of the teachings of Arāḍa in the *Buddhacarita*.

Arāḍa and not Aśvaghoṣa as Expounder

The modern studies of the *Buddhacarita* account have not led to its proper evaluation in the history of Sāṁkhya. While analysing it scholars always emphsise the text, the *Buddhacarita*, attributing the account to Aśvaghoṣa, with a very casual reference to Arāḍa, but without giving him credit for the authorship of the principles. Hence, these views are ascribed to the first century of the Christian era, and not to the times of Arāḍa.

No doubt, our source of information for this account of Sāṁkhya in the *Buddhacarita*, composed by Aśvaghoṣa. The question, now, is whether the date of the composition of the text is to be taken as the date also of its original exposition by Arāḍa. There is no reason for believing that Aśvaghoṣa created the details of the system and attributed them to Arāḍa. He could not have gained anything from this nor have added to the glory of Budha and Buddhism. There was

10. XII. 45.
11. *Buddhacarita*, XII.45-67.

a justification for it if Arāḍa had been a great celebrity, enjoying a respectable following even in the times of Aśvaghoṣa. Aśvaghoṣa was expected to imagine the details and weave a system, if Arāḍa had actually influenced Buddha's thought. Hence, we cannot say that Aśvaghoṣa authored these principles. He is to be given credit for presenting an account of the teachings of Arāḍa. We have reasons to believe that in doing so Aśvaghoṣa tried to be faithful to the original exposition by Arāḍa. We can allow Aśvaghoṣa, as a poet, under the exigencies of his poetic composition, to omit some details. But, cannot visualise that he took any liberty with the details of the teachings and the use of technical terms.

The way modern scholars have mixed up Arāḍa and Aśvaghoṣa is noticed in their discussion of the absence of a reference to *guṇa*s in the *Buddhacarita*. Keith,[12] on this ground, observes that Aśvaghoṣa expounds a school of Sāṁkhya which does not speak of the *guṇa*s. The explanation offered by P. Chakravarti[13] is revealing. He points out that the account is brief and ignores many fundamental doctrines of Sāṁkhya, such as *satkārya* theory and the *pramāṇa*s and their varieties, and that Aśvaghoṣa was writing a *kāvya* and not a philosophical treatise. To prove that Aśvaghoṣa was not ignorant of the *guṇa* theory Chakravarti adds that in Canto XXVI of the *Budhacarita* the doctrine of the *guṇa*s is refuted. It is not realised that the question is not whether Aśvaghoṣa knew the *guṇa* theory. The fact is that in Canto XII, which purports to present Arāḍa's views on Sāṁkhya, the theory is not mentioned, which would mean that, according to Aśvaghoṣa, Arāḍa did not assign it any place in his account. Larson[14] says that the absence of a reference to *guṇa*s means that Aśvaghoṣa describes 'a view of Sāṁkhya which has no need of a *guṇa* theory' and not that he was unaware of it. He, thus, confines his discussion to Canto XII of the text, but does not think in terms of Arāḍa, attributing the authorship of the principles to Aśvaghoṣa. H.S. Joshi[15] differs from all these

---

12. *Sāṁkhya System*, pp. 25-6.
13. *Op.cit.*, p. 110.
14. *Op.cit.*, p. 107.
15. *Sāṁkhyayoga-darśana kā Jīrṇoddhāra*, p. 240.

scholars in recognising Arāḍa as representing the nineteenth sub-branch of the main branch of Sāṁkhya.

A Case for Arāḍa

It may possibly be argued that Aśvaghoṣa was not expected to have on access to the original views of Arāḍa. We do not find an account of the views of Arāḍa in any other source. The Mokṣadharmaparva in the *Mahābhārata* has preserved the views of several Sāṁkhya teachers. In some cases these accounts are introduced as ancient history. But the relevant portions in the *Mahābhārata* are by no means exhaustive. We know of many Sāṁkhya teachers whose views are not recorded in the Epic. Arāda was one such teacher.

Arāḍa and a Sāṁkhya School

An important reason for this neglect was possibly that Arāḍa did not belong to any distinct Sāṁkhya school, nor did he set-up a school of his followers. J.A.B. van Buitenen speaks of the Sāṁkhya-Yoga in the *Buddhacarita* representing a separate tradition. On the basis of the similarities between the doctrines of Caraka-Pañcaśikha and Aśvaghoṣa, Larson suggests an old tradition of Sāṁkhya-Yoga in Caraka-Pañcaśikha and Aśvaghoṣa. P. Chakravarti also speaks of a common school of Sāṁkhya influencing Aśvaghoṣa, Caraka, the Epic and the authorities cited in the *Yogabhāṣya*. But, these modern theories are not supported by any specific mention of a Sāṁkhya school, to which Arāḍa belonged or a common school influencing Arāḍa and others. The lists of Sāṁkhya teachers, recorded independently by a number of texts, do not contain the name of Arāḍa. The list of teachers-students in some commentaries on the *Sāṁkhyakārikā* may imply Sāṁkhya traditions representing Sāṁkhya schools, but Arāḍa is conspicuous by his absence in them. In the *Buddhacarita* Arāḍa himself says that Jaigīṣavya, Janaka and Vr̥ddha-Parāśara also held the views which he preached. This has the appearance of a Sāṁkhya tradition; but, there is no clear reference to a school and its expounder. All the three teachers were contemporaries, possibly senior, of Arāḍa. Arāḍa simply suggests that all these four had similar, but not identical, views.

The absence of reference to Arāḍa or his views in later records suggests that he did not establish a school. Though negative evidence cannot be conclusive, as it can never be exhaustive, the fact that the *Yuktidīpikā* is silent about Arāḍa is not without significance.

It may be argued that the early Pāli literature does not contain a detailed account of the teachings of Arāḍa which could have served as the basis for Aśvaghoṣa. In the Canonical literature there is no known reference which may require an elaborate treatment of the views of Arāḍa. The *Majjhimanikāya*[16] has a reference to Alāra-kalāma, who may be identified with Arāḍa, Alāra-kalāma, when asked by Buddha, says that he had reached up to the plane of *akiñcana* (naught). In the *Buddhacarita* Arāḍa describes the final stage as *akiñcanya*. This establishes a link between the account in the *Buddhacarita* and the Pāli canonical literature and indicates the possibility of Arāḍa's exposition looking back to pre-Buddha times.[17]

Arāḍa's Philosophical Views

Arāḍa begins by defining *sattva* (being) to mean only *prakṛti* (primary matter), *vikāra* (modifications), birth, death and old age (XII.17). *Prakṛti* consists of *pañcabhūtas* (five elements), *ahaṁkāra* (ego-principle), *buddhi* (intellect) and *avyakta* (unseen power).[18] The *vikāras* include the five senses, the five objects of the senses, the five organs of action, and the *manas* (mind).[19] That which is conscious is called *kṣetrajña* (knower of the field), because it knows the field.[20] *Vyakta* is that which is subject to birth, old age, disease and death; its reverse is known to be *avyakta*. *Ajñāna* (ignorance), *karman* (activity) and *tṛṣṇā* (desire) are the causes of the cycle of

16. 26-*Ariyapariyesanasutta*.
17. Keith, *op.cit.*
18. P. Chakravarti, *op.cit.*, p. 110.
19. *Buddhacarita*, XII.39 — *hetvābhāva phalābhāva iti vijñātumarhasi.*
20. *Kārikā*, 47-8.

existence.[21] He, who abides in these three, cannot transcend existence. Arāḍa mentions eight reasons why the self gets involved in existence and suffering and explains them. These are: *vipratyaya* (misunderstanding), *ahaṁkāra* (wrong attribution of personality), *saṁdeha* (confusion of thought), *abhisaṁplava* (wrong conjunction), *aviśeṣa* (lack of discrimination), *anupāya* (wrong means), *saṁga* (attachment) and *abhyavapāta* (falling away) (24-32). *Avidyā* (ignorance) is described as five-fold; its varieties, *tamas*, *moha*, *mahāmoha*, *tāmiśra*, and *andhatāmiśra*, are enumerated and explained (33-37). For abandoning the rushing torrent of birth and death and obtaining the everlasting sphere the *kṣetrajña* has to acquire right knowledge which means properly discriminating the group of four, *pratibuddha* (intelligent), *apratibuddha* (one who lacks intelligence), *vyakta* (seen) and *avaykta* (unseen) (40-41). The state of liberation is the condition of *parama-brahma* (supreme absolute) who is described as being without any attribute, as real and immutable (42).

This is followed by an account of 'another' method. Though it is not named as such, it signifies *yoga*. Here we have an account of the practices and techniques of *yoga*. The practice of four kinds of meditation gradually leads one to emancipation.

Evaluation of Arāḍa's Views

In discussing the philosophical system of Arāḍa we cannot make the absence of a reference to any point our basis. The brief account is not expected to do justice to the details of the system. The absence may be purely accidental, or possibly the point was not so elaborately discussed as to attract the notice of Aśvaghoṣa. The prominent Sāṁkhya principles, which are mentioned as not occurring here, are the *guṇa* theory,[22] the theory of *satkārya*, the *pramāṇas* and their varieties,[23] and the *tanmātras*. It may, however, be pointed out that the theory of *satkārya* is clearly implied, when Arāḍa says

21. XII.308.5, 7, 17; XII.306.44; XII.307.48.
22. XII.318.
23. *Op. cit.*, pp. 103-7.

that if the cause is absent (*hetvābhāva*).[24] It is quite likely that some points were present in a nascent form, but had not been elaborated into a full philosophical principle.

There are some distinctive views in the account given by Arāḍa which are opposed to the general understanding of the Sāṁkhya philosophy. The first is the concept of *sattvas*. *Sattvas* are quite different from the *tattvas*, which characterise the Sāṁkhya system. They signify basic realities and include *puruṣa*, *prakṛti*, birth, death and old age. Second, *prakṛti*, here, differs from its classical notion in Sāṁkhya, where it signifies one of the two basic categoires. Prakṛti is conceived as a plural notion and includes within it *pañcabhūtas*, *ahaṁkāra, buddhi,* and *avyakta*. Third, Arāḍa does not use the technical term *puruṣa*. Instead, he speaks of *kṣetrajñas* as individual selves. Fourth, though essentially dualistic, the account does not specifically mention the concept of dualism of *puruṣa* and *prakṛti*. The use of the term *ātma-cintaka* for the teachers of the system is also significant. Besides individual selves, Arāḍa refers to the Cosmic Self or *parama-brahma*. Fourth, Arāḍa distinguishes between *kṣetra* and *kṣetrajña* on one hand, and between *vyakta* and *avyakta* on the other. Fifth, *avyakta* is neither higher than *prakṛti*, nor identical with it, but is a constituent of *prakṛti*. Sixth, Arāḍa classifies *prakṛti* and its evolutes into two: *prakṛti* which is eightfold, and *vikāra* (modification), which comprises the ten organs, *manas* and the five objects of the senses. Seventh, Arāḍa mentions the five objects of senses as *tattvas*. Eighth, Arāḍa regards *ajñāna*, *karma* and *tṛṣṇā* as the cause of the cycle of existence. He enumerates eight factors for the same and goes on to define them. Ninth, Arāḍa mentions *avidyā* (ignorance) as being five-fold and enumerates its varieties. According to the *Sāṁkhyatattvakaumudī*, Vārṣagaṇya laid down the concept of five-fold *avidyā*. We find that the *Sāṁkhyakārikā*[25] lists there five varieties not as *avidyā* but as *viparyaya*, classifying these varieties into further sub-varieties. Tenth, the use of the terminology of *vyakta* and *avyakta, pratibuddha* and *apratibuddha* is another

24. *Op.cit.*, pp. 108-9.
25. P. Chakravarti, *op.cit.*, p. 109.

distinctive characteristic of Arāḍa's system. The term *avyakta* is found in some other accounts of Sāṁkhya principles. *Vyakta*, as opposed to *avyakta*, can be recognised, but it is not evidenced in other parallel accounts of Sāṁkhya. The terms *pratibuddha* and *apratibuddha* have parallels in the accounts of Sāṁkhya attributed to Vasiṣṭha[26] and Yājñavalkya[27] in the *Mahābhārata*. The Epic references use the terms *buddha*, *apratibuddha* and *budhyamāna* and show slight difference in their specific meanings.

Features of Early Sāṁkhya in Arāḍa's Exposition

In the account of Sāṁkhya Arāḍa expounds there are many features which refer to an early stage in the history of Sāṁkhya, much earlier than the standardisation brought about by Īśvarakṛṣṇa. In the first place, here Sāṁkhya and Yoga are intrinsically connected. They are not two different systems, but two different ways in the same system. The account refers to the stage of Sāṁkhya-Yoga in the history of Sāṁkhya. This stage is evidenced by the *Gītā* and many chapters in the Śāntiparva of the *Mahābhārata* claiming to represent ancient history.

Second, P. Chakravarti[28] has pointed out some striking similarities between the system expounded by Arāḍa and the account found in the Śārīrasthāna of the *Caraka-saṁhitā*. These include classification of *avyakta* and its evolutes into two groups, counting the objects of senses as *tattvas*, omission of *tanmātras*, distinction between *kṣetra* and *kṣetrajña* and *avyakta* and *vyakta*, enumeration of eight factors for causing worldly existence, and the identification of the stage of literation with *Brahman*.

The date of Caraka is a subject of controversy. The whole text of the *Caraka-saṁhitā* cannot be assigned to one specific date; portions belonging to different periods are found mixed up in the text. Traditionally also three distinct layers are recognised in it. Caraka is credited with the revision of the text, originally written

---

26. G.J. Larson, *op.cit.*, pp. 107-8.
27. *Loc. cit.*
28. XII.67.

by Agniveśa. Agniveśa presents the Sāṁkhya principles as expounded by Ātreya. Later, the text as revised by Caraka was completed by Dṛḍhabala. Thus, the account of Sāṁkhya found in the *Caraka-saṁhitā* is to be assigned to the period of Agniveśa or even earlier to that of Ātreya.

Third, P. Chakravarti[29] points out the close relation between Arāḍa's Sāṁkhya and the Sāṁkhya accounts in the *Mahābhārata*. This includes the concepts of *vyakta* and *avyakta*, technical terms such as *pratibuddha*, *apratibuddha* and the like, the classification of *tattva*s into two groups of eight primary constituents and sixteen modifications, the negation of the *tanmātra*s, and the mentioning of ignorance (*ajñāna*), activity (*karma*) and desire (*tṛṣṇā*) as the cause of the cycle of existence.

In the case of the *Mahābhārata* also chronology is a very vexed problem. Generally the broad time-bracket of 400 BC to AD 400 is suggested, but it is believed that the text had received its present form by the end of the second century. Here also three main stages in the growth of the text, admitted by tradition, are *Jaya*, *Bhārata* and *Mahābhārata*. Many chapters in the Śāntiparva are among the latest to be added to the text, possibly sometime between 200 BC and AD 200. But the date of their incorporation in the text need not be the date of their composition also in all the cases. The account found in them may look back to earlier times. In some cases, including the chapters of the Sāṁkhya account, we have an explicit statement that they are part of ancient history. Hence, the close similarity, on certain important points, between Arāḍa's exposition and the Sāṁkhya chapters in the *Mahābhārata* envisages an early date for Arāḍa.

Date of Arāḍa

The suggestion that Aśvaghoṣa (Arāḍa), Caraka, the Epic and the authorities cited in the *Yogabhāṣya* were influenced by a common school of Sāṁkhya[30] or that Caraka, Pañcaśikha and Aśvaghoṣa (Arāḍa) represent and old tradition in a fluid or changing condition

29. XII.229.
30. U.V. Shastri, *op.cit.*, pp. 584-92.

which was influenced by a common Sāṁkhya-Yoga[31] makes a case for Arāḍa being an early Sāṁkhya teacher; but this is not helpful in determining his date. Larson[32] narrows the scope slightly when he describes Aśvaghoṣa's (Arāḍa's) treatment as representing 'a somewhat later version of the kinds of speculation found in Caraka-Pañcaśikha'. This line of argument, though not very definitive, indicates that Arāḍa belonged to the same phase of Sāṁkhya which witnessed Pañcaśikha and Ātreya (or Agniveśa) and that possibly he was a little later than these. But, there is no evidence which may help us calculate the time-gap separating Arāḍa from his elder contemporaries.

We come to a similar conclusion about the chronological position of Arāḍa with the help of the testimony of the *Buddhacarita*.[33] On his own admission, Arāḍa did not precede Jaigīṣavya, Janaka and Vṛddha-Parāśara. We know from the *Mahābhārata*[34] that Jaigīṣavya was a senior contemporary of Devala and Āvāṭya and was possibly a contemporary of Pañcaśikha also.

Janaka was associated with Mithilā. We find reference to several kings with the name of Janaka. The Mokṣadharmaparva of the *Mahābhārata* connects Janaka with the exposition of Sāṁkhya.[35] Janaka, the philosopher king, is known from the Upaniṣads also. Videha, with its capital at Mithilā, later became a constituent member of the federal republic of Saṁvajjī. Janaka, as the king of Videha, has to be placed before its incorporation in Vajjī. This would place Janaka in pre-Buddha times.

Vṛddha-Parāśara is generally identified with Pañcaśikha.[36] Pañcaśikha was one of the earliest Sāṁkhya teachers. He was the pupil of Āsuri, who himself was Kapila's direct disciple. The

31. *Mbh.*, XII.320.24.
32. XII.220-2, 224.
33. P. 175.
34. *Op.cit.*, p. 113.
35. XII.218.32-3.
36. XII.23.

Mahābhārata[37] refers to him as a revered Sāṁkhya teacher, Janaka being his pupil. The *Yuktidīpikā* mentions him as the teacher of Janaka, Vasiṣṭha and many others. P. Chakravarti points out that 'Pañcaśikha passed as a mythical figure even in the days of Buddha'.

The account of the dialogue between Janaka and Pañcaśikha, as recorded in the *Mahābhārata*, would suggest that all these philosophers were not necessarily much separated in time from one another. They were contemporaries, as senior or junior, with the result that one could react to the views of another. In this account Pañcaśikha is mentioned as reporting that some people regard *avidyā*, *karma* and *tr̥ṣṇā* as the cause for the rebirth. In the *Buddhacarita* Arāḍa expresses the same view in almost identical terms. Pañcaśikha does not name the author of the view he is going to refute, but it can be easily surmised that he is most likely referring to the views of Arāḍa. There is nothing improbable in it. If there are contemporaries, a senior may as well refer to the views of his junior. This is quite compatible with the evidence of the *Buddhacarita* in which Arāḍa refers of Jaigīṣavya, Janaka and Vr̥ddha-Parāśara also holding views expounded by him.

Conclusion

The above discussion indicates that Arāḍa is to be associated with early Sāṁkhya teachers who belonged to pre-Buddha time. The *Buddhacarita* very clearly says that he was a senior contemporary of Buddha. On this basis we may place Arāḍa around the period 600-520 BC, which is not incompatible with other available references to him.

Thus, was see that Arāḍa was a pre-Buddha Sāṁkhya philosopher. He belonged to a phase of Sāṁkhya history when

37. P. Chakravarti, *op. cit.*, p. 114 takes it to be an allusion to the doctrine of Buddhism and hence argues that the reference will require Pañcaśikha to be placed after Buddha. It is to be noted that for comparison Chakravarti refers to as passage in Candrakīrti's *Mādhyamakavr̥tti*.

Sāṁkhya-yoga had a joint form. Sāṁkhya had not acquired the fixed character, which came to be associated with its name. Arāḍa possibly did not formulate a school of his own, but had his distinctive views, which, on many points, differed not only from the later standardised version of Sāṁkhya but also from the views of some of his contemporaries.

8

Early Sāṁkhya Ācāryas

Paurika

YUKTIKDĪPIKĀ ON PAURIKA

THE name of Paurika as a Sāṁkhya teacher is known from the *Yuktidīpikā*.[1] He is included in the list of teachers who fill up the gap between Pañcaśikha and Īśvarakr̥ṣṇa. The *Yuktidīpikā*[2] preserves a quotation from his treatise. According to this passage, for each *puruṣa* there is a separate *pradhāna* (*prakr̥ti*), which creates its own body (*śarīra*) and other *tattvas*. When their *pradhāna*, endowed with *mahat* and *śarīra*, prevails, other objects also exist; with its disappearance others also disappear. In this quotation Paurika is referred to as a Sāṁkhya teacher (*sāṁkhyācārya*).

ṢAḌDARŚANASAMUCCAYA EVIDENCE

It is interesting to find that cuṇaratnasūri, in his commentary on the *Ṣaḍdarśanasamuccaya*,[3] attributes the theory of the plurality

1. P. 175.
2. *maulikyasāṁkhyā hyātmānamātmānaṁ prati pr̥thakpradhānaṁ vadanti, uttare tu sāṁkhyāḥ sarvātmasvapyekaṁ nityaṁ pradhānamiti prapannāḥ* I — p. 169
3. *pratipuruṣamanyat pradhāṇaṁ śarīrādyarthaṁ karoti* I *teṣāñca māhātmyaśarīrapradhānaṁ yadā pravarttate tadetarāṇyapi, tannivr̥ttau ca teṣāmapi nivr̥ttiḥ, iti paurikaḥ sāṁkhyācāryo manyate* II — p.169

of *prakṛtis* to ancient teachers of Sāṁkhya. According to this passage, the *maulikya*-Sāṁkhyas expound that for each *ātman* (*puruṣa*) there is a separate *pradhāna*, but the later (*uttara*) Sāṁkhyas uphold that in all the *ātmans* there is only one permanent *pradhāna*.

The two references to the same theory of the plurality of *prakṛtis* may be equated. This would suggest that Paurika was among the early Sāṁkhya teachers. This implication has been opposed by U.V. Shastri,[4] followed by A.P. Mishra.[5] Shastri takes *maulikyas* in the literal sense of *mūla* meaning origin. According to him, there is no evidence that Kapila, Āsuri and Pañcaśikha, the first three Sāṁkhya teachers, subscribed to the theory of plurality of *prakṛtis*. He suggests that the reading *maulikya* for Paurika as a mistake on the part of Guṇaratnasūri, who had no knowledge of the Sāṁkhya teacher Paurika and imagined a dichotomy, on the question of *prakṛti*, between the earlier and later Sāṁkhya teachers.

We do not find any reason to reject the clear testimony of Guṇaratnasūri and seek shelter under the imagined explanation. We know from independent sources that the history of Sāṁkhya reveals wide difference of opinion on several important issues, indicating that earlier Sāṁkhya teachers upheld views which were radically different from those expounded by later Sāṁkhya teachers. This difference is often underlined by referring to the unique views of *ādya-sāṁkhyas* or *vṛddha-sāṁkhyas*.

There is a phonetic similarity between *paurika* and *maulikya*. But whereas *paurika* is in the singular number, *maulikya* has been used in the plural. The difficulty arises when we take the term *maulikya* strictly literally as referring to the earliest teachers or to the founder exponents. There is no problem if the term is interpreted to mean 'ancient' or 'early'. The natural meaning of the reference in the commentary of Guṇaratnasūri is that, among early Sāṁkhya teachers, there were many who subscribed to the theory of the plurality of *prakṛtis*. *Paurika* was not done in expounding this

4. *Sāṁkhyadarśana kā Itihāsa*, pp. 629-31.
5. *Sāṁkhyadarśana kī Aitihāsika Paramparā*, p. 17.

principle, though his was possibly the best known presentation.

DATE OF PAURIKA

We do not have any information about Paurika, his life and times. Paurika was his name, but we cannot be sure about his background, the social or geographical group implied by the derivative meaning of the term.

The date of Paurika is not known. The *Yuktidīpikā* mentions him as being post-Pañcaśikha and pre-Īśvarakr̥ṣṇa in time. This list of Sāṁkhya teachers in the *Yuktidīpikā* has no pretensions to a chronological order; hence the position of Paurika in the list cannot be used for calculating his date. The author of the *Yuktidīpikā* seems to discuss earlier views on various Sāṁkhya to pies. This in itself may suggest an early date for Paurika. This is supported by the fact that in the *Yuktidīpikā* he is referred to with a due show of respect as a *sāṁkhyācārya*. The attribution of Paurika's distinctive view to the *Maulikyasāṁkhyas* by Guṇaratnasūri will also strengthen the suggestion that Paurika was one of the early Sāṁkhya teachers.

The *Yogabhāṣya* on the *Yogasūtra* helps us considerably narrow down the limits for the date of Paurika. Vyāsa, in his commentary,[6] quotes from Vārṣagaṇya an argument to refute the theory of the plurality of *prakr̥ti*. He says that there is no case for separate ultimate causes (*mūlapr̥thakatvam*) because there is no differences in form (*mūrti*), interposition (*vyavadhi*) and class (*jāti*). It seems that the theory of the plurality of *prakr̥ti* had a fair currency among the Sāṁkhya philosophers. Among these thinkers Paurika enjoyed a prominent position. Thus, Paurika may reasonably be placed before Vārṣgaṇya. No doubt, the date of Vārṣagaṇya has not been fixed with certainty. But definitely he is known to have been an early Sāṁkhya teacher, who founded a school of his principles. In any case, the evidence of the *Yogabhāṣya* helps us in preparing a chart of relative chronology for early Sāṁkhya teachers.

---

6. *mūrtivyavadhijātibhedābhāvannāsti mūlapr̥thakatvamiti varṣagaṇyaḥ* I — III. 53

G.J. Larson and R.S. Bhattacharya[7] place Paurika in the time-bracket of AD 100-300. They envisage that in the phase of Sāṁkhya as a technical philosophical system culminating in the *Sāṁkhyakārikā* there was a sub-phase of pre-*Kārikā* Sāṁkhya which included Paurika, Pañcādhikaraṇa and Patañjali. We have pointed out that the proposed time-bracket errs on the side of being late and have suggested 500-400 BC roughly for Pañcādhikaraṇa.[8] This may hold good for Paurika as well. This is supported by the fact, pointed out above, that Guṇaratnasūri ascribes to the Maulikyasāṁkhyas the principle of plurality of *prakṛtis*, which is known to be the characteristic view of Paurika.

Larson and Bhattacharya place Vārṣagaṇya also in this time-bracket. We have elsewhere argued for an earlier date for Vārṣagaṇya.[9] Paurika seems to be senior to him. The criticism of the theory of plurality of *prakṛtis* by Vārṣagaṇya[10] would require us to place Paurika around 450 BC.

Pañcādhikaraṇa

SOURCES

The name of Pañcādhikaraṇa does not occur in any ancient text listing Sāṁkhya philosophers. The *Māṭharavṛtti*, *Jayamaṅgalā* and the Chinese translation of Paramārtha's commentary do not include his name in the lineage of Sāṁkhya scholars between Pancaśikha and Īśvarakṛṣṇa. The list of sages belonging to the Sāṁkhya tradition who are entitled to *tarpaṇa* is also without his name. In the *Mahābhārata* we have names of many Sāṁkhya scholars, but Pañcādhikaraṇa does not occur here. We do not know of any text attributed to him.

It is only the *Yuktidīpikā* on the *Sāṁkhyakārikā* which refers to the views of Pañcādhikaraṇa at eight places.[11] Besides this,

7. *Encyclopaedia of Indian Philosophies*, Vol. IV — Sāṁkhya, pp. 9-13.
8. See *under hdg. Pañcādhikaraṇa*.
9. See *infra* chapter 17.
10. Vyāsa on III.53.
11. P. 175.

Pañcādhikaraṇa and his principles find a place in some texts independent of the Sāṁkhya stream. Padmapāda, in his commentary on the *Prapañcasāratantra*;[12] refers to the views of the followers of Pañcādhikaraṇa about the *kṣetrañja* entering the womb through the blood and semen of his parent. A second reference has been traced in the *Nareśvaraparīkṣa*.[13] A third reference is found in the commentary of Helārāja, the son of Bhūtirāja, on the *Vākyapadīya*.[14] It quotes a passage about the position of the Sāṁkhya believers of the philosophy of Pañcādhikaraṇa.

NAME

In the absence of any specific detail about Pañcādhikaraṇa, we cannot say anything about him, his background, the times to which he belonged, and his writings. The fact that the Sāṁkhya tradition, recorded by the *Yuktidīpikā*, is confirmed by three independent sources leaves no doubt about the historicity of Pañcādhikaraṇas. The *Nareśvaraparīkṣā* mentions the name as *Pañcāṅgādhikaraṇa*. P. Chakravarti has no doubt about his being Pañcādhikaraṇa.[15]

The name Pañcādhikaraṇa sounds a little queer. But, that is no

---

12. U.V. Shastri, *Sāṁkhyadarśana kā Itihāsa*, pp. 632-3, lists these passages, also A.P. Mishra, *Sāṁkhyadarśana kī Aitihāsika Paramparā*, p. 180; I. *Yuktidīpikā*, p. 108, line 4; II. p. 108, lines 7-8; III. p. 108, lines 13-15; IV. p. 108, lines 15, 17; V. p. 114, lines 1-3; VI. p. 132., lines 28-29; VII. p. 114, lines 10-16; VIII. p. 147, lines 22-4; p. 148, lines 1-2; G.J. Larson and R.S. Bhattacharya, *Encyclopedia of Indian Philosophies*, Vol. IV — *Sāṁkhya*, p. 130 analyse only six of the passages.

13. *atrāpi cetanādhātorāgatiṁ bahudhāviduḥ* । *retuḥ śoṇitajaṁ prāhureke'nye māturāhṛtāt*, — I. 94-7. Commentary — *retaḥ śonitajamiti pañcādhikaraṇānāṁ pakṣaḥ* । See P. Chakravarti, *Origin and Development of the Sāṁkhya System of Thought*, pp. 294-5; also pp. 133, fn.6.

14. *Kashmere Series of Texts and Studies*, p. 19. *nanvārthahitākāra-viśeṣasaṁvedanātmano'rthaviśeṣvyavasthāpakatvam, ato naiṣa doṣaḥ iti pañcāṅgādhikaraṇāḥ* । *yadāha* — *'tadbhogyapratibimbasya grāhaṇaṁ bhoga ātmani' iti*, see P. Chakravarti, *op. cit.*, p. 133, fn.5.

15. III.53 (Anantasayana Sanskrit Granthavali), p. 68. *Infra*, fn.24, U.V. Shastri, *op. cit.*, p. 633.

reason for dismissing it as fictitious. We have historical references to names still more queer. The suspicion is no doubt increased by the reading Pañcāṅgādhikaraṇa recorded in the *Nareśvaraparīkṣā*.

Whether Pañcādhikaraṇa was the original name or it was given to the person later on account of some speciality of his cannot be decided. U.V. Shastri[16] suggests that, as in the case of Pañcaśikha, the name Pañcādhikaraṇa was also appended later for some special reason. *Adhikaraṇa* signifies office and ancient texts and epigraphs refer to *adhikaraṇas* of a judicial or administrative nature. As *pañca* prefixed to *adhikaraṇa* did not carry much sense to the author of the *Nareśvaraparīkṣā* who may have replaced *pañca* with *pañcāṅga*. *Adhikaraṇa* has many other meanings, namely, relation, reference, connection, a receptacle, subject, substratum; location, place; and topic, subject or complete argument. As we have seen subsequently, Pañcādhikaraṇa had special views about the nature, number and function of *karaṇas* (organs). One wonders if this was, in some way, the reason for giving him this name.

AN EARLY SĀṀKHYA PHILOSOPHER

There are some indications of Pañcādhikaraṇa being early Sāṁkhya philosopher. The *Yuktidīpikā*[17] at one place says that according to Patañjali, Pañcādhikaraṇa and Vārṣagaṇa *mahat* originates out of *pradhāna*. If the order of enumeration is any indication of the chronological position, Pañcādhikaraṇa has to be placed later than Patañjali but earlier than Vārṣagaṇa. But, possibly the author of the commentary did not mean a chronological sequence in the names; He arranged them according to the importance. In any case, Pañcādhikaraṇa is to be regarded an early Sāṁkhya philosopher like Patañjali and Vārṣagaṇa.[18]

The *Yuktidīpikā* quotes the Sāṁkhyavṛddhas as arguing that the sense-organs are the products of *ahaṁkāra* and criticising the

16. *Op. cit.*
17. *Op. cit.*, p. 631.
18. Passage no.1—*patañjali-pañcādhikaraṇa-varaṣagaṇānāṁ pradhānāt mahānutpadyata iti* ।

view that the sense-organs are material.[19] Now, according to the *Yuktidīpikā* itself, Pañcādhikaraṇa formulated the view that the sense-organs are material. The criticism of this view by the elder Sāṁkhya philosophers[20] implies that Pañcādhikaraṇa was earlier than these philosophers, or in any case, was their contemporary, preferably a senior one. The term Sāṁkhyavṛddhas refers to Sāṁkhya philosophers who belonged to earlier stages in the history of the Sāṁkhya philosophy. The designation Ādya-Sāṁkhya or Maulikya-Sāṁkhya refers to the earlier form of Sāṁkhya as distinguished from its later exposition, which found its classical form in the *Sāṁkhyakārikā*. We can, hence, place Pañcādhikaraṇa in the post-Pañcaśikha period, which witnessed a rich growth and wide variety of principles. He most likely belonged to an early phase in this period, before any significant attempt at systematisation and standardisation was made.

PAÑCĀDHIKARAṆA AS A TĀNTRIKA

The *Yuktidipikā* at one place refers to Pañcādhikaraṇa as a *tāntrika*.[21] U.V. Shastri[22] recognised the possibility of the reference indicating the time to which Pañcādhikaraṇa belonged, but did not work out its implications. *Tāntrika* here does not refer to the popular usage or the term signifying one proficient in rites and cult of Tāntricism. Of all the commentaries on the *Sāṁkhyakārikā* the

---

19. See *infra*, chapter 17.

20. *evaṁ hi sāṁkhyavṛddhā āhuḥ — āhaṁkārikāṇīndriyāṇi arthaṁ sādhayitumarhanti nānyathā । tathā hi kārakaṁ kārakatvādeva prāpyakāri bhavati । bhautikāni cendriyāṇi kathaṁ prāpyakārīṇi dūravartini viṣaye bhaveyuḥ, āhaṁkārikāṇāṁ tu teṣāṁ vyāpakatvāt . . . bhautikatve hi yatparimāṇāṁ karaṇam tatprarimāṇaṁ grāhyaṁ gṛhṇīyāt* । — p. 123. The quotation occurs also in *Nyāyamañjarī*, Vol. II, p. 49.

21. The two points are: if sense-organs are material, they cannot perceive an object lying at a distance, and they can receive only such objects as are equal to them in magnitude; but actually they can receive objects which are bigger or smaller.

22. Passage no. 6 — *karaṇaṁ . . . daśavidhamiti tāntrikāḥ pañcādhikaraṇaprabhṛtayaḥ*.

Yuktidīpikā attaches much significance to the concept of *tantra*, explaining its technical meaning and demonstrating that its characteristic features and rules (*yukti*) are applicable to the *Sāṁkhyakārikā*. *Tantra* means a treatise or a systematic exposition. *Tantrayukti* refers to the rules governing the exposition of a system or the presentation of a writing. The very title of the commentary *Yuktidīpikā* indicates its primary objective to highlight the application of *tantrayukti*s to the original *Sāṁkhyakārikā*.[23] The earlier Sāṁkhya texts were often designated as *tantra*s. The *Sāṁkhyakārikā* uses the term *tantra* for the exposition of the principles by Pañcaśikha.[24] The additional verse of the *Sāṁkhyakārikā*, as recorded by Māṭhara, uses the term *tantra* for the earlier presentation of Sāṁkhya views, of which the *Sāṁkhyakārikā* claims to be a reflection as it were in a mirror.[25] The Jain canonical texts mention *ṣaṭṭitaṃtaṃ* as one of the early expositions of Sāṁkhya principles.[26] The *Yuktidīpikā* in referring to the earlier treatises on Sāṁkhya composed by Vindhyavāsin and other treatises on Sāṁkhya composed by Vindhyavāsin and other teachers, uses the expression *tantrāntara*.[27] It seems that the term *tantra* was often used as a technical term for the early treatises on Sāṁkhya. *Tāntrika* would, thus, refer to the author of an early Sāṁkhya treatise. The application of the term to Pañcādhikaraṇa suggests that, according to the author of the *Yuktidīpikā*, Pañcādhikaraṇa was an early Sāṁkhya philosopher, who had composed a treatise designated as a *tantra*.

WORK OF PAÑCĀDHIKARAṆA

There is no mention of the exact title of the treatise composed by Pañcādhikaraṇa. The ancient sources simply refer to the name of Pañcādhikaraṇa. The passages in the *Yuktidīpikā* and other sources

23. *Op. cit.*, pp. 633-4.
24. *Yuktidīpikā*, p. 3, lines 16-17.
25. *tena ca bahudhā kṛtaṁ tantram* ।
26. *tantrasya ca bṛhanmūrterdarpaṇasaṅkrāntamiva bimbam* ।
27. *Kalpasūtra* and *Anuyogadvārsūtra*, See U.V. Shastri, *op. cit.*, pp. 96-7.

recording the views of Pañcādhikaraṇa do not seem to quote his actual words in most of the cases. Some passages clearly mention his views very briefly, without the least suggestion that they are quotations from him. Passage nos. 1, 2, 4 and 6 are of this category. The reference in Padmapāda's commentary on the *Prapañcasāra-tantra* is of a similar nature. A comparison of passage nos. 3 and 5 shows that, though they refer to the views of Pañcādhikaraṇa, they are not in the form of his actual words; they represent his views, but the formulation is by the author of the *Yuktidīpikā*. Passage no. 3 ends with the expression *iti pañcādhikaraṇaḥ*, which may suggest that the preceding sentence is reproduced from the treatise of Pañcādhikaraṇa. Passage no. 5 is introduced by the expression *yaḥ pañcādhikaraṇapakṣaḥ* and ends with *iti*. The two passages communicate the same view and have many common words. But, they are not identical. There are major differences in expression and the order of points made in them. Evidently, both cannot be quotations from Pañcādhikaraṇa's treatise. If one of the two is to be treated as taken from the original text, the preference should be for passage no. 3. The other passage purports to present the stand of Pañcādhikaraṇa but not in his actual words.

Passage nos. 7 and 8 are of a slightly different nature. Both are introduced by the expression *pañcādhikaraṇasya tāvat*. The expression *iti* does not occur at the end of passage no. 7, but we find *yathā jñānamevaṁ dharmādayo'pi iti*. That passage no. 7 records the views of Pañcādhikaraṇa is confirmed by Padmapāda, who very briefly refers to the view by the expression *retaḥ-śoṇitajaṃ* parallel to *śukraśoṇitam* in passage no. 7. As in the case of the six passages discussed above, these two may also be treated as presenting the views of Pañcādhikaraṇa, but the formulation was made by the author of the *Yuktidīpikā*, without necessarily borrowing sentences from the original. In passage no. 8 there are two verses introduced respectively by the expressions *āha ca* and *atra tu tattvaiḥ sahotpattyaviśeṣāt sāṁsiddhikamabhedenāha*. These verses appear to have been borrowed from the original text of Pañcādhikaraṇa in support of the presentation of his views in prose by the author of the commentary.

The passage occurring in the *Nareśvaraparīkṣā* has two parts. The first mentions the views of Pañcādhikaraṇa as *ato naiva doṣaḥ iti pañcādhikaraṇaḥ*. Immediately after this we have the sentence *yadāha—'tadbhogya-pratibimbasya grahaṇam bhoga ātmani' iti*. It is clear that whereas the first part summarises the stand of Pañcādhikaraṇa in the words of the author of the *Nareśvaraparīkṣā*, the second reproduces the actual words of Pañcādhikaraṇa.

In Helārāja's commentary on the *Vākyapadīya* we have a reference to the views of some philosophers followed by the sentence '*kṛtapariniṣṭhitā . . . tirobhavanti*' with *iti pañcādhikaraṇa-darśanasthānāṁ sāṁkhyānāmabhyupagamaḥ* suffixed to it. Clearly the sentence is intended to be an actual quotation from a work of the Pañcādhikaraṇa school.

To summarise, we can be sure about the actual words of Pañcādhikaraṇa only in the case of two verses quoted in the *Yuktidīpikā* (passage no. 8), a sentence in the *Nareśvaraparīkṣā*, and another in Helārāja's commentary on the *Vākyapadīya*. There is a possibility that passage no. 3 also reproduces Pañcādhikaraṇa's words. Passage nos. 5, 7 and 8 represent Pañcādhikaraṇa's views faithfully, but the presentation has been done by the author of the *Yuktidīpikā*, who possibly borrowed freely words and expressions from the original. The remaining passage nos. 1, 2, 4 and 6 and the commentary of Padmapāda mention Pañcādhikaraṇa's views very briefly.

HIS PHILOSOPHICAL VIEWS

These passages and surviving quotations indicate some important features of the philosophical system expounded by Pañcādhikaraṇa.

First, according to Pañcādhikaraṇa, *mahat* is produced from *pradhāna*. This was the view of Patañjali and Vārṣagaṇya also. The *Yuktidīpikā* says that some philosophers hold that from *pradhāna* is produced another *tattva* whose form cannot be described and that *mahat* is produced from this *tattva*. Pañcādhikaraṇa formulated his view in opposition to this (passage no. 1), Second, according to Pañcādhikaraṇa the number of *karaṇa*s or organs is ten (passsage no. 6). This is in violent contrast to the *Sāṁkhyakārikā*, which mentions thirteen organs, ten external and three internal. The *Yuktidīpikā* records the difference of opinion among Sāṁkhya philosophers on this point. Vārṣagaṇya and Vindhyavāsin regard the number to be eleven. Patañjali considers only twelve organs. The available passages do not enumerate the ten organs recognised by Pañcādhikaraṇa. Possibly he considered only the ten external organs, five sensory organs and five motor organs. In passage no. 5 the words *antaḥkaraṇe bāhye ca* standing for *karaṇam* in passage no. 3 indicate that Pañcādhikaraṇa divided the *karaṇa*s into two — internal and external. But, here again there is no specification of the *karaṇa*s of the two types.

Pañcādhikaraṇa has formulated a very distinctive view about the sense-organs (*indriyāṇi*). He regards them to be material products (*bhautikāni*).[28] This is opposed to the general Sāṁkhya view that the sense-organs are the modification of *ahaṁkāra*, thus differentiating the organs from their physiological sites in the material parts of the body. The cryptic reference to the view of Pañcādhikaraṇa does not specify the grounds for propounding the view and other details of its implications. The *Yuktidīpikā* records the arguments against Pañcādhikaraṇa's view as advanced by other Sāṁkhya philosophers. The argument is based on the position that the organs function only when they come into contact with the object of perception (*prāpyakārī*). The physical organ being material cannot bring about the perception of an object lying at a distance. The sense-organs as material substance can perceive objects which are equal to them in magnitude. That they are pervasive as products of *ahaṁkāra* accounts for their perceiving all objects, whether big or small.

Pañcādhikaraṇa makes a significant departure from the views of other Sāṁkhya philosophers about the functioning of the organs. According to him, the *karaṇa*s by nature are without any impression left on them (*nirlikhitasvarūpa*). They are like an empty village or a dry river (*śūnyagrāmanadīkalpa*). The natural (*prākṛta*) and

---

28. P. 4, lines 7-8.

acquired (*vaikṛta*) knowledges are received from an external stimulus, which is an influx from the *pradhāna* (*prakṛti*) (passage no. 3).[29] In passage no. 5 the internal and external *karaṇas* are mentioned as being like the dried river and then an additional detail is added *sāttvika-sthityātmakṛtamapratyayasyāvasthānam*.[30]

Another passage (no. 4) is also in connection with the functioning of the *karaṇas*.[31] According to Vārṣagaṇya, when the *karaṇas* function abnormally, the influx comes into them from the *pradhāna*, but, in the ordinary course, they act from within. As opposed to this, Patañjali regards them as always acting from within, whereas Pañcādhikaraṇa holds that they always act on the basis of influx coming from outside.

Pañcādhikaraṇa's views on the theory of knowledge are recorded in greater details (passage no. 7). According to him, *jñāna* (knowledge) is of two kinds: *prākṛta* (natural) and *vaikṛta* (acquired). The *prākṛta* kind is classified into three: *tattvasamakāla*, *sāṁsiddhika* and *ābhiṣyandika*. *Tattvasamakāla*, is that kind of knowledge which appears in the *tattva* (evolute of the *prakṛti*) *mahat* at the very moment of its manifestation from the *prakṛti*.[32] *Sāṁsiddhika* and *ābhiṣyandika* are two kinds of knowledge of a body whose objects and organs have been produced. *Sāṁsiddhika* (innate) knowledge appears along with the composite presence of objects and organs. This is illustrated by the knowledge which the great sage (Kapila) had. His knowledge was innate. As against this, in the case of *ābhiṣyandika* (caused) knowledge the objects and the organs are innate, but it appears on account of another cause or stimulus

---

29. Passage no. 2 — *bhautikānīdriyāṇīti pañcādhikaraṇamatam* ।

30. *tathā karaṇaṁ nirlikhita-svarūpam śūnyagrāmanadīkalpam, prākṛtavaikṛtikāni tu jñānāni prerakāṅgasaṅgṛhītāni pradhānādāgacchanti ceti pañcādhikaraṇaḥ* ।

31. *anayoścābhidhānād yaḥ pañcādhikaraṇapakṣaḥ — prākṛta-vaikṛtānāṁ jñānānāṁ pradhānavat (pradhānāt) śuṣkanadīsthānīyāntaḥkaraṇe bāhye ca prerakajñānāṁśakakṛta upanipātaḥ tathā ca sātvikasthityātmakṛtamapratyayasya-vasthānamiti tat pratikṣipataṁ bhavati* ।

32. *karaṇāṇāṁ . . . svabhāvātivṛttiḥ . . . sarvāparata itipañcādhikaraṇah* ।

(*karaṇāntara*). The *vaikṛta* (acquired) knowledge is of two kinds: *sva-vaikṛta* (self-acquired) and *para-vaikṛta* (acquired from other sources). The *sva-vaikṛta* knowledge is called *tāraka* or acquired by self-reasoning. *Tāraka* is the first of the eight *siddhis*, recognised in Sāṁkhya. The remaining seven *siddhis* fall under the *para-vaikṛta* kind of knowledge, which, here, is described as acquired by the other *siddhis* (*siddhyantarāṇi*). A verse is quoted which enumerates three kinds of knowledge. *Vaivarta* is coeval with *tattva* (*tattvasamam*). *Ābhiṣyandika* is the second. *Vaikṛta* is the third and is called *ṣaṭkauśika* (caused by physical body possessing six sheaths). Not differentiating *sāṁsiddhika*, on account of the similarity resulting from its emergence along with the *tattvas*, a verse is quoted to the following effect: *Vaikṛta* is of two kinds. Of these, *sva-vaikṛta* is *tāraka*. *Para-vaikṛta* is of seven types, designated as *sattvārāma*, etc. As is the case with *jñāna* so is the case with *dharma*, etc.[33]

Helārāja mentions the Sāṁkhya views associated with the philosophy of Pañcādhikaraṇa in connection with the standpoint of some that those belonging to the past time (*atītādhva*) appear in later times on the revolving of the cycle (*parāvartta*) of the world. According to this, the dispositions (*bhāva*), which after being completely accomplished (*kṛtapariniṣṭhita*), have entered the folds of the *prakṛti* (*pradhānaprasevāntargata*) reveal themselves (*uddarśayantyātmānam*) in course of time (*yathākālam*), and again at the time of the dissolution (*pralaya*) they disappear in that itself (*tattraiva tirobhavanti*).[34]

---

33. It means that the moment the evolute of *prakṛti* is manifested, its knowledge emanates in it simultaneously. This is a significant point. It regards an object and its knowledge as correlated. It discards the view that an object exists, but its knowledge may be absent; both exist together; one cannot exist without the other.

34. *pañcādhikaraṇasya tāvat — dvividhaṁ jñānaṁ — prākṛtikaṁ vaikṛtikaṁ ca | prākṛtikam trividham — tattvasamakālaṁ sāṁsiddhikamābhiṣyandikaṁ ca || tatra tattvasamakālaṁ — saṁhataśca mahāṁstattvātmanā mahati pratyayo bhavati | utpannakāryakaraṇasya tu sāṁsiddhikamābhiṣyandikaṁ ca bhavati ||*

Another significant principle expounded by Pañcādhikaraṇa is that of *vaivarta-śarīra* (passage no. 7). It is a subtle medium or intermediate body which serves as the vehicle for the migration of *puruṣa* from one embodiment to another. It seems that Pañcādhikaraṇa viewed it as the distinguishing mark of the individual personality of the *puruṣas*. Pañcādhikaraṇa does not explain the nature of this *vaivarta-śarīra*. It cannot be equated with the organs (*karaṇas*), which are mentioned separately and as distinct from it. Possibly he took it to be constituted of *mahat* (*buddhi*), *ahaṁkāra*, *manas* and the *tanmātras* (subtle elements). According to Pañcādhikaraṇa, at the time of the sexual intercourse between the parents the *vaivarta śarīra*, integrated with the organs (*karaṇāviṣṭa*), enters into the semen and blood. After the entry it gradually develops as ovum and other stages. With the development of the parts and becoming sensitive it comes out of the womb of the mother. On account of the merit and demerit (*dharmādharma*) it has performed during the period of the enjoyment (*upabhoga*) of six *siddhis* (*ṣaṭsiddhi*) it remains in the world. It retains its existence uptil the body perishes as a result of the exhaustion of merit and demerit. If the organs (*karaṇas*) (during the embodiment) have been sanctified through virtuous deeds (*dharmasaṁskṛtam*), the subtle medium (*sūkṣma-śarīra*) migrates to heaven (*dyudeśa*). If the organs retain impressions of demerits, the subtle medium goes to hell (*yātanā-sthāna*) or the world of animals (*tiryag-yoni*). The admixture of merits and demerits leads to the world of human beings. Thus, the *sūkṣma-śarīra* serves as

---

→ *sāṁsiddhikaṁ yat saṁhatavyūhasamakālaṁ niṣpadyate, yathā paramarṣerjñānam* । *ābhiṣyandikam ca saṁsiddhakāryakaraṇasya kāraṇāntareṇotpadyate* ।। *vaikṛtaṁ tu dvividhaṁ — svavaikṛtam paravaikṛtañca* ।

svavaikṛtaṁ tārakam, paravaikṛtaṁ siddhyantarāṇi । *āha catattvasamaṁ vaivarttaṁ tatrābhiṣyandikam syāt* ।।

vaikṛtamatastṛtīyaṁ ṣāṭkauśikametadākhyātam । *atra tu tattvaiḥ sahotpattyaviśeṣāt sāṁsiddhikamabhedenāh — vaikṛtamapi ca dvividhaṁ svavaikṛtaṁ tatra tārakaṁ bhavati* ।

syāt saptavidhaṁ paravaikṛtam sattvarāmādi nirdiṣṭam. iti ।*yathā jñānamevaṁ dharmādayo'pi iti* ।।

the vechicle of *puruṣa* in his migration (*ātivāhika*) and has the capacity of holding and seizing (*dhāraṇaprāpaṇa*) the sense-organs (*indriyas*). It is always enveloped (*pariveṣṭyate*) by the physical body (*vāhyenāpāyinā*) at the time of the birth and is forsaken (*parityajyate*) by the same at the time of the death.[35]

The *Nareśvararpaīkṣā* records the view of Pañcādhikaraṇa about *bhoga* (enjoyment). *Bhoga* is the experiencing of the desirable and undesirable modifications of *buddhi* received through ṣense-organs. According to Pañcā(ṅgā)dhirakaṇa, on account of the special awareness of improper objects of senses (*arthāhitākāraviśeṣa-saṁvedanāt*) there is a special arrangement for the perceived objects (*arthāviśeṣavyavasthāpakatvam*) of soul (*ātmanaḥ*). This is supported by a quotation which says that *bhoga* is the receiving in the *ātman* of the reflection of the object of experience (*tadbhogyapratibimbasya grahaṇam bhoga ātmani*).

HIS FOLLOWERS

There is evidence to show that the philosophical system expounded by Pañcādhikaraṇa did not die out with him. His views were retained by his followers, who represented a separate school of thought. Though the *Yuktidīpikā*, in all the passages under consideration, reproduces the views of Pañcādhikaraṇa himself, the *Nareśvaraparīkṣā* refers to the view as that of Pañcā(ṅgā)-dhikaraṇas (*pañcāṅgsidhikaraṇāḥ*). Padmapāda also mentions the view as the viewpoint of the Pañcādhikaraṇas (*pañcādhikaraṇānāṁ pakṣaḥ*). Helārāja in his commentary refers to the stand of the followers of Sāṁkhya who follow the philosophical system of Pañcādhikaraṇa.

From these references it is clear that the philosophical system of Pañcādhikaraṇa was upheld by his followers in later times. We cannot be sure about the times up to which they had a real

35. *kecittu manyante — atītādhvavarttino'pi punaḥ punaḥ kālāntare jagata parāvartteṣūdbhavanti* I *'kr̥taparinistṣhitā hi bhāvāḥ pradhānaprasevakāntargatā yathākālamuddarśayantyātmānaṁ, punaḥ pralaye tatraiva tirobhavanti' iti pañcādhikaraṇadarśana-sthānāṁ sāṁkhyānā(maya) mabhyupagamaḥ* II

existence. The views of Pañcādhikaraṇa were available to the author of the *Yuktidīpikā* commentary. In later times, though they were not accessible in original, there were philosophers who subscribed to them.

CONCLUSION

The reasons for the work and system of Pañcādhikaraṇa not surviving in a substantial manner are not difficult to imagine. The standardisation of the Sāṁkhya system attempted from time to time, culminating in the most effective and systematic one presented by Īśvarakṛṣṇa, had the natural effect of expelling and suppressing the memories of earlier expositions. Pañcādhikaraṇa did not belong to the stream of Sāṁkhya system which was continued by Īśvarakṛṣṇa. He was radically opposed to this stream on a number of important issues and could not be accomodated in the subsequent flow of the system. Pañcādhikaraṇa had his own views about the evolutes of *pradhāna* (*prakṛti*), number and functioning of the *karaṇa*s, nature of *indriya*s, migration of *vaivarta-śarīra* from one embodiment to another, and the theory of knowledge. The Sāṁkhya lineage of Pañcaśikha ignored him, which relegated him and his system to the realm of obscurity.

DATE OF PAÑCĀDHIKARAṆA

G.J. Larson and R.S. Bhattacharya, though admitting that 'it is difficult to ascertain even rough approximations' of the dates of Pañcādhikaraṇa, Paurika and Patānjali, suggest the time-bracket of AD 100-300.[36] In place of the phase of Classical Sāṁkhya, they

36. *pañcādhikaraṇasya tāvat — vaivarttaṁ śarīraṁ mātāpitṛsaṁsargakāle karaṇāviṣṭam śukraśoṇitamanupraviśati* | *tadanupraveśācca kalalādibhāvena vivardhate* ||

vyūḍhāvayavaṁ tūpalabdhapratyayaṁ māturudarānniḥsṛtya yau dharmādharmau ṣaṭsiddhyupabhogakāle kṛtau tadvaśādavatiṣṭhate | *yāvattatkṣayāt śarīrapātastastāvat* || *yadi dharmosaṁskṛtaṁ karaṇaṁ tato dyu deśaṁ sūkṣmaśarīreṇa prāpyate, tadviparyāttu yātnāsthānaṁ tiryagyoniṁ vā, miśrībhāvena mānuṣyam* | *evamātivāhikaṁ sūkṣmaśarīramindriyāṇām dhāraṇaprāpaṇasamarthaṁ nityaṁ bāhyenāpāyina pariveṣṭyate parityajyate ca* ||

speak of the phase of Sāṁkhya as a technical philosophical system. They divide it into two sub-phases, pre-*Kārikā* Sāṁkhya and *Kārikā* Sāṁkhya. As contrasted with the later sub-phase, represented by the followers of Vārṣagaṇya, including Vindhyavāsin and Īśvarakṛṣṇa, they suggest the date AD 100-300 for the earlier sub-phase accomodating two groups: (a) Paurika, Pañcādhikaraṇa, Patañjali and other early philosophical *ācāryas* and (b) Vārṣagaṇya. This is based on the dates proposed for Vindhyavāsin and Īśvarakṛṣṇa and the evidence of the *Yuktidīpikā* indicating 'a rich fabric of internal debate involving such teachers as Paurika, Pañcādhikaraṇa, Patañjali, Vārṣagaṇya, and various schools such as the "followers of Vārṣagaṇya."'.[37]

There is, however, no evidence for calculating the time-gap separating the older Sāṁkhya teachers from the *Sāṁkhyakārikā* and the *Yuktidīpikā* and for determining the relative chronology of the teachers. The suggestion of an internal debate among these teachers creates an impression about their contemporaneity. It is not unlikely that the teachers belonged to different dates and expounded their views without any criticism of another view.

The *Yuktidīpikā* mentions Paurika, Pañcādhikaraṇa and Patañjali as belonging to the gap between Pañcaśikha and Īśvarakṛṣṇa. In this list there are eleven names, but they cannot be taken to represent a chronological sequence in the *Yuktidīpikā*. Pañcādhikaraṇa is designated as a *tāntrika*,[38] which possibly indicates that he belonged to an early period in the history of Sāṁkhya, when the system or a text expounding it was called a *tantra*. Again, as we have pointed out,[39] according to *Yuktidīpikā*, the *Sāṁkhyavṛddhas* criticise the theory that the sense-organs are material,[40] which view the *Yuktidīpikā* itself attributes to Pañcādhikaraṇa.[41]

---

37. *Encyclopaedia of Indian Philosophies*, ed. by K. Potter, Vol. IV — *Sāṁkhya*, pp. 9-13.
38. P. 132, see *supra* under 'Pañceādhikaraṇa as a Tāntrika'.
39. See *supra* under 'An early Sāṁkhya Philosophy'.
40. P. 123.
41. P. 108.

Pañcādhikaraṇa, thus, would appear to be among the early *Sāṁkhyuavṛddhas*. He was possibly close to the times of Pañcaśikha. The time-bracket suggested by Larson and Bhattacharya errs on the side of being late. We would place him around 500-450 BC.[42]

Ulūka

ULŪKA AS A SĀṀKHYA TEACHER

The name of Ulūka as a Sāṁkhya teacher is testified by two commentaries on the *Sāmkhyakārikā*.[43] Paramārtha's commentary, which is available in Chinese translation, and the *Māṭharavṛtti* include his name in the list of Sāṁkhya teachers who form the teacher-pupil tradition after Pañcaśikha and before Īśvarakṛṣṇa. The *Yuktidīpikā*[44] and the *Jayamaṅgalā* do not mention his name.

Śrutadevasūri, in his commentary on the *Yaśastilakacampū*,[45] paraphrases Sāṁkhya as Ulūkadarśana, which shows the importance attached to be contributions of Ulūka to the development of Sāṁkhya as a philosophical system. In the Jain text *Tattvārtharājavārtika*[46] the *akriyāvādins* are said to comprise of eighty-four different schools. The list of teachers named here includes Ulūka along with many others who were exponents of Sāṁkhya.

The epic-Purāṇic tradition remembers Ulūka as an ancient sage. In the *Mahābhārata*,[47] Ambā, the daughter of the King of Kāśī, feeling wronged by Bhīṣma, resorts to severe penance and

42. See *supra* under 'Paurika' for Paurika and *infra* chapter 14 for Patañjali
43. *Kārikā*, 71.
44. The *Yuktidīpikā* includes Mūka in its list. The editor expresses doubt about the reading. Mūka is not evidenced as a Sāṁkhya teacher by any other source.
45. Vol. III. p. 111.
46. I.5, p. 51, U.V. Shastri, *Sāṁkhyadarśana kā Itihāsa*, p. 609 refers to the *Tattvārthaślokavārttika* (chapter VIII, p. 474) as classifying 363 systems (*vādas*) into four, of which the second *akriyāvāda* includes 180. Ulūka and Kapila are mentioned in this list separately.
47. Udyoga (v). 186.26.

then visits important pilgrimage centres in the Vatsa country. The holy hermitage of Ulūka is included in this list. We do not have details about the achievements of Ulūka for which he received respect.

The *Vāyu Purāṇa*[48] mentions Ulūka, along with Akṣapāda, Kaṇāda and Vatsa, as *yogātman*, *mahātman*, pure and with unsoiled mind. All these are well-known philosophers. In the early phase of its history Sāṁkhya was a composite system with Yoga, hence this reference does not go against the Sāṁkhya connections of Ulūka.

HIS PHILOSOPHICAL VIEWS

There is no Sāṁkhya text written by Ulūka, or do we have quotations referring to his views. But the available references provide some glimpse of his principles.

Śrutadevasūri describes the philosophical system of Ulūka, identified with Sāṁkhya, as having *satkārya* as its second name. The Sāṁkhya theory of causation believes in the effect being existent in the cause. We do not know when and how it came to require its full exposition. The possibility of the Sāṁkhya principle of causation, even in a rudimentary form, being expounded by Ulūka cannot be denied.

There are various shades of views covered by the name *akriyāvāda*, depending on the emphasis envisaged by the meaning assigned to *akriyā* or non-action, it may be interpreted as advocating a fatalist view or an apathy to moral actions. The Jain sources do not go into its details, with the result that we are left into a state of uncertainty about the principle of *akriyā* laid down by Ulūka.

According to the *Rasavaiśeṣikasūtra*[49] followers of Ulūka regard sense-organs as elemental products. This is in opposition to the followers of Vārṣagaṇya who consider them to be the products of *ahaṁkāra*. Such a difference among the followers of Ulūka and

48. (A.S.S.) p. 169, verses 2-4.

49. *ahaṁkārikānīti vārṣagaṇyāḥ(ṇaḥ) aulūkyāḥ punar bhautikāni* | — III. 2, p. 124.

Vārṣagaṇya about the sense-organs being evolutes of the *mahābhūtas* or *ahaṁkāra* is attributed by Uddyotkara[50] to the followers of Yoga and Sāṁkhya respectively. Combining the testimonies of the *Rasavaiśeṣikasūtra* and Uddyotakara we find that Ulūka, on this point, was closer to the Yoga as compared with Sāṁkhya. But this difference of opinion is not the distinguishing feature of Yoga and Sāṁkhya. Possibly the difference characterised two schools of Sāṁkhya.

The testimony of *Rasavaiśeṣikasūtra* is significant in showing that in the Sāṁkhya circles the followers of Ulūka maintained their separate identity on account of their distinctive views on certain important issues.

HIS DATE

H.S. Joshi[51] places Ulūka around 675 BC. His calculation is based on the fact that in the Chinese translation of Paramārtha's commentary on the *Sāṁkhyakārika* Ulūka is named after Garga, who, according to Joshi, is to be assigned the date *c.* 825 BC.[52] But, there is a major flaw in Joshi's argument. Though he accepts the testimony of Paramārtha for taking Garga to have been a predecessor of Ulūka, he rejects the principal statement of Paramārtha making Pañcaśikha a predecessor of Garga, Ulūka and others. The date *c.* 825 BC, proposed for Garga by Joshi, cannot be accepted. Joshi arrives at this date on the basis of two references to the views of Gārgya by Yāska (700 BC according to Joshi). But, the views of Gārgya, quoted by Yāksa, relate to grammar and poetics. There is no ground for identifying this Gārgya with Garga, the Sāṁkhya teacher.

Both the *Māṭharavṛtti* and Paramārtha place Ulūka in the chronological gap between Pañcaśikha and Īśvarakṛṣṇa. The lists of Sāṁkhya teachers for this gap, as given by the four commentaries

---

50. On *Nyāyasūtra*, I.1.29—*bhautikānīndriyānīti yogānām, abhautikānīti sāṁkhyānām.*

51. *Sāṁkhyayogadarśana kā Jīrṇoddhāra*, p. 63.

52. *Ibid.*, pp. 61-2.

on the *Sāṁkhyakārikā*, are so different in names and numbers that they evidently do not record a set order of remuneration, nor can they be interpreted as showing a chronological sequence. Moreover, we cannot determine the period to be assigned to each one name. The *Māṭharavṛtti* names Bhārgava before Ulūka. It is only Paramārtha who refers to the transmission of the knowledge of Sāṁkhya from one to the next teacher. He says that Pañcaśikha gave it to Ho-kia and Ho-kia to Ulūka. This will suggest that Ulūka was in the second generation after Pañcaśika, bringing him close to the time of Buddha. But, possibly Paramārtha has woven the names into a chronological sequence of direct teacher-student relationship. In the present state of our knowledge we cannot be precise in placing Ulūka in the post-Pañcaśikha phase of Sāṁkhya.

If, however, Ulūka is to be identified with the philosopher who formulated the Vaiśeṣika philosophy, then he is to be placed earlier than Kaṇāda, who laid down the Vaiśeṣika system in the form of *sūtra*s.

9

New Beginnings by Jaigīṣavya and Āvaṭya

Jaigīṣavya

SOURCES

JAIGĪṢAVYA was among the earliest Sāṁkhya philosophers and enjoyed a high respect in the Sāṁkhya-Yoga circles. He is known from the *Mahābhārata*,[1] the Purāṇas (*Kūrma*,[2] *Vāyu*[3] and *Padma*[4]), *Īśvaragītā*,[5] Aśvaghoṣa's *Buddhacarita*,[6] Vyāsa's *Yogabhāṣya*[7] and Vācaspati's *Tātparyaṭīkā*,[8] and *Tattvavaiśāradī*.[9]

REPUTATION AS A SĀṀKHYA-YOGA TEACHER

The references show that Jaigīṣavaya enjoyed a high veneration. In

---

1. XII.318.59-62; XII.229.3-25; IX.50.6-56.
2. I.47.17-9; I.52.5
3. XXIII.131-2.
4. *Padma Purāṇa*.
5. XI.128.
6. XII.67.
7. II.55; III.18.
8. III.2.42.
9. On *Yogabhāṣya*, II.5; H.S. Joshi, *Sāṁkhyayogadarśana kā Jīrṇoddhāra*, p. 57 mentions Vācaspati's *Sāṁkhyatattvakaumudī* on *Kārikā* 2 and Vijñānabhikṣu's *Sāṁkhyapravacanabhāṣya* on V.32. But these do not refer to Jaigīṣavya.

the Śāntiparva of the *Mahābhārata*[10] he is referred to as endowed with the highest knowledge (*mahāprājña*). In the Śalyaparva[11] account he is mentioned as the high-souled one (*mahātmā*) and the great sage (*mahāmuni*), and Devala addresses him as the venerable one (*bhagavān*). The *Yogabhāṣya* on the *Yogasūtra*[12] mentions Jaigīṣavya twice as the venerable one (*bhagavataḥ* and *bhagavān*). It refers to his having acquired the knowledge arising out of intuitional wisdom (*vivekajaṁ jñānam*). Vācaspatimiśra, in his commentary *Tattvavaiśāradī*,[13] pays respect to Jaigīṣavya, mentioning him as the great sage (*parama-ṛṣi*) and adding that he expounded the view which was the stand of the author of the *Yogasūtra*. The *Kūrma Purāṇa*[14] testifies to the high veneration enjoyed by him. He is mentioned as one of the incarnations of Mahādeva in the *kali*-age and is referred to by the appellation *yogīndra* (foremost among *yogins*).

Jaigīṣavya was respected as an eminent Sāṁkhya teacher. In the Śāntiparva[15] Gandharva Viśvāvasu gives a list of eminent authorities of Sāṁkhya from whom, he learnt the principles of the system. The list includes some mythical names along with certain highly reputed historical teachers. Jaigīṣavya is one of these historical figures. In the *Buddhacarita* of Aśvaghoṣa Arāḍa expounds his principles, which evidently represent Sāṁkhya philosophy, and adds that these principles were expounded also by Jaigīṣavya, Janaka and Vṛddha-Parāśara.[16] The Sāṁkhya connections of Jaigīṣavya are clearly pronounced in the *Īśvaragītā*,[17] which mentions Jaigīṣavya and Pañcaśikha as the pupils of Kapila.

---

10. XII.229.4.
11. II. 50.53-5.
12. III.18
13. On *Yogabhāṣya*, II.55 — *sūtrakārābhimatam vaśyatāṁ parama-ṛṣi sammatāmāha — cittaikāgryāditi*
14. I.52.5.
15. *Mbh.*, XII.318.59-62.
16. XII.67.
17. XI.128.

According to P. Chakravartti,[18] Jaigīṣavya was 'a teacher of Yoga and not of pure Sāṁkhya'. His connections with Yoga are prominently evidenced in the *Kūrma Purāṇa*. The epithet *yogīndra* is used for him,[19] and his hermitage is described as the abode of great *yogins*.[20] Some references in the *Mahābhārata* clearly imply that he was a *yogin* of great spiritual powers. At one place, when Devala approaches Jaigīṣavya, the latter is described as a true *yogin*, without anger and joy (*akrudhyantam-ahṛṣyantam*).[21] In the Śalyaparva[22] Devala is said to have taken to the ascetic ways impressed by the powers of the austerities of Jaigīṣavya which were borne out of Yoga. The account of the dialogue between Āvāṭya and Jaigīṣavya in the *Yogabhāṣya*[23] prominently refers to Jaigīṣavya observing through his Yogic power the sufferings caused by birth in the ten cycles of creation.

The surviving references to the philosophical principles of Jaigīṣavya relate to topics, which are traditionally taken to belong to the Yoga system. Thus, he is said to have expounded the principles of *dhāraṇā*, and to have laid down that sense-control (*indriyajaya*) is actually non-perception (*apratipatti*) which results from the concentration of *citta* (*cittaikāgrya*). References to his views are found in sources which belong to the Yoga system, namely the *Yogabhāṣya* and the *Tattvavaiśāradī*. Vācaspatimiśra pays him a high compliment by designating him as *parama-ṛṣi* and observing that he upholds the view which is expounded by the author of the *Yogasūtra*.

A.P. Mishra[24] argues that the references to Jaigīṣavya expounding on topics belonging to the Yoga system do not show that he was not connected with Sāṁkhya. According to him, though the

18. *Op. cit.*, p. 127.
19. I.52.5.
20. I.47.17-19.
21. *Mbh.*, XII.229.4.
22. *Ibid.*, IX.50.53
23. On *Yogasūtra*, III.18.
24. *Sāṁkhyadarśana kī Aitihāsika Paramparā*, pp. 155-7.

views attributed to Jaigīṣavya are not avowed Sāṁkhya principles, they emanated originally from known Sāṁkhya views on certain important issues. Thus, when in the Śāntiparva Jaigīṣavya preaches Devala to realise the permanent position of Brahmā, distinct from *prakṛti*, remaining unaffected by praise and blame alike, he refers to *puruṣa* untouched by the three *guṇa*s and the opposite feelings of hate, joy and sorrow, etc. This is essentially a Sāṁkhya principle.

Mishra further refers to the dialogue between Āvāṭya and Jaigīṣavya as reported in the *Yogabhāṣya*. Here Jaigīṣavya is represented as saying that the highest form of contentment, derived from the mastery over the *prakṛti*, is nothing but pain, when compared to the bliss of liberation. Thus, according to Mishra, Jaigīṣavya establishes that world and life are full of suffering. Mishra infers that Jaigīṣavya was the foremost teacher, who, visualising the truth of the basic principles of Sāṁkhya, through his highest *yogic* powers, expounded them clearly. Mishra describes Jaigīṣavya as the foremost among principal Sāṁkhya-Yoga teachers of very early times.

Jaigīṣavya belonged to a very early period in the history of Sāṁkhya, when it was so intrinsically interwoven with Yoga that the two could not be separated. This was the characteristic feature of the Sāṁkhya system in that stage of its evolution and Jaigīṣavya naturally reflected it. Another possibility is that among the many Sāṁkhya schools there was one which emphasised the joint nature of Sāṁkhya and Yoga. Possibly Jaigīṣavya was the foremost exponent of this school. His characteristic emphasis was possibly carried forward by his disciples Āvāṭya and Devala among others.

Work-composition

H.S. Joshi says that Jaigīṣavya wrote entitled the *Dhāraṇāśāstra*.[25] P. Chakravartti[26] also refers to him as the author of the *Dhāraṇāśāstra*. Both base this view on the testimony of

---

25. *Op. cit.*, pp. 57-8. He describes the contents of this work. But neither the text is available nor is there any reference to its contents in any ancient text.

26. *Op. cit.*, p. 128.

Vācaspatimiśra's commentary *Tātparyaṭīkā* on the *Nyāyasūtra*.[27] Though the reference does prove that Jaigīṣavya wrote a treatise expounding his views on *dhāraṇā*, we cannot be sure about its title. *Dhāraṇāśāstra* is the subject of his work; it need not be the title of his work. This follows from the fact that Vācaspatimiśra himself refers to *Dhāraṇāśāstra* as expounded by Jaigīṣavya and others. Clearly *Dhāraṇāśāstra* signifies a subject or discipline and not the title of a book.

All available reference to the views of Jaigīṣavya are in prose. Whether they are actual expressions from Jaigīṣavya's treatise or are presentations of his views by the author or text quoting him cannot be determined. The probability is in favour of the second alternative; but, it has to be admitted that, in doing so, the secondary sources have retained significant words and expressions used by Jaigīṣavya. We cannot rule out the possibility that Jaigīṣavya employed verses also to formulate his views, but there is no undoubted evidence in support of it.[28]

In the *Mahābhārata*[29] the dialogue between Jaigīṣavya and Devala is in verses. This, however, does not mean that Jaigīṣavya presented his views in verses. The use of verses was a compulsion on account of the form of the *Mahābhārata*. These verses cannot be said to have formed a part of the treatise composed by Jaigīṣavya. Lakṣmīdhara, in his *Kṛtyakalpataru*,[30] reproduces these nineteen verses in the *Mahābhārata*, but attributes them to Jaigīṣavya, which would create the impression that both Lakṣmīdhara and the compiler of the relevant section in the *Mahābhārata* borrowed the verses in question from the original treatise of Jaigīṣavya. But, we know that, in some similar cases, Lakṣmīdhara reproduces verses from the *Mahābhārata*, but does not mention the *Mahābhārata* as the source and attributes them to the celebrated personally referred

27. III.2.42; *Dhāraṇāśāstraṁ Jaigīṣavyādiproktam.*

28. H.S. Joshi, *op. cit.*, p. 58 says that the *Dhāraṇāśāstra* of Jaigīṣavya contained verses. But in the absence of any definite evidence, the view can be neither confirmed nor rejected.

29. *Mbh.*, XII.22.5-25.

30. *Mokṣakāṇḍa*, pp. 228-9.

to in the account.[31] The account of the Devala-Jaigīṣavya dialogue cannot be construed to prove that Jaigīṣavya formulated his ideas in his treatise by composing verses. It is to be noted that in a similar account of the dialogue between Jaigīṣavya and his disciple Āvaṭya, as recorded by Vyāsa in his commentary on the *Yogasūtra*, the views are expressed in prose.

PHILOSOPHICAL VIEWS

In the absence of actual quotations from the writings of Jaigīṣavya or detailed references to his views on important issues, we are not in a position to formulate the Sāṁkhya system presented by him. The only reference, which can be taken to represent his view, is found in the *Yogabhsāṣya*.[32] Here it is said that, according to Jaigīṣavya, sense-control consists in the non-perception of the objects, which stage is realised through the full concentration of the *citttas*.

In line with this is the reference, made by Vācaspatimiśra, to Jaigīṣavya having expounded the *Dhāraṇāśāstra*.[33] We cannot hazard any guess about the actual opinion expressed by Jaigīṣavya on different topics connected with the subject of *dhāraṇā*.

The account of the dialogue between Āvāṭya and Jaigīṣavya, as recorded by Vyāsa in the *Yogabhāṣya*,[34] represents Jaigīṣavya as

31. *Journal of Ancient Indian History*, Vol. XIII, pp. 57-64.
32. II.55 — *cittaikāgryādapratipattireveti jaigīṣavyah* |
33. *Tātparyaṭikā* on *Nyāyasūtra*, III.2.42.
34. On *Yogasūtra*, III.18 — *atredamākhyānaṁ śrūyate bhagavato jaigīṣavyasya saṁskārasākṣātkaraṇād daśasu mahāsargeṣu janmapariṇāmakramamanupaśyato vivekajam jñānaṁ prādurabhavat* | *atho bhagavān āvaṭyastamudharasthamuvāca — daśasu mahāsargeṣu bhavyatvādanabhibhūtabuddhisatvena narakatiryaggarbhaṁ sambhavaduḥkhaṁ sampaśyatā devamamanuṣyeṣu punaḥ punarutpadyamānana sukhaduḥkhayoḥ kimadhikamupalabdhamiti? bhagavantamāvaṭyaṁ jaigīṣavya uvāca — daśau . . . yat kiñcidanubhūtaṁ tat sarvaṁ duḥkameva pratyavaimi* | *bhagavānāvaṭya uvāca — yadidamāyuṣmataḥ pradhānavaśitvamanuktamaṁ ca santoṣasukhaṁ kimidamapi duḥkhapakṣe nikṣiptamiti? bhagavān jaigīṣavya uvāca — viṣayasukhāpekṣayai-*

→

enunciating the principle of birth in the world being essentially suffering. He is said to have observed, in the ten cycles of creation, pain arising from hell and birth for both gods and human beings. According to him, even the mastery over the *prakṛti*, which is the highest form of contentment, is to be placed in the category of pain. The joy of contentment (*santoṣa-sukha*) is invaluable only as compared to the pleasures of sensation. When it is compared to the bliss of liberation, it is also nothing but pain. This is the nature of *buddhi*. It comprises of three *guṇa*s. The form of suffering is the thread of craving (*tṛṣṇā*). By the cessation of the suffering caused by craving follows joy, incessant and suitable in all respects, which is termed as happiness (*sukha*). It is to be noted that the reality of suffering is the starting point of Sāṁkhya.[35] It is emphasised by Īśvarakṛṣṇa in his introductory verses.[36] This was, possibly, an important feature of Sāṁkhya thought even in its early formulations.

In the Śalyaparva chapter Devala approaches Jaigīṣavya to enquire from him the path for emancipation (*mokṣadharma*) and is taught the method of Yoga.[37] In another chapter in the Śāntiparva the narrative of Devala and Jaigīṣavya occurs in connection with people who follow the path for emancipation (*mokṣadharma*) and achieve the position of *Brahman*.[38] In this narrative there is nothing by way of metaphysics. What Jaigīṣavya preaches belongs to the domain of ethics. Even if another person does him wrong, one should always do him well and always think well of him. One should refrain from hoping and not worry about the past; he should act in the present. Control the senses, conquer anger, strive for acquiring knowledge, and do not harm anybody by thought, speech or action.

→ *vedamanuttamaṁ santeṣasukhamuktaṁ kaivalyāpekṣayā duḥkhameva buddhisattvasyāyaṁ dharmastriguṇaḥ triguṇaśca pratyayo heyapakṣe nyasta iti duḥkhasvarūpastṛṣṇātantustṛṣṇā-duḥkhasantānāpagamāttu prasannamabādhāṁ sarvānukūlaṁ sukhamidamuktamiti* ||

35. *Sāṁkhyakārikā*, *kārika* 1.
36. A.P. Mishra, *op. cit.*, p. 155.
37. IX.50.53-7.
38. XII.229.2-5.

If people blame me or praise me, I do not become small or great by that. One should think that all such people actually describe themselves only. Those, who lead their life in this manner, add to their happiness. In this way one realises Brahmā, who is sublime and is definitely distinct from *prakṛti*. The passage, thus, establishes the primacy of *pruruṣa*, as distinct from *prakṛti*. It advocates the ethical norms of conduct, similar to the one laid down in the *Gītā*, as characteristic of a man of steadfast knowledge (*sthitaprajña*).

In the *Buddhacarita*[39] Arāḍa remarks that Jaigīṣavya also upheld the principles which he has expounded. From this it can be inferred that there was a general similarity in the exposition of Sāṁkhya by Jaigīṣavya and Arāḍa. We can use the account of Sāṁkhya available in the *Buddhacarita* for Jaigīṣavya also, but only in the broadest sense. We do not know the details of the actual presentation made by Jaigīṣavya and the manner in which he differed from Arāḍa.

Thus, the principal features of the philosophical system of Jaigīṣavya, which are projected by the cryptic and indirect references in later texts, are those which are to be expected in the early stages of the history of Sāṁkhya. The emphasis on the basic reality of the concept of suffering, the primacy of *puruṣa* as distinct from *prakṛti*, the joint presentation of Sāṁkhya and Yoga, and the underlining of the unruffled ethical conduct as *mokṣadharma* are some points in his presentation which can be easily identified.

DATE

H. S. Joshi[40] places Jaigīṣavya around 525 BC. This is deduced from Jaigīṣavya being taken to be a disciple of Pañcaśikha, whose date, as suggested by Joshi, was around 550 BC. Joshi calculates these dates on the basis of a statement in the *Kathāsaritsāgara* mentioning Vyāḍi, a disciple of Varṣa (or Vārṣagaṇya) as a contemporary of Nanda. He takes the date of Vyāḍi to be *c*. 375-350 and that of

---

39. XII.67.
40. *Op. cit.*, p. 58.

Vārṣagaṇya to be *c.* 400 BC. He places Pañcaśikha long before Vārṣagaṇya, on the ground that the latter brought out a revised account of *Saṣṭhitantra*, which was originally expounded by Pañcaśikha.

This view is based on a late tradition making Vyāḍi a contemporary of Nanda king and describing him as a disciple of Varṣa, who is identified with Vārṣagaṇya. Even if all this is accepted, there is no valid argument for postulating a gap of only 150 years between Pañcaśikha and Vārṣagaṇya.

There are other indications also which help us determine the date of Jaigīṣavya. According to the *Kūrma-Purāṇa*, Jaigīṣavya was a contemporary of Pañcaśikha and not his disciple, both being the disciples of Kapila. We also know that his example was emulated by Devala. There is an account of a dialogue between Devala and Jaigīṣavya, in which Jaigīṣavya preaches ethical ideas to Devala. Jaigīṣavya is reported to have answered the philosophical queries of his disciple Āvaṭya. One tradition, as recorded in the *Kūrma Purāṇa*, represents Sāṁkhya, Manohara, Kauśika, Kṛṣṇa, Sumanas and Vedavāda as the chief disciples of Jaigīṣavya. Thus, we have a long list of the disciples of Jaigīṣavya. From other sources we find people having names of Sāṁkhya, Kauśika and Kṛṣṇa; but we cannot be sure if they were also Sāṁkhya philosophers, as required by the context of the reference. Of these, no doubt, Kṛṣṇa propounds Sāṁkhya-Yoga principles in the *Gītā*, but the known sources do not associate Jaigīṣavya with Kṛṣṇa at any stage of his career. Āvaṭya, who was closely associated with Jaigīṣavya, and is referred to by the *Yogabhāṣya* with respect as *bhagavān*, is not known from any other source. Thus, the only disciple of Jaigīṣavya who can be helpful in fixing his date is Devala.

The above analysis shows that Jaigīṣavya is to be placed not before Pañcaśikha but certainly before Devala.

According to the *Kūrma Purāṇa*, both Pañcaśikha and Jaigīṣavya were the pupils of Kapila. The *Mahābhārata* mentions that Devala received spiritual teaching from Jaigīṣavya. The combined testimony of these two texts will make all the three, Pañcaśikha, Jaigīṣavya and Devala, contemporaries. U.V. Shastri[41] resolves the apparent incongruity by suggesting that as Pañcaśikha is reported to have enjoyed an unusually long life, he could have been, in the later part of his life, a senior contemporary of Jaigīṣavya, who also may have acquired a long life and, in his turn, in his old age, was a senior contemporary of Devala.

Apparently there is nothing inherently improbable in the explanation which envisages a long life for two of the early Sāṁkhya teachers, who are known to have acquired spiritual powers through the practice of *yoga*. But, there is a weak link in the chain of argument. It is clear that Jaigīṣavya was one of the early Sāṁkhya teachers. Whether he was a direct disciple of Kapila, as stated in the *Kūrma Purāṇa*, cannot be confirmed. It is quite likely that the *Kūrma Purāṇa* has mixed up the chronological position of these early Sāṁkhya teachers. We know that a long established tradition, which is accepted by Īśvarakṛṣṇa also, unequivocally says that Kapila had preached Sāṁkhya principles to Āsuri, who communicated them to Pañcaśikha. There is no independent confirmation of the teacher-student relationship between Kapila and Pañcaśikha. Thus, though there is a strong possibility of Jaigīṣavya also being one of the early Sāṁkhya teachers, his contemporaneity with Pañcaśikha as a co-pupil cannot be accepted as proven.

The *Buddhacarita*[42] of Aśvaghoṣa provides an important clue to the date of Jaigīṣavya. Arāḍa names Jaigīṣavya, Janaka and Vṛddha-Parāśara as upholding the philosophical views expounded by him. According to the *Buddhacarita*, Buddha, before his enlightenment, approached Arāḍa and sought from him the knowledge for overcoming miseries. Arāḍa expounded his philosophy and then made a reference to Jaigīṣavya and others. The historicity of Janaka and Vṛddha-Parāśara, as teachers of Sāṁkhya, is confirmed by other independent sources. This evidence of the *Buddhacarita* indicates that Jaigīṣavya was not later than Arāḍa.

41. *Op. cit.*, 598-9.
42. XII.67.

He could have been a contemporary of Arāḍa. Most likely he was senior to Arāḍa. In any case, Jaigīṣavya will be placed earlier than Buddha.

The evidence, which we have discussed above, clearly shows that Jaigīṣavya enjoyed the reputation of being an eminent Sāṁkhya philosopher of very early times. His deification as an incarnation of Śiva and the reference to his demonstrating his *yogic* powers to Rudra and Umā are indicative of the same. In the *Vyāsabhāṣya* on the *Yogasūtra* the account of the dialogue between Āvaṭya and Jaigīṣavya is mentioned as an *ākhyāna*, which shows that Jaigīṣavya was considered to belong to very early times.

In the Śāntiparva the account of the dialogue between Devala and Jaigīṣavya is introduced as ancient history (*itihāsam purātanam*).[43] Clearly Jaigīṣavya flourished several centuries before the composition of this and similar other chapters dealing with Sāṁkhya. In another context in the Śāntiparva[44] Jaigīṣavya is mentioned along with certain mythical personalities and very eminent Sāṁkhya philosophers of a very early time, from whom Gandharva Viśvāvasu claims to have learnt Sāṁkhya.

Thus, we may conclude that Jaigīṣavya was not only earlier than Aśvaghoṣa, but preceded the Mokṣadharma chapters in the Śāntiparva by several centuries. He appears not to have preceded Pañcaśikha. He was definitly earlier than Āvaṭya, Buddha, Arāḍa and Devala. The date of Buddha is generally accepted to be 583-463 BC. Devala and Arāḍa are referred to as senior contemporaries of Buddha. Jaigīṣavya, as a teacher of Devala and a predecessor of Arāḍa, can be located around 650 BC.

Āvaṭya

The name of Āvaṭya as a Sāṁkhya teacher is known only from the *Yogabhāṣya* of Vyāsa, a commentary on the *Yogasūtra*.[45] He is

---

43. *Mbh.*, XII.229.3
44. *Ibid.*, XII.318.59-62.
45. III.18. For the original passage see *supra* fn. 34.

mentioned as a follower (*anucara*) of Jaigīṣavya. In the passage under reference he is referred to as *bhagavān* at three places. This shows the high respect which he commended in Sāṁkhya-Yoga circle.

We do not find any reference to any text written by him or to any of his philosophical views. From the passage under reference he appears to have had a highly alert intelligent mind. He asks Jaigīṣavya to tell, on the basis of his having observed, in the ten cycles of creation, pain arising from hell and birth, out of pleasure and pain which is larger among gods and human beings. He further asks Jaigīṣavya if the highest joy of contentment (*santoṣa-sukha*) is also to be placed to the credit of pain.

We do not have any means to determine, the views upheld by Āvaṭya. But, if we believe that his views were similar to those of his teacher, we can hazard that he accepted the principles which Jaigīṣavya communicated to him and which we have indicated above.

Padmapāda, in his commentary on the *Prapañcasāratantra*,[46] detailing the various views about the process of the descent of *puruṣa* into the womb, mentions one saying that this takes place due to pious hankering of the parents for a child and their consequent observance of restriction in food and movement in confirmity with the religious injunctions.[47] Padmapāda attributes this view to Āpadya and others (*Āpadyādayaḥ*). The editor, taking *Āpadyādayaḥ* to be a corrupt reading, corrected it as *Ātreyādayaḥ*, but without giving any reason for it. C. Chakravarti[48] points out that a manuscript in the Royal Asiatic Society of Bengal[49] has the reading *Āvadyādayaḥ* and suggests that the original reading was *Āvaṭyādayaḥ*. If this is to be accepted, it will mean that Āvaṭya had his own peculiar views on many points, including the nature of the *puruṣa* as he is born in the world.

---

46. I.94-7.
47. *karmaphalamiti apatyārthināṁ yathoktāhāravihāra śraddhādyāti śayād garbhaṁ praviśatītyāpadyādayaḥ* ।
48. *Op. cit.*, p. 295, fn.1.
49. G.8543, fol. 17b, 1.5.

10

Vasiṣṭha and the Sāṁkhya-Yoga School

Sources

THE name of Vasiṣṭha as a Sāṁkhya teacher is known from the *Yuktidīpikā*. In it Pañcaśikha is said to have expounded Sāṁkhya to many, Janaka, Vasiṣṭha and others.[1] No other authentic Sāṁkhya text mentions Vasiṣṭha. We do not know of a Sāṁkhya text attributed to Vasiṣṭha. The only confirmation of Vasiṣṭha as a Sāṁkhya teacher is found in the Mokṣadharma section of the Śāntiparva of the *Mahābhārata*, chapters 302 to 308, wherein Vasiṣṭha is represented as explaining Sāṁkhya principles to king Karāla Janaka.

It may be mentioned here that Śaṅkara, in his commentary on the *Brahmasūtra*,[2] refers to Devala and some other authors of Dharmasūtra as using Sāṁkhya principles in their texts. Vasiṣṭha is also the author of a *Dharmasūtra*. The testimony of Śaṅkara is confirmed in the case of Devala. We cannot be sure if Śaṅkara intended to include Vasiṣṭha in this test. The *Vasiṣṭha-dharmasūtra* consists of thirty chapters, of which the ninth and tenth deal respectively with rules for forest hermits and *saṁnyāsins*. But, these do not contain any account of the Sāṁkhya-Yoga principles and practices. It is only in chapter XXVI that the virtue of *prāṇāyāma* as a purifier is mentioned. This clearly cannot justify Vasiṣṭha

---

1. *bahubhyo janaka — vasiṣṭhādibhyaḥ samākhyātam* | — p. 175.
2. I.4.28.

being referred to as a Sāṁkhya teacher. Thus, our only evidence for the Sāṁkhya views of Vasiṣṭha in the Mokṣadharmaparva of the *Mahābhārata*.

Philosophical Views of Vasiṣṭha

Vasiṣṭha, in expounding the Sāṁkhya system, speaks of twenty-five categories. He enumerates the twenty-four categories as the *prakṛti* and its evolutes, and adds that Viṣṇu is the twenty-fifth category. But, in no later reference Viṣṇu is mentioned as the twenty-fifth category. It is *puruṣa* who is referred to as the twenty-fifth category. Vasiṣṭha maintains that there are only twenty-five categories. But, in chapter XII.308 a twenty-sixth category is introduced.

Vasiṣṭha traces the course of creation through Brahmā, who is formless *svayambhuva* but creates Brahmā with a form. He is known under various names Hiraṇyagarbha, Mahān, Viriñci, Aja, Vicitrarūpa, Viśvātmā, Ekākṣara and Viśvarūpa. Under the influence of evolution (*vikriyā*) he creates himself as *ahaṁkāra* and *prajāpati* characterised by it.

In the subsequent account Vasiṣṭha describes creation of twenty-four *tattva*s in terms of *prakṛti* and its evolutes. He names the transformation of *prakṛti* from *avyakta* to *vyakta*, as *vidyā-sarga*. *Mahat* and *ahaṁkāra* are designated as *avidyā-sarga*. The appearance of subtle elements from *ahaṁkāra* is termed as *bhūta-sarga*. The simultaneous appearance of the group of ten from *ahaṁkāra*, namely the five gross elements (*vāyu*, *jyoti*, *ākāśa*, *āpa* and *pṛthivī*) and their subjects (*śabda*, *sparśa*, *rūpa*, *rasa* and *gandha*) is the *vaikṛta-sarga*. The fifth, the *bhautika-sarga*, is the simultaneous creation of *manas*, the five sense-organs (*buddhīndriya*) and the five organs of action (*karmendriya*).

The world, made of the twenty-four *tattva*s, is termed as *vyakta* and is also named as *kṣara*, being destroyed constantly. Different from it is the *tattva* which is *akṣara*. Viṣṇu is the twenty-fifth *tattva*. The *Pañcaviṁśatika* is beyond *tattva*s (*nistattva*), but is called a *tattva*, because of its association with the *tattva*s (*tattvasaṁśrayaṇa*).

In the very next verse the twenty-fifth *tatttva* is described as *amūrta* and eternal (*nitya*). Though without form, it is present in all the bodies. It is not subjected to creation and dissolution; in conjunction with the *prakṛti* it also assumes attributes, though really it is without attributes (*nirguṇa*).

Chapter 303 is devoted to a detailed exposition of the idea that the *jīva*, on account of its association with the *prakṛti*, in its ignorance, considers itself to be the doer of actions and the enjoyer of their consequences. He takes birth in different forms. But, in reality it is *prakṛti* which performs good or bad deeds and bears their consequences. *Prakṛti* is without *liṅga*s (*aliṅga*). Its existence is to be inferred. Likewise the existence of *puruṣa* is also to be inferred.

Chapter 304 further discusses the downfall of *jīva* associating with ignorant people on account of the *prakṛti*. Like the moon with sixteen *kalā*s the *jīva* cannot overcome the effect of its association with the sixteenth, the *prakṛti*, which is like *amā* of the moon. The *jīva*, ignorant about the twenty-fifth *tattva*, which is pure, becomes impure.

In chapter 305 Vasiṣṭha dispels the doubts raised by Janaka about the relationship between *kṣara* (*puruṣa*) Janaka himself regards it to be similar to the relationship between a female and a male. Vasiṣṭha emphasises the need for the correct understanding of the sacred texts. The *guṇa*s and the eight constituents of a body are created out of *prakṛti* but are not characteristic of *akṣara* which is formless. Vasiṣṭha says that the product is similar to the cause. He repeats that *kṣara* and *akṣara* are to be inferred, the *prakṛti* through its *liṅga*s, the twenty-fifth *tattva* being *aliṅga*. He points out that whereas *akṣara* remains one and the same (*ekatva*), the *kṣara* assumes various forms (*nānātva*). The *ekatva* of the twenty-fifth *tattva* is the correct view, its *nānātva* is the wrong view.

In chapter 306 Janaka further clarification. Vasiṣṭha spells out Sāṁkhya and Yoga separately. In the Yoga practices (*yogakṛtya*) he mentions *dhyāna* (meditation) to be of the greatest importance. *Dhyāna* is of two kinds: concentration of mind (*ekāgratā manasaḥ*) and *prāṇāyāma*. Vasiṣṭha spells out the distinctive qualities of a *yogī* who sees the *parama ātman*.

In his account of Sāṁkhya Vasiṣṭha mentions *prakṛti* or *avyakta* as the first, from which is created *mahat*. From *mahat* is created *ahaṁkāra*, from which come out the five (subtle) *bhūta*s. These are the eight *prakṛti*s. The sixteen evolutes (*vikāra*) are the five *jñānedriya*s, five *karmendriya*s, *manas* and the five gross *bhūta*s. The order of dissolution is in the reverse order. In the *pralaya* (dissolution) the *prakṛti* is one (*ekatva*) and in the creation it assumes numerous forms (*bahutva*). The *avyakta* is called *kṣetra*. The twenty-fifth *tattva*, the *mahānātmā*, is called *adhiṣṭhātā* as it resides in the *kṣetra*. He is also called *kṣetrajña* (or *jñātā)* (knower of *kṣetra*) and *puruṣa*. *Avyakta* is *jñāna* and the twenty-fifth *tattva* is *jñeya*. In Sāṁkhya there are twenty-four *tattva*s, the twenty-fifth is different from the *tattva*s. The twenty-fifth *tattva* is *budhyamāna*. When it knows itself, it becomes *kevala*. *Avyakta* is *sarva*. The twenty-fifth *tattva* is different from *sarva* (*asarva*). It knows, it is free from the cycle of birth.

In chapter 307 Vasiṣṭha explains the nature of *puruṣa* and *prakṛti* by employing pairs of opposite terms. Thus, he speaks of *vidyā* and *avidyā*. *Avidyā*, here, does not refer to the five *avidyā*s (ignorance) in other Sāṁkhya accounts. *Avyakta* is referred to as *avidyā* and the twenty-fifth *tattva* as *vidyā*. In the case of the twenty-four *tattva*s, the *prakṛti* and its evolute, each succeeding *tattva* is described as *avidyā* in relation to the preceding one, which is referred to as *vidyā*.

Vasiṣṭha distinguishes between *avyakta* and the twenty-fifth *tattva* by describing the former as *jñāna*, whereas the latter is designated as *jñeya* in one sense and *vijñāta* in another. He says that both these are to be termed alike as *akṣara* and *kṣara*. Both are without beginning and eternal, creation and dissolution are only the characteristics of *avyakta*, which hence is designated as *akṣara*. On account of the creation of its evolutes it is called *kṣara*. The *mahat* and other evolutes are created by the coming together of *puruṣa* and *prakṛti*, hence, the twenty-fifth *tattva* is also called *kṣetra* because it resides in *mahat* and other evolutes. When the evolutes are dissolved, *prakṛti* becomes one; *kṣetrajña* is also dissolved in the *parama ātman*. When the *puruṣa* realises the nature of the *prakṛti* and its own difference from the latter, then it obtains its pure nature.

In the concluding verses of the chapter Vasiṣṭha says that the Sāṁkhya recognises only twenty-five *tattvas*, but the Yoga admits *budhyamāna* and *buddha* as two different *tattvas*.

In chapter 308 Vasiṣṭha explains the categories of *budhyamāna* and *buddha*. The *avyakta* is called *apratibuddha*, because it does not know the *parama ātman*. The twenty-fifth *tattva* is termed as *budhyamāna*, because it knows the *avyakta*, but does not know the twenty-sixth *tattva*, the *buddha*, who is pure (*vimala*), infinite (*aprameya*) and eternal (*sanātana*). This *brahman* knows the twenty-fifth and the twenty-fourth *tattvas*. When the *budhyamāna* realises its difference from the *avyakta* and acquires the pure and highest knowledge, it reaches *budhatva* and recognises that it is the twenty-sixth *tattva*.

Vasiṣṭha concludes by emphasising the principle of the difference between *puruṣa* and *prakṛti* and of the *nānātva* and *ekatva* of *puruṣa*. He lays down the qualities of a person entitled to receive this knowledge. He describes it as the supreme knowledge (*brahma param*), which is the essence of all knowledge (*sarvajñānasya tattvārtham*).

Distinctive Feature of Vasiṣṭha's Views

The exposition of Sāṁkhya by Vasiṣṭha has several distinctive features. It is based on the dualism of the conscious and the unconscious *tattvas*. Though the terms *puruṣa* and *prakṛti* occur at places, Vasiṣṭha prefers to use the term *pañcaviṁśaka* and *avyakta*. He employs sets of words to bring out the distinction between *prakṛti* and *puruṣa*: *kṣara*, *akṣara* *kṣetra* and *adhiṣṭhātā*, and *jñāna* and *jñātā* or *jñeya*. This would refer to a period, long before the fixity of terms, which followed the standardisation introduced by Īśvarakṛṣṇa.

A similar fluidity is to be noticed in regard to the terms *vidyā* and *avidyā*. In the Sāṁkhya system *avidyā* (ignorance) has a special meaning. *Avidyā* is said to be of five kinds. But Vasiṣṭha uses *avidyā* in juxtaposition to *vidyā*. It is does not refer to any special type of ignorance. It signifies something false, non-existent or having a semblance of reality. *Vidyā* refers to something true, existent and real. This is why among the evolutes of *prakṛti* an earlier *tattva* is called *vidyā*, whereas the succeeding one is described as *avidyā*. This feature also refers to a period earlier than the period of the acceptance of the technical meaning of *avidyā* as ignorance.

The Sāṁkhya system presents *prakṛti* and its evolutes into two groups the *aṣṭaprakṛtis* (eight *prakṛtis*) and the *ṣoḍaśa vikāras* (sixteen evolutes). Vasiṣṭha classifies the evolution of *prakṛti* and twenty-three *tattvas* into five stages: *vidyā-sarga*, *avidyā-sarga*, *bhūta-sarga*, *vaikṛta-sarga* and *bhautika-sarga*. The *Sāṁkhyakārika*[3] refers to two types of *sargas*: *liṅga* and *bhava*, and then adds *bhautika-sarga* as a third. In an earlier *kārika* (46) it speaks of the *pratyaya-sarga*. Of the five types of *sargas*, it is only the *bhautika-sarga* which occurs in the *Sāṁkhyakārikā*, but its connotation differs readically from that of Vasiṣṭha. It is only the *liṅga-sarga* in the *Sāṁkhyakārika* which covers the *sargas* of Vasiṣṭha, but in a very different manner. The *Ahirbudhnyasaṁhitā*,[4] in describing the sixty topics of *Sāṁkhya-tantra,* has a different scheme. It divides the elements into two *maṇḍalas*, *prākṛta* and *vaikṛta*, of which the thirty-two in the first division include *guṇa-tantra*, *akṣara-tantra*, *prāṇa-tantra*, *kartṛ-tantra*, *sāmi-tantra*, *jñāna-tantra*, *kriyā-tantra*, *mātra-tantra* and *bhūta-tantra*. But, these are not described in terms of *sargas*. This feature also refers to an early stage in the history of Sāṁkhya long before it adopted the broad classification into two groups: *prakṛti* and basic *tattvas* and the sixteen evolutes visibly characterising the world.

The most significant feature of Sāṁkhya presented by Vasiṣṭha is the acceptance of a twenty-sixth (*ṣaḍviṁśaka*) *tattva*, the *buddha*.

---

3. *Kārikā*, 52-3.
4. XII.19-30.

This is all the more important, because Vasiṣṭha, after describing the twenty-four *tattva*s, mentions the twenty-fifth (*pañcaviṁśaka*) *tattva* in great details, and then adds that there are only twenty-five *tattva*s and no other *tattva* beyond it.

There is a close affinity and connection between the twenty-fifth and twenty-sixth *tattva*s. Both are to be contrasted with the twenty-fourth *tattva* (*caturviṁśaka*), the *avyakta* which is devoid of consciousness (*apratibuddha*). The twenty-fourth *tattva* is *buddhyamāna*. It knows the *avyakta*, but does not know the *buddha*. It has the potentiality of knowing the *buddha*. In association with the *avyakta* it identifies itself with the *avyakta* and its evolutes. When it realises its own nature and its difference from *avyakta*, it realises that it is *buddha* and becomes *buddha*. Vasiṣṭha emphasises that, though included in the list of *tattva*s, the twenty-fifth is different from the *tattva*s.

The Sāṁkhya system subscribes to the view of plurality (*anekatva*) of *puruṣa*s. Vasiṣṭha differs from it in a significant manner. He holds that the twenty-fifth *tattva* is characterised by both *ekatva* and *nānātva*. It is one, but in association with the *kṣetra*, the *avyakta* and the evolutes with their *guṇa*s, it considers itself to have numerous forms. The *nānātva* is removed when it realises its distinction from the *prakṛti*. In this sense the twenty-fifth *tattva* of Vasiṣṭha signifies the individual *jīva*. It is like *ātman* in the Upaniṣads, which is the same as the *brahman*, but it has to realise its oneness with *brahman*. Thus, the twenty-fifth and twenty-sixth *tattva*s detailed by Vasiṣṭha differ from the concept of *puruṣa* in the standardised Sāṁkhya and are very close to the idea of *ātman* and *brahman* in the Upaniṣads. As rightly pointed out by P. Chakravarti,[5] Vasiṣṭha has tried 'to reconcile the Sāṁkhya theory of the plurality of the spirits with the doctrine of unity'.

Vasiṣṭha presents an account of creation which differs radically from the philosophical view of creation and dissolution through *prakṛti*. He refers to Brahmā or Hiraṇyagarbha, known under various names, who, subjecting himself to the process of evolution

5. *Origin and Development of the Sāṁkhya System of Thought*, p. 48.

(*vikriyā*), creates *ahaṁkāra* and *prajāpati* characterised by *ahaṁkāra*. Then he narrates the process of creation with *avyakta* becoming *vyakta*. Evidently, Vasiṣṭha takes shelter under the concept of Brahmā Hiraṇyagarbha to explain the evolution from the *avyakta*.

Vasiṣṭha says that the existence of *prakṛti* and the *aliṅga* (*ātman*) is to be known through inference. The *prakṛti* is inferred from its evolute *liṅgas*. The argument here is only in a nascent form; it is not properly and systematically developed. We know that Īśvarakṛṣṇa advancese arguments for the existence of *prakṛti* and *puruṣa*. In this respect Vasiṣṭha evidently represents an early stage in the history of Sāṁkhya system.

Vasiṣṭha in History

In evaluating the role of Vasiṣṭha in the history of the Sāṁkhya system we have to identify him and locate him in time.

Traditionally Vasiṣṭha is described as the son of Brahmā. The family lineage after Vasiṣṭha is Śakti Parāśara and Vyāsa. In the *Viṣṇu Purāṇa*[6] Vasiṣṭha is referred to as the family preceptor of Ikṣvāku (*ikṣvāku-kulācārya*), who was the son of Vaivasvata Manu. The name of Vasiṣṭha occurs in connection with many important events in the history of Ikṣvāku family, which are far removed from one another.[7] According to a narrative found in the *Rāmāyaṇa* and *Viṣṇu Purāṇa*,[8] on account of a mutual clash both Nimi, the twelfth son of Ikṣvāku, and Vasiṣṭha the family priest and the son of Brahmā, died by cursing each other. Through the blessings of Brahmā Vasiṣṭha was reborn from the semen of Mitra-Varuṇa in Urvaśī. The *Rāmāyaṇa* adds that Ikṣvāku reappointed Vasiṣṭha as the family preceptor. Next, Vasiṣṭha was requested by Triśaṅku, belonging to the twenty-seventh generation of Ikṣvāku, to transmit him to the heaven in his human body through sacrifice.[9] Vasiṣṭha

6. IV.2.17.
7. *Uttara* chapters, 55-6.
8. IV.5.
9. *Rām.*, Bāla, 57.10-12.

is reported to have participated in many sacrifices performed by Daśaratha,[10] who was in the thirty-second generation after Triśaṅku. Evidently no single person can be expected to have such a long life as to be present in all the events separated from one another by centuries. Possibly different persons with the same name have been mixed up in these accounts. It is not unlikely that all the family preceptors of the Ikṣvākus were alike named as Vasiṣṭha, referring to their family.

The question remains: who was the Vasiṣṭha the Sāṁkhya teacher. U.V. Shastri,[11] relying on the appellation Maitra-Vāruṇi given to Vasiṣṭha in the *Mahābhārata*,[12] regards him to be the same sage who had a quarrel with Nimi. He says that Karāla Janaka, to whom Vasiṣṭha expounded Sāṁkhya, was the son of Nimi, either Mithi Janaka or his brother. The designation Maitrāvāruṇi is incongruous and ill suits the Vasiṣṭha under study. A. P. Mishra[13] suggests that, on account of the similarity of name, this adjective used for the contemporary of Nimi, was applied to the later Vasiṣṭha. Possibly, it was not a case of mistaken identity. To add to the prestige of the exposition of Sāṁkhya by Vasiṣṭha and assign it a respectable antiquity Vasiṣṭha was connected with Brahmā, and, in the process, was described as the son of Mitra-Varuṇa.

In the list of *r̥ṣis* Pargiter[14] mentions Vasiṣṭha as the family preceptor of king Sudāsa of the Sūryavaṁśa. This Vasiṣṭha was the father of Śakti and grandfather of Parāśara. Sudāsa was in the twelfth generation after king Sagara of the Ikṣvāku dynasty. Rāmacandra belonged to the twelfth generation after Sudāsa. A.P. Mishra[15] considers Vasiṣṭha under reference to be a contemporary of Sudāsa. But, when according to this view Karāla Janaka is located in the royal family of Videha as a contemporary of Vasiṣṭha

---

10. *Rām.*, 10, 14.
11. *Sāṁkhyadarśana ka Itihāsa*, p. 588.
12. XII.302.9.
13. *Sāṁkhya-Darśana ki Aitihāsika Paramparā*, p. 147.
14. *Ancient Indian Historical Tradition*, p.
15. *Op. cit.*, pp. 146-7.

and Sudāsa it leads to chronological confusion. In the dynastic list of Videha, we find several kings having the name of Janaka, which seems to have been used as a family name. But the name Karāla does not appear in this list. Rāma, in the twelfth generation after Sudāsa, married Sītā, the daughter of Janaka Śīradhvaja. Kuśadhvaja was the younger brother of Śīradhvaja. Dharmadhvaja Janaka, mentioned in the Mokṣadharmaparva of the *Mahābhārata*[16] is taken to have been a son of Kuśadhvaja. There is no evidence for placing Karāla Janaka in the times of Sudāsa, twelve generations before Rāma and Janaka Śīradhvaja. Hence, the suggestion for identifying the Sāṁkhya Vasiṣṭha with Vasiṣṭha, a contemporary of Sudāsa, remains unconfirmed. The suggestion creates a serious problem. Vasiṣṭha, as a contemporary of Sudāsa, will be twelve generations before Rāma. This will be in violent conflict with the testimony of the *Yuktidīpikā* naming Vasiṣṭha as one of the disciples of Pañcaśikha.

There is some evidence to indicate that Vasiṣṭha, the Sāṁkhya teacher, was a historical being and not a mythological sage. The *Yuktidīpikā* records that Vasiṣṭha was one of the disciples to whom Pañcaśikha had communicated the Sāṁkhya principles. In the Mokṣadharmaparva Bhīṣma narrates to Yuidhiṣṭhira the dialogue between Vasiṣṭha and king Karāla Janaka as an ancient historical narrative (*itihāsam purātanam*) and not as a legend or myth. This is strengthened by the fact that Vasiṣṭha is stated to have expounded the Sāṁkhya principles to Karāla Janaka, a historical personality, and in the process explained the doubts raised by him. Janaka often appears as a general name for kings of Videha with their capital at Mithilā. The name of Karāla Janaka does not figure in the Purāṇic list of kings. But it is well-known that the Purāṇic lists suffer from defects of omission and commission. In this case we have the testimony of independent sources confirming the existence of a king named Karāla Janaka. In the *Majjhima Nikāya*[17] Buddha tells Ānanda that Karāla Janaka did not follow the holy path and did not become an ascetic. The *Nimi-Jātaka* (Jātaka No. 541) records that

16. XII.320.4.
17. Mahādeva, Suttanta, 83.

Nimi's son Kalāra Janaka brought his line to an end. The *Arthaśāstra*[18] refers to Karāla Vaideha (king of Videha), who was destroyed along with his kinsmen and kingdom on account of the forceful seizure of a brāhmaṇa girl. It can be easily seen that Karāla Vaideha refers to Karāla Janaka, Janaka being a common name given to kings of Videha. The reference occurs as an instance of historical cases of kings perishing on account of their immoral deeds. Aśvaghoṣa in his *Buddhacarita*[19] mentions Karāla as Maithila. This evidently refers to Karāla Janaka. The appellation Maithila is a paraphrasing of Vaideha applied to him by Kauṭilya. Another passage in the *Buddhacarita*[20] says that Karāla Janaka took away a brāhmaṇa maiden and gained nothing but ruin; still he did not give up passion. Aśvaghoṣa seems to have followed the evidence of the *Arthaśāstra* or another earlier source or tradition which Kauṭilya had himself used. Aśvaghoṣa mentions Karāla Maithila along with Daṇḍaka. It is significant that Kauṭilya also refers to the cases of King Daṇḍakya Bhoja and Karāla Vaideha together as instances of kings perishing along with their kinsmen and kingdom on account of entertaining a sinful desire for a brāhmaṇa maiden.

His Date

There has been no serious effort to determine the date of Vasiṣṭha. One indication is the Mokṣadharmaparva in which Bhīṣma refers to the dialogue between Vasiṣṭha and Karāla Janaka as an ancient narrative. Bhagavaddatt[21] places Vasiṣṭha 40-50 years before the Mahābhārata War in the times of Nimi II, mentioning Karāla Janaka as his son. If any reliance is placed on the evidence of the *Mahābhārata*, Vasiṣṭha will be much earlier. Bhīṣma himself had enjoyed a long life before he lay on the arrow-bed in the Mahābhārata War. It is to be noted that the account in the Mokṣadharmaparva

18. I.6.5.
19. XI.31.
20. IV.80.
21. *Bhāratavarṣa kā Itihāsa*, p. 160; referred to by U.V. Shastri, *op. cit.*, p. 587.

is not part of the original story. It was inserted in the Epic at a very late stage. Hence the date of events and persons referred to in this account cannot be inferred with reference to the characters of the original story. Thus, the account need not be an ancient narrative long before Bhīṣma. We can say that it was considered an ancient history at the time of the composition of the relevant chapters or their insertion in the Epic. Hence, on the testimony of these chapters in the Mokṣadharmaparva, Vasiṣṭha, the Sāṁkhya teacher cannot be placed before the times of Bhīṣma in the Epic story. As we have pointed out earlier, the author of the chapters in the Mokṣadharmaparva, for giving prestige to Vasiṣṭha, the expounder of Sāṁkhya principles to a historical king named Karāla Janaka, equated him with the sage of legendary fame, venerated as a son of Brahmā. In the same process the account of his dialogue with Karāla Janaka was introduced by Bhīṣma as an ancient narrative.

In fixing the date of Vasiṣṭha, the Sāṁkhya teacher, we need not take all the details of the legendary references to Vasiṣṭha, the ancient sage. On this basis U.V. Shastri[22] places him in the beginning of the *tretā* age. This creates serious problems arising out of the traditional account about the association of Vasiṣṭha with Ikṣvāku, Nimi, Sagara, Sudāsa and Rāma. Likewise, there will be difficulty about Pañcaśikha and his chronological position with regard to Kapila. Pañcaśikha will, then, have to be assigned as exceptionally long life to become the contemporary of Kapila, Āsuri and his own many students, such as Jaigīṣavya, Janaka, and Vasiṣṭha.

The date of Vasiṣṭha can be narrowed down to limits with tolerably dependable approximation. The starting point for our calculation is the statement in the *Yuktidīpikā* associating Vasiṣṭha with Pañcaśikha, a historical person, from whom he is said to have received the knowledge of Sāṁkhya. This would make Vasiṣṭha a junior contemporary of Pañcaśikha. The *Mahābhārata* account of the dialogue between Vasiṣṭha and Karāla Janaka will likewise make Karāla Janaka a junior contemporary of Vasiṣṭha.

On a superficial view the testimony of the *Yuktidīpikā* appears

22. *Op. cit.*, p. 588.

to be a little confusing. It mentions Janaka first Vasiṣṭha next as having received the exposition from Pañcaśikha. But, this Janaka is not to be confused with Karāla Janaka. In the *Mahābhārata* itself we have a reference to another Sāṁkhya teacher named Dharmadhvaja Janaka who claims to have been a student of Pañcaśikha.[23] It has been suggested that this Dharmadhvaja Janaka was possibly the son of Kuśadhvaja, a younger brother of Śīradhvaja Janaka, the father of Sītā.[24] Thus, Janaka mentioned by the *Yuktidīpikā* as a direct student of Pañcaśikha could not have been the same as Karāla Janaka, a student of Vasiṣṭha.

The association of Karāla Janaka with Vasiṣṭha helps us fix the date of Vasiṣṭha with a certainty which is unfortunately not found in the history of Indian philosophy. Karāla Janaka was in the historical memory of the people in the times of the *Arthaśāstra*, *Jātaka*s and *Majjhima-nikāya*. He does not seem to have been far removed from the times of the Buddha. The combined testimony of the *Jātaka*, *Arthaśāstra* and *Buddhacarita* records the historical fact that the Janaka dynasty ended with Karāla[25] Janaka. It is generally believed that the Vajji republic of Vaiśālī was founded on the ruins of the Videha kingdom. Yogendra Mishra fixes the end of the Janaka dynasty of Videha and the foundation of the Vajji republic in about 725 BC.[26] On this basis, Vasiṣṭha, the Sāṁkhya teacher, may be placed roughly in 775-700 BC.

His Place in Sāṁkhya History

According to the *Yuktidīpikā*, Pañcaśikha had expounded Sāṁkhya

23. *Mbh.*, XII.320.4
24. A.P. Mishra, *op. cit.*, p. 144. According to *Viṣṇu Purāṇa*, IV.5.29 Kuśadhvaja was the brother of Śīradhvaja, but *Bhāgavata Purāṇa*, IX.23.39 mentions him as the son of Śīradvaja.
25. Karāla, meaning terrible, was possibly a nick-name which the king earned on account of his immoral deeds. We have parallel examples of Kālāśoka in Indian history and of Ivan the Terrible in the history of Russia.
26. *An Early History of Vaiśāli*, pp. 98-102. See also *Comprehensive History of Bihart* Vol. 1, Part I. ed. by B.P. Sinha, p. 225.

to Vasiṣṭha. We do not know the details of this exposition. The philosophical principles propounded by Pañcaśikha are not available in their original form. There is no surety about his authorship of the texts which are sometimes attributed to him. There are many passages, quoted from his work scattered in later commentaries besides the chapters in the Mokṣadharmaparva. Though the full system presented by him cannot be reconstructed, we do get an idea of some of the significant points made by him. In the case of Vasiṣṭha, as we have pointed out, our knowledge is confined to the seven chapters in the Mokṣadharmaparva. A comparison of the expositions attributed to the two Sāṁkhya teachers shows that, besides general similarities, there is no significant oneness in respect of special points. It would seem that, though Vasiṣṭha learnt the basic principles of Sāṁkhya from Pañcaśikha, he developed his own system. This possibly gave him the prestige of an independent teacher of Sāṁkhya.

The Mokṣadharmaparva chapters project this image of Vasiṣṭha. The chapters do not make the slightest allusion to his indebtedness to Pañcaśikha, though in the case of some other thinkers there is an avowed declaration to their association with Pañcaśikha. Vasiṣṭha claims that he made efforts to please the eternal Brahmā Hiraṇyagarbha and from his mouth received the knowledge.[27] Later, Bhīṣma repeats that the high-souled sage Vasiṣṭha got this knowledge from Hiraṇyagarbha. Nārada obtained it from Vasiṣṭha. Bhīṣma says that he himself acquired it from Nārada. By introducing Hiraṇyagarbha as the originator of the Sāṁkhya principles, expounded by him, and by not referring to any human teacher. Vasiṣṭha claims a high prestige for his system and also originality for himself.

The significant point of departure is the fact that Hiraṇyagarbha is mentioned as the originator of Sāṁkhya, whereas the general tradition associates Hiraṇyagarbha with the exposition of Yoga. The association of Hiraṇyagarbha suited the new formulation of Sāṁkhya principles which Vasiṣṭha attempted, and which differed

27. *Mbh.*, XII.308.40.

from the exposition offered earlier by Pañcaśikha. Vasiṣṭha uses Hiraṇyagarbha as the bridge to connect Sāṁkhya and Yoga. He himself brings out this point in the introductory verses of his exposition to Karāla Janaka.[28] He refers to Hiraṇyagarbha and mentions the various names under which he is known. In the Yoga system he is designated as *mahān*. Vasiṣṭha adds that in the *Sāṁkhyaśāstra*. Hiraṇyagarbha is referred to under various names.

Our discussion suggests that Vasiṣṭha had created an independent school of Sāṁkhya. The separate line of transmission through Nārada to Bhīṣma is recorded in the *Mahābhārata*.[29] The subsequent history of the school after Bhīṣma is not mentioned. The *Mahābhārata* has recorded his exposition to Karāla Janaka. The continuation of the school after Karāla is not known. The unfavourable remark made by the Buddha in the *Majjhima-nikāya* shows that the salutary principles were lost upon Karāla Janaka. In the *Mahābhārata* Vasiṣṭha remarks that he has presented the illuminating knowledge clearly with the desire for the good of his disciples (*śiṣya*).[30]

The real significance of the exposition of Sāṁkhya by Vasiṣṭha in the Mokṣadharmaparva and also of other accounts of Sāṁkhya in the section has often not been appreciated. Thus, Hopkins[31] dismisses the Epic Sāṁkhya as the hybrid hotch-potch of the genuine Sāṁkhya. Keith,[32] likewise, observes that the Epic does not ascribe the doctrine of *Brahman* to the Sāṁkhya proper. Such views suffer from a preconceived obsession to identify Sāṁkhya with its form in the *Sāṁkhyakārikā* and to take Sāṁkhya to be fixed and unchanging. The possibility of a change or development in the long course of Sāṁkhya history is not duly recognised. Likewise, it is fallacious to take the *Mahābhārata* as one unified text and to synthesise all the various accounts of Sāṁkhya in it as

28. *Mbh.*, XII.302.18-20.
29. *Ibid.*, XII.308.44-6.
30. *Ibid.*, XII.307.45.
31. *The Great Epic of India*, p.
32. *Sāṁkhya System*, p. 57.

being uniformly one. At different period portions have been accommodated in the text. All the Sāṁkhya views recorded in it are not to be processed as representing just one view by ironing out the inconvenient details and differences. Within the Sāṁkhya system itself in the early phases of its history there were a number of schools or sub-systems with widely divergent views even on some vital points. The exposition by Vasiṣṭha represents one such school. P. Chakravarti[33] terms it as the Sāṁkhya-Yoga school of the Epic.

It is clear that whatever synthesis Vasiṣṭha forged and the points he emphasised, he considered himself to be basically a Sāṁkhya teacher. This is indicated by the concluding verses of chapter 307[34] in which at the end of his discourses he says that he has expounded the Sāṁkhya philosophy, which is very wide (*bṛhat*), and that he has described the highest *tattva* in Sāṁkhya in the proper manner. He admits the separate nature of Sāṁkhya and Yoga as two systems. When Karāla Janaka wants him to expound the two separately, he does so.[35] But in the separate account of Yoga he emphasises only the practice (*yoga-kṛtya*) of *dhyāna*, including *prāṇāyāma*.

Vasiṣṭha places Sāṁkhya and Yoga together.[36] The two are treated as in separable.[37] Vasiṣṭha says that whatever the seekers of Yoga observe that the followers of Sāṁkhya about: he alone is wise who sees Sāṁkhya and Yoga to be one.[38] Later on he repeats that whatever is *Sāṁkhyaśāstra* that is also Yoga philosophy.

Vasiṣṭha goes a step further and attempts a fusion of Sāṁkhya with Yoga. He does not merely present the two together. This can be seen in chapters 307 and 308. In verse 47 of chapter 307 Vasiṣṭha says that, according to the Sāṁkhya, there is no *tattva* beyond the twenty-fifth, but, in the following verse he adds that, according to the Yoga philosophy, there are the *tattva*s of *buddhyamāna* and

33. *Op. cit.*, p. 51.
34. XII.307.45-47.
35. *Mbh.*, XII.305, 5-46, See also XII.307.44.
36. *Ibid.*, XII.305.18;31.
37. *Ibid.*, XII.305, 33 — *sāṁkhyayoga ca kuśalaḥ* ।
38. *Ibid.*, XII.305.19.

buddha. In chapter 308 Vasiṣṭha explains, in some details, the concepts of *apratibuddha*, *budhyamāna* and *buddha*. In concluding verses he remarks that, according to the Sāṁkhya philosophy, the concept of *nānātva* is that in the light of *prabuddha*, the twenty-sixth *tattva*, the *jīva* is *budhyamāna* (knows the *apratibuddha*), but is also *abuddhimān* (does not know the *buddha*).

Conclusion

Thus, we see that Vasiṣṭha was a Sāṁkhya philosopher who belonged to the eighth century BC (*c*. 775-700 BC). He had learnt Sāṁkhya principles from Pañcaśikha and, in turn, had discoursed his views to Karāla Janaka and others. Because of his important contributions in the field of philosophical thought, he was given an honoured position and was mixed up with the ancient sage Vasiṣṭha of legendary fame.

Vasiṣṭha belonged to an age when Sāṁkhya and Yoga had become very close. Vasiṣṭha accommodated some important points of Yoga into his presentation of Sāṁkhya principles and also introduced some new features. He gave Hiraṇyagarbha a high place as the originator of the Sāṁkhya views which he expounded. He mooted the concept of the twenty-sixth *tattva buddha*, or supreme soul. In his account he used many pairs of terms to refer to *prakṛti* and *puruṣa*: *kṣetra* and *kṣetrajña* or *adhiṣṭhātā*, *kṣara* and *akṣara*, and *jñāna* and *jñātā* or *jñeya*. He argued for the principle of unity as characterising the plurality of *puruṣa* (or *jīva*). His concept of *budhyamāna* and *buddha*, with *budhyamāna* realising his differences from *apratibuddha* (*prakṛti*) and oneness with *buddha*, and becoming *buddha* has parallel in the Upaniṣadic concepts of *ātman* and *brahman*.

Vasiṣṭha used inference (*anumāna*) to prove the existence of *prakṛti* and *puruṣa*. He classified the appearance of *prakṛti* and its evolutes into five stages of creation (*sarga*s).

After the standardisation of Sāṁkhya by Īśvarakṛṣṇa the school of Vasiṣṭha gradually lost its force, leaving only a brief memory in the *Mahābhārata*.

11

Asita-Devala Chapter in the Mahābhārata

Introduction

THE Mokṣadharmaparva in the Śāntiparva of the *Mahābhārata*, chapter 275[1] gives an account of the views of Asita-Devala. The narrative has several clearly recognisable elements of the Sāṁkhya system. The last but one verse refers to the knowledge of Sāṁkhya as essential for wiping out the effects of *puṇya* (merit) and *pāpa* (sin).[2] Asita-Devala is recognised as a Sāṁkhya authority. In the *Mahābhārata* itself Asita-Devala is connected with Sāṁkhya through Śiva,[3] who is described as imparting Sāṁkhya.[4]

But the chapter has not received due attention from modern authorities on Sāṁkhya. S.N. Dasgupta, E. Johnston and E. Frauwallner have not taken note of this presentation of Sāṁkhya in their publication. A.B. Keith[5] dismisses it by remarking that "the details of this version deviate more and more from any normal schedule, the organs of knowledge being reckoned at eight".

---

1. Gita Press, Gorakhpur, In Poona Critical Edition it occurs as chapter 267.
2. Verse 38.
3. XII.18.8.
4. XIII.14.198; XIII.17.63.
5. *History of Sāṁkhya Philosophy*, p. 47.

P. Chakravarti[6] points out that it differs to a considerable extent from the orthodox Sāṁkhya. As contrasted with these, studies of Sāṁkhya in Hindi take a more direct notice of this chapter.[7] But some recent studies of Sāṁkhya as enunciated in the *Mahābhārata*,[8] do not recognise the separate existence of this chapter. Taking the accounts of Sāṁkhya in different chapters of the Śāntiparva to present one uniform picture, they do not work out the possibility of variations reflecting the differences in the views of various authors of the Sāṁkhya system.

E.W. Hopkins[9] was the first to present an account of the contents of the chapter, but he did not attempt its proper assessment for the history of Sāṁkhya.

Contents of the Chapter

The introductory verse of the chapter refers to the intention of the author to present Asita-Devala's views on the creation and destruction of the creatures (*bhūtānām prabhavāpyayam*). Nārada wants to know from whence the universe, consisting of mobile and immobile objects, is created and in whom does it merge at the time of final destruction (*pralaya*) (verses 1-3).

Asita says that there are five great essences from which *kāla*

---

6. *Origin and Development of the Sāṁkhya System of Thought*, pp. 44, 128.
7. U.V. Shastri, *Sāṁkhyadarśana kā itihāsa*, 2nd edn., p. 606; A.P. Mishra, *Sāṁkhyadarśana kī aitihāsika paramparā*, pp. 157-8; U. Kushwaha, *Sāṁkhyadarśana aur āyurveda*, p. 16; H.S. Joshi, *Sāṁkhya-yoga darśana kā jīrṇoddhāra*, pp. 64, 216-7; G.S. Musalgaonkar, *Sāṁkhya-tattva-kaumudī* (4th edn.), Introduction, pp. 46-7.
8. Ram Suresh Pandey, *Mahābhārata aur purāṇon men sāṁkhya-darśana*, p. 347; Ram Chandar Singh, *Āyurvedikasaṁhitāon ke prakāśa men mahābhārata men nihita sāṁkhya-yoga prasthāna kī vajñānika samīkṣā*. Thesis submitted for Ph.D. Degree of Banaras Hindu University, 1981.
9. *The Great Epic of India*, pp. 155-7.

creates creatures moved by *bhāva*.[10] These five gross elements are eternal, indesctructible and unchangeable, and are by nature possessed of mighty energy.[11] They are water, space, earth, wind and heat, *kāla* being the sixth. There is nothing higher than these. If any one asserts the existence of anything else, then his assertion would be idle. These five, *kāla*, *bhāva* and *abhāva* make the eight eternal *bhūta*s which function in the creation and dissolution of all beings (*bhavatyayau*). A creature, when destroyed, is divided into these five once again. The body is made of earth, the ear from air, the eye from the sun, the breath from the wind, and the blood from water (verses 4-11).

Verses 12 to 22 give an account of organs of knowledge and of action and their attributes (*jñāna-ceṣṭendriya-guṇa*s). There are five senses which are the organs of knowledge: eye, nose, ear, skin and tongue, with their functions of sight, hearing, smelling, touch and taste, and their *guṇa*s (constituents) as colour, smell, taste, touch and sound (verses 12-14). But these *guṇa*s are copmprehended by the *kṣetrajña*[12] (soul) and not by senses (verse 15). *Citta*

---

10. Verse 4 of Critical Edition has the following reading:
yebhyaḥ sr̥jati bhūtāni kālo bhāvapracoditaḥ ।
mahābhūtani pañceti tānyāhurbhūtacintakāḥ ।।
Some versions read *kāle* for *kālo* and hence postulate that *praramātmā*, understood here, is the subject of the verb *sr̥jati*. The reading in verse 5 is *kālo bhāvapracoditaḥ*; it confirms the reading *kālo* in verse 4. Some versions have *ātma* — in place of *bhāva* — in verse 5. This is inconsistent and confusing. Hopkins translates the two phrases as meaning 'impelled by being' and 'impelled by soul'. *Bhāva* is also a crucial term. It has been taken to mean 'the desire for becoming many'. 'the desire for existence as many'. But the term occurs later in verses 25 to 28 to signify the three states of mind: *sattva*, *tamas* and *rajas*.

11. Verse 6 — *mahatastejaso rāśin*.
The expression has sometimes been interpreted to mean the rays of effulgent *mahat*. But a careful analysis shows that in the scheme of creation no superior force, *mahat* or *paramātman*, is given any place. Hopkins takes it to signify a group (*rāśi*) of great effulgence.

12. Other terms, used for *kṣetrajña* in the following verses, are *dehī*, *śarīrin*, *kṣetrī* and *jantu*.

(perception)[13] is higher than the group of sense (*indriya-saṁghāta*). *Manas* (mind) is higher than *citta*. *Buddhi* (intellect) is higher than *manas*. *Kṣetrajña* is higher than *buddhi*. A creative first becomes aware (*cetayate*) of different objects through the senses, then pondering (*vicārya*) with the mind he determines (*vyavasyati*) them (verses 16-17). The eight organs of knowledge (*jñānendriyas*) and *citta*, the group of five senses (*indriya-saṁghāta*), *manas* and *buddhi* (verse 18). *Pāṇi* (hands), *pāda* (feet), *pāyu* (anal duct), *mehana* (membrum virile) and *mukha* (mouth) are the five organs of action (*karmendriya*) with their respective functions. *Bala* (muscular power) is the sixth organ of action[14] (verses 19-22).

Verses 23 to 27 bring out the difference between sleep and dream and refer to the three *bhāvas*.[15] When, on account of *śrama* (exertion) the organs cease to perform their function, it is said that the person sleeps (*svapiti*). If the organs cease to function, but the mind does not do so and enjoys the objects (*viṣayān*), it is the act of dreaming (*svapna-darśanam*). There are three *bhāvas*: *sāttvika*, *rājasika* and *tāmasika*; they are lauded when they are exhibited in action (*karmayuktān praśaṁsanti*). Happiness (*ānanda*), success (*karmāṇāṁ siddhiḥ*), knowledge (*pratipatti*), and absence of attachment (*paragati*) are the attributes (*nimittāni*) of *sāttvika bhāva* (in the wakeful stage): they reapper in memory (during sleep). In creatures, whatever *bhāvas* (*sāttvika*, *rājasika* or *tāmasika*) are based on *vidhi* (action), their passage from one *bhāva* into another (waking and sleeping)[16]

---

13. *Citta* is not properly defined here. Some other systems of philosophy mention it as of a higher order than *buddhi*. Here it possibly refers to vague awareness, mere sensation or indefinite perception. Verse 17 attributes to the *indriyas* the function which derivatively should have belonged to *citta* (*cetayate*).

14. Here the reading is *ṣad etāni vācā samyag yathā mama*. The Critical Edition reads *yathāgamam* which would mean that Devala claims to have named six organs of action.

15. The verses, particularly 25 to 27, have been variously interpreted as the account is not very lucid.

16. The term *bhāva* in verse 27 has been used in two different senses — first, for one of the three *bhāvas* (*sāttvika*, *tāmasika* and *rājasika*) and later for one of the two stages of sleep and dream.

is agreeable and constant and can be directly apprehended (verses 23-27).

There are seventeen *guṇa*s (constituents) including fourteen *indriya*s and three *bhāva*s. The *dehī*, who is in the body, is the eighteenth. He is eternal. All these *guṇa*s are attached to the *śarīrin* (*dehī*): when he disappears, the *guṇa*s also disappear along with the body. This body made of five primal *bhūta*s (elements) is only a temporary union (*sannipāta*). Along with the *śarīrin* the *guṇa*s number one and eighteen.[17] Along with *ūṣman*[18] the body composed of five *bhūta*s becomes a combination (*saṁghāta*) of twenty *guṇa*s. The *mahat*[19] along with *vāyu*[20] upholds the body (verses 28-31).[21]

In the destruction of the body (*deha-bhedane*) *vāyu* is the instrument of *mahat*, which alone is effective.[22] Upon the exhausation of *puṇya* and *pāpa* a creature is resolved into the five elements in the same manner as it is created. Propelled by *puṇya* and *pāpa* he enters in due course of time a body resulting from his acts.[23] The *kṣetrī*, urged on by *kāla* (time), migrates from one body to another

---

17. *ekaśa daśa cāṣṭau ca guṇāḥ saha śarīriṇām* ।
The text does not make clear the identification of this one (*eka*) besides the eighteen referred to in verse 28.

18. *Uṣman*, thus, becomes the twentieth element. But its exact nature is not defined. The commentator takes it to mean the internal heat of the stomach.

19. *Mahat*, which is evidently different from *kṣetrajña* or *dehī*, has not been explained in the text.

20. Possibly *vāyu* here stands for *ūṣman*. But in *Mbh.*, XII.219.9 *ūṣman* and *vāyu* are differentiated.

21. In the Critical Edition the grouping of lines differs slightly. Its verse 30 consists of three lines; verse 30+31a. Accordingly, its verse 31=31b+32a; verse 32=32b+33a. It drops 33b and condenses verse 34 to form its verse 33 of one line only. Its verses 34 to 38 are equivalent to verses 35 to 39 of the Gita Press edition.

22. Verse 32 — *tasya prabhāvayuktasya nimittam dehabhedane*. The Critical Edition reads *tasyāsya bhāva*. The line has been interpreted differently, because it is not clear which element is denoted by *tasya* and which element is considered to be *nimitta*.

23. Verse 33 — The Critical Edition drops this line.

abandoning them in succession.[24] Those who are enlightened have a definite knowledge (*niścita-niścayaḥ*) and do not grieve; those, who are ignorant, see connexions (*sambandha-darśinaḥ*)[25] (where they do not exist) and experience grief. The *dehī* is not related to anybody else nor is anybody related to him. He alone is eternal, but, in the body, he is subjected to happiness and misery. He is never born, nor does he die. After giving up the body, he sometimes succeeds in attaining the highest end. After exhausting the *karma*, he destroys the body subject to *puṇya* and *pāpa* attains to *Brahmatva*. The knowledge of Sāṁkhya (*sāṁkhya-jñānam*)[26] is propounded for the exhaustion of *puṇya* and *pāpa*; by their exhaustion is realised the highest end in *Brahma-bhāva* (verses 32-39).

Asita-Devala and Devala

In the Devala chapter the introductory verse refers to the interlocution between Nārada and Asita-Devala. The second verse mentions Nārada approaching Devala. In the following verse Nārada poses his philosophical query and the reply is introduced by the expression *asita uvāca*. The colophon of the chapter refers to the dialogue between Nārada and Asita. Clearly the author of the chapter took the names Asita-Devala, Devala and Asita to signify one and the same person. A similar use of the names is seen in other parts of the *Mahābhārata*. In chapter 229 of the Śāntiparva verse 3 refers to the interlocution between Asita and Jaigīṣavya, but the following verse mentions Jaigīṣavya addressing Asita-Devala. Later in the chapter we find the introductory phrase *devala uvāca*.

Devala is mentioned in some other Parvas of the *Mahābhārata*. At places the name appears also as Asita-Devala, which leads to the

24. Verse 34 —

    hitvā hitvā hyayaṁ praiti dehād dehaṁ kṛtāśrayaḥ ।
    kālasaṁcoditaḥ kṣetrī viśīrṇād vā gṛhād gṛham ।।

    The Critical Edition compresses it into one line by omitting the words from *praiti* to *kālasaṁcoditaḥ* and thus a reference to the role of *kāla* in this context is avoided.
25. The Critical Edition reads *saṁbhandhimāninaḥ*.
26. Critical Edition — *sāṁkhyam jñānam*.

conclusion that the same person has been named both as Devala and Asita-Devala.

There is, however, some evidence mentioning Asita and Devala as two different persons. Thus, in the *Gītā*[27] Asita and Devala are named as two different sages. A.P. Mishra[28] points out that in the Śāṇḍila *gotra* the *pravaras* are Śāṇḍilya, Asita and Devala,[29] of which Asita was earlier than Devala. Relying on the testimony of the *Śatapatha*, as quoted in the *Nirṇayasindhu*, he takes Asita to have been the father of Devala. He, therefore, suggests that the reading Asita-Devala in the *Mbh.*, XII.229.3-4 is to be amended as Āsita-Devala. But, this is not the solitary reference to Asita-Devala. In the *Mahābhārata* itself[30] there are many passages where the names Asita, Devala and Asita-Devala are interchangeable. In all these cases Asita and Asita-Devala cannot be corrected to read Āsita and Āsita-Devala respectively.

There is an undoubted tradition about Asita and Devala being the names of two different sages.[31] How the two names were fused into one is not known. It is not unlikely that, in the beginning, to distinguish him from other persons with the name Devala, the Sāṁkhya teacher was designated as Āsita-Devala. The *Mahābhārata* evidence envisages more than one Devala.[32] In course of time the appellation Āsita came to be transformed into the name Asita. The early Jain texts also record the two traditions Asie Davila (= Asita-Devala) as one person and Asita and Devala being two persons.[33] Here the name of Asita appears as Asiya (= Asita). Possibly the second tradition was misled by the form Āsita-Devala to conjecture the name Asita for Āsita.

---

27. X.13.
28. *Op. cit.*, pp. 157-8.
29. Kamalākarabhaṭṭa's *Nirṇayasindhu*, p. 386.
30. S. Sorensen, *Index of Proper Names in the Mahābhārata*, s.v. *Asita-Devala* and *Devala*.
31. *Mbh.*, XII.47.7 for Asita as a sage.
32. S. Sorensen, *loc. cit.*
33. See Appendix II. Śīlāṅka in his commentary on *Sūtrakr̥tāṅga*, I.1.3.4. took the expression Asita-Devila to imply two different persons Asita and Devala.

It is, however, clear that later on Devala was often referred to as Asita-Devala. Asita is sometimes used as an appellation for Devala and sometimes stands for him. Apparently, the earlier association with Asita, the name of his father, was forgotten. Possibly Asita came to be used as an adjective qualifying Devala. We have a parallel case in the name of Kṛṣṇa Dvaipāyana.

The *Mahābhārata* records some interesting details about Devala or Asita-Devala. He was a famous sage and was the son of Pratyūṣa, a Vasu.[34] At another place he is mentioned as the elder brother of sage Dhaumya and as having participated in the serpent sacrifice of Janamejaya.[35] He was present at the coronation of Yudhiṣṭhira along with other sages,[36] addressed Yudhiṣṭhira on the Añjana mountain.[37]

To evaluate the significance of the present chapter (hereinafter referred to as Devala chapter) we may look into its context. The general framework of the Śāntiparva is an interlocution between Yudhiṣṭhira and Bhīṣma. Yodhiṣṭhira implores Bhīṣma to educate him on many questions of a political, social, moral and religious nature. About half of the chapters (174 to 365) are traditionally taken to form a distinct sub-section of the Śāntiparva and are designated as Mokṣadharmaparva. The present chapter occurs in the Mokṣadharmaparva. Its immediate connection is to be seen in the opening verse of chapter 273 wherein Yudhiṣṭhira asks Bhīṣma how a man becomes sinful (*pāpātmā*), how he performs virtous acts (*dharmam*), how he attains renunciation (*nirvedam*), and how he attains emancipation (*mokṣam*). Chapter 273 contains the explanation given by Bhīṣma. In the opening verse of chapter 274 Yudhiṣṭhira requests Bhīṣma to enlighten him about the means (*upāya*) for attaining emancipation. Chapter 275 is not introduced by any question posed by Yudhiṣṭhira. Bhīṣma, on his own, says that in this connexion is cited the old narrative (*itihāsam purātanam*)

34. I.66.26.
35. I.53.8; 182.2.
36. II.53.10.
37. II.78.15.

of the interlocution (*saṁvādam*) between Nārada and Asita. This narrative in its turn is introduced by saying that Nārada asked Devala about the origin and destruction (*prabhavāpyayam*) of the creatures (*bhūtānām*). In the following verses Asita presents his views. In chapter 273 Yudhiṣṭhira asks Bhīṣma how to dispel the craving for material gains (*arthodbhava tṛṣṇā*) which led him to perpetrate many sinful deeds.[38]

Apparently, it seems that the point raised in the beginning of chapter 273 is covered by chapters 273 and 274, after which the narrative is resumed in chapter 276, without requiring the details in chapter 275. The first verse in chapter 274 seems to connect it with the preceding two chapters by the introductory verses *atraivodāharantīmam*. Of course, we do not have an introductory verse in which Yudhiṣṭhira poses a corollary question about any point enunciated by Bhīṣma in the preceding chapter, requesting him for clarification or elaboration. Hence, it may be argued that chapter 275 was not part of the original scheme of chapterisation, but was added subsequently. But, this is not a compelling argument. At many other places in the Śāntiparva the main speaker himself resumes the thread of the narrative and does not wait for any question by the second person. In this case, the concluding verses (33 to 39) in the chapter deal with the question of emancipation, thus connecting it with the subject-matter of chapter 273 and 274. Hence, it is quite likely that chapter 274 formed a part of the Mokṣadharmaparva of the Śāntiparva, along with chapters 273 and 274 right from the time of the early formulation of the Śāntiparva.[39]

Differences with Sāṁkhyakārikā

P. Chakravarti[40] points out important differences which the present narrative has with the orthodox version of Sāṁkhya. First, Asita-Devala gives a prominent place to time (*kāla*) in the process of creation, but orthodox Sāṁkhya rejects time as a separate entity.

---

38. XII.1.4.
39. XIII.18.17-18.
40. *Op. cit.*, p. 45.

Second, he speaks of eight elements, the five gross elements, time, entity and non-entity, of which entity and non-entity are not recognised in orthodox Sāṁkhya. Third, Asita-Devala refers in an ascending order to the sense-organs, *citta*, *manas*, *buddhi* and *kṣetrajña*, but the difference among *citta, manas*, *buddhi* is not made clear. Fourth, the present account ignores *ahaṁkāra* and *prakṛti*. Fifth, Asita-Devala speaks of eight organs of knowledge, power as the sixth organ of action, and the stage of *Brahman* as the final achievement.

The failure of modern scholars to evaluate properly the present narration of Sāṁkhya attributed to Asita-Devala is due to their over-obsession with the nature of Sāṁkhya as found in the *Sāṁkhyakārikā*. The standardisation of the Sāṁkhya system attempted by Īśvarakṛṣṇa and the prestige and recognition accorded to his text threw other early Sāṁkhya texts into the background, with the result that gradually they were lost to the world of scholarship. The *Sāṁkhyakārikā*, being the only available early text of Sāṁkhya, created, in some quarters, a wrong impression that the Sāṁkhya has changed little in its long course of history.[41] Though the fallacies of such an opinion were exposed long back, the unacknowledged impression has persisted that the classical presentation of Sāṁkhya by Īśvarakṛṣṇa is the real Sāṁkhya and that details of the Sāṁkhya system given by him had been the distinguishing features of Sāṁkhya from the very beginning. Many scholars have attempted to trace the historical evolution of Sāṁkhya up to the times of Īśvarakṛṣṇa,[42] but often they have not overcome the presumption of a static and stereotyped Sāṁkhya system. They

41. According to Garbe, *Die Sāṁkhya-Philosophie*, Īśvarakṛṣṇa presents the original form of Sāṁkhya propounded first by Kapila as a complete and well-planned system which for more than a dozen centuries did not undergo any important change in its essential doctrines.

42. For pre-Classical Sāṁkhya see H. Oldenberg, "Zur Geschichte der Sāṁkhya-Philosophie" in *NGGW*, 1918; A.B. Keith, *The Sāṁkhya System*; F. Edgerton, "The Meaning of Sāṁkhya and Yoga" in *AJP*, 1924, pp. 1-46; *The Beginning of Indian Philosophy*. Prominent among those who refer to stages in the pre-Classical Sāṁkhya are S.N. Dasgupta, *A History of Indian Philosophy*, Vol.I, pp. 208-73; E.A. →

ascribe to some Sāṁkhya celebrities minor changes within the overall structure reconstructed by Īśvarakṛṣṇa. In the pre-Īśvarakṛṣṇa period it is only in the case of Pañcaśikha that some innovations have been identified. It has not been possible to delineate the different stages in the development of Sāṁkhya up to the times of Īśvarakṛṣṇa and to determine the contributions of different authors. The difficulty is primarily on account of the non-availability of the texts composed by the ancient authorities. We have a few stray quotations from some of the many Sāṁkhya celebrities who preceded Īśvarakṛṣṇa.

The possibility of wide variations in the views of Sāṁkhya scholars before Īśvarakṛṣṇa is now generally admitted. These differences are not restricted to minor points of details, even on facts of fundamental importance there is a wide range of conflicting views.

An analysis of the passages relating to the Sāṁkhya system preserved in the *Mahābhārata* also shows that the period covered by the Mokṣadharmaparva of Śāntiparva witnessed a very wide and popular currency of Sāṁkhya system, which was not characterised by a fixed and rigid formulation of the principles, but instead embraced a rich variation of views. This sub-section clearly records that according to the learned people the Sāṁkhya system possesses a vast literature,[43] which is also recognised as having a high antiquity.[44]

In the Mokṣadharmaparva section itself there are many accounts of the Sāṁkhya system, conflicting among themselves and differing from the principles propounded in the *Sāṁkhyakārikā*.

→ Johnston, *Early Sāṁkhya*, and E. Frauwallner, *History of Indian Philosophy*, Vol. I, pp. 217-321. For a critical evaluation of various historical studies of Sāṁkhya, see G.J. Larson, *Classical Sāṁkhya*, pp. 7-72. Larson (*ibid.*, pp. 77-156) himsef traces the historical development of pre-Classical Sāṁkhya through two broad stages of Ancient Speculations and Proto-Sāṁkhya Speculations.

43. XII.307.47.

44. XII.301.114.

Early Character of the Devala Chapter

It is clear from the text of the Devala chapter that Devala belonged to a period long before the composition of the Śāntiparva. In the opening verse of the chapter the interlocution between Nārada and Asita-Devala is described as an old narrative (*itihāsam purātanam*). In the second verse Devala is described as old (*vṛddham*) and foremost among the wise people (*buddhimatām varam*). By the time of the composition of the chapter Devala had come to enjoy a long established reputation as one of the foremost thinkers whom Nārada approached for seeking enlightenment.

Another significant point about the narrative is that in describing the five great elements it refers to the authority of the *bhūta-cintakas*.[45] Likewise, later in verse 18 the *jñānendriyas* are enumerated on the authority of the *adhyātma-cintakas*. This would refer to a period when different schools of philosophy had not assumed their distinct personalities and separate existence. Different opinions were grouped on the basis of the topics and characteristic opinion. The early Buddhist and Jain literature reflect such a situation.[46] They refer to a plethora of philosophical and religious views on various metaphysical entities and problems. The traditional schools of Indian philosophy, cannot be distinctly recognised in any one of them. In the Devala chapter also we do not find a reference to any system of philosophy other than the Sāṁkhya. The philosophers are here grouped into two: those who deliberate about the elements or material world (*bhūta-cintakas*) and those who deliberate about spirit or self (*adhyātma-cintakas*). This shows that Devala and his exposition of Sāṁkhya refer to an early period, long before the formalisation of philosophical views into distinct systems.

Comparison with the Devaladharmasūtra

Our effort to determine the authenticity of the views of Devala in

45. Verse 4.
46. Rhys Davids, *Buddhist India*, pp. 238ff; B.M. Barua, *History of Pre-Buddhist Indian Philosophy*; R.N. Mehta, *Pre-Buddhist India*, pp. 332ff; G.C. Pande, *Origin of Buddhism*, pp. 338ff.

the Devala chapter is bulked down by the absence of the original text composed by Devala. We know,[47] on the authority of Śaṅkara,[48] the great Advaita philosopher, that Devala had composed a Dharmasūtra text in which he had adopted the Sāṁkhya philosophy, Aparārka, in his commentary on the *Yājñavalkya-smṛti*, and Lakṣmīdhara, in his *Kṛtyakalpataru*, reproduce many passages which deal with several aspects of Sāṁkhya and Yoga. This confirms the genuineness of the tradition of Sāṁkhya principles being expounded by Devala.

But the views expressed in the Devala chapter do not have parallels in the extracts from the *Devaladharmasūtra*.[49] There is no resemblance between the two sources in terms of style, sentences or phrases. We cannot trace any significant similarity in the ideas expressed in them. On the contrary, there is a wide divergence of opinion on important points. The new features in the ideas of the Devala chapter, pointed out by P. Chakravarti, which are not known to occur in any known Sāṁkhya work, are conspicuous by their absence in the available passages of the *Devaladharmasūtra*.

We cannot take shelter under the pretext that, the full text of the original *Devaladharmasūtra* being not available, there is a possibility of the new features occurring in its portions which have been lost. The main points in the Sāṁkhya views of Devala are adequately covered in the available extracts. We do not rule out the possibility that some lost passages gave a more detailed exposition of some points. But, in the present case, it is not a question of minor variations in details in the two accounts of Devala's views. Some of the points discussed in the Devala chapter are covered in the available extracts, but the treatment in the two sources shows wide differences.

---

47. See our article "Was there a Devaladharmasūtra?" in the *Journal of the Ganganath Jha Kendriya Sanskrit Vidyapeeth*, Vol. XXXVII, pp. 189-97.
48. On *Vedāntrasūtra*, I.4.28.
49. See *infra* chapter 12.

Kāla in the Devala Chapter

Kāla does not find any place in the account in the *Devaladharmasūtra*, but in the Devala chapter it has an important role. *Kāla* is among the six great elements. It is *kāla*, which moved by *bhāva*, creates creatures from the five great elements. No doubt, in the classical Sāṁkhya *kāla* has not been assigned an important position. But, this is not a valid ground for suspecting the authenticity of the Devala chapter. On the contrary it goes to establish that the chapter reflects an early stage in the evolution of Sāṁkhya. The *Śvetāśvatara Upaniṣad*, which is known to contain an early exposition of the Sāṁkhya system, refers to seven main topics, of which *kāla* is the first, the remaining six being *svabhāva*, *niyati*, *yadṛcchā*, *bhūta*s, *yoni*, and *puruṣa*.[50] This Upaniṣad says that some people designated *prakṛti* as *kāla* and condemns them as being illusioned.[51] The account of *kāla* in the Devala chapter is very near the description of *kāla* in the *Śvetāśvatara Upaniṣad*. Possibly this account of *kāla* was current in the period before the composition of this Upaniṣad; later *kāla* came to be gradually dropped from the Sāṁkhya scheme. The *Mahābhārata* and some Purāṇas, in their account of Sāṁkhya, record echoes of the early Sāṁkhya formulation with *kāla* occupying a prominent position.[52] In one account in the *Mahābhārata*[53] the order of evolution in the reverse order is *pṛthivi*, *āp*, *tejas*, *pavana*, *vyoma*, *manas*, *buddhi*, *kāla*, and Viṣṇu (*puruṣa*). Here *kāla* is mentioned in place of *prakṛti*. Another account in the *Mahābhārata* has *prakṛti* in place of *kāla* of the earlier account.[54] But, here *kāla* is described as being instrumental in the transformation of the *tattva*s.[55] The account, narrated by Sulabhā to Janaka, mentions *kāla* as the twentieth *guṇa* which is the cause

50. I.2.
51. VI.1.
52. Hari Shankar Joshi, *Sāṁkhya-yoga darśana kā jīrṇoddhāra*, pp. 213-21.
53. XII.206.10-12.
54. XII.210.25-9.
55. XII.211.11.

of the creation and dissolution of beings.[56] The account in the *Kūrma Purāṇa* describes *kāla* as eternal and without a beginning; it indicates the connection between two events.[57] In this narrative, in the order of evolution *kāla*, *pradhāna* and *puruṣa* are the first to issue out of *avyakta*.[58] The *Viṣṇu Purāṇa* contains an account in which Parāśara instructs Maitreya. Here *kāla* is used for *puruṣa* as it stands aloof when *prakṛti* is in the state of equilibrium of *guṇas*.[59] *Kāla* occurs in two separate accounts in the *Bhāgavata Purāṇa*. In one, *kāla* is mentioned as the twenty-fifth *tattva*.[60] It is *kāla* which imparts *ceṣṭā* to *prakṛti* in its state of equilibrium.[61] *Ceṣṭā* here signifies commotion or the urge towards creation. The second account in the *Bhāgavata Purāṇa* mentions several new *tattvas*: *dravya*, *karma*, *kāla*, *svabhāva*, *jīva* and *brahma* (Vāsudeva).[62] It further says that the commotion in the equilibrium of *guṇas* is caused by *kāla*.[63]

Thus, in Sāṁkhya there was an early tradition about *kāla*.[64] Though it ceased to be fashionable, especially after the classical formulation of Sāṁkhya, its memory survived in the *Mahābhārata* and Purāṇas. In this early tradition *kāla* was included in the list of *tattvas* sometimes standing for *prakṛti* and sometimes signifying *puruṣa* who sets into motion the process of evolution by affecting

---

56. XII.320.110.
57. II.3.8.
58. II.3.1.
59. *Viṣṇu Purāṇa*, I.2.27.
60. III.16.26.
61. *Ibid.*, III.26.17.
62. II.5.14.
63. *Ibid.*, II.6.22.
64. *Sāṁkhyapravacanasūtra*, I.12 describes *kāla* as being all-pervading and eternal (*vyāpino nityasya*) and related to all *puruṣas* (*sarvasambhandhāt*).

    Though some scholars take it to be an ancient text composed by Kapila himself or by Pañcaśikha, modern scholars generally dismiss it as a later text.

the equilibrium of *guṇa*s characterising *prakṛti*. This is quite in line with the Devala chapter, wherein *kāla* is included in the list of *tattva*s and is described as starting the process of creation.

It is not unlikely that the *Sāṁkhyakārikā* itself contained a reference to the high position enjoyed by *kāla* in the earlier accounts of the Sāṁkhya. B.G. Tilak has reconstructed the missing verse in the original set of seventy verses forming the *Sāṁkhyakārikā*.[65] It refers to *īśvara*, *kāla* and *svabhāva* being mentioned by different groups of earlier thinkers. Possibly later, when the Sāṁkhya philosophy was standardised and got fixed, this verse was dropped because it pronounced views which them were considered to be totally opposed to Sāṁkhya.

Here it may be noted that though verse 9 of the Devala chapter mentions the five great elements *kāla*, *bhāva* and *abhāva* as the eight elements, (*bhūtāni*), which are eternal (*śāśvatāni*) in the creation and dissolution of the creatures, in verse 6 it names only six of them: the five elements and *kāla*. We do not find anything parallel to this in the *Devaladharmasūtra*. But there is a case for this being based on an earlier genuine tradition. Before the categories in Sāṁkhya were standardised as twenty-four or twenty-five there were varying accounts about their number and names. Sometimes the purpose or context of enumeration was an important consideration. Thus, Hiraṇyākṣa, in propounding his view that a creature as also his diseases originate from six *dhātu*s, points out that earlier Sāṁkhya teachers held that a creature is the combination of six *dhātus*.[66] From the context it seems that the six *dhātu*s comprised of the five *bhūta*s and *ātman*. Of course, here we have *ātman* in place of *kāla* of the Devala chapter. This difference can possibly be explained through the peculiar context of the two cases.

---

65. *Sanskrit Research*, vol. 1, pp. 107-17 cited by Chakravartti, *op. cit.*, pp. 156-7:
kāraṇan īśvaram eke bruvate kālaṁ pare svabhāvaṁ vā ।
prajāḥ kathaṁ nirguṇato vyaktaḥ kālaḥ svabhāvaśca ।।
66. *Caraka*, Sūtra, 25.15.

Thus, it is quite likely that the Devala chapter actually records an early view attributed to Devala.[67]

Bala in the Devala Chapter

The inclusion of *bala* as the sixth organ of action does not affect the genuineness of the Sāṁkhya account in the Devala chapter.[68] No doubt the extracts from the *Devaladharmasūtra* do not have any matching reference. But in the Śāntiparva chapter 219, which purports to record the view of Pañcaśikha, one of the earliest Sāṁkhya teachers, we have an identical enumeration of six organs of action, *bala* being the sixth.[69]

Nature of Presentation in the Śāntiparva Chapters

In evaluating the authenticity of the Devala chapter we must keep in mind the nature of the epic text and its style of presenting the views of others. The *Mahābhārata* claims to be encyclopaedic in character,[70] but it is not in the form of a digest. It does not collect passages as quotations from other texts. Though, at many places, it presents the view of sages and other important persons as their utterances (*uvāca*), clearly the presentation is not in their original words, having a uniform format, style and metre. The author of the Śāntiparva chapters has presented the views of others in his own words, accommodating them in his style and planning of chapters. Naturally there is bound to occur considerable changes in the formal expression of the views.

Standardisation of Sāṁkhya

The standardisation of Sāṁkhya philosophy by Īśvarakṛṣṇa has

---

67. The reading in the Critical Edition is *ātmapracoditaḥ*. This would suggest that for the author of the Devala chapter it is *ātman* and not *kāla* which is important here. We may also note the use of the term *rāśi* in both the texts in this context.
68. Verse 22.
69. *Mbh.*, XII.219-20.
70. *Ibid.*, XVIII.5.50.

been the greatest obstacle in the way of a proper understanding of the historical evaluation of the Sāṁkhya system. It pushed into oblivion earlier presentations of the Sāṁkhya principles. Even before Īśvarakṛṣṇa some other thinkers tried to introduce order and uniformity in the existing versions of Sāṁkhya principles. Though we cannot determine all these stages and their significant features, there are traces of attempts at systematisation that preceded Īśvarakṛṣṇa.[71]

In the *Sāṁkhyakārikā* Īśvarakṛṣṇa himself indicates that his was not the first and only attempt at systematisation of the Sāṁkhya philosophy. His brief reference[72] to the early history of the transmission of Sāṁkhya notes that Pañcaśikha expanded or modified that *tantra* (*tena ca bahudhā kṛtam tantram*). We can say, on the basis of this succinct remark, that Pañcaśikha reorganised the Sāṁkhya system. His contribution was either in the form of an elaboration of the Sāṁkhya philosophy or the preparation of a detailed text. Pañcaśikha gave a definite shape and order to the Sāṁkhya principles as its first systematiser.

Śaṅkara, the author of the *Jayamaṅgalā* commentary on the *Sāṁkhyakārikā*, quotes *saṁgrahakāra* as enumerating ten *mūlikārthas* in a verse.[73] This *saṁgrahakāra* was evidently a Sāṁkhya author who systematised the Sāṁkhya philosophy and codified it.[74] He possibly introduced an element of standardisation.

In the *Gītā*,[75] in the beginning of the concluding chapter, five causes indispensable for the completion of all sorts of actions are referred to on the authority of Sāṁkhya. P. Chakravarti[76] takes the word *kṛtānta* to mean 'established conclusion' and infers that Sāṁkhya was systematised before the composition of the *Gītā*.

---

71. See *infra*, chapter 19.
72. *Kārikas*, 69-71.
73. On *kārikā*, 51.
74. "The Mūlikārthas in Sāṁkhya", *Indian Historical Review*, Vol. pp.
75. XVIII.13.
76. *Op. cit.*, p. 56.

The close similarity in the presentation of Sāṁkhya in three different sets of chapters in the Śāntiparva[77] has led Frauwallner[78] to infer that all these are different versions of one and the same text. We may suggest that before the time of the composition of the Mokṣadharmaparva a certain amount of standardisation in the formulation of Sāṁkhya[79] had been achieved, which served as the basis for the accounts in the three sets of chapters.

Systematisation of Sāṁkhya in the Mokṣadharmaparva

The Devala chapter is also to be placed in the phase of systematisation of Sāṁkhya as recorded in the Mokṣadharmaparva. Frauwallner did not notice that though the Devala chapter does not have passages identical with the Ur-text for the three sets of chapters, the presentation of Sāṁkhya in this chapter resembles the arrangement in the Ur-text. Frauwallner[80] reconstructs the structure of the Ur-text. 'It begins with the description of the elements, their qualities and the formulation of beings or principles out of the elements. In the second place, there follows a description of the sense-organs and the psychical organs and the role of the most important among them, of knowledge (*buddhiḥ*) is described at great length. With that is joined easily the theory of the states (*bhāvāḥ*) of knowledge on which the bondage of the soul depends. That leads again to the description of bondage, to the mention of release through the knowledge of the soul and to the description of the released. Then the text once more harks back to the character

---

77. *Mahābhārata,* XII.194; XII.247-9; XII.287 (= 285 of Gita edn.).
78. *History of Indian Philosophy*, Vol. I, p. 227.
    Hopkins, *op. cit.*, pp. 157-62, also had noted that they are based on one Sāṁkhya text.
79. Frauwallner, *op. cit.*, p. 228 remarks: 'Nothing can be gathered with regard to the origin and the period of origin of these texts'. But, he points out that the original text 'must have enjoyed special esteem and unusual dissemination' (*ibid.*) and that the great deviations of these versions give 'an evident impression of their having led a separate existence for a long time before they were taken into the great collection of the Mokṣadharma' (*ibid.*, p. 227).
80. *History of Indian Philosophy*, Vol. I., p. 230.

of releasing knowledge and ends resundingly with a comparatively lengthy description of release, the end being underlined or distinguished effectively with a change in metre.' The Devala chapter has the same broad outline. Possibly the systematisation of Sāṁkhya, attempted sometime before the Mokṣadharmaparva, was adopted by some Sāṁkhya scholars in the subsequent period. In this process, it was natural that many individual features and details of the views were ironed out to conform to the plan of the systematiser.

We have independent testimony to the fact that Devala systematised and codified the Sāṁkhya philosophy. In one extract from the *Devaladharmasūtra*,[81] there is an introductory remark that it has abridged the voluminous and profound texts, composed earlier on Sāṁkhya and Yoga and presented with arguments and proper arrangement, and has described them according to topics. Thus, Devala in his Dharmasūtra attempted in his own way a codification of the Sāṁkhya system.

Differences with the Devaladharmasūtra

But the question still remains: how to explain the differences between the *Mahābhārata* version of Devala's views and the account of the Sāṁkhya system in the *Devaladharmasūtra*. We offer an explanation: Devala was an ancient sage. He was respected for his views on various philosophical problems. He was recognised as an early Sāṁkhya authority. But, in the formative period in the history of Sāṁkhya, his views had not assumed the form of a distinct treatise. Some amount of standardisation was introduced by Pañcaśikha. The Ur-text in the Mokṣadharmaparva, was either part of the process of systematisation started by Pañcaśikha or synchronised with it. One cannot be dogmatic about the chronological relationship between Pañcaśikha's writings and the Ur-text in the Mokṣadharmaparva. Possibly the two were not far removed in time from one another. It is not unlikely that, as a result of the influence of the systematisation, some features of the Sāṁkhya of Devala

81. Aparārka on *Yājñavalkya*, Prāyaścitta, 109.

were ironed out. The *Mahābhārata* chapter could not give a complete account of the views of Devala; it followed the outline laid down by the systematisation in the Ur-text.

When the *Devaladharmasūtra* was composed, its author, in presenting the Sāṁkhya system, did not adopt Devala's views as recorded in the *Mahābhārata*. There can be two explanations of his doing so. First, the Śāntiparva (or the Mokṣadharmaparva) of the *Mahābhārata*, with its present chapters, was possibly not available to the author of the *Devaladharmasūtra*. The composition of the *Devaladharmasūtra* is to be placed long before that of the Śāntiparva of the *Mahābhārata*.[82] Another explanation can be that the author of the *Devaladharmasūtra* did not consider the Śāntiparva chapter to represent fully and faithfully Sāṁkhya views of the Devala.

The difference between the two accounts possibly originated from their differing aims and scopes. Whereas the Devala chapter presents Devala's views on Sāṁkhya within the framework of the systematisation in the Ur-text in the Śāntiparva, the *Devaladharmasūtra* records briefly the important details in the Sāṁkhya philosophy. The first is characterised by a definite orientation and emphasis, whereas the second gives a complete account of Sāṁkhya as it had come to be systematised by that time.

Authenticity of Devala Chapter — Points of Contact with the Devaladharmasūtra

A sympathetic analysis of the Devala chapter would indicate certain points of contact with the *Devaladharmasūtra*, particularly when contrasted with the *Sāṁkhyakārikā*. First, the original intention of the Devala chapter was to describe the creation and dissolution of the elements (*bhūtānām prabhavāpyayam*) from which this world of mobile and immobile things is created and in which the elements are merged at the time of dissolution (*pralaya*).[83]

---

82. But this may create another problem. If the *Devaladharmasūtra* had been composed before the Śāntiparva assumed its present form, then we will have to explain why the author of the Śāntiparva did not follow the *Devaladharmasūtra* in expounding Devala's Sāṁkhya.

83. Verses 2-3.

In the original *Devaladharmasūtra* also this topic was specifically described. In the passages from the *Devaladharmasūtra* in the *Kṛtyakalpataru*[84] we have an account of the order of creation (*utpatti-krama*). The parallel quotation in Aparārka refers to both the order of creation (*utpatti-krama*) and the order of dissolution (*apyaya-krama*). The *Sāṁkhyakārikā*[85] refers to the emergence of *mahat* from *pravṛti* and of *ahaṁkāra* from *mahat* and then to the two-fold creation (*dvividhaḥ sargaḥ*) from *ahaṁkāra*: the group of eleven (*manas* and ten organs) and the five *tanmātras* (subtle elements). There is no reference to the order of dissolution.[86] Incidentally it may be noted that like the *Devala-dharmasūtra*, the Devala chapter also uses the word *apyaya* for dissolution.

Second, the Devala chapter has very distinctive views on emancipation and other related points.[87] It says that urged by the *puṇya* (merits) and *pāpa* (sins) the *kṣetrin* enters the body resulting from his acts. Urged on by *kāla*, it migrates from one body to another. The enlightened ones, endowed with certainty of knowledge, are not given to grief over this; but the fools, who envisage permanent relationship, indulge in grief. The *dehī* is not related to another, nor any one belongs to him; he alone is eternal and, when in the body, he is subject to happiness and misery. He is never born, nor does hem ever die. After leaving this body, sometimes he attains the highest end (*paramāṁ gatim*). Through the exhaustion of *karma* he overcomes the body, which results from merit and sin, and, after giving up the body, attains to Brahmā (*brahmatvam upagacchati*). Upon the exhaustion of merit and sin, he achieves the highest end by attaining the status of Brahmā (*brahmabhāve param gatim*).

Here the description of the *dehī* and the reference to the attainment of *brahmatva* or *brahma-bhāva* as the highest end are

---

84. Mokṣa-kāṇḍa, p. 101.
85. *Kārikās*, 22-4.
86. *Kārikā* 69 says that the secret knowledge expounded by the great sage (Kapila) analyses the existence, origin and termination of all beings (*sthityutpattipralayāḥ*).
87. Verses, 33-39.

not in conformity with the position generally taken in Sāṁkhya. One explanation can be that here Sāṁkhya has an overcoating of Vedānta. The resemblance with the ideas propounded in the *Gītā* is too apparent to require any detailed exposition. But, similar views are found in many other chapters of the Mokṣadharmaparva section and are attributed to more than one thinker. This general agreement may reflect the views accepted by the author of the concerned chapters or else it was generally accepted view in that particular stage in the history of Indian philosophical thought.

We can particularise the explanation. The ideas in the Devala chapter reflect the views of Sāṁkhya-Yoga of those times. In view of the differences in the opinion of modern scholars about the history of the Sāṁkhya and Yoga systems, particularly their relationship, we will not invlove ourselves into a discussion whether the Devala chapter belongs to the period which witnessed attempts at the fusion of the two systems or to the period when there was an attempt to assert the individuality of the Sāṁkhya against the current practice of bracketing it with Yoga.

The synthesis of Sāṁkhya principles with Yoga ideas is the characteristic feature of the Devala chapter. The chapter faithfully projects this characteristic of the philosophy propounded by Devala.[88] We are fortunate in having in the extracts from the *Devala-dharmasūtra* an outline of its section of Sāṁkhya-Yoga, at places with the fullest details.

U.V. Shastri[89] has collected only prose passages from the *Devaladharmasūtra*, as quoted by Aparārka[90] and Lakṣmīdhara.[91]

88. *Mahābhārata*, XII.229 gives an account of the teachings which Devala is said to have received from his teacher Jaigīṣavya. These teachings have much in common with the verses in the Devala chapter which we are discussing here. This would be another argument in favour of the authenticity of the views attributed to Devala in the Devala chapter.
89. *Sāṁkhyadarśana kā itihāsa*, pp. 600-5.
90. On *Yājñavalkyasmṛti*, Prāyaścitta, 109.
91. *Kṛtyakalpataru*, Mokṣa-kāṇḍa, pp., 7, 8, 21, 49, 50, 84, 100f., 109, 124, 165, 168, 170, 173, 174, 181, 212, 216.

But, the original text contained verses as well.[92] In the Mokṣa-kāṇḍa of the *Kṛtyakalpataru* itself we have many verses, sometimes in the form of a long connected quotation. As a illustration of verses containing ideas similar to those of the Devala chapter referring to the nature of *dehī* and to *brahmatva* as the highest aim we may mention quotations from the *Devaladharmasūtra* on *ariṣṭa* and *utkrānti*.[93]

Third, in the Devala chapter there is no specific reference to the number of categories being twenty-four or twenty-five. First among eight eternal elements are included[94] the five great elements,[95] *kāla*, *bhāva* and *abhāva*. Later we have a reference to seventeen *guṇa*s consisting of the *indriya*s and the *bhāva*s.[96] In earlier verses the *indriya*s are enumerated as being fourteen (eight *jñānedriya*s —*cakṣus*, *nāsikā*, *karṇa*, *tvac*, *jihvā*, *citta*, *manas* and *buddhi*[97] and six *karmendriya*s —*pāṇi*, *pāda*, *pāyu*, *mehana*, *mukha* and *bala*).[98] The second line of the verse referring to seventeen *guṇa*s introduces *dehī* as the eighteenth.[99] In the following verse the *guṇa*s, including the *śarīrin*, are mentioned as being nineteen.[100] The immediately following line increases the number to twenty by adding *ūṣmā* (heat).[101] It is apparent that the number of categories had not been rigidly fixed as twenty-five. This would refer to a time long before the standardisation introduced by Īśvarakṛṣṇa. The number of categories was fixed as twenty-five quite sometime before

---

92. Our reconstruction of the *Devaladharmasūtra* is to appear shortly.
93. Our article, "Devala on Ariṣṭas", in *Indological Studies*, Prof. D.C. Sircar Commemoration Volume, (ed. by S.K. Maity and V. Thakur), pp. 141-2.
94. Verse 9.
95. *Ibid.*, verse 7.
96. Verse 28.
97. Verses 12 and 18.
98. Verses 19 and 22.
99. Verse 28.
100. Verse 30—*ekaśca daśa cāṣṭau ca guṇāḥ saha śarīriṇā*. But the break-up of the *guṇa*s into three groups of one, ten and eight is not clear.
101. Verse 31.

Īśvarakṛṣṇa. We know that an earlier tradition enumerated sixty items (*ṣaṣṭhitantra*) as constituting Sāṁkhya. The quotations from the *Devaladharmasūtra* reflect an intermediary stage when the enumeration of categories was still in a fluid state. The number of categories as mentioned in the Devala chapter is not found here. Instead Sāṁkhya is defined in terms of the twenty-five *tattvas*.[102] But in enumerating the *tattvas* the groupings do not clearly add to the number twenty-five. Actually they are presented in such a manner that they can lead to different totals. Moreover, the *Dharmasūtra* enumerated fifty *pratyayas* along with ten *mūlikārthas* which form the sixty elements of the *ṣaṣṭhitantra*.

Fourth, another notable points about the account of Sāṁkhya in the Devala chapter is the enumeration of *jñānendriyas* as being eight, namely, five organs, *citta*, *manas* and *buddhi*.[103] No other Sāṁkhya text gives a parallel account of the *jñānendriyas*. The *Sāṁkhyakārikā* mentions the *buddhīndriyas* (organs of ascertainment or sense-organs) as being eye, ear, nose, tongue and skin.[104] But the Devala chapter is not in total disagreement with the generally accepted Sāṁkhya stand. In later Sāṁkhya accounts it was possibly retained in a slightly modified form. The *Sāṁkhyakārikā*[105] speaks of thirteen *karaṇas* (instruments), grouped into two, *antaḥkaraṇas* (internal organs) and *bāhya* (external) *karaṇas*. The internal organs are *buddhi*, *ahaṁkāra* and *manas*, whereas the ten external organs include five sense-organs and the five organs of action. The *karaṇas*, internal and external, are bracketed because they have similar or complementary functions to perform. *Kārikā* 27 says that *manas* (mind) is of the nature of both sense-organs and organs of action. The mind is characterised by the function of *saṁkalpa* (reflection). It is designated as an *indriya* because it has a function similar to those of the senses (*indriyam ca sādharmyāt*). The function of all the thirteen *karaṇas* is described

102. Aparārka on *Yājñavalkya*, Prāyaścitta 109; *Kṛtyakalpataru*, Mokṣa, p. 100.
103. Verse 18.
104. *Kārikā*, 26. See also *kārikā*, 34.
105. *Kārikās*, 32-5.

as being seizing, holding and manifesting (*āharaṇadhāraṇa-prakāśakaram*).[106] One important difference between the internal and external *karaṇa*s is that whereas the external *karaṇa*s function in present time, the internal *karaṇa*s function in all the three times (past, present and future).[107] The external organs are known as the context (or sphere) of the three internal *karaṇa*s (*bāhyaṁ trayasya viṣayākhyam*).[108] *Kārikā*s 34 and 35, read together, bring out how the functions of the internal *karaṇa*s are complementary to those of the external *karaṇa*s. Of the two, the sense-organs and the organs of action, the functions of the sense-organs are more analogous to those of three internal organs. Whereas the sense-organs perform the basic work of mere sensing, the *buddhi* and other internal *karaṇa*s comprehend all the objects; the three internal *karaṇa*s are the chamberlain, whereas the remaining ten are the doors.[109] In the light of this it will not be incongruous to postulate that in an earlier account of Sāṁkhya the three internal *karaṇa*s were grouped with the five external sense-organs and were designated as eight *jñānedriya*s.

The account in the *Devaladharmasūtra* is not much different from that in the *Sāṁkhyakārikā*. It also refers to the classification under *buddhīndriya*s and *karmendriya*s and then mentions the ten *indriya*s, *buddhi*, *ahaṁkāra* and *manas* as *karaṇa*s, divided into two: *antaḥkaraṇa*s and *bahiṣkaraṇa*s.[110]

The *Yuktidīpikā* quotes the opinion of the followers of Vṛṣagaṇa who accept only *buddhi* as an *antaḥkaraṇa* and thus maintain that the *karaṇa*s are eleven in number.[111] Thus, it would seem that the final acceptance of *buddhi*, *ahaṁkāra* and *manas* as three *antaḥkaraṇa*s was the result of a long process and that at some intermediate stage only *buddhi* was admitted as a *karaṇa*. The

106. *Kārikā*, 32.
107. *Kārikā*, 33.
108. *Ibid*.
109. *Kārikā*, 35.
110. Aparārka on *Yājñavalkya*, Prāyaścitta, 109; *Kṛtyakalpataru*, Mokṣa, p. 101.
111. Page 132. It further records that Pañcādhikaraṇa and some others regard the number to be ten only.

Sāṁkhyakārikā makes a special mention only of *manas* (and not *buddhi* and *ahaṁkāra*) as an *indriya*. Possibly this represents the survival of an earlier view parallel to that of Vārṣagaṇyas.

Thus, the ascription of the account of *jñānendriyas* to Devala in the *Mahābhārata* chapter may be based on a genuine earlier tradition.

Musalagaonkar's Late Date for Devala

G.S. Musalagaonkar[112] takes note of both the Devala chapter in the *Mahābhārata* and the extracts from Devala in Aparārka. But, he is not worried about the evident conflict in the two accounts. He makes no attempt to reconcile them. He takes them both to be genuine accounts of the enunciation of Sāṁkhya philosophy by Devala. He is concerned about the chronological compatibility. He does not suggest any definite date which may satisfy the requirements of the two cases, but seems to argue in favour of a date around the third century of the Christian era. He refers to Kane who mentions Devala as being contemporary of Bṛhaspati and Kātyāyana and hence belonging to the period between the fourth and sixth centuries.[113] To reconcile this date with the date of the Devala chapter Musalagaonkar labours to lower down the date of Devala associated with the *Mahābhārata*. U.V. Shastri places Devala before the second century BC by which date the *Mahābhārata*, with many references to Devala, is supposed to have received its present form. To counter it Musalagoanker refers to the view of Winternitz that the *Mahābhārata* received its final form in the fourth century AD.[114] Likewise, he interprets the reference in the *Māṭharavṛtti*[115] to Devala and others (*prabhṛti*) preceding Īśvarakṛṣṇa in the *History*

112. *Sāṁkhya-tattva-kaumudī*, Introduction, pp. 46-7.

113. *History of Dharmaśāstra*, Vol. I, (1st edn.) pp. 121, 215 (= 2nd edn. 284, 502). It is not clear how Musalagaonkar equates it with the third century of the Vikrama era. Kane, *op. cit.*, (2nd edn.), p. 488 places Bṛhaspati between AD 200 and 400.

114. *History of Indian Literature*, pp. 465-75.

115. On *Sāṁkhyakārikā*, 12 — *kapilādāsuriṇā prāptamidaṁ jñānam* । *tataḥ pañcaśikhena, tasmāt bhārgavolūkavālmīkihārīta-devaloprabhṛtī-nāgatam* ।।

of Sāṁkhya to suggest that Devala came before Īśvarakṛṣṇa and not to indicate a very ancient date for him.

But, the chronological gap remains. Whatever date we may accept for the Mokṣadharmaparva section, Devala and his version of Sāṁkhya in it have to be placed long before its composition.[116] Likewise, the Sāṁkhya tradition given by the *Māṭharavṛtti* includes Devala in the list of famous sages, Bhārgava, Ulūka, Vālmīki, Hārīta and others, quite distinct from reputed Sāṁkhya authorities Kapila, Āsuri and Pañcaśikha. Thus, Māṭhara evidently envisages that Devala was quite removed from the time of Īśvarakṛṣṇa. Here again even the most recent date suggested for Īśvarakṛṣṇa will ill suit the date which Kane suggests for Devala.

Actually, in fixing the date for Devala, Kane has been over cautious. On the ground that Devala verses on partition, inheritance and women's rights over *strīdhana* are cited by Aparārka and the *Smṛticandrikā*, he places Devala, the jurist, in the period of the great jurists Bṛhaspati and Kātyāyana. But, this is only the lower limit inferred from the fact that *vyavahāra* verses of Devala are quoted by Aparārka and the *Smṛticandrikā* and does not preclude an earlier date for Devala, the jurist.

In this connexion the important point is that the Sāṁkhya views of Devala are found in the *Devaladharmasūtra*. This fact was noticed by Śaṅkara, the great Advaita philosoher, and is corroborated by actual *sūtra* passages on Sāṁkhya quoted by Aparārka and Lakṣmīdhara from Devala. Kane had not recognised the possibility of the existence of a *Devaladharmasūtra* when the first edition of the first volume of his *History of Dharmaśāstra* was published. In the second edition Kane argues for two Devala texts: a *Devalasmṛti* in verses and a *Devaladharmasūtra*.[117] According to him, this Dharmasūtra 'dealt with most of the topics that are discussed in the Dharmasūtras of Gautama, Āpastamba, Baudhāyana, Hārīta and others and also some matters in detail such as Sāṁkhya and

116. See *supra*, und 'Asita-Devala and Devala' section.

117. *History of Dharmaśāstra*, Vol. I, 2nd edn., p. 283.

Yoga'.[118] Hence for considering the Sāṁkhya views of Devala found in the Śāntiparva the relevant text is the *Devaladharmasūtra* and not the *Devalasmṛti*.

The probable date for the *Devaladharmasūtra*, which also contains an account of Sāṁkhya, will not violently clash with the generally accepted date for the Śāntiparva. The Devala chapter in the *Mahābhārata* will roughly belong to this time-bracket. But, it is quite likely that it preserves memories of an earlier period.

Devala in History

The Brāhmaṇical tradition at places glorifies Devala into a mythological sage, but there is no doubt that he was a historical person and belonged to an early period of Indian history.[119] He is mentioned alike in the Jain, Buddhist and Brāhmaṇical sources, which, at times, show points of similarity.

As we have pointed out above, Śaṅkara mentions him as the author of a Dharmasūtra. The *Māṭharavṛtti* refers to him as a Sāṁkhya philosopher. The *Gītā* names him as a revered sage. The *Mahābhārata* refers to him at many places in Ādi, Sabhā, Śalya, Śānti and Anuśāsana *parvas*. In the epic his dialogues with both Nārada and Jaigīṣavya are given and some details about his personal life are recorded.

The Buddhist tradition refers to him as being senior to the Buddha. The Aśvalāyanasutta in the *Majjhima-nikāya*[120] mentions him as a reversed sage. Buddhaghoṣa refers to him as a Bodhisattva.[121]

Asita-Devala was known to the authors of the *Isibhāsiyāim*[122]

---

118. *History of Dharmaśāstra*, Vol.I, 2nd edn., p. 282.
119. Sagarmal Jain, *Ṛṣibhāṣita: eka adhyayana*, pp. 27-30.
120. Vol. II, p. 154.
121. *Mahāvaṁsa*, II.785.
122. Adhyayana, 3.

and *Sūyagaḍa*.[123] The *Isimaṇḍala* also mentions him in *gāthā* no.[124] The *R̥ṣimaṇḍala-vr̥tti*, belonging to the thirteenth-fourteenth centuries, gives a detailed account of his life.

The Jain tradition, referring to his status as a householder in his early life, confirms the account in the Śalyaparva, chapter 50 of the *Mahābhārata* before he met Jaigīṣavya. The *Mahābhārata* account about the dialogue between Nārada and Devala receives an interesting confirmation from the *Indriyajātaka* which mentions Nārada as a younger brother of Devala whom the latter preaches. The *Isibhāsiyāim* also seems to indicate the contemporaneity of Nārada and Devala, when it includes them as the first and third *r̥ṣis* in its collection of the views of fourty-five *r̥ṣis*. The inclusion of Devala in the *Isibhāsiyāim* indicates that he belonged to a much earlier time than the *Isibhāsiyāim*, whose composition is placed between the fifth and third centuries BC.

All this indicates that Devala was a historical person, who was a senior contemporary of Buddha and, possibly, also of Mahāvīra. He was a junior contemporary of Jaigīṣavya, a disciple of Pañcaśikha. His association with Nārada will also favour his placement in earlier times. For Devala a date around 650 BC may not be wide off the mark.

But, this does not mean that all the texts claiming to record his views were also of this date. We do not have the original exposition made by Devala, though the relevant secondary sources may be based on it. These are to be dated separately and independently.

---

123. I.1.3.4.

124. Sagarmal Jain, *op. cit.*, p. 9.

12

Sāṁkhya in the Dharmasūtras — The Devaladharmasūtra

Introduction

THE *Māṭharavṛtti*[1] on the *Sāṁkhyakārikā* includes the name of Devala in the teacher-student lineage between Pañcaśikha and Īśvarakṛṣṇa. The *Mahābhārata* provides confirmation of the Sāṁkhya connections of Devala.[2] Śaṅkara, the great Advaita philosopher, in his commentary on the *Brahmasūtra*[3] has pointed out that Devala and some other authors of Dharmasūtras have adopted Sāṁkhya principles. The Dharmasūtra of Devala not being available, the testimony of Śaṅkara has not been duly considered. There are quotations from Devala in the Aparārka on the *Yājñavalkyasmṛti*[4] and the Mokṣa-kāṇḍa of Lakṣmīdhara's

1. On *kārikā*, 71.
2. See *supra*, chapter 11.
3. I.4.28.
4. Aparārka on *Yājñavalkya*, Prāyaścitta, 109.

athāto dharmavarjitvānna tiryagyonyāṁ puruṣārthopadeśaḥ I *devamanuṣayordvividhaḥ puruṣārthaḥ* I*abhyudayo niḥśreyasamiti* I

tayorabhyudayaḥ pūrvoktaḥ I *dvividhaṁ niḥśreyasaṁ sāṁkhyayogāviti* I

pañcaviṁśatitattvajñānaṁ sāṁkhyam I *viṣayebhyo nivarthyā'-bhiprete'rthe manaso'vasthā (pa)naṁ yogaḥ* I *ubhayatrāpavargaḥ phalam* I *janmaraṇaduḥkhayoratyantā' bhāvo' pavargaḥ. etau sāṁkhyogau cādhikṛtya yairyuktitaḥ samayateśca pūrvapraṇītāni viśālāni gambhīrāṇi tantrāṇīha saṁkṣipyoddeśato vakṣyante* I

→

Kṛtyakalpataru.[5] These deal with Sāṁkhya principles. On the basis of these quotations we have argued that there was a

---

→ *tantra sāṁkhyānāmekā mūlaprakṛtiḥ । sapta prakṛtivikṛtayaḥ । pañca tanmātrāṇi । ṣoḍaśa vikāraḥ pañca pañcendriyāṇi । arthāśca । pañca bhūtaviśeṣaḥ । trayodaśa karaṇāni । trīṇyantaḥkaraṇāni । catasraścatasro mātṛjāḥ pitṛjāśca kośāḥ । pañca vāyuviśeṣaḥ । trayo guṇāḥ । trividho bandhāḥtrayo bandhanetavaḥ । dvau bandharāgau । trīṇi pramāṇāni । trividhaṁ duḥkham । caturvidhaḥ pratyayasargaḥ । tathā viprayayaḥ pañcavidhaḥ । aśaktiraṣṭāviṁśatividhā । siddhiraṣṭavidheti pratyayabhedāḥ pañcāśat ।*

astitvamekatvamathārthavattvaṁ parārthamanyatvamatho nivṛttiḥ ।
yogo viyogo bahavaḥ pumāṁsaḥ sthitiḥ śarīrasya ca śeṣavṛttiḥ ।।
iti daśamūlikārthāḥ ।

atha mūlaprakṛtiravyaktam । mahānahaṁkāraḥ pañca tanmātrāṇīti prakṛtivikṛtayaḥ । śabdatanmātraṁ sparśa(tan)mātraṁ rasatanmātraṁ rūpatanmātraṁ gandhatanmātramiti tanmātrāṇi । dvividhānindriyāṇi । bhūtaviśeṣāśca vikārāḥ । cakṣuḥśrotraghrāṇa-jihvātvaco buddhīndriyāṇi । rūpaśabdagandharasa-sparśāsteṣāmrthāḥ । vākpāṇipādapāyūpasthāḥ karmendriyāṇi । bhāṣaṇaṁ kriyā gamanamutsarga ānanda eṣāṁ karmāṇi । vāyvagnyabākāśapṛthivyo bhūtaviśeṣāḥ । daśendriyāṇi buddhyahaṁkāramanāṁsi ca karaṇāni । teṣu manobudhyahaṁkārā-ścāntaḥkaraṇāni । daśa bahiṣakaraṇānindriyāni ca । guṇasāmyalakṣaṇamavyaktaṁ pradhānaṁ prakṛtirvidhāna-mityanarthāntaram । adhyavasāyalakṣaṇo mahān buddhirmatirūpa-tabdhirityanarthāntaram । abhimānalakṣaṇo'haṁkāro'bhimāna ityanarthantāram ।

na pūrvapūrvikā prakṛtiḥ prakṛtermahānutpadyate । tato'haṁkāraḥ ahaṁkārāttanmātrāṇīndriyāṇi ca ।। tanmātrebhyo viśeṣā ityutpattikramaḥ । yo yasmādutpasyate sa tasmiṃilīyata iti vā'pyayakramaḥ ।।

5. *Kṛtyakalpataru*, Mokṣa, pp. 7, 8, 21, 49, 50, 59, 84, 100, 109, 124, 156, 168, 170, 173, 174, 181, 212 & 216.

Kṛtyakalpataru, Mokṣa, pp. 100-1

tatra sāṁkhyānamekā mūlaprakṛtiḥ । saptaprakṛtivikṛtayaḥ । mahadahaṁkārau, pañcatanmātrāṇi, ṣoḍaśa vikārāḥ । pañca pañcendriyāṇi । arthāśca pañcabhūtaviśeṣāśca । trayodaśa karaṇāni । teṣāṁ trīṇyantaḥkaraṇāni । daśa bahiḥkaraṇāni ।।

atha mūlaprakṛtiravyaktam । mahānahaṁkāraḥ pañca tanmātrāṇīti prakṛtivikṛtayaḥ । śabdatanmātraṁ, sparśatanmātram, rūpatanmātraṁ, rasatanmātraṁ । gandhatanmātramiti

→

Devaladharmasūtra.[6] S.C. Banerji[7] also includes Devala in his list of authors of Dharmasūtras. Kane[8] has also admitted that there was a *Devaladharmasūtra*.

Among the modern authorities on Sāṁkhya P. Chakravarti,[9] though mentioning Devala as a Sāṁkhya teacher on the basis of the Mokṣadharmaparva, does not take notice of the extracts from the *Devaladharmasūtra* dealing with Sāṁkhya. P.V. Kane, in his *History of Dharmaśāstra*,[10] reproduces the passage recorded by Aparārka. G.J. Larson and R.S. Bhattacharya,[11] in their recent most standard work on Sāṁkhya, have not included Devala in the list of Sāṁkhya teachers and have not taken any notice of the extracts from the *Devaladharmasūtra*. As against this, Sāṁkhya

---

→ *tanmātrāṇīti* | *dvividhāni indriyāni mano bhūtaviśeṣāśca vikārāḥ* || *cakṣuḥśrotraghrāṇajihvātvaco buddhīndriyāṇi* | *rūpaśabdagandharasasparśāsteṣāmarthāḥ* || *vākpāṇipādapāyūpasthāḥ karmendriyāṇi* | *bhāṣaṇaṁ kriyā gamanamutsargaḥ prītiriti karmendriyārthāḥ* | *vāyvagnyābākāśapṛthivyo bhūtaviśeṣāḥ* | *daśendriyāṇi buddhyahaṁkāramanāṁsi ca karanāṇi teṣāṁ manobuddhyahaṁkārāścāntaḥkaranāṇi* | *daśa bahiḥkaraṇāni indriyāṇi ca* || *guṇasāmyalakṣaṇamavyaktaṁ pradhānaṁ prakṛtiḥ vidhānamityanarthāntram* | *adhyavasāyalakṣaṇo mahān buddhirmatirūpalabdhirityanarthāntram* | *abhimānalakṣaṇo'haṁkāro vaikāriko'haṁkāriko'bhimān ityanarthāntaram* | *sattāmātralakṣaṇāni tanmātrāṇi* | *svānugrahalakṣaṇānīndriyāṇyakṣānīndriyāṇyucyante* | *saṁkalpalakṣaṇaṁ manaḥ* | *indriyārthalakṣaṇā viṣayaviśeṣa bhūtānīryanarthāntaramiti* | *sarvapūrvikā prakṛtiḥ* | *prakṛteḥ mahānutpadyate* | *mahato'haṁkāraḥ* | *ahaṁkārātanmātrāṇi indriyāni cat* | *tanmātrebhyo viśeṣā ityutpattikramaḥ* ||

6. "Was there a Devaladharmasūtra?" Baladeva Upadhyaya Felicitation Volume, *Journal of the Ganganatha Jha Kendriya Sanskrit Vidyapeeth*, Vol. XXXVI (1981), pp. 189-97. Also P.V. Kane, *History of Dharmaśāstra*, 2nd edn. Vol. I, part 1, pp. 283-4.
7. *Dharmasūtras*, pp. 53, 247-57.
8. *History of Dharmaśāstra*, Vol. I, 2nd edn., pp. 282-3; Vol. V, pp. 1353, 1380-1, 1431-2.
9. *Origin and Development of the Sāṁkhya System of Thought*, pp. 44, 127.
10. Vol. V, pp. 1380-81.
11. *Sāṁkhya*.

studies in Hindi have often referred to this account of Sāṁkhya. U.V. Shastri[12] took pains to record the passages as quoted by the Aparārka and Lakṣmīdhara. His lead has been followed among others, by A.P. Mishra,[13] Musalagaonkar,[14] and Usha Kushwaha.[15] But, none of these scholars has subjected the Sāṁkhya views expressed in the extracts to a critical analysis.

The *Devaladharmasūtra* has not been reconstructed through the available extracts.[16] U.V. Shastri[17] has collected many prose passages. Some prose passages are noted by S.C. Banerji.[18] An analysis of passages dealing with some specific topics shows the high value of this source.[19]

Philosophical Passages in the Devaladharmasūtra

The surviving passages show that the section in the *Devaladharmasūtra* which concerned Sāṁkhya began with a reference to *puruṣārthas* (goals of human life). It classifies *puruṣārthas* into two *abhyudaya* (prosperity) and *niḥśreyas* (highest bliss). The reference says that the earlier section of the text dealt with *abhyudaya*, whereas the present one aimed at covering *niḥśreyas*.

Niḥśreyas comprises of Sāṁkhya and Yoga. Sāṁkhya is the knowledge of twenty-five categories (*pañcaviṁśati-tattva-jñāna*). Yoga is the fixing of the mind on the desired goal after turning it away from objects of senses (*viṣayebhyas nivarttyā'bhipre*

---

12. *Sāṁkhyadarśana kā itihāsa*, pp. 600-5.
13. *Sāṁkhyadarśana kī aitihāsika paramparā*, p. 159.
14. *Sāṁkhyatattvakaumudī*, Introduction, p. 47.
15. *Sāṁkhyadarśana aur āyurveda*, p. 16.
16. Our reconstruction will be published separately.
17. *Op. cit.*, pp. 600-5.
18. *Op. cit.*, pp. 247-57.
19. Our article "Devala on Ariṣṭas" in *Indological Studies*, Prof. D.C. Sircar Commemoration Volume (ed. by S.K. Maity and U. Thakur), pp. 141-2; "Devaladharmasūtra on Aiśvarya", in *Śrī Dineśacandrikā: Studies in Indology* (D.C. Sircar Felicitation Volume), pp. 153-8; "Devaladharmasūtra on Varṇas and Jātis", in *Dr. R.N. Dandekar Felicitation Volume*, pp. 239-45.

manaso'vasthāpanam). *Apavarga* (absolution) is the fruit of both Sāṁkhya and Yoga. It means the total disappearance (*atyantā'-bhāva*) of the sufferings.[20]

The text says that on Sāṁkhya and Yoga there are extensive (*viśāla*) and profound (*gambhīra*) *tantras* composed earlier with the help of ratiocination (*ukti*) and tradition (*samaya*), and that they have been summarised (*saṁkṣipya*) and presented according to their subjects (*uddeśa*).[21]

The Sāṁkhya envisages one *mūla-prakṛti* (primeval matter) seven *prakṛti-vikṛtis* (modifications of *prakṛti*) *mahat* (the great one) and *ahaṁkāra* (ego),[22] five *tanmātras* (subtle elements), sixteen *vikāras* (products), five *indriyas* (organs) (of *jñāna*) and five (*indriyas* of *karma*), *arthas* (five objects of senses), five *bhūtaviśeṣas* (gross elements), thirteen *karaṇas* (instruments of action) of which three are internal (*antaḥkaraṇa*) and ten external (*bahiḥkaraṇa*) or the *indriyas*.[23]

The enumeration is continued further in the passage quoted by Aparārka. There are four *kośas* (vestures) each born of the father and the mother; five (*vāyu-viśeṣas*) (special winds), three *guṇas* (properties or constitutents), two types of *bandhas* (bondage), three *bandhahetus* (cause of bondage), the two *bandha* (bondage) and *rāga* (affection), three *pramāṇas* (sources of correct knowledge), three types of *duḥkha* (suffering). The passage further says that the *pratyaya-sarga* (intellectual creation) is of four types. *Viparyaya*

---

20. Lakṣmīdhara does not reproduce this introductory passage as prefacing the account of Sāṁkhya (*Kṛtya.*, Mokṣa, pp. 100-1) but quotes it later (*ibid.*, p. 165) in another context.

    Kṛtyakalpataru, Mokṣa, p. 165.

    devamanuṣyahoḥ dvividhaḥ puruṣārtho' bhyudayo niḥśreyasamiti I *tayorabhyudayaḥ pūrvoktaḥ dvividhaḥ niḥśreyasamiti sāṁkhyayogau. pañcaviṁśatitattvajñānam sāṁkhyaṁ* I *viṣayebhyo nivṛtyā'-bhiprete'rthe manaso'vasthāpanaṁ yogaḥ* I *ubhayatrāpa-vargaḥ phalam* I I

21. Lakṣmīdhara omits this passage.
22. Aparārka omits *mahadaṁkārau*.
23. Aparārka omits *daśa bahiḥkaraṇāni indriyaṇi ca*.

(wrong notion) is of five kinds. *Aśakti* (incapacity) is of twenty-eight kinds. *Tuṣṭi* (contentment) is of nine kinds. *Siddhi* (perfection) is of eight kinds. Thus, there are fifty divisions of *pratyaya*.

Existence (of *prakṛti*, *astitva*),[24] its singleness (*ekatvam*) (and) objectiveness (*arthvattvam*); subserviency (of *prakṛti* on *puruṣa*, *parārtham*), distinctiveness (of *puruṣa* from *prakṛti*, *anyatvam*), inactivity (*nivṛtti*),[25] conjuction (of *puruṣa* and *prakṛti*, *yoga*), disjunction (of *puruṣa* from *prakṛti*, *viyoga*), plurality of *puruṣa* (*bahavaḥ pumāṁsaḥ*)[26] and the existence of body along with the unmanifest nature of *prakṛti* (*sthitiḥ śarīrasya ca śeṣavṛttiḥ*).[27] These are the ten *mūlikārthas* (radical categories).

In the following passage we find an explanation and elaboration of the categories mentioned above. Thus, *mūla-prakṛti* is described as *avyakta*. *Mahat*, *ahaṁkāra* and five *tanmātras* are referred to as the *prakṛti-vikṛtis*. The *tanmātras* are those of *śabda* (sound), *sparśa* (touch), *rasa* (taste), *rūpa* (form) and *gandha* (smell). The *indriyas* are of two types. The *bhūta-viśeṣas* are the *vikāras* (products). Eyes, ears, nose, tongue and skin are *buddhīndriyas* (the sense-organs). *Rūpa*, *śabda*, *gandha*, *rasa* and *sparśa* are their *arthas* (objects). *Vāk* (speech, here signifying mouth), *pāṇi* (hands), *pāda* (feet), *pāyu* (anus) and *upastha* (organ of generation) are the *karmendriyas* (organs of action). *Bhāṣaṇa* (speaking), *kriyā* (doing), *gamana* (going), *utsarga* (excretion) and *ānanda* (joy, here coitus) are their *karmas* (actions). *Vāyu* (air), *agni*, (fire), *āp* (water) *ākāśa* (ether) and *pṛthivī* (earth) are the *bhūta-viśeṣas*. The ten *indriyas*, *buddhi* (intellect), *ahaṁkāra* (ego) and *manas* (mind) and the *karaṇas*. Of these *manas*, *buddhi* and *ahaṁkāra* are the *antaḥkaraṇas*. The ten *bahiṣkaraṇas* are the *indriyas*.

The passage goes on to explain the categories in terms of their *lakṣaṇa* (characteristics) and *arthāntara* (synonyms). The *avyakta* is

24. *Rājavārtika* as quoted in the *Sāṁkhyatattvakaumudī* of Vācaspati (on *Sāṁkhyakārikā* 72) mentions it as *pradhānāstitvam*.
25. *Rājavartika* mentions it as *akartṛtvam*.
26. *Rājavartika* has *anaikyam*.
27. *Rājavartika* has only *śeṣavṛttiḥ* which is not properly explained. Possibly it refers to the unmanifest form of *prakṛti*.

characterised by the equilibrium of *guṇas* (*guṇasāmya*), and *pradhāna*, *prakṛti* and *vidhāna* are the synonyms. *Mahat* is characterised by *adhyavasāya* (ascertainment) its synonyms are *buddhi*, *mati* and *upalabdhi*. *Ahaṁkāra* is characterised by *abhimāna* (self-conceit), *vaikārika*, *ahaṁkāra* and *abhimān* are the synonyms.

The text goes on to explain the other categories in a similar manner. Aparārka has omitted this passage, but Lakṣmīdhara records a part of it. The *tanmātras* are characterised by mere existence (*sattā-mātra*). The *indriyas* are characterised by acceptance of their objects (*svānugraha*). The eyes (*akṣa*) are said to be *indriyas*. The *manas* is characterised by volition (*saṁkalpa*). The *viṣaya-viśeṣas* are characterised as the objects of the *indriyas* (*indriyārtha*); they are synonymous with *bhūtas* (elements).

The next passage deals with the process of evolution and dissolution. For evolution the term used is *utpatti*. The passage in Aparārka says that there is no preceding category before *prakṛti* (*na pūrvapūrikā prakṛtiḥ*). The passage as recorded by Lakṣmīdhara says that *prakṛti* precedes all the categories (*sarvapūrvikā*). From *prakṛti* is evolved *mahat*. From the later is evolved *ahaṁkāra*. From *ahaṁkāra* are evolved the *tanmātras* and the *indriyas*. From the *tanmātras* are evolved the *viśeṣas*. The passage dealing with the process of dissolution (*apyaya-krama*) is found only in Aparārka. It says that a category is dissolved into the category from which it evolves.

The passage quoted by Aparārka ends here. The parallel passage in the *Kṛtyakalpataru* also does not go beyond this. But, the *Kṛtyakalpataru* records some other passages in other contexts which can be connected with the main passage as they elaborate and explain the points in it. Thus, one passage[28] deals with the three

28. *Kṛtyakalpataru*, Mokṣa, p. 124.
prakṛtibandho vaikārikabandho dakṣiṇābandha iti bandhatrayī I *tatrā'vyaktādibhiraṣṭābhirbandhaḥ (prakṛtibandhaḥ)* I *indriya-irindriyārtheṣu bandho vaikārikabandhaḥ* I *iṣṭāpūrttādibhirbandho dakṣiṇābandhaḥ* I *tatra prakṛtiṣu bandho devatānāṁ dakṣinā-bhirāśramiṇāṁ vaikārairaneṣāṁ dharmo' jñānāṇi ca bandhahetavaḥ* II

bandhas and the *bandhahetus*. The *vaikārika bandha* is caused by the *indriyas* in their objects. The *bandha* caused by *iṣṭāpūrtta* (sacrifices, digging wells, etc., and other acts of charity) and others is called the *dakṣiṇābandha*. The *bandha* in the *prakṛtis* characterises the gods (*devatānām*), that caused by *dakṣiṇas* characterises the people of the four *āśramas* (*āśramiṇām*) and that caused by *vaikāras* the other beings. The ignorances (*ajñānāni*) are the cause of *bandha*.

The *Devaladharmasūtra* gave much coverage to the topic of the defects of thought of action which are sinful and result in the bondage of man. The emphasis on metaphysical topics has tended to reduce the importance of these portions. In the *Devaladharma-sūtra* there was an exhaustive account of demerits caused by sin (*pāpa-doṣa*). They arise out of mind, speech and body (*manovākya-śarīraja*). The text lists the various types of *pāpa-doṣas* arising out of the three sources. U.V. Shastri[29] has not reproduced all the relevant passages. He gives only the introductory passage up to the listing of twelve types of *pāpa-doṣas* arising out of mind.

Another passage in the text dealt with the subject of *kaṣāya* (passion).[30] *Rāga* (affection) *dveṣa* (abhorrence) and *moha* (attachment) are called *kaṣāyas*. They can be eradicated (*apakarṣaṇa*) through five types of *tapas* (austerities) characterised by *yama* and *niyama* and also through the knowledge of the categories (*tattva-jñāna*). This is the burning of *kaṣāyas* (*kaṣāya-pacana*).

The text discussed separately the subject of final goal or emancipation. The full details of the account are not available, but one can form an idea of its nature from the surviving two passages.

---

29. *Op. cit.*, p. 603. *Kṛtyakalpataru*, Mokṣa, p. 84.
athātaḥ pāpadoṣān manovākyaśarīrajān vyākhyāsyāmaḥ | *tatra moharāgadveṣamānalobhamadaśokamamatvā'haṁkārabhaya-harṣamoghavittāmoghacintāśceti dvādaśa mānasāḥ* ||

30. *Kṛtyakalpataru*, Mokṣa, p. 168.
rāgadveṣamohāḥ kaṣāyā ucyante | *teṣām yamaniyamalakṣaṇena tapasā pañcavidhena tattvajñānena cāpakarṣaṇam* |*kaṣāyapācanam* ||

One passage says that *prayojanas* (purpose or objective) are of four types: *sāyujya* (identical unity) *sālokya* (residing in the same heaven), *prakṛtiaya* (merging in the *prakṛti*) and *mokṣa* (liberation). It defines *sāyujya* as being through the acquisition of supernatural powers (*aiśvaryāvāpatiyuktyā*) *ekajalpa*[31] with Hiraṇyagarbha, Nārāyaṇa, Śiva, Mahendra, Soma, Sūrya, Skanda, Jyeṣṭhā, Umā, Devī and other divinities.[32] In the extant passages there is no explanation of the other *prayojanas*.

Another quotation purports to describe the condition of a liberated person according to sāṁkhya (*iti sāṁkhyam*).[33] The special term for such a person does not occur in it. Obstracted from the world (*nivṛtta*), being without *guṇas* (*nirguṇa*), with his *bandhas* broken (*chinna-bandha*), released from the suffering of birth, old age and death, is as if asleep (*suptavat*), intoxicated (*mattavat*), or having inhaled the smoke of poison (*viṣadhūmapānavat*) such a person devoid of *sattva* and other *guṇas* (*sattvādihīna*) and based in the *tanmātras* (*tanmātrāvasthita*), achieves the final (*ekāntika*) highest bliss (*parama-sukha*).

Devala classifies *śarīra* (body) into three: *devatā* (god), *mānuṣa* (man) and *tiryak* (animal).[34] He lists in detail the characteristic features, qualities and defects, o the three. The classification is of

---

31. U.V. Shastri is not sure of the expression. We wonder if it is intended to mean 'getting the same name'. Other possible reading can be *ekakalpa*, *ekatalpa*, but they do not adequately cover the expression *sāyujya*.
32. *Kṛtyakalkpataru*, Mokṣa, p. 8 —
sāyujyam sālokyaṁ prakṛtilayo mokṣaśceti caturvidhaṁ prayojanam. teṣāmaiśvaryāvāptiyuktyā hiraṇyagarbhanāyaṇaśivamahendra-somasūryaskandajyeṣṭhomādevīprabhṛtīnāṁ devatānāmai-kajalpaṁ(?)sāyjyam ||
33. *Kṛtyakalpataru*, Mokṣa, p. 7 —
sa tathā nivṛtto nirguṇaśchinnabandho janmajarāmaraṇa-duḥkhavinirmuktaḥ suptavat mattavat viṣadhūmapānavat sattvādihīnaḥ tanmātrāvasthitaḥ paramasukhamaikāntika-madhigacchatīti sāṁkhyam ||
34. *Kṛtyakalpataru*, Mokṣa, p. 109.

central importance, because the account of *puruṣārthas* and the following exposition of Sāṁkhya and Yoga are based on it.

Aparārka does not record the passages dealing with Yoga. They are found in the *Kṛtyakalpataru*. There is no consolidated account of the principles of Yoga parallel to that of Sāṁkhya. The surviving passages indicate that this section was comparatively longer and more detailed. The style in the two cases has similarities, with differences on account of the nature of the topics covered.

Before taking up an analysis of passages dealing with Yoga, we may refer to some others which relate to allied topics, but do not come strictly under Yoga. One passage[35] lists some noble qualities and conduct, without referring to the context. Another passage deals with the rules relating to a *parivrājaka*.[36] A third passage deals with the duties and rules for a *yati*.[37] A fourth passage describes in details the conduct to be followed when the *yati* goes for *bhikṣā* (begging).[38] Evidently these passages were connected with the section of the *dharmasūtra* which described the rules concerning the *āśramas*. In this case the third and the fourth designated here as *parivrājaka* and *yati*, in place of *vānaprastha* and *saṁnyāsa* respectively.

The passages expounding principles of Yoga have not been recorded. We have disjointed passages describing *prāṇāyāma*, *pratyāhāra, dhāraṇā* and *dhyāna*.

Prāṇāyama is said to be of three types *kumbha*, *recana* and *pūraṇa*. The passage goes on to explain *udvāta*, *prāṇa*, *apāna*, *vyāna*, *udāna* and *samāna*.[39]

Two passages define *pratyāhāra* and *dhāraṇā*.[40] The fourth passage is a long one and covers all the important aspects of *dhyāna*.[41]

---

35. *Kṛtyakalpataru*, Mokṣa, p. 21.
36. *Ibid.*, p. 49.
37. *Ibid.*, p. 50.
38. *Ibid.*, p. 59.
39. *Ibid.*, Mokṣa, p. 170.
40. *Ibid.*, pp. 173, 174.
41. *Ibid.*, p. 181.

A passage lists ten *upasargas* (hindrances or trouble) for a *yogin*.[42]

We have a long passage on the eight properties (*guṇas*) of *aiśvarya* (high spiritual powers).[43] In Yoga they are well-known as *siddhis*. The eight *aiśvaryas* are listed as *aṇimā* (becoming small as an atom), *mahimā* (increasing size at will), *laghimā* (assuming lightness at will) *prāpti* (obtaining anything) *prākāmya* (irresistible will) *īśitva* (superiority), *vaśitva* (controlling one's self) and *yatrakāmāvasāyitva* (entering a place according to will). There are broadly classified into two: the first three relating to the body (*śārīra*) and the remaining five to the organs (*aindriya*). The nature of the eight powers is explained in the same style in which the terms in the Sāṁkhya passages are treated. *Yatrakāmāvasāyitva* is said to be of three types: *chāyāveśa* (entering the shadow), *avadhyānāveśa* (entering the mind of a distant person) and *aṅgapraveśa* (entering the body) which also are duly explained. The passage refers to entering into a material object (*mūrtta-dravya*) by the power of *yatrakāmāvasāyitva* to be possible through a very high *aiśvarya*. The concluding sentence says that having obtained these *aiśvarya* properties a person having eradicated sin (*uddhṛtakalmaṣa*), having destroyed doubt (*chinna-saṁśaya*), having himself perceived the truth (*pratyakṣadarśī*), knowing the all-including *dharma* (*dharmapravarajña*) and knowing that all this rooted in falsehood (*kūṭastha sarvamidam*, is non-existent (*asat*) and not lasting (*anitya*), by himself obtains peace (*śānti*). This is known as the obtaining of *aiśvarya* (*aiśvaryāvyāpti sic. — āvāpti*).

Features of Devala's Exposition

We have discussed[44] the contributions of Devala, in his *Dharmasūtra*, in systematising Sāṁkhya and introducing an element of standardisation.

Devala has a very distinctive style. He first gives a summarised

42. *Kṛtyakalpataru*, Mokṣa, p. 212.
43 *Ibid.*, p. 216.
44. See *infra* chapter 19.

account of the Sāṁkhya principles. He, then explains the categories eleborating them by listing their components. Where necessary he adds further details. Thus he first mentions *mahat*, *ahaṁkāra* and the five *tanmātras* as the *prakṛti-vikṛtis*. Then he enumerates the five *tanmātras*. The most distinctive nature is demarcated and described.

Sāṁkhya is defined as the knowledge of the twenty-five categories. But the categories are not listed in a compact form. It can, however, be seen that they include *prakṛti*, seven *prakṛti-vikṛtis* and sixteen *vikāras*. *Puruṣa* is implied as the twenty-fifth *tattva*, but has not been mentioned in the surviving extracts. Likewise, in the case of the sixteen *vikāras* the two types of *indriyas* and the five *arthas* or *bhūta-viśeṣas* are mentioned, but not the *manas*. This is only accidental, because later in connection with the *karaṇas*, *manas* is included in the three *antaḥkaraṇas*. Later *manas* is explained separately as characterised by *saṁkalpa*.

Devala has given two separate expositions of Sāṁkhya. The first is in the form of twenty-five categories. In the second he mentions fifty *pratyayas*, classified into four *pratyaya-sargas*, five *viparyayas*, twenty-eight *aśaktis*, nine *tuṣṭis* and eight *siddhis*. Immediately following this is a verse enumerating ten *mūlikārthas*. Thus, in the second case we find a reference to sixty (fifty+ten) principles. Devala gives primary to the exposition of twnety-five categories, but retains the earlier tradition of sixty principles (*ṣaṣṭhitantra*). He makes a departure from the earlier tradition inasmuch as he enumerates the sixty principles, but does not label them as such. Īśvarakṛṣṇa also expounds Sāṁkhya through twenty-five categories and describes the fifty *pratyaya-sargas*. But, he omits the ten *mūlikārthas* altogether, and, thus, even though proclaiming his faith fulness to the *ṣaṣṭhitantra*, deviates from it in a marked manner.

Devala represents an intermediate stage between the early tradition of *ṣaṣṭhitantra* and the later standardisation introduced by Īśvarakṛṣṇa. The *ṣaṣṭhitantra* included ten *mūlikārthas* and fifty *pratyaya-sargas*. Later, Sāṁkhya came to be described in terms of the categories, whose number was standardised as twenty-five. Devala accepted the definition of Sāṁkhya as expounding the twenty-five categories. He retained the earlier tradition of *ṣaṣṭhitantra* also. He chose to emphasise the central position of twenty-five categories and diluted the importance of the *ṣaṣṭhitantras* by not designating the sixty principles as *ṣaṣṭhitantra* even while enumerating them. Īśvarakṛṣṇa will be placed much later in the sequence of development. Though repeating his avowed allegiance to the *ṣaṣṭhitantra* principles, he does not follow its system of enumeration. He deviates from it and adopts the system of twenty-five categories. It is a truncated *ṣaṣṭhitantra* which Īśvarakṛṣṇa retains. He expounds the *prartyaya-sargas*, but omits altogether the vital account of ten *mūlikārthas*.

In his account of Sāṁkhya Devala mentions some details which generally are not duly emphasised. Thus, he refers to *kośas*, four created by the mother (*mātṛja*) and four by the father (*pitṛja*). He also mentions five types of special winds (*vāyu-viśeṣa*). In both the cases the cryptic passages are not followed by a detailed exposition of their constituent elements.

Devala assigns an important position to the evolution and dissolution of the categories. For those the technical terms used are *utpatti-krama* and *apyaya-krama*. According to him, *mahat*, the *tanmātras* and the *indriyas* evolve from *ahaṁkāra*. The *viśeṣas* (elements) evolve from the *tanmātras*. The reversal of the process is dissolution, in which a category dissolves into the one from which it evolves.

Here there is no specific reference to the evolution of *manas* from *ahaṁkāra*, but it seems to be included in the *indriyas*. Devala envisages two separate lines of evolution from *ahaṁkāra*, one, the *indriyas* (including the *manas*) and the second of the *tanmātras*. The sequence of evolution leads to the emergence of gross elements (*bhūta-viśeąsas*) from the subtle elements (*tanmātras*).

According to Īśvarakṛṣṇa, the original formulation of Sāṁkhya principles by Kapila considered the question of creation, sustenance and dissolution of the world.[45] The accounts of Sāṁkhya principles

45. *Sāṁkhyakārikā*, 69.

associated with some early teachers in the Mokṣadharmaparva also contain passages dealing with this topic, in which is entwined the process of the emergence of *tattvas*. The replacement of the description of the creation and dissolution of the world by an account of the evolution of categories from *prakṛti* appears to be a feature of Sāṁkhya in a later period when it was identified with tweny-five *tattvas*. In Devala we have only the treatment of the philosophical problem of evolution of categories, without any reference to the process of creation of world.

U.V. Shastri[46] points out that in the *Devaladharmasūtra* passage, as quoted in the Aparārka, there are four *sūtras* which are idential with *sūtras* in the *Tattvasamāsasūtra*[47] and three others are identically similar.[48] Three other *sūtras* can also be traced[49] in the *Tattvasamāsasūtra* with the difference that the order of words is reversed. Shastri adds that in the case of the third category of three *sūtras* the *Sāṁkhyaṣaḍādhyāyī* (=*Sāṁkhyapravacanasūtra*)[50] has expressions which are identical with those in the *Devaladharma-sūtra*. He adds that the *Sāṁkhyaṣaḍādhyāyī* has four other *sūtras*[51] which have close parallels in the *Devaladharmasūtra*.

On the basis of this, analysis Shastri argues for the authenticity and early date of the two texts, *Sāṁkhyaṣaḍādhyāyī* and the *Tattvasamāsasūtra*. According to him, the *Sāṁkhyaṣaḍādhyāyī* was the main text, whereas the *Tattvasamāsasūtra* was in the form of a list of the contents of the former. He argues for the *Devaladharmasūtra* being indebted to the *Sāṁkhyaṣaḍādhyāyī*. A.P. Mishra[52] suggests that if Devala did not derive his *sūtras* from these texts, he was indebted to some early text in the form of an exposition based on these texts which was attempted by Pañcaśikha

46. *Op. cit.*, pp. 263-4.
47. Sūtras, 2, 16, 19, 22.
48. *Ibid.*, p. 4, 10, 21.
49. *Ibid.*
50. III.38-40.
51. I.61; II.13, 16, 38; III.37.
52. *Op. cit.*, pp. 159-60

or some other author. H.D. Sharma[53] objects that the suggestion of Devala being indebted to the *Sāṁkhyasūtra* texts is based on the assumption that the latter were earlier in date; but this has to be proved and not assumed. Those, who consider the *Sāṁkhya-pravacanasūtra* and the *Tattvasamāsasūtra* to be later texts, suggest that Devala possibly drew from some other text which is presently lost. Shastri holds that two *sūtra* texts of Sāṁkhya were ancient texts, though they were touched in later times. Devala himself admits that he borrowed from earlier texts. Shastri says that instead of imagining an unknown text one should admit the obvious that Devala borrowed from the *Sāṁkhyasūtras*. He advances evidence for an early date for Devala to suggest an even earlier date for the two Sāṁkhya texts.

For the present we will not enter into a discussion about the date of the two Sāṁkhya texts. What is significant is the use of *sūtras* by Devala. In many branches of Sanskrit learning the early formulations were often as *sūtras*. U.V. Shastri[54] collects evidence referring to some early presentations of Sāṁkhya principles in the *sūtra* form: Vidyāraṇya's commentary on the *Sūtasaṁhitā*, Vardhamāna's commentary on Udayana's *Nyāyakusumāñjali*, Vācaspatimiśra's commentary *Sāṁkhyatattvakaumudī*, *Gopālatāpinī Upaniṣad*, *Garbhopaniṣad* and Gauḍapāda's commentary on *Sāṁkhyasaptati*. This is clearly brought out by many quotations recorded in the *Yuktidīpikā*. The Sāṁkhya view presented in the *Suśruta-saṁhitā* follows the *sūtra* style. Siddharṣi in his *Upamitibhavaprapañca-kathā*[55] (dated AD 904) presents Sāṁkhya principles in *sūtras*. The *Bhagavadajjukīya*, which is referred to in the Mamandoor inscription of the Pallava King Mahendravikramavarman (AD 650) expounds Sāṁkhya principles in *sūtras*.[56] Thus, the *sūtras* characteristic of in which Devala's exposition of Sāṁkhya point to its early date in Sāṁkhya history.

---

53. *Sāṅkhyatattvakaumudī*, Introduction, p. 23.
54. *Op. cit.*, pp. 230-68.
55. P. 666-7.
56. T.R. Chintamani in *Journal of Oriental Research*, April 1928.

Devaladharmasūtra in the History of Sāṁkhya

An analysis of the passages of the *Devaladharmasūtra* shows parallelism with the *Sāṁkhyakārikā* both in the topics covered and the details of the views, which does not leave any doubt about the exposition being genuine Sāṁkhya, and confirms the testimony of Śaṅkarācārya. This emphasises the need for giving due importance to the Devala evidence for reconstructing the nature of Sāṁkhya and its historical development. The proper evaluation of Sāṁkhya in historical perspective is seriously handicaped by the fact that we have only one ancient Sāṁkhya text, the *Sāṁkhyakārikā*. The other two available Sāṁkhya texts, the *Tattvasamāsasūtra* and the *Sāṁkhyapravacanasūtra*, have a suspect value as compositions of an early period. We do have stray quotations of the views of some Sāṁkhya teachers. The accounts of Sāṁkhya principles in the *Caraka-saṁhitā*, *Buddhacarita* and the Mokṣadharmaparva section in the *Mahābhārata* have their own limitations as sources for the history of Sāṁkhya, because, though containing views of earlier Sāṁkhya teachers, they are presented by others in a later period. The *Devaladharmasūtra* has the advantage of being the original formulation of its own author. Moreover, though the complete text is not available, the surviving passages provide an idea of its main features. Here we do not have a mere collection of stray sentences but a compact account of the important aspects of the system in a summarised form, and the detailed treatment of some points seems to have dropped out.

This source will serve as a corrective to several views expressed by modern scholars to cover the gaps in the history of Sāṁkhya caused by paucity of relevant evidence. Thus Johnston has attempted a history in terms of the emergence and development of terms and principles. But, there is a need to associate these ideas with their expounders. In this context the testimony of Devala is of great significance, because now we know of a definite stage when Devala codified in a summarised form the Sāṁkhya principles expounded in earlier texts. Some modern scholars have attributed certain principles to individual Sāṁkhya teachers. In some cases they have taken recourse to imagination for crediting Pañcaśikha, Āsuri,

Vārṣagaṇya or Īśvarakṛṣṇa for their authorship. If a principle ascribed to a teacher of a date later than Devala occurs in the *Devaladharmasūtra*, then the attribution cannot valid. A suggestion, associating a principle with an earlier teacher, receives support from its occurrence in the Devala extracts.

Date of the Devaladharmasūtra

The date of the *Devaladharmasūtra* has not been fixed. P.V. Kane is silent about it.[57] Musalagaonkar[58] places it in the third century of the Vikrama era. He bases his view on partial evidence. It is to be noted that there are several Dharmaśāstra texts associated with the name of Devala. Besides the well-known *Devalasmṛti* in ninety verses, which was composed in the eighth century, there were, according to Kane, two ancient texts, a *Devalasmṛti* and a *Devaladharmasūtra*, which are now lost and are known only through quotations in later commentries and digests. When Kane published the first edition of the first volume of his *History of Dharmasāstra*, he did not recognise the separate existence of a *Devaladharmasūtra*. At that time the date which he proposed for Devala applied to Devala, the author of the Smṛti. This date has been applied by Musalagaonkar to Devala, the author of the *Dharmasūtra*, also. The date of the *Devaladharmasūtra* has to be discussed independently and separately.

Devala was an ancient sage. The Buddhist tradition mentions him as being elder to the Buddha, but it does not refer to his views and contributions which may lead to his identification as the author of a Dharmasūtra. The Jain text *Isibhāsiyāim* devotes a section to the views of Asita-Devala.[59] In this text Asita-Devala is recognised as one of the ancient sages, all of whom did not necessarily belong to the Jain tradition. The account in the text could have been a modified presentation of the views of Devala. But, we cannot be sure about it actually occurring in the *Devaladharmasūtra*. In the

---

57. *History of Dharmaśāstra*, 2nd edn., Vol. I, part I, pp. 282-3.
58. *Sāṁkhyatattvakaumudī*, Introduction p. 47.
59. See Appendix, II.

Mokṣadharmaparva section in the Śāntiparva of the *Mahābhārata* Devala appears as an ancient Sāṁkhya teacher who was a pupil of Jaigīṣavya, who, in his turn, was a disciple of Pañcaśikha. His views are presented in one chapter. We recognise Sāṁkhya views of Devala represented in the format of the Mokṣadharmaparva, but it will be difficult to accept them as being faithful to the exposition in the *Devaladharmasūtra*.[60]

The evidence discussed above helps us in indicating a rough upper limit for Devala, the Sāṁkhya teacher. But, it cannot suggest the date of the *Devaladharmasūtra*.

The date of this text is to be fixed on its own. The quotations from it occurring in the Aparārka and the *Kṛtyakalpataru* provide a lower limit. This may be pushed considerably by the reference to its Sāṁkhya expositions by Śaṅkarācārya. Śaṅkara implies that it was an early text, which was little known and little consulted as a source for Sāṁkhya system. This will place the *Devaladharmasūtra* long before Śaṅkara and certainly earlier than the commonly known writings on Sāṁkhya. We cannot ascertain all these texts referred to by Śaṅkara. Possibly he had in his mind the *Sāṁkhyakārikā* and the commentaries on it and the Mokṣadharmaparva section in the Śāntiparva. This provides an argument to push back the lower limit.

The very fact that the text is a Dharmasūtra narrows down the time-bracket for it. There is no traditional list of Dharmasūtras. It is, however, recognised that, besides the available Dharmasūtras, there were quite a few others. The known Dharmasūtras are generally placed in the time-bracket of 500 BC to AD 200, which may hold good for the text under consideration.

This is not a place for a lengthy discussion on the dating of the Dharmasūtras. The upper limit of 500 BC is generally suggested on the assumption that the Dharmasūtras belong to the post-Buddha phase of history. The argument is that, to contain the overflow of asceticism released by Buddhism, the theory of four *āśrama*s was

---

60. See *supra* chapter 11.

formulated, accomodating *saṁnyāsa* as the fourth *āśrama*. It is said that this task was accomplished by the Dharmasūtras. But the thesis of a post-Buddha origin of the *āśrama* system is presumptuous. The system had its origin in the period of the later Vedic texts. It does not seem to have acquired a fixed form even in the Dharmasūtras. There are variations in the nomenclature of the *āśrama*s and the order of their enumeration. Hence the upper limit is not so sacrosant as it is taken to be and may require adjustments.

There is no accpeted definition of Dharmasūtra in terms of its nature, scope and contents. An analysis of the available Dharmasūtra works shows that, besides trating topics, which are covered by Smṛti texts, they covered the subject of *mokṣa*. On account of this approach the Dharmasūtras are found dealing with topics relating to Sāṁkhya and Yoga. In course of time the coverage of Sāṁkhya-Yoga seems to have gradually decreased. The extent to which the Mokṣa-kāṇḍa section of a Dharmasūtra covers various topics indicates its position in the chronological order of the Dharmasūtras. In this respect the *Devaladharmasūtra* is distinctive in giving the widest coverage to Sāṁkhya and Yoga. From the available extracts it is clear that there were two main divisions or books in this text. One dealt with the *puruṣārtha* of *abhyudaya* and related to Smṛti topics. The other concerned *niḥśreyas*, of which *apavarga* was objective. Sāṁkhya and Yoga both lead to *apavarga*. The text goes on to cover exhaustively topics relating to Sāṁkha and Yoga. Other Dharmasūtras dealt with only a few topics, mostly relating to Yoga. This would suggest that the *Devaladharmasūtra* was among the earliest Dharmasūtras.

Some of the Dharmasūtras are associated with specific Vedic *śākhā*s. But this affiliation is not known for other Dharmasūtras. The *Devaladharmasūtra* is not claimed by any Vedic *śākhā*. This was possibly a reason for the text not being preserved in its fullness by the tradition. Among the Kalpasūtras the Dharmasūtras, as compared with the Śrautasūtras and the Gṛhyasūtras, do not seem to have always emerged in the association of particular *śākhā*s, but were possibly adopted subsequently by them. Here also the earlier Dharmasūtra texts differed from the later ones. The detailed exposition of Sāṁkhya by the *Devaladharmasūtra* may have stood in the way of its adoption by a Vedic *śākhā*. Though this is not a very definitive argument, it favours an early position for the *Devaladharmasūtra* in the list of the Dharmasūtras.

The internal evidence of the text does not provide clues for fixing its date. It does not mention any specific author, text or historical person. It does, however, refer to earlier *tantra*s on Sāṁkhya and Yoga, extensive and profound, which were summarised by the author to present his account. This implies the presence of a rich Sāṁkhya literature, some of which were designated as Tantra. The Mokṣadharmaparva mentions the views of a number of Sāṁkhya philosophers, but their original writings have not survived. In the earlier times there was a text, generally named as *Ṣaṣṭhitantra*. The text and its author cannot be identified. Pañcaśikha is credited with expanding the Sāṁkhya system. Some scholars believe that he was the author of the *Ṣaṣṭhitantra*. Some texts are circulated under the name of Kapila, but the ascription is not certain. The claims of *Sāṁkhyapravacanasūtra* and *Tattvasamāsasūtra* as early Sāṁkhya texts are suspect. The avowed assertion of its author ill, inany case, place the *Devaladharmasūtra* after the *Ṣaṣṭhitantra* phase of Sāṁkhya.

There are two indications for an early date of this text. First, it is in the *sūtra* style, which brackets it with references to some early formulations of Sāṁkhya in the form of *sūtras*.[61] Second, the text belongs to the phase of Sāṁkhya history, when its exposition in terms of sixty principles had come to be replaced by its identification with twenty-five categories.[62] The way the author retains an account of the earlier presentation of Sāṁkhya principles shows that not much time had elapsed after the formulation of the twenty-five categories and it had not completely ousted the earlier system. The author refers to sixty principles, fifty *pratyaya-sarga*s and ten *mūlikārtha*s, without combining them to form a single unit of sixty. The later Sāṁkhya tradition retained fifty *pratyaya-sarga*s out of

61. See *supra* under section "Features of Devala's Exposition".

62. See *supra*, under section "Features of Devala's Exposition".

the sixty. The *Sāṁkhyakārikā* discusses them elaborately. But the ten *mūlikārthas* are omitted in standard accounts of Sāṁkhya.[63] A verse attributed to *saṁgrahakāra* by Śaṅkara, the author of the *Jayamaṅgalā* commentary on the *Sāṁkhyakārikā*, enumerates them.[64] Devala has a direct and clear knowledge of the *mūlikārthas*. He was not far removed from the times when the concept of the *mūlikārthas* was a common knowledge.

We have noted that Jain and Buddhist traditions remember Devala as an ancient sage. The Mokṣadharmaparva has a more pointed knowledge of Devala as a Sāṁkhya teacher. We have made a comparative study of the Sāṁkhya principles in the Devala chapter in the Mokṣadharmaparva and the *Devaladharmasūtra*. The author of the Devala chapter had a knowledge of the Sāṁkhya views of Devala, but we cannot prove that he based his presentation on the account in the Dharmasūtra.[65] From the Mokṣadharmaparva we know that Devala was a pupil of Jaigīṣavya, who in his turn learnt Sāṁkhya from Pañcaśikha. We have argued for *c*. 650 BC as the date of Jaigīṣavya.[66]

Thus we can infer that Devala may be placed around 600 BC and the composition of the Dharmasūtra associated with his name may be dated around 550-500 BC.

---

63. See our article "The Mūlikārthas in Sāṁkhya", *Indian Historical Review*, Vol. pp.
64. See *supra* chapter 19.
65. See *supra* chapter 11.
66. See *supra* chapter 9.

13

Sāṁkhya and the Hārītadharmasūtra

Hārīta as a Sāṁkhya Teacher

THE name of Hārīta as a Sāṁkhya teacher is known from the *Yuktidīpikā*[1] and *Māṭharavṛtti*,[2] two commentaries on the *Sāṁkhyakārikā*. He is not mentioned in any other source, nor are his views referred to or his treatise quoted in them.

The list of Sāṁkhya teachers in the *Yuktidīpikā* begins with the name of Hārīta.[3] The position of Hārīta in this list cannot be suggestive of his chronological position. Opposed to this is the evidence of the *Māṭharavṛtti*, places Hārīta as the third in its list of four Sāṁkhya teachers between Pañcaśikha and Īśvarakṛṣṇa.

Hārīta as a Smṛti Writer

Hārītā is known as a Smṛti writer. He have two sets each of *Vṛddha-Hārīta-smṛti* and *Laghu-Hārīta-smṛti* included in the two collections of Smṛtis published by Jivananda and Anandasrama. The *Laghu-Hārīta-smṛti* of the Anandasrama collection is a small text of 117 verses on topics falling within the recognised scope of a Smṛti. The *Laghu-Hārīta-smṛti* in the Jivananda collection[4] has about 250

---

1. P. 175.
2. On *kārikā*, 71.
3. As pointed out by the editor, the lacuna before the name in the manuscript suggests that the list had another name before Hārīta.
4. Vol. I, pp. 177-93.

verses grouped in seven chapters. Besides the duties of the four *varṇas* and *āśramas*, it deals with Yoga also.

The *Vṛddha-Hārīta-smṛti* in the two collections is the same, with a very minor difference in chapterisation. This Smṛti contains about 2600 verses. The Jivananda collection[5] arranges the verses into eight chapters. The Anandasrama collection breaks the first two chapters of Jivananda collection into five chapters and, thus, has a total of eleven chapters. The *Vṛddha-Hārīta-smṛti* deals with the *nitya* and *naimittika* rites of the *varṇas* and *āśramas* and also such philosophical subjects as the nature of the individual self, the Supreme self, and the means of attaining *mokṣa*.

P.V. Kane[6] regards *Vṛddha-Hārīta-smṛti*, a professedly Vaiṣṇavite text, to be a comparatively late work. The *Laghu-Hārīta-smṛti* of the Anandasrama collection contains some verses which are ascribed to Hārīta in Aparārka and the *Smṛticandrikā*. Kane[7] suggests that several Smṛti texts were compiled and ascribed to Hārīta, 'probably because they were based more or less on the *Hārītadharmasūtra*'.

Evidently, when the *Yuktidīpikā* and the *Māṭharavṛtti* included Hārīta in their lists of Sāṁkhya teachers, they did not have in their mind any of these *Hārītasmṛti* texts. On the contrary, when the *Laghu-Hārīta-smṛti* (of the Jivananda collection) and the *Vṛddha-Hārīta-samṛti* were compiled, their authors may have been influenced by the reputation of Hārīta as a Sāṁkhya teacher to include portions relating to Yoga, the nature of the individual self, Supreme Self and the means of attaining *mokṣa*.

Hārītadharmasūtra

Kumārila, in his *Tantravārttika*,[8] mentions Hārīta as a *sūtrakāra* on *dharma*. The original text is not available, but numerous

---

5. Vol. I, pp. 194-409.
6. *History of Dharmaśāstra*, Vol. I, part 1, p. 135.
7. *Op. cit.*, p. 135.
8. P. 179.

quotations from it, preserved in the medieval commentaries and *nibandhas* indicate that it was a very extensive text in mixed prose and verse, which 'dealt exhaustively with the same topics as are dealt with in other Dharmasūtras'.[9] S.C. Banerji has attempted a reconstruction of the *Hārītadhadrmasūtra*,[10] but, in his monograph *Dharma-sūtras*,[11] he confines himself to prose passages of Hārīta.

Vamanasastri Islampurkar reported a manuscript of the *Hārītadharmasūtra* at Nasik.[12] But, the manuscript has not been published, nor has it been critically analysed. Kane[13] suggests that this Dharmasūtra text was associated with the *Black Yajurveda*.

Hārīta is quoted as an authority in the Dharmasūtras of Baudhāyana, Āpastamba and Vasiṣṭha.[14] This indicates that he was among the early Dharmasūtra writers and was held in high esteem. The allusion to Hārīta as a Sāṁkhya teacher was possibly intended to refer to the *Hārītadharmasūtra*. This is suggested by the fact that the list of four Sāṁkhya teachers, named in the *Māṭharavṛtti*, has Hārīta immediately before Devala, who was a Dharmasūtra writer. Śaṅkara, the great Advaita philosopher, in his commentary on the *Vedāntasūtra*,[15] points out that Devala and some other Dharmasūtra writers adopted Sāṁkhya principles in their works. Aparārka and Lakṣmīdhara (*Kṛtyakalpataru*) quote passages from Devala giving an account of Sāmkhya principles.[16] This confirms the testimony of Śaṅkara and makes a case for some other Dharmasūtra writers also dealing with Sāṁkhya in their works. Hārīta was one of these Dharmasūtra authors.

---

9. Kane, *op. cit.*, pp. 127-36.
10. *Journal of Oriental Institute*, Vol. VIII, 1958, pp. 14-37. But a more thorough search will reveal many more passages and a bigger volume.
11. P. 257-89.
12. Jolly, *Hindu Law and Custom*, pp. 8-9. See also Kane, *op. cit.*, pp. 125-6.
13. *Op. cit.*
14. Kane, *op. cit.*, pp. 127-8.
15. I.4.28.
16. U.V. Shastri, *Sāṁkhyadarśana kā itihāsa*, pp. 600-5.

Extracts from Hārītadharmasūtra

U.V. Shastri[17] collects nine prose passages of Hārīta quoted in the Mokṣa-kāṇḍa of Lakṣmīdhara's *Kṛtyakalpataru*. These passages do not contain anything, specifically belonging to the Sāṁkhya system,[18] and hence have been ignored by modern scholars.[19] The interest of Aparārka and Laksmīdhara was only in Dharmaśāstra material. The absence of passages dealing directly with Sāṁkhya cannot be used for ruling out their occurrence in the original text of the *Hārītadharmasūtra*.

A minute analysis of the available passages does suggest that the *Hārītadharmasūtra* dealt with Sāṁkhya material also. The passages reproduced by U.V. Shastri relate to the *vānaprastha* stage and the *yati-dharma*. In the scheme of classification envisaged by the *nibandhas* the Mokṣa-kāṇḍa is to contain provisions about the *vānaprastha* and the *saṁnyāsa āśrama*. Treatment of Yoga and the associated philosophy of Sāṁkhya will be covered by the Mokṣa-kāṇḍa. The classification of topics in this *kāṇḍa* is to be according to the scheme of a Dharmaśāstra text and not a treatise on Sāṁkhya. In the available passages there are indications of Sāṁkhya-Yoga accounts.

The first passage refers to the *vānaprastha*, its divisions and sub-divisions. The second passage mentions practices to be followed by an ascetic for annihilating himself (*ātmānaṁ kṣapayat*). The introductory remarks indicates clearly that in the preceding portion Hārīta had made statements about the desire of an ascetic of Sāṁkhya and Yoga to merge himself with the Brahmā.[20] It says that, desiring emancipation (*apavarga*), he should retire to the forest (*araṇya-gamana*). The fifth passage mentions the rules to be

---

17. *Op. cit.*, pp. 606-7.
18. P. 22, 26, 42, 52, 53, 60, 81, 82, 174.
19. A.P. Mishra, *Sāṁkhyadarśana kī aitihāsika paramparā*, p. 160, refers only to the *Laghu-Hārīta-smṛti* of the Jivananda collection, but dismisses it as without any bearing on Sāṁkhya.
20. *sāṁkhyayogayorbhikṣorbrahmalayecchaprāptiva-canāntaram hārītaḥ* ।— p. 42.

followed by him. The sixth chapter discusses in detail how he is to observe (*vyavahārtvyam*) *ahiṁsā*. The seventh passage relates to the rules for begging (*bhikṣā*) and eating food. The seventh passage deals with the birth of desire on account of craving (*saṁkalpāt kāma*) and advises the control of *kāma* by being without craving (*asaṁkalpa niyamanam*). Likewise, the eighth passage says that anger (*krodha*) is in the form of *tamas* and its control is through forbearing (*kṣamā*). The ninth passage is also significant. It discusses the various stages of *dhyāna* and *samādhi*.

Hārīta in the Mokṣadharmaparva

We can, hence, infer that Hārīta in his Dharmasūtra discussed not only the rules and practice of Yoga, but also some related theoretical principles of Sāṁkhya which could not find a place in the surviving quotations because of the nature of the *nibandha* work quoting from his text.

The *Mahābhārata* testifies to the high position enjoyed by Hārīta as a sage. He held Yudhiṣṭhira in high regard.[21] He came to see Bhīṣma when he lay on the bed of arrows.[22] In the Mokṣadharmaparva section of the Śāntiparva there is a chapter (278) in which Bhīṣma, in replying to Yudhiṣṭhira's query about the conduct, character and knowledge for attaining the position of *Brahman* which is beyond *prakṛti*, narrates the ancient history (*itihāsam purāthanam*) of the account given by Hārīta, Hārīta describes the *dharma* for the *parivrājaka āśrama*. According to Hārīta, a sage (*muni*) should leave his house and become an ascetic. He should remain unchanged in gain and loss and unconcerned for desires (*kāmeṣu nirapekṣaḥ*). He should not see, think or speak ill, should never utter ill of others. He should not do *hiṁsā* to any living being. He should have friendliness (*maitrāyaṇagataḥ*) and never enmity (*vaira*). He should forbear those who speak ill of him and, without becoming angry, should speak well. The proper conduct for begging in the village and the food to be accepted are laid down. He

---

21. Vana III.26-3.
22. *Mbh.*, XII.47.7.

is to take up his abode in a secluded place. He is to maintain equanimity and always remain satisfied. Observing the impermanance of the material thing (*bhautika*) and the appearance and destruction of the *bhūtas*, he is to keep his *ātman* controlled (*praśāntātman*). He is to keep the *vega* (on rush) of his speech, the *vega* of *krodha* (anger) of his mind, the *vega* of *hiṁṣā* and the *vega* of his stomach and the organ of generation (*udaropastha*). For those, who know, it leads to *mokṣa*, and for the ignorant it is mere effort (*śrama*). This is the complete vehicle for emancipation (*mokṣayāna*) for the learned. He, who follows it, achieves the shining world (*lokastejomayaḥ*) and he merits the highest position (*antyāya kalpata*).

Conclusion

The teachings attributed to Hārīta in the Śāntiparva chapter have similarities with the Dharmasūtra passages attributed to him in regard to the points covered and the details of the provision. The form of presentation in the present case is in verse and accounts for the two references not being closely similar. The teachings of Hārīta in the Śāntiparva are in conformity with the stage of composite Sāṁkhya-Yoga. This account refers to an early phase of Sāṁkhya. This is evidenced by the Śāntiparva itself which mentions the exposition by Hārīta to be an ancient history. In the introductory verse[23] we have a reference to *prakr̥ti* and the permanent *Brahman* beyond *prakr̥ti*. This shows that, according to the author of the chapter, Hārīta was a Sāṁkhya teacher.

---

23. *Mbh.*, XII.278.1.

14

Patañjali as a Sāṁkhya Ācārya

Introduction

THE *Yogasūtra* of Patañjali is a masterly treatise on Yoga. Not only in India but elsewhere also scholars and followers of Yoga study the text with profound veneration. In the process Patañjali has received the highest respect. His name has become synonymous with Yoga.

The *Yuktidīpikā* records six passages referring to Patañjali's views on Sāṁkhya topics. As this goes against the established image of Patañjali, scholars have refused to take notice of them. The only exceptions are P. Chakravarti,[1] U.V. Shastri[2] and A.P. Mishra,[3] who assign them to another Patañjali, different from the author of the *Yogasūtra*. In this way they have accepted a Patañjali as a Sāṁkhya teacher. G.J. Larson and R.S. Bhattacharya[4] in their recent study of admitted Patañjali to the list of Sāṁkhya teachers.

Sources

On the Sāṁkhya views of Patañjali U.V. Shastri[5] has collected

1. *Origin and Development of the Sāṁkhya System of Thought*, pp. 133-5, 290.
2. *Sāṁkhyadarśana kā itihāsa*, pp. 614-29.
3. *Sāṁkhyadarśana kī aitihāsika paramparā*, pp. 182-9.
4. *Encyclopedia of Indian Philosophies*, ed. by K. Potter, Vol. IV, pp. 129-30.
5. *Op. cit.*, pp. 623-4. See also A.P. Mishra, *op. cit.*, pp. 188-9; G.J. Larson and R.S. Bhattacharya, *op. cit.*, p. 130 refer to four passages in the *Yuktidīpikā*.

seven passages from the *Yuktidīpikā*, one from the *Yogasūtrabhāṣya* of Vyāsa, and one from Śaṅkara's commentary on the *Brahmasūtra*. P. Chakravarti[6] traces one passage in Padmapāda's commentary on the *Prapañcasāratantra*.

The first passsage[7] in the *Yuktidīpikā* says that 'hence the *ahaṁkāra* does not exist' is the view of Patañjali for he holds that egoism (*asmi-pratyaya*) is the function of *mahat* (intellect).

The second *Yuktidīpikā* passage[8] is directly connected with then first. It says that Patañjali, Pañcādhikaraṇa and the Vārṣagaṇas (the followers of Vārṣagaṇya) hold that from *pradhāna* is evolved *mahat*. It repeats the argument that egoism is the function of *mahat*.

The third passsge,[9] which refers to the various views about the source of influx when the organs act, says that, according to Patañjali, they always act from within.

The seventh passage[10] repeats this view in a negative manner. It says that, on account of the three-fold *bhāvas*, the senses do not always act from within, as held by Patañjali.

The fourth passage[11] says that according to Patañjali the *karaṇas* (organs) are twelve.

The fifth passage[12] referss to the view of Patañjali about the

6. *Op. cit.*, p. 134.
7. *evaṁ tarhi naivāhaṁkāro vidyata iti patañjaliḥi* । — p. 32
8. *mahato'smi pratyayasvarūpatvābhyupagamāt* । *patañjali-pañcādhikaraṇavārṣagaṇānāṁ pradhānāt mahānutpadyata iti . . . mahato'smipratyaya-kartṛtvābhyupagamāt* ।। — p. 108.
9. *karanānām . . . svabhāvātivṛttiḥ . . . sarvā svata iti patañjaliḥ* ।
10. *evaṁ trividhabhāvaparigrahāt . . . na sarvaṁ svataḥ patañjalivat* । — pp. 148-9.
11. *karaṇaṁ dvādaśavidhamiti patañjaliḥ* । — p. 132.
12. *pātañjale tu sūkṣmaśarīram yat siddhikāle pūrvam-indriyāṇi bījadeśaṁ nayati; tatra tatkṛtāśayavaśāt dudeśaṁ yātanāsthānaṁ vā karṇāni prapya nivartate* । *tatra caivaṁ yuktāśayasya karmavaśādanyadutpadyate yadindriyāṇi bījadeásaṁ nayati tadapi nivartate, śarīrapāte cānyadutpadyate, evamanekāni śarīrāṇi* ।। — p. 144.

   We have followed the free translation given by P. Chakravarti, *op. cit.*, pp. 290-1.

migration through the subtle body (*sūkṣma-śarīra*). In the period of the enjoyment of the benefits of the six *siddhis* this body transmits the ten organs into the seed of *karman*, so that they are integrated with the merit and demerit of the individual. At the termination of *siddhi*, when death becomes inevitable, this body pushes the integrated organs so that they get in touch with the parental seed of the next birth. Simultaneously with death the subtle body automatically disappears. The migration into the higher or lower world is determined by the merit and demerit acquired during the period of *siddhi*. In the next life also the individual derives a fresh subtle body through the operativeness of his *karman*. In this life also the process is repeated. The new subtle body transmits the organs into the seed of *karman* and pushes them to get in touch with the parental seed of the next birth. In this way the series of the subtle bodies continues.

The sixth passage in the *Yuktidīpikā*[13] reproduces only the penultimate sentence of the preceding passage. It simply says that at the death the subtle body disappears. Again in the next life another subtle body is created.

The eighth passage, which occurs in the *Yogabhāṣya*[14] of Vyāsa, defines *dravya* (substance) is the aggregate of components, which are inseparably connected with one another.

The ninth passage listed by U.V. Shastri occurs in Śaṅkara's commentary on the *Brahmasūtra*.[15] It records an extract from the *Yogaśāstra* saying that Yoga is the means for the understanding of the *tattvas*; thus, Yoga has been accepted as auxiliary for the way to proper realisation. Śaṅkara does not attribute the passage to Patañjali. We have a clear reference to *Yogaśāstra* as the source. The extract does not occur in the *Yogasūtra* and could have been

13. *yattavat patañjaliḥ āha — sūkṣmaśarīraṁ vinivarttate punaścānyadutpadyate* I — p. 145.

14. *ayutasiddhāvayava-bhedānugataḥ samūho dravyamiti patañjaliḥ* I — III. 44.

15. *yogaśāstre'pi — atha tatvādarśanopāyaḥ yogaḥ iti samyagdarśanābhyupāyatvenaiva yogo'ṅgīkriyate* I I — II. 1.3.

taken from another text on Yoga. Shastri does not spell out his argument for attributing it to Patañjali.

The tenth reference to Patañjali's Sāṁkhya view is to be found in Padmapāda's commentary on the *Prapañcasāratantra*. On the process of the descent of *puruṣa* into the womb the *Prapañcasāra-tanta* refers to a number of views. The process of the descent of the pure self into the womb of the mother along with the individual self of the father is explained by the simile of the transmission of light from one lamp to another.[16] Padmapāda says that this is the view of Patañjali, Dhanvantari and others. He adds that it is not only the individual self of the father that descends into the womb, but that of the mother also does so through her menstrual blood discharged at the time of sexual operation.[17] Thus, the passage refers to Patañjali's view about the transmigration from one body to another and deals with part of the point covered in the passage no. five in the *Yuktidīpikā*.

R.S. Bhattacharya[18] refers to a sentence of Patañjali quoted by Lakṣmīdhara in his commentary on the *Saundaryalaharī*. Here Patañjali is mentioned as *bhagavat*. The passage deals with the *cakras*. Bhattacharya does not accept it to be from the *Yogasūtra* of Patañjali. Its occurrence in the Sāṁkhya work of Patañjali is equally suspect.

Works Attributed to Patañjali

There are many texts circulated under the name of Patañjali.[19] Of these we do not consider here the *Mahābhāṣya* on the *Aṣṭādhyāyī* and the lexicon attributed to Vāsuki by Hemacandra in the *Abhidhāna-cintāmaṇi*. Likewise, we have not discussed the

---

16. *dīpād dīpāntaraṁ yathā* | — I. 97.
17. *dīpād dīpāntaramiti patañjalidhanvantaryādipakṣah* | *tat paraṁ dhāma tasya piturātmā kaścidevaṁ brūta* | *ityuttaratrānvayaḥ* | *raktavyatikṛtāditi strayātmano'pi saṅkrāntidarśitā* |
18. *An Introduction on the Yogasūtra*, p. 100 — *svādhiṣṭhāne saṁhāraḥ ṣaḍbindukṛtaḥ* ||
19. U.V. Shasti, *op. cit.*, pp. 614-15.

redaction of the *Caraka-saṁhitā* done by Patañjali and the *Nidānasūtra* (or *Chandovīciti*) attributed to Patañjali. Al-Bīrūni profusely quotes from the Book of Patañjali, which we have analysed to show that is was a famous work on Yoga composed possibly in the second century BC.[20]

There is a text named the *Paramārthasāra* attributed to Patañjali.[21] Its editor Suryanarayan Sharma Shukla identifies this Patañjali with the famous author of the *Yogasūtra*. No cogent argument has been advanced in support of the view. It rests on the common name Patañjali.

There is reason to believe that the Patañjali, quoted in the *Yuktidīpikā*, could also not have been the author of the *Paramārthasāra*.[22] Verse 83 of the *Paramārthasāra*[23] occurs in the *Yuktidīpikā*[24] also. The *Yuktidīpikā* does not attribute the verse either to the *Paramārthasāra* of Patañjali, suggesting that the author of the *Yuktidīpikā* borrowed it from some earlier source to which the *Paramārthasāra* was also indebted. There are major differences between Patañjali, the author of the *Paramārthasāra*, and Patañjali quoted in the *Yuktidīpikā*. Whereas in the *Yuktidīpikā* Patañjali holds that the *karaṇas* are twelve in number, in the *Paramārthasāra* they are said to be thirteen. Likewise, Patañjali as quoted in the *Yuktidīpikā* believes that there is a subtle intermediate body which is created and destroyed like the physical body, but the *Paramārthasāra*[25] says that with each *puruṣa* there is a subtle body from the beginning of the creation which lasts till the dissolution or appearance of true knowledge.

---

20. See Appendix III.
21. Edited by Suryanarayan Sharma Shukla. Acyuta Grantha Mālā, Varanasi. Earlier Pub. Anantaśayana Granthamālā. The author is referred to as Ādhāra or Śeṣa-jagadādhāra. Patañjali is regarded as the incarnation of Śeṣanāga. Hence Patañjali is taken to be its author.
22. U.V. Shastri, *op. cit.*, pp. 622-3.
23. *vr̥kṣāgrāccyutavādo yadvadanicchannara kṣitau patati* | *tadvad guṇapuruṣajño'nicchannapi kevalī bhavati* ||
24. With the reading *prattyeva* in place of *kṣitau patati* on p. 25.
25. Verses 11-13, 17.

Bhattacharya on Patañjali Only as a Yoga Writer

R.S. Bhattacharya oppose the view that there was another Patañjali, different from the author of the *Yogasūtra*, who was a Sāṁkhya teacher. He does not consider the evidence of the sentences in the *Yuktidīpikā* recording the distinguishing views of Patañjali. The reason adduced by him is that 'the drift of all these sentences is not quite clear to us'.[26] This is a virtual admission by Bhattacharya of the force of the argument in favour of Patañjali being a Sāṁkhya teacher. The sentences are not ambiguous and clearly state Patañjali's special views on certain points in Sāṁkhya system. Bhattacharya has failed to trace parallels of these views in the *Yogasūtra*. We have an independent confirmation of the authenticity of the *Yuktidīpikā* quotation in at least one case. Passasge no. 7 listed above presents in some detail Patañjali's view about the transmigration of individual through subtle body. In the *Prapañcasāratantra* we find several views on the subject. Padmapāda, in his commentary says that one of these views is held by Patañjali and Dhanvantari. He adds more details emphasising a particular point in the view as found in the *Yuktidīpikā*. Padmapāda had no need to produce the actual words of Patañjali and all the details, but the description does not leave any doubt about the identity of the view in the two references.

Bhattacharya takes points to prove that Patañjali's view about *dravya*, as quoted in the *Vyāsabhāṣya*, cannot prove that there was a second Patañjali who was a Sāṁkhya teacher. He admits that the passage defining *dravya* is not found in the *Yogasūtra*, nor is the term *dravya* used in it. But, he argues, the idea of aggregate is in perfect accordance with the view-point of the *Yogasūtra*. According to him, the sentence under reference was part of the oral teachings of Patañjali, the author of the *Yogasūtra*, which could not be included in the original text. He offers another explanation suggesting that Patañjali himself wrote a *vṛtti* on his *Yogasūtra* and the present sentence occurred in it. His alternative suggestion is that a person of the Patañjali *gotra*, who was a follower of the

26. *Op. cit.*, p. 100.

Yoga philosophy, composed a work on *Yogasūtra* which contained the sentence quoted in the *Vyāsabhāṣya*.

In his keenness to controvert the Sāṁkhya associations of the extract and to establish its connections with the Yoga tradition, Bhattacharya adopts stands which are self-defeating, besides being totally conjectural. The sentence defining *dravya* in the characteristic manner does not occur in the *Yogasūtra*. To suggest that it was part of the oral teachings of Patañjali which could not be included in the text even at a later stage is highly presumptuous. Likewise, the suggestion that the sentence was part of the *vṛtti* composed by Patañjali himself is equally speculative, without any evidence in its support. To accept the sentence as a part of the *vṛtti* we have to trace a context in the *Yogasūtra* were the particular extract has a relevance. The second explanation offered by Bhattacharya virtually concedes the point that the *Yogasūtra* and the work in which the sentence occurred were two different works written by two people belonging to the Patañjali *gotra*. This amounts to a tacit admission of the basic point which Bhattacharya proposes to criticise. It is clear that he is not prepared to accept the obvious interpretation of the extract as belonging to a text by a Patañjali different from the author of the *Yogasūtra*. The evidence of the *Yuktidīpikā* makes a case for this Patañjali being a Sāṁkhya teacher.

Date of Patañjali

There is no definite indication about the date of Patañjali. The reference to Patañjali and his views in the *Yuktidīpikā* suggest that he was among the early Sāṁkhya teachers. The *Yuktidīpikā*[27] includes him in the list of Sāṁkhya teachers belonging to the gap between Pañcaśikha and Īśvarakṛṣṇa. There are eleven names in this list, but the position of a teacher in it is no indication of his comparative chronology. We cannot be sure of the years to be assigned to each teacher. The possibility cannot be ruled out that some of the teachers were contemporaries. But, in any case, it is significant that in this list of Patañjali appears along with teachers, such as Pañcādhikaraṇa and Vārṣagaṇya, who were senior names in the history of Sāṁkhya.

27. P. 175.

We have discussed the evidence for the date of Pañcaśikha.[28] In the post-Pañcaśikha period, if we take into account the possible dates for Pañcādhikaraṇa, Hārīta and Vāṣagaṇya we may place Patañjali, the Sāṁkhya teacher, in the bracket 500-400 BC.

G.J. Larson and R.S. Bhattacharya[29] place Patañjali along with Paurika and Pañcādhikaraṇa in the time-bracket of AD 100-300. We have pointed out that this errs on being late and have suggested 500-450 BC for Pañcādhikaraṇa and Paurika.[30]

The occurrence of a quotation from Patañjali in the *Yogabhāṣya* of Vyāsa does not mark any improvement over the testimony of the *Yuktidīpikā*, because of the late date of Vyāsa. But, U.V. Shastri,[31] who places Vyāsa very early, in any case earlier than Patañjali, the Sāṁkhya teacher, the author of the *Mahābhāṣya* and the redactor of Caraka, explains the sentence as added on the margin by a later reader of the *Vyāsabhāṣya*, which was later incorporated in it by a subsequent copyist. Thus, Shastri does not consider the evidence of the *Vyāsabhāṣya* to have any bearing on the date of Patañjali, the Sāṁkhya teacher. Though we do not agree with Shastri about the comparative date of the *Vyāsabhāṣya* and the interpretation of the presence of the extract from Patañjali in it, it is not of any use in improving upon the evidence of the *Yuktidīpikā* in fixing the date of Patañjali.

Shastri[32] favours the date second century BC for Patañjali, the Sāṁkhya teacher. He considers him to be different from the author of the *Yogasūtra*, but identifies him with the author of the *Mahābhāṣya* and the redactor of the *Caraka-saṁhitā*. This view is

---

28. See *supra* chapter 7, under section "Date of Arāḍa". He was later than Āsuri but earlier than Jaigīṣavya and Devala and was a senior contemporary of Arāḍa and Janaka, which may favour the time bracket *c*. 700-650 BC.
29. *Op. cit.*, pp. 9-13.
30. See *supra* chapter 8, under sections "Paurik — Date of Paurika" and "Pañcādhikaraṇa — Date of Pañcadhikaraṇa".
31. *Op. cit.*, p. 629, fn.1.
32. *Op. cit.*, pp. 626-9.

based on two assumptions — first, Patañjali, the author of the *Yogasūtra*, is different from Patañjali, the Sāṁkhya teacher, and second, Patañjali, the author of the *Mahābhāṣya*, cannot be identified with the author of the *Yogasūtra*. Hence, Patañjali, the Sāṁkhya teacher, is identified with the author of the *Mahābhāṣya*. This, according to Shastri, was the basis for the tradition identifying Patañjali as an authority in three disciplines of spiritualism, medicine and grammar.

We do not propose to discuss here the ancient tradition identifying the three Patañjalis, the authors of texts in three different areas. This much, however, is generally conceded that Patañjali, the author of the *Yogasūtra*, cannot be identified with the author of the *Mahābhāṣya*. About the identification of Patañjali, the author of a text on philosophy (*manas*) in the tradition there is no unanimity among scholars. The case of the author of the *Yogasūtra* is not favoured by modern scholars. Elsewhere,[33] we have suggested the possibility that he is the author of the text on Yoga quoted by Al-Bīrūnī.

Patañjali on Sāṁkhya and Yoga

Here we concentrate on the problem of the identification of the Sāṁkhya teacher Patañjali and consider other related issues from this angle. U.V. Shastri, A.P. Mishra and P. Chakravarti, who distinguish between Patañjali, the Sāṁkhya teacher, and the author of the *Yogasūtra*, depend on the non-availability of the *Yuktidīpikā* extracts in the *Yogasūtra*. We have seven extracts in the *Yuktidīpikā* which cover four points in Sāṁkhya philosophy: the evolution of *mahat* from *pradhāna* but without the intermediacy of *ahaṁkāra*; the number of *karaṇa*s being only twelve; the senses always acting from within, without an influx of impetus from outside; and the transmigration of individual from one body to another through a subtle body. If we had a larger number of extracts on a few more topics, the comparison would have been more convincing.

---

33. See Appendix III.

We suggest that the association of Patañjali with both Sāṁkhya and Yoga does not necessarily mean that there were two Patañjalis. Sāṁkhya and Yoga are two allied systems. In an earlier stage in the history of the development of Sāṁkhya they were fused together to form a single unit. The exposition of the Sāṁkhya system by many thinkers, such as Yājñavalkya and Vasiṣṭha, presented as old narratives (*itihāsam purātanam*) in the *Mahābhārata*, contains an account of both Sāṁkhya and Yoga principles. The same teacher could claim to belong to both Sāṁkhya and Yoga. This seems to have been the case with Patañjali. He was essentially a Sāṁkhya teacher. At a later stage in his life he concentrated on Yoga. Thus, the Sāṁkhya and Yoga views of Patañjali do not imply two different philosophers having the same name. They can be explained as referring to two phases in the development of the philosophical ideas of the same person.

Patañjali possibly did not compose a major work on Sāṁkhya. He did not establish a separate Sāṁkhya school of his followers. With the many early Sāṁkhya teachers and their works the Sāṁkhya views of Patañjali did not have much chance of surviving in their full form. The rejection of his views by later Sāṁkhya thinkers, who gave the system a standard form, was effective in pushing his Sāṁkhya views into oblivion. Only a few of these, which were significantly unique, survived the long course of time. The greater prestige of his classic composition on Yoga was another reason for his Sāṁkhya views not receiving primacy.

In this connection the views of S.N. Dasgupta[34] are very significant. He points out that the *Maitrāyaṇī*, *Śvetāśvatara* and *Kaṭha Upaniṣads* of *Kṛṣṇa Yajurveda*, where we find reference to Yoga methods, are the only ones where we find clear references also to the Sāṁkhya tenets, though the Sāṁkhya and Yoga ideas do not appear there as related to each other or associated as parts of the same system. But there is a remarkable passage in the *Maitrāyaṇī* in the conversation between Śākyāyana and Bṛhadratha where we find that the Sāṁkhya metaphysics was offered in some quarters to

34. *A History of Indian Philosophy*, Vol. I, pp. 227-9.

explain the validity of the Yoga processes, and it seems therefore that the association and grafting of the Sāṁkhya metaphysics on the Yoga system as its basis, was the work of the followers of this school of ideas which was subsequently systematised by Patañjali.

Later, in dealing with Yoga, Dasgupta refers to the Pātañjala school of Sāṁkhya as forming its subject and adds that

> Patañjali was probably the most notable person for he not only collected the different forms of Yoga practices, and gleaned the diverse ideas which were or could be associated with the Yoga, but grafted them all on the Sāṁkhya metaphysics, and gave them the form in which they have been handed down to us. Vācaspati and Vijñānabhikṣu, the two great commentators on the *Vyāsabhāṣya*, agree with us in holding that Patañjali was not the founder of the Yoga, but an editor. Analytic study of the *sūtra*s also brings home the conviction that the *sūtra*s do not show any original attempt, but a masterly and systematic compilation which was also supplemented by fitting contributions. The systematic manner in which the first three chapters are written by way of definition and classification shows that the materials were already in existence and that Patañjali only systematised them. There was no missionising zeal, no attempt to overthrow the doctrines of other systems, except as far as they might come in, by way of explaining the system. Patañjali is not even anxious to establish the system, but he is only engaged in systematising the facts as he had them.

Thus, we see that Patañjali was essentially a Sāṁkhya teacher. In those times Sāṁkhya and Yoga were often taken together. The Sāṁkhya school, to which Patañjali belonged, gave Yoga a systematic basis by strengthening its metaphysical aspect of Sāṁkhya and also systematising and consolidating Yoga. Patañjali contributed to both Sāṁkhya and Yoga. His contributions to Yoga outclassed his earlier expositions of Sāṁkhya. Patañjali, the Sāṁkhya teacher, and Patañjali, the Yoga author, are not two different persons, but two aspects, or rather phases, of the life and activities of one and the same person.[35]

Chronological Consideration for the Identity of Patañjali, the Sāṁkhya Ācārya and Yogasūtrakāra

The identity of the two Patañjalis is not vitiated by chronological considerations. Earlier scholars, in the absence of a certainty about the date for Patañjali, the Sāṁkhya teacher, and Patañjali, the Yoga writer, used the argument to differentiate between the two Patañjalis. But, a careful consideration shows that chronological compatibility is in favour of identifying the two Patañjalis.

We have shown above that Patañjali, the Sāṁkhya teacher, may be placed in the rough time-bracket of 500-400 BC. The date for the composition of the *Yogasūtra* is difficult to determine. On the basis of the equation with the author of the *Mahābhāṣya*, scholars often placed Patañjali, the author of the *Yogasūtra*, in the second century BC.[36] Earlier scholars, who rejected this equation, placed Patañjali after the *Mahābhāṣya*.[37]

R.S. Bhattacharya, though frankly admitting that there is nothing in the *Yogasūtra* to help us determine its date with a considerable amount of precision,[38] places Patañjali earlier than 500 BC.[39] Bhattacharya mentions several indirect considerations for an early date: the Pātañjala *śākhā* of the *Sāmaveda*, Patañjali as a *gotra* name in the *Matsya Purāṇa*, Patañjali being mentioned by

35. *Bhāgavata Purāṇa*, though a late Purāṇa, mentions Patañjali in its list of the *siddhas* along with Āsuri (VI.15.14)—*āsuriḥ sa-patañjaliḥ*. This may refer to a tradition which clubs Patañjali with earlier Sāṁkhya teachers.

36. Max Müller, *Six Systems of Indian Philosophy*, p. 410; *Cultural Heritage of India*, Vol. III, p. 14; S.N. Dasgupta, *A History of Indian Philosophy*, I, p. 212; Kane, *History of Dharmaśāstra*, V, p. 1399.

37. Woods, *Yoga Philosophy*, Introduction, p. xix (fourth or fifth century). Jacobi, *JAOS*, XXI (later than AD 450); Keith, *Sāṁkhya System*, p. 70 (later than the third century).

38. *Op. cit.*, p. 109.

39. *Op. cit.*, p. 112.

Kātyāyana, some *Tripiṭaka* passages presuming *sūtra*s of the *Yogasūtra*, some older Purāṇas in chapters, which are definitely not later, containing passages which are based on the *sūtra*s of the *Yogasūtra*s, and the peculiar usage of certain terms.

But the absence of a reference to Patañjali by the Buddha and the early Pāli literature and the silence of the Mokṣadharmaparva to his views on Yoga will suggest that Patañjali did not acquire celebrity in the earlier period. Hence a date a little later, between 500 and 400 BC will appear more reasonable.

Thus, indirect evidence points to the same rough period for Patañjali in both Sāṁkhya and Yoga traditions, suggesting that both refer to the same person.

15

Sāṁkhya Schools

Classification into Four Streams

H.S. JOSHI has attempted a reconstruction of Sāṁkhya-Yoga philosophy in terms of its teachers and schools.[1] He treats Sāṁkhya and Yoga as forming a unity, but is alive to their separate traditions. He gives primacy to Sāṁkhya, but assigns separate sections to Yoga, its teachers, texts and schools. Of the two parts of his monograph, the first entitle 'History' is devoted to the history of teachers. The second part is termed as Sambhrānta Sāṁkhya. Sambhrānta Sāṁkhya is not a paraphrase of Classical Sāṁkhya, *sambhrānta* here signifies 'expanding' and 'spreading'. This part discusses the forms Sāṁkhya assumed in course of its spatial and chronological expansion.

In both the parts the grouping has been termed as streams (*dhārās*). The first speaks of four streams,[2] but the classification is based neither on strictly chronological grounds, though a claim is made to that effect, nor on views or principles. The names of teachers in the four streams do not represent schools or systems. They are grouped rather mechanically and involve a confused overlapping. The first stream begins with Kapila and includes such teachers as were connected with the line of followers after him or the chronological sequence thereafter, namely Āsuri, Voḍhu,

1. *Sāṁkhyayogadarśana kā jīrṇoddhāra*.
2. *Op. cit.*, p. 40.

Pañcaśikha, Jaigīṣavya, Āvaṭya, Vārṣagaṇya (Varṣa, Vṛṣa or Vṛṣagaṇa) and Vyāḍi. The second stream consists of teachers who were contemporaries of teachers other than Kapila in the first list. These are Yāska, Ulūka, Vṛddha-Parāśara, Śrīkṛṣṇa, Bhīṣma, Arjuna and Śuka. The third list mentions Vedic and Purāṇic sages and philosophers. These include Hiraṇyagarbha. Brahmā, Rudra and Manu and the progenies of Brahmā or Manu who are represented as expounding Sāṁkhya in the *Mahābhārata* and the Purāṇas. Other names are Śuka, Ātreya, Asita, Devala, Ārṣṭiṣeṇa, Parāśara, Vyāsa, Punarvasu, Raibhya, Vāmadeva, Gautama, Akṣapāda, Janaka, Sulabhā, Karāla Janaka, Āśvalāyana, Kuśika, Vatsa, Ikṣvāku, Vivasvān and Kaṇāda. In this list the names, other than those of Vedic sages and philosophers are Śuka, Akṣapāda, Kaṇāda, Sulabhā, Āśvalāyana, Vatsa, Raibhya and Punarvasu. The fourth stream consists of teachers, contemporaries of Īśvarakṛṣṇa, either as senior or as junior. The names included in this list are Mārkaṇḍeya, Patañjali, Vindhyavāsa, Agniveśa (?), Rudraka, Kumāra Gaya and Arāṭ.

The 'contents', which presents a rather detailed account of the chapterisation in the book, gives a slightly different scheme of classification. Here the second stream consists of only Garga, Yāska and Ulūka. The third stream is divided into two sub-groups. The first sub-group includes Vṛddha-Parāśara, Kṛṣṇa, Bhīṣma and Śukra (?) of the second stream, along with Asita-Devala, Ārṣṭiṣeṇa, Parāśara and Vyāsa of the third stream. The second sub-group is that of Vedic-Purāṇic teachers and includes the names of Bhṛgu, Marīci, Aṅgirā, Pracetā, Kratu, Sanatkumāra, Sanātana, Sana, Sanaka, Sanandana, Pulastya, Kaśyapa, Nārada, Vasiṣṭha, Ikṣvāku and Atri and retains Śuka of the second stream. These new names are evidently those of the progenies of Brahmā. Likewise, the fourth stream is made to include Akṣapāda, Kaṇāda, Kuśika, Āśvalāyana and Vatsa of the third stream also. The details in chapter 3 of the book follow this scheme of the contents.

It is not correct to treat these four lists of teachers as representing four streams, branches or schools of Sāṁkhya. They are four convenient groups, but without any consistent basis or criterion.

The first group consists of recognised Sāṁkhya teachers, the second of teachers who were contemporaries of Sāṁkhya philosophers coming after Kapila, and the fourth of teachers who were senior or junior contemporaries of Īśvarakṛṣṇa. The third list is a mixed one containing mythological names and Vedic and Purāṇic sages and personalities associated with Sāṁkhya.

In the second part of the book, chapters 11 to 15 present the systems or schools of Sāṁkhya-Yoga classified as five streams (*dhārās*), which are further subdivided into sub-branches (*upaśākhās*). Of these, the fifth stream relates to Yoga philosophers. The remaining four refer to systems of Sāṁkhya philosophy. They are classified on the basis of their characteristic principles.

Branches of Sāṁkhya

The first three streams are designated as *Ahorātra-śākhā, Kāla-śākhā* and *Atri-śākhā*, whereas the fourth one is named as the *Pradhānastambha*. These are further subdivided into sub-branches, four of Ahorātra, seven of Kāla, five of Atri, and twenty of the Pradhāna.

AHORĀTRA ŚĀKHĀ

The first stream expounds its principle in terms of creation and dissolution termed as *ahorātra*, the night referring to the stage when the *prakṛti* (Brahmā) is in equilibrium, whereas the day signifies the agitation of *prakṛti* and the beginning of the process of creation or evolution. This stream is based on the line *śrīśca te ca lakṣmī patnyāvahorātre*. The first sub-branch of this stream is found first in the Pariśiṣṭa in the *Nirukta*[3] of Yāska. The second sub-branch is represented by the Ahorātrayoga in the *Gītā*.[4] The *Durgāspataśatī* in the *Mārkaṇḍeyapurāṇa* expounds the principles of the third sub-branch in its section entitled *Prādhānika rahasya*. Chapter 1 in the *Manusmṛti* presents the principles of the fourth

---

3. *yuyaṁ sahasraparyantamahanyad brahmaṇo vidiḥ* |
rātriṁ yugashasrānatāṁ tehorātra vide janāḥ ||
4. X.12-27.

sub-branch. The fifth sub-branch finds expression in the *Vāyu Purāṇa*.[5]

KĀLA ŚĀKHĀ

The second stream includes *kāla* in the list of *tattvas*. The earliest acceptance of *kāla* as a *tattva* is found in the *Śvetāśvatara Upaniṣad*.[6] The first sub-branch of this school, as expounded in the *Mahābhārata*,[7] names *puruṣa* as Viṣṇu and *prakṛti* as *kāla*, and, without recognising *mahat*, traces *manas* and *ahaṁkāra* directly from *buddhi*. The second sub-branch (as expounded in the *Mahābhārata*[8]) mentions *prakṛti* in the place of *kāla*, naming it as *avyakta* also. It describes *kāla* as the cause of the transformation of all the *tattvas* and objects. It believes in six *mahābhūtas*, but does not name the sixth one. The third sub-branch is presented by Devala in the *Mahābhārata*.[9] Here *kāla* is mentioned as distinct from both *prakṛti* and *puruṣa*. The teachers of this sub-branch are named as *bhūta-cintaka* and *adhyātma-cintaka*. This sub-branch designates the *tattvas* as *rāśis*. It numbers the *mahābhūtas* as eight, adding *kāla*, *bhāva* and *abhāva* to the well-known five, and, parallel to them, numbers the *jñānendriyas* also as eight adding *citta*, *manas* and *buddhi* to the well known five ones. It numbers the *tattvas* variously as sixteen, seventeen, eighteen, twenty and twenty-five by adding new ones. In its scheme the inclusion of *ūṣmā* as a *tattva* (eighteenth) is very significant. The fourth sub-branch is described in the *Kūrma Purāṇa*.[10] Its teachers are referred to as *tattva-cintaka* and *brahmavādī*. According to it, both *kāla-pradhāna* and *puruṣa* emanate from *avyakta*, *kāla* which represents the connection between two events (*saṁyogaja*), is described as *anādi*. The fifth sub-branch, recorded in the *Viṣṇu Purāṇa*,[11] was expounded

5. Chapter 5.
6. *kālaṁ tathānye parimulyamānāḥ* |
7. XII.210.8-46
8. XII.213 (221).
9. XII.281 (275).
10. Chapter 2, part 2.
11. I.2.27.

by Parāśara to Maitreya. According to it, in the stage of equilibrium in *prakṛti*, *puruṣa* remains aloof from it, and is termed as *kāla*. The sixth sub-branch is found in the *Bhāgavata Purāṇa*[12] and is communicated by Kapila[13] to Devahūti. Here *kāla* is mentioned as the twenty-fifth *tattva*, which causes stirrings in the *prakṛti* in its stage of equilibrium. The seventh sub-branch is also found in the *Bhāgavata Purāṇa*.[14] It accepts a number of new *tattvas*, such as *dravya*, *karma*, *kāla*, *svabhāvya*, *jīva* and *brahma* or Vāsudeva.

ATRI-SIDDHĀNTĪYA ŚĀKHĀ

The third stream is designated as *atri-siddhāntīya*. It investigated into the functioning of the internal and external organs. It is found mainly in the texts on *Āyurveda*. Atri was the earliest authority in *Āyurveda* and is included in the list of Sāṁkhya teachers. The first sub-branch of this stream is recorded in the *Nirukta*. According to it, by following the path of *dharma*, anybody can become Īśvara or become immortal; getting involved in passions a man suffers repeated births and deaths. The second sub-branch made remarkable advancements in the area of *pañca-mahābhūtas*, physics and botany. It expounded the principle of life even in plants.[15] The third sub-branch finds a detailed exposition in the two Saṁhitā texts associated with the names of Caraka and Suśruta.

MUKHYASTAMBHĪYA ŚĀKHĀ

The mainstream of Sāṁkhya is termed as *mukhya-stambhīya*, *pradhāna-stambhīya* or *kāpilīya*. It covers all the important expressions of Sāṁkhya principles. Joshi lists twenty sub-branches of the mainstream.

---

12. III.16.26; III.26.17-30.
13. Joshi, *op. cit.*, pp. 219-20 takes this Kapila to be different from Kapila, the Sāṁkhya philosopher.
14. II.5.14; II.6.22-31.
15. *Mbh.*, XII.184.10-18.

Sub-branches

The first three sub-branches are indicated when Sanatkumāra refers to the views mentioning the number of *tattvas* as twenty-three or twenty-four, whereas he himself takes them to be twenty-five.[16] The fourth sub-branch is represented by Yājñavalkya who mentions the *tattvas* to be twenty-six.[17] The fifth sub-branch mentions the order of creation as *akṣara*, *khaṁ*, *vāyu*, *jyoti*, *jala*, *jagati* and *jagat*,[18] without assigning any place to *puruṣa*, *brahmā*, *mahat* or *ahaṁkāra*. The six sub-branch[19] presents three cycles of evolution and dissolution. Here we find four terms *akṣara*, *jñāna*, *pañca ākṛti* and *sūkṣma*, which are used in a special sense, not found elsewhere. In the third cycle the term *ātmā* signifies *puruṣa*. This sub-branch presents an elaborate order of *tattvas*.

The seventh sub-branch[20] is characterised by a special terminology about *puruṣa*. *Mahāpuruṣa* is its twenty-fourth *tattva*, *mahāpuruṣa-vaikṛta* or *mahādeva* is the twenty-fifth *tattva*, and *bhagavān* (*puruṣottama*) is the twenty-sixth *tattva*. Its order of evolution is also distinctive.

The eighth sub-branch[21] designates the *tattvas* as *bhāvas* and describes all of them as evolutes of *svabhāva*. Allied to this is the ninth sub-branch,[22] which holds the order of evolution to be *mahābhūta*, *cetanā*, *ātmā*, *manas* (*ahaṁkāra*) and *buddhi*. The tenth sub-branch[23] is also associated with the *svabhāvavādins*. The order of evolution according to this sub-branch is *indriyas*, *pañca-tanmātras*, *manas* (*ahaṁkāra*) and *buddhi*. *Buddhi* is also described as *ātmā* in human beings. In all these sub-branches no place is assigned to *mūla-prakṛti* and *puruṣa*.

---

16. Joshi *op. cit.*, p. 228. *Mbh.*, XII.165.26-27 cannot be traced in the Gita Press edn.
17. *Mbh.*, XII.318.72-84.
18. *Ibid.*, XII.200-01 canot be traced in the Gita Press edn.
19. *Ibid.*, XII.202.11, 12, 22, 24.
20. *Ibid.*, XIII.168.1-3, 25, 28.
21. *Ibid.*, XII.222.23, 25.
22. *Ibid.*, XII.237.45-6.
23. *Ibid.*, XII.246.3-4.

The eleventh sub-branch was expounded by Vasiṣṭha.[24] It speaks of two types of creations: *bhūta-sarga*, relating to *pañca-tanmātras* and *pañca-mahābūtas*, and *bhautika-sarga* concerning five *karmendriyas* and five *jñānendriyas*. It assigns the highest place to *hiraṇyagarbha*, also designated as *buddhi*, *mahat* and *virañji*. Joshi[25] prefers to designate it as *hiraṇyagarbha* sub-branch.

The twelfth branch[26] resulted from the dressing-up of Sāṁkhya, in the garb of Vaiṣṇavism. According to it, in the beginning there was only *jñāna*, from which came out *pradhāna*, *triguṇa mahāmāyā*, or *vaiṣṇavī-prakṛti*, which is also designated as *svabhāva*.

The thirteenth sub-branch, as known from the *Manusmṛti*,[27] represents the most developed form of Sāṁkhya-Yoga. According to it, in the beginning there was only darkness, which was the state of equilibrium. First emerged the Svayambhū (*puruṣa*), who created water, in which he sowed seeds which became the golden egg. From it emerged Brahmā, who divided the egg into two parts. The order of evolution is *buddhi*, *manas* (*triguṇātmaka*), *ahaṁkāra*, *tanmātra*, *mahābhūta*, *mana*, *jñānendriyas* and *karmendriyas*.

The fourteenth sub-branch also represents a developed stage and is found in the *Vāyu Purāṇa*.[28] The dark stage is termed as *pradhāna* and *prakṛti*. From it emergence *mahat*, variously named as *manas*, *mahat*, *mati*, *brahmā*, *puraḥ*, *buddhi*, *khyāti*, *īśvara*, *prāṇa*, *citti*, *smṛti*, *saṁvid* and *vipuri*. The three *guṇas* develop in it and are termed as *liṅga*, The *kṣetrajña* resides in it. When the *rajas guṇa* is predominant, *ahaṁkāra* is evolved, and when the *tamas guṇa* is predominant, *pañca-tanmātras* are evolved from which come out *pañca-mahābhūtas*.

---

24. *Mbh.*, XII.302.18, 25-8.
25. *Op. cit.*, p. 233. He points out that the term *hiraṇyagarbha*, which signified a Vedic deity, was also used for *buddhi tattva*, but the Purāṇic writers identified him with Brahmā Virañji.
26. *Mbh.*, XII.238.17-21.
27. I.5-20.
28. III.4, 9-11.

The fifteenth sub-branch is recorded in the *Brahma Purāṇa*.[29] It presents a detailed account of the developed system. It is expounded by Vasiṣṭha to Karāla Janaka. It mentions *buddhi-tattva* as the *parama-tattva* and the *ātma-tattva*. All the *tattva*s are characterised by several *guṇa*s and each has its own *vidyā*.

The sixteenth sub-branch is found in the *Devībhāgavata Purāṇa*. Here also the Sāṁkhya-Yoga system is superimposed by Vaiṣṇava terminology. The Purāṇa gives many names for *prakṛti*; *tapas*, *tamas*, *jaḍatā*, *jñāna*, *māyā*, *pradhāna*, *prakṛti*, *śakti*, *ajā*, *citta* and *saṁvitta*. The creation is said to be natural and automatic. In the beginning there was only *citta*. The Devī claims to be *citta* and, in conjunction with *puruṣa*, produces *ahaṁkāra* and the subsequent evolutes. *Avidyā* is also described as *māyā* and *sattvātmikā*. *Īśvara*, when reflected in it, is called *jīva*.

The seventeenth sub-branch, as traced in the *Mahābhārata*,[30] has a distinctive character. Here the *guṇa*s of the *pañca-mahābhūta*s are said to be six, *mūrti* being the sixth, though in actual enumeration only four are named. The *tattva*s include four *mahābhūta*s and six *guṇa*s, with *citta* as the eleventh and *buddhi* as the twelfth. This sub-branch omits *ākāśa* as a *tattva* and *salida* as a *guṇa*.

The eighteenth sub-branch, found in the *Kūrma Purāṇa*,[31] has been termed by Joshi as *Māheśvara Sāṁkhya-Yoga*. It is presented by Śiva himself. The order of the *tattva*s, in an ascending sequence, is *indriya*s, *manas*, *ahaṁkāra*, *mahat*, *avyakta*, *puruṣa*, *prāṇa*, *vyoma*, *agni* (Śiva or *īśvara*).

The nineteenth sub-branch is found in the *Buddhacarita*[32] of Aśvaghoṣa. It is presented by Arāḍ (Arāḍa). The Sāṁkhya philosophers are designated as *ātma-cintaka*s. *Puruṣa* or *ātmā* is termed as *kṣetrajña* and also as *vyakta*, as distinguished from *avyakta*. *Ajñāna*, *karma* and *tṛṣṇā* are the three causes of birth.

29. 235.16; 238.2, 4-5; 242.82; 243.2, 4-6; 262.83.
30. XII.219.12, 34.
31. (A.S.S) Vol. 2, p. 463.
32. XII.17-39.

There are five causes of *avidyā*; *vipratyaya*, *ahaṁkāra*, *saṁdeha*, *abhisamplava*, *aviśeṣa* and *anupāya* and six effects of it: *tama*, *moha*, *mahāmoha*, *tāmiśra*, *avapāta* and *andhatāmiśra*. The system subscribes to the principle of *satkāryavāda*.

The twentieth sub-branch is traced in the *Agni Purāṇa*.[33] According to it, Brahmā entered *puruṣa* and *prakṛti*, which was followed by an explosion in *mahat*, and *ahaṁkāra* appeared as an evolute. The creation which followed is of three types, *vaikārika*, *taijasa* and *bhūtādi*.

Evaluation of the Scheme of Classification

Joshi has not indicated the rationale for the classification into streams and their sub-branches. There is no uniform ground of classification even of the four streams. The first stream in identified as subscribing to the principle of creation and dissolution termed as day and night (*ahorātra*). The second stream is characterised by its acceptance of *kāla* as a *tattva*. The third stream is not distinguished in terms of its principles, but for its occurring in Āyurvedic texts, which are believd to have originated with Atri.

The fourth stream is designated as the main, principal or Kāpila stream. Its distinguishing features are not indicated. Though Joshi lists twenty sub-branches of it, he does not take cognizance of the variations in principles associated with Sāṁkhya teachers from Āsuri to Īśvarakṛṣṇa. The commentaries on the *Sāṁkhyakārikā* record a wide range of views on several important points in Sāṁkhya philosophy. These could have represented schools or branches and sub-branches of Sāṁkhya. Joshi lists the twenty sub-branches on the basis of accounts found in the *Mahābhārata*, the Purāṇas (*Vāyu*, *Brahma*, *Devībhāgavata*, *Kūrma* and *Agni*), *Manusmṛti* and *Buddhacarita*. The sub-branches are identified with the help of varying criteria, for example, the number of *tattva*s, terminology, order of evolutes, name of narrator, Vaiṣṇava influence, and the extent of the elaboration of the system. It can be seen that, if the

33. (A.S.S) chapter 18, p. 40.

type of criteria adopted in the case of the first three streams is applied to the sub-branches under the fourth stream, some of these can also be conveniently grouped as streams, for example, *svabhāvavāda* stream, and Vaiṣṇava stream. If a system appears in several sources in slightly varying form of development, the references represent one stream only and are not to be interpreted as indicating different branches or sub-branches. This holds good for the sub-branches listed under the streams of *ahorātra siddhānta* and *Atri-siddhānta* also. Likewise, a few sub-branches in the fourth stream are described as developed or elaborate. This cannot be the ground for labelling them as different sub-branches. The distinction is to be made only on the grounds of some distinguishing principles, the use of a special terminology, and the role of *tattvas*.

In identifying the streams and their sub-branches one point is to be kept in mind. If a text under study proposes to expound Sāṁkhya principles, then only we can accept accounts in it as representing schools and sub-branches of Sāṁkhya. In the *Mahābhārata* we have several undoubted references to the exposition of Sāṁkhya principles, in some cases as the utterances of known Sāṁkhya authorities. It is necessary to differentiate between a school of Sāṁkhya and the adoption of Sāṁkhya principles by other systems. Thus, if in the *Manusmṛti*, *Gītā* or any *Purāṇa* we have accounts, which have some parallels to Sāṁkhya principles, with also some deviations from them, we are not to interpret them as referring to schools of Sāṁkhya, but as evidence of Sāṁkhya influence in other spheres of thought.

There is a basic difficulty in identifying the schools of Sāṁkhya. For this we require an account of the main principles of these schools. But the available sources do not provide the necessary evidence. Generally we find a brief allusion to some important views on a particular point. It is only in a very limited case that a few passages refer to the views of a given Sāṁkhya teacher.

Eighteen Sāṁkhya Schools

J. Takakusu[34] points out that, according to Chinese tradition, there

34. "A Study of Paramārtha's Life of Vasubandhu", *JRAS*, 1905, p. 49.

were eighteen Sāṁkhya schools. The Chinese testimony is based on the authority of Kuei-chi, a pupil of Hsuan Tsang, who belonged to the later part of seventh century AD. In his commentary on his teacher's treatises Kuei-chi says that there were eighteen Sāṁkhya schools or groups. Takakusu translates the relevant passage to mean. "The Sāṁkhya school was formerly split up into eighteen groups, the head of which was 'Ba-li-sha', meaning 'Rain'. His associates were all called the 'Rain-host' (Vārṣagaṇya)." The Chinese source does not name these schools, nor does it specify their distinguishing principles. E.H. Johnston[35] suggests that eighteen may well be a round number, but argues that Indian evidence would support the statement. No Indian text confirms the tradition about eighteen schools of Sāṁkhya. Johnston points out that Vyāsa, in his commentary on the *Yogasūtra*,[36] mentions eight theories on the subject of the reason for the union between *puruṣa* and *prakṛti*. In support of his view Johnston refers to the schools of Pañcaśikha and Vārṣagaṇya.

Sāṁkhya Schools Identified by Kushwaha

The testimony of Kuei-chi leaves no doubt that several Sāṁkhya schools were recognised in the seventh century AD. Usha Kushwaha[37] confirms the historicity of the tradition about eighteen Sāṁkhya schools with the help of the Purāṇas, especially the *Bhāgavata Purāṇa*. She presents a list of twenty-one schools named after the number of the *tattva* they accept as *ekatattvavādī, tritattvavādī,* etc., the others subscribing to four, five, six, seven, nine, eleven, thirteen, sixteen, seventeen, twenty-three, twenty-four, twenty-five, twenty-six, twenty-eight, thirty, thirty-three, twenty-six, thirty-seven or fifty-one *tattvas*. The *Bhāgavata Purāṇa* in Chapter XI.22 indicates thirteen schools. Those advocating twenty-three, twenty-eight, thirty and thirty-three *tattvas* are mentioned on the evidence respectively of *Bhāgavata Purāṇa*, III.6.1-2, XI.19.14, XI.24.1-8

35. *Early Sāṁkhya*, p. 2.
36. II.23.
37. *Sāṁkhyadarśana aur āyurveda*, pp. 3-6.

and II.5.18-31. The three schools referring to one, six and twenty-three *tattvas* are listed on the basis of the *Caraka-saṁhitā*, Śārīrasthāna, chapter 1. The two schools advocating thirty-six and fifty-one *tattvas* are identified on the evidence of the *Śiva Purāṇa*.

It is to be noted that no ancient text offers a consolidated list of all these schools. In most of the cases the appellations are not mentioned in the original texts. Usha Kushwaha coins the names after calculating the number of *tattvas* mentioned in the passage. In many cases the texts do not refer to any connection between the enumeration to the *tattvas* and the Sāṁkhya system. Further, the basis of the distinction among the schools is just the mechanical fact of the number of *tattvas*. From the commentaries on the *Sāṁkhyakārikā* we learn that there were sharp differences on several important issues in the Sāṁkhya principles, but they are not taken into account in the formation of the schools as determined by U. Kushwaha. But, this does not mean that we deny the existence of Sāṁkhya schools. They are indicated in ancient sources, but it is difficult to trace them, fix their designations, and determine their characteristic views.

Frauwallner on Schools

Frauwallner admits that Sāṁkhya as a philosophical system was split into many schools. But he actually mentions only three of them. According to him, of these the most important was the philosophical school of Sāṁkhya in its narrow sense. He, however, regards even Pañcaśikha, who stands at the head of this school, to be no less shadowy than Kapila and Āsuri. In the classical time of the system he places decisive names, Vr̥ṣagaṇa, Vārṣagaṇa, Vārṣagaṇya, and Vindhyavāsī, a late representative of the school, naming Mādhava as the last of the olden times. Frauwallner names the school of the Classical Yoga as the second direction of the Sāṁkhya school and envisages a third representing a Tāntric tradition direction headed by Pañcādhikaraṇa.

Yoga is closely connected with Sāṁkhya. They are sometimes described as two aspects of the same system and as being complimentary. But, the two have their own spheres of emphasis. They are by no means identical, nor can one be described as a branch of the other. No doubt there were teachers who presented the two systems jointly representing a distinct Sāṁkhya-Yoga school.

Frauwallner is not justified in postulating a Tāntric direction of Sāṁkhya as a third school of Sāṁkhya. This is based on a late tradition referring to Pañcādhikaraṇa as a Tāntrika. As we have shown, the term *tāntrika* is not used in the popular sense of one following the Tāntric system. Tantra here signifies a Sāṁkhya exposition. Pañcādhikaraṇa is thus mentioned here as a Sāṁkhya teacher who presented his views in the form of a Tantra.

Thus, Frauwallner has not tried to identify the schools in Sāṁkhya system. He includes all the Sāṁkhya teachers from Pañcaśikha to Mādhava as representing the main Sāṁkhya system. He does not mention the sub-schools in Sāṁkhya by grouping the teachers.

Sāṁkhya Lineage of Īśvarakṛṣṇa

Īśvarakṛṣṇa traces the lineage of the Sāṁkhya teachers from its first expounder Kapila. He names Āsuri as the disciple of Kapila and Pañcaśikha as the disciple of Āsuri. He does not name the Sāṁkhya philosophers who followed Pañcaśikha, but implies a vast literature and a wide variety of views. The fact that Īśvarakṛṣṇa confines himself to only the first three Sāṁkhya philosophers and asserts that his formulation is faithful to the earlier exposition made by Pañcaśikha shows that he definitely differed from many prevailing accounts of Sāṁkhya. Possibly, there were several traditions and Īśvarakṛṣṇa attempted to revive the lineage of Pañcaśikha, though he made some modifications in the process. Īśvarakṛṣṇa, who introduced an element of standardisation is responsible, to a very large extent, for wiping out the memories of the earlier schools.

Īśvarakṛṣṇa mentions only three names, but evidently the wide period separating him from Pañcaśikha witnessed a long line of Sāṁkhya teachers, who may have belonged to different schools.

The *Yuktidīpikā*[38] very effectively projects it by remarking that as the Sāṁkhya system was propounded by Kapila in the beginning, it is not possible to delineate even in hundreds of thousands of years the lineage of its teachers, as is done in the case of other Śāstras. Evidently the long line of eminent Sāṁkhya teachers is expected to have expounded a wide range of views, and not to repeat monotonously a set an fixed system of thought.

Sāṁkhya Lineage between Pañcaśikha and Īśvarakṛṣṇa

For the lineage of teachers between Pañcaśikha and Īśvarakṛṣṇa the *Yuktidīpikā* mentions the names of Hārīta, Būddhaḷi, Kairāta, Paurika, Ṛṣabheśvara, Pañcādhikaraṇa, Patañjali, Vārṣagaṇya, Kauṇḍinya and Mūka(?). A lacuna in the manuscript of the text before the name of Hārīta suggests that it mentioned some other names as well, which possibly were dropped by the scribe's mistake at some stage. According to the *Māṭhara* commentary, Bhārgava, Ulūka, Vālmīki, Hārīta and Devala belonged to the period of the gap. The *Jayamaṅgalā* commentary mentions the names of only Garga and Gautama. All these commentaries suffix the word *prabhṛti* (and the like) to their lists, implying thereby that the lists are by no means exhaustive. Surprisingly, these three lists do not contain common names, with the solitary exception of Hārīta mentioned by the *Yuktidīpikā* and the *Māṭharavṛtti*. This may be interpreted to suggest that the lists represent separate traditions or lineages. But, it will be intriguing, then, that the number of teachers in the three lists is widely varying, ten, five and two, which cannot be expected to cover independently three schools of Sāṁkhya. In all these three lists the lineage is connected ultimately with Īśvarakṛṣṇa, which raises the question of explaining how he could be the lineal descendant of three separate schools.

Though it is asserted by the three commentaries that Īśvarakṛṣṇa received the knowledge of Sāṁkhya through teacher-student lineage (*śiṣya-paramparā*), we cannot establish the

38. *adyo te śāstrasya bhagavato'gre pravṛtvād na śātrāntarasat vaṁśaḥ śakyo varṣasatasahasrairapyākhyātum* | — p. 175.

chronological connection among the various names in the three lists. We are not sure even about the order of sequence in them. It is not certain that each succeeding name was that of a disciple of the person immediately preceding it. The commentaries do not assert it. The *Māṭharavṛtti*, however, clearly says that Īśvarakṛṣṇa received the system from Bhārgava, Ulūka, Vālmīki, Hārīta, Devala and others.

It is only Paramārtha, who, in his commentary, specifically refers to the lineal connection, when he mentions the names as forming a bridge between Pañcaśikha and Īśvarakṛṣṇa. He says that the knowledge of Sāṁkhya was transmitted by Pañcaśikha to Ho-kia, by Ho-kia to Ulūka, by Ulūka to Po-p'o-li, and by Po-p'o-li to Īśvarakṛṣṇa, Ho-kia (= Japanese version Kat'-kia) may signify Garga, and Po-p'o-li (= Japanese version Bat'-ba-li) may stand for Bāddhali. Here a direct lineage is envisaged. But, the long period between Pañcaśikha and Īśvarakṛṣṇa cannot be covered only by three teachers in succession, namely Garga, Ulūka and Bāddhali, unless we choose to place Īśvarakṛṣṇa long before the time generally assigned to him. Evidently there were many other Sāṁkhya teachers in this lineage. Paramārtha mentions only three of them, and also commits the mistake of postulating a direct lineage among the five teachers from Pañcaśikha to Īśvarakṛṣṇa.

Sāṁkhya — Earlier and Later

The differences in the various forms of Sāṁkhya exposition were so pronounced that they were perceptible even to non-Sāṁkhya thinkers. In the *Caraka-saṁhitā*[39] we have a reference to the exposition by the *ādyasāṁkhya*. It shows that the earliest exposition of Sāṁkhya was considered to be different from the Sāṁkhya which came to be developed later. Thus, a broad distinction was maintained between the earlier and the later Sāṁkhya. Scholars generally agree that the Sāṁkhya system of philosophy, found in the *Caraka-saṁhitā*, represents an older form of Sāṁkhya, which was different

39. Sūtra 25.10 — *sāṁkhyairādyaiḥ saṁparikīrtitāḥ* ।

from the Classical Sāṁkhya of Īśvarakṛṣṇa,[40] and refer to it as the *ādya-sāṁkhya*. It is interesting to find that the Jain scholar Guṇaratnasūri, in his commentary on the *Ṣaḍdarśana-samuccaya*, speaks of the original or *maulikya-sāṁkhya*. According to him, the *maulikya-sāṁkhya* teachers postulate separate *pradhāna* (*prakṛti*) for each *ātman*, whereas the later ones (*uttara*) propound one eternal *pradhāna* for all the *ātmans*. Thus, a characteristic principle of the earlier Sāṁkhya system was the doctrine of the plurality of *prakṛtis*, whereas the later Sāṁkhya subscribed to the tenet of a single *prakṛti*.

We cannot say definitely if the *ādya-sāṁkhya* or *maulikya-sāṁkhya* was organised as a distinct school which had its separate existence even in later times after Sāṁkhya came to believe in one *prakṛti*. We do not know whether the original Sāṁkhya system was maintained by its followers in later times, or it existed only in texts to be referred to as an object of history. The evidence of the *Caraka-saṁhitā* suggests that the *ādya-sāṁkhya* continued to receive the allegiance of scholars in later times.

A similar distinction is maintained in the Sāṁkhya system on the ground of the belief in God or the rejection of the principle. We propose to discuss the problem in the following chapter.

Yuktidīpikā on Divergent Views in Sāṁkhya System

The *Yuktidīpikā* provides clear evidence for the existence of Sāṁkhya teachers and schools subscribing to views opposed to the principles expounded in the *Sāṁkhyakārikā*. This commentary aims at vindicating the views of Īśvarakṛṣṇa with the help of cogent arguments. It meets the criticism and contrary views of non-Sāṁkhya systems. At places, it refers to the views expressed by earlier Sāṁkhya authorities, and, after a proper analysis and

---

40. S.N. Dasgupta, *A History of Indian Philosophy*, Vol. I, pp. 213-14. Usha Kushwaha, *Sāṁkhyadarśana aur āyurveda*, pp. 240-2 makes a detailed study of the similarities and dissimilarities between the two to infer the characteristic features of the *ādya-sāṁkhya* in the Āyurveda texts. See pp. 240-2.

arguments, upholds the position taken by Īśvarakṛṣṇa. Some of these views are attributed to individual philosophers, whereas a few are specifically ascribed to the followers of a thinker. The reference to the followers maintaining a view shows that the thinker established a school which survived even after his death. Some instances referred to below are only illustrative and by no means exhaustive.

SENSE-ORGANS — NATURE AND FUNCTIONING

At one place the *Yuktidīpikā*[41] says that, according to some teachers, the sense-organs have no fixed magnitude and are modified into the shape of the object, whose impression they receive; others are of the view that the sense-organs are limited; while in the opinion of Vindhyavāsin they are pervasive.

The *Yuktidīpikā* refers to the difference of opinion among Sāṁkhya teachers about the nature of the organs. It quotes the opinion of Pañcādhikaraṇa that the organs are material products.[42] As a criticism of this view, the *Yuktidīpikā* reproduces the view of earlier Sāṁkhya teachers (*Sāṁkhyavṛddhas*), who argue on the basis of the fact that the organs are *prāpyakārī*, which means that they function only when they come in contact with their objects. The organs perceive objects lying at a distance. They perceive all objects, great or small, irrespective of the magnitude of the organs. All this is possible only when the organs are considered to be pervasive. This shows that the organs are not material products, but are the products of *ahaṁkāra*.[43]

On the question of perception the *Yuktidīpikā* quotes the view of Vindyavāsin that it is the coming into contact of organs with the objects and is free from imagination (indeterminate) (*avikalpika*).[44] It again refers to the opinion of other teachers who hold that general cognition (*sāmānya-jñāna*) of an object belongs to the organs

41. P. 108.
42. P. 108.
43. P. 12.
44. P. 4.

(*indriyas*) and special cognition (*viśesa-jñāna*) to the intellect (*buddhi*).[45]

The *Yuktidīpikā* mentions the opinion of several Sāṁkhya teachers about the number of organs.[46] Thus, Pañcādhikaraṇa takes the number to be ten, but the followers of Vārṣagaṇya mentions eleven organs. Vindhyavāsin holds the same opinion. According to Patañjali, there are only twelve organs, because he does not consider *ahaṁkāra* to be a separate entity, including it within *buddhi*.

The *Yuktidīpikā* refers to the view of a teacher who holds that the motor organs grasp, *manas* and *ahaṁkāra* retain, while the sensory organs and *buddhi* illumine the objects.[47] It criticises those who hold that the sensory organs illumine the objects.[48]

As against the view of Īśvarakṛṣṇa that the organs operate successively in apprehending all percepts, past or not visible, the *Yuktidīpikā* says that the ancient teachers maintained that in the case of present percepts there is a simultaneous operation of the organs.[49]

CLASSIFICATION OF KNOWLEDGE

The *Yuktidīpikā*[50] mentions elaborately the views of Pañcadhikaraṇa and Vindhyavāsin on the classification of knowledge which differ considerably from that of Īśvarakṛṣṇa. Pañcādhikaraṇa classifies knowledge into two heads—*prākṛta* (natural) and *vaikṛta* (acquired). *Prākṛta* is subdivided into three classes — *tattvasama*, *sāṁsiddhika* and *abhisyandika*. *Vaikṛta* is sub-divided into two classes — *sva-vaikṛta* or *tāraka* and *para-vaikṛta*. Vindhyavāsin disregards both *tattvasama* and *sāṁsiddhika*. According to him, knowledge cannot be innate; it is to be acquired. It does not function out of its own accord.

---

45. P. 121.
46. Pp. 108, 132.
47. P. 122.
48. P. 122.
49. P. 130.
50. Pp. 147-8.

BHOJA

Another point, on which the *Yuktidīpikā*[51] records differing views, relates to *bhoga*, whereas some teachers hold that everything is experienced in the *mahat* (*buddhi*), according to Vindhyavāsin, it is experienced in *manas* (mind). Some teachers hold that reflection (*saṁkalpa*), self-appropriation (*abhimāna*) and ascertainment (*adhyavasāya*) are distinctly separate; according to Vindhyavāsin they are one. Vārṣagaṇya is of the view that when the organs function abnormally, the influx comes into them directly from the *pradhāna* (*prakṛti*), but, in the ordinary course, they act from within. Patañjali says that they always act from within, but Pañcādhikaraṇa holds that they always act on the basis of influx from outside. According to Pañcādhikaraṇa, the organs by their nature are without any impression left in them and are like an empty village or a dry river. Whenever there is an external stimulus of knowledge, they receive automatically an influx from the *pradhāna*; it is only then that the organs can operate.

ORDER OF EVOLUTION

The *Yuktidīpikā* records differing views among earlier Sāṁkhya teachers about the order of evolution. Vindhyavāsin regards *ahaṁkāra* as also the five subtle elements as evolving from *mahat*.[52] But, Patañjali. who does not consider *ahaṁkāra* to be a separate category, holds that egoism characterises *mahat*.[53]

TRANSMIGRATION OF PURUṢA

The best illustration of the importance of the *Yuktidīpikā* is found in the passage wherein it discusses different views about the *puruṣa* adopting a physical body and migrating from one existence to another. Pañcādhikaraṇa holds the view that *puruṣa*, in his migratory state, is associated with a subtle body (*vaivarta śarīra*),

---

51. P. 108.
52. P. 108.
53. P. 32.

which enters the blood and semen of parents at the time of their intercourse. It then reaches the womb, forms the embryo, which develops into an avum, foetus, etc., and is then released from the womb as a child. The physical body, thus derived, is retained so long as the fruition of merit and demerit is not completely exhausted. The subtle body, after its separation from the physical body, migrates to heaven, hell, world of plants or animals or the world of human beings, according to merit and demerit acquired. The subtle body has the capacity to hold and seige the sense-organs; it is enveloped by the latter at the time of a new birth and is forsaken by the same at death. Patañjali holds that the subtle body varies with ach birth. For enjoying the benefits of the six *siddhis* the body transmits the ten organs into the seed of *karman*, which results in the integration of the organs with the merit and demerit of the individual. On the termination of *siddhis* this body pushes the integrated organs from behind, so that the latter may get themselves in touch with the parental seed of the next birth. As soon as this is accomplished, simultaneously with death the subtle body disappears. The migration into the higher or lower world is determined by the merit or demerit acquired during the period of *siddhi*. In the next life another fresh subtle body is received through good or bad *karman*. In this way the series of subtle bodies continues till the stock or merit and demerit is exhausted. According to Vindhyavāsin, the sense-organs are ubiquitous and hence there can be no movement of them from one embodiment to another. Fresh birth means only the manifestation of sense-organs in the medium of the parental seed. Death is the withdrawal of this manifestation. Thus, there is no existence of any subtle intermediate body. The *Yuktidīpikā* discusses these views and, in support of Īśvarakr̥ṣṇa's stand, shows that, by maintaining a subtle intermediate body, the problems connected with the process of migration of the *puruṣa* from one embodiment to another can be satisfactorily solved.[54]

EVOLUTION FROM AHAṀKĀRA

On the question of the evolution of *tattvas* from *ahaṁkāra*, the

---

54. On *kārikā*, 41.

Yuktidīpikā[55] refers to the view of an ancient Sāṁkhya text (*śāstra*), but without giving its name. The *ahaṁkāra* is considered to be threefold, *vaikārika*, *taijasa* and *bhūtādi*, according as it abounds respectively in *sattva*, *rajas* and *tamas*. According to this text, the *bhūtādi*, when the *vaikārika* (*sattva*) element is predominant in them and they are excited by the *taijasa*, follow the *vaikārika* for bringing about differentiation in their evolutes. In the same manner the *vaikārika*, when the *bhūtādi* (*tāmasa*) element is predominant in them and they are excited by the *taijasa*, follow the *bhūtādi* for bringing about differentiation in their evolutes. This is a significant way of emphasising the role of *guṇa*s in determining the nature of the evolutes emerging from *ahaṁkāra* and classifying them into subjective and objective series. This emphasis was not retained by later teachers but was reasserted by the *Yuktidīpikā*.

PRATYAYA-SARGA

The *Yuktidīpikā*[56] describes a concept of *pratyaya-sarga* (volitional evolution) which is different from that of the *Sāṁkhyakārikā* (46). It refers to an earlier Sāṁkhya text as Śāstra. The title of the text and the name of its author are not mentioned. Evidently it refers to an ancient system of Sāṁkhya principles. This evolution is after the evolution beginning with *mahat* and ending in the five gross elements (*viśeṣa*). This evolution springs from the will of what is variously termed as *Māhātmya-śarīra* and *Brahman*. Having derived his physical body, equipped with the organs, from the *prakṛti* at the beginning of a cycle of creation. He had a strong desire to procreate progenies who may do His work and may know Him, others and themselves. From His desire sprang from the main stream (*mukhya-srota*s) five gods. But He was not satisfied. Then He created twenty-eight gods from the horizontal (*tiryak*) stream, but He was not satisfied even with them. From the upward (*ūrdhva*) stream nine gods were created. But He did not think that His purpose was served. Then from the downard (*arvāk*) source He created eight

55. P. 116.
56. P. 112.

gods. This is a significant view of *pratyaya-sarga* which seems to have been accepted by earlier Sāṁkhya teachers, but was modified in presentation by later teachers.

EVOLUTION OF TATTVĀNTARA FROM PRAKṚTI

It may be noted here that the *Yuktidīpikā*[57] refers to an earlier Sāṁkhya view, different from the usually accepted version of Sāṁkhya. Whereas generally *mahat* is believed to have evolved from *prakṛti*, some teachers held that from *prakṛti* first emanates another *tattva* (*tattvāntara*) of indistinct form (*anirdeśya-svarūpa*). *Mahat* evolves from this nebulous *tattva*. Evidently this squence of evolution could not find acceptance in the general Sāṁkhya circle and was hence dropped.

SCHOOLS IN YUKTIDĪPIKĀ

At on place the *Yuktidīpikā* says that, according to Patañjali, Pañcādhikaraṇa and the Vārṣagaṇas *mahat* is evolved from *pradhāna* (*prakṛti*). Besides their common view on the point, the formal institutional connection among the three is not indicated. The names do not shown any order of chronology or importance. Available evidence shows that Patañjali did not precede Pañcādhikaraṇa. Vārṣagaṇas were the followers of Vārṣagaṇya. It is not known why, as in the case of Patañjali and Pañcādhikaraṇa, the name of Vārṣagaṇya is not mentioned and instead his followers are referred to. It is not unlikely that Patañjali and Pañcādhikaraṇa did not found an independent Sāṁkhya school, whereas the philosophical views of Vārṣagaṇya were not only preserved but developed and popularised by his followers.

Here we may note the interesting fact that the *Yuktidīpikā* quotes the views of several Sāṁkhya teachers, Pañcaśikha, Vārṣagaṇya, Patañjali, Paurika, Pañcādhikaraṇa and Vindhyavāsin. But, in no case does it refer to the views of the followers of these teachers. The only exception is that of Vārṣagaṇya. Of the thirteen

57. P. 108.

passages referring to the views associated with this philosopher, it is only in four cases that we have an attribution to him personally.[58] In the remaining nine passages the views are attributed to the followers of Vārṣagaṇya. It seems that there was a strong group of the followers of Vārṣagaṇya who had preserved his philosophical views. The school possibly maintained its individual identity even after the standardisation effected by Īśvarakṛṣṇa. In the case of other Sāṁkhya teachers we do not have the evidence to suggest that they founded a separate system of Sāṁkhya with its own group of adherents. From other sources we do learn of some Sāṁkhya teachers such as Yājñavalkya, Vasiṣṭha, Pañcādhikaraṇa, Jaigīṣavya and Pañcaśikha as expounding their views to individuals, but this is not sufficient proof for their distinct schools. Of these it is Pañcaśikha for whom we have reference to the largest number of disciples. Possibly all these established their own separate schools.

Conclusion

The reference to the Sāṁkhya school being split up into eighteen groups, as made by Kuei-chi, is to explained in the light of the above-mentioned facts, as gleaned from the *Yuktidīpikā*. Kuei-chi mentions Ba-li-sha meaning Rain (Varṣa) as the head of the eighteen groups. The obvious question is how can an individual be the head of eighteen groups. It seems that in the process of the recording of the fact in the Chinese and its translation now, certain elements have been introduced which have confused the original statement. Possibly Kuei-chi wanted to record that the Sāṁkhya school was divided into eighteen groups of which the chief was the one founded by Vārṣagaṇya. In his time also, it seems, the school was known as that of the Vārṣagaṇas, as indicated by the *Yuktidīpikā*. Not fully familiar with the background of the formation of the name Vārṣagaṇa from Vārṣagaṇya, Kuei-chi seems to have given explanations which create confusion.

The above discussion shows that though there were quite a few

58. P. 108, lines 9, 15-16. Vṛṣagaṇavīra on p. 90 clearly alludes to him. The reading *bhagavān Vārṣagaṇaḥ* on p. 72 seems to be the scribe's mistake for *Vārṣagaṇyaḥ*.

groups of Sāṁkhya thinkers, with their distinctive views, they could not retain their separate existence as independent schools. Of these the school associated with the name of Vārṣagaṇya had the most pronounced character and enjoyed a longer existence.

One word about eighteen as the number of Sāṁkhya schools according to Kuei-chi. Kuce-chi does not mention any school, excepting that of the Vārṣagaṇas. In Indian tradition several numbers have a hallowed sanctity and are adopted for classification and grouping. Eighteen is one such number. There are eighteen Purāṇas, eighteen Upapurāṇas, eighteen Parvas in the *Mahābhārata*, eighteen *vidyās* and eighteen Vyavahārapadas. Here the number may be imaginary and not actual, and was possibly intended to imply a large number of schools.

We may also note that the Buddhist canonical literature speaks of eighteen schools in Buddhism. This could have influenced the Chinese Tradition to mention Sāṁkhya also being divided into eighteen schools.

16

Sāṁkhya — Seśvara and Nirīśvara

Introduction — Philosophy and Religion

In ancient India philosophy is found emerging generally as an adjunct of religion. Philosophical thought did not exist in isolation. There are, no doubt, passages of sublime metaphysical heights. But philosophy seldom arose in abstraction. It is in the context of religious needs that philosophical speculation had its birth. The practical requirements of religion were often provided with an intellectual background or speculative justification through philosophical thinking. The need for escape from the sufferings of life and the urge for salvation led to various methods and ways. These methods or systems tried to rationalise their approach by presenting a philosophy dealing with the problems of life and world, the causes of suffering, and the way to overcome suffering. F. Edgerton[1] underlines this characteristic of Indian thought by describing it as "practical in its motive". It seeks truth "not as an abstract and in itself; it is for the sake of the salvation which that truth is believed to bring with it".

Among the issues, which the philosophical systems are supposed to deal with, the nature and role of God occupies an important position. In certain respects it becomes a distinguishing feature of the system. The question is important in respect of the Sāṁkhya system as well.

1. "The Meaning of Sāṁkhya and Yoga", *American Journal of Philology*, XLV, L, No. 117, 1924, p. 1.

Sāṁkhya — Atheistic

From very early times the Sāṁkhya view about God has been debated and discussed. The classical exposition of Sāṁkhya in the *Sāṁkhyakārikā* does not contain any mention of God. For this reason Sāṁkhya is labelled as an atheistic system. Denial of God is taken to be a distinguishing feature of Sāṁkhya. It is often pointed out that the twin systems of Sāṁkhya and Yoga subscribe to the same philosophical views; the main point of difference between the two is that, whereas Yoga upholds the position of God and assigns him a dominant role in its scheme, Sāṁkhya does not mention God in its philosophical system. The atheistic nature of Sāṁkhya is taken to be such a prominent characteristic of the system, that scholars often describe it as a non-Vedic philosophy. Scholars go to the extent of branding Sāṁkhya as being anti-Vedic and suggesting its origin from a non-Vedic source. Modern scholars have a complete faith in the atheistic nature of Sāṁkhya philosophy. This view of modern scholars has conditioned their treatment of the Sāṁkhya philosophy, giving it a particular slant and direction.

Here we do not propose to discuss the question of Sāṁkhya being Vedic or non-Vedic in all its fulness. We propose to concentrate only on one vital aspect of the problem relating to the Sāṁkhya position about God.

For a proper study of the question we have to analyse its different aspects and dimensions. We are required to begin with the views of modern authorities on Sāṁkhya and then to go on to the references in the ancient works, with a final scrutiny of the opinions expressed in Sāṁkhya texts. Here we will restrict ourselves to an analysis of the interpretations and explanations offered by modern authorities of Sāṁkhya.[2]

Modern scholars are so much obsessed with the notion of Sāṁkhya being atheistic that at times they have failed to do justice to the references to the contrary in ancient texts. They are inclined

---

2. We have used with advantage G.J. Larson, *Classical Sāṁkhya*, pp. 16-72, 245-56 for his critical review of interpretations of Sāṁkhya by modern scholars.

to explain such passages in a number of ways. They would not change their fixed view about the atheistic nature of Sāṁkhya even when faced with clear references opposing it. They postulate several stages in which Sāṁkhya was changed its stand on the question of God. According to them, Sāṁkhya before it acquired its classical atheistic form at the hands of Īśvarakṛṣṇa, underwent transformation from atheistic to theistic and from theistic to atheistic. They do not subscribe to a set pattern of transformation. They suggest varying patterns, according to their views about the original nature of Sāṁkhya.

GARBE'S VIEWS

Richard Garbe, among the earliest scholars to attempt a detailed study of Sāṁkhya, underlined its atheistic character. According to him, Sāṁkhya does not have any place for a god or gods.[3] Garbe holds that Sāṁkhya, in its principal features, is the work of one man, Kapila,[4] and that it has not undergone any remarkable alternation in its history.[5] The denial of God was one of the main features of the original Sāṁkhya of Kapila.[6]

Garbe requires us to believe that Sāṁkhya emerges suddenly in its full-grown form without any antecedents. We will not discuss all the fallacies in his arguments. The basic defect in Garbe's interpretation of Sāṁkhya is his reliance mainly on the *Sāṁkhya-pravacanasūtra*, as explained by Aniruddha and Vijñānabhikṣu. He ignores the other Sāṁkhya texts and references to Sāṁkhya in other ancient works and hence comes to a historically indefencible position. He fails to appreciate the historical significance of the testimony particularly of the Middle Upaniṣads (*Kaṭha* and *Śvetāśvatara*), the Mokṣadharmaparva chapters in the Śantiparva of the *Mahābhārata*, the *Gītā*, and the *Manusmṛti*. He does not recognise the possibility of Sāṁkhya acquiring its classical form in

---

3. *Die Sāṁkhya Philosophie*, pp. 253 ff.
4. *Ibid.*, pp. 46-50.
5. Garbe (ed.), *Sāṁkhya Sūtra Vṛtti*, Introduction, p. iv.
6. *Die Sāṁkhya Philosophie*, p. 26.

the *Sāṁkhyakārikā* through a process of historical change and of there being an early Sāṁkhya or pre-classical Sāṁkhya, which differed from the classical Sāṁkhya even in respect of certain vital points. Garbe could not give any place to the suggestion that Sāṁkhya was theistic at least in some quarters and at a certain stage of its history.

Stages in Sāṁkhya History — Consideration of Atheism

Later scholars, who were conscious of the historical argument and evidence, formulated several stages in the growth of Sāṁkhya philosophy, in which its view of God was a determining feature. One such early scholar was Joseph Dahlmann. He argues that the philosophical portions in the *Mahābhārata* contain the original form of Sāṁkhya.[7] In that stage Sāṁkhya and Yoga were not two separate systems.[8] As Sāṁkhya-Yoga they were one system, which was theistic.[9] Dahlmann was still under the spell of Garbe's influence. He took the original Sāṁkhya, found in the Epic, to be identical with the Classical Sāṁkhya with one or two exceptions.[10] Though the Epic Sāṁkhya has similarities with the Classical Sāṁkhya, the differences, though not many, are significant in nature. The theistic nature is one of the striking features of the Epic Sāṁkhya.

Paul Oltramare, like Garbe, interprets Sāṁkhya as a unified entity with little change in its long history from the earliest times to the *Sāṁkhyapravacanasūtra* and its commentaries. But he shows a departure from Garbe in some important respects. According to him, the Sāṁkhya dualism is not in terms of matter and spirit, but of Being and Becoming.[11] More importantly, Oltramare offers a more rational explanation of the atheism of Sāṁkhya. The philosophy of dualism of Being and Becoming suits the atheistic nature of

---

7. *Die Sāṁkhya Philosophie als Naturlehre and Erlosungslehre*, pp. 1-19.
8. *Ibid.*, pp. 5-10.
9. *Ibid.*, pp.12-13.
10. *Ibid.*, pp. 6-7.
11. *L' Histoire des Idées theosophiques dans L' Inde*, Tome Premier: "La Theosophie Brahmanique", pp. 221-30.

Sāṁkhya better than does the dualism of matter and spirit. The distinction between Becoming and Being does not admit the existence of a third entity as an all-encompassing god. But this does not rule out individual gods. According to Oltramare, the atheism of Sāṁkhya does not deny the existence of these gods. On the contrary he takes the concept of Becoming to include these gods appearing in the traditional Indian pantheon.[12] They do not clash with the formulation of Sāṁkhya principles. They do not have any relevance to the problems of creation and man's salvation. The merit of Oltramare's view is that he recognises that Sāṁkhya does not propound total atheism; its principles do not leave any place for a creator God who is also the ultimate refuge.

Hermann Oldernberg, with his sound knowledge of the Vedas and other Sanskrit texts, was in a position to reconstruct to origin and early history of Sāṁkhya. He distinguishes the Classical Sāṁkhya from its earlier formulation, which he terms as *vor-Klassische Sāṁkhya* (pre-classical Sāṁkhya). This can be traced in the Middle and Younger Upaniṣads (*Kaṭha*, *Śvetāśvatara* and *Maitrayāṇīya*) and in the philosophical portions of the *Mahābhārata* (*Gītā* and Mokṣadharmaparva[13]). The *Kaṭha Upaniṣad* does not represent a fully theistic system. Its *puruṣa* is like *Brahman*.[14] The pre-Classical Sāṁkhya in the *Śvetāśvatara Upaniṣad* and the *Bhagavad Gītā* acquires a more theistic form.[15]

Though A.B. Keith interprets Sāṁkhya as derived out of the speculations in the Vedas, *Brāhmaṇas* and Upaniṣads,[16] he does not think in terms of pre-classical Sāṁkhya formulations. He holds, that Sāṁkhya as a system is not found much before some later portions of the Mokṣadharmaparva.[17] He notices that the Middle

---

12. *L' Histoire des Idées theosophiques dans L' Inde*, pp. 268-71.
13. "Zur Geschichte der Sāṁkhya-Philosophie", *Nachrichten von der Königlichen Gesellschaft der Wissenschaften zu Göttinge*, Philologisch-historische Klasse aus dem Jahre, 1917, p. 218.
14. *Ibid.*, p. 223.
15. *Ibid.*, pp. 226ff, 233ff.
16. *The Sāṁkhya System*, p. 8.
17. *The Sāṁkhya System*, p. 65.

Upaniṣads (*Kaṭha*, *Śvetāśvatara*, *Muṇḍaka*; *Īśa*, etc.) tend to be theistic or even absolutistic. Keith, who considers the denial of the Absolute and the emphasis on individual soul (*puruṣa*) as one of the two Key Notions Sāṁkhya, does not take the formulations in the Middle Upaniṣads to be Sāṁkhya at all. What he takes to be the characteristics of Sāṁkhya are actually features which were standardised by Īśvarakṛṣṇa. It is to be noted that the meaning of the term Sāṁkhya has changed in course of centuries and with it the characteristics and contents of Sāṁkhya principles have varied. There is a case for recognising the historical possibility of a growth and change in Sāṁkhya philosophy. The standardisation of Sāṁkhya philosophy by Īśvarakṛṣṇa has overshadowed the earlier enunciation of Sāṁkhya principles. It will not be valid to equate Sāṁkhya only with what is generally described as the Classical Sāṁkhya. considering the long history of Sāṁkhya, we will have to admit several stages in its evolution. If we cannot identify all these stages, we have to recognise at least two broad phases of pre-classical Sāṁkhya and classical Sāṁkhya.[18]

These observations are applicable also to Keith's discussion of the testimony of the Epic, Keith holds that there are many kinds of speculations in the Mokṣadharmaparva and other philosophical portions of the Epic.[19] He describes only a few passages,[20] which mention twenty-five categories and clearly deny God or an Absolute, as representing Sāṁkhya. He refuses to recognise the other passages as testifying to the Sāṁkhya system. But, he does admit that all these passages have a dominant theistic tinge, with many Vedāntic ideas.[21] As Keith refuses to connect these passages with Sāṁkhya,

18. G.J. Larson and R.S. Bhattacharya, *Sāṁkhya* (Encyclopaedia of Indian Philosophies, Vol. IV) point out that the classical Sāṁkhya or the technical philosophical Sāṁkhya has a long history divided into broad phases of pre-Kārikā and Kārikā Sāṁkhya. The first, on early phase, includes older *ācāryas* and Vārṣagaṇya. The second, the later phase, inculdes the followers of Vārṣagaṇya including Vindhyavāsin and Īśvarakṛṣṇa.
19. *Op.cit.*, pp. 36ff.
20. *Mbh.*, XII.289.1 ff; XII.294.297ff.
21. *The Sāṁkhya System*, pp. 36-7.

there is no question of his admitting that Sāṁkhya had a theistic phase in its history. Like Garbe, he considers Sāṁkhya to be basically atheistic.

Edgerton on Sāṁkhya being Non-theistic

F. Edgerton holds that originally the term Sāṁkhya signified a method of salvation by knowing, without any reference to the content of knowing.[22] According to him, in the Upaniṣads and the Epic Sāṁkhya has this meaning; it does not imply any system of metaphysical truth whatsoever.[23] It was only with the formulation in the *Sāṁkhyakārikā* that the name Sāṁkhya came to be associated with a particular system of thought, 'with the doctrines of plurality of souls and no world soul'.[24] Edgerton is among the few scholars who have controverted the popular view that Sāṁkhya was atheistic or non-absolutistic.

Though Edgerton is justified in suggesting that Sāṁkhya originally was a method of salvation by knowing, he shuts his eyes to the rich evidence, particularly in the Upaniṣads and the Mokṣadharmaparva chapters of the *Mahābhārata*, about the circulation of Sāṁkhya as a philosophical system long before the *Sāṁkhyakārikā*. Edgerton ignores the fact that the *Sāṁkhyakārikā* itself refers to a rich and long history of Sāṁkhya as a system before its own times.[25] By taking the fully developed formulation in the *Sāṁkhyakārikā* to be the earliest form of Sāṁkhya he adopts a position which is similar to Garbe's presentation of Sāṁkhya as a monolithic system. Thus, he rules out the possibility of Sāṁkhya undergoing any significant transformation and fails to appreciate the Upaniṣadic and Epic passages with a theistic slant.

Edgerton's explanation of the term *anīśvara* in *Mahābhārata*,

---

22. *The Beginnings of Indian Philosophy*, pp. 24ff; "The Meaning of Sāṁkhya and Yoga", *op.cit.*, p. 16.
23. "The Meaning of Sāṁkhya and Yoga", *op.cit.*, p. 32.
24. *Ibid.*, p. 34.
25. *Kārikas*, 71-3.

XII.289.3 as meaning 'soul' or 'highest self' and not 'he who has no lord' is valid objection to the view which sees in the *Mahābhārata* passage a reference to Sāṁkhya being atheistic. But, what could not receive due attention from Edgerton is the fact that the question of Sāṁkhya being atheistic or not is to be discussed primarily on the basis of the references in the specific texts of Sāṁkhya. It has to be admitted that the enunciation of Sāṁkhya principles in the *Sāṁkhyakārikā* has no place for theism. Edgerton does not vindicate his view about Sāṁkhya not being atheistic by explaining the system as found in the *Sāṁkhyakārikā* and other texts of Sāṁkhya.

Use of Early Texts for Sāṁkhya History

Among the scholars, who have appreciated the historical value of the Upaniṣads, Mokṣadharmaparva, *Gītā* and other early texts and have formulated several stages in the history of the growth of Sāṁkhya, the names of S.N. Dasgupta, E.H. Johnston and E. Frauwallner stand out prominent. Sometimes they define these stages in terms of their being theistic or atheistic. The sequential order of these phases varies on account of the differences in the chronological position of these texts and their relative importance as suggested by the scholars.

Dasgupta, envisages three stages. On the basis of the contents of the *ṣaṣṭhitantra*, as described in the *Ahirbudhnyasaṁhitā*, he suggests that originally Sāṁkhya was theistic. The second stage, as represented in the *Caraka-saṁhitā* and the doctrines of Pañcaśikha in *Mahābhārata*, XII.219, was atheistic, Īśvarakṛṣṇa's *Sāṁkhya-kārikā* represents the third and final stage characterised by atheism.[26]

Johnston also identifies five phases which can be reduced to three prominent stages.[27] According to him, the *Sāṁkhyakārikā* gives the classical form of Sāṁkhya which represents the fifth phase. The first four phases are to be placed before the *Sāṁkhyakārikā*. Johnston changes the order of the first two stages

26. *A History of Indian Philosophy*, Vol. I, pp. 219-21.
27. *Early Sāṁkhya,* pp. 81-8.

describing the first as the early atheistic, the second an intermediate theistic, and the third a later atheistic. The first stage contains two phases and is represented by the *Kaṭha Upaniṣad* recording an incomplete form of Sāṁkhya and later by a more systematic form probably of the Vārṣagaṇya school. The second, theistic stage, is found in the *Śvetāśvatara Upaniṣad* and the *Bhagavad Gītā*. In the third stage, which occurred before the appearance of the classical Sāṁkhya, the atheistic schools formulated their principles in such a way as to reconcile the changes made in the preceding theistic phase. Some of this reformulation is attributed to the Pañcaśikha school.

A serious difficulty with Johnston's formulation is the larger use which he makes of imagination with very slender evidence in his support. His reconstruction of the history of Sāṁkhya is based on the study of certain key terms, their use and modification. He does not have definitive texts representing the various phases which he identifies. In his study Johnston has violently discarded the known chronological indications. Thus, there is no valid argument in support of the association of the later school of Vārṣagaṇya with the second phase and of the earlier Pañcaśikha school with the fourth phase.

Frauwallner[28] determines five stages in the development of Sāṁkhya. According to him, the original *Grund* text of the three passages in the Mokṣadharmaparva in the Śāntiparva of the *Mahābhārata*[29] represents the first articulation of Sāṁkhya theory, being a further working out of the Upaniṣadic doctrine of the self. The second stage, associated with Pañcaśikha, witnessed the articulation of most of the later classical Sāṁkhya, including the introduction of the theory of evolution and other related doctrines. The third stage, associated with Vārṣagaṇya, was characterised by the addition of further doctrines, particularly the introduction of the sixty topics (*ṣaṣṭhitantra*). The classical formulation in the *Sāṁkhyakārikā* is the final stage.

---

28. *History of Indian Philosophy*, pp.
29. XII.194 = 247-49 = 287 (Critical edition XII.187 = 239-40).

Frauwallner does not mention the concept of God as the distinguishing feature of any of these four stages. His total refusal to see in the Upaniṣads actual Sāṁkhya speculation, his limited use of the rich Mokṣadharmaparva passages and his ignoring the theistic references have pushed to the background this important aspect of Sāṁkhya.

Ralationship with Yoga

In Indian tradition Sāṁkhya and Yoga are often bracketed together. They have much in common. Certain aspects are emphasised in one, while some others are detailed in the other. H. Zimmer does not take them to be two different systems. According to him, the two make up one system of theory and practice. The Sāṁkhya represents the theoretical dimension of the system and the Yoga its practical.[30] One can easily visualise that from this it will be easy to connect the theistic view with the practice and the atheistic view with the theory of the system.

Two recent studies by J.W. Hauer[31] and Mircea Eliade[32] have a similar view on this question. Both have Yoga as their main concern. Naturally they approach Sāṁkhya from the side of Yoga. They over emphasise the Yoga connections and, thus, are not in a position to do justice to the independent elements in the nature and development of Sāṁkhya.

According to Hauer, a type of proto-Yoga circulating among the Vrātyas was taken over by Brāhmaṇism. Sāṁkhya is a later development within that Yoga tradition which emphasised speculation and intuitive philosophical examination of the Yogic state of consciousness. Later there arose some other basic differences between Sāṁkhya and Yoga. Hauer notices this atheistic and dualistic character of Sāṁkhya as early as the times of *Mahābhārata*, XII.289.[33]

---

30. *Philosphies of India*, p. 280.
31. *Der Yoga* (Stuttgart, 1958).
32. *Yoga: Immortality and Freedom.* Its English translation by Willard R. Trask (New York); also appeared in 1958.
33. *Loc. cit.*, pp. 208-9.

Eliade finds Yoga and Sāṁkhya to be very much alike. Among the very few essential differences between the two, one is that whereas Sāṁkhya is atheistic, Yoga is theistic.[34] Eliade fails to recognise any variation in this characteristic of Sāṁkhya, because he takes Sāṁkhya in the Mokṣadharmaparva and other earlier works to refer not to any system, but to any kind of metaphysical knowledge.[35] Even at a very early stage in the history of modern Sāṁkhya scholarship some scholars were critical of characterisation of Sāṁkhya as an atheistic system. They pointed out that the early texts of the system do not make a clear denial of the existence of God, being generally silent on this issue. Some scholars go on to offer a philosophical explanation of this silence. The Sāṁkhya texts do not explicitly mention God, not because they do not believe in His existence, but because they do not find a rationally justified role for Him in their philosophical system.

Sāṁkhya as Theistic

Max Müller[36] points out that the *Tattvasamāsa* and the *Sāṁkhyakārikā* do not explicitly subscribe to atheism. In neither of the two texts there is any specific denial of the existence of a god or gods.

With A.K. Mazumdar the attempt to explain the atheistic character of Sāṁkhya swings to another extreme. He does not find any conflict between the theistic passages in Sāṁkhya and the atheistic arguments advanced in the commentaries and other later Sāṁkhya texts. According to him,[37] the so-called atheistic arguments become really theistic when interpreted properly. But, this is overstretching the explanation. The fact remains that Classical Sāṁkhya is atheistic in expounding its principles. The atheistic character of Sāṁkhya is taken for granted by the commentators. They are at pains to explain it as issuing out of the compulsions of

---

34. *Loc. cit.*, p. 7.
35. *Ibid.*, pp. 148-9.
36. *The Six Systems of Indian Philosophy*, pp. 302ff.
37. *The Sāṁkhya Conception of Personality*, p. 1.

the philosophical stand of Sāṁkhya and as not conflicting with the requirements of religious sects to which they themselves belonged.

Appreciation of Sāṁkhya Stand

Modern scholarship generally speaking has been appreciative of the Sāṁkhya view on God. Sāṁkhya, as a philosophical system, does not have a place for God. Rational argument, when strictly applied to the Sāṁkhya principles, cannot justify a philosophical acceptance of God. Sāṁkhya is to be commended for rationally following its principles. It has been bold enough not to be swayed by other considerations in its philosophical exposition. It has extended its arguments to their logical ends.[38]

G.J. Larson has presented a very critical and convincing study of the history and meaning of Sāṁkhya. He takes into account the full range of the history of Sāṁkhya, though emphasising its classical formulation by Īśvarakr̥ṣṇa. He makes a judicious and critical use of the studies attempted by earlier scholars.[39] He is aware of the desirability of a historical study of the development of Sāṁkhya.[40] He himself attempts an interpretation of the historical development of Classical Sāṁkhya.[41] Before Īśvarakr̥ṣṇa's Classical Sāṁkhya he envisages only two phases. In the first, termed as Ancient Speculations and covering the Vedas and the oldest Upaniṣads, he traces many motifs, ideas and structures of thought which were later assimilated into Sāṁkhya context. The second phase of proto-Sāṁkhya speculations includes the *Kaṭha*, *Śvetāśvatara, Maitrī* and other later Upaniṣads, Caraka and Pañcaśikha, Aśvaghoṣa's *Buddhacarita,* Mokṣadharmaparva and *Gītā*. He notices a variety of traditions, without attempting a chronological scheme. In the texts of this phase "monistic trends

38. Sovani, *A Critical Study of the Sāṁkhya System*, p. 4. "There was no place for Him in the system and Indian thinkers and Indian followers were bold enough to carry their conclusions to the logical ends."
39. *Classical Sāṁkhya*, pp. 16-72, 245-56.
40. *Ibid.*, pp. 73-5.
41. *Ibid.*, pp. 77-163.

frequently parallel or subsume dualistic tendencies, and many passages are given theistic emphasis".[42] According to Larson, in this phase we may place "the emergence of a specific doctrine of twenty-five principles, comprehended from an evolutionary perspective, basically dualistic, nonthesistic and emphasising salvation by knowing".[43]

Sāṁkhya Being Non-Theistic

Larson takes a mid-way stand. He does not discuss the question of Sāṁkhya being theistic or atheistic. According to him, Sāṁkhya was non-theistic, and not atheistic. That is how he explains the term *anīśvara* in *Mahābhārata*, XII.289.3.[44] He translates the expression *anīśvaraḥ katham mucyet* as "how can he who has no lord be saved?" in the sense of "how can *puruṣa* be saved for whom an *īśvara* is irrelevant?" Larson is of the view that this approach explains the position of the *Sāṁkhyakārikā* on the question of theism. The text does not deny the existence of gods, in *kārikā*s 53 and 54 they are mentioned, but within the realm of *prakṛti*. These gods are, thus, irrelevant from the point of view of salvation. This non-theistic stand seems to have characterised Sāṁkhya for a long period. According to Larson, the earliest attempt to set forth a clearly atheistic doctrine is to be seen in the *Sāṁkyapravacana-sūtra*.[45]

Larson is justified in hesitating to attempt a historical presentation of the development of Sāṁkhya principles. The paucity of relevant texts of earlier periods and the uncertainty about the chronological position of the available references will deter any such attempt. But, there are enough indications of a broad outline of the chronological sequence of development and, following the lead of some earlier scholars, Larson could have attempted it.

Larson's view that Sāṁkhya had a non-theistic stand is based

42. *Classical Sāṁkhya*, p. 139.
43. *Ibid.*, p. 142.
44. *Ibid.*, pp. 132-5.
45. I.92-4.

mainly on the testimony of the Mokṣadharmaparva verse. He does not discuss in any detail the evidence of other Sāṁkhya texts, making only a brief reference to *kārikās* 53 and 54 of the *Sāṁkhyakārikā*. His opinion that this non-theistic character of Sāṁkhya persisted from the times of the Mokṣadharmaparva and was changed into an atheistic one only by the *Sāṁkhyapravacana-sūtra* cannot be upheld. Larson places the *Sāṁkhya pravacanasūtra* after the fourteenth century, but before the sixteenth century.[46] A perusal of the commentaries of the *Sāṁkhyakārikā* will show that the current view was that Sāṁkhya was atheistic and that they considered all possible objections to the atheistic argument. As an illustration we may refer to the discussions in the *Yuktidīpikā*.[47] P. Chakravarti[48] is inclined to place the commentary not before the first half of the seventh century and not later than the eighth century.

Latika Chattopadhyaya's Reconciliation

Latika Chattopadhyaya has made a very reasonable and convincing analysis of God in the Sāṁkhya.[49] She does not restrict herself to the *Sāṁkhyakārikā*, but studies the other Sāṁkhya texts, commentaries and relevant passages in the Upaniṣads, *Mahābhārata* and the Purāṇas. She takes due cognizance of the fact that Sāṁkhya makes provision for the divine parsonality in some form or other.[50] Reconciling the theistic fragments of Sāṁkhya with its atheistic arguments, she says:

The bifurcation of the Sāṁkhya system into theism and

46. *Classical Sāṁkhya*, p. 164.
47. (Ed. by P. Chakravarti), pp. 84-8.
48. *Origin and Development of the Sāṁkhya System of Thought*, pp. 161-2. A recent study concludes that it cannot be much later than the late seventh or early eighth century. Laron and Bhattacharya, *op. cit.*, p. 228.
49. *Self in Sāṁkhya Philosophy*, Calcutta, 1982, pp. 157-98. I am grateful to Dr. Smt. Chattopadhyaya for kindly presenting me a copy of this work.
50. *Self in Sāṁkhya Philosophy*, pp. 166-72.

> atheism points respectively to the position of subordination in which either of the two, reasoning and belief, is put. The atheistic arguments discernible in Sāṁkhya cannot prove conclusively that their authors are necessarily without any belief in a divine being; what they prove in reality is that Sāṁkhya, as a philosophy, cannot include within its fold anything like God that cannot be arrived at through a process of reasoning.[51]

Sāṁkhya explains the whole world process by means of two principles, *prakṛti* and *puruṣa*. By substituting evolution for creation, it dispenses with the creator God. The God does not have a function to justify his own existence in Sāṁkhya.[52] Sāṁkhya tries to deduce the various *tattvas* through the power of inference, which is applied for arriving at God also 'and herein lies the root of the Sāṁkhya denial of God'.[53] Dr. Chattopadhyaya stresses "the fact that God in the theistic philosophical systems enters through the passage of belief and not through that of reasoning. The fragments of the theistic Sāṁkhya, along with the treatment of God in the Yoga, mark also this dominance of belief over reasoning, although alien to the Sāṁkhya-Yoga structure."[54]

Chattopadhyaya brings out the relation and distination between Sāṁkhya and Yoga.[55] She criticises the common assumption that Yoga is the theistic counterpart of the atheistic Sāṁkhya. The real distinction between the two is that Yoga is based on practice, while Sāṁkhya is concerned mainly with theory. On account of its concern for practical attainments Yoga "has to include within its sphere some new elements which, although unamenable to logic are indispensable for the Yoga practice. God is one such element in the Yoga".[56] Her final summing up offers the most convincing

51. *Self in Sāṁkhya Philosophy*, pp. 172-3.
52. *Ibid.*, pp. 157-63.
53. *Ibid.*, p. 174.
54. *Ibid.*, p. 177.
55. *Ibid.*, pp. 180-2.
56. *Ibid.*, p. 177.

explanation of the apparently intriguing and conflicting Sāṁkhya standpoint and statements about God. "Contrary to the popular belief, we should rather note that in course of history the Sāṁkhya has relaxed at times its reationalistic vigour and adopted itself to the practical demand for a personal God."

Conclusion

Thus, we see that the earlier studies on Sāṁkhya suffer from a number of fallacies and mistakes and hence could not arrive at an explanation which may be both philosophically valid and historically correct. Some scholars identify Sāṁkhya principles with the enunciation in a particular text. Some others dismiss the presentation of Sāṁkhya views in earlier texts, sometimes in non-Sāṁkhya associations, as not relevant for their study. The Yoga associations of Sāṁkhya also have sometimes coloured the interpretations advanced by modern scholars. Whereas some scholars consider Sāṁkhya philosophy to be fixed and unchanging, others postulate a unilinear development for it. The attempts at determining the stages in the development of Sāṁkhya in terms of its views on God are vitiated by the neglect of the chronological position of the sources and the thinkers involved.

But the most serious mistake arises out of a failure to appreciate that Sāṁkhya system did not have a monolithic form in all the periods of its history. No doubt the standardisation effected by Īśvarakṛṣṇa provided a frame-work within which the later writers and commentators attempted minor variations or elaborations. It is to be realised that Sāṁkhya had a very rich and varied formulation in the pre-Īśvarakṛṣṇa period. It will not be correct to say that in this long period there were chronologically earlier or later phases of theisitic and atheistic Sāṁkhya, one ousting and replacing the other completely. Theistic and atheistic traditions seem to have co-existed in different circles. Theistic views have been recorded in some of the Upaniṣads and in the Mokṣadharmaparva. They also recur later in the Purāṇas and the commentaries on account of the sectarian involvements of their authors.

Sāṁkhya and Yoga are allied systems which, at times, have been taken to form a unity. They, no doubt, have their differences as well. In Yoga the practical side is more pronounced. In Sāṁkhya the philosophical aspect is more prominent. As a system based on reason Sāṁkhya does not find any argument to support of His existence; in the process of evolution the creator God does not have any role to play, and for salvation also. He is not relevant. Hence Sāṁkhya does not mention God. But, when Sāṁkhya also partakes of the nature of a practical method, it refers to a god or gods.

Thus, Sāṁkhya is to be labelled as bing theistic, non-theistic or atheistic according to the point of view from which we consider it. But, no one designation will hold good absolutely. It may vary with the text and the age concerned.

17

Vārṣagaṇya, A New Sāṁkhya Tradition

Introduction

SOME modern scholars assign Vārṣagaṇya a high place among ancient Sāṁkhya authorities and atribute to him important contributions in the history of formulation of Sāṁkhya principles. The ancient texts, however, do not confirm such an estimate of Vārṣagaṇya. Īśvarakṛṣṇa, in his brief account of the history of Sāṁkhya, does not include Vārṣagaṇya in the list of Sāṁkhya celebrities.[1] But, this can be explained as being casual and dictated by the requirements of the limited space in the verse. It is, however, significant that not many lists of Sāṁkhya celebrities contain the name of Vārṣagaṇya. In the Śāntiparva of the *Mahābhārata*[2] Viśvāvasu, the king of the Gandharvas, after listening from Yājñavalkya the account of the twenty-five categories (*pañcaviṁśam*) poses before him his confusion about the true knowledge, as the latter had acquired the knowledge of Sāṁkhya and the discipline of Yoga. The context of the account in the chapter, the categories enunciated in it, and the names of the sages listed show that here Vārṣagaṇya has been mentioned as one of the Sāṁkhya authorities.[3]

The Sāṁkhya tradition does not preserve a full account of its

1. *Sāṁkhyakārikā*, 69-71.
2. (Gita Press edition) XII.318.58-61.
3. The adjective used for Vārṣagaṇya is *dhīmataḥ*. It may be just casual to suit the requirements of metre. The respect shown by the adjective does not indicate any thing specific.

early history. Taking advantage of the expression *śiṣya-paramparā*, occurring in the *Sāṁkhyakārikā*,[4] the commentators have supplied a list of Sāṁkhya teachers to fill up the gap. The name of Vārṣagaṇya does not occur in the lists given in *Māṭharavṛtti* and *Jayamaṅgalā*. Paramārtha also does not mention Vārṣagaṇya in the list of Sāṁkhya teachers between Pañcaśikha and Īśvarakṛṣṇa.[5] The *Yuktidīpikā* says that the long history of the lineage of teachers (*vaṁśaḥ*) cannot be enumerated.[6] When referring to the gap, it mentions only Janaka and Vasiṣṭha.[7] But, later names several Sāṁkhya teachers, including Vārṣagaṇya.[8]

Vṛṣagaṇa, Vārṣagaṇas and Vārṣagaṇya

In the ancient texts we have three names Vṛṣagaṇa, Vārṣagaṇāḥ and Vārṣagaṇya. But these names should not create any confusion about their identity.[9] From Vṛṣagaṇa we can have the form Vārṣagaṇya to refer to the son of Vṛṣagaṇa.[10] Likewise, Vārṣagaṇāḥ is a derivative of Vṛṣagaṇa in the sense of a disciple or follower of Vṛṣagaṇa.[11]

The *Ārṣānukramaṇī* attributes the authorship of three *ṛcās* in

4. *Kārikā*, 71.
5. Takakusu, *La Samkhya Karika*, p. 148, fn. 3 corrects Po-p'o-li of the Chinese source to be a mistake for Po-li-so, Japanese Bat-li-sha, Sanskrit Vṛṣa. Aswami, in his Sanskrit restoration of the Chinese translation of Paramārtha, follows Takakusu and enumerates the list of teachers and disciples between Pañcaśikha and Īśvarakṛṣṇa as Gārgya, Ulūka, and Vārṣagaṇa (p. 98). U.V. Shastri *Sāṁkhya-darśana kā itihāsa*, pp. 518-19 restores Po-po-li as Kapila, but this creates many more problems than it hopes to solve. All this exercise is unnecessary. Po-p'o-li or Bat'-ba-li in the Japanese version is equated with Baddhali mentioned by the *Yuktidīpikā* as a Sāṁkhya teacher.
6. On *Kārikā,* 70, p. 175.
7. *Ibid.*
8. *Ibid.*
9. U.V. Shastri, *op. cit.*, p. 522, fn. 1.
10. Pāṇini IV.1.105 — *Gargādi-gaṇa*. Vṛṣagaṇa + *Yañ* (in the sense of *apatya*).
11. Vṛṣagaṇa + *aṇ* (in the sense of *tad adhīta, tad veda*) Paṇini, IV.2.59.

the *Ṛgveda*[12] to Vṛṣagaṇa. Considering the manner in which the Vedic tradition has been preserved with meticulous care, there is a good case for the historicity of Vṛṣagaṇa, though we may have reservations about the actual period in which he is to be placed. The *Ārṣānukramaṇī* indicates that it took him to be a historical person and not a mythological figure. It mentions him as the son of Vasiṣṭha.[13] But, the hymns do not support the suggestion that Vṛṣagaṇa was actually the composer of these hymns. One of the hymns[14] has *vṛṣagaṇa* in the plural, which suggests that here it could not have been the name of a person.

The *Lāṭyāyana Śrautasūtra*[15] mentions the views of Vārṣagaṇya. The views of Vārṣagaṇya are referred to at several places in the *Nidānasūtra* attributed to Patañjali[16]. Though Vārṣagaṇya in these two sources seems to the same person[17], he need not have been identical with Vārṣagaṇya of the Sāṁkhya tradition, because the two texts referred to above do not contain any statement of Vārṣagaṇya which may have any connexion with Sāṁkhya.

Pāṇini[18] includes Vṛṣagaṇa in the *Gargādi gaṇa*. This would result in the formation of the name Vārṣagaṇya in the sense of a progeny of Vṛṣagaṇa. Thus, it seems that both the names Vṛṣagaṇa and Vārṣagaṇya were quite well-known in the times of Pāṇini. But, Pāṇini does not give any details to identify Vṛṣagaṇa and Vārṣagaṇya. Patañjali[19] also mentions the name of Vārṣagaṇya, but without providing any information which may help his identification. There will be no chronological difficulty in identifying Vārṣagaṇya as an ancient teacher of the Sāṁkhya tradition.

---

12. IX.97.7-9.
13. *Vṛṣagaṇa Vāsiṣṭhaḥ*. It may also imply that there were more than one people with this name, hence the need to distinguish by mentioning the name of father.
14. IX.97.8.
15. X.9.10.
16. (Ed. by Kailash Nath Bhatnagar), pp. 33, 34, 62, 76, 96, 104.
17. U.V. Shastri, *op.cit.*, p. 610.
18. IV.1.105.
19. On I.1.51, *Vārttika*, 2.

No text written by Vārṣagaṇya is available. The ancient texts do not refer to the name of the work composed by him. The quotations from his writings occurring in commentaries do not leave any doubt about his composition being a Sāṁkhya text.[20] Such quotations occur also in works belonging to some philosophical systems other than Sāṁkhya.[21] Vācaspatimiśra[22] is the only writer, who, in introducing one quotation from Vārṣagaṇya refers to him as enunciating *Yogaśāstra*. In view of the undoubted testimony of many texts of diverse traditions which associate Vārṣagaṇya with Sāṁkhya, Vācaspatimiśra seems to be wrong when he describes Vārṣagaṇya as propounding *Yogaśāstra*.[23] But Vācaspatimiśra was possibly not without some reason in his support. Vārṣagaṇya seems to have belonged to a period when Sāṁkhya and Yoga formed a single unit. In view of the Yoga portions in the work written by Vārṣagaṇya, later writers associated him with Yoga. There can be another explanation for the reference in Vācaspatimiśra's *Bhāmatī*. As has been demonstrated by P. Chakravarti,[24] the theoretical portions of the *Yogabhāṣya* are based upon the system of Vārṣagaṇya and his followers. Thus, there was a living tradition in the circle of Yoga which gave a high respect to the views of Vārṣagaṇya. This was possibly the basis of the statement made by Vācaspatimiśra about Vārṣagaṇya as an expounder of *Yogaśāstra*.[25]

---

20. Quotations occurring in *Yuktidīpikā*, *Sāṁkhya-tattvakaumudī*, *Vyāsabhāṣya* on *Yogasūtra* and *Bhāmatī* on *Vedāntasūtra*. See U.V. Shastri, *op.cit.*, pp. 611-14.
21. *Vyāsabhāṣya* on *Yogasūtra*, III.53, *Nyāyavārttika-tātparyaṭīkā*, I.1.4; Padmapāda's commentary on the *Prapañcasāratantra*, I.94-7; *Rasavaiśeṣikasūtra*, III.2, p. 124; *Abhidharmakośa Bhāṣya* of Vasubandhu. See P. Chakravarti, *Origin and Development of the Sāṁkhya System of Thought*, p. 136.
22. *Bhāmatī* II.1.3, *ata eva yogaśāstraṁ vyutpādayitāha sma bhagavān vārṣagaṇyaḥ* I
23. Vijñanabhikṣu on *Brahmasūtra*, I 1.4 attributes the verse in question to Vyāsadeva. Vyāsa *on Yogasūtra*, IV.13 quotes the verse with the reading *māyeva*.
24. *Op.cit.*, pp. 138-41.
25. P. Chakravarti, *op.cit.*, p. 125.

The quotations in later writings are attributed either to Vārṣagaṇya or to the Vārṣagaṇas (*Vārṣagaṇāḥ*, *Vārṣagaṇānām*). We do not find any opinion or statement of Sāṁkhya being ascribed to Vr̥ṣagaṇa.[26] The *Yuktidīpikā* at one place[27] quotes the authority of a Vr̥ṣagaṇavīra. No other source confirms the name of Vr̥ṣagaṇavīra as a Sāṁkhya writer. U.V. Shastri[28] aptly takes it to signify Vārṣagaṇya, *vīra* meaning son.

The use of the name Vārṣagaṇa in plural implies that here we have a reference to a school or group of students, disciples or followers. But, in the absence of definite evidence about Vr̥ṣagaṇa having been a Sāṁkhya teacher, it is difficult to believe that he founded a school of his followers. It is Vārṣagaṇya who was reputed as a Sāṁkhya authority. Hence, Vārṣagaṇas may refer to his followers. There is nothing irregular about the formation of the expression Vārṣagaṇa to denote a follower alike of Vr̥ṣagaṇa and Vārṣagaṇya. This is provided for by Pāṇini.[29]

In the absence of any authentic information about the history of the school associated with Vārṣagaṇya, it is not possible to attribute the views recorded as those of Vārṣagaṇas to any specific person and to place them in a chronological sequence. It will not be illogical to suggest that these followers of Vārṣagaṇya were maintaining views originally propounded by Vārṣagaṇya. So, for the purposes of our study of the history of Sāṁkhya, we may attribute to Vārṣagaṇya not only the quotations under his specific name but also those which are recorded as the views of the Vārṣagaṇas. It must, however, be emphasised that, in the case of views ascribed to Vārṣagaṇas the origin may be attributed to Vārṣagaṇya, but their enunciation in the available developed from was evidently the work of his followers.

---

26. U.V. Shastri, *op. cit.*, p. 613 says that some of the statements in the name of Vārṣagaṇya occur in the *Yuktidīpikā* actually under the name of Vr̥ṣagaṇa.
27. See *infra*, fn. 64.
28. *Op. cit.*, p. 613, see also P. Chakravarti, *op.cit.*, p. 137.
29. IV.2.III — *kaṇvādibhyo gotre*.

Contributions of Vārṣagaṇya

We cannot hazard any guess about the scope and contents of the text written by Vārṣagaṇya, its arrangement and division of topics. From the available quotations it seems to have been characterised by a strange mixture of verses, *sūtras*, longer passages, and sometimes a discussion of other's views and vindication of the Sāṁkhya position. In the absence of relevent evidence we cannot determine if all this was Vārṣagaṇya's own contribution or some portions containing discussion and elaboration were supplied by his followers.

Johnston[30] assigns Vārṣagaṇya and his school an important place in the history of Sāṁkhya. In his scheme of five phases Vārṣagaṇya represents the second phase, which belonged to the interval between the *Kaṭha Upaniṣad* and the *Śvetāśvatara Upaniṣad*. In this phase Sāṁkhya received a more systematic form. Johnston mentions many new principles as being enunciated in this period, but does not check if they occur in the quotations attributed to Vārṣagaṇya. Moreover, there is no evidence to indicate that Vārsagaṇya appeared in such an early period of the history of Sāṁkhya, long before the times of Pañcaśikha and even earlier than the theistic phase of Sāṁkhya recorded in the *Śvetāśvatara Upaniṣad*.

The important role of Vārṣagaṇya in the history of Sāṁkhya is based on the testimony of later commentators who quote Vārṣagaṇya as propounding important principles on certain vital points concerning Sāṁkhya philosophy.[31]

An important contribution of Vārṣagaṇya was the doctrine of *pañcaparvā avidyā*,[32] or five ignorance causing the union of soul

---

30. *Yuktidīpikā*, pp. 39, 67, 72, 95, 102, 108, 132, 133, 145, 170; Vyāsa on *Yogasūtra*, III. 53, IV.13; *Nyāyavārttika*, I.1.5; *Nyāyavārttikatātparyaṭīkā* (Vijainagar edn.) p. 155; *Sāṁkhyatattvakaumudī* on 47; *Bhāmatī* on *Brahma-sūtra*, II.1.3.
31. *Sāṁkhyatattvakaumudī* on 47.
32. XII.33.

with physical elements. This principle occurs in the *Buddhacarita*.[33] On this basis Johnston[34] infers that the Sāṁkhya doctrines, as recorded in the *Buddhacarita*, were enunciated by Vārṣagaṇya. But, the argument is not convincing. The *Buddhacarita* is silent about the source from which it derived its account of the Sāṁkhya principles. The fact that Vārṣagaṇya is mentioned as a teacher of the *pañcaparvā avidyā* does not mean that all the accounts of Sāṁkhya, in which a reference to *pañcaparvā avidyā* occurs, were written by Vārṣagaṇya. The doctrine could as well have been accepted and retained by subsequent writers. A fundamental objection will be that, though Vārṣagaṇya is referred to as a teacher of the *pañcaparvā avidyā,* it has not been claimed that he was the first or the only expounder of the doctrine. It is not unlikely that the doctrine formed a part of the Sāṁkhya system from an earlier time and Vārṣagaṇya elaborated it or gave further importance to it. Hence, it will not be logical to attribute all the Sāṁkhya principles as enunciated in the *Buddhacarita* to Vārṣagaṇya.

Another notable contribution attributed to Vārṣagaṇya by Keith[35] and Frauwallner[36] is the authorship of the *Ṣaṣṭhitantra*. This is based on the fact that Vācaspatimiśra, supported by the commentator Balarāma, mentions Vārṣagaṇya's verse about the nature of *guṇa*s as occurring in a work called *Ṣaṣṭhitantra*. Another argument advanced by Frauwallner is that Vācaspatimiśra attributes to Vārṣagaṇya a quotation about the *pañcaparvā avidyā*. The five *avidyā*s are the five *viparyaya*s included in the fifty *pratyaya-sarga*s, which were part of the formulation of *ṣaṣṭhitantra*s. Hence Vārṣagaṇya is to be credited with the formulation of *ṣaṣṭhitantra*. The second argument is not definite. We cannot be sure when the five *avidyā*s were included in the *pratyaya-sarga*s. The fifty *pratyaya-sarga*s are mentioned in the *Devaladharmasūtra*. The concept of *ṣaṣṭitantra* seems to have circulated before Vārṣagaṇya's time. Significantly Īśvarakṛṣṇa, who loudly proclaims

33. *Early Sāṁkhya*, p. 8.

34. *Ibid.*, pp. 82-4.

35. *The Sāṁkhya System*, p. 77.

36. *History of Indian Philosophy*, Vol. I. p. 252.

his faithfulness to *ṣaṣṭhitantra*, does not refer to the name of Vārṣagaṇya. The attribution is opposed to the testimony of other sources which credit Kapila, or more commonly Pañcaśikha, with the authorship of *Ṣaṣṭhitantra*. We have no definite solution of the tangle. In view of the more likely attribution of *Ṣaṣṭhitantra* to an earlier author, it may be suggested that Vācaspatimiśra is wrong in saying that Vārṣagaṇya's verse in question occurs in a text named *Ṣaṣṭhitantra*. He, possibly by mistake, used the title of an earlier work for Vārṣagaṇya's text. P. Chakravarti[37] has offered a novel explanation to reconcile the conflicting evidence. According to him, the original *Ṣaṣṭhitantra* was the work of Pañcaśikha; Vārṣagaṇya simply revised it. But, there is no evidence to support this suggestion. If we are not to reject any one of the conflicting traditions, we may postulate that *Ṣaṣṭhitantra* was the work of Pañcaśikha, the case of Kapila being uncertain in view of the mythological elements in the accounts and that Vārṣagaṇya also chose to name his text as *Ṣaṣṭhitantra* in consideration of the central position of the sixty topics in the system of Sāṁkhya. It would seem that Sāṁkhya is earlier times was virtually identified with *Ṣaṣṭhitantra*.

In this connection it is interesting to note that some of the quotations from Pañcaśikha occurring in Vyāsa's *Yogasūtrabhāṣya* are attributed by the *Yuktidīpikā* to Vārṣagaṇya.[38]

U.V. Shastri[39] challanges the ascription of the original *Ṣaṣṭhitantra* to Vārṣagaṇya. He argues that according to Vārṣagaṇya[40] in the *ādisarga* the *pradhāna*, not influenced by *puruṣa*, has the quality of not being conscious, which is totally opposed to a statement on the point attributed to the *Ṣaṣṭhitantra* by the *Māṭharavar̥tti* and the *Gauḍapādabhāṣya*[41] saying that *pradhāna* is influenced by *puruṣa*.

---

37. *Op.cit.*, pp. 126-7.
38. P. Chakravarti, *op.cit.*, p. 115.
39. *Op.cit.*, pp. 613-14.
40. *Yuktidīpikā*, p. 102. See *infra* fn. 49.
41. On *Sāṁkhyakārikā*, 17—*puruṣādhiṣṭhitaṁ pradhānaṁ pravarttate*. U.V. Shastri, *op. cit.*, points out that this is also the view of *Sāṁkhyaṣaḍādhyāyī* (or *Sāṁkhyapravacanasūtra*) I.61.

The passage, containing a criticism of the Vaiśeṣika theory of atoms, is attributed to Vārṣagaṇya by Vyāsa.[42] This creates problems. It would imply a late date for Vārṣagaṇya, providing for the formulation of Vaiśeṣika as a separate system of philosophy and also for the emergence of the practice of inter-school debates and discussions, when the formulation of one's own principles was not enough, and a system was required to criticise the views of others and to define one's own position. This would ill suit the chronological position of Vārṣagaṇya as the author of a *Ṣaṣṭhitantra* and the original propounder of some important principles Sāṁkhya. Īśvarakṛṣṇa[43] claims that he omitted *paravāda* in his work. This tacitly implies that *paravāda* was a notable feature of some of the Sāṁkhya texts written before his times. There would be no difficulty in placing Vārṣagaṇya's text, with a passage criticising Vaiśeṣika theory of atoms, before the times of Īśvarakṛṣṇa. But, when we come to determine how much time elapsed between Vārṣagaṇya and Īśvarakṛṣṇa, we cannot be on sure grounds.

Some other quotations in later works also appear in the nature of discussions defending the Sāṁkhya position against criticism by others. Thus, in answering the objection as to how a single entity can contain contradictory characteristics of pleasure, pain and delusion, Vārṣagaṇya argues that the forms and functions are contradictory only when they are in their intensity; the ordinary ones can coexist with those that are in their intensity.[44] Likewise, in one quotation[45] the Vārṣagaṇas seem to be arguing against the concept of the immutable eternity of an object. It says that even the entire universe (*trailokya*) enters into its past stage as it is not absolutely eternal, but it does not lose its existence completely; it lies in its primary cause in a talent stage, and hence cannot be perceived. The *vināśa* (destruction) is of two types, that of the

42. *Yogasūtrabhāṣya*, III.53.
43. *Sāṁkhyakārikā*, 72 — *paravādavivarjitaścāpi*.
44. *Yuktidīpikā*, p.72 — *tathā ca bhagavān vārṣagaṇyaḥ* — *rūpātiśayā vṛtyatiśayācca parasparena viruddhyante, sāmānyāni tvatiśayaiḥ saha pravartante* ।
45. *Yuktidīpikā*, p. 67.

tattvas at the time of the *pralaya* and that of others as temporary transformation. It is well-known that one point of criticism of the Sāṁkhya system by the Buddhists is that they maintain the existence of a *dharmī* (abiding principle) manifesting itself through its *dharma* (properties). The present quotation seems to offer the explanation anticipating this criticism.

We can form some idea of the important principles enunciated by Vārṣagaṇya. One such view was the refutation of the plurality of *prakṛti*.[46] The *Yogasūtrabhāṣya* quotes Vārṣagaṇya to the effect that "since there is no difference as to limitation-in-extent or by reason of intervening-space or of species, there is no distinction in the (primary) root (or things)". This assumes significance, because it marks an important land-mark in the history of the evolution of Sāṁkhya principles. From Guṇaratnasūrī's commentary on the *Ṣaḍdarśana-samuccaya*[47] we learn that whereas the ancient teachers of Sāṁkhya subscribed to the principle of plurality of *prakṛtis*, later teachers believed in one eternal *pradhāna*.

Vārṣagaṇya seems to have discussed in detail the nature of *pradhāna* (or *prakṛti*) and to have defended the Sāṁkhya position. In the *Yuktidīpikā*[48] we have two quotations on this point. In one quotation the analogy (*dṛṣṭānta*) of the relation between male and female has been referred to. The followers of Vārṣagaṇya mention that the interaction between *prakṛti* and *puruṣa* might be compared to the manner in which man and women become sexually aroused by contemplating or noticing their unconscious bodies. U.V. Shastri[49] points out that this was on early analogy used in Sāṁkhya circles

46. *Yogabhāṣya*, III. 53 — *mūrtivyavadhijātibhedābhāvānnāsti mūlapṛthakatvamiti vārṣagaṇyaḥ* ।

47. *Sāṁkhya section — Maulika — sāṁkhyā hyātmānamātmānaṁ prati pṛthakpradhānaṁ vadanti, uttare tu sāṁkhyāḥ sarvātmasvapyekaṁ nityaṁ pradhānamiti prapannāḥ* ।

48. *tathā ca vārṣagaṇāḥ paṭhanti — pradhānapravṛttirapratyayā puruṣeṇāparigṛhyamāṇā"disarge vartate iti* । — p. 102.
vārṣagaṇānāntu yathā strīpuṁśarīramacetanānāmuddiśyetaretaram-pravṛttistahā pradhānasyetyayaṁ dṛṣṭāntaḥ । — p. 170.

49. *Op. cit.*, pp. 590-1.

and is mentioned in the *Mahābhārata*,[50] the *Ṣaḍādhyāyī*[51] (*Sāṁkhyapravacanasūtra*) and the *Māṭharavṛtti*.[52]

According to the other quotation, the followers of Vārṣagaṇya maintain that *pradhāna* functions from the very beginning of creation quite independently of *puruṣa*.

Vārṣagaṇya evidently had discussed the nature of *puruṣa* as well. This is indicated by a quotation in the *Yuktidīpikā*,[53] but there is no possibility of our being able to determine the points which Vārṣagaṇya detailed about *puruṣa*. Here the followers of Vārṣagaṇya are quoted as maintaining, on the question of the relationship between *puruṣa* and *buddhi*, that the *puruṣa*, having come upon the *vṛtti*s of *buddhi*, conforms itself to those transformations.

A discussion of the nature of the *guṇa*s formed an important feature of the treatment of Sāṁkhya by Vārṣagaṇya. In one verse attributed to him by Vācaspatimiśra he refers to the ultimate nature of the *guṇa*s which cannot be directly perceived, but can be inferred with the help of their visable manifestation.[54] On the question of the three *guṇa*s, though apparently different, cooperating together to bring about manifestation, the *Yuktidīpikā*[55] quotes Vārṣagaṇya. The quotation says "When the *rūpa*s and *vṛtti*s are developed to their full extent, they, of course, oppose one another, but ordinary *rūpa*s and *vṛtti*s are able to function in cooperation with the more intense or fully developed ones."

---

50. XII.310.12.
51. II.9.
52. On *Kārikā*, 21.
53. *tathā ca vārṣagaṇāḥ paṭhanti — "buddhivṛttyāviṣṭo hi pratyaya-tvenānuvarttamānāmanuyāti puruṣaḥ" iti* । — p. 95.
54. The verse is quoted, without mentioning the source, by *Yogasūtrabhāṣya*, IV.13. —

    guṇānāṁ paramaṁ rūpaṁ na, dṛṣṭipathamṛcchati ।

    yattu dṛṣṭipathaṁ prāptaṁ tanmāyaiva sutucchakam ।।

    It is Vācaspatimiśra (*Bhāmatī* on *Brahmasūtra* II.1.2. 3. who ascribes it to *Yogasūtra* of Vāraṣagaṇya.
55. *vārṣagaṇānaṁ pradhānāt mahānutpadyate* — p. 72.

Vārṣagaṇya possibly devoted considerable space to a discussion of the evolution of *tattvas* from *pradhāna*. The first to evolve from *pradhāna* is *mahat*.[56] Vārṣagaṇya brings out the characteristic qualities of *mahat*. One passage quoted in the *Yuktidīpikā* mentions the view of the followers of Vārṣagaṇya that there is one general *mahat* derived from *prakṛti*.[57] According to the second passage,[58] the followers of Vārṣagaṇya say that *mahat*, which is mere *liṅga*, cannot be comprehended; it is not to be distinguished in the form of effect and cause; it appears as another *tattva* with distinct characteristics. The emphasis given to *ahaṁkāra* by the followers of Vārṣagaṇya is recorded in the *Rasvaiśeṣikasūtra*.[59]

By the time of Vārṣagaṇya the concept of *tanmātras* had come to acquire an important place in the Sāṁkhya system. But, it did not settle down to a fixed position. According to the *Yuktidīpikā*, whereas some took the *tanmātras* to have a uniform single form, Vārṣagaṇya described them as having more than one form.[60] This means that "each subsequent subtle element is made up of its own unique essence in combination with the essences of its predecessors so that *śabda* is pure sound, *sparśa* is pure contact plus pure sound, *rūpa* is pure form plus pure contact plus pure sound, and so forth".

Vārṣagaṇya made significant contributions to the concept of *karaṇas*. According to the *Yuktidīpikā*, the followers of Vārṣagaṇya give the number of *karaṇas* to be eleven,[61] differing from others who mention thirteen *karaṇas*, consisting of five organs of action, five organs of knowledge[62] and three internal *karaṇas*. In another passage the *Yuktidīpikā* quotes Vārṣagaṇya about the nature of the

---

56. *Yuktidīpikā*, p. 108.
57. *sādhāraṇo hi mahān prakṛtitvāt iti vārṣagaṇānāṁ pakṣaḥ* I—p. 140.
58. *yadi yathā vārṣagaṇā āhuḥ — liṅgamātro mahānasaṁvedyaḥ kāryakāraṇarupeṇāviśiṣṭo viśiṣṭalakṣaṇena tathā syāt tatvāntaram* I —p. 133.
59. III.2, p. 124 — *āhaṁkārikāṇīti vārṣagaṇyāḥ (ṇāḥ). aulukyāḥ punarbhautikāni* I
60. *ekarūpāṇi tanmātrāṇītyanye ekottarāṇīti vārṣagaṇyaḥ* I — p. 108.
61. *Yuktidīpikā*, p. 133 — *karaṇam . . . ekādaśavidham iti vārṣagaṇāḥ* I
62. *Yuktidīpikā*, p. 132 refers to Pañcādhikaraṇa and others mentioning only ten.

karaṇas.[63] It says that the extraordinary accomplishments of the *karaṇas* are empowered from without through the inherent power of *prakṛti*, whereas ordinary functioning occurs from within.

The Vārṣagaṇas maintained an independent stand on the question of the *kṣetrajña* (soul) appearing in a body. Padmapāda says that, according to them, it enters the embryonic body through the juice prepared from the food taken by the mother.[64]

The work composed by Vārṣagaṇya contained an account of the sources of knowledge (*pramāṇa*). The nature of the different *pramāṇas* and their justifications were possibly dicussed. In one quotation *pratyakṣa* is defined by the followers of Vārṣgaṇya as the activity of ears and other sense-organs.[65] Another quotation in the *Nyāyavārtika* defines *anumāna*[66] as ariving at, on account of the perception of one aspect of an established relation, the other aspect of a relation. The *Yuktidīpikā*[67] attributes to Vṛṣagaṇavīra the view that the knowledge of an object, which is not immediate and is obstructed, can be acquired through signs and scriptures and quotes two verses defining *pratyakṣa* as the knowledge resulting from the direct contact between senses and objects; the same is known as *smṛti* when it goes beyond senses and is available through *bhāvanā*; the knowledge through *bhāvanā* later reappearing through senses is called *pratyabhi jñāna*.

---

63. *karaṇānāṁ mahatī svabhāvātivṛttiḥ pradhānāt svalpā ca svataḥ iti vāṣagaṇyaḥ* I — *Yuktidīpikā*, p. 108

64. Padmapāda on *Prapañcasāratantra*, I.94-7 — *(kṣetrajñaḥ) māturā-hṛtādāhārād yo rasaḥ pākajaḥ taddvāreṇa garbhaśarīraṁ viśatīti vārṣagaṇāḥ*.

65. *Yuktidīpikā*, p. 39 — *śrotrādivṛttiriti vārṣagaṇaḥ* I

66. *Nyāyavārtika*, I.1-5 — *sambandhādakasmāt pratyakṣa-tāccheṣasiddhiranumānam* I

67. On *Kārikā*, 30, p 130 — *tathā ca vṛṣagaṇavīreṇāpyuktaṁ bhavati . . . anāgatavyavahita — viṣayajñānaṁ tu liṅgāgamābhyām* I *āha ca — viṣayendriyam jātam punarbhāvanayā smṛtiḥ* II

U.V. Shastri, *op.cit.*, p. 613, fn. reproduces only the first verse and expresses doubt about its being attributed to Vṛṣagaṇavīra.

Vasubandhu,[68] in his *Abhidharmakośa*, attributes to the followers of Vārṣagaṇya the theory of *Satkāryavāda*: "According to them there is neither production of something new nor extinction of something existent, what exists is always existent, what does not exist will never become existent." The *Yuktidīpikā*[69] in a quotation attributes to the Vārṣagaṇas a discussion in support of the position that the entire universe form its stage of manifestation enters the stage of past; but it does not lose its existence; it lies in its latent stage in its primary cause and hence cannot be perceived. The nature of *vināśa* in the of *tattva*s differs from that in the cases of other objects.

Asaṅga or Maitreya-Asaṅga (fourth century) in his *Yogācārabhūmi* attributes to Vārṣagaṇya this view. He says: 'As to the nature of the doctrine according to which the effect exists in the cause, a certain śramaṇa or brāhmaṇa holds this opinion saying that the effect in fact exists perpetually through perpetual time and constantly through constant time; such a one is Vārṣagaṇya.[70] Though the view is in effect the same as that attributed to Vārṣagaṇya by Vasubandhu, there is a clear difference in the wording of the exposition. The quotation given by Vasubandhu is supported by other sources. It would follow that Asaṅga is referring to the views of Vārṣagaṇya, but not in his original words.

---

68. See Stcherbatsky, *Central Conception of Buddhism,* p. 75. *Yogasūtrabhāṣya,* IV.12 quotes the first portion as *na asati sataḥ saṁbhavaḥ na ca asti sato vināśa iti* I Vātsyāyana (*Nyāyasūtrabhāṣya*, I.1.29) attributes to the Sāṁkhya philosophers this part, though worded slightly differently.
69. D. Seyfort Ruegg in *Indo-Iranian Journal*, Vol. VI (1962), pp. 137-40.
70. *tathā ca vārṣagaṇāḥ paṭhanti — "tadetat trailokyaṁ vyakterapaiti na sattvāt* I *apetamapyasti vināśapratisedhāt* II *saṁsargāccāsya saukṣmayaṁ saukṣmyāccānupalabdhiḥ* I *tasmād vyaktyapagamo vināśaḥ* I *sa tu dvividhaḥ — asargaraplayāt tatvānāṁ, kiñcitkālāntarā-vasthānāditateṣām iti."* — p. 67.

    The quotation occurs with some changes in the *Yogasūtrabhāṣya*, III.13.

Omission of Vārṣagaṇya

Earlier we have pointed out that the name of Vārṣagaṇya does not occur in the lists of ancient Sāṁkhya authorities, even though authentic quotations recording his views are found in several works. The omission of his name by Īśvarakṛṣṇa could, no doubt, have been due to the limitation of space. But, there was possibly another reason. The development of Sāṁkhya from Kapila to Pañcaśikha was in a specific direction. The period after Pañcaśikha witnessed a rich growth of Sāṁkhya literature and a multiplicity of views on different points. No single list can claim to be exhaustive. The compilers of the lists had their own reasons for including some names and omitting others. We offer a possible explanation for Īśvarakṛṣṇa omitting the name of Vārṣagaṇya. Whereas Īśvarakṛṣṇa follows the tradition which began with Kapila, Āsuri and Pañcaśikha, Vārṣagaṇya adopts a different view on some important issues.[71] It is not unlikely that Īśvarakṛṣṇa did not mention the name of Vārṣagaṇya as be considered him an outsider to Sāṁkhya tradition mentioned by him and to which he himself belonged.

Vārṣagaṇya in the Chinese Tradition

The Chinese tradition preserves some interesting information about Vārṣagaṇya and his importance in the history of Sāṁkhya. There are two slightly different accounts in Chinese sources. One account is found in Paramārtha's *Life of Vasubandhu* (*Vasubandhucarita*).[72] The other account is given by Kuei-chi, the pupil of Hsuan Tsang.[73]

According to Paramārtha, Vārṣagaṇya was a sage of the Sāṁkhya school and was known mythologically as the "King of the Nāgas". Vindhyavāsa, who learned the Sāṁkhya system from Vārṣagaṇya, revised the content of the system and composed some couplets summarising the revised doctrines. Paramārtha refers to a debate between Vindyavāsa and Buddhamitra, the Buddhist,

71. A.P. Mishra, *Tattvakaumudīprabhā*, Introduction, p. 22.
72. J. Takakusu, "Life of Vasubandhu", *Toung Pao*, July 1904.
73. J. Takakusu, *La Sāṁkhya Karika*, Introduction, pp. 38-40.

who was the teacher of Vasubandhu. The account makes Vārṣagaṇya a contemporary not only of Vindhyavāsa, Buddhamitra and Vasubandhu but also of Vikramāditya and his crown-prince Bālāditya, who later became a patron of Buddhism.

Kuei-chi refers to the important position of Vārṣagaṇya in the history of Sāṁkhya. The Sāṁkhya school was formerly split up into eighteen groups, the head of which was 'Ba-li-sha', meaning 'rain' (*varṣa*). His associates were all called the 'Rain-host' (Vārṣagaṇya). The 'Gold-seventy' (*Hiraṇyasaptati*) is the work of them.[74] Kuei-chi further refers to a debate between a Sāṁkhya teacher and a Buddhist, for which the Sāṁkhya teacher composed in seventy verses a treatise called the "Gold-seventy"[75]. The Chinese tradition identifies the "Gold seventy" with the *Sāṁkhya-śāstra* or the Chinese version of the *Sāṁkhyakārikā*.[76]

The events and persons mentioned in the two accounts are identified. Takakusu[77] and following him, Garbe[78] and Keith[79] identify Vindhyavāsa with Īśvarakṛṣṇa.

The identification, if accepted, will bring Vārṣagaṇya very close to Īśvarakṛṣṇa in time and will provide clues to the date of Vārṣagaṇya. The dates of Vikramāditya (identified with Candragupta II or Skandagupta), his son Bālāditya, Buddhamitra, Vasubandhu, Vindhyavāsa and Īśvarakṛṣṇa, all become relevant to us. The dates for the composition of Paramārtha's *Life of Vasubandhu* and the Chinese translation of *Sāṁkhyakārikā* will have important bearing on the subject. Apparently, there is a case for reading in Paramārtha's account of the Sāṁkhya writings of Vindhyavāsa a reference to the *Sāṁkhyakārikā* and for identifying "Gold-Seventy"

---

74. Takakusu, "A study of Paramārtha's Life of Vasubandhu, and the Date of Vasubandhu", *JRAS*, 1905, p. 49.
75. *Ibid.*, 72.
76. Takakusu, "La Sāṁkhyakarika" (I), pp. 38-40.
77. *Bulletin de l Ecole Francaise d Extreme Orient,* IV, p. 59; *Toung Pao* July, 1904, pp. 47-51.
78. *Die Sāṁkhya Philosophie*, pp. 77-83.
79. *History of Sāṁkhya Philosophy*, p. 73.

(*Hiraṇyasaptati* or *Suvarṇasaptati*) with the *Sāṁkhyakārikā* which contains seventy *kārikās*.[80] But, there are serious difficulties in accepting the identification.[81] The *Yuktidīpikā* clearly distinguishes between Vindhyavāsin and Īśvarakṛṣṇa.[82] Moreover, the views of Vindhyavāsin, as preserved in other texts,[83] are totally opposed to what Īśvarakṛṣṇa says on those points.[84] Larson[85] is justified in opposing the identification on the ground that the *Sāṁkhyakārikā* is not a polemical text and could not have been written for the purposes of a debate. His suggestion that the Chinese tradition has identified two separate texts or events is quite plausible. A tradition about a debate between a Buddhist and Sāṁkhya teacher, who belonged to the school of the followers of Vārṣagaṇya, and was possibly Vindhyavāsa, became mixed up with the subsequent composition of the *Sāṁkhyakārikā* or the *Sāṁkhyasaptati* by Īśvarakṛṣṇa.[86]

Date of Vārṣagaṇya

All this helps us determine roughly the place of Vārṣagaṇya in the broad outlines of the history of Sāṁkhya. If the ascription of the same passage to both Pañcaśikha and Vārṣagaṇya is taken to be factually correct, we may infer that Vārṣagaṇya possibly adopted pasages from Pañcaśikha. Thus, Vārṣagaṇya will have to be placed after Pañcaśikha, possibly not much removed in time from him. The value of the Chinese sources lies in establishing that Vārṣagaṇya belonged to the period before Vindhyavāsa, who is said to have rewritten the book composed earlier by Vārṣagaṇya. When the Chinese tradition mentions Vindhyavāsa as studying with his

80. *Sāṁkhyakārikā*, 72 — *saptatyāṁ kila ye'rthāḥ* |
81. H.D. Sharma, "The Sāṁkhya teachers", *Festschrift Mori Winternitz*, pp. 228-9.
82. P. 4.
83. *Yuktidīpikā*, p. 108; Kumārila's *Ślokavārtika*, pp. 293, 704; Bhoja on *Yogasūtra*, IV.22; Medhātithi on Manu I.45; Guṇaratna on *Sarvadarśanasaṁgraha*, pp. 102, 104; *Syādvādamañjarī* (Chowkhamba), p. 117.
84. Gopinath Kaviraj, *Jayamaṅgalā*, ed. by H. Sharma, Introduction. p. 7.
85. *Classical Sāṁkhya*, p. 155.
86. For a detailed analysis of the Chinese evidence see *infra* chapter 18.

teacher Vārṣagaṇya, it possibly means that he belonged to the school of Vārṣagaṇya. If the passage is literally interpreted as referring to Vindhayavāsa as the direct disciple of Vārṣagaṇya, it would make Vārṣagaṇya the senior contemporary of Vindhyavāsa.

There is no positive indication of the date to which Vārṣagaṇya belonged. Later tradition does record the name of a Vedic sage as Vṛṣagaṇa. If we postulate that Vṛṣagaṇa and his son Vārṣagaṇya were known to Pāṇini, they will have to be placed quite sometime before Pāṇini, but we cannot determine the precise duration of this gap. In the *Mahābhārata* Viśvāvasu, the Gandharva king, includes Vārṣagaṇya in the long list of sages and scholars from whom he learnt Sāṁkhya. Clearly the list does not have any pretensions to maintaining a chronological sequence.[87] Hence, we cannot deduce anything about the date of Vārṣagaṇya from his position in this list. We can only infer that at the time of the incorporation of this particular chapter in the Mokṣadharmaparva of the Śāntiparva of the *Mahābhārata* Vārṣagaṇya enjoyed the reputation of being an ancient Sāṁkhya authority. Considering the various problems in fixing the date of the *Mahābhārata* in general and of the Śāntiparva (and the Mokṣadharmaparva section) in particular, we will not be wide off the mark if we place Vārṣagaṇya, the Sāṁkhya authority mentioned in it, as being not later than the fifth-fourth centuries BC.[88] The dates generally suggested for Pāṇini will also not go against this

---

87. Hare Viśvāvasu claims that later (*tadanantaram*) he acquired the knowledge not only from the sages and scholars named by him but also from Rudra, Viśvarūpa gods, pitṛs and the demons—*Mbh*, XII.318.62-3. In the names enumerated by Viśvāvasu Jaigīṣavya appears first and his own father Kaśyapa is mentioned last. The name of Kapila, occurring in the middle and after Jaigīṣavya, Asita, Devala, Parāśara, Vārṣagaṇya, Bhṛgu and Pañcaśikha, shows the disturbed chronological sequence of names in the list.

88. U.V. Shastri, *op.cit.*, pp. 609-11, fn. 2 on the basis of the *Mahābhārata* reference places Vārṣagaṇya before the Mahābhārata War. We need not discuss this view, because it involves a confusion between the Mahābhārata War and the composition of the *Mahābhārata* text. Shastri places Vārṣagaṇya before Pāṇini and Buddha. It may be conceded that Vārṣagaṇya came before Pāṇini, but Shastri's argument for placing him before Buddha is not convincing.

date. A respectable antiquity for Vārṣagaṇya is indicated, when authors, not only of Sāṁkhya works[89] but also of other philosophical systems,[90] venerate him with the honourable appellation of *bhagavān*.

The recorded facts about the history of the Sāṁkhya are not helpful in fixing the date of Vārṣagaṇya. Among the commentators the author of the *Yuktidīpikā* alone includes him in the list of Sāṁkhya teachers who preceded Īśvarakṛṣṇa. We cannot be sure that the names are listed in the correct historical sequence. It may, however, be noted that Vārṣagaṇya appears after Hārīta, Bāddhali, Kairata, Paurika, Ṛṣabheśvara, Pañcādhikaraṇa and Patañjali but before Kauṇḍinya and Mūka. This will give him a late date, specially when Patañjali, apparently associated more closely with Yoga, is placed in the second century BC, on the basis of his identification with the author of the *Mahābhāṣya*.[91]

Vārṣagaṇya in Isibhāsiyāim

Modern scholars have failed to notice the important information which the Jain tradition records about Vārṣagaṇya. In the *Isibhāsiyāim*[92] section (*ajjhayana-adhyayana*) 18 deals with the views of Varisava (*Varisava-kaṇhena arhatā isiṇā buitam*). In the body of the section the name of the *ṛṣi* is easily identified with Vārisakaṇhā referred to in the *Ṭhāṇāṅga*.[93] Walther Schubring[94] takes Vārisakaṇhā and Varisavakaṇha to be based on Vārṣagaṇya. In the Sanskrit *ṭīkā* on the *Isibhāsiyāim*[95] the name of the *ṛṣi* is

---

89. *Yuktidīpikā*, p. 72; *Sāṁkhyatattvakaumudī* on *Kārikā* 47.
90. *Bhāmatī* on *Vedāntasūtra*, II.1.3.
91. See *supra* chapter 14 where we have suggested that Patañjali, the Sāṁkhya teacher, is to be placed in the bracket *c.* 500-400 BC.
92. L.D. Series 54, ed. by Walther Schubring, pp. 34-7.
93. 390a. On this basis Sagarmal Jain, *Ṛṣibhāṣita: Eka Adhyayana* (Jaipur, 1988), pp. 54-5 restores the name as Vāriṣeṇa Kṛṣṇa. The editors of the Prakrit Bharati edition equate *Varisava* with Varṣapa, but ignore the second part *Kaṇha*. In the first *Saṁgrahaṇī* of the text the reading is *Varise Kaṇhe*.
94. *Isibhāsiyāim*, Introduction, p. 4.
95. P. 140.

restored as Vārṣagaṇya. The presentation of the views of the *ṛṣi* in the present case, as also in other cases, has been conditioned by the uniform pattern of the structure of the section, the style of repeating set phrases and sentences, particularly in the introductory part and the conclusion, and the retention of peculier Jain concepts of eighteen *pāpa-karmas* with related terms *pāṇātivāeṇa*, *pariggaha*, *arati* and *micchādaṁsaṇa*. The attempt, on the part of the author, to weave the different sections of the text into a unified whole and not to leave it to assume the character of a mere collection diverse views, is indicated in the present section by a reference to the created beings bearing the consequences of their evil deeds and remaining in the cycle of worldly existence as mentioned in the ninth section (*ṇavamuddesagameṇam*). Even with this limitation, we can get a rough idea of some of the characteristic views of the *ṛṣi* and the terminology used by him. The opening sentence of the section says that the soul (*jīve*), which does not have self-control (*ayate*), uses strong means or violence (*vajjam*).[96] By not resorting to sinful acts, beginning with killing beings and going up to false philosophy, and by controlling the five sense-organs, including ears, he gives up violence and overcomes the punishment of cutting of hands and feet and attains eternally the auspicious abode (*sivamacala-jāva ciṭṭhanti*).[97] To illustrate the statement that in ordinary circumstances strong means are used a verse is reproduced saying that the bird uses the blows of its beak and the water-carrier uses thong and ropes.[98]

As no text written by Vārṣagaṇya is available, we cannot check the correctness of the views and passages ascribed to him in the *Īsibhāsiyāim*. The available quotations from his work are very few and hence no conclusion can be drawn on the basis of the absence

---

96. *ayate khalu bho jīve vajjaṁ samādiyati.*

97. *pāṇāivātaveramaṇenaṁ jāva micchādaṁsaṇasall-averamaṇeṇaṁ soinya 5-ṇiggaheṇaṁ ṇo vajjaṁ samajjiṇittā hatthaccheyaṇāiṁ pāyaccheyaṇāim jāva domaṇastāiṁ vītivatittā sivamacala — jāva ciṭṭanti.*

98. *sakuṇī saṁkupayaghātaṁ ca varattaṁ rajjugaṁ tahā* । *vārisattadharo ccaiva vibhāgammi vihāvae* ॥

of any quotation parallel to the passages in the *Īsibhāsiyāim*. The views ascribed to different *ṛṣis* appear to be qenuine and authentic, though their presentation is affected by the fixed pattern of structure and style of expression and the attempt to accommodate them within the framework of Jain principles.[99] The expressions *ayate*,[100] *jīva*, *soindiya 5-ṇiggaheṇaṁ* and *sivamacala* could very well have been taken from Vārṣagaṇya's work. Some texts and passages recording an early phase of Sāṁkhya, when it was closely connected with Yoga, have parallel concepts and terms. On the basis of the analysis of other sections[101] we can take the verse to have been based on the original writing of Vārṣagaṇya.

The historical identity of most of the *ṛṣis*, whose views are collected in the *Isibhāsiyāim*, is clear. Some of them are, no doubt, taken from the Brāhmaṇical tradition about semi-historical sages.

The *Isibhāsiyāim*, though not included in the list of Jain Āgama texts, enjoys a high respect being classed as a *Kālīya* text, which is approved for the study-hours in the daily time-table. It looks like an early text in the category of the *Āyāra*, *Sūyagaḍa*, *Uttarājjhāyā* and *Dasaveyāliya*. It breathes an atmosphere free from sectarian orthodoxy, which developed in later phases of the history of Jainism. It has to be placed long before the times of the *Viyāhapannatti*. It appears to be more under the influence of Pārśvanātha.[102] Thus, the *ṛṣis*, whose views are recorded in the text, were possibly either earlier than Mahāvīra or were his close contemporaries. They could not have belonged to a period long after Mahāvīra.[103] Sagarmal Jain, in his recent study of the text demonstrates that it was composed sometime between the fifth century BC and third century BC. Thus, is Vārṣagaṇya is to be identified with Varisavakanha of the *Isibhāsiyāim*, he is to be placed by the fifth-fourth centuries BC.

---

99. See Appendix II.
100. It is derived from the root *yam* 'to control, restrain' and reminds us of the term *yati* meaning 'one who has controlled his passions'.
101. See Appendix II.
102. *Ibid.*
103. See Appendix II.

A earlier date is not ruled out by the evidence of the *Isibhāsiyāim*.

Conclusion

In the history of Sāṁkhya Vārṣagaṇya belongs to the gap between Pañcaśikha and Īśvarakṛṣṇa. He expressed significant views on some important points, sometime taking a stand different from that of the mainstream, represented by Kapila, Āsuri and Pañcaśikha, which was supported and strangthened later by Īśvarakṛṣna. He is to be placed in the phase before Īśvarakṛṣṇa, which was characterised by the writing of *ākhyāyikā*s and *paravāda*. Vārṣagaṇya also wrote in the form of these categories, challenging the views of other systems and defending the Sāṁkhya position against the criticism of others.

18

Vindhyavāsin and the Emergence of Classical Sāṁkhya

VINDHYAVĀSIN[1] occupies an important place in the history of Sāṁkhya. On certain vital points in the Sāṁkhya philosophy he expounded his distinctive views, radically opposed to the standardised system presented by Īśvarakṛṣṇa. He is engulfed in controversies about his very identity. Modern scholars have expressed doubt about his name, the period when he flourished, and his relationship with Īśvarakṛṣṇa. The confusion is increased by the ancient Chinese sources, which provide conflicting evidence amenable to varying interpretations.

Name

In the Chinese tradition in Paramārtha's *Vasubandhucarita* (Life of Vasubandhu) the name occurs as Vindhyavāsa.[2] In ancient Indian texts it is generally spelt as Vindhyavāsin.[3] Kumārila mentions two readings, Vindhyanivāsa[4] and Vindhyavāsin[5] at two

---

1. We have followed the form Vindhyavāsin evidenced in Indian sources, but, in referring to the accounts of Paramārtha and Kuei-chi, have used the name Vindhyavāsa.
2. Takakusu, "A Study of Paramārtha's Life of Vasubandhu" and the Date of Vasubandhu, *JRAS* (1905), 47-50; "La Sāṁkhyakārikā, étudiée à la lumière de sa version chinoise (I)", *BEFEO*, Tome IV Hanoi, 1904, pp. 407.
3. U.V. Shastri, *Sāṁkhyadarśana kā itihāsa*, pp. 521-6, 636-8.
4. *Ślokavārtika*, Akṛtivāda 76.
5. *Ślokavārtika*, Ātmavāda 62.

different places. Umbeka in his commentary[6] explains Vindhyanivāsa as standing for Vindhyavāsin. Medhātithi[7] gives the name of the Sāṁkhya philosopher as Vindhyavāsa. The variant forms of the name create a doubt about the original name and its significance. G.J. Larson,[8] without discussing the question, uniformly adopts the name as Vindhyavāsa. A.B. Keith[9] takes Vindhyavāsin and Vindhyavāsa as two distinct persons, the first being a Sāṁkhya teacher and the second a Mīmāṁsā teacher. But, this distinction is misplaced. Medhātithi and Paramārtha both very clearly mention Vindhyavāsa also as a Sāṁkhya teacher.

RUDRILA

Kamalaśīla, in his commentary on the *Tattvasaṁgraha*,[10] quotes a verse which shows that Rudrila was the original name[11] and the appellation Vindhyavāsin (an inhabitant of the Vindhya mountains) was fully justified in his case, because, he like a beast, considered curd and milk to be the same. But, the name Rudrila is mentioned only in this source; it is not confirmed by any other ancient record. U.V. Shastri[12] points out another reading of the second line of the verse in question as *vadatā vindhyavāsitvaṁ khyāpitaṁ vindhyavāsinā*. This demolishes the suggestion that Rudrila was the original name of the philosopher. This reading gives a happier meaning. According to it, by saying that curd is the same as milk and milk is the same as curd, Vindhyavāsin has demonstrated his being an inhabitant of the Vindhya mountain (a beast). Here there is a play on the name Vindhyavāsin. This gives a natural form of expression to the verse and proves that Vindhyavāsin was the real

---

6. On *Ślokavārtika*, Akṛtivāda 76.
7. On *Manu*, I.55.
8. *Classical Sāṁkhya*, pp. 141-4.
9. *Karmamīṁmāmsā*, p. 59.
10. *Tattvasaṁgrahapañjikā*, p. 22, line 26.
11. P. Chakravarti, *Origin and Development of the Sāṁkhya System of Thought*, p. 144; Also U.V. Shastri, *op. cit.*, p. 633; A.P. Mishra, *Sāṁkhyadarśana kī aitihāsika paramparā*, p. 173.
12. *Op. cit.*, p. 639, fn. 14.

name of the philosopher. The form Vindhyavāsin is not queer as a name. Similar names are evidenced in the ancient period, and the name enjoys currency even in modern times. Thus, we do not see any reason for rejecting the continuous Indian tradition naming the Sāṁkhya philosopher as Vindhyavāsin.

ASSOCIATION WITH VINDHYA

The vavant forms, *nivāsa*, *vāsa* and *vāsin*, suffixed to Vindhya suggest that they were possibly to intended to refer to the abode of the Sāṁkhya philosopher in the Vindhya region. This would imply that Vindhyavāsin or Vindhyavāsa was not the original name. The Sāṁkhya philosopher came to be designated by this appellation. It stuck to his name and gained such a wide currency that it pushed his original name into oblivion.

According to Paramārtha's "Life of Vasubandhu"[13] was Pi-li-cha-kia-na, the teacher of Vindhyavāsa, who was associated with the Vindhya mountain. He was the king of the Nāgas. He assumed the form of a sage and lived at the foot of the Vindhya mountain. This would mean that Vindhyavāsa came to be associated with the Vindhya mountain through his teacher. Paramārtha further says that, when Vasubandhu learnt about the defeat of his teacher Buddhamitra at the hands of Vindhyavāsa, he came to Ayodhyā from Puruṣapura (Peśāwar) to challenge Vindhyavāsa to a debate. He could not meet Vindhyavāsa. He searched for him and at last learnt about his death in the Vindhya mountain. In Paramārtha's account the Vindhya mountain is associated with Vindhyavāsa in two ways — his teacher lived at its foot and he himself died there. In the Chinese account these two elements were possibly inserted on the basis of the literal meaning of the name Vindhyavāsa. Both the facts are flimsy creations of imagination. We can understand that when Vindhyavāsa was not accepted as a regular name tradition. The two details were inserted to suit its literal meaning. Both are not intrinsically connected with the person and career of the Sāṁkhya teacher. Considering the distance of space, and

13. *JRAS*, 1905, pp. 33-53.

possibly of time involved, we can explain such concoctions. In the account of Paramārtha Vindhyavāsa is retained as the name of the Sāṁkhya scholar; there is no suggestion of a different original name and of the appellation. Vindhyavāsa being acquired later on account of an association with the Vindhya mountain.

VINDHYAVĀSIN AND VYĀḌI

The confusion is further confounded by the fact that in some grammatical texts Vyāḍi is also referred to as a Vindhyavāsin. On this basis Tanusukaram Sharma[14] identifies Vindhyavāsin with Vyāḍi. It has been shown that Vyāḍi was the real name of the scholar.[15] He was also known as Vindhyavāsin, possibly because of his abode in the Vindhyas, Vindhyavāsin was not his regular name. H.S. Joshi[16] speaks of two Vindhyavāsins, Vyāḍi as Vindhyavāsin I and Vindhyavāsa, the senior contemporary of Vasubandhu, as Vindhyavāsin II. But, there is no need for postulating two Vindhyavāsins. The earlier teacher was named as Vyāḍi. He was not named as Vindhyavāsin. It is the later teacher, whose Sāṁkhya affiliations are well established, who was known as Vindhyavāsin. We find in Vācaspatimiśra's commentary *Tattvavaiśāradī* a reference to a sage named Māṇḍavya who had achieved spiritual powers (*siddhis*) by the use of *rasāyana*. He was also designated as Vindhyavāsin.[17]

IDENTIFICATION OF VINDHYAVĀSA WITH ĪŚVARAKṚṢṆA

Some modern scholars have added to the existing confusion by identifying Vindhyavāsin with Īśvarakṛṣṇa, the author of the *Sāṁkhyakārikā*. The statements about Vasubandhu and Vindhyavāsa create serious chronological difficulties, especially about the relative position of Vindhyavāsa and Īśvarakṛṣṇa, to tide

---

14. *Māṭharavṛtti* (Chowkhamba Sanskrit Series), Introduction, pp. 3-4.
15. P. Chakravarti, *op. cit.*, pp. 142-4.
16. *Sāṁkhyayogadarśana kā jīrṇoddhāra*, p. 59.
17. *Vyāsabhāṣya* on *Yogasūtra* IV.1 — *yathā māṇḍavyo munīrasāyanopayogād vindhyavāsīti* |

over which Takakusu[18] too Īśvarakṛṣṇa and Vindhyavāsa as the same man. The suggestion was accepted by Garbe,[19] A.B. Keith[20] and B.G. Tilak.[21] The supposed conflict arising out of the Chinese accounts and the chronological problems issuing out of it can be resolved.[22] The suggestion that Vindhyavāsa and Īśvarakṛṣṇa are identical arose due to a mixing up of the accounts of Paramārtha and Kuei-chi. According to Paramārtha, Vindhyavāsa had re-worked the Sāṁkhya system which he had learnt from his teacher Vārṣagaṇya and had composed some couplets summarising the revised doctrines. He further says that Vasubandhu, who could not engage Vindhyavāsa in a debate as the latter had died, composed the *Paramārthasaptati* as a rejoinder to the Sāṁkhya doctrines. According to Kuei-chi, a Sāṁkhya teacher, for the purposes of his debate with a Buddhist, composed the "Gold Seventy", a text in seventy verses. He further refers to the *Paramārthasaptati* as a rejoinder composed by Vasubandhu.[23] Modern scholars, who identify Vindhyavāsa with Īśvarakṛṣṇa, rely on the fact that in the catalogue of Nanjio the "Gold Seventy" is the *Sāṁkhyaśāstra* or the Chinese version of the *Sāṁkhyakārikā*.[24]

But there are several weak links in this chain of arguments. Kuei-chi does not mention the name either of Vindhyavāsa or of Īśvarakṛṣṇa. The only name, or rain occurring in his account, is that of Varṣa (Ba-li-sha or Rain). Kuei-chi does not attribute the authorship of the "Gold Seventy" to any of these two. Actually he refers to this text as the work of the associates of Varṣa, who were called Vārṣagaṇya (Rain-host). The text composed by Īśvarakṛṣṇa is named as the *Sāṁkhyakārikā*. This text cannot be identified with the "Gold Seventy" mentioned by Kuei-chi. The Indian tradition over the centuries retains the name *Sāṁkhyakārikā* uniformly

18. *JRAS*, 1905, pp. 33-53.
19. *Die Sāṁkhya Philosophie,* pp. 77-83.
20. *The Sāṁkhya System*, pp. 76-7.
21. *Gītārahasya* (1938, 6th edn.), p. 188, fn.
22. See *infra* under "Chiness Account about Vindhyavāsa".
23. Takakusu in *BEFEO*, *op. cit*., pp. 38-40.
24. Takakusu, in *JRAS*, *op.cit*., p. 47.

without any indication that it was ever called the *Saptati*, *Sāṁkhyasaptati* or *Suvarṇa* (or *Hiraṇya*)-*saptati*. It is only *kārikā* 72, whose attribution to Īśvarakṛṣṇa is not beyond suspicion, which refers to all the subjects of the *ṣaṣthitantra* being present in the *saptati* (seventy verses). But this cannot be construed to suggest the title *Saptati* for the text. Kuei-chi himself makes two different statements about the "Gold Seventy". At one place he refers to it as the work of the Vārṣagaṇyas. In another context he says that a Sāṁkhya teacher composed the treatise the "Gold Seventy" for the purposes of a debate with a Buddhist.

The identification of Vindhyavāsin with Īśvarakṛṣṇa has been suggested to overcome the confusion and chronological difficulties presented in the Chinese sources. The Chinese texts seem to associate the composition of the "Gold Seventy" with the name of Vindhyavāsin whereas Nanjio's Catalogue mentions the *Sāṁkhyakārikā* of Īśvarakṛṣṇa, known as the *Sāṁkhyaśāstra*, to be the "Gold Seventy". We have shown[25] that there is no compelling reason to accept the suggested identification of the Gold Seventy with the *Sāṁkhyakārikā*. The confusion in the Chinese texts can be resolved in a better manner without taking recourse to the theory of identification of Vindhyavāsa with Īśvarakṛṣṇa.

The long philosophical tradition in India does not contain the slightest indication of the two names standing for one and the same person. In Indian texts the philosophical views ascribed to Vindhyavāsin on many an important are so violently opposed to those of Īśvarakṛṣṇa that they would amount to that person blowing hot and cold at the same time. On this subject the testimony of the *Yuktidīpikā* is very clear. At many places, in discussing the philosophical position of Īśvarakṛṣṇa, it refers to the view of Vindhyavāsin, which was opposed to Īśvarakṛṣṇa and goes on to maintain the opinion of Īśvarakṛṣṇa.[26] The position is made very clear when it says that Īśvarakṛṣṇa does not describe *jijñāsā* and

25. See *infra* under section "The Date of Vindhyavāsin — Vindhyavāsin and Īśvarakṛṣṇa — Kaṇagasattrī".

26. See U.V. Shastri, *op.cit.*, pp. 638-9; A.P. Mishra, *op.cit.*, p. 175.

other members of a syllogistic reasoning, because they have already been discussed by Vindhyavāsin and other authoritative teachers.[27] If the two had been identical the logical explanation on the part of the *Yuktidīpikā* would have been to point out that Īśvarakṛṣṇa has discussed this in another work of his.

Later Indian texts refer to the characteristic views of Vindhyavāsin. They were familiar with Īśvarakṛṣṇa. But, nowhere do they hint at the two being identical. Ancient scholars like Haribhadrasūri refer to both Vindhyavāsin and Īśvarkṛṣṇa respectively. S.N. Dasgupta[28] points out that Guṇaratna mentions Īśvarakṛṣṇa and Vindhyavāsin as two authorities[29] and that the *anuṣṭubh* verse of Vindhyavāsin quoted by him [30] cannot be traced as belonging to Īśvarakṛṣṇa.

Chinese Account about Vindhavāsa

Larson and Bhattacharya offer a new interpretation of the Chinese evidence to determine the comparative sequence of Vārṣagaṇya, Vindhyavāsin, Vasubandhu and Īśvarakṛṣṇa and suggest their chronology. This has led them to conclude meaningful changes in the history of Sāṁkhya and the specific role of these philosophers.

Out of the two accounts by Paramārtha and Kue-chi they consider the one of Paramārtha to be more reasonable and reliable. According to them, Vārṣagaṇya was an earlier teacher. Vindhyavāsin was his pupil in the sense that he belonged to the tradition of Vārṣagaṇya. Vindhyavāsin revised Sāṁkhya in his *Sāṁkhyaśāstra*. He had a debate with Buddhist philosophers who preceded Vasubandhu. Vasubandhu composed *Paramārthasaptati* as a rejoinder to the *Sāṁkhyaśāstra* of Vindhyavāsin. The *Sāṁkhyakārikā* is not a polemic text connected with the debate with the Buddhists. It was an 'in-house' document whose audience was made up of followers of Sāṁkhya. The chronological sequence

27. P. 4.
28. *A History of Indian Philosoply*, Vol. I, p. 218, fn. 3.
29. *Tarkarahasyadīpikā*, pp. 102, 104.
30. *Ibid.*, p. 104.

which Larson and Bhattacharya thus reconstruct is: Vārṣagaṇya *c.* AD 100-300 but probably earlier rather than later. Followers of Vārṣagaṇya (*vārṣagaṇāḥ*) *c.* AD 300-400, Vindhyavāsin *c.* AD 300-400 and Īśvarakṛṣṇa *c.* AD 350-450.

The baffling controversy about the history of Sāṁkhya in relation to the times and contributions of Vindhyavāsin has been caused by the confusing Chinese accounts. The confusion is created mostly by the Catalogue of Nanjio and the Chinese translation of Paramārtha's *Vasubandhucarita* (Life of Vasubandhu). In this connection the testimonies of Hsuan Tsang and his pupil Kuei-chi have not been properly analysed.

CONFUSION CREATED BY PARAMĀRTHA

The prevailing confusion is the creation mostly of Paramārtha's "Life of Vasubandhu". Paramārtha refers to Vindhyavāsa as a pupil of Vārṣagaṇya, but, at the same time, makes him a contemporary of Vasubandhu by saying that he participated in a debate with Vasubandhu's teacher Buddhamitra. Paramārtha possibly did not possess an authentic knowledge about Vindhyavāsa and his position in the history of Sāṁkhya. He possibly laboured under the impression that the "Gold Seventy" was the work of Īśvarakṛṣṇa. Modern scholars start with Paramārtha's testimony as their main source. They try to see reason in it and explain conflicting evidence. Paramārtha commits major mistakes on certain vital points. Earlier scholars did not reject Paramārtha's testimony. Larson[31] has boldly recognised the contradictions in the garbled account of Paramārtha.

KUEI-CHI'S ACCOUNT

In contrast with Paramārtha, Kuei-chi move is dependable. Kuei-chi clearly says that the "Gold Seventy" (*Hiraṇyasaptati*) is the work of Rain-host (Vārṣagaṇya), the associates of the Sāṁkhya teacher Ba-li-ṣa (Varṣa).[32] Evidently the treatise *Hiraṇyasaptati* is attributed by him to Vārṣagaṇas, who were the followers of a

31. *Op.cit.*, pp. 142-4.
32. Takakusu in *JRAS*, *op.cit.*, p. 49.

Sāṁkhya teacher. Kuei-chi was possibly misled by the form Vārṣagaṇa to imagine that the founder of the Sāṁkhya school was Varṣa, not realising that the form Vārṣagaṇa is derived from Vārṣagaṇya, the name of the founder of the school. Here Kuei-chi does not name the follower of Vārṣagaṇya who wrote the "Gold Seventy". There is a strong possibility of his being Vindhyavāsin. The testimony of Paramārtha about Vindhyavāsa being a follower of Vārṣagaṇya receives support from the fact that Vindhyavāsin, on several important points, holds the same view as was enunciated by Vārṣagaṇya.[33]

In another context Kuei-chi refers to a debate between a Sāṁkhya teacher and a Buddhist. The Sāṁkhya teacher is said to have composed, for the purposes of the debate, a treatise in seventy verses called the "Gold Seventy". The Sāṁkhya teacher defeated the Buddhist. Later Vasubandhu composed the *Paramārthasaptati* as a rejoinder.[34] In this account the names of the Sāṁkhya teacher and the Buddhist are not mentioned. But, if the "Gold Seventy" of this reference is the same as the "Gold Seventy" in the other reference by Kuei-chi, the inference may be drawn that the Sāṁkhya teacher was a Vārṣagaṇa or Vindhyavāsin himself. Vasubandhu is also associated with the debate. His *Paramārthasaptati* is mentioned as a rejoinder to the Sāṁkhya principles. But, the point, which remains unanswered, is the gap separating the rejoinder from the debate: did Vasubadhu write his treatise immediately after the debate, or there was a long gap between the two events. The reference, by no means, necessitates the writing of the "Gold Seventy" to closely followed by the composition of the *Paramārthasaptati*.

EXPLANATION OF PARAMĀRTHA'S ACCOUNT

Here we may again refer to Paramārtha's "Life of Vasubandhu". According to Paramārtha, Vārṣagaṇya was a Sāṁkhya teacher. His pupil Vindhyavāsa learned Sāṁkhya from him but re-worked the content of the system and also composed some couplets summarising the revised doctrines. Vindhyavāsa in a debate defeated the Buddhist

33. See *infra* under section "Vindhyavāsin and Vārṣagaṇya".
34. Takakusu in *BEFEO*, *op.cit.*, pp. 38-40.

Buddhamitra, who was the teacher of Vasubandhu. Vasubandhu could not challenge Vindhyavāsa in a debate, as the latter had died in the mean time. As a rejoinder to the Sāṁkhya doctrine Vasubandhu composed the *Paramārthasaptati*.

In Paramārtha's account Vindyavāsa is closely connected with both Vārṣagaṇya and Vasubandhu, which causes an unbridgeable gulf. But, in both the cases the chronological connections are not as definite as they are made out. In the account Vārṣagaṇya is mentioned as a mythological being. Some scholars, in their attempt to bring Vindhyavāsa nearer in time to Vasubandhu, say that Vindhyavāsa was not the direct disciple of Vārṣagaṇya, but was a pupil in the Sāṁkhya tradition started by him. Takakusu suggests that the original Sanskrit name for the Chinese expression under reference could be either Varṣagaṇa or Vārṣagaṇa. If it is Varṣagaṇa, it would mean that Paramārtha, in naming the founder of the Vārṣagaṇas imagined a Sāṁkhya sage of this name committing a mistake similar to that of Kuei-chi, when he imagined Varṣa as the founder of a Sāṁkhya school. If it is Vārṣagaṇa, then it yields a happier meaning. Vindhyavāsa, now, becomes a pupil of Vārṣagaṇa, which means a follower of Vārṣagaṇya. The way the teacher of Vindhyavāsa is mystified suggests that Vindhyavāsa lived long before Paramārtha.

PARAMĀRTHA ON VINDHYAVĀSA'S CONTRIBUTION

Paramārtha refers to Vindhyavāsa as re-working the contents of the system received from his teacher and as presenting the revised doctrines in some couplets. Both these statements can be supported, though not directly. The philosophical views of Vindhyavāsin, as recorded in later texts, do not appear to be in his original words. On the basis of these references, we cannot come to any definite conclusion about the form of the treatise composed by Vindhyavāsin. It may, however, be noted that Guṇaratnasūri, in the *Ṣaḍdarśana-samuccaya*,[35] quotes a verse of Vindhyavāsin.[36] Kamalaśīla, in his

35. P. 104.

36. *Vyomavatī* (Chowkhamba), p. 521 also quotes the verse, but without any reference to the source.

commentary on the *Tattvasaṁgraha*,[37] quotes a verse, without referring to its author, which P. Chakravarti[38] takes to be a quotation from Vasubandhu's *Paramārthasaptati*, admitting that there is no conclusive evidence in its support. We cannot be sure, but it is possibile that the first line of this verse was borrowed from Vindhyavāsin's text.

Both the statements about Vindhyavāsin re-working the contents of the system and presenting his exposition in verses tacitly refer to the composition of the "Gold Seventy" or the *Kanakasaptati* by Vindhyavāsin. The very name of this treatise indicates that it was composed in verses. In confirmation of the other statement P. Chakravarti[39] refers to a few points where Vindhyavāsin deviates from the views of his predecessors. If we take Paramārtha's account to refer to Vindhyavāsin re-working the doctrine of his own teacher and not of other predecessors, than we are confronted with the close similarity between Vidhyavāsin and Vārṣagaṇya on several points and have to seek another explanation of the statement. We know that the earliest known exposition of Sāṁkhya was in the form of the *Ṣaṣṭhitantra*.[40] In the *Yuktidīpikā* other expositions of Sāṁkhya have been termed as *tantrāntara*s. Vindhyavāsin marked a departure from the earlier practice of *tantra*s by presenting his views in seventy verses and started the series of *saptati*s. Vasubandu emulated Vindhyavāsin, but entitled his treatise as *Paramārthasaptati* in opposition to the *Kanakasaptati* of the rival Sāṁkhya system. Īśvarakṛṣṇa paid allegiance to the tradition of the *ṣaṣṭhitantra*, but presented his views in seventy verses, thus combining the features of the two important Sāṁkhya streams of *ṣaṣṭhitantra*s and *saptati*s. Paramārtha was possibly so much obsessed with the general currency of the *Sāṁkhyakārikā* in *saptati* verses that with only a dim vision of Vindhyavāsin and the obscurity of his *Kanakasaptati*, overshadowed by the

37. P. 22.
38. *Op. cit.*, p. 147.
39. *Op. cit.*, p. 145.
40. Scholarly opinion is devided on recognising the *Tattvasamāsaśutra* and the *Sāṁkhyasūtras* as early texts of Sāṁkhya.

Sāṁkhyakārikā, he refrained from making an unequivocal statement about Vindhyavāsin composing the "Gold Seventy".

THE CATALOGUE OF NANJIO

The Catalogue of Nanjio was far removed in time from the early texts of Sāṁkhya. At that time authentic information about these texts was not available in China. The text of the *Kanakasaptati* and its author were not duly known. It is, therefore, quite plausible that the *Sāṁkhyakārikā*, a text in seventy verses, was identified with the *Kanakasaptati* and referred to as "Gold Seventy".

VINDHYAVĀSIN'S PARTICIPATION IN A DEBATE WITH A BUDDHIST

G.J. Larson[41] has offered a very plausible explanation to resolve the confusion about the debate between a Sāṁkhya teacher and a Buddhist, the role played by Vindhyavāsa and Vasubandhu in it, the composition of a text named the "Gold Seventy", and its identification with the *Sāṁkhyakārikā* of Īśvarakr̥ṣṇa. According to him, 'the Chinese tradition has tended to identify two separate texts or events. On the one hand, there was probably a tradition which involved a debate between a Sāṁkhya teacher and a Buddhist, and there is no reason to doubt that the Sāṁkhya school involved was that of the followers of Vārṣagaṇya, one of whom was a certain Vindhyavāsa. At a later time this tradition became associated with the composition of the *Sāṁkhyasaptati* or the Chinese version of the *Sāṁkhyakārikā*. The latter text was probably composed by Īśvarakr̥ṣṇa sometime after the reported debate, perhaps as a final summary of the Sāṁkhya position. This conclusion would support the Chinese tradition concerning a debate, at least in its main outline, and would eliminate the necessity of equating the *Kārikā* with the text or couplets used in the context of the debate.

Vindhyavāsin and Vārṣagaṇya

Takakusu, relying on the testimony of Paramārtha, took

41. *Op. cit.*, p. 144.

Vindhyavāsa to be a disciple of Vārṣagaṇya. In the Chinese translation of Paramārtha's account, the name of the teacher appears as Pi-li-cha-kia-na. In Japanese the name has been transliterated as Bi-ri-sha-gaṇa. According to Takakusu, the original name was either Vṛṣagaṇa or Vārṣagaṇa.

The Chinese translation of Paramārtha's commentary on the *Sāṁkhyakārikā*, explaining the tradition of teachers and disciples, referred to in the penultimate *kārikā* mentions Īśvarakṛṣṇa as the disciple of Po-po-li. Takakusu took Po-po-li to stand for Varṣa.[42] Belvalkar[43] suggested that the original Sanskrit name of this teacher of Īśvarakṛṣṇa was Devala. U.V. Shastri[44] argues, without being dogmatic, that the Chinese expression possibly stood for Kapila. P. Chakravarti,[45] relying on the Japanese transliteration of the name as Bat'-ba-li, takes it to correspond to Bāddhali, mentioned in the *Yuktidīpikā*.[46] Evidently this evidence does not have any bearing on the subject under discussion.

On the testimony of Paramārtha a Vindhyavāsa, as a disciple of Vārṣagaṇya, is placed in a in a period after Vārṣagaṇya.

The idealogical connection between Vārṣagaṇya and Vindhyavāsin is to be accepted. Though we have only a few fragmentary references to the views of Vārṣagaṇya and Vindhyavāsin, the tradition, as recorded in the *Yuktidīkikā* and other texts, shows that, on some important points, the two had a remarkably identical view.[47] These relate to the number of *karaṇa*s being eleven, to *pratyakṣa* being characterised as *srotrādi-vṛtti*, and to the nature of *anumāna*.

If we accept that Vindhyavāsa was the disciple of Vārṣagaṇya,

---

42. *BEFEO*, *op.cit.*, p. 148, n.3. The equation is a far-fetched on Po-p'o-li = Po-so-li = Po-li-so = Va-li-so = Varṣa.
43. *Bhandarkar Commemoration Valume*, p.
44. *Op. cit.*, pp. 520-1.
45. *Op. cit.*, pp. 131-2.
46. P. 175. Also mentioned in *Tattvārtha-Rājavārttika*, p. 51.
47. U.V. Shastri, *op.cit.*, pp. 521-6; P. Chakravarti, *op.cit.*, pp. 138-41.

his date, as the junior contemporary of Vārṣagaṇya, will approximate to the date of the latter. The date of Vārṣagaṇya is not precisely known, but he seems to have been one of the early Sāṁkhya teachers.[48] This association of Vindhyavāsa with Vārṣagaṇya is difficult to reconcile with Paramārtha's account, which makes Vindhyavāsa an elder contemporary of Vasubandhu, who has to be placed in the middle of the fourth century.[49]

To reconcile this apparent conflict, U.V. Shastri[50] suggests that the reference to Vindhyavāsa as the pupil of Vārṣagaṇya does not mean that he was a direct disciple of the latter, Vārṣagaṇya was the teacher (*guru*) of Vindhyavāsa in the sense that Vindhyavāsa belonged to the school (*sampradāya*) founded by Vārṣagaṇya.

It seems that the Chinese tradition, ignorant about the rules governing the formation of a term to refer to the followers of Vārṣagaṇya,[51] imagined explanations based on the literal meaning of the component parts of the name Vārṣagaṇya. According to the rules of the Sanskrit grammar, a follower of Vārṣagaṇya is designated as a Vārṣagaṇa. Kuci-chi, the pupil of Hsuan Tsang, in his ignorance, split the appellation Vārṣagaṇa into two *vārṣa* (relating to Varṣā) and *gaṇa* (host). As a corollary to this, he imagined a Sāṁkhya philosopher with the name Varṣa and applied Vārṣagaṇa to refer to a follower of Varṣa.[52]

Extending this explanation to the account given by Paramārtha, P. Chakravarti argues that possibly Paramārtha failed to understand

---

48. *Supra*, chapter, 17. See Chakravarti, *op.cit.*, p. 135, Belvalkar in *Bhandarkar Commemoration Volume*, p. 177 holds that both Vindhyavāsa and Vṛṣa or Vārṣagaṇya followed Īśvarakṛṣṇa.
49. See under section "The Date of Vindhyavāsin — Contemporaniety with Vasubandhu".
50. *Op. cit.*, pp. 515-27.
51. U.V. Shastri, *op.cit.*, p. 522, fn. 1. See also P. Chakravarti, *op. cit.*, pp. 156-8.
52. P. Chakravarti, *op. cit.*, pp. 136-7, points out a similar mistake on the part of Kuei-chi explaining the word *kapila* to mean 'red', adding that Kapila, the propounder of Sāṁkhya, was so called because his complexion was red.

the real meaning of the term Vārṣagaṇa, which he found being applied to Vindhyavāsa. This appellation was intended to mean that Vindhyavāsa was a follower of Vārṣagaṇya. Paramārtha imagined a Sāṁkhya philosopher of the name Vr̥ṣagaṇa to explain the derivative form of the appellation current for Vindhyavāsa. The date of Vindhyavāsa cannot be determined on the basis of the restoration of the name Vr̥ṣagaṇa in the account of Paramārtha proposed by Takakusu, because there is no other evidence to confirm the historicity of a Sāṁkhya philosopher names Vr̥ṣagaṇa.

Takakusu made an alternative suggestion that the original Sanskrit form of the Chinese name of the teacher of Vindhyavāsa was Vārṣagaṇa. Vārṣagaṇa means a follower of Vārṣagaṇya. If we accept that Vindhyavāsa was a pupil of Vārṣagaṇa and not directly of Vārṣagaṇya, it steers clear of many problems. It provides for a gap between Vārṣagaṇya and Vindhyavāsin and also explains the similarities in the philosophical ideas of Vindhyavāsin and Vārṣagaṇya.

Thus, we see that the date of Vindhyavāsin is not to be bracketed with that of Vārṣagaṇya. He seems to have been separated from Vārṣagaṇya by more than one generation.

Vindhyavāsa and Vasubandhu

The real difficulty is created by Paramārtha, when he associates Vindyavāsa with a debate with Vasubandhu's teacher Buddhamitra. It is to be noted that no Chinese account connects Vasubandhu and Vindhyavāsa directly. According to Paramārtha, Vasubandhu could not engage Vindhyavāsa in a debate, because the latter had died, and Vasubandhu had to write a rejoinder to the Sāṁkhya doctrines. In the account given by Kuei-chi there is no reference to a debate between the author of the "Gold Seventy" and Vasubandhu. The latter is simply said to have composed his *Paramārthasaptati* later as a rejoinder to the Sāṁkhya doctrines. It appears that there was a chronological gap between Vindhyavāsa and Vasubandhu, so that the two could not meet personally. The fact that Vasubandhu composed his treatise as a rejoinder would indicate merely that he belonged to a later date.

VINDHYAVĀSA'S BUDDHIST ADVERSARY

It is only Paramārtha who names the Buddhist adversary of Vindhyavāsa as Buddhamitra and refers to him as the teacher of Vasubandhu. But, the name of Buddhamitra as Vasubandhu's teacher is not confirmed by any independent source. According to Hsuan Tsang, Manoratha was the teacher of Vasubadhu. Kuei-chi does not mention the name of Vasubandhu's teacher, because there was no need for him to do so. Manoratha, as a vehement critic of Sāṁkhya principles, is known from the *Yuktidīpikā*. The *Yuktidīpikā*, is establishing the validity of the Sāṁkhya principles, first presents faithfully the views and arguments of the opponents of the Sāṁkhya. After criticising the opponent's wrong view of bondage in two couplets, it expounds the Sāṁkhya view and in the concluding remark, says that 'by this the intention of Manoratha will be frustrated.[53] This exposes the mistake in Paramārtha's statement that Vindhyavāsa engaged in a debate with Vasubandhu's teacher named Buddhamitra.

Excepting this allusion to Manoratha as a critic of the Sāṁkhya system, the *Yuktidīpikā* does not name any other anti-Sāṁkhya Buddhist philosopher. P. Chakravarti,[54] however, points out that at one place the *Yuktidīpikā*[55] vehemently criticises the view of Vasubandhu. This has led Chakravarti[56] to take three couplets, occurring in the *Yuktidīpikā*[57] as a criticism of the Sāṁkhya theory of the *guṇa*s and its view of bondage and liberation by its opponents to be quotations from the *Paramārthasaptati*.[58] According to him

---

53. *Yuktidīpikā*, p. 107 — *tasmād viphalatāṁ yātu manoratha-manorathaḥ* |
54. *Op. cit.*, p. 150.
55. Pp. 135-7 (notes).
56. *Op. cit.*, pp. 150-3.
57. Pp. 72, 107.
58. According to the Chinese tradition, Vasubandhu wrote the *Pramārthasaptati* as a rejoinder to the Sāṁkhya principles. But, in the *Yuktidīpikā* it is Vasubandhu's teacher Manoratha who is named preeminently for his criticism of the Sāṁkhya views. This would mean that both the teacher and the pupil wrote separate matrical treatises →

the *Yuktidīpikā* is a rejoinder of the *Paramārthasaptati*. He says that the author of the *Yuktidīpikā* gives a fitting reply to the arguments of Vasubandhu and establishes the validity of the *Kārikā* of Īśvarakṛṣṇa. He argues:

> Had Vasubandhu actually written his *Paramārthasaptati* with a view to refuting the treatise of Vindhyavāsa, the author of the *Yuktidīpikā* would never take so much trouble in pleading the case of Īśvarakṛṣṇa. In that case, he would certainly write a commentary on the treatise of Vindhyavāsa, instead of the *Kārikā* of Īśvarkṛṣṇa.

TREATISES AND THE DEBATE

Chakravarti bases his view on the equation of the *Sāṁkhyakārikā* of Īśvarakṛṣṇa with the "Gold Seventy", in opposition to which Vasubandhu, according to Kuei-chi, wrote his *Paramārthasaptati*. We have shown[59] that the *Sāṁkhyakārikā* cannot be identified with the "Gold Seventy", which really stands for the *Kanakasaptati*. The author of the *Yuktidīpikā* argues to maintain Sāṁkhya principles against their criticism by opponents. He chose that *Sāṁkhyakārikā*, because it was the most standard and the latest account of Sāṁkhya. It may be pointed out that couplets or views (which Chakravarti attributed to the *Paramārthasaptati*) criticising Sāṁkhya are confined to a few points and are not found in a sizeable number of cases (as will be expected if the *Yuktidīpikā* had been a rejoinder of the *Paramārthasaptati*). We find that the author of the *Yuktidīpikā* on a given principle discusses various points of view, including those of other Sāṁkhya schools.

→ criticising Sāṁkhya principles. Explaining it, Chakravarti, *op. cit.*, p. 152 says that 'the teacher himself did not write any such treatise, and it was Vasubandhu who in his Paramārtha-Saptati tried to restore the fame of his teacher, and in doing so it would be natural on the part of the pupil to ascribe sometimes even his arguments to his teacher Manoratha and thus to make the position of the teacher more safe which made Manoratha the target of attack by the author of the *Yuktidīpikā*.

59. See *infra*, under section "The Date of Vindhyavāsin — Vindhyavāsin and Īśvarakṛṣṇa — Sāṁkhyakārikā as Kanakasaptati".

The sequence of the composition of the relevant texts, according to Chakravarti, will be the *Sāṁkhyakārikā* (or "Gold Seventy"), then its criticism by Vasubandhu in the *Paramārthasaptati*, and finally the *Yuktidīpikā* as a rejoinder to the *Paramārthasaptati*. The "Gold Seventy", however, is not the *Sāṁkhyakārikā*, but is an earlier work named the *Kanakasaptati*, possibly written by Vindhyavāsin. Now, there can be two possible sequences of the relevant texts depending on the relative chronology, which we accept for Vasubandhu and Īśvarakṛṣṇa. If Vasubandhu was earlier, then we have to postulate that, sometime after the composition of the *Kanakasaptati* by Vindhyavāsin of the Vārṣagaṇa school of Sāṁkhya, the Buddhist stand was vindicated by Vasubandhu in his *Paramārthasaptati*. He was followed by Īśvarakṛṣṇa, who tried to maintain the principles of the *Ṣaṣthitantra*, but presented them in the form of a *Saptati*. Īśvarakṛṣṇa, in his presentation, deliberately eschewed all criticism and arguments. This lacuna in the Sāṁkhya account was filled up by the author of the *Yuktidīpikā*, who gave arguments in support of the Sāṁkhya principles, rebutting the criticism of the opponents. If, however, we take Īśvarakṛṣṇa to have preceded Vasubandhu, the position will be slightly changed. After Vindhyavāsin formulated in the *Kanakasaptati* his views, different on certain points from the mainstream of the Sāṁkhya, Īśvarakṛṣṇa thought it prudent to re-establish the original tradition, associated with the *Ṣaṣthitantra,* but chose to do so only in seventy verses, as was done in the *Kanakasaptati*. Following the fashion of the *saptati*s in the Sāṁkhya circles, Vasubandhu presented the Buddhist point of view in his *Paramārthasaptati*. The *Yuktidīpikā* took up the task to demonstrate the rationality on the Sāṁkhya principles. We cannot show our preference for either of the two possibilities, because, though we have, besides the testimony of Paramārtha, other independent indications for the date of Vasubandhu, the only limit in the case of Īśvarakṛṣṇa is provided by the fact that Parmārtha's commentary on his *Sāṁkhyakārikā* was translated in Chinese between AD 557 and 569.

ASSOCIATING VINDHYAVĀSA WITH VASUBANDHU

The intriguing question remains: why should Paramārtha bracket

Vindhyavāsa with Vasubandhu in a debate. Larson has explained the conflicting account by saying that here two separate events have been mixed up. Vindhyavāsa was engaged in a debate with a Buddhist in earlier times. His name was dragged down by Paramārtha to the debate in the times of Vasubandhu. We know that the Buddhist philosophers, for several centuries, had engaged in philosophical discussions with teachers of Sāṁkhya, Nyāya and Vaiśeṣika systems, which added to the richness and logical ordering of philosophical ideas. It is not unlikely that the accounts, in some cases, confused the names of the actual participants. When Paramārtha associated Vindhyavāsa with the debate in the times of Vasubandhu, there was possibly a basis for such a confusion to be created. Chakravarti[60] points out that the Buddhist tradition refers to an earlier, Vasubandhu. Yaśomitra mentions the view of a Vasubandhu named as Sthavira Vasubandhu and Vṛddhācārya Vasubandhu.[61] Possibly he belonged to the times of Vindhyavāsin and was the pupil of Buddhamitra. Paramārtha could have been led by the contemporaneity of this Vasubandhu with Vindhyavāsin to associate Vindhyavāsa with the debate in the times of Vasubandhu, the famous Buddhist scholar.

The Date of Vindhyavāsin

The date of Vindhyavāsin is a very vexed problem. It is fixed on the basis of three arguments: his contemporaneity with Vasubandhu, the later texts referring to him and his views, and his relative position *vis-a-vis* Īśvarakṛṣṇa.

CONTEMPORANEITY WITH VASUBANDHU

According to the Chinese version of Paramārtha's *Vasubandhucarita* ("Life of Vasubandhu"), Vindhyavāsa defeated the Buddhist scholar Buddhamitra in a debate and, when Vasubandhu wanted to challenge Vindhyavāsa in a debate, he found that Vindhyavāsa was

60. *Op. cit.*, p. 153.

61. *sphuṭārthābhidharmakośavyākhyā* (Tokyo), p. 280, lines 6-7, p. 35, line 20.

dead.[62] This would indicate that Vindhyavāsa was a senior contemporary of Vasubandhu. The date of Vasubandhu will help us fix, with rough approximity the date of Vindhyavāsa. But, unfortunately Vasubandhu cannot be precisely located. Takakusu[63] placed Vasubandhu in *c*. AD 420-500. According to N. Péri,[64] Vasubandhu is to be placed a century earlier than this date. Takakusu's date will make Vasubandhu a contemporary of King Skandagupta (*c*. AD 452-480), whereas Péri's date points to Candragupta II (*c*. AD 380-415). Both these kings are known to have assumed the title of Vikramāditya. But, according to Paramārtha, Vikramāditya's crown prince was Bālāditya, who later patronised Buddhism. It may be noted that in either case the Gupta king is not known to have Bālāditya as his crown prince. The only Gupta king designated as Bālāditya is Narasiṁhagupta, the son of Purugupta and the grandson of Kumāragupta I, but his date is generally fixed around AD 510-530. His father Purugupta is not known to have assumed the *biruda* of Vikramāditya and his date will be rather late for other considerations.[65] The earliest date for Vasubandhu, as suggested V.A. Smith,[66] is AD 280-360. The date of Vindhyavāsa is taken to be a generation or two earlier than the date of Vasubandhu, but we do not know of a Vikramāditya and his son Bālāditya in this time-bracket to suit the requirements of the case.

The Indian tradition also offers a clue to the date of Vasubandhu Vāmana, in his *Kāvyālaṁkārasūtravṛtti*,[67] quotes the second half of a verse saying that 'this very son of Candragupta, young and shining like the Moon (Candraprakāśa), a patron of men of letters, fortunately successful in his efforts, has now become king'. Vāmana, in his comments, says that here the expression *āśrayaḥ kṛtadhiyām*

62. Takakusu, in *BEFEO*, *op. cit.*, pp. 47-50.
63. Takakusu in *JARAS*, *op. cit.*, p. 53.
64. *BEFEO*, XI, pp. 356ff.
65. A.S. Altekar's suggestion, based on numismatic evidence, of two Narasiṁhagupta Bālādityas, the first being earlier in date, is not supported by other independent evidence.
66. *The Early History of India,* Appendix IV.
67. III.2.2, p. 86.

(a patron of men of letters) refers to the ministership of Vasubandhu (*Vasubandhu-sācivyopakṣepaparatvāt*). This would make Vasubandhu a contemporary of the son of king Candragupta and Vindhyavāsa a contemporary of Candragupta himself. In the Gupta fimily there are two kings with the name of Candragupta:[68] Candragupta I, who is glorified as the founder of the Gupta Empire, and Candragupta II, the most renowned king of the Gupta dynasty, who is known by his title of Vikramāditya. P. Chakravarti favours the claim of Candragupta II to be the Candragupta under reference. His argument is that in Pramārtha's account, Vikramāditya is said to have given at Ayodhyā three lakhs of gold to Vindhyavāsa for defeating Buddhamitra in a debate, which suits his identification with king Candragupta II Vikramāditya. But, the details about the son of Candragupta, as recorded in the verse quoted by Vāmana, suit Samudragupta (the son of Candragupta I) and not Kumāragupta I (the son of Candragupta II). We know from his Allahabad Pillar Inscription that Samudragupta had to assert himself against the other claimants to the throne and that he was a patron of men of letters. It is difficult to choose between the two alternatives for the identification of Candraguptra. In either case Vindhyavāsa, a generation earlier than Vasubandhu, will be placed in the fourth century AD, there being a difference of some seventy or eighty years between the two possibilities. Vasubandhu occupies a high position in the history of Buddhism. Originally a Sarvāstivādin, he accepted Yogācāra under the influence of his elder brother. He wrote several authoritative books. He was an expert of logic and wrote books (*Vādahṛdaya, Vādavidhi* and *Vādavidhāna*) with *vāda* (science of disputation) as part of their name. As the abbot of Nālandā he had a long and distinguished career, and had a large company of disciples, who became very famous. Diṅnāga, the great logician, was one of them. Thus, a date in the middle of the fourth century seems to be reasonable for him. Vindhyavāsa may, thus, belong to the close of the third and first half of the fourth century AD.

---

68. Some modern historians interpret the numismatic evidence to suggest a third Candragupta. Even if we accept the theory he will belong to the period of the decline of the Guptas, which will not suit the reference to the achievements of his son, including his patronage of men of letters.

But we have shown[69] that Vindhyavāsin did not engage in a debate with Vasubandhu's teacher, was much earlier than Vasubandhu and possibly was involved in an earlier debate with another Buddhist, Parmārtha's account can be construed to prove that Vindhyavāsin was not later than Vasubandhu.

INTERNAL AND EXTERNAL EVIDENCE

The treatise of Vindhyavāsin in its full form is not available, hence no argument for his date can be built on the basis of the internal evidence of his work. The external evidence of references to Vindhyavāsin or his views in later works helps us bring down the limit for his date. The Chinese tradition referring to Vindyavāsa does indicate that he was later than Vārṣagaṇya, the famous Sāṁkhya philosopher. Vindhyavāsa was known as a follower of Vārṣagaṇya.[70] He was not a direct disciple of Vārṣagaṇya, but possibly was not much removed from him. Vārṣagaṇya was an early Sāṁkhya teacher, but his precise date is not known.

Vindhyavāsa is mentioned by Pramārtha. Parmārtha translated the *Sāṁkhyakārikā* between AD 557 and 569. If we postulate a gap of at least 100-150 years to account for the type of fanciful statements made by Paramārtha about Vindhyavāsa, we cannot place him later than the fifth century AD.

We have listed below the references to the views of Vindhyavāsin occurring in later works. Of these the *Yuktidīpikā*, a commentary on the *Sāṁkhyakārikā*, and the *Ślokavārttika* of Kumārila are the earliest. The uncertainty about the date of the composition of the *Sāṁkhyakārikā* and the chronological order of the different commentaries on it creates difficulties for attempts at fixing the date of the *Yuktidīpikā*. According to Larson,[71] it was written 'sometime during or prior to the eighth century AD'. Estter A. Solomon,[72]

69. See *supra* under section "Vindhyavāsa and Vasubandhu — Vindhyavāsa's Buddhist Adversary".
70. See *supra* under section "Vindhyavāsin and Vārṣagaṇya".
71. *Op. cit.*, p. 280.
72. *The Commentaries of the Sāṁkhyakārikā — A Study,* Ahmedabad, 1974.

who has made a comparative study of the various commentaries on the *Sāṁkhyakārikā* places the *Yuktidīpikā* in the fifth century AD. Kumārila was a senior contemporary of Śaṅkara, the great Advaita philosopher. Kumārila is generally placed in the seventh century.

These indications provide a lower limit to the date of Vindhyavāsin. When the *Yuktidīpikā* commentary refers to the views of Vindyavāsin, it implies that he was a Sāṁkhya authority of considerable respectability. This line of evidence would not favour for Vindhyavāsin any date later than the third century AD.

VINDHYAVĀSIN AND ĪŚVARAKṚṢNA

The date of Vindhyavāsin is sometimes determined in relation to that of Īśvarakṛṣṇa. In this connection scholars have considered all the three possibilities: Vindhyavāsin is identified with Īśvarakṛṣṇa, is said to have preceded Īśvarakṛṣṇa, or else is taken to have followed him.

Takakusu, on the basis of his theory of the indentification of Vindhyavāsa around AD 450.[73] But, as we have seen[74] the theory of the identification of the two cannot be accepted.

Vindhyavāsa after Īśvarakṛṣṇa

Belvalkar[75] had placed both Vārṣagaṇya and Vindhyavāsa after Īśvarakṛṣṇa. He suggests that Vindhyavāsa possibly composed the *Hiraṇyasaptati* as a commentary on the *Kārikās* of Īśvarakṛṣṇa. This view is too speculative to deserve much serious consideration. It is based on a conjectural explanation to find a way out of the apparently conflicting statements in the Chinese sources.

U.V. Shastri[76] also places Īśvarakṛṣṇa before Vindhyavāsa. His view is not based on any independent consideration of the principles

73. *JRAS*, *op. cit.*, p. 53.
74. See *supra* under section "Name — Identification of Vindhyavāsa with Īśvarakṛṣna".
75. *Bhandarkar Commemoration Volume,* p. 177.
76. *Op. cit.*, pp. 530-3.

expounded by the two or any textual reference to their comparative chronological position. He argues by accepting the date *c.* AD 250 for Vindhyavāsa,[77] as proposed by Belvalkar. He places Īśvarakr̥ṣṇa several centuries before this on three main arguments (a) Īśvarakr̥ṣṇa's *Sāṁkhyakārikā* is referred to as the *Kaṇagasattarī* in the Jain text *Anuyogadvārasūtra*, generally dated towards the close of the first century of Christian era, (b) the *Māṭharavr̥tti* a commentary on the *Kārikā*, is earlier than Vindhyavāsa, and (c) Īśvarakr̥ṣṇa is earlier than the first Śaṅkarācārya whose date is 509 BC.

We would not enter into any long discussion about the date of Īśvarakr̥ṣṇa, but will certainly point out the major flows in the arguments advanced to indicate an early date for Īśvarakr̥ṣṇa.

Saṁkhyakārikā as Kanakasaptati

The first argument for placing Īśvarakr̥ṣṇa earlier is based on the identification of his *Sāṁkhyakārikā* with "Gold Seventy" (*Hiraṇyasaptati*) of the Chinese sources and also with *Kaṇagasattarī*, mentioned in the Jain text *Anuyogadvārasūtra*. As a first step in the chain of this argument, the *Sāṁkhyakārikā* is also designated as the *Sāṁkhyasaptati,* because there are seventy verses in it. In the second step, the *Sāṁkhyakārikā* or the *Sāṁkhyasaptati* is designated as *Hiraṇyasaptati* ("Gold Seventy"). And, finally, the *Hiraṇyasaptati* is identified with the *Kaṇagasattarī* of the *Anuyogadvārasūtra.*[78]

In the Indian tradition the *Kārikā*s are emphasised in the title of the treatise composed by Īśvarakr̥ṣṇa. Though the text contains seventy (*saptati*) verses, this aspect has seldom been underlined. In

---

77. Shastri, *op. cit.*, pp. 640-1 places Vindhyavāsin in the sixth century BC, calculating on the basis of the date 509 BC for the birth of Śaṅkarācārya.

78. P. Chakravati, *op. cit.*, p. 148 independently suggests the identification of the "Gold Seventy" with *Śāṁkhyasapatati* (= *Sāṁkhyakārikā*) or *Kaṇagasattarī* (= *Kanakasaptati*). See also A.B. Dhruva, in *Proceedings and Transactions of the First Oriental Conference*, Poona, Vol. 2, p. 270; Gopinath Kaviraj, Introduction, p. 7 (H. Sharma, ed., *Jayamaṅgalā*).

certain circles the name *Sāṁkhyasaptati* could have been in circulation, but a specific reference to this is wanting.

This Chinese tradition designates the treatise of Īśvarakṛṣṇa as *Sāṁkhyaśāstra* and identifies the "Gold Seventy" with it. But this is done only by the Catalogue of Nanjio. It is not confirmed by earlier Chinese sources. Paramārtha, in his "Life of Vasubandhu" does not refer to the "Gold seventy". Hsuan Tsang also is silent about it. It is only Kuei-chi who mentions the "Gold Seventy", but he attributes it to the Vārṣagaṇas and not to Īśvarakṛṣṇa. Kuei-chi refers to a fanciful story about the treatise being so named. According to him, the king rewarded the author with gold for his victory in the debate. There is no reference in any Indian text to the *Sāṁkhyakārikā* being designated as the *Hiraṇyasaptati* also, nor to a Sāṁkhya text being so named on account of the gold paid to its author. The Chinese tradition has preserved a garbled and confused account of diverse pieces of information in the early history of Sāṁkhya.[79] Apparently, not convinced about the authenticity of the Chinese account naming the Sāṁkhya text as the "Gold Seventy" and its identification with the *Sāṁkhyakārikā*, Belvalkar suggests that the Sāṁkhya text under reference, came to be named as the *Hiraṇyasaptati*, because Sāṁkhya assigns an important place to the concept of Hiraṇyagarbha in its scheme.[80] Clearly, the contemplated role of Hiraṇyagarbha in Sāṁkhya philosophy is not proven, and then it is not such an important principle as to impart the Sāṁkhya text the name *Hiraṇyasaptati*. U.V. Shatri[81] suggests an alternative explanation for designating the *Sāṁkhyakārikā* as the "Gold Seventy". According to him, Kapila was the original

---

79. See P. Chakravarti, *op. cit.*, p. 137; also p. 153; G.J. Larson, *op. cit.*, pp. 143-4; U.V. Shastri, *op. cit.*, pp. 512-3.

80. Belvalkar in *Bhandarkar Commemoration Volume,* pp. 176-7, suggests that Vindhyavāsin wrote the commentary *Hiraṇyasaptati* on the *Sāṁkhyakārikā* of Īśvarakṛṣṇa, but on account of a mistake on the part of later writers the name of commentator was used in place of the author of the original text, and that of the author of original text replaced that of the commentator. The suggestion is highly conjectural. Fora a criticism See U.V. Shastri, *op. cit.*, pp. 529-30.

81. *Op. cit.*, p. 528.

expounder of the Sāṁkhya system which Īśvarakṛṣṇa presented in the *Sāṁkhyakārikā*. Kapila literally means the golden colour, hence, in deferance to the founder of the Sāṁkhya system, the *Sāṁkhyakārikā* came to be named as the *Hiraṇyasaptati*. But, the explanation is fanciful and far-fetched; it does not explain why, of all the various texts, not authored by Kapila but by other Sāṁkhya teachers, the *Sāṁkhyakārikā* alone should retain a reference to the name of Kapila. Then, it is difficult to understand why, in place of a direct reference to Kapila, an indirect allusion to him, through one of the meanings of his name, should be made.

In Kuei-chi's account the "Gold Seventy" is associated with a debate between a Sāṁkhya teacher and a Buddhist. G.J. Larson[82] correctly observes.

> It is quite difficult to believe that *Sāṁkhyakārikā* was written for purposes of a debate. It is not a polemical text. Indeed, in *Kārikā* LXXII it is expressly set forth that the text is a simple summary of doctrine without illustrative stories or arguments against opponents.

Thus, there is no valid ground for indentifying the *Sāṁkhyakārikā* with the "Gold Seventy" (*Hiraṇyasaptati*). Hence there will be no justification for the final step of indentifying it with the *Kaṇagasattarī* mentioned in the *Anuyogadvārasūtra* and then inferring the date of Īśvarakṛṣṇa.

Kaṇagasattarī

The *Anuyogadvārasūtra* lists a number of ignorant, false and irresponsible philosophies and texts. It mentions *Kaṇagasattarī* along with *Kāvilaṁ*, *Logāyatan*, *Saṭṭhiyantaṁ* and *Māṭharapurāṇa-vāgaraṇanāḍagāi*. Before *Kaṇagasattarī* we have the names of *Bhārahaṁ, Rāmāyaṇam, Bhīmasurukhaṁ, Kodillayaṁ* and *Ghoḍayamuham*. The list does not refer to Jain texts and systems. We have the names of *Bhārata*, *Rāmāyaṇa*, *Kauṭilyam* (*Koḍillayaṁ*) *Vaiśeṣika* (*Vaiśeṣiyam*) and Buddhism (*Buddhasāsaṇam*). The

82. *Op. cit.*, p. 144. He claims that this point 'no one sems to have noticed'.

order of enumeration does not show any arrangement or proper grouping. Māṭhara, if standing for a Sāṁkhya teacher, is inconveniently placed as part of a compound along with *Purāṇavāgaranaṇāḍagāï*. Likewise, the presence of *Logāyataṁ* in between *Kāvilaṁ* and *Saṭṭhiyantaṁ* is difficult to explain otherwise.[83] The insertion of *Besiyaṁ*, *Vaiśeṣiyaṁ* and *Buddhasāsanaṁ* between *Kaṇagasattarī* and *Kāvilaṁ* shows that the order of enumeration is totally haphazard. *Kaṇagasattarī* does not go directly with the Sāṁkhya *Kāvilaṁ* and *Saṭṭhiyantaṁ*. It is more closely associated with *Ghoḍayamuham*, *Veṣiya*, *Vaiśeṣiya* and *Buddhasāsana*. Either the *Kaṇagasattarī* was connected with an independent philosophical system, or else it belonged to a school of Sāṁkhya, different from the main school of Kapila and the *Ṣaṣṭhitantra*. As Īśvarakṛṣṇa emphatically proclaims his idealogical allegiance to Kapila, Āsuri and Pañcaśikha, who most likely authored the *Ṣaṣṭhitantra*, the *Kaṇagasattarī* which precedes *Kāvila* and *Saṭṭhiyanta*, cannot be the *Sāṁkhyakārikā* of Īśvarakṛṣṇa.

Īśvarakṛṣṇa after Vindhyavāsin

Shastri[84] argues that the vehemence, with which Vindhyavāsin rejects the concept of a subtle intermediate body, shows that he came after Īśvarakṛṣṇa, who propounds it. But, the argument is presumptuous. We do not have the original text written by Vindhyavāsin. Later texts merely refer to his view against the concept of a subtle intermediate body. We have here two views on the subject. There is no reason to believe that Īśvarakṛṣṇa was the only Sāṁkhya philosopher to subscribe to the concept of the intermediate body. We do not have evidence for making any positive assertion about the relative chronology of Vindhyavāsin and Īśvarakṛṣṇa. Interestingly, B. Bhattacharya,[85] on this very

83. *Lokāyata*, literally meaning 'current among the people', may appear to be qualifying the following name *Saṭṭhiyanta*. But, here we have an enumeration of independent names; there is no reason why the term may not be taken to refer to the Lokāyata school of philosophy.

84. *Op. cit.*, p. 640.

85. *Journal of Indian History*, Vol. VI, p. 36.

evidence, argues that Īśvarakṛṣṇa devotes three *kārikās* (39-41) to a refutation of Vindhyavāsin's views on subtle body. U.V. Shastri,[86] points out that not three *kārikās*, but only *kārikā* 40 concerns subtle body and this cannot, in any way, be construed to indicate that Īśvarakṛṣṇa wrote this *kārikā* as a rebuttal of Vindhyavāsin. Actually, a comparison of the views of the two Sāṁkhya philosophers does not yield any tangible evidence for their relative chronological position.

A.P. Mishra[87] subscribes to the view that Vindhyavāsa followed Īśvarakṛṣṇa. He does not advance any argument to support his view, but criticises the arguments advanced for placing Vindhyavāsa before Īśvarakṛṣṇa. For *pūrva-pakṣa* he mentions three arguments. The first is based on Paramārtha's account about Vasubandhu. No doubt the account does not make a specific mention of Īśvarakṛṣṇa and considering the vagueness and contradictions involved, it cannot be used for a definite assertion about the relative chronological position of Vindhyavāsa and Īśvarakṛṣṇa. The second argument, based on the equation of Vindhyavāsin with Vyāḍi, is equally untenable, because Vindhyavāsin was not another name of Vyāḍi; the latter came to be designated as a *vindhyavāsin* on account of his abode in the Vindhyas.

A.P. Mishra admits the force of the third argument. The author of the *Yuktidīpikā* argues that the *jijñāsā* and other members of the syllogistic reasoning are not expounded by Īśvarakṛṣṇa because Vindhyavāsin and other teachers have expounded them in their treatises and they are respected as authoritative by Sāṁkhya philosophers. But, to maintain his view of Īśvarakṛṣṇa being earlier, Mishra tries to explain away this argument. He says that the author of the *Yuktidīpikā* advances two arguments to explain the absence of an account of *jijñāsā* and other members in the *Sāṁkhyakārikā*. First, *jijñāsā* and others are parts of *anumāna*. Īśvarakṛṣṇa has discussed *pramāṇa*. *Jijñasā* and others are inherently implied in it, hence they have not been separately

86. *Op. cit.*, pp. 530-1.
87. *Op. cit.*, pp. 171-3.

discussed. Mishra argues that this is the main argument and the second argument, based on their exposition in the treatises of Vindhyavāsin and others, is secondary. In the face of the main argument the secondary argument is not to be given importance.

Mishra has not recognised the fact that the two arguments are separate and independent. One does not replace or oust the other. The merit and historical value of the two are to be considered separately. The second argument does not leave any scope for doubting the earlier chronological position of Vindhyavāsin. Actually, the way the author of the *Yuktidīpikā* refers to the views of earlier scholars to supplement the treatment in the *Sāṁkhyakārikā* leads to the clear inference that Vindhyavāsin and other teachers, whose views he mentions, were earlier than Īśvarakr̥ṣṇa.

P. Chakravati[88] gives another argument to prove that Vindhyavāsin was a predecessor of Īśvarakr̥ṣṇa. He points out that in the Jain text *Pramāṇamīmāṁsā*[89] perception is defined as *śrotrādivr̥ttiravikalpikā* by the early Sāṁkhya teachers, whereas Īśvarakr̥ṣṇa defines it as *prativiṣayādhyavasāya dr̥ṣṭam*. We know that the first definition was expounded by Vindhyavāsin. This shows that, as compared with Īśvarakr̥ṣṇa, Vindhyavāsin was considered to be an early Sāṁkhya teacher and hence was certainly earlier than Īśvarakr̥ṣṇa.

Conclusion

Thus, we see that Vindhyavāsin preceded Paramārtha and the author of the *Yuktidīpikā* by several centuries. He was definitely earlier than Īśvarakr̥ṣṇa and Vasubandhu. But, we cannot be sure about the time-gap separating him from these two. It is quite likely that he was earlier than the *Anuyogadvārasūtra*. We can postulate a span of at least hundred years for his reputation to settle down, for being recognised as one of the three main Sāṁkhya authorities, along with Kapila and the *Ṣaṣthitantra*. He followed Vārṣagaṇya on many points. Possibly he belonged to Sāṁkhya school founded

88. *Op. cit.*, p. 149.
89. P. 39.

by Vārṣagaṇya. He could have been an immediate disciple of Varṣagaṇya, but, in any case, was not far removed from him.

Taking into consideration all these facts, it can be suggested that Vindhyavāsin flourished in a period when Sāṁkhya principles were being actively debated and discussed. The standardisation, which is designated as the Classical Sāṁkhya, had not settled down. Thus, for Vindhyavāsin a date towards the beginning of the second century BC will meet the requirements of the case.

Vindhyavāsin' Philosophical Views

An analysis of the passages in later texts[90] referring to the views of Vindhyavāsin helps us get an idea of some of his distinguishing principles.[91] This account will, by no means, be exhaustive, but can project his main contributions as recognised by later writers.

The most significant point expounded thus was about the *antarabhavadeha* or the subtle intermediate body. Kumārila, in his *Ślokavārttika*,[92] in a verse says that Vindhyavāsin has rejected the concept of the subtle intermediate body, there being no reason in favour of its existence. This is confirmed by Medhātithi,[93] who says that Vindhyavāsin and other Sāṁkhya teachers do not subscribe to the intermediate existence. He does not quote the actual view of Vindhyavāsin. He says that some believe that there is a subtle intermediate body, which passes on to the other birth, whereas others do not uphold it. He quotes a couplet of Vyāsa (addressed to a king) to the effect that after the destruction of the body the organs enter another body, hence there is no intermediate existence of a subtle body between two manifest bodies. After this there is a reference to Vindhyavāsin and other Sāṁkhya teachers also rejecting

90. Collected by U.V. Shastri, *op. cit.*, pp. 638-40. There are 20 passages. A.P. Mishra, *op. cit.*, pp. 174-6 lists 19 omitting No. 1 in Shastri's list.
91. See A.P. Mishra, *op. cit.*, pp. 176-8; P. Chakravarti, *op. cit.*, p. 141.
92. Sūtra 5, verse 62 —
antarabhavadehastu niṣiddha vindhyavāsinā |
tadestitve pramāṇaṁ hi kiñcidavagamyate ||
93. On *Manu*, I.55.

the intermediate existence. The *Yuktidīpikā* presents Vindhyavāsin's point of view, possibly in its own words and not those of Vindhyavāsin.[94] It says that the sense-organs are ubiquitous, hence there is no special case for their movement from one embodiment to another. Fresh birth only means the manifestation of the sense-organs in the shape of the parental seed; the withdrawal of this manifestation results in death. Thus, there is no case for the existence of a subtle intermediate body.

Here we may refer to a minor detail which has not been mentioned in the passages collected by Shastri and Mishra. Śaṅkara in his *Prapañcasāratantra*,[95] refers to several views about the process of the descent of *puruṣa* into the womb. One of the view says that this is due to the all-pervasiveness of the individual soul (*kṣetrajña*). Padmapāda, in his commentary, adds that this is the point of view of Vindhyavāsin.[96]

A second set of distinctive views of Vindhyavāsin relate to the concept of enjoyment or experience (*bhoga*) on the part of *puruṣa*. Guṇaratnasūri, in his commentary on Haribhadrasūri's *Ṣaḍdarśanasamuccaya*,[97] quotes a couplet of Vindhyavāsin expounding the concept of *bhoga*. It says that *puruṣa* makes the mind (*manas*) as if conscious by virtue of its proximity to him, without himself undergoing any modification, just as a red *javā* flower makes the crystal look as if red by virtue of its proximity to it. This very concept is noted by the *Yuktidīpikā*.[98] It says that, whereas other teachers maintain that everything is experienced in

---

94. P. 144, lines 20-22—*vindhyavāsinastu vibhutvādindriyāṇāṁ bījadeśe vṛttyā janma । tattyāgo maraṇam ।। tasmānnāsti sūkṣmaśarīram । tasmānnirviśeṣaḥ । saṁsāra iti pakṣaḥ ।।*

95. *kecidasya paraṁ dhāmno vyāptimeva pracakṣate* । — I. 94-7

96. *vindhyavāsī tvevaṁ bhogamācaṣṭe* ।
"puruṣo'vivṛtātmaiva svanirbhāsamacetanam ।
manaḥ karoti sānnidhyādupādhiḥ sphaṭikamyathā", iti ।। — p. 104.
See Vyomavatī, pp. 521-2, for its explanation.

97. P. 108, line 12 — *tathā'nyeṣāṁ mahati sarvārthopalabdhiḥ manasi vindhyavāsinaḥ* ।

98. *paraṁ dhāmno vyāptimiti vindhyavāsipakṣaḥ* ।

the *mahat* (*buddhi*), in the opinion of Vindhyavāsin they are experienced in the mind (*manas*). This concept is also expressed in a slightly different manner in another fragmentary passage attributed to Vindhyavāsin by Bhoja in his commentary on the *Yogasūtra*.[99] This cryptic allusion is to be explained to mean that it is the *buddhi* (*sattva*) which is afflicted by *rajas*, but the *puruṣa* also appears to be afflicted inasmuch as he is reflected in the *buddhi*.

On the subject of *bhoga* the *Śāstravārttāsamuccaya-syādvādakalpalatā*,[100] a commentary on the *Śāstravārttāsamuccaya*, attributes a view which is different from the principle expounded above. The *Śāstravārttāsamuccaya* (III.27) in a couplet, says the *bhoga* on the part of the *puruṣa* is not the *bhoga* by the body, as expounded by earlier scholars (*pūrvasūris*) it arises by reflection, as in the case of a mirror. The commentary adds that here *pūrvasūris* refers to Vindhyavāsin and others. Clearly here the original view of Vindhyavāsin has not been detailed. The commentary adds that the view laid down in the verse was upheld by many earlier scholars, including Vindhyavāsin. As we have seen, Vindhyavāsin does not take this stand. He does not emply the analogy of reflection in the minor. He mentions the analogy of the crystal, which, on account of the proximity of a red *javā* flower, appears to be red. The concept of *bhoga* in terms of *pratibimbodaya* is attaributed to Āsuri and not to Vindhyavāsin. Guṇaratnasūri, in his commentary on the *Ṣaḍdarśanasamuccaya*,[101] quotes a verse of Āsuri. The verse says that the *buddhi* also assumes the form of the sense-organs, as they are modified into the shape of their respective objects on coming in contact with them; there arises a flow of *sattva* in the *buddhi* which becomes transparent like the self-luminous *puruṣa*, and then the

---

99. IV.22 — *anenaivābhiprayeṇa vindhyavāsinoktam* ।
"satyatapyatvameva puruṣatapyatvam" iti ॥

100. On III.27, p. 109, line 8 —
dehabhogena naivāsya bhāvato bhoga iṣyate ।
pratibimbodayāt kintu yathoktaṁ pūrvasūribhiḥ ॥
pūrvasūsibhiḥ vindhyavāsyādibhiḥ ।

101. *vivikte dṛkpariṇatau buddhau bhogo'sya kathyate* ।
pratibimbodayaḥ svacche yathā candramaso'smbhasi । — p. 104

puruṣa is seen reflected in the *buddhi*, just as the moon is reflected in the transparent water; this is called the *bhoga* of the *puruṣa*. There is an apparent difference between the two concepts of *bhoga*. Clearly the commentary on the *Śāstravārttāsamuccaya* by mistake attributes to Vindhyavāsin the meaning of *bhoga* which was expounded by Āsuri.

Another significant deviation from other Sāṁkhya teachers, which Vindhyavāsin made, is recorded in the *Yuktidīpikā*.[102] It says that, whereas other teachers of Sāṁkhya are of the view that *saṁkalpa* (reflection), *abhimāna* (self-appropriation) and *adhyavasāya* (ascertainment) are distinctly separate entities, Vindhyavāsin lays down that these are identical.

Kamalaśīla, in his commentary *Tattvasaṁgrahapañjikā*,[103] quotes a verse of an author, opposed to the Sāṁkhya system, who ridicules Vindhyavavāsin for his theory of causation. According to this verse, Vindhyavāsin, whose real name was Rudrila, demonstrated his beast-like ignorance as an inhabitant of the Vindhya mountain, when he said that the curd is the same as milk and the milk is the same as curd. We have suggested above[104] that the alternative reading of the second line would indicate that in place of Rudrila the original name of the Sāṁkhya philosopher was Vindhyavāsin and that the first line of the verse in some form appeared in Vindhyavāsin's original work. The reference shows that Vinddhyavāsin had expounded the Sāṁkhya theory of causation, according to which the cause is not materially different from the effect.

Vindhyavāsin makes a significant departure from the stand of

102. P. 108, lines 12-13 —
saṁkalpābhimānādhyavasāyanānātvamanyeṣām ekatvaṁ vindhyavāsinaḥ ।

103. P. 22, line 26 —
yadeva dadhi tatkṣīraṁ yatkṣīraṁ taddadhīti ca ।
vadatā rudrilenaivaṁ khyāpitā vindhyavāsitā ।।

104. P. 108, lines 6-7 —
mahataḥ ṣaḍaviśeṣaḥ sṛjyante pañcatanmātrāṇyahaṅkāraśceti viṇdhyavāsimatam ।

the other Sāṁkhya teachers in respect of the order of appearance of the evolutes. Many Sāṁkhya thinkers regard the five *tanmātras* (subtle elements) to have evolved from *ahaṁkāra*. But, according to Vindhyavāsin, the five *tanmātras* and *ahaṁkāra* are non-specific the specific, charateristic of their respective properties being not manifest, and both alike come out of *mahat*. This view of Vindhyavāsin is recorded in the *Yuktidīpikā*.[105]

Vindhyavāsin holds a distinctive view on the number of organs. Whereas Īśvarakṛṣṇa later standardised the number of *karaṇas* as thirteen, earlier thinkers proposed different numbers. In this respect Vindhyavāsin agrees with Vārṣagaṇya and names eleven *karaṇas*. Of these, five are motor organs, five sensory organs and also *manas*. This is recorded by the *Yuktidīpikā*.[106]

In the Sāṁkhya system an important place is assigned to the question of the magnitude of the sense-organs (*indriyas*). Some thinkers hold that when the sense-organs receive the particular impression of an object, they are modified into the shape of that object. Some others are of the view that the sense-organs are of limited magnitude. As against these, Vindhyavāsin is of the opinion that sense-organs are pervasive. This viewpoint of Vindhyavāsin is also known from the *Yuktidīpikā*.[107]

The most significant views of Vindhyavāsin, as preserved by later writers, relate to the topic of theory of knowledge. The

---

105. P. 108, line 11 — *karaṇamapi . . . ekādaśakamiti vindhyavāsī* ।

106. P. 108, line 10 — *indriyāṇi saṁskāraviśeṣayogāt parigṛhītarūpāṇīti kecit paricchinnaparimāṇīnityapare vibhūnīti vindhyavāsimatam* ।।

107. P. 148, lines 10-14 —

vindhyavāsinastu nāsti tatvasamaṁ sāṁsiddhikaṁ ca ।

kiṁ tarhi? siddhirūpameva । *tatra paramarṣerapi sargasaṅghātavyūhottarakālameva jñānam niṣpadyate, yasmād gurumukhābhipratipatteḥ pratipatsyata iti* । *apītyāha — "siddhaṁ nimitaṁ naimittikasyānugrahaṁ kurute nāpurvamutpādavyati"* *iti* । *nimittanaimittikabhāvaścaivamupapadyate* । *tatra nimittanaimittikabhāvaścaivamupapadyate* ।

tatra paramarṣeḥ peṭustūktaḥ anyeṣām kiliṣṭa ityayaṁ viśeṣaḥ ।

sarveṣāṁ tu tārakādyaviśiṣṭam ।

Yuktidīpikā[108] has a long passage analysing Vindhyavāsin's view about the different varieties of knowledge. Here the *Yuktidīpikā* presents Vindhyavāsin's viewpoint, but in its own words. Possibly Vindhyavāsin's own words have been freely used here, but it is difficult to locate them.[109] According to this passage, Vindhyavāsin does not accept *tattvasama* (knowledge which appears in a *tattva* or evolute of the *prakr̥ti* at the very moment of its manifestation) and *sāṁsiddhika* (knowledge which exists innately in a composite body consisting of the organs and their objects) types of knowledge. Knowledge cannot be innate; it is to be acquired. Even in the case of Kapila, the most revered sage, the knowledge reveals in a subsequent period after he emerges into existence, for he is said to have received it through oral transmission by his teacher, and in this way knowledge will be revealed in future also. By this Vindhyavāsin means that a stimulus as an efficient cause brings out an already existing object into revelation. It helps to manifest the substance existing in a latent form in the material cause, but it does not produce anything not existing before. The connection between the stimulus or efficient cause and the substance latent in the material cause arises in this manner. In the case of the revered sage Kapila there is quick transmission of knowledge, which is unparalleled, whereas in the case of ordinary beings the transmission is obstructed and is difficult. This is the difference. In the case of knowledge acquired by reasoning (*tāraka*) and other acquired ones, there is no difference of opinion.

The *Yuktidīpikā* quotes a passage, defining the various sources of knowledge[110] as occurring in other *tantra*s (*tantrāntareṣu*). Scholars generally interpret it as taken from the writings of

---

108. U.V. Shastri, *op. cit.*, p. 638, fn. 1 identifies the fragment between *apītyāha* and *iti* as being Vindhyavāsin's own.

109. P. 4, lines 10-12 —
pratyakṣādinyapi ca tantrāntareṣūpadiśyante — "śrotrādivr̥ttiḥ pratyakṣam । *sambandhādekasmāccheṣasiddhiranumānam* । *yo yatrābhiyuktaḥ karmaṇi cāduṣṭaḥ sa tarāptaḥ tasyopadeśah āptavacanam" iti* ।

110. *Yuktidīpikā*, p. 4. lines 7-8. For the passage see *infra* fn. 114.

Vindhyavāsin. This inference is based on the fact that the *Yuktidīpikā*, in the preceding lines, refers to Vindhyavāsin and others as expounding in the *tantrāntaras*.[111] Moreover, as we see below, there are other references to Vindhyavāsin defining *pratyakṣa* and *anumāna* in this manner and using similar expressions. The form of the passage shows that it is an actual quotation and not a formulation by the author of the *Yuktidīpikā*. But, it remains inexplicable why he should mention the *tantrāntaras* as the source and not name specifically any one writer or text. This is further intriguing when we find that he was familiar with Vindhyavāsin and his views. A possible explanation can be that these definitions of the sources of knowledge appeared in not only Vindhyavāsin's treatise but also in a few other Sāṁkhya texts and that he wanted to emphasise points which were common to all these texts.

According to this passage, *pratyakṣa* (perception) is the functioning of the sense-organs, ear and others. *Anumāna* is the realisation is all remaining cases on the basis of a relation perceived previously. One is authority (*āpta*) for that sphere with which he is specially associated and is without blemish in his action. His injunctions are known as authoritative statements (*āpta-vacana*).

Later texts attribute to Vindyavāsin statements about *pratyakṣa* and *anumāna* which are in consonance with the definitions laid down in the *Yuktidīpikā*. Thus, Abhayadevasūri, in his commentary[112] on Siddhasanadivākara's *Sanmatitarka*, quotes the definition of *pratyakṣa* as given by Vindhyavāsin. Here also *pratyakṣa* is described as the functioning of the sense-organs, but it is further elaborated by saying that this functioning is indeterminate (*avikalpikā*). Thus, according to Vindhyavāsin, *pratyakṣa*, in terms of modern psychology, will be termed as indeterminate perception, wherein there is a mere awareness of the

111. P. 533, line 2 —
śrotrādivṛttiravikalpikā iti vindhyavāsipratykṣalakṣaṇam ||

112. P. 423, line 22 —
etacca yathoktam—pratyakṣadṛṣṭasambandhamanumānaṁ viśeṣato dṛṣṭamanumānamityevaṁ vindhyavāsinā gaditam ||

object perceived, without determining its attributes or specific nature. Whether the expression *avikalpikā* was dropped deliberately in the *Yuktidīpikā* is not known. But, if it was so, the author possibly wanted to emphasise the point which Vindhyavāsin had common with other philosophers of the Vārṣagaṇa school, to which he belonged.

Likewise, in the case of *anumāna* Kamalaśīla, in his *Tattvasaṁgrahapañjikā*,[113] quotes the definition as pronounced by Vindhyavāsin. Here also the definition found in the *Yuktidīpikā* is retained, but with a point of elaboration. In this passage it is stated that *anumāna* is based on the actual perception of connection; *anumāna* is that which is based on the observation of the specific (*viśeṣatodr̥ṣṭam*).

In line with this is a verse in which Kumārila[114] describes *pramāṇatā* or validity of knowledge as laid down by Vindhyavāsin. It arises out of the awareness of an object whose existence is being suspected (*sandihyamānasadbhāvavastubodhāt*) and is based on the observation of the specific (*viśeṣa-dr̥ṣṭam*).

From the *Yuktidīpikā*[115] we get an indirect reference to an important part of the contents of Vindhyavāsin's treatise. It says that Īśvarakr̥ṣṇa is silent about the ten members in a purely syllogistic reasoning, because Vindhyavāsin and other teachers, who are accepted as authoritative, had expounded *jijñāsā* (desire to know) and other syllogistic members in their respective treatises. Clearly the account of these syllogistic members given by

---

113. *Ślokavārtika*, p. 393, verse 143 —
sandihyamānasadbhāvavastubodhāt pramāṇatā ।
viśeṣadr̥ṣṭametacca likhitaṁ vindhyavāsinā ॥

114. P. 4, lines 7-8 —
kiñca tantrāntarokteḥ tantrāntareṣu hi vindhyavāsiprabhr̥tibhirācāryairupadiṣṭāḥ pramāṇaṁ taste prācāryā ityataścānupadeśo jijñāsādīnām ॥

115. P. 76 lines 14-15 —
nahi vaḥ sāmānyaṃ dravyādarthāntarabhūtamasti sārūpyamātre sāmānyaparikalpanāt ।

Vindhyavāsin was considered to be authoritative in Sāṁkhya circles. These ten members are (1) *jijñāsā* (desire to know), (2) *saṁśaya* (doubt), (3) *prayojana* (purpose), (4) *śakyaprāpti* (possibility of a solution), (5) *saṁśayavyudāsa* (dispelling of the doubt), (6) *pratijñā* (proposition), (7) *hetu* (reason), (8) *dṛṣṭānta* (exemplification), (9) *upasaṁhāra* (application), and (10) *nigamana* (conclusion).

The concept of *sāmānya* is an important principle in Sāṁkhya. In the *Yuktidīpikā*[116] it is interpreted to mean the similar or common characteristic of the individuals belonging to the same class or community; it has no separate existence apart from the substance. P. Chakravarti[117] holds that this view was originally held by Vindhyavāsin. Though the suggestion is quite likely, there is no positive textual reference to confirm it. The author of *Yuktidīpikā* does not say that he is quoting Vindhyavāsin or referring to his views.

The *Sāhityamīmāṁsā*[118] mentions Vindhyavāsin's views of *sāmānya*. According to Vindhyavāsin, *sāmānya* is the attribute, which is inseparable from individuals known earlier and is recognisable in later individuals. *Sāmānya* is the same as *sādṛśya*, the two words have the same meaning. Kamalaśīla, is his commentary *Tatvasaṁgrahapañjikā*,[119] says that Vindhyavāsin is of the view that *sārūpya* means *sādṛśya*. Vindhyavāsin has used all the three terms — *sāmānya, sādṛśya* and *sārūpya*. The central term was *sāmānya* Vindhyavāsin equated it with *sādṛśya*. In this connection he also used the term *sārūpya*, but took *sārūpya* also to mean *sādṛśya*. Thus, he equated *sārūpya* with *sāmānya* and explained both as meaning *sādṛśya*.

116. *Op. cit.*, p. 248.
117. *vindhyavāsinastu — pūrvavyaktayavacchinnamapūrvavyaktau pratīyamānaṁ sāmānyameva sādṛśyam | tadekaśabdavācyam iti matam ||* p. 43.
118. P. 636, line 7 —
sārūpyaṁ sādṛśyaṁ vindhyavāsīṣṭam |
119. *Op. cit*, pp. 248-50.

P. Chakravarti[120] analyses Vindhyavāsin's view on *sāmānya*, as referred to by Kumārila in the *Ślokavārtika*. While discussing his own view of *sāmānya* meaning universal,[121] Kumārila refers to the views of teacher who takes *sāmānya* to mean *piṇḍasārūpya*. Finally he mentions this teacher to be Vindhyavāsin. He poses these question if *sāmānya* signifies *sārūpya* of *piṇḍa*s then what does *sārūpya* mean according to this teacher.[122] Kumārila remarks that if the term *sārūpya* means 'sameness of form' (*samānarūpabhāva*), then it is the same as *jāti* propounded by Kumārila himself; if, however, it means *sādṛśya* (similarity), then the question arises as to 'whose', 'with whom' and 'how' this 'similarity' occurs. By way of his concluding remark, Kumārila says that Vindhyavāsin in his work has used the term *sārūpya* as meaning 'sameness of form' and as an entity not absolutely different from the individuals that comprise a class. Kumārila adds that due to ignorance others call it *sādṛśya* or similarity.[123] P. Chakravarti[124] justifiably questions the faithfulness of Kumārila's account to the original view of Vindhyavāsin. Kumārila's conception of *sāmānya* differs from that of Vindhyavāsin. Kumārila here makes an attempt to explain *sārūpya* 'in such a way as may be helpful to support his won doctrine of universal'.

It seems that Vindhyavāsin used primarily the term *sāmānya*, signifying the common characteristic of individuals belonging to the same class. He explained it as implying *piṇḍasārūpya* (sameness of form). He also used the word *sādṛśya* to explain the terms

---

120. Akṛtivāda verses 65-76.

121. Akṛtivāda 65 —
sārūpyameva sāmānyaṁ piṇḍānāṁ yena kalpyate ।
tena sārūpyaśabdena kiṁ punaḥ pratipadyate ॥

122. *tena nātyantabhino'rthaḥ sārūpyamiti varṇitam* ।
granthe vindhyanivāsena bhrānteḥ sādṛśyamucyate ॥

123. *Op. cit.*, pp. 249-50.

124. According to Paramārtha, Vindhyavāsa had reworkded the Sāṁkhya system, which he had learnt from his teacher. The Tibetan sources also refer to his altering the Sāṁkhya according to his own view. See Wassilief, *Buddhismus*, p. 240.

sāmānya and *sārūpya, sādṛśya* referring to the same characteristics of all the individuals forming a class.

Thus, we see that Vindhyavāsin radically differed from the Sāṁkhya view, which came to be standardised later by Īśvarakṛṣṇa. His distinctive views relate to the principles of *antarābhavadeha*, the descent of the *kṣetrajña* in the womb, *bhoga*, identify of *saṁkalpa*, *abhimāna* and *adhyavasāya*, theory of causation, the order of evolutes, number of *karaṇas*, magnitude of the *indriyas*, the theory of knowledge, the nature of *pratyakṣa, anumāna* and *āpta-vacana*, ten members of syllogistic reasoning, and *sāmānya*.

Frauwallner attributes two major doctrinal changes to Vindhyavāsin. First, a new interpretation of the three-fold division of the *antaḥkaraṇas*. He replaces *buddhi* (the faculty of knowledge) by *mahat* (the great principle). It is the first general form in which the *prakṛti* unfolds itself. It is mere existence, a mark or sign and represents the first inequality in the distribution of the qualities of the *prakṛti* through which the equilibrium in it is given up. It is neither a psychical organism nor a product. Out of it originate the *ahaṁkāra* and the five *tanmātras* and the total elemental world. According to Vindhyavāsin, there are only eleven psychical organs — ten sense-organs and the *manas*. The *manas* unites in itself all functions which had been formerly attributed to the three *antaḥkaraṇas*. Second, the psychical organs are infinitely large. The sense-organs touch the distant objects during perception. This explains how the senses perceive objects which are larger or smaller than the physical organs. From this Vindhyavāsin draws the inference that there is no subtle body which wanders in the cycle of births. In the case of rebirth the all-prevailing psychical organs cease their work in their abode of the former body and assume it again in the abode of the new body.

Frauwallner also notes that Vindhyavāsin made efforts for the explanation of the idea of *sāmānya* (commonness) and sought to define it more sharply as *sārūpya* (similarity).

Vindhyavāsin seems to have enjoyed a key position in the history of Sāṁkhya. He belonged to the school of Vārṣagaṇya, but gave it a new exposition. There is no definite evidence about the continuation of his views in subsequent times and their impact on later thinkers.

G.J. Larson and R.S. Bhattacharya say that, like Vindhyavāsin, Īśvarakṛṣṇa was also a follower of the Vārṣagaṇya school and was familiar with the views of Vindhyavāsin. In presenting a standardised account of Sāṁkhya, he dispelled the cobweb of conflicting views of earlier teachers. In his final account he did not accept some of the view of Vindhyavāsin and chose to adopt another tradition. Vindhyavāsin, however, influenced the future course of philosophical development in a marked manner in another direction.

P. Chakravarti and Frauwallner have pointed out close similarities in the exposition of views by Vindhyavāsin and the *Yogasūtra* as commented by Vyāsa. Besides strikingly parallel numerous expressions in the two, Larson and Bhattacharya have emphasised three main points of contact: (a) The reduction of the functions of *buddhi, ahaṁkāra* and *manas* to *ekatva* (oneness) correlates with Yoga's notion on *citta*, (b) The all-pervasiveness of the sense capacities eliminating the need for a subtle body is paralleled by the all-pervasiveness of *citta* in Yoga eliminating the need for a subtle body; (c) The interpretation of *sāmanya* and *jāti* as *sārūpya* (similarity) is common to both. From this Larson and Bhattacharya hazard the guess that Vindhyavāsin's revision of Sāṁkhya eventually became the classical Yoga philosophy of Patañjali and Vyāsa which they term as Pātañjala-Sāṁkhya in contrast to *Kārikā*-Sāṁkhya. They place Patañjali's *Yogasūtra* in the period *c.* AD 400-500.

It is not the place to discuss the date of the *Yogasūtra*, but it appears to be considerably later. There is an inherent correlation between Sāṁkhya and Yoga, one adopting from the other. But the spheres of the two are demarcated. In the Mokṣadharmaparva section, Sāṁkhya and Yoga are often treated together, but there is no doubt about their specific areas and topics. Yoga has its own independent history of development. All this has culminated in the Classic formulation of Yoga in the *Yogasūtra*. It does not mean that the possibility of influences from other traditions and consequent changes is denied. Vyāsa pointed out parallels from the Sāṁkhya stream or Vindhyavāsin, but that does not amount to admitting borrowing or influence. The Yoga tradition, barring the references in the *Vyāsabhāṣya*, does not assign any high position to Vindhyavāsin. By the time of Patañjali Yoga had acquired a distinct form and identity. It will be a case of over-simplification to designate the Yoga of Patañjali as Pātañjala-Sāṁkhya. It does not acquire the character of Sāṁkhya; it remains Yoga.

19

Epilogue

Systematisation and Standardisation of Sāṁkhya

Introduction

THE long history of Sāṁkhya, from its first appearance to the composition of the *Sāṁkhyakārikā* by Īśvarakṛṣṇa, is rich in its contents and projects interesting contours of change. It witnessed a long line of very eminent thinkers, who made significant contributions to the growth of Sāṁkhya philosophy. They seem to have produced a voluminous literature on the subject. There was a remarkable efflorescence of Sāṁkhya principles. The wide variety of ideas would have baffled the ordinary believer in Sāṁkhya philosophy by their conflicting statements on certain basic issues. All this must have created a need for synthesising the plethora of views and presenting a standardised account of the principles. Some thinkers must have realised the practical necessity for a coherent, compact and summarised account of the principles, easy to comprehend and communicate.

There is evidence to indicate that this type of exercise was attempted by a number of scholars in the ancient period. Much of the voluminous Sāṁkhya literature being not available, the details of all the landmarks in the history of systematisation, standardisation and summarising cannot be delineated and the thinkers, who did it, cannot be identified and described. We have some references to a few such attempts at this on-going process in Sāṁkhya history. Even the brief references are enough to dispel the erroneous general impression that Sāṁkhya was propounded as a set system, with fixed principles in all respects. The Sāṁkhya is, thus, envisaged as a monolithic structure, with a unilinear development, often in the form of elaboration and clarification of principles expounded earlier.

Standardisation by Īśvarakṛṣṇa

Of the various attempts at standardisation the most outstanding was the one offered by Īśvarakṛṣṇa.[1] He claims to have studied all the writings of his predecessors and to have duly understood them. He says that he received the knowledge handed down through the line of teachers and taughts. He makes a pointed reference by name only to the first three Sāṁkhya teachers, possibly to indicate his faithfulness to the original formulation of Sāṁkhya. He is at pains to assert that he is not deviating from the *ṣaṣṭhitantra*. The *ṣaṣṭhitantra* seems to have been the earliest recorded account of Sāṁkhya principles. Īśvarakṛṣṇa treats it as the ancient and most respected version of Sāṁkhya. He claims that he presents in a summarised form the principles propounded in the *ṣaṣṭhitantra*.

The exercise done by Īśvarakṛṣṇa was so successful that it received ready recognition. As contrasted with earlier accounts of Sāṁkhya, mostly in *sūtras*, Īśvarakṛṣṇa chose to present his principles in the *āryā* metre. The ease and fluency of the metre were convenient for memorising the account. The style and choice of terms and expressions were qualities which added to the merit of the *Sāṁkhyakārikā*. In presenting a summary of the important principles of Sāṁkhya. Īśvarakṛṣṇa says that he has avoided the illustrative tales (*ākhyāyikā*) and controversy with opponents (*paravāda*). This must have weeded out long details appearing in many texts.

The *Sāṁkhyakārikā* does not have the mechanical character of a summary. It has its own positive qualities. Though he claims to present the principles of *ṣaṭhitantra*, Īśvarakṛṣṇa clearly deviates

1. See *supra* Chapter 1.

from its arrangement. He presents the twenty-five *tattvas* and the fifty *pratyaya-sargas*. On many issues, he seems to have taken his own personal stand. In several cases he adds some details and some arguments.

The recognition accorded to the standardised account in the *Sāṁkhyakārikā* is evidenced by the number of commentaries which were written on it and the Chinese translation of the commentary of Paramārtha. This version forestalled any new attempt to formulate Sāṁkhya principles. Sāṁkhya came to be identified with it. Modern scholars have been so much obsessed with it that some of them have closed their eyes to the historical realities of Sāṁkhya before this formulation. They designate it as Sāṁkhya or orthodox, pure or classical Sāṁkhya and refuse to accept as Sāṁkhya any deviation from it.

The standardisation not only prevented fresh, original texts on Sāṁkhya, other than commentaries on it, but also overshadowed earlier expositions. It is a natural phenomenon observed in many spheres of literary writings that a classic text eclipses earlier works to the extent that they are pushed into the background and are slowly and gradually forgotten and thus lost for ever. We find that in the history of Sāṁkhya the earlier attempts at systematisation and standardisation did not completely drive out earlier works. It speaks of the merit of the standardisation brought about by Īśvarakṛṣṇa that many of his predecessors were reduced to shadowy figures and their writings have survived as a few quotations retained by the commentaries.

Standardisation by Pañcaśikha

Īśvarakṛṣṇa, though the last but the most effective systematiser of Sāṁkhya, is important for the history of Sāṁkhya in recording the significance of the first attempt of this nature. He says that Pañcaśikha expanded the *tantra* (*bahudhā kṛtaṁ tantram*). The term *tantra* has two distinct meanings of a doctrine and scientific treatise. Ancient commentators have interpreted the pithy remark according to the meaning assigned by them to the word *tantra*.

Bahudhā likewise, can he interpreted variously. It can refer to the elaboration of the doctrines, and also to its diversification and modification. When *tantra* is used in the sense of a treatise, the passage signifies that Pañcaśikha composed a voluminous text.

The reference is to be interpreted in the light the role which is assigned to Kapila and his direct disciple Āsuri. Though later texts ascribe passages, texts and doctrines to Kapila and also principles and passages to Āsuri, there is no undoubted evidence detailing their views and writings. Īśvarakr̥ṣṇa makes it clear that Kapila for the first time proclaimed the Sāṁkhya doctrine, which had remained esoteric earlier. He made an oral exposition to Āsuri.[2] This is confirmed by several independant sources.[3] It goes to the credit of Āsuri that he faithfully preserved the teachings of Kapila and communicated it to his own disciple.[4] Īśvarakr̥ṣṇa does not attribute any formal text to Kapila. He merely mentions two important points in his principles, the primacy of *puruṣa* (*puruṣārtha*) and the existence, origin and termination (*sthityutpattipralaya*) of all beings (*bhūtānām*). It can be surmised that Kapila concentrated on these two aspects of his doctrine but did not elaborate them. As can be expected in such cases, the exposition was nebulous and was not spelt out with all the implications. Āsuri is not known to have made any improvement in the principles or their exposition.

Pañcaśikha for the first time recorded the teachings of Kapila and thus gave them a shape. In this process he discussed in details the various issues in the doctrine. He can be expected to have covered several aspects of the problems, and given them a full and exhaustive character. The treatise, which he composed, was an elaborate one. It seems quite likely that he expounded the principles in terms of sixty elements. Thus, *ṣaṣṭhitantra* was the name of his text and also referred to the most significant feature of his exposition. We can imagine that Pañcasikha not only diversified the principles

2. *Sāṁkhyakārikā*, 69-70.
3. See *Bhāgavata Purāṇa* I.3.10; (also *Garuḍa Purāṇa*) *Mbh.*, XII.326-8; Vyāsa on *Yogasūtra* I.25.
4. *Mbh.*, XII.220.10.10;225.24. See our article on Āsuri in *Chinnaswami Centenary Volume* (Varanasi, 1990) pp. 35-52.

and elaborated them but also prepared a voluminous text, which expounded the doctrines in terms of sixty topics.

The merit of the systematisation offered by Pañcaśikha was duly recognised. It was accorded importance as being highly valuable. In the Jain tradition we find that the *saṭṭhiyanta* is mentioned separately along with *Kāvilaṁ* (=*Kāpilam*).[5] It became the standard version of Sāṁkhya. The example of Pañcaśikha was followed by other systems of thought. The *Ahirbudhnyasaṁhitā* shows that the Pāñcarātra system also presented its principles in the form of sixty points. This text makes an interesting reference to several ways of enumerating sixty points.[6] The importance of the *ṣaṣṭhitantra* in the Sāṁkhya tradition is apparent from the fact that later thinkers were keen to proclaim their faith in the *ṣaṣṭhitantra*. Īśvarakṛṣṇa is not the only philosopher who did it. If the ascription of a *ṣaṣṭhitantra* to Vārṣagaṇya is correct, it would indicate that he thought it necessary to re-affirm the *ṣaṣṭhitantra* doctrine and went to the extent of preparing another text with the same title.

Saṁgrahakāra

The *Jayamaṅgalā* commentary on the *Sāṁkhyakārikā* quotes the verse enumerating the ten fundamental principles (*mūlikārtha*) of Sāṁkhya, as being of the *saṁgrahakāra*.[7] The verse occurs in some other sources,[8] but nowhere do we find its author being named. The name of this *saṁgrahakāra* is not known from any other text. Apparently he codified the Sāṁkhya doctrines and thus tried to introduce a system in the diffused expositions of the doctrines. It is baffling why the other texts quoting the verse have not cared to name the source, when, in many other cases, they mention the

5. *Anuyogadvārasūtra,* 41 — *kāvilaṁ logāyataṁ saṭṭiyantaṁ* |
6. XII.29 — *ṣaṣṭhitantrāṇyathaikaikamṣāṁ nānāvidhaṁ mune* |
7. On *Sāṁkhyakārikā,* 51.
8. See our article "Daśamūlikārtha in Sāṁkhya", in *Indian Historical Review*, Vol.

original authority.[9] The reference in the *Jayamaṅgalā* implies that the identity of the codifier was well known in the times of its author and hence he did not recognise the need for naming him.

The enumeration of the ten fundamental principles is implied in the exposition of the sixty points. Hence, it is not unlikely the Pañcaśikha, who expounded the sixty principles, was the author of the verse in question and is to be identified with the *saṁgrahakāra*. But, then the question will arise why did the author of the *Jayamaṅgalā* commentary, though familier with the name of Pañcaśikha, chose not to mention him by name, but referred to him by the designation *saṁgrahakāra*. It is to be noted that there is no other reference to support the use of the term *saṁgrahakāra* for Pañcaśikha.

The verse in question is quoted by Devala in the account of Sāṁkhya in his *Devaladharmasūtra*.[10] It is, thus, clear that the *saṁgrahakāra* preceded Devala. It is not unlikely that, though Pañcaśikha enumerated the ten basic principles, he did not use a verse for doing so. We do not have the original work written by Pañcaśikha, but the surviving quotations do not favour the possibility of its being in verses. Possibly, some later Sāṁkhya scholar attempted a condensed account of the voluminous presentation of Pañcaśikha and he adopted verses as the medium of expression. We find the names of many Sāṁkhya philosophers who belonged to the period after Pañcaśikha, but before Devala.[11] We admit that in the present state of our knowledge we cannot identify this unnamed codifier of Sāṁkhya.

---

9. *Sāṁkhyatattvakaumudī* on *kārikā* 72 quotes it on the authority of *Rājavārtika*, which is also a commentary. We are not sure of the author of the *Rājavārtika*. Clearly Vācaspatimiśra had no access to the original work of the *saṁgrahakāra* and hence quotes the verse from a secondary source.
10. U.V. Shastri, *Sāṁkhyadarśana kā itihāsa*, p. 600.
11. *Māṭharvṛtti* on *kārikā* 71 — Bhārgava, Ulūka, Vālmīki and Hārīta.

Systematisation by Devala

Devala was another Sāṁkhya philosopher who attempted a synthesis of the circulating diversified theories and offered a compact and coherent account. His presentation appeared in the Dharmasūtra which he composed. This text gave a prominent coverage to the principles of Sāṁkhya and Yoga. These portions were of a great value for the understanding of the Sāṁkhya principles. Śaṅkara, in his criticism of the Sāṁkhya, says that exposition of the system in the *Devaladharmasūtra* and other Dharmasūtras are also to be taken notice of.[12] Though the complete text of this *dharmasūtra* is not available,[13] long passages from it have been preserved as quotations in Aparārka's commentary on the *Yājñavalkyasmṛti* and in the *Kṛtyakalpataru* of Lakṣmīdhara.[14]

Devala says that the voluminous and serious treatises, composed earlier with proper reasoning and conclusions, have been presented here in a summarised form in a purposeful manner.[15] Devala helps us in restoring several lost links in the history of Sāṁkhya.[16]

Devala stands at a crucial juncture in the history of Sāṁkhya. The earlier formulation of *ṣaṣṭhitantra* was still current, but along with it another account in terms of the *tattva*s had gained currency. Devala strikes a synthesis between the two. He defines Sāṁkhya in terms of the twenty-five *tattva*s. But, at the same time mentions the *ṣaṣṭhi* principles. It is clear that he gives primacy to the concept of Sāṁkhya as the knowledge of twenty-five *tattva*s. But, he does not mention *ṣaṣṭhitantra*. He enumerates the fifty *pratyaya-bheda*s and then adds the ten *mulikārtha*s. Thus, though Devala synthesises

---

12. On *Brahmasūtra*, I.4.28 —
devalaprabhṛtibhiśca kaiściddharmasūtrakāraiḥ svagranthe-ṣvāśritaḥ |
13. Our own reconstruction of the text is to be published shortly.
14. See U.V. Shastri, *op. cit.*, pp. 600-5.
15. *etau sāṃkhyayogau cādhikṛtya yairyuktitaḥ samayataśca pūrvapraṇītāni viśālāni gambhirāṇi tantrāṇīha samkṣipyoddeśato vakṣyante* |
16. See *supra* chapter 12.

the two traditions about the presentation of Sāṁkhya doctrines, he shows a definite decline in the importance of the *ṣaṣṭhitantra* version.

Another important aspect of standardisation and synthesis forged by Devala is about the relationship of Sāṁkhya with Yoga. It brackets Sāṁkhya and Yoga. It says that the highest good (*niḥśreyas*) is two-fold and consists of Sāṁkhya and Yoga.

Devala presents a synthesis of views about God. Sāṁkhya is often criticised as being atheistic. Some modern scholars admit that Sāṁkhya view has changed from atheistic to theistic and then finally again to atheistic. We have demonstrated that both the theistic and atheistic points of view were present in Sāṁkhya, and one of the two was projected depending on the context of the points being discussed. Devala synthesises the two trends by presenting them in their proper background. He describes the process of creation and evolution from *prakṛti*, but does not provide any place to god (*īśvara*) in it. But, he does not hide his belief in god in other contexts. In describing the three forms of person, he mentions the *devalaśarīra* along with the *mānuṣaśarīra* and the *tiryagyoniśarīra*. Likewise, in his account of the various systems, Devala refers to *sāyujya* as community with the main deities whom he actually names.

In his attempt at systematisation Devala adopts the effective form of *sūtras*, in which the compact and condensed expression does not give any scope for any discussion or debate. Another characteristic of Devala's style is the enumeration of the components of any principle or element. He also explains the doctrines with the help of pithy phrases. At places, he takes recourse to the listing of various technical terms used for a concept as synonyms (*anarthāntara*).

The date of Devala cannot be fixed precisely. He was a disciple of Jaigīṣavya, who, in his turn, was a disciple of Pañcaśikha. The Buddhist tradition places him before the Buddha. We may place him roughly around 600 BC.

Mahābhārata on Systematisation

The *Mahābhārata* also bears traces of attempts at synthesis and systematisation on one hand, and standardisation of the account on the other. The deviations from the classical Sāṁkhya recorded in the *Mahābhārata* have been explained variously by modern scholars, as representing an early stage in the emergence of Sāṁkhya or as a later stage when a Vedāntic colouring was applied to the Sāṁkhya principles. It is now generally admitted that the *Mahābhārata* preserves accounts of Sāṁkhya in early stages of its formulation. What is generally not appreciated is that the *Mahābhārata* is not a mere unintelligent collection of diversified and conflicting accounts of Sāṁkhya doctrines. We find that some of the Sāṁkhya teachers, whose views are recorded in the *Mahābhārata*, attempted to reconcile and synthesise conflicting stands on some of the Sāṁkhya principles. Along with this, it seems that the compilers of the *Mahābhārata* tried to coordinate the accounts to present a standardised version.

Attempts of Yājñavalkya and Vasiṣṭha

Illustrations of attempts at synthesis are to be found in the accounts of Sāṁkhya associated with Yājñavalkya and Vasiṣṭha. Vasiṣṭha[17] mentions twenty-five categories and maintains that there is no *tattva* beyond the twenty-fifth.[18] He says that Viṣṇu is to be regarded as the twenty-fifth *tattva*.[19] He adds that the twenty-fifth category or *puruṣa* is not a separate *tattva*; through delusion it embraces the *tattvas* and hence is regarded as a separate *tattva* and, though without any form, in conjunction with the *prakṛti*, it takes the latter's attributes as its own.[20] In XII.308 Vasiṣṭha mentions the twenty-sixth category and introduces the concepts of *apratibuddha*, *budhyamāna* and the *buddha*. The *apratibuddha* is the *prakṛti*. The *budhyamāna* is the twenty-fifth category, the

---

17. *Mbh.*, XII.302-7.
18. XII.302.47.
19. XII.302.38.
20. XII.302.38-40.

puruṣa or the *jīva* (individual soul). The *buddha* is the twenty-sixth category or the liberated soul.[21] The twenty-fifth category becomes one with the twenty-sixth, on recognising that he is not different from the latter and on not apprehending anything by his own *buddhi* (intelligence).[22] The present account in the *Mahābhārata* shows an attempt 'to reconcile the Sāṁkhya theory of the plurality of the spirits with the doctrine of unity'.[23] We also notice an attempt to fuse the Sāṁkhya and Yoga doctrines. Vasiṣṭha mentions the doctrines of *buddha, apratibuddha* and *budhyamāna* as characteristic of Yoga and refers to the twenty-sixth category[24] later he observes that the Sāṁkhya expounds the doctrine of the twenty-sixth category and uses the terms *prabuddha* and *budhyamāna*.[25]

The features characterising the Sāṁkhya exposition by Vasiṣṭha are, also to be observed in the account associated with Yājñavalkya. Here chapters XII.310-315 deal with Sāṁkhya and chapters XII.316-19 with Yoga. In chapter XII.318 he mentions the twenty-sixth category and the concepts of *apratibuddha*, *budhyamāna* and *buddha*. But, Yājñavalkya himself observes that the twenty-sixth category is advocated by the Sāṁkhya and Yoga.[26] The concept of the twenty-sixth category is not to be associated with the Yoga only. According to P. Chakravarti, this doctrine was advocated by the Sāṁkhya-Yoga school of the Epic.[27] The testimony of Vasiṣṭha and Yājñavalkya is to be interpreted as showing that an attempt was made to synthesise Sāṁkhya and Yoga, the two parallel and supplimentary systems of thought.

It will be difficult to fix the date of the synthesis attempted by Vasiṣṭha and Yājñavalkya. These are the names of ancient sages,

21. XII.308.5-7.
22. XII.308.16-18.
23. P. Chakravarti, *Origin and Development of the Sāṁkhya System of Thought*, p. 48.
24. XII.307.48.
25. XII.308.17.
26. *Mbh.*, XII.319.77-9.
27. *Op. cit.*, p. 51

but there is no definite evidence to place them in historical chronology. Both are known as authors of reputed Dharmaśāstra texts. Vasiṣṭha plays an important role in the *Rāmāyaṇa* story. Yājñavalkya enjoys a place of high respect in the philosophical system of the Upaniṣads. On the basis of their associations with kings of Videha we have proposed *c.* 975-900 BC as the date for Yājñavalkya[28] and *c.* 775-700 BC as the date for Vasiṣṭha.[29] We may suggest that this systematisation occurred in the period of the Upaniṣads.

Grund Text in the Mokṣadharmaparva

Hopkins had pointed out the close similarity in several passages in the Mokṣadharmaparva section of the Śāntiparva. At times many verses are identical in them.[30] P. Chakravarti[31] points out that three different chapters (XII.194, 247, 285), in expounding *adhyātma*, which is actually a statement of the main principles of Sāṁkhya, present the same details and, at several places, in identical verses. Chakravarti takes this to suggest that these verses were taken from a common source. E. Frauwallner[32] takes the three sets of chapters in the Mokṣadharmaparva section, namely XII.194, 247-9 and 287, as being so closely related as to be the three versions of one text, which he refers as *epischen Grund text des Sāṁkhya*. According to him, it originated before the writing of the Mokṣadharmaparva. Frauwallner takes it to be the first articulation of Sāṁkhya theory and places it in the period after the oldest Upaniṣads and roughly contemporary with the rise of Buddhism.

It is to be noted that the Mokṣadharmaparva is full of chapters presenting Sāṁkhya doctrines. In many cases we have the names of a particular Sāṁkhya teacher as expounding them. In the

---

28. See *supra* chapter 5.
29. See *supra* chapter 10.
30. *The Great Epic of India*, p.
31. *Op. cit.*, pp. 54-6.
32. "Untersuchungen zum Mokṣadharma", *WZKM*, XXXII (1925), pp. 179-206.

present instance we have three sets of chapters, of which Vyāsa is the narrator of one and Bhīṣma of the other two. It is clear that these two do not present the system as expounded by some earlier thinkers. These are not three separate accounts given by three different philosophers. It is not easy to comprehend why Bhīṣma should expound Sāṁkhya twice in identical verses in the same text and why should the compiler include identical verses (and chapters) in three places in the same Mokṣadharmaparva. If there was a *Grund* text or an original, why should three corrupt versions of it be accommodated in the same section. Because the names of the authors of these chapters, or of the expounders of the three versions of the doctrine, are not known, we cannot describe them as three versions of one and the same text. We suggest that the three presentations of the system were made at three places in the section, which, being of the same period and covering the same ground, had naturally many common points and similar expressions. The standardisation was effected by the compiler of the Mokṣadharmaparva section and he used some expressions and even verses at more than one place. We argue that these doctrines represent an early stage in the history of Sāṁkhya, but they are by no means its earliest form. We are of the view that some of the expositions attributed to the early Sāṁkhya philosophers in the *Mahābhārata* are possibly based on some early traditions and hence are earlier than the *Grund* text set of chapters. The standardisation in the chapters of the *Grund* text was effected by the compiler of the Mokṣadharmaparva. It did not require much change in the views and contents; it was effected more in its form and extent. The date of this standardisation will be roughly the same as the date of Mokṣadharmaparva section in the Śāntiparva of the *Mahābhārata*.

Gītā Reference to Standardisation

The *Gītā* contains a very clear reference to a standardisation affected in the Sāṁkhya system. In the eighteenth chapter it mentions five causes (*kāraṇāni*), which are requisite for the successful completion (*siddhi*) of any action. It says that these are enunciated in the *kṛtānta sāṁkhya*.[33] This expression means 'Sāṁkhya whose conclusions have been established'. It shows that the Sāṁkhya had diverse and conflicting views, which were systematised and a final statement of the position was established. On the basis of this reference, it can be inferred that sometime before the composition of the *Gītā* the divergent Sāṁkhya views were reconciled to arrive at a settled conclusion.

The date of this systematisation is difficult to settle. The date of the composition of the *Gītā* is itself a subject of wide differences in views. Without claiming a precise date for it, we can only say that the systematisation was brought about before the composition of the *Gītā*. We may further hazard the guess that this was possibly different from and later than the systematisation recorded in the Mokṣadharmaparva and associated with the names of Vasiṣṭha and Yājñavalkya and the one represented by the three chapters suggesting a *Grund* text.

The above study demonstrates that the view of Sāṁkhya system being expounded in all its details from the very beginning and remaining static and fixed in later times does not stand the test of historical scrutiny. The system has evolved and grown in course of time and, on many occasions, the diversity of views were reconciled and a compact and coherent system was presented. We cannot trace all such attempts and different stages. But the few which can be detected indicate the possibilities of its history.

---

33. XVIII.13 —
pañcemāni mahābāho kāraṇāmi nibodha me ।
sāṁkhya kṛtānte proktāni siddhaye sarvakarmaṇām ॥

Appendix I

Voḍhu

Voḍhu as Sāṁkhya Teacher

VOḌHU was an early Sāṁkhya teacher.[1] The *Vāmana Purāṇa*[2] mentions his name as one of the early Sāṁkhya philosophers. His name occurs in the list of Sāṁkhya teachers in the *Gauḍapādabhāṣya*.[3] The traditional list of sages entitled to *tarpaṇa* contains the names of Sāṁkhya teachers, Voḍhu being one of them.[4]

---

1. H.S. Joshi, *Sāṁkhyayogadarśana kā jīrṇoddhāra*, pp. 53-4, 37-8, 32-3 says that his name occurs in the list of Sāṁkhya teachers in the *Mahābhārata* and Chinese and Tibetan tradition and in the *Vāyu Purāṇa* list of *yogins*. Keith, *The Sāṁkhya System*, pp. 51-2 also mentions the reference to his name in the Epic and the Chinese translation of the commentary on the *Sāṁkhyakārikā*. We do not find the name of Voḍhu in the *Mahābhārata* and the *Vāyu Purāṇa*. We are not aware of a Tibetan tradition on this point. The Chinese tradition evidently refers to the Chinese translation of Paramārtha's commentary of the *Sāṁkhyakārikā*. The sequence of Sāṁkhya teachers between Pañcaśikha and Īśvarakṛṣṇa, according to this source, is Ho-Kia, Ulūka and Po-p'o-li. Voḍdhu is not mentioned here. Possibly Joshi takes Po-p'o-li to stand for Voḍhu. But, this is totally misconceived. Po-p'o-li is rendered as Bat-ba-li in the Japanese version, which, according to P. Chakravarti, *op. cit.*, p. 132, corresponds to Bāddhali of the *Yuktidīpikā* list. Keith suggests the name of Viḍhu in place of Ulūka, but there is no cogent reason in its favour.
2. XXXIV. 38.
3. *Gauḍapādabhāṣya*
4. *Atharvaveda Pariśiṣṭa*.

The appearance of Voḍhu's name in the *tarpaṇa* list shows that he was revered as an eminent Sāṁkhya philosopher, to whom a grateful posterity pays homage to remind itself of its indebtedness to him. All these names are those of early sages which shows that Voḍhu is to be assigned a place in the early history of Sāṁkhya philosophy. In the *Vāmana Purāṇa* the name of Voḍhu is mentioned as a Sāṁkhya philosopher along with its first two celebrities, Kapila and Āsuri.

Absence of Reference

There is no reference to any work composed by Voḍhu. The later texts do not quote any passage from his work. Nor do we find any reference to his views on any of the problems.

Īśvarakṛṣṇa mentions the names of only Kapila, Āsuri and Pañcaśikha in the early history of Sāṁkhya.[5] The absence of a reference to Voḍhu can be explained on the ground that he did not belong to the philosophical lineage of Kapila continued by Āsuri and Pañcaśikha. He possibly represented a different tradition in Sāṁkhya.

Historicity

The *Vāmana Purāṇa* mentions Voḍhu as the son of Dharma and Hiṁsā. Such a mythological origin does not disprove the historicity of the person; it was intended to emphasise his importance in a figurative manner. Among the traditional names of early Sāṁkhya teachers, Keith concedes historical reality to Voḍhu. In the manual for *tarpaṇa* Voḍhu, along with six others, is mentioned as the seven human beings (*sapta manuṣyas*) entitled to it.

Senior to Āsuri

The position of Voḍhu in the *tarpaṇa* list of Sāṁkhya sages shows a variation. In one list he appears after Kapila and in another after Āsuri.[6] The tradition that Kapila communicated his views to Āsuri,

5. *Sāṁkhyakārikā*, 70.
6. H.S. Joshi, *op. cit.*; Keith, *op. cit.*

who, in his turn, taught them to Pañcaśikha, would suggest that Voḍhu did not precede Āsuri. It may be argued that Āsuri taught Sāṁkhya principles to more than one disciple. Of these, Pañcaśikha founded a school, but possibly Voḍhu did not establish an independent school.

It is, however, to be noted that there is no inherent difficulty in placing Voḍhu before Āsuri. Voḍhu was an early Sāṁkhya teacher being mentioned along with Kapila and Āsuri. Becasue he differed from the Sāṁkhya tradition of Kapila down to Pañcaśikha, his chronological position was remembered vaguely and hence his name was differently located in the list of Sāṁkhya teachers.[7] The suggestion of Voḍhu being a senior contemporary of Āsuri is supported by the evidence of the *Vāmana Purāṇa* which names Sāṁkhya teachers in the sequence of Kapila, Voḍhu and Āsuri.

Weber on Voḍhu

Weber[8] had identified Voḍhu with the Buddha. According to him, the orthodox tradition had corrupted Buddha into Voḍhu. Voḍhu, it is to be noted, cannot be the Prākr̥t form of Buddha. The Buddha himself had favoured the use of Prākr̥t. The name of Buddha in texts of Sanskrit and Prākr̥t alike always appears as Buddha.

There is no justification for suggesting Voḍhu to be a corrupt form of Buddha. In ancient records we have several instances of such queer names. It was only in the infancy of Indological studied that such fanciful suggestions could be offered. With the progress of research the separate identity of Buddha and Voḍhu cannot cause a misgiving.

---

7. According to Keith, *op. cit.*, it would be unwise to place any faith on these evidences of chronology.
8. Cited by Garbe, *Sāṁkhya Philosophie*, p. 72.

Appendix II

Asita-Devala in Isibhāsiyāi

Isibhāsiyāi — An Ancient Jain Text

THE *Isibhāsiyāi* (*R̥ṣibhāṣitāni*)[1] is one of the most ancient Jaina āgamic works. *Ṭhāṇaṅga* (*Sthānāṅga*)[2] mentions it as the third chapter of the *Paṇhāvāgaraṇāim* (*Praśnanavyākaraṇa*), the tenth *aṅga*. But the text of the *Paṇhāvāgaraṇāim*, being a post-Gupta replacement of the original, does not contain this chapter. The *Samavāyaṅga*[3] also knows the *Isibhāsiyāi* and describes it as containing forty-four *ajjhayaṇa* (*adhyayana*). This tallies with the form of the *Isibhāsiyāi* which has fortyfive sections.[4] The text evidently was of considerable significance to the Jainas, because the scholiast, who wrote the *Āvassayanijjutti* (*Āvaśyaka-niryukti*)

---

1. *Isibhāsiyāim. A Jaina Text of Early Period,* ed. by Walther Schubring L.D. Series 45, Ahmedabad, 1974. It was originally published in *Den Nachrichten der Wissenschaften zu Gottingen*, 1942, pp. 489-576. The Sanskrit commentary was published in the same *Akademie*, 1951, pp. 21-52. The second edition of the text published from Hamburg in 1969 contains its German translation as well. Prakrit Bharati Series No. 46 offers the text with translation in English and Hindi.
2. *Sthāna*, 10, *sūtra* 755.
3. *Samavāya* 44.
4. According to Schubring, *op. cit.*, p. 2, the difference in the number of sections is to be explained by the fact that section no. 20 of the text does not correspond to the pattern of other sections, each of which is associated with the utterence of a *r̥ṣi*. There is no such explanation of the *Vihimaggapavā* (Ś 1363 = AD 1441) of Jinaprabha mentioning fifty as the number of sections in it.

(erroneously taken as the celebrity, Bhadrabābu), expresses his resolve to write a *nijjutti* on it also.[5] The *Sūyagaḍa* (*Sūtrakṛtāṅga*)[6] names certain earlier "Mahāpuruṣa Arhats" who evidently belonged to the Vedic tradition and achieved the position of Arhats by resorting to ways and practices which generally are not approved by Jainism. The term *iha* used here refers to Jaina canonical literature. But the author of the commentary explains it to signify *Ṛṣibhāṣita* and other texts (*Ṛṣibhāṣitādau*). The text commanded respect in Jaina literature. It was accepted as a *kālīya* text, which, though not included in the *aṅgas*, was approved for the study hours in the daily time-table.[7]

On the basis of 'numerous indisputably genuine early reminiscences in language and style' Schubring places it in the category of the most ancient Jaina *āgamas* such as the *Āyāra* (*Ācāra*, particularly its first part, the *Bambhacerāim*), the *Sūyagaḍa* (*Sūtrakṛta*), the *Uttarajjhāyā* (*Uttarādhyayana*) and the *Dasaveyāliya*[8] (*Daśavaikālika*). The *Isibhāsiyāi* doubtless has parallels in language and expression with these four texts. In the number of stanzas, the predominace of *ślokas* and the extent of prose the *Isibhāsiyāi* is closest to the *Dasaveyāliya*; in the diversity of the metres it is like the *Dasaveyāliya*, *Uttarajjhāyā* and *Sūyagaḍa*.[9] Like the *Bambhacerāim*, our text is characterised by an intermingling of prose with verse, in which 'whole stanzas, half stanzas and single *pādas* alternate with unmetrical executions'.

The author of the text, as ascertained by Schubring, was close to Jina Pārśva from the doctrinal standpoint. This is indicated by the greater importance given to Pārśva in devoting a rather long passage for expounding his dictum.[10] The text, moreover, does not separate the fourth and fifth vows seprately as was the case with the *Cāturyāma-dharma* preached by Pārśva before Vardhamāna

5. *Āvassaya-nijjutti*, II.6.
6. *Ibid.*, III.4.1-4 — *ete puvviṁ mahāpurisā āhitā iha saṁmatā* ।
7. *Nandī* (Agamodaya Samiti) 202b; *Pakkhiya* (Devchand Lalbhai Pustakoddhara), 4, 66a.
8. *Op. cit.*, p. 2.
9. *Ibid.*, p. 7.
10. Section 31, pp. 66-9.

Mahāvīra. The *Isibhāsiyāi* was evidently still under the influence of Pārśva. It fuses the fourth and fifth vows into one.

The text breathes an atmosphere of liberal attitude which may have characterised the early days in the history of Jainism. It pays respect to many thinkers and religious leaders outside the Jaina fold by collecting their sayings to form a canonical work. Some of these belonged to the Vedic or Brāhmaṇical tradition. We also find Maṁkhaliputta[11] (Maskariputra Gośāla) and the Buddhists Mahākāsava[12] (Mahākāśyapa) and Sāiputta (Śāriputra)-*buddha*.[13] There are, in the text, certain views which could not have been tolerated in later days of Jainism, when orthodoxy had settled down and anything inconsistent with the set doctrines, dogmas and practices could not expect an honourable reference. Section 20 introduces an anonymous *utkaṭa-vādin* place of a *ṛṣi* and mentions, with a fair show of approval, his materialism. We have an 'unjinistic' recognition of farming as *divvā kisī*[14] and a reference to cosmogonic theories, including one about the origin of the world from water.[15] Likewise, orthodox Jainism of later times could not have accepted the equation of Pārśva, Mahāvīra, and latter's adversary Gośāla Maskariputra, alike as *pratyekabuddha*s, which we find in our text. These 'strange things' in the text explain, according to Schubring, why it fell into 'nearly complete oblivion'[16] and created uncertainty about it in later writings. This exemplified by the confusion about it in Haribhadra's commentary on the *Āvassayanijjutti*. In it the *Isibhāsiyāi* is identified at one place[17] with the canonical *Paiṇṇa* (*Prakīrṇaka*) named *Devindatthaya* (*Devendra-stava*), and in another[18] with the *Uttarajjhāyā*. We already have referred to the later confusion about the number of sections in the text.

11. Section 11.
12. Section 9.
13. Section 38.
14. Sections 26 and 32.
15. Section 37 — *savvamiṇaṁ purā udagamāsi tti* ।
16. *Op. cit.*, p. 9.
17. On *Āvassaya-nijjutti*, II.6.
18. *Ibid.*, VIII.5.

A pointer to date of the text is the reference to Gośāla Maskariputra. The *Viyāhapannatti*[19] (*Vyākkyā-prajñapti*) (*c.* second-third century AD) represents him as a renegade disciple of Mahāvīra, but in our text he does not suffer from any such humiliation. On the contrary he enjoys an honoured position as a *pratyekabuddha*. This transformation in his status in Jaina perception must have taken a long period. Thus, the *Isibhāsiyāi* is to be place a few centuries before the selfsame (and other passages are similar in vein and style) in the *Viyāhapannatti*.

Characteristics of the Text

The emphasis on ethical thought is the main characteristic of the text. It brings out the common points in the ethical ideas of the early religions of different traditions. The metaphysical and doctrinal details and differences, which dominate later sectarian and scholastic texts, did not receive any importance from the author of this text. This also is a significant pointer to the early date of the text.[20]

R̥ṣis in the Text

Our text purports to collect the views of *r̥ṣis*. Generally the word *r̥ṣi* is used for a sage. It is supposed to be synonymous with *muni*. But, in our text it is employed in the special sense of a *pratyekabuddha*, A *pratyekabuddha* is a person, who, having realised the highest knowledge, acquired the status of the *buddha* for himself but, unlike the *buddha*, did not found a school or community. That the *pratyekabuddhas* of our text had no intention to teach, though they had their own characteristic views, is clear from the fact that the word *buitam* (dictum) and not *pannattam* (teaching) is used for them.[21] Under the name of *r̥ṣi* or *pratyekabuddha* the text records the views of forty-five thinkers, though in one case the actual name of the *r̥ṣi* is not mentioned.

---

19. On *Āvassaya-nijjutti*, 15.
20. Sagarmal Jain, *R̥ṣibhāṣita: Eka Adhyayana* Jaipur, 1988, p. 9 places the text between the fifth and third centuries BC.
21. Schubring, *op. cit.*, p. 2.

The text does not give enough details to identify the *ṛṣis* or to locate them in time and place in all the cases. However, some of them can be easily identified with personalities mentioned in early texts of Brāhmaṇical tradition, for example, Jaṇṇavakka (= Yājñavalkya), Bāhuya (= Bāhuka or Nala), Soriyāyaṇa (= Sauryāyani), Addālaka (= Uddālaka) and Aruṇa Mahāsālaputta (= Āruṇi). The Brāhmaṇa association is clear in the cases of Piṅga, Isigiri (Ṛṣigiri) and Sirigiri (Śrīgiri) who are called *māhaṇa-parivvāyaga* (*brāhmaṇ-parivrājaka*).[22] Other names in this category are Asiya Davila (= Asita Devala), Aṅgarisi Bharaddāya (= Aṅgiras Bhāradvāja), *deva* Nārāya (= *devarṣi* Nārada),[23] Divāyaṇa (= Dvaipāyana) and Mātaṅga. Vāu (= Vāyu), Soma, Jama (= Yama) and Varuṇa are the four Lokapālas (Regents of the Quarters) in the Brāhmaṇical pantheon from very early times. Some names, for which we cannot adopt a very definite view (but some of them can still be identified), are Madhurāyaṇa (= Mathurāyaṇa), Tārāyaṇa (= Tārāgaṇa, more probably sage Nārāyaṇa), Āriyāyaṇa, Varisava-Kaṇha (= Varisakaṇha or Vārṣagaṇya, the ancient Sāṁkhya teacher). About Harigiri, Kumbhaputta. Pupphasālaputta, Rāmaputta (correctly Rāmagutta), Gāhāvaiputta (= Gāthāpatiputra) Taruṇa, Ketaliputta[24] and Vidu (= ? Vidura) we are less certain. Besides Vaddhamāna (= Vardhamāna Mahāvīra) and Pāsa (Pārśva), we have Maṁkhaliputta (= Gośāla Maskariputra), Sāiputta (= Śāriputra) Buddha and *mahai* Mahākāsava (= Mahākāśyapa). Vajjiyaputta possibly also had a Buddhist association and belonged to the Vajji republic.[25] Vāgalacīri (= Vakkalacīri), Jaina Ṛṣyaśṛṅga, enjoyed a place of high respect in the eyes of the author of the text being referred to as *viyatta bhagavaṁ* and *uggatava*. The other names in the text are Metajja (Maitreya), Bhayāli, Sāṁjai

22. Ambaḍa is also called *parivvāyaga*. His interlocutor is Jagaṁdharāyaṇa (= Yaugaṁdharāyaṇa).

23. Schubring, *op. cit.*, pp. 4-5 prefers to identify him with prince Nārāya of Bāravaī.

24. Schubring, *op. cit.*, p. 4 suggests it to be a perplexity varient of Tetaliputta in section 10.

25. Schubring (*ibid.*) describes him as the head of the school of the Vātsī-putras, i.e., Vatsīputra.

(= ? Sañjaya),[26] Dagabhāla,[27] Vārattaya Addaga, Indanāga (Indranāga) and Vesamaṇa (Vaiśravaṇa).

Some of these names occur in some other Jaina texts as well. The *Sūyagaḍa*[28] (*c.* second century BC) mentions Asita, Devala, Dvaipāyana, Parāśara, Nami-videhi Rāmagupta, Bāhuka and Nārāyaṇa as *mahāpuruṣa* who achieved the highest knowledge, even though they followed ways not approved by Jainism. Confirmation of the names from other Jaina writings and non-Jaina texts makes a strong case for the historicity of most of the names mentioned in the *Isibhāsiyāi*. In the case of some others, we can postulate a quasi-historical existence, as they were handed down by a long and persistent tradition. (The four Lokapālas and Vaiśravaṇa are of course Vedic divinities).

In section 3 the name of the *ṛṣi* in the introductory prose passage is Asiya Davila. The concluding prose sentence mentions him simply as Davila. Schubring[29] feels no difficulty in taking Asita Devala to be the original of Asiya Davila. There cannot be any objection to equating Asiya with Asita. But Devala, as the original of Davila, is not so easy to explain. However, considering the major changes occurring in the name of other sages in the text and the form Davila (as intermediary between Devala and Davila), the restoration is to be accepted.

Here I intend to discuss the identity of "Asita Devala" with particular reference to his characteristic ideas as stated in the *Isibhāsiyāi*.

At the very outset it is to be pointed out that, though Asita Devala is mentioned as the name of a single person, the *Sūyagaḍa*[30]

26. Schubring, *op. cit.*, p. 7 equates him with a king whose name is Sanskritised as Saṁyata.
27. Schubring (*ibid.*) identifies him with Gaddabhāli, the teacher of *Saṁjaya = Saṁyata*.
28. I.3.4.1-4.
29. *Op. cit.*, p. 5.
30. I.3.4.3 —

āsile devile ceva dīvāyaṇa mhānrisī ।
ṇarāsare sagaṁ bhoccā bīyāṇi hariyāṇi ॥

makes Asita and Devala two different persons. The commentator Śīla-sūri (*c.* third quarter of the ninth century AD) falls in line with the *Sūyagaḍa*.[31] There is some other Jaina evidence in support of Asita alone being the name of an individual. The *Isimaṇḍala* instead mentions the name as *Devilāsuta*.[32] There is no doubt that the *Isimaṇḍala* has Asita Devala of the *Isibhāsiyāi* in mind, because the introductory phrases in the two cases are closely parallel.[33] In Brāhmaṇical tradition Asita Devala sometimes appears as one single name. But Devala alone is generally used as the name for an ancient sage respected as an authority alike in the *Āyurveda* and the Sāṁkhya, besides being a Smṛti writer. Hence, we would not involve ourselves in the discussion whether there were more than one Devala, or the first Devala made contributions to many areas of knowledge. The varied contributions of Devala are reflected in the quotations from the *Devaladharmasūtra* surviving in medieval commentaries and digests.

The main burden of the teaching of Asita Devala in the *Isibhāsiyāi* is the cessation of all moral impurities or sins (*savvalevovarata*). The introductory prose passage begins by saying that those who are contaminated by moral impurities (*levovalittā*) revolve for a long time in this ocean of world. It seems that after *saṁsārasāgaraṁ* the expression *aṇupariyaṭṭanti* is missing. Likewise, in the following sentence the word *levovaratā* also seems to have been dropped.[34] The second sentence says, by way of contrast, that the person whose moral impurities have ceased,

---

31. *api ca āsilo nāma maharṣistathā devilo dvaipāyanaśeca tathā parāśarākhya ityevamādayaḥ bījaharitādiparibhogādeva siddhā iti śrūyate* ǀ
32. Here it is said that king Devilāsuta nearly married his own daughter. We do not have any confirmation of this fact about Asita, Devala, or Asita Devala from any other source and are not in a position to offer any explanation of it.
33. The *Isibhāsiyāi* has *bhaviyavvaṁ khalu bho savvalevāvratenaṁ*, whereas the *Isimaṇḍala* reads *bhaviyavvam bho khalu savva-kāma-virena'eyam ajjhayaṇaṁ bhāsittu devilāsuya rāyarisi siva suhaṁ patto* ǀ
34. Schubring, *op. cit.*, p. 103.

having crossed the world, reaches a permanent abode and remains there. A number of adjectives describe the happy state of such a person. The text adds that, 'having resolved to become a man free from all moral impurities, Asita Davila, the *arhat-ṛṣi*, (thus) said'. The eleven verses which follow are supposed to record the teachings of Davila.

Thus it begins: He, who does violence (*vihiṁsate*) to the life of a small or big being, has his soul over-dominated by attachment and malignity (*rāgadoṣābhibhūtappā*) and he is contaminated by sinful acts (*lippate pāvakammuṇā*)[35] (verse 1). He, who takes any belongings (*pariggahaṁ giṇhate*), whether little or considerable, is contaminated by sinful acts on account of the guilt of stupefication caused by greed (*gehīmucchāya doseṇaṁ*)[36] (verse 2). He, who expresses anger (*kohaṁ*), on his own or for another person, is contaminated by sinful acts on account of the chains caused by it (verse 3).

After this we have a note saying: 'In this manner up to *micchādaṃsaṇasalla*.[37] The term appears as the last in the list of eighteen *pāpas* recognised in the Jaina tradition[38] and signifies a false philosophy of life.

Verse 4 enumerates as moral impurities (*leva*) killing a living thing (*pāṇātivate*), saying untruth (*aliyavayaṇaṃ*), stealing or taking what has not been given away (*adattaṁ*), intercourse (*meḥuṇagamanaṃ*) and amassing property (*pariggahaṁ*). Verse 5 mentions anger (*kohe*), conceit (*māṇo*), deceit (*māyā*), and greed (*lobho*) as moral impurities which are of various forms or types (*bahuviho*, *bahuvidhavidhīe* and *bahuvidhā*). Hence, having considered them to be the cause for augmenting sinful acts, one should be a noble seeker of the best goal and should become a

35. Verse 2 has *lippae* place of *lippate*.
36. Here and in verse 8 *gehī* is to be rendered as *gṛddhi*, from the root *gṛdh* to covet, desire, strive after greedily.
37. *Salla* (= *Śalya*) meaning a spear, dart or arrow also stands for an extraneous substance lodged in the body and giving it very great pain. Figuratively it signifies any cause of poignant or heart-rending grief. The word also means sin or crime.
38. A.M. Sethiya, *Jaina Siddhānta bola saṁgraha*, Vol. 3, p. 182.

wandering ascetic for vigorous efforts[39] (verse 6). As milk is destroyed after being associated with poison, attachment and malignity are the destroyer after being associated with poison, attachment and malignity are the destroyer of continence (*bambhacera*) (verse 7).[40] As the best of milk by stupefication is turned into curd, so the sinful acts increase on account of the guilt of greed (verse 8).[41] The Jungle trees in a forest, when burnt by the wild fire, grow again, but, in the case of people exhumed by the fire of anger, it is very difficult to be free from unhappiness (verse 9).[42] Even the fiercely burning fire can be extinguished by water, but the fire of delusion cannot be extinguished by all the water in the sea (verse 10).[43] He, who has realised the nature of the shackles of birth and death, has broken the (cycle of) birth and death and is free from the dust (of action), achieves final beatitude (verse 11).[44]

At the end we have a summarised sentence,[45] the full form of

---

39. *tamhā te taṁ vikiṁcittā pāvakammapavaḍḍhaṇam uttamaṭṭhavaraggāhī vīriyattāe parivvae* ।
40. *khīre dūsiṁ jadhā pappa viṇāsamuvagacchati* ।
    evaṁ rāgo va doso vā bambhaceraviṇāsaṇā ।।
41. *jadhā khīraṁ padhāṇaṁ tu mucchaṇā jāyate dadhiṁ* ।
    evaṁ gehippadoseṇaṁ pāvakammaṁ pavaḍḍhatī ।
42. *raṇṇe davaggiṇā daḍḍhā rohaṁte vaṇapādavā* ।।
    kohaggiṇā tu daḍḍhāṇaṁ dukkhā dukkhāṇam ṇa ṇivattatī ।।
    The Sanskrit Ṭīkā cannot make out any sense in the second line of the verse and remarks: *munestu krodhāgninā dagdhānāṁ duḥkhānāṁ nivartanaṁ pratyāgamo na bhavati* । *kastu nāma duḥkhānāṁ pratyāgamamicchedityaspaṣṭam* ।।
    The commentator fails to notice that in the earlier two verses also the comparisons are not completely parallel in the use of the expressions, even though the main points are clear. The Prakrit Bharati edition translates the line as meaning 'so does the reviving vice, thanks to the wrathfulness of man'.
43. *sakkā vaṇhī ṇivāretuṁ vāriṇā jalito bahiṁ* ।
    savvodahijaleṇāvi mohaggī duṇṇivārao ।।
    The Sanskrit Ṭīkā does not take any notice of verses 10 and 11.
44. *jassa ete pariṇṇātā jātīmaraṇabaṁdhaṇā* ।
    se chinnajātimaraṇe siddhiṁ gacchati ṇīrae ।।
45. *evaṃ se buddhe . . . ṇo puṇaravi iccatthaṃ havvamāgacchati tli bemi* ।

which appears earlier at the end of the first section. The fuller sentence is to be translated thus: 'I say, "Thus becoming enlightened, indifferent (to worldly attachment), freed from sins, restrained, taking all objects to be the same, and a renouncer,[46] he does not come again for the activities of this (world)." '

We have to discuss the extent to which these passages represent Asita Devala's own words and ideas. According to Schubring the whole text was composed by one single author; the parallelism in the structure of the individual chapters proves this 'not less than the throughout uniform style and the numerous self-quotations'.[47] He admires the text as being original and attractive.[48] The 'charm of novelty' of the text reveals itself when contrasted with the 'uniform creation' of contemporary parallel texts which are only 'more or less cleverly and transparently composed compilations'. Our author has adorned the passages borrowed from the words of the *ṛṣis* by covering them with 'the plumage of its own'. This has camouflaged the original words of these *ṛṣis* to such an extent that their disciples 'would indeed have stood perplexed before these splinters from the thought workshop of the master'.

Exposition of the Views

For determining the original views and expressions of any *ṛṣi* in this text, we have to concentrate on the motto and the exposition parts of the concerned section. The sections do not show a uniform style in regard to these two. They are in any of three forms, prose, verses, or both mixed together. The variation is more noticeable in the case of motto.[49] The variations, as against a stereotyped uniformity, may be construed to show that the form and expressions in the different sections result from the peculiarities in the original expression of the teachings of the different *ṛṣis*.

---

46. *Tāi* may be rendered as either *tyāgī* or *trayī*. In the second case it will mean protector.
47. Schubring, *op. cit.*, p. 9.
48. *Ibid.*, pp. 8-9.
49. Schubring, *op. cit.*, p. 3.

Devala Section

The nature of the text compelled the author to make 'greater borrowings' from the original. Schubring has suggested that in the motto and exposition portions, stanzas, in a metre other than the *śloka*, would generally appear to have been borrowed by the author from some other source. Likewise, some prose passages are parallel to passages in other texts and were 'more or less conscious reminiscence'.[50] These two criteria of the metre of the stanzas and the expression in the prose passages do not help us much in the case of the section on Devala and we will have to analyse the content of the section for internal indications.

In the section we notice a visible attempt to cast Devala's ideas into the mould of Jainism. Schubring[51] points out that verse III.1 and III.2 of the text deal respectively with the guilt effected by *prāṇātipāta* and *parigraha*, i.e., the violation of the first and fifth *mahāvratas* (vows) in Jainism. The second of the four manuscripts of the text, which Alsdorf photographed in Jain Bhandar in 1957, inserts three verses between lines *a* and *b* of verse 2.[52] They refer to the guilt effected by the violation of the second (speaks the untruth — *musaṁ bhāsae*), third (takes what is not given — *adinnaṁ geṇhai*) and fourth (enjoys intercourse — *mehuṇaṁ sevai*) vows. According to Schubring,[53] these verses 'do not make the expression of an old text'. He admits that the insertion of these stanzas, relating to the second, third and fourth vows, is logical in itself. But, considering the approach of the author in a parallel situation in an

---

50. Schubring, p. 9.
51. *Op. cit.*, p. 126.
52. *Ibid.*, pp. 126-27
jo musaṃ bhāsae kiṁci appaṁ vā jaï vā bahuṃ ।
appaṇa' aṭṭhā parassa vā lippae pāve-kammaṇā ॥
adinnaṁ geṇhaï jo . . . ( ) . . . ।
mehuṇaṁ sevaï jo u tericchaṁ divvaṁ māṇusaṁ ।
rāga-dosa abhibhūya' appā lippae pāva-kammaṇā ॥
53. *Ibid.*, p, 127. He refers to the metrical defect in lines 2, 3 and 5 and to the use of *kammaṇā* instead of *kammuṇā* of verses 1-3.

earlier section of the text (I.19ff), where he mentions only the first, third and fourth vows, we can say that it was not imperative on his part to include these five lines to cover the second, third and fourth vows. The Sanskrit Ṭīkā and Prakrit Bharati edition also do not take cognizance of these five lines. It seems that somebody, with a view to fitting the stanzas into the Jaina formulation of *mahāvrata*s, added these lines.

An analysis of the subsequent portions of the text makes it clear that the author did not have the model of the *mahāvrata*s in his mind. In verse 3 he refers to the expression of anger (*kohaṁ*) as a factor causing contamination with sinful acts, on the same footing as the killing of beings and the taking of belongings. Verse 3 is followed by the expression *evaṁ jāva micchādaṁsaṇasalle*. The author, thus, intends to cover factors, the first three being mentioned in the first three verses, which go up to *micchādaṁsaṇasalle*. The Jaina tradition mentions eighteen *pāpa-karmas*.[54] Of these the first is *prāṇātipāta* (verse 1 of our text), the second, third and fourth are respectively *mṛṣāvāda, adattādāna* and *maithuna* (five lines in the manuscript mentioned above), the fifth is *parigraha* (verse 2 of our text), the sixth is *krodha* (verse 3 of our text) and the eighteenth is *mithyā-darśanaśalya*.[55] Thus, according to the author of the text, Devala also spoke about the eighteen *pāpa-karma*s, beginning from *prāṇātipāta* and ending with *mithyādarśanaśalya*. The intention of the author becomes quite clear when in verses 4-5 he enumerates the guilt-contaminations as *pāṇātivāto aliyavayaṇaṁ, adattaṁ, mehuṇagamanaṁ, pariggahaṁ, koho, māṇo, māyā* and *lobho*, which occur in the same order as the first nine *pāpa-karma*s in the Jaina tradition. Clearly, he was straining hard to present Devala's verses on *lepa*s within the pattern of Jaina enumeration of *pāpa-karma*s.

---

54. A.M. Sethiya, *op. cit*.
55. From the seventh to the seventeenth we have *māna, māya, lobba, rāga, dveṣa, kleśa, abhyākhyāna, piśunatā, paraparivāda, rati-arati* and *māyā-mṛṣā*.

Approach and Style of the Author

Schubring points out quite a few mistakes and contradictions in the text,[56] some of which were due to the defective tradition on which the author drew, while he was doubtlessly responsible for some others. It is, however, not possible to fix the responsibility on the author or tradition in each case. But, it is to be noted that the author was not satisfied to work as a mere cataloguer or compiler of the views of others. He had a definite plan or purpose and he asserted his rights as an author to realise it. As pointed out earlier, he wanted to emphasise the ethical parts in the teachings of the thinkers. The omission of other aspects of their teachings was bound to project a partial or lopsided picture of their total teachings. In his effort to project the ethical problems of the ideas of his predecessors, with the view to bringing home the homogenity and universality of the ethical core of different religions, our author could have inadvertently, and in some cases deliberately, ironed out the divergent details. This possibly happened in the case of Devala's teachings also.

The attempt on the part of the author to present the teachings of Devala to suit his convenience is to be seen in the structure of the section. Like all other sections in the text it has three distinct parts: the motto, the exposition separated from it by the name of the *r̥ṣi*, and the conclusion. No amount of reasoning will convince anyone to believe that all the forty-four *r̥ṣi*s formulated their views in the stereotyped form in which they occur in our text. This holds good for the section on Devala also. The absurdity is apparent in the case of the concluding sentence. Though it purports to be an utterance of a particular *r̥ṣi*, it has a set formula of words, so much so that the author dispenses with the formality of reproducing it in full in all the sections and instead gives the opening and concluding expression. Clearly the sentence recording the concluding resolve of the different

---

56. *Op. cit.*, p. 11: 'wavering in the judging of the *riddhi* (9 and 45), and the error concerning the *agandhana* (45), the repeated use of the same motto in 26 and 32, the transformation of current names, the R̥ṣi Ketaliputta besides Tetaliputta'.

ṛṣis could not have been identical, even if we admit the closest similarities in their views. Thus, in the present section also we see the working of the hands of the author who wanted to present Devala's teachings according to his scheme and structure.

The very first line of the introductory prose passage shows that the central point in Devala's teachings is *leva* (*lepa*), contamination of sin. Verses 4 and 5 confirm it. The first three verses explain *leva* by employing the descriptive expression *lippata pāvakammuṇā* as the refrain. Later on, verses 6 and 8 also speak of the *pāvakamma* getting augmented.

Comparison with Devaladharmasūtra

The original work of Devala is not available. On the basis of quotations in later works we can reconstruct some parts of the erstwhile *Devaladharmasūtra*.[57] The text, it is revealed, possessed one full chapter concerning *pāpa-doṣas*. *Prāyaścitta*, doubtless, had formed an important part of the *dharmaśāstra* literature. But only a few Smṛtis refer, and that too very briefly, to the *pāpas*. The account of *pāpa-doṣas* in the *Devaladharmasūtra* is without any parallel in any other Brāhmaṇical text. It classifies *pāpa-doṣas* broadly into three on the basis of their origin from mind, speech, or body. These three are further divided respectively into twelve, six and four sub-types. Each of these is first defined and explained in prose passages in the form of *sūtras*. They are followed by verses explaining or illustrating in a more popular style the nature of the different *pāpa-doṣas*. Thus, the chapter of *pāpa-doṣas* would appear to be one of the more significant portions of the *Devaladharmasūtra*. It was quite proper, then, on the part of the author of the *Isibhāsiyāi* to include an account of the contamination casused by sin on the basis of the treatment of the subject by Devala.

We have seen above that in the first three verses of our text there was a deliberate attempt to accommodate Devala's views in the Jaina pattern. But, even in this process, the original kernel of Devala's writings peeps out. Thus, in the first two verses, though

57. Our reconstruction is to be published separately.

the violations of the vows of *ahiṁsā* and *aparigraha* are treated, it is clear that the original emphasis was on *rāga-doṣa* (attachment and malignity) and *gehī* (greed) as factors causing contamination of sinful acts. The author could not pursue this exercise of his for long, probably because there was not enough material in Devala's verses amenable to the Jaina scheme. He included a verse on *koho* (anger) and finally gave up the exercise by remarking that in this way it goes up to *micchādaṁsaṇasalla*.

This incongruity becomes still more clear in the subsequent verses. Verse 8 again refers to the increase in sinful acts on account of the guilt of *gehī* (greed). *Gehī* (*Skt. gr̥ddhi*) does not appear in the Jaina list of eighteen *pāpas*. It does not occur in the *Devaladharmasūtra* either. But, we find that in the extant quotations from Devala, the verses describing *lobha* contain three which bring out the significance of *tr̥ṣṇā* or *tr̥ṣā*. We cannot rule out the possibility that some of the lost verses contained a similar reference to *gr̥ddhi*. Further onward, in verse 10, the *pāpa*, which has been underlined, is followed by *moha*. *Moha* also does not figure in the Jaina list of the 18 *pāpa-sthānakas*. But it has been included by Devala in the list of twelve *pāpa-doṣas* which arise out of the mind.

Verses 6 and 11, though touched by the author of the *Isibhāsiyāi*, retain words with a specific usage characteristic of the Brāhmaṇical tradition to which Devala belonged. The second line of the verse 6 reads: *uttamaṭṭhavaraggāhi vīriyattāe parivvae.* In the expression *uttamaṭṭha, aṭṭha* has been used in the sense of one of the pursuits of life (*puruṣārthas*). In the Jaina texts the usual term in such a context would be *esaṇā*. The expression *uttamaṭṭha* here stands for *mokṣa* which is described as the highest or ultimate pursuit of life. The verb *parivvae* is to be derived from the Sanskrit verb *parivrāj*[58] and is to be connected with the words *parivrajyā, parivrāj, parivrāja* and *parivrājaka*. They refer to a wandering mendicant, recluse, or ascetic who has renounced the world. In the religious atmosphere prevailing at the time of the appearance of the Buddha, the order

58. For a similar use of the verb *pravraj* see *Jābālopaniṣad*, 4 — *vanī bhūtvāpravrajet; Baudhāyanadharmasūtra*, II.10.2,18 — *brahmo-caryavān pravrajatrityekeṣām* ।

of the *parivrājakas* was fairly prevalent. In the wake of the popularity of the Śramaṇic systems, the Brāhmaṇical tradition made an effort to contain and control it by recognising it as the fourth stage of life (*āśrama*). The fourth *āśrama* in later times was generally termed *saṁnyāsa*, but in earlier times the appellation *parivrājaka* seems to have been more in vogue. In one surviving except from the *Devaladharmasūtra*,[59] the duties and rules relating to a *parivrājaka* are prescribed. Thus, it can be seen that verse 6 of our text advises that pursuing the ultimate *puruṣārtha* (*mokṣa*) one should become a *parivrājaka* (enter the fourth *āśrama*) and exert himself.[60]

Verse 11 says that he who has understood the nature of the chains of birth and death, breaks the cycle of birth and death and is taintless, attains *siddhi*. The word *siddhi* in a general sense often means fulfilment or success. But it has a restricted and specialised meaning as well. In the Yoga system *siddhi* (or *aiśvarya-guṇa*) refers to suprerhuman powers or faculties, which are supposed to be eight in number. The *Devaladharmasūtra* evidently contained a detailed account of the Yoga and Sāṁkhya systems.[61] Here *siddhi* seems to have been used in the technical sense common to the Yoga system and the *Devaladharmasūtra*.

Verse 7 reveals the original words of Devala which seem to have escaped the changing hands of the author of the *Isibhāsiyāi*. It describes *rāga* (attachment) and *dosa* (*dveṣa* malignity) as the destroyer of *bambhacera* (*brahmacarya*). The use of the term *bambhacera* is significant. It stands for the first stage or order in the life of an individual (*āśrama*), the life of celibacy passed by a brāhmaṇa boy in studying the Vedas, or celibacy, chastity, etc. The context, however, does not have any reference to the first stage of

---

59. *Kṛtyakalpataru,* Mokṣa p. 49.
60. *Vīriyattāe* (Skt. *vīryārtham*) may be taken to make an indirect allusion to Jainism. Mahāvīra is the name of the twenty-fourth *tīrthaṁkara* of the Jainas, who is often glorified as the real founder of Jainism.
61. Śaṅkara on *Vedāntasūtra*, I.4.28. One of the earliest full account of the eight *siddhis* is associared with the *Devaladharmasūtra*. Our article "Devaladharmasūtra on Aiśvarya", in *Śrī Dineśacandrikā: Studies in Indology* (D.C. Sircar Felicitation Volume), pp. 153-8.

life alone. Likewise, the passage will not yield a happy meaning if *brahmacarya* restricted to celibacy inasmuch as there is no direct and intimate connection between *dveṣa* and *caryā* on the one hand and celibacy on the other. Among the many meanings of *Brahman* are 'Supreme Being', 'religious austerities', and 'intellect'. The *caryā* of *Brahman* will, theafore, signify religous study or self-restraint. This use of the term *brahmacarya* in this verse appears to have survived from the original verse of Devala.[62]

Early Features of the Section

Against the background of these indications of the original Brāhmaṇical core of Devala surviving the Jaina revision, we may refer to certain features of style and structure, which, though not conclusive, are compatible with the known features of Devala's writings in the available excerpts.

First is the introductory prose passage. It is admitted that this portion of the text was intended to introduce the views of a *ṛṣi* and hence would appear to have been formulated mostly by the author of the text. As against the other sections in the text associated with other *ṛṣis*, whose original writings are not available, the section under study is to be compared with the views of Devala as recorded in a *dharmasūtra* named after him. This *dharmasūtra* was partly in prose *sūtras* and partly in verses. The surviving prose passages of the *Devaladharmasūtra* show a peculiar style. We often find long sentences, wherein the details are in the form of adjectives qualifying the main noun.[63] This is also a feature of the introductory prose passage in the section associated with Devala. In the partly damaged second sentence we have several words qualifying *saṁsārasāgaraṁ* and *ṭhāṇam*. The style comes out beautifully in the third sentence which has a long string of adjectives describing the characteristic of a *savvalavovarae* person. We cannot argue, in the absence of the full

62. This seems to have been the original and early meaning of the term *brahmacarya*. This will be an indicator of an early date for Devala.

63. See, for example, passages on the four *varṇas* in our article on "Devaladharmasūtra on Varṇas and Jātis", in *Dr. R.N. Dandekar Felicitation Volume*, Delhi 1984, pp. 239-45.

text of the *Devaladharmasūtra*, that these expressions or sentences occurred in the original, but, we can suggest that the author of our text possibly tried to present the introduction, which purports to record the motive or resolve of Devala, in the peculiar style he noticed as characterising the prose passages in Devala's original work.

Another prominent feature of the style of the *Devaladharmasūtra* is that it first enumerates all the important points or subdivisions in a summarised form and then in subsequent verses elaborates, explains, and illustrates them. Although the full text of the *Devaladharmasūtra* is unavailable, in all the cases where we are able to reconstruct a chapter, this style is evident. In our text the section on Devala also seems to possess this characteristic. This point is all the more significant because our author was not under any obligation to reproduce all the passages from Devala's original. He was presenting the views of Devala, within the frame-work of his text and the task taken up by him. Verses 1-3 followed by the remark *evaṁ jāva micchādaṁsaṇasalle* show that the author cut short the portions dealing with the enumeration of the factors causing *pāvas*. Verses 4-5 retain the style of enumeration in a pronounced manner. The subsequent verses (6-11) are evidently in the nature of further explanation and elaboration of the points or factors listed in the earlier verses. To illustrate our point, we may refer to verses 8 and 9 which bring home the force of *gehī* and *koha* mentioned as factors causing *pāva* in verses 2 and 3. A comparison of the phrasing of verses 2 and 8 will show the intrinsic connection between the two.[64] This similarity in the style suggests that our author had before him the original *Devaladharmasūtra* from which he drew. No doubt it may be argued that this characteristic is shared by early Indian thought as projected in some of the earlier works belonging to different branches of learning. However, it must be remembered that it was not an invariate feature of Indian thought and texts, and, when compared with texts of a similar nature, the *Devaladharmasūtra* has it in a very pronounced manner.

---

64. Both employ the terms *mucchā, gehi, doseṇam* and *pāvakamma* in a specific sense.

A few other features of the passage attributed to Devala in our text may also be noted. We are conscious that they are found associated with many other early texts and are not so characteristic of the passages surviving in the name of Devala to drive home the connection between the two only on the basis of these features.

The first is the metre *śloka* employed in our text. Though the metre has been used in the *Devaladharmasūtra* also, it is the most convenient and popular metre for this type of writings and occurs in Sanskrit, Pāli and Prākṛt texts alike.

The second pronounced feature noticeable in our text is the repetition of the same phrases in the fourth part of the verse as refrain. In verses 1 to 3 we find the word *lippate pāvakammuṇā* being repeated thus. In verses 4 and 5 *levo* occurs seven times evidently for emphasising its importance. This feature can also be seen in many other texts with a religious, philosophical, dialectical, or ethical theme which resort a similar style for creating greater effect.

Another significant feature of the style in our text is the use of homely simile and illustration for clarifying the point. In verses 7 to 10 the illustrations are derived from the phenomena of milk being destroyed as a result of contamination with poison, milk turning into curd, forest trees being burnt by jungle fire and fire being controlled with the help of water. This feature is characteristic of many early Indian texts, particularly those which have to explain a difficult philosophical idea in an easy manner or which seek to create greater impact in emphasising the importance of a religious or ethical precept.

Appendix III

Al-Bīrūnī on Patañjali

Book of Patañjali

Al-Bīrūnī refers to the Book of Patañjali (*Kitāb Pātañjala*) and gives long quotations from it.[1] He mentions it as a very famous book,[2] as one of the three main texts for understanding the spiritual views of the Hindu, the other two being the *Sāṁkhya* of Kapila and the *Gītā*. According to Al-Bīrūnī,[3] the text is about 'the emancipation of the soul from the fetters of the body'. At another place[4] he describes the book to be 'on the search for liberation and for the union of the soul with the object of its meditation'. The way Al-Bīrūnī refers to it, along with the Sāṁkhya work of Kapila, suggests that he regarded the book to be an important source for the allied discipline of Yoga. This creates the expectation that Al-Bīrūnī was referring to the *Yogasūtra* of Patañjali.

Different from Yogasūtra

But, there is a world of difference in the structure of Patañjali's book, as mentioned by Al-Bīrūnī, and the known form of the *Yogasūtra*. Moreover, as pointed out by Sachau,[5] the philosophical

---

1. Sachau, *Alberuni's India*, *s.v.* Patañjali.
2. *Ibid.*, I, p. 29.
3. I, p. 8.
4. I, p. 132.
5. II, p. 264.

system of Al-Bīrūnī's Patañjali 'differs in many points essentially from that of the Sūtras'. It is only in a very few cases that Sachau could trace remote parallels in the *Yogasūtra*.[6] The possiblity of Al-Bīrūnī confusing between the commentary on Patañjali's *Yogasūtra* and its original text and adding details taken from the commentary is also ruled out. Sachau points out that 'the extracts given in the *Indica* stand in no relation with the commentary of Bhoja Rājā, although the commentator here and there mentions ideas which in a like or similar form occur in Alberuni's work'. This holds good for all other commentaries on the *Yogasūtra*, none of which contains passages similar to those quoted in Al-Bīrūnī's, account.

The importance of Patañjali's *Ygasūtra* is so deep-rooted that people are not willing to appreciate the unequivocal testimony of Al-Bīrūnī. They do not accept the obvious possiblity that there was another text on the subject which was also attributed to Patañjali. Thus, P. Chakravarti[7] is not prepared 'to assume the existence of a different philosopher of the name of Patañjali other than the author of the Yogasūtra'. His argument is that Al-Bīrūnī's translation scarcely observes fidelity to the the original text. But, Chakravarti himself holds that Patañjali mentioned in the *Yuktidīpikā* was different from Patañjali, the celebrated authority on Yoga.

We may accept the possibility of minor variations in the translation, but not a total transformation of the very nature of the text. The *Yogasūtra* is in the form of aphorisms, but the Book of Patañjali, as referred to by Al-Bīrūnī, is not presented in aphorisms. Moreover, according to Al-Bīrūnī, the Book was in the form of conversation between the pupil and his master; the pupil asks questions about philosophical issues and the master expounds the principles to him.[8] Al-Bīrūnī records[9] that the Book referred to certain tales, of Nandikeśvara being transferred into paradise in

6. Vol. II, p. 233, (*Yogasūtra* II.27 — seven kinds of enlightenment); II, p. 287 (*Yogasūtra* IV.38 — liberation; *ibid.*, III.42, 44, 45 — faculties of a perfect Yogin).
7. *Origin and Development of the Sāṁkhya System of Thought*, p. 134.
8. I, pp. 27-9, 55-6, 81.
9. I, p. 93.

his human shape, and of Indra being changed into a serpent for his incest. We can speculate about nature and contents of the book of Patañjali from the fact that extract from a commentary on it (*Mufassar Kitāb Patañjala* or *Mufassar Pātañjala*)[10] quoted by Al-Bīrūnī[11] 'are all of them not of a philosopher, but of a plainly Purāṇic character, treating of cosmographic subjects, the *lokas*, Mount Meru, the different spheres, etc.' This shows that either these topics were included in the original book of Patañjali itself or else they were additional information supplied by the commentator. There is no known commentary on the *Yogasūtra* of this nature. In any cases, the text of the Book of Patañjali seems to have been different from Patañjali's *Yogasūtra*.

Due importance has not been attached to the unimpeachable testimony of Al-Bīrūnī. Al-Bīrūnī[12] clearly says that, for preparing his *Indica*, he translated into Arabic two books one called *Sāṁkhya* and another called *Patañjali* (*Pātañjala*?). He says that these two books contain most of the elements of the belief of the Hindus and adds: 'I hope that the present book will enable the reader to dispense with these two earlier ones.' Al-Bīrūnī, thus, claims to have had the full text of the book, to have read it and translated it, and to have faithfully represented its views. Hence, there should be no doubt about Al-Bīrūnī using a text ascribed to Patañjali, but different from Patañjali's *Yogasūtra*.

Philosophical Views in the Book of Patañjali

Here we summarise the philosophical views expressed in the extracts from the book as recorded by Al-Bīrūnī.[13]

---

10. The name of the commentator is not mentioned by Al-Bīrūnī. Sachau suggests it to be Balabhadra (II, p. 264). But, Al-Bīrūnī himself shows that Balabhadra have specialised in the area of astrology and astronomy. See Vol. I, pp. 156, 305, *s.v.* Balabhadra.
11. I, pp. 232, 234, 236, 238, 248.
12. I, p. 8.
13. R.K. Chaube, *India as Told by the Muslims*, pp. 50-6 lists ten extracts. He splits our passage I into two (no. 1 and 2) and mentions our III (B) as a separate entry (no. 5). He does not take any notice of our III (C) →

I. The first, a long passage recording the conversation between the pupil and the master,[14] says that the worshipped one, by the worship of whom blessing is obtained, 'is he who, being eternal and unique, does not for his part stand in need of any human action for which he might give as a recompense either a blissful repose, which is hoped and longed for, or a troubled existence, which is feared and dreaded. He is unattainable to thought, being sublime beyond all unlikeness which is abhorrent and all likeness which is sympathetic. He by his essence knows from all eternity. *Knowledge*, in the human sense of the term, has as its object that which was *unknown* before, whilst *not knowing* does not at any time or in any condition apply to God. He is height, absolute in the idea, not in *space*, for he is sublime beyond all existence *in any space*. He is the pure absolute good, longed for by every created being. He is the knowledge free from the defilement of forgetfulness and not knowing. As he knows he no doubt also speaks. The difference between him and the *knowing* sages who have *spoken* of their *knowing* is time, for they have learned in time and spoken in time, after having been not knowing and not speaking. By speech they have transferred their knowledge to others. Therefore their speaking and acquiring knowledge take place in time. And as divine matters have no connection with time, God is *knowing*, *speaking* from eternity. It was he who spoke to *Brahman*, and to others of the first beings in different ways. On the one he bestowed a book; for the other he opened a door, a means of communicating with him, a third one he inspired so that he obtained by cognition what God bestowed upon

---

→ and IX. On p. 89 of his monograph, R.K. Chaube gives a quotation from Patañjali: 'He who enters upon the world with a virtuous character thought not liberated, after death is not lost, but is rewarded, in the next life.' We cannot trace the quotation in Al-Bīrūnī's *Indica*. On p. 83 of Al-Bīrūnī the account of *mokṣa* according the Sāṁkhya has only the first half of this sentence, and the remaining passage describes the way he is rewarded in the world.

14. I, pp. 27-9. He have not retained the format of the conversation, the question posed by the pupil, and the answer given by the Master. Instead, we have presented the view by integrating the question and the answer.

him. His knowing is the same from all eternity, for ever and ever. As he has never been not-knowing, he is *knowing* of himself, having never acquired any knowledge which he did not possess before. He speaks in the Veda which he sent down upon *Brahman*: 'Praise and celebrate him who has spoken the Veda, and was before the Veda.'

To the question how can he be worshipped to whom the perception of the senses cannot attain the master says: "His name proves his existence, for where there is a report there must be something to which it refers, and where there is a name there must be something which is named. He is hidden to the senses and unperceivable by them". However, the soul perceives him, and thought comprehends his qualities. This meditation is identical with worshipping him exclusively, and by practising it uninterruptedly beatitude is obtained.

II. The second passage[15] says: 'The soul, being on all sides tied to ignorance, which is the cause of its being fettered, is like rice in its cover. As long as it is there, it is capable of growing and ripening in the transition stages between being born and giving birth itself. But if the cover is taken off the rice, it ceases to develop in this way, and becomes stationary. The retribution of the soul depends on the various kinds of creatures through which it wanders, upon the extent of life, whether it be long or short, and upon the particular kind of its happiness, be it scanty or ample.

To the question about the condition of the spirit, when it has a claim to a recompense or has committed a crime, and is then entangled in a kind of new birth either in order to receive bliss or to be punished, the master says: "It migrates according to what it has previously done, fluctuating between happiness and misfortune, and alternately experiencing pain or pleasure."

To the question, what happens if a man commits something which necessitates a retribution for him in a different shape from that which he has committed the thing, and if between both stages there is a great interval of time and the matter is forgotten, the

15. I, pp. 55-6.

master answers: 'It is the nature of action to adhere to the spirit, for action is its product, whilst the body is only an instrument for it. Forgetting does not apply to spiritual matters, for they lie outside of time, with the nature of which the notions of long and short duration are necessarily connected. Action, by adhering to the spirit. Frames its nature and character into a condition similar to that one into which the soul will enter on its next migration. The soul in its purity knows this, thinks of it, and does not forget it; but the light of the soul is covered by the turbid nature of the body as long as it is connected with the body. Then the soul is like a man who remembers a thing which he once knew, but then forgot in consequence of insanity or an illness or some intoxication which overpowered his mind. Do you not observe that little children are in high spirits when people wish them a long life, and are sorry when people imprecate upon them a speedy death? And what would the one thing or the other signify to them, if they had not tasted the sweetness of life and experienced the bitterness of death in former generations through which they had been migrating to undergo the due course of retribution?

III. The third extract relates to the opinion of the author of the book of Patañjali about *mokṣa*.[16] There are three passages with intervening information and comments. We cannot dogmatise that they are in a running order. The first extract is specifically attributed to the author of the book of Patañjali. The second extract is attributed to the Hindus, but, at its end, Al-Bīrūnī remarks: "This is what *Patañjali* says about the knowledge which liberates the soul." This makes it certain that the second extract, giving the Hindu view, was also taken from Patañjali. The third extract is not in the form of an actual quotation. It gives the view of the Hindus. Immediately after this extract we have a quotation from the *Gītā* indicating that the earlier extract refers to the view of another text, most likely the book of Patañjali, as in the case of the second extract.

(*A*) The consideration of thought on the unity of God induces man to notice something besides that with which he is occupied. He who

16. I. pp. 68-70.

wants God, wants the good for the whole creation without a single exception for any reason whatever, but he who occupies himself exclusively with his ownself, will for its benefit neither inhale, breathe, nor exhale it (*śvāsa* and *praśvāsa*). When a man attains to this degree, his spiritual power prevails over his bodily power, and then he is gifted with the faculty of doing eight different things by which detachment is realised; for a man can only dispense with that which he is able to do, not with that which is outside his grasp. These eight things are:

1. The faculty in man of making his body so thin that it becomes invisible to the eyes.
2. The faculty of making the body so light that it is different to him whether he treads on thorns or mud or sand.
3. The faculty of making his body so big that it appears in a terrifying miraculous shape.
4. The faculty of realising every wish.
5. The faculty of knowing whatever he wishes.
6. The faculty of becoming the ruler of whatever religious community he desires.
7. That those over whom he rules are humble and obedient to him.
8. That all distances between a man and any far-away place vanish.

(*B*) If a man has the faculty to perform these things, he can dispense with them, and will reach the goal by degrees, passing through several stages:

1. The knowledge of things as to their names and qualities and distinctions, which, however, does not yet afford the knowledge of definitions.
2. Such a knowledge of things as proceeds as far as the definitions by which particulars are classed under the category of universals, but regarding which a man must still practise distinction.

3. This distinction (*viveka*) disappears, and man comprehends things at once as a whole, but within time.
4. This kind of knowledge is raised above *time*, and he who has it can dispense with names and epithets, which are only instruments of human imperfection. In this stage the *intellectus* and the *intelligens* unite with the *intellectum*, so as to be one and the same thing.

(*C*) According to the Hindus, the organs of the senses have been made for acquiring knowledge, and the pleasure which they afford has been created to stimulate people to research and investigation, as the pleasure which eating and drinking afford to the taste has been created to preserve the individual by means of nourishment. So the pleasure of *coitus* serves to preserve the species by giving birth to new individuals. If there were not special pleasure in these two functions, man and animals would not practise them for these purposes.

IV. The fourth passage[17] relates to the practical path leading to *mokṣa*. The passage is not in a continuous running form. It relates to the three parts of the path of liberation. In the first part we find an actual extract from the book of Patañjali followed by paragraphs from the *Viṣṇu Dharma* and the *Gītā*. In the case of both the second and the third parts the first paragraph is not referred to as an extract from the book of Patañjali, but, in both the accounts, they are followed, as in the case of the first part, by further details from the *Gītā*. On the analogy of the first part, we can take the first paragraphs of the second and third parts to be based on the Book of Patañjali. Hence we may reconstruct the fourth passage as follows:

We divide the path of liberation into three parts:

(i) The *practical* on (*kriyā-yoga*), a process of hebituating the senses in a gentle way to detach themselves from the external world, and to concentrate themselves upon the internal one, so that they exclusively occupy themselves with *God*. This is in general the path of him

17. I, pp. 76-80.

who does not desire anything save what is sufficient to sustain life.

(ii) The second part of the path of liberation is renunciation (the *via omissionis*), based on the knowledge of the evil which exists in the changing things of creation and their vanishing shapes. In consequence the heart shuns them, the longing for them ceases, and a man is raised above the *three primary forces* which are the cause of actions and of their diversity. For he who accurately understands the affairs of the world knows that the good ones among them are evil in reality, and that the bliss which they afford changes in the course of recompense into pains. Therefore he avoids everything which might aggravate his condition of being entangled in the world, and which might result in making him stay in the world for a still longer period.

(iii) The third part of the path of liberation which is to be considered as instrumental to the preceding two is *worship*, for this purpose, that God should heep a man to obtain liberation, and design to consider him worthy of such a shape of existence in the metempsychosis in which he may effect his progress towards beatitude.

V. At the end Al-Bīrūnī[18] remarks: "The author (Patañjali) adds to the three parts of the path of liberation a fourth one of an illusory nature, called *Rasāyana*, consisting of alchemistic tricks with various drugs, intended to realise things which by nature are impossible. Al-Bīrūnī does not give the details of the views of Patañjali on *Rasāyana* as a path leading to *mokṣa*."

In a later chapter Al-Bīrūnī[19] mentions his reference, recorded above, on the authority of Patañjali, that one of the methods leading to liberation is *Rasāyana*.

---

18. I, p. 80.
19. I, p. 189.

VI. According to Al-Bīrūnī this passage[20] occurs in the end of the Book of Patañjali. In it the Master describes to his pupil the nature of liberation: "If you wish, say, Liberation is the cessation of functions of the *three forces*, and their returning to that home whence they had come. Or if you wish, say, It is the return of the soul as a knowing being into its own nature."

VII. Al-Bīrūnī, referring to the Book of Patañjali, says[21]: Speaking of a man who restrains his senses and organs of perception, as the turtle draws in its limbs when it is afraid, he says that" 'he is not fettered, because the fetter has been loosened, and he is not liberated, because his body is still with him'.

VIII. Al-Bīrūnī[22] points out another passage in the same book which does not agree with the theory of liberation as expounded above. 'The bodies are the snares of the souls for the purpose of acquiring recompense. He who arrives at the stage of liberation has acquired, in his actual form of existence, the recompense for all the doings of the past. Then he ceases to labour to acquire a title to a recompense in the future. He frees himself from the snare, he can dispense with the particular form of his existence, and moves in it quite freely without being ensnared by it. He has even the faculty of moving wherever he likes, and if he like, he might rise above the face of death. For the thick, cohesive bodies cannot oppose an obstacle to his *form* of existence (as e.g. a mountain could not prevent him from passing through). How, then, could his body oppose an obstacle to his soul?

IX. Al-Bīrūnī,[23] after quoting ancient Greek authors, Ammonius, Pythagoras, Socrates and Proclus, says that the Hindus hold similar views about nature. He quotes the conversation between Arjuna and Vāsudeva, which would imply the *Gītā* as the source. The next paragraph appears as an extract, clearly differentiating it from the first. At the end of the quotation Al-Bīrūnī adds that the

20. I. p. 81.
21. I, p. 82.
22. I, pp. 8-83.
23. I, p. 87.

doctrine of Patnãjali is akin to that of the Sūfī. This would indicate that Al-Bīrūnī took the second paragraph to be an extract from the work of Patañjali. This reads as follows:

> *Brahman* is the upper roots of this tree, its trunk is the Veda, its branches are the different doctrines and schools, its leaves are the different modes of interpretation, its nourishment comes from the *three forces*, the tree becomes strong and compact through the senses. The intelligent being has no other keen desire but that of felling this tree, i.e., abstaining from the world and its vanities. When he has succeeded in felling it, he wishes to settle in the place where it has grown, a place in which there is no returning in a further stage of metempsychosis. When he obtains this, he leaves behind himself all the pains of heat and cold, and coming from the light of sun and moon and common fires, he attains to the divine lights.

Thus the main thrust of the philosophical ideas of Patañjali, as underlined by the extracts given by Al-Bīrūnī,[24] includes the following topics: the nature of God to be worshipped and the difference between him and the knowing sages; soul and its transmigration through its acts; the eight spiritual powers (*aṣṭa-siddhi*s) four stages of knowledge to be acquired; organ of senses; three paths of liberation: *kriyā-yoga*, *jñāna-yoga* and *bhakti-yoga*, with *rasāyana* as the fourth; nature of liberation (*mokṣa*) and the liberated man, and the *Brahman*.

Comparison with Yogasūtra

In the extracts there are certain views, which have their parallels in the *Yogasūtra*. These relate to the idea of soul, the idea of metempsychosis, the eight *siddhi*s, the four stages of meditation, and liberation.[25] These similarities show that the Book used by Al-Bīrūnī was a genuine work of Yoga.

---

24. S.N. Dasgupta, *History of Indian Philosophy*, Vol. I, pp. 233-6 is the only scholar to study these extracts but strangely is apologetic in referring to it and increasing the confusion.

25. S.N. Dasgupta, *op. cit.*, p. 234.

There is no similarity in the expression and presentation of the two texts, indicating that Al-Bīrūnī did not use the *Yogasūtra* for his account. By way of difference in the two texts, S.N. Dasgupta[26] refers to certain important points in the *Yogasūtra* which are either absent or totally minimised. These are: The importance of *yama* and *niyama*, the value of Yoga discipline as a separate means of salvation, and the significance of Yoga as control of mental states (*cittavr̥ttinirodha*). These are, no doubt, important points in the Yoga system expounded in the *Yogasūtra*. But, it can always be argued that the negative argument is not conclusive, because Al-Bīrūnī is not expected to give an account of the whole text or a faithful summary of its contents. It cannot be ruled out that he failed to appreciate the significance of some vital points.

The real difference is in the change in the emphasis and the introduction of new points. Thus, the conception of God in the Book has been made so important that He is the only object of meditation and absorption in Him is the goal. Second, liberation and Yoga are defined as absorption in God. More importantly, the Book introduces the concept of *Brahman* as an *aśvattha* tree with roots upwards and branches below (*ūrddhvamūla āvāk śākhā*) following the Upaniṣadic tradition. Another very significant difference is the introduction of *rasāyana* as a means of salvation.

Book of Patañjali an Independent Text

It is, thus, clear that the Book of Patañjali used by Al-Bīrūnī was an independent text. S.N. Dasgupta[27] describes it as 'a new modification of the Yoga doctrine on the basis of Patañjali's *Yogasūtra* in the direction of Vedānta and Tantra', as 'the transition link through which the Yoga doctrine of the *sūtra*s entered into a new channel in such a way that it could be easily assimilated from there by later developments of Vedānta, Tantra and Śaiva doctrines'. Thus, according to Dasgupta, the Book represents modification of Yoga to bring it nearer to Vedānta and Tantra.

26. *Op. cit.*, p. 235.
27. *Op. cit.*, p. 253.

But, no available text represents Yoga in the manner the Book does. There is a text named *Paramārthasāra*, which is attributed to Patañjali.[28] There are, however, no similarities between the *Paramārthasāra* and the Book in terms of the contents and the structure.

P. Chakravarti[29] refers to a manuscript of a text entitled *Yogadarpaṇa* attributed to Patañjali. It is mentioned in Rai Bahadur Hiralal's *Catalogue of Sanskrit & Prākṛt Manuscripts in the Central Provinces and Berar.*[30] The details of the text and its contents are not known, hence nothing definite can be pronounced about its identification with the Book.

It is to be admitted that the text used by Patañjali cannot be traced.

S.N. Dasgupta[31] places the composition of this text 'within the first 300 to 400 years of the Christian era'. On the basis of the reference to *rasāyana* as a means of salvation, he places its author after Nāgārjuna. He identifies him with the author of the *Pātañjalatantra* 'who has been quoted by Śivadāsa in connection with alchemical matters and spoken of by Nāgeśa as '*Carake Patañjaliḥ*'.[32] Al-Bīrūnī seems to be confused when he attributed to Patañjali, the author of the Book, a reference to *rasāyana* as a means of salvation. Al-Bīrūnī, when he quotes Patañjali about the way for the achievement of salvation, very clearly mentions three paths. It was a later addition on the part of Al-Bīrūnī to mention alchemy as the fourth path. This did not occur in the Book. The references to Patañjali in medical texts created a confusion in the mind of Al-Bīrūnī and he attributed to Patañjali, the author of the Yoga text, an advocay of *rasāyana*.

---

28. U.V. Shastri, *Sāṁkyadarśana kā itihāsa*, p. 622.
29. *Op. cit.*, p. 134.
30. Nagpur, 1926. No. 4432.
31. *Op. cit.*, p, 236.
32. *Op. cit.*, p. 235.

Tradition about Patañjali as an Author on Yoga

Dasagupta further argues that in the tradition identifying Patañjali, the author of the *Mahābhāṣya*, with Patañjali, the authority on Yoga, the latter is to be equated with Patañjali quoted by Al-Bīrūnī. In his support he refers to the testimony of Bhoja and Cakrapāṇi. Bhoja, in his commentary on the *Yogasūtra*,[33] suggests that out of the three works connected with Patañjali one was a text on Yoga dealing with *cetas*. Cakrapāṇi, in his commentary on the *Caraka-saṁhitā*, refers, among the three writing of Patañjali, to one work, apparently on Yoga, dealing with *manas*.[34] Leaving aside the much debated question of the identification of the three (or two) persons referred to in the tradition as pointing to one and the same Patañjali, we confine ourselves to the author on Yoga. Dasgupta seems to argue that as the reference does not mean the author of the *Yogasūtra*, it may suggest Patañjali as quoted by Al-Bīrūnī. In the references there is nothing which may favour either of the two possibilities; both are guesses of equal merit. Hence, we cannot be sure that Patañjali of these references is Patañjali mentioned by Al-Bīrūnī.[35]

Thus, we cannot adduce any conclusive evidence for fixing precisely the date of Patañjali's text quoted by Al-Bīrūnī. We are sure only that by the time of Al-Bīrūnī (and possibly of Bhoja and Cakrapāṇi) it was recognised as a famous work. It is to be placed long after the composition of the *Yogasūtra*. There is no evidence to narrow this wide time-bracket.

---

33. *Bhojavṛtti*, verse 5.
34. U.V. Shastri, *op. cit.*, p. 621.
35. Both Bhoja and Cakrapāṇi use the expression *Pātañjala*. In Al-Bīrūnī also the name of the Book is mentioned as Book of Pātañjali, Book of Pātañjala or Patañjala. It seems that the text mentioned by Bhoja, Cakrapāṇi and Al-Bīrūnī was commonly known as Pātañjala and hence is to be distinguished from Patañjali's *Yogasūtra*. But, not much weight can be given to this argument inasmuch as the *Yogasūtra* is also often referred to as Pātañjala.

Patañjali's Text Mentioned in Kṛṣṇacarita

The three introductory verses in the *Kṛṣṇacarita*, attributed to king Samudragupta, speak of three scholarly compositions by the foremost sage Patañjali.[36] The third verse mentions a text named *Yogadarśana* composed by him,[37] which is described as a poem full of the highest bliss, mervellous, expounding the Yoga, and destroyer of the blemishes of the mind. The verse clearly refers to the title of the text as *Yogadarśana*.[38] R.S. Bhattacharya[39] is very sure that this refers to the *Yogasūtra* of Patañjali. He explains *kāvya* as an adjective menaing *varaṇīya*, attractive, graceful, charming, and amends *mahānandamaya* as *mahāyogamaya* (dealing with *mahāyoga,* the highest form of Yoga). But, there is no need for this learned exercise against the natural and obvious meaning of the verse. The title of the composition is clearly given as the *Yogadarśana*. It is said to be in verses (*kāvya*). It is described as a marvellous text (*adbhuta*), which is full of the highest bliss (*mahānandamaya*). It is in the nature of explanation of *yoga* (*yogavyākhyānabhūta*) and destroys the blemishes of *citta*. The reference to the text as a poem which gives highest *ānanda* implies its literary pleasures also, besides the philosophical happiness. The expression *vyākhyāna*, meaning special exposition or explanation, will not have a happy application to the cryptic *sūtra*s in the *Yogasūtra*. Bhattacharya does not accept the unequivocal reference to a poetical composition on Yoga by Patañjali on the ground that there is no evidence to prove the existence of such a work. This argument proceeds in the reverse order. The logical course is to accept the testimony of the *Kṛṣṇacarita* about a poetical work on Yoga by Patañjali and then to admit that no such work is now available.

---

36. U.V. Shastri, *op. cit.*, p. 617; R.S. Bhattacharya, *An Introduction to the Yogasūtra*, pp. 79-81.
37. *mahānandamayaṁ kāryaṁ yogadarśanamadbhutam* ।
yogavyākhyānabhūtaṁ tad racitaṁ cittadoṣaham ।।
38. Y. Mimamsaka, *Saṁskṛta vyākaraṇa śāstra kā itihāsa*, I, p. 334; II. p. 380 takes the name to *mahānanda* or *mahānandamaya* explaining *yogadarśana* to mean dealing with supernormal powers (*siddhis*).
39. *Op. cit.*

We hazard the guess that possible the text was the one used by Al-Bīrūnī as the Book of Patañjali for presenting the Yoga system. The suggestion is conditioned by a few limitations. Al- Bīrūnī does not directly refer to the form of the text, nor does he give a summary of its total structure. The translation, howsoever carefully done, cannot give a true idea of the literary merit of the original. But, it is to be noted that, as different from a general philosophical text, it contained Purāṇic stories also. Parallel to the adjective *adbhuta* we find Al-Bīrūnī referring to his text as a very famous work. The detailed exposition of the philosophical points through conversation and discussion will be happily covered by the expression *vyākhyāna* used in the *Kṛṣṇacarita*. The translation from Sanskrit into Arabic and then from Arabic into English do not provide scope for the literary merit of the original to surface. Even within this limitation, one can visualise that its style of presentation was effective and gripping.

Date of The New Text

The form and style of the new text were different from those of philosophical *sūtras*, *saṁhitās*, *bhāṣyas* and *vṛttis*. We find interesting similarities with the chapters expounding philosophical ideas, specially Sāṁkhya and Yoga principles, in the Mokṣa-dharmaparva of the Śāntiparva of the *Mahābhārata*. The latter appear in the form of a dialogue between a person asking questions about philosophical points and a teacher (*ācārya*) expounding the principles. In many cases they are introduced as ancient narratives (*itihāsam purātanam*) and sometimes contain earlier events and stories to illustrate or explain a point. The presentation is in verses. The style is impressive; it takes recourse to similes and analogies. Some of the verses have a literary quality and can be a credit to any poet and his poetry. The original text used by Al-Bīrūnī seems to have been characterised by all those qualities which mark the philosophical poetry preserved in the Mokṣadharmaparva.

The above discussion provides due to determine the date of Patañjali, the author of the Yoga text drawn upon by Al-Bīrūnī,. The high reputation of the text in the times of Samudragupta, the author of *Kṛṣṇacarita*, points to a date quite sometime before the middle of the fourth century. The parallelism in form and style with the chapters in the Mokṣadharmaparva will suggest the time-bracket of fourth century BC to the first century AD. Thus, we will not be erring much, if we suggest a date in the second century BC.

Conclusion

Incidently this brings this Patañjali very close to the date generally proposed for Patañjali, the author of the *Mahābhāṣya*. The identity of Patañjali, the author of the *Yogasūtra*, with Patañjali, the grammarian, has been keenly debated, with widely divergent views accepting or rejecting it. The question of difference in philosophical views and of the chronological gap have been raised. We do not propose to discuss the issue presently. The chronological compatibility of the two texts created the tradition that Patañjali authored books in three different fields. The long continuation of the tradition explains the prestige of Patañjali, the author of a Yoga text, in the time of Al-Bīrūnī. Later, people, not familiar with this text, took Patañjali, the author of the *Yogasūtra* to be the Patañjali of the tradition.

The non-availability of the text under study is a great loss to philosophical studies of ancient India. One fervently wishes its being ferretted out from some Bhandar of manuscripts.

Appendix IV

Vyāḍi, the Vindhyavāsin

Vyāḍi as a Sāṁkhya Teacher

THE *Kathāsaritsāgara*[1] makes a definite reference to Vyāḍi as a teacher (*ācārya*) of Saṁkhya-Yoga. This receives support from the fact that Umbeka, in his commentary on the *Ślokavārttika*[2] of Kumārila, attributes to Vyāḍi a statement that *sāmānya* (universality) is the same as *piṇḍa-sārūpya* (similarity) A second reference to the views of Vyāḍi is made by Syalikanātha in his commentary on the *Bṛhati*[3] of Prabhākara. According to him, Vyāḍi was an advocate of Vyaktivāda.

But, no genuine Sāṁkhya text mentions the name of Vyāḍi. The lists of Sāṁkhya teachers, who cover the gap between Pañcaśikha and Īśvarakṛṣṇa, as given by the commentaries on the *Sāṁkhyakārikā*, are not known to contain his name. But, it may be argued that these lists are by no means exhaustive. Vyāḍi's name is conspicuous by its absence among the Sāṁkhya teachers mentioned by Viśvāvasu in the Mokṣadharmaparva section of the Śāntiparva in the *Mahābhārata* and the numerous *yogins* enumarated in the *Vāyu Purāṇa*. Possibly Vyāḍi did not found a separate school of Sāṁkhya, and the followers of other schools did not attach much value to his views.

1. I.2.
2. Akṛtivāda, 65.
3. I.3.33.

His Versatile Personality

The memory of Vyāḍi as a teacher of Sāṁkhya-Yoga survived down to the times of Somadeva, the author of the *Kathāsaritsāgara*, which indicates his importance. As we have seen above, in the Mīmāṁsā circle some of his significant views were remembered long after him. He was a versatile man and made important contributions in some other areas, besides Sāṁkhya philosophy. He was an eminent grammarian, respected for his contributions in this field. Possibly this aspect of his personality overshadowed his work in the field of Sāṁkhya.

The *Kathāsaritsāgara* emphasises the importance of Vyāḍi as a grammarian and lexicographer. He is said to have composed a commentary called *Saṁgraha* on the *sūtra*s of Pāṇini and compiled a lexicon (*kośa*). It is stated that he was a predecessor of Patañjali. The statements in the *Kathāsaritsāgara* receive confirmation from other sources. Kātyāyana, in his *Vārttika*,[4] refers to Vyāḍi. Patañjali, in his *Mahābhāṣya*,[5] refers to this text. Bhartṛhari, in his *Vākyapadīya*,[6] mentions that the *saṅgraha* was a huge text, which was impossible for ordinary grammarians to grasp. The reference to Vyāḍi's name in the ancient lexicons[7] suggests his importance, which, to some extent, was possibly on account of his composing one of the early lexicons.

Al-Bīrūnī[8] records a story of a certain Vyāḍi, who lived in the city of Ujjain in the time of king Vikramāditya. He devoted his life to the study of the science of *rasāyana* and finally succeeded in preparing the concoction, with which he made gold and flew to any place he liked. He is said to have composed famous books on this science. This Vyāḍi is difficult to identify. The garbled tradition has difficulties about chronology. But, if his being credited with acquiring

---

4. On I.2.64 (45).
5. P. 6.
6. II.484, 488.
7. *Trikāṇḍaśeṣa*, II.3.24-5; *Abhidhānacintāmaṇi*, III.5.6.
8. I.189-91.

spiritual powers and composing books, has a semblance of the memory of the Vyāḍi we are discussing, this will be another indication of his versatile achievements.

His Views

The available sources record only two specific views of Vyāḍi, namely *vyaktivāda* and the theory of the equation of *sāmānya* with *sārūpya*. According to P. Chakravarti,[9] 'all the tenets and doctrines ascribed to Vyāḍi in the Sanskrit literature, speak more or less of grammatical speculations and none of them falls under the province of pure Sāṁkhya'. He does note that Vyāḍi agrees with Sāṁkhya in regard *sāmānya* to be nothing but *sārūpya*, but adds that this principle 'is mainly concerned with grammatical speculation and (*sic*. has) very little to do with Sāṁkhya proper'. But, this is ignoring a specific testimony to maintain one's views. It is to be realised that in India several branches of learning, such as grammer, poetics, philosophy and medicine, often taper into a common problem and a common view at a higher level. It will be doing Indian system a wrong, if the water-tight compartmentalisation, being followed in modern times, is applied to it. The references imply that, on some points, Vyāḍi expressed his views with perallels in the Sāṁkhya system which were noted by followers of an allied system. Whether Vyāḍi did this as a part of his grammatical work, or separately as an exposition of Sāṁkhya, is a point which is difficult to determine and has only a scholastic value.

Yyāḍi Identified with Vindhyavāsin

Tanusukharam Sharma[10] identifies Vyāḍi with Vindhyavāsin. His main argument is that some lexicons mention Vindhyavāsin as a synonym of Vyāḍi. His second argument is that Umbeka, in his commentary on the *Ślokavārttika*, attributes the view of *sāmānya* being not different from *piṇḍa-sārūpya* to Vyāḍi at one place and

---

9. *Origin and Development of the Sāṁkhya System of Thought*, p. 143.
10. *Māṭharavṛtti* (Chowkhamba Sanskrit Series), Introduction, pp. 3-4.

to Vindhyavāsin at another.[11] He further argues that, whereas according to Syalikanātha Vyāḍi was an advocate of *vyaktivāda*, Kumārila[12] attributes it to Vindhyavāsin.

The suggestion appears to be convincing and has found many supporters. B. Bhattacharya,[13] however, rejects the proposed identification. U.V. Shastri[14] and P. Chakravarti[15] independently argue against the identification. Their contention is that *vindhyavāsin* is an appellation meaning 'one who lives in the Vindhya region', it was applied to both Vyāḍi and a Sāṁkhya teacher, whose original name was Rudrila, U.V. Shastri explains this argument by pointing out that in the lexicons the synonym for Vyāḍi is not always *vindhyayvāsin*, but is also *vindhyastha* and *vindhyanivāsin,* which shows that Vindhyavāsin was not his second name. He further points out that, besides these two teachers designated as *vindhyavāsin*, there was a third person, a certain sage named Māṇḍavya, who was also called *vindhyavāsin*. To bring out the separate identity of the two persons with the appellation *vindhyavāsin*, Charkavarti points out that whereas one was a Sāṁkhya teacher, the other, namely Vyāḍi, was a grammarian.

To distinguish between Vyāḍi and Vindhyavāsin Shastri and Chakarvarti point out the long gap of several centuries in the possible dates of the two. Vyāḍi is to be placed many centuries before Christ, which is too early a date for Vindhyavāsin.

Joshi on Vindhyavāsin I and Vindhavāsin II

To reconcile the conflicting pieces of information and to circumvent the chronological inconvenience. H.S. Joshi[16] says that there were two Vindhyavāsins, whom he designates as Vindhyavāsin I and Vindhyavāsin II. He identifies Vindhyavāsin I with Vyāḍi and

11. Akṛtivāda, 76.
12. *Ślokavārtika*, Akṛtivāda.
13. *Journal of Indian History*, Vol. VI, p.
14. *Sāṁkhyadarśana kā itihāsa*, pp. 533-5.
15. *Op. cit.*, pp. 142-4.
16. *Sāṁkhyayoga darśana kā jīrṇoddhāra*, p. 59.

Vindhyavāsin II with Vindhyavāsin, the author of the commentary *Hiraṇyasaptati* on the *Sāṁkhyakārikā* of Īśvarakr̥ṣṇa. The suggestion involves much unnecessary exercise. Vindhyavāsin was not a regular name of Vyāḍi. It is only the lexicons which point out that he had his abode in the Vindhya region. By naming him as Vindhyavāsin I we will only introduce an element of confusion in otherwise simple and clear evidence. The philosophical views, quoted under the name of Vindhyavāsin, are all to be attributed to one and the same person.

His Date

The only clue to the date of Vyāḍi is found in the *Kathāsaritsāgara*: Here Vyāḍi is mentioned as a contemporary on Nanda, to have written a commentary on the *sūtras* of Pāṇini and to have been a predecessor of Patañjali. His chronological position in the history of grammatical literature, confirmed by references in the *Vārttika* and the *Mahābhāṣya*, suggests that he belonged to a period later than Pāṇini but earlier than Patañjali and Kātyāyana. By Nanda, the *Kathāsaritsāgara* evidently means a king of the Nanda dynasty, which is generally assigned to the date *c*. 362-322 BC. Thus, Vyāḍi may be placed in the middle of the fourth century BC.

Conclusion

In the *Kathāsaritsāgara* Vyāḍi is referred to as a disciple of *bhagavān* Varṣa. On this basis Vyāḍi is to be placed in the school of the followers of Vārṣagaṇya. Vindhyavāsin, the famous Sāṁkhya teacher, is known to have been a prominent follower of the school of Vārṣagaṇya. It may be hazarded that the attribution of the same views to both Vyāḍi and Vindhyavāsin and the reference to Vyāḍi having his abode in the Vindhya region indicate the Vārṣagaṇya affiliation of Vyāḍi.

Appendix V

An Early Buddhist Account of Sāṁkhya

Introduction

H.D. SANKALIA is one of the very few scholars to take note of the account of Sāṁkhya philosophy given by Hsuan Tsang along with his own objections against some central points in Sāṁkhya. This is an important piece of evidence for the history of Sāṁkhya system, but strangely enough no standard study of the Sāṁkhya philosophy refers to it.

Hsuan Tsang and His Soures

The renowned Chinese traveller and scholar enjoys a place of importance in the annals of Indian history. His account of India and his life and works are considered to be reliable sources for the study not only of Buddhism but also for social and religious history of India in general. Hsuan Tsang visited India during the reign of king Harṣavardhana. He was born in AD 600 in Chin Lin in the Honan province. Ordained as a Buddhist monk in AD 622, he left for India in AD 629. He reached Kashmir in AD 631. He visited several places, staying at some for months and years. He started on his return journey in AD 643 and reached his country in AD 645.[1]

The accounts of Hsuan Tsang's travel to India and the narrative of the places visited by him are available in the form of three books.

1. *The University of Nalanda*, Madras, 1934, pp. 194-7.

The *Si-Yu-Ki*[2] was written by Hsuan Tsang himself. P.C. Bagchi has translated the *Sha-Kia-fang-che*,[3] which records the description as its author had heard from Hsuan Tsang. It is useful inasmuch as it, at places, supplements the information in the *Si-Yu-Ki*. But, both these texts do not contain much biographical details about Hsuan Tsang. For this we have to turn to the third text *The Life of Hiuen Tsiang* by the Shaman Hwui-li as translated by S. Beal.[4]

The *Life* is only the first part of a fuller Chinese work "History of the Master of the Law of the three Piṭakas of the "Great Loving Kindness Temple" in ten chapters. The first five chapters were written by Hui-li. Hui-li was one of the disciples of Hsuan Tsang. He had received much of his information from Hsuan Tsang himself. The biography written by Hui-li covered Hsuan Tsang's life up to his Indian travels. Hui-li wrote in AD 648-649. After his death, in AD 670 or a little later, the account was revised, enlarged and edited by Yan-t' sung, one of the followers of Hui-li. He added an introduction and five new chapters dealing with Hsuan Tsang's life and activities after his return to China. He published the complete work in ten chapters in AD 688.[5] Yen-t'sung's five chapters have not been rendered into English.

The Narrative

The relevant narrative belongs to the period of about two years of his stay at Nālandā after his return from his travels in western India but before he went to Kāmarūpa on the invitation of its king Kumārarāja and then came to Harṣavardhana and attended the Mahāmokṣapariṣad at Prayāga in AD 643. In this period he had two important discussions, one with Siṁharaśmi, a Buddhist monk of Nālandā, and the other with a brāhmaṇa scholar.

This brāhmaṇa was a Lokatiya (Shun-si sect). He came to

---

2. *Si-Yu-Ki, Buddhist Records of the Western World*, London, 1884.
3. Visva-Bharati, Santiniketan, 1959.
4. London, 1884. New edn. 1911. Enlarged Indian edn. Delhi, 1972.
5. Julian, *Histoire de la vie de Hiouenthsang et de ses voyages l'dans Inde*, Paris, 1853, Preface, p. lxxix.

dispute with the Nālandā. He challenged them by hanging forty theses at the Temple gate. When for several days there was no response. Hsuan Tsang asked an attendant in his quarters to pull down the document, to tear it in pieces, and trample it under foot. The brāhmaṇa had heard of the fame of Hsuan Tsang and did not dare to go into dispute with him. Hsuan Tsang asked him to come and discuss the points. He debated with the brāhmaṇa in the presence of Śīlabhadra and with all the priests as witnesses. Hsuan Tsang criticised the practices and way of life of the heretical sects of the Bhūtas, Nirgranthas, Kāpālikas and the Jutikas or the Chingkias (Chudinkas). The philosophical schools whose views are actually mentioned are the Sāṁkhyas (Saṁkhyas) and the Vaiśeṣikas. But, he rebuts in detail only the principles of the Sāṁkhya Śāstra. The Brāhmaṇa, unable to reply, was silent. In terms of his anouncement before the debate, he volunteered to offer his head to his victor. Hsuan Tsang spared his life and bade him act as his servant and follow his directions. Later he liberated the Brāhmaṇa, who, filled with joy, went to Kāmarūpa and told king Kumārarāja about Hsuan Tsang.

Account of Sāṁkhya as Pūrva-pakṣa

The account of the Sāṁkhya philosophy presented by Hsuan Tsang, evidently as *pūrva-pakṣa* in the debate, reads as follows:

> As to the heretics called Sāṁkhyas (*sho-lun*), they establish twenty-five principles; from *prakṛti* or *mūla-prakṛti*, proceeds *ahaṁkāra*; from this proceed the five subtle particles (called *tanmātra*); from these the eleven[6] organs (of sense and action). These twenty-four all minister to and cherish the *soul* (*ātman*), which accepting and using the help thus given, excludes and removes itself. This being done, then the 'soul' remains pure and uncontaminated.

6. The passage reproduced by Sankalia by mistake reads 'seven' in place of 'eleven' which creates confusion.

Criticism of Sāṁkhya by Hsuan Tsang

The criticism which Hsuan Tsang advanced against the Sāṁkhya system occupies more space.

But now, to rebut the principles of the Sāṁkhya-Śāstra; you say that in the presence of your twenty-five principles, the character of 'soul' is distinct and diverse, but by intermingling with the other twenty-four it becomes substantially and intimately one. And you say that nature (*prakṛti*) is hypostatised[7] by union with the three *guṇas* of *sattva*, *rajas* and *tamas* and by intermingling of these three there is perfected the *mahat* and the other twenty-three principles, thus you affirm that these twenty-three principles are perfected by the three *guṇas*. But if you constrain your *mahat* and the others, to lay hold of the three, and so to become perfect, as in the case of a crowd or a forest and without this intermingling they are false, how then do you say that 'all things are true' (substantially true)?

Again, *mahat* and the rest, being each perfected by the three, then each one so perfected is the same as the whole, but if each is the same as the whole, then the office of each ought to be the same, and then, where is the force of the three forming the substence of all? Again, if one is the same as all, then the mouth and the eye functions, and so on, are the same as the functions of nature.

Again, if each function discharges the duties of all, then the mouth and the ear, and so on, ought to smell perfumes and see colours; for if not, what is the meaning of the assertion that the three *guṇas* make one common substance. How can any sensible man formulate such principles?

But again, *prakṛti* and *ātman*, both being eternal, ought to be in their hypostases identical; how, then can one, in distinciton from the other, by intermingling, produce *mahat*, and so on?

---

7. Here the passage quoted by Sankalia mistakingly reads 'hypnotised' for 'hypostatised'. According to the *Oxford English Dictionary*, this verb is dervied from the noun 'hypostasis' which in Metaphysics stands for 'underlying substance, opposite to attributes or to what is unsubstantial'.

But again, with respect to the nature of *ātman*, if it is eternal, then it is the same as *prakṛti* — but if they are the same then what need of speaking of *ātman*? and then the *ātman* is not able to accept the aid of the twenty-four principles, and so there can be no possibility of establishing the different offices of 'subject' and 'object'.

Authenticity of the Narrative

It is to be noted that Julian omits the section dealing with the debate between Hsuan Tsang and the brāhmaṇa scholar. But that does not create any doubt about the authenticity of the account. The passages, that precede the present narrative as well as those that follow, form a connected account. It does not appear from the context that the present passages have been interpolated. Julian does not record his reasons for omitting the passage. It is not unlikely that Julian could not find much sense in the Chinese version on account of his inability to find a dependable description of Sāṁkhya philosophy and to restore technical words and expressions in that system. As we have pointed out later, S. Beal also felt serious difficulty in translating the section.

Discrepencies in the Account of Sāṁkhya

Sankalia admires Hsuan Tsang for presenting 'strikingly original and unique' refutation of Sāṁkhya and for probing 'the very vitals of the system'. He admits that Hsuan Tsang's criticism of the Sāṁkhya system, on the ground that the *ātman* is futile, being identical with *prakṛti* and hence incapable of intermingling with it, 'dazzles us at first sight'. But he goes on to add that 'a little examination of his objections' shows that Hsuan Tsang 'assumes to much'. Sankalia points out serious defects in Hsuan Tsang's arguments and observes that there is no reason why Hsuan Tsang's 'opponent should have been silenced and accepted defeat'. He concludes that Hsuan Tsang's refutation 'though strikingly origninal, is unconvincing'.

MISTAKES BY THE BIOGRAPHER

Sankalia admits the possibility of 'a mistake in the translation', or his biographer not being 'able to represent his master's views well'. But the second explanation is not very plausible. The present *Life* of Hsuan Tsang is as handed down by Yen-t'sung. He took the account of Hsuan Tsang's life as written by Hui-li and not only added details relating to the period after the death of Hsuan Tsang but also revised and enlarged the earlier account. We cannot deny the possibility of some changes creeping into the original account prepared by Hui-li. But Yen-t'sung was not far removed from the times of Hsuan Tsang. Hsuan Tsang died in AD 670. The complete work was published by Yen-t'sung in AD 688. He possibly started the work of addition and revision in AD 670 or shortly after. Yen-t'sung was the pupil of Hui-li. Hui-li in his turn was an intimate disciple of Hsuan Tsang. Hui-li's close association with Hsuan Tsang enabled him to have facts directly from his Master. He was in a position to get his account checked and confirmed by Hsuan Tsang. Thus the chances of Hui-li's account being not faithful in recording Hsuan Tsang's observations and criticism seem to be remote.

DEFFICULTIES OF TRANSLATION

We admit the possibility of the translation not being able to communicate exactly the account given by Hsuan Tsang and the criticism extended by him. Translation by itself is a difficult task. Every language has its own specialities. The terms and words in one language have their special connotation in the social and cultural ethos of the people using the language. Another language cannot easily provide exact parallels for the expressions in one language. The difficulty becomes still more pronounced when we deal with philosophical ideas. In the present case the terms in the Sāṁkhya system have a specialised meaning. We cannot be sure whether Hsuan Tsang communicated appropriate Chinese equivalents for Sāṁkhya terminology. The peculiar nature of the Chinese script creates serious difficulties for a modern English translator, particularly on account of the changes in pronunciation and the uncertainty about the English word being able to capture the exact meaning of the original Sanskrit term out of its many variant possibilities, especially when the intermediary Chinese expression is also susceptible to various shades of similar but not identical connotation. S. Beal himself admits that in translating the account of the Sāṁkhya system the difficulty has been very great.[8] He depended on the Chinese version of the *Sāṁkhyakārikā* and consulted Colebrooke's account of Sāṁkhya.[9] Beal very candidly records: "I offer my translation as tentative only."[10] To illustrate, we may point out that in the account of Sāṁkhya the twenty-fifth principle is translated by Beal as 'soul' for which he restores the original term as *ātman*. Later on he added the expression 'personal existence' in the footnote to be nearer to the Chinese rendering. We know that the term generally used by Sāṁkhya in this context is *puruṣa*. We cannot fix the responsibility for introducing this confusion on Hsuan Tsang, Hui-li, Yen-t'sung or Beal.

In Hsuan Tsang's rebuttal of the Sāṁkhya doctrine Beal, at many places, uses the word 'perfect', both as verb and adjective. The word does not seem to be used in its common, general sense. Here it signifies 'completed' or 'made up of'. The choice of this particular expresion by Beal was possibly dictated by the actual Chinese expression used in the original. Whether the mistake was introduced by one of the three Chinese writers, on account of employing a term which was not very appropriate, or Beal selected an inappropriate English word by picking one out of the many possible shades of meaning of the Chinese term, cannot be determind. But, this creates confusion about the precise criticism advanced by Hsuan Tsang. We cannot rule out the possibilitiy of similar mistakes in some other passages and expressions.

FORMULTION BY HSUAN TSANG HIMSELF

Hsuan Tsang does not mention the source from which he derived his account of the Sāṁkhya system. The context of the philosophical debate between the brāhmaṇa scholar and Hsuan Tsang will not

8. *Op. cit.*, p. 162, fn. 2.
9. *Miscellaneous Essays.*
10. *Loc. cit.*, p. 164, fn. 1.

require a reference to the original Sāṁkhya text. Actually, among the known early accounts of Sāṁkhya there is none which can be said to be totally reflected in Hsuan Tsang's account.

It seems that Hsuan Tsang himself formulated the present summarised account of Sāṁkhya. He does not attempt a complete and exhaustive statement of all the important aspects of Sāṁkhya philosophy. He mentions only three important points — the twenty-five principles, the evolution of principles from *prakr̥ti*, and the nature of *ātman*. It is clear from the objections raised by Hsuan Tsang that there were other important points in the Sāṁkhya system which he did not include in his summarised version. One such point concerns the three *guṇas* and their relations with the *prakr̥ti* and the other principles. The original, on which Hsuan Tsang relied, most likely referred also to the characteristics of *puruṣa* and *prakr̥ti*.

ACCOUNT REPRESENTS SĀṀKHYA DEVELOPMENTS IN A PARTICULAR PERIOD

The account of the Sāṁkhya system and its refutation by Hsuan Tsang contains a serious discrepancy. If the original Chinese account by Hsuan Tsang was available to the translator S. Beal and his translation is faithful, we will have to infer from the conflicting and inconsistent statements about the number of principles that Hsuan Tsang is confused and confusing. The account of Sāṁkhya mentions twenty-five principles. From *prakr̥ti* to the eleven organs we have twenty-four principles and *ātman* becomes the twenty-fifth. In the criticism in the opening sentence *ātman* is mentioned first as the twenty-sixth principle and then as the twenty-fifth.[11] In

11. S. Beal, *op.cit.*, p. 163 — " . . . in the presence of your twenty-five principles, the character of *soul* is distinct and diverse, but by intermingling with the other twenty-four it becomes substantially and intimately one". One possible explanation can be that when Hsuan Tsang speaks of 'in the presence of your twenty-five principles' he possibly wants to mean 'out of the twenty-five principles (including the *ātman*)'. Likewise, we will have to explain the expressions 'the *mahat* and other twenty-three principles' occurring later on to me '*mahat* and other twenty-three principles totalling twenty-three'.

the following sentence we have a reference first to the *prakṛti* and than to *mahat* and the other twenty-three principles,[12] which will make *ātman* the twenty-sixth principle. There are, no doubt, varying accounts about the number of principles recognised in Sāṁkhya. But the present account does not show that Hsuan Tsang is referring to this state of affairs in the Sāṁkhya tradition. It is an obvious case of confusion in calculating and recording the number.

It may be argued that Hsang Tsang represents the Sāṁkhya philosophy of his times and that certain aspects of Sāṁkhya, which are not mentioned by him, had not been evolved by that time. This type of explanation has been offered by some scholars for the nature of Sāṁkhya in some early texts. Sāṁkhya is one of the oldest philosophical systems in India. Its early history is abscure and we do not have authentic accounts of Sāṁkhya belonging to the period before Īśvarakṛṣṇa. We have indications that even in the Sāṁkhya circles there was a multiplicity of opinions on several important points. It is now admitted that the Sāṁkhya philosophy has changed and grown in course of time. Hence scholars interpret the account of Sāṁkhya in a particular text, for example the Upaniṣads, *Mahābhārata*, *Buddhacarita* and *Caraka-saṁhitā*, as either reflecting a particular stage in the evolution of the Sāṁkhya system or recording the views circulating in one of the many schools in Sāṁkhya.

But this explanation does not hold good in the present case. In the case of some earlier texts, we need not always take the account to describe the whole of the Sāṁkhya philosophy. These texts possibly gave only those details of Sāṁkhya which they considered to be relevant to their context. If a particular point or detail does not occur in any earlier text, it does not necessarily mean that it did not exist at that time. The explanation that Hsuan Tsang's version reflects Sāṁkhya at a particular stage of its evolution or a school of Sāṁkhya will not be valid. After Īśvarakṛṣṇa standardised the Sāṁkhya system there was little scope for multiplicity of opinions

---

12. *S. Beal,* op. cit., p. 163, but the immediately following clause refers only to 'these twenty-three principles'.

on the same point to persist or for new developments and changes to be introduced. Sāṁkhya is not known to have changed or grown for several long centuries after it was standardised by Īśvarakṛṣṇa. Hsuan Tsang has to be placed much later than Īśvarakṛṣṇa. If Hsuan Tsang's account reveals any major variation from the classical Sāṁkhya, it cannot be explained in any manner other than its being a deliberate omission or a mistake on the part of Hsuan Tsang.

Hsuan Tsang Studies Sāṁkhya in India

Hsuan Tsang acquired a deep knowledge of the Sāṁkhya system in India. A commentary on the *Sāṁkhyakārikā* had been translated into Chinese before Hsuan Tsang's time. This was done by Paramārtha from AD 557 to 569.[13] We do not know the extent to which it had gained circulation in China and whether Hsuan Tsang had access to it. As Chinese monks, with a mastery of Sanskrit and a thorough knowledge of philosophy, were scarce before Hsuan Tsang's time, it is difficult to believe that he could acquire a knowledge of the Sāṁkhya principles before leaving for India. As a child brought up in the Confucian tradition, at the age of thirteen he went to live with his brother Chang-tsi, a Buddhist teacher at Ising-tu convent in Loyang. Hsuan Tsang was selected as a Buddhist monk. In search of peaceful conditions he went to different places in China. Finally he reached Ch'eng-tu in the south-west. Hsuan Tsang had some knowledge of even non-Buddhist literature.[14] He

---

13. Kuei-chi ascribes the commentary to Vasubandhu. See J. Takakusu, "La Samkhya Karika", *BEFEO* Tome IV, 1905, Introduction, p. 38. B. G. Tilak, *Sanskrit Research*, Vol. I, No. 2, p. 108 had taken it to be the commentary by Gauḍapāda. S.K. Balvalkar regards the *Māṭharavṛtti* to be the original of the Chinese translation. The view has been controverted by A.B. Keith, *A History of Sanskrit Literature*, p. 488, but has been forcefully supported by U.V. Shastri, *Sāṁkhya-darśana kā itihāsa*, pp. 546-66. N. Ayyaswomi Sastri, *Suvarṇa-saptatiśāstra*, Introduction, p. 42, considers another ancient, now lost Māṭharabhāṣya to have served as the basis, P. Chakravarti, *Origin and Development of the Sāṁkhya System of Thought*, p. 160 resolves the controversy by describing both the Chinese commentary and the *Māṭharavṛtti* as 'indebted to a common source'.
14. S. Beal, *Life*, p. 7.

was ordained as a monk in AD 622. In AD 629 he started on his journey to India.

From the account of Hsuan Tsang's travels in India and the scholars with whom he studied it appears that he had not acquired any fair knowledge of Sāṁkhya in China. He learnt Sāṁkhya from Indian teachers in India. Among the subjects studied at Nālandā Sāṁkhya occupied an important place.[15] Hsuan Tsang remained 'first and last for two years' with Jayasena, a profound Buddhist scholar living on the hill called Hastivana. Jayasena is described as 'the admiration of the period'. He had made a deep study of the Yogaśāstra. He 'completely mastered' both from 'beginning to end' all the numerous works of non-Buddhist scholars, 'exhausted these inquiries root (*leaf*) and branch' and 'studied all of them both within and without'.[16] It seems that Sāṁkhya was one of the subjects over which he acquired mastery.[17]

Hsuan Tsang's Interest in Sāṁkhya

It seems that in his controversy with the eminent Buddhist monk Siṁharaśmi the question uppermost in the mind of Hsuan Tsang was to rebut the Sāṁkhya stand. Siṁharaśmi had rearranged the Prāṇyamūlaśāstra and the Sataśāstra with the object 'to refute the principles of the Yoga'. Hsuan Tsang opposed the Prāṇyamūla and Sataśāstra and approved of the Yoga. According to him, the founders

---

15. S. Beal, *Life*, p. 112.
16. *Ibid.*, pp. 153-4.
17. The translation mentions "the medicinal art, magic and arithmetic". In an earlier context (*loc. cit.*, p. 112) the list of non-Buddhist subjects studied at Nālandā names "the *Cikitsāvidyā*, the works on Magic (*Atharvaveda*), the Sāṁkhya". The three names in the two lists are parallel. Whereas in the earlier list the translator has been able to restore the original Sanskrit names, in the subsequent list he was led astray by the literal meaning of the Chinese terms. Sāṁkhya is derived from *saṁkhyā* meaning number. It is quite likely that the Chinese translator in his effort to remin closer to the original term Sāṁkhya used a term referring to which has been translated by Beal into arithmetic.

of these doctrines followed one thought, and were not mutually at variance, or opposed. Hsuan Tsang's biographer records:

> Hiuen-Tsiang aimed by the assertions of the Prāṇyamūla and Sataśātra simply to overthrow the conclusions of the Sāṁkhya.

It is pertinent to enquire why Hsuan Tsang gives so much importance to Sāṁkhya and the refutation of its principles. Sāṁkhya, no doubt, occupies an important place among the ancient philosophical systems. It is one of the earliest systems and enjoyed a high respectability.

Scholars hold widely divergent views about the relationship between Buddhism and Sāṁkhya. Some trace Buddhist influence on the origins of Sāṁkhya. But some others believe that Sāṁkhya is older than the birth of Buddhism. Some scholars identify Sāṁkhya as one of the factors which contributed to the origin of Buddhism. There is a general tendency to trace both Sāṁkhya and Buddhism to the same non-Vedic source, often designated as Śramaṇa tradition. Sāṁkhya is not named in any of the early Buddhist texts. But some scholars identify some of the philosophical ideas mentioned in the Buddhist canonical literature as being Sāṁkhya. A tradition in Buddhist circle, persisting up to the times of Aśvaghoṣa, mentions Sāṁkhya principles among the teachings which the Buddha is said to have learnt from Arāḍa a teacher before he actually received enlightenment; but, it does not admit that Arāḍa belonged to the Sāṁkhya school or that he taught Sāṁkhya principles. Whether such a tradition arose in later times in view of the popularity and prestige of Sāṁkhya or it was an honest tradition continuing from the early days of Buddhism cannot be decided.

There is a long history of doctrinal debates between Sāṁkhya philosophers and Buddhist scholars. Paramārtha in his *Life of Vasubandhu* (*Vasubandhucarita*) available in its Chinese translation records that Vindhyavāsa, who had revised the doctrine of his teacher, defeated Buddhamitra, the teacher of Vasubandhu, in a debate. Vasubandhu came from Puruṣapura to challange Vindhyavāsa for a further debate. But he found the heretic adversary dead in the mountain. To refute the revised work of Vindhyavāsa Vasubandhu composed *Paramārthasaptati* in seventy verses.[18] A similar account of a debate between a Buddhist and a Sāṁkhya teacher is recorded by Kuei-chi, a pupil of Hsuan Tsang. He is silent sbout the names of the two. According to him, the Sāṁkhya teacher revised the Sāṁkhya doctrine and presented it in his composition "Gold Seventy" in seventy couplets. In opposition to this Vasubandhu composed the treatise entitled *Paramārthasaptati*.[19] We have shown that the two accounts do not refer to one and the same debate and have discussed the identification of the Sāṁkhya teacher and the Buddhist scholar, the texts written by them and the period to which they belonged.[20]

Hsuan Tsang's Critical Arguments

One must admire the intellectual keenness of Hsuan Tsang. He understands the essentials of the Sāṁkhya philosophy and presents them very succinctly. His criticism reveals a very sharp brain. He makes a frontal attack on the fundamental points in the Sāṁkhya system. His arguments are so original and persuasive that they seem to brook no opposition. The first point, which they establish, is that the dualism of *prakṛti* and *ātman* has no logical basis. The criticism of the evolution of twenty-three principles from *prakṛti* and of the differentiation between various created beings on the basis of the theory of three *guṇa*s is incisively scathing.

But a closer scrutiny of the arguments advanced by Hsuan Tsang shows that they are not convincing and definitive.

Hsuan Tsang has a very subtle way of building up his argument against Sāṁkhya. To the original position of Sāṁkhya he adds in innocent looking auxiliary statement. From this he derives an inference which is clearly not maintainable. Thus, he ridicules Sāṁkhya as maintaining an illogical position. The auxiliary point,

---

18. Takakusu, *Toung Pao*, July, 1904.
19. Takakusu, "La Sāṁkhya-kārikā", Introduction, pp. 38-40.
20. See *supra* chapter 18.

so ceverly introduced by Hsuan Tsang, has no authenticity for the Sāṁkhya. No authoritative Sāṁkhya text adopts this position.

Hsuan Tsang concentrates his criticism on three important points in Sāṁkhya: (1) the nature of *ātman* and its relationship with the other categories, (2) the theory of *guṇas*, and (3) the separate identity of *ātman* and *prakṛti*.

NATURE OF ĀTMAN AND ITS RELATIONSHIP WITH OTHER CATEGORIES

He attributes to Sāṁkhya the view that the character of *ātman* is distinct and different from other principles, but, by intermingling with other twenty-four principles, it becomes substantially and intimately one. This is oversimplifying the case[21] and, thus, presenting it as inherently self-contradictory and ridiculous. The first part of the statement is correct. The *puruṣa* is characterised as being different and divergent (*viparyāsa*) from *prakṛti*. *Puruṣa* is witness (*sākṣī*), solitary (*kevala*), indifferent (*madhyastha*), spectator (*dṛṣṭṛ*) and non-agent (*akartṛ*). This character of *puruṣa* is the essential thing. It is not radically changed. Sāṁkhya does not maintain that, as a result of the association with *prakṛti*, there is any fundamental change in the character of *puruṣa*. On the contrary Sāṁkhya holds that, as a result of this conjunction of *puruṣa* and *prakṛti*, the unconscious (*acetana*) *prakṛti appears* to be conscious (*cetanavat*) and the indifferent (*udāsīna*) *puruṣa* appears as if it is the agent (*kartā*). The two retain their nature. As a result of the conjunction the two *appear* to be what they are not. The object of the conjunction of the two is clearly mentioned as being the realisation on the part of the *puruṣa* and the solitariness of the *prakṛti*. Thus, unless it is suggested that Hsuan Tsang possibly records the view accepted by one particular section of the Sāṁkhya philosophers, which, on account of the standardised version of the *Sāṁkhyakārikā*, has not come down to us, we will have to infer that Hsuan Tsang has misrepresented the Sāṁkhya stand. We cannot be assertive in deciding whether Hsuan Tsang honestly misunderstood the

21. *Sāṁkhyakārikā*, 19-21.

Sāṁkhya view or deliberately misrepresented it to expose it to redicule and criticism.

THEORY OF GUṆAS

The second point of criticism relates to the important role of *guṇa*s in the Sāṁkhya philosophy. On account of its importance Hsuan Tsang gives a detailed treatment to its analysis. His criticism is that *mahat* and other twenty-three principles are made of the three *guṇa*s, but, if one analyses them, one does not find the *guṇa*s. This point, it must be said, has not been clearly made out. Another point, which also has not been fully developed, is that, whereas Sāṁkhya propounds all things to be true, *mahat* and other principles are false without the intermingling of the three *guṇa*s. Hsuan Tsang criticises at length the Sāṁkhya theory of the evolution of *mahat* and other principles by the combination of the three *guṇa*s. He ridicules the assertion that the three *guṇa*s make one common substance. He argues that if all these twenty-four principles are made of the three *guṇa*s, they all must be the same. If they all are the same, the office of all these should be the same and their functions also should be the same. In that case each one of these should discharge the functions of all others. Then the mouth, the ear and others should also be able to smell perfumes and see colours. Clearly, here Hsuan Tsang attributes to Sāṁkhya statements which are not known to have been made in authoritative Sāṁkhya texts. Thus, Sāṁkhya does not assert that all things are true and that *mahat* and other twenty-three principles are false without the intermingling of the three *guṇa*s. Likewise, it is wrong to attribute to Sāṁkhya the statement that the three *guṇa*s make one common substance. The basic defect in the criticism is that Hsuan Tsang does not seem to have appreciated the true import of the theory of *guṇa*s. Dr. Sankalia[22] has distinctly pointed out that Hsuan Tsang's objection "is thoroughly opposed to the chemical principles on which the Sāṁkhya system is based". The components of a group or compound are not completely identical with it. No single element in the group can be a substitute for it. The group or compound is formed only by a combination of the

22. *Op. cit.*, p. 196.

components. Here, what is important is the fact of combination.[23] Ther nature of the combination depends on the ratio in which the component elements are present and on the fact as to which element dominates in the combination. *Mahat* and all other principles are not the same, because the three *guṇa*s are not present in them in the some ratio. They all differ from one another inasmuch as they are dominated by a particular *guṇa* and the ratio in which the three *guṇa*s mingle in them varies. Thus, though *mahat* and other evolutes of *prakr̥ti* alike formed by a combination of the three *guṇa*s, they have their own peculiar ratio of the component *guṇa*s and have a particular *guṇa* as the predominant one. The *Sāṁkhyakārikā*[24] very aptly remarks that the unmanifest cause or *prakr̥ti* operates in the form of the three *guṇa*s and, by combination undergoing transformation, is diversified according to the differences severally of the other *guṇa*s depending on the principal *guṇa,* as does water (*salilavat*). The commentary *Sāṁkhyatattvakaumudī* by Vācaspatimiśra, explaining *salilavat*, says that simple water shed by the clouds, coming into contact with various situations, is modified as sweet, sour, bitter, pungent or astringent, in the character of the juice of the coconut, palm, *bel*, *karañja*, *āmalaka*, wood apple, etc.

SEPARATE IDENTITY OF ĀTMAN AND PRAKR̥TI

An important point in Hsuan Tsang's criticism is based on his premise "*prakr̥ti* and *ātman*, both being eternal, ought to be in their hypostases identical". From this he derives three points sofcriticism: (1) How can one of these, namely *prakr̥ti*, in distinction from the other, produce *mahat* and other principles? The implication is that then the evolution of principles, *mahat* and downwards, could as well have been from the *ātman*; (2) If *prakr̥ti* and *ātman* are the

23. Sankalia, *loc cit.*, remarks "Because, if our is constituted by the five elements, it does not mean that our body is as good as and equal to every one of the elements. Only when the five elements combine that the body can be created, and Hsuan Tsang seems to have missed this point."

24. *Kārikās*, 14-16.

same, then there is no need for mentioning *ātman* separately; *ātman* does not have any justification for existing as a separate principle; and (3) If the two are identical, then how can we maintain that there are two different offices of *subject* and *object*. How can than *ātman* be in a position to accept the aid of the twenty-four principles?

There is a basic defect in Hsuan Tsang's criticism. He confuses between the adjectives 'eternal' and 'all-pervasive'. They are neither synonymous nor identical in import. They envisage totally different criteria. Whereas 'eternal' refers to time, 'all-pervasive' refers to space. What is eternal need not be all-pervasive and what is all-pervasive need not be eternal. The one does not exclude the other. Hence the assertion that *prakr̥ti* and *ātman* are eternal does not necessarily mean that they are coeval and identical.

Actually the starting point of the criticism is not justified. The attribution to the Sāṁkhya system the view that both *prakr̥ti* and *ātman* are eternal has to be appreciated properly. The Sāṁkhya, no doubt, regards *puruṣa* and *prakr̥ti* (or *pradhāna*) as the two primary principles. They are not differentiated from the other principles on the ground of being eternal. The criterion is that of being evolvent or evolute. *Prakr̥ti* (evolvent) is described also as *mūla-prakr̥ti* (root evolvent), because it is non-evolute (*avikr̥ti*). The seven principles, beginning with *mahat*, are the evolutes of the evolvent (*prakr̥ti-vikr̥tis*). The sixteen other principles are evolutes (*vikāra*). *Puruṣa* is placed in an altogether separate category, being neither an evolvent nor an evolute.[25] The *Sāṁkhyakārikā* lists the distinguishing features of the *vyakta* (*mahat* and other evolutes) and the *avyakata* (*pradhāna* or *prakr̥ti*). The *avyakta* has characteristics quite opposite to those of the *vyakta*. The *vyakta* is described as being dependent on a cause (*hetumat*), non-eternal (*anitya*) and non-pervading (*avyāpi*).[26] The quality of being eternal is not to be associated with both *vyakta* and *avyakta*. On the contrary, whereas *vyakta* is non-eternal (*anitya*), *avyakta* is eternal

25. *Sāṁkhyakārikā*, 3.
26. *Ibid.*, 10-11.

(*nitya*). Likewise, the two are not all-pervading. Whereas *vyakta* is non-pervading, *avyakta* is pervading. In *kārikā* 11 certain characteristics are associate with both *vyakta* and *pradhāna* (*avyakta*). *Puruṣa* is reverse of both *vyakta* and *avyakta* in respect of these attributes (mentioned in *kārikā* 11), yet it is similar to the *pradhāna* (or *avyakta*) in respect of certain other characteristics mentioned in the preceding *kārikā*.[27] On the basis of *kārikā* 10 we may infer that the characteristics which *puruṣa* has in common with *pradhāna* are: being without a cause, being eternal, being pervading, being immutable, single, and independent. Thus, Sāṁkhya does not derive the quality of all-pervasiveness from the quality of being eternal. It ascribes to *puruṣa* and *pradhāna* several characteristics which are not necessarily connected with one another. These include the characteristics of being eternal and pervading. Here *vyakta* is described as being *avyāpi* and hence *avyakta* or *prdhāna* as also *puruṣa* will be *vyāpi*. *Avyāpi* means limited or finite, whereas *vyāpi* will mean unlimited or infinite. It is quite likely that Hsuan Tsang does not mean to derive *vyāpi* from *nitya*. He was well awere of the characteristics of *puruṣa* and *pradhāna* or *avyakta* and argued that how can the two alike be *vyāpi*; only one can be *vyāpi*. We will have to infer that Hsuan Tsang has not been able to state his point clearly.

When Hsuan Tsang criticises Sāṁkhya for making one of the two, *puruṣa* and *prakṛti*, 'subject' and the other 'object'. He possibly refers to the description of *vyakta* and *pradhāna* as *viṣaya*,[28] and of *puruṣa* as reverse of this. His argument is that if the two are identical how can one be 'subject' and another be 'object'. But Sāṁkhya clearly mentions the distinguishing features of the two. Though they have certain common characteristics, they have equally important points of differences. In any case, the reference to *viṣaya*

27. *Tadviparītastathā ca pumān*. All the commentators agree in taking this expression to mean that *puruṣa* is reverse of both *vyakta* and *pradhāna* in respect of attributes mentioned in *kārikā* 11, but is similar (*tathā ca*) to the *pradhāna* in respect of attributes in *kārikā* 10. They explain *ca* in *tathā ca* as having the sense of *api* (even yet).
28. *Sāṁkhyakārikā*, 11.

and its *viparīta* shows that Hsuan Tsang had a more detailed knowledge of Sāṁkhya than is reflected in his summarised account.

We have earlier referred to the problem of identifying the original Sāṁkhya text used by Hsuan Tsang. It is very difficult to be sure, through the English translation of the Chinese account, about the technical Sanskrit terms and expressions meant by him. He designates *prakr̥ti* also as *mūla-prakr̥ti*, groups the evolutes in a certain manner,[29] and refers to the qualities of being *nitya* and *vyāpi* for *prakr̥ti* and *ātman*[30] and to the distinction between the two as *viṣaya* and its opposite.[31] All this would suggest that Hsuan Tsang was relying on the *Sāṁkhyakārikā*. There are, no doubt, certain points and details which are not referred to in the *Sāṁkhyakārikā*. The use of the term *ātman* for *puruṣa* is one such.

Explanation

If the difficulty caused by the translation is not deemed to be a valid explanation, then we have three possible explanations: (a) Hsuan Tsang consulted some other texts as well, (b) Hsuan Tsang could not appreciate the niceties and subtleties of the Sāṁkhya system, (c) Hsuan Tsang deliberately gave the present account. We have referred to these points in the foregoing discussion. The possibility of Hsuan Tsang not restricting his study of the Sāṁkhya to just one text cannot be ruled out. Hsuan Tsang had an inquisitive mind and had an insatiable appetite for books. The earlier texts and accounts of Sāṁkhya are not expected to have been completely ousted immediately after the composition of the standardised account in the *Sāṁkhyakārikā*. We do not attach much weight to the explanation accusing Hsuan Tsang of inability to understand the Sāṁkhya properly. Hsuan Tsang was a versatile scholar. He had a philosophical mind. His knowledge was not confined to his own religion. He had acquired a deep understanding of the finer points and details of philosophies. A valid explanation of the differences

29. Cf. *Sāṁkhyakārikā*, 3.
30. Cf. *Ibid.*, 10-11.
31. Cf. *Ibid.*, 11.

which Hsuan Tsang's version reveals from the commonly accepted description of the Sāṁkhya system is that the account refers to a debate between Hsuan Tsang and his brāhmaṇa antagonist. In a debate one can take the liberty of giving a twist to the case made by his opponent. This is not on account of any ignorance on the part of the debator. Nor can this be interpreted as being dishonest.

Conclusion

To conclude, Hsuan Tsang offers the first critical account of Sāṁkhya by a non-Sāṁkhya scholar. This speaks highly of the wide range of his interest and his versatile scholarship. His original criticism reveals the philosophical sharpness and brilliance of his mind.

Index